CONNECT FEATURES

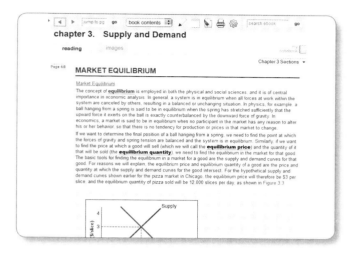

eBook

Connect includes a media-rich eBook that allows you to share your notes with your students. Your students can insert and review their own notes, highlight the text, search for specific information, and interact with media resources. Using an eBook with Connect gives your students a complete digital solution that allows them to access their materials from any computer.

Tegrity

Make your classes available anytime, anywhere. With simple, one-click recording, students can search for a word or phrase and be taken to the exact place in your lecture that they need to review.

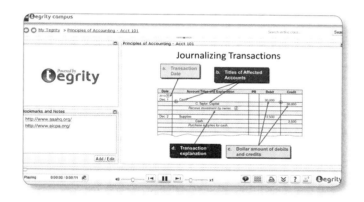

Connect Insight

The first and only analytics tool of its kind, Connect Insight is a series of visual data displays, each of which is framed by an intuitive question and provides at-a-glance information regarding how an instructor's class is performing. Connect Insight is available through Connect titles.

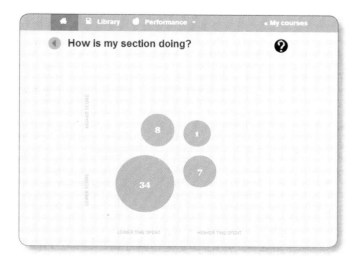

EASY TO USE

Learning Management System Integration

McGraw-Hill Campus is a one-stop teaching and learning experience available to use with any learning management system. McGraw-Hill Campus provides single sign-on to faculty and students for all McGraw-Hill material and technology from within the school website. McGraw-Hill Campus also allows instructors instant access to all supplements and teaching materials for all McGraw-Hill products.

Blackboard users also benefit from McGraw-Hill's industry-leading integration, providing single sign-on to access all Connect assignments and automatic feeding of assignment results to the Blackboard grade book.

The **Best** of **Both Worlds**

POWERFUL REPORTING

Connect generates comprehensive reports and graphs that provide instructors with an instant view of the performance of individual students, a specific section, or multiple sections. Since all content is mapped to learning objectives, Connect reporting is ideal for accreditation or other administrative documentation.

At a Glance Insights — Assignment Results & Statistics Reports — Student Performance Reports — Item Analysis Reports — Category Analysis Reports — At-Risk Student Reports — LearnSmart Reports

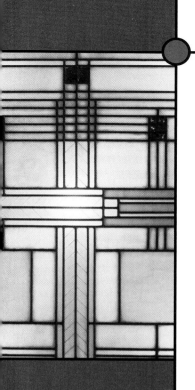

PRINCIPLES OF

MACRO-
ECONOMICS

Sixth Edition

THE McGRAW-HILL SERIES IN ECONOMICS

ESSENTIALS OF ECONOMICS

Brue, McConnell, and Flynn
Essentials of Economics
Third Edition

Mandel
Economics: The Basics
Second Edition

Schiller
Essentials of Economics
Ninth Edition

PRINCIPLES OF ECONOMICS

Asarta and Butters
Principles of Economics,
Principles of Microeconomics,
and Principles of Macroeconomics
First Edition

Colander
Economics, Microeconomics, and
Macroeconomics
Ninth Edition

Frank and Bernanke
Principles of Economics,
Principles of Microeconomics,
Principles of Macroeconomics
Sixth Edition

**Frank, Bernanke, Antonovics,
and Heffetz**
Brief Editions: Principles of
Economics, Principles of
Microeconomics, Principles of
Macroeconomics
Second Edition

Karlan and Morduch
Economics, Microeconomics, and
Macroeconomics
First Edition

McConnell, Brue, and Flynn
Economics, Microeconomics, and
Macroeconomics
Twentieth Edition

McConnell, Brue, and Flynn
Brief Editions: Microeconomics and
Macroeconomics
Second Edition

Miller
Principles of Microeconomics
First Edition

Samuelson and Nordhaus
Economics, Microeconomics, and
Macroeconomics
Nineteenth Edition

Schiller
The Economy Today,
The Micro Economy Today,
and The Macro Economy Today
Fourteenth Edition

Slavin
Economics, Microeconomics,
and Macroeconomics
Eleventh Edition

ECONOMICS OF SOCIAL ISSUES

Guell
Issues in Economics Today
Seventh Edition

Sharp, Register, and Grimes
Economics of Social Issues
Twentieth Edition

ECONOMETRICS

Gujarati and Porter
Basic Econometrics
Fifth Edition

Gujarati and Porter
Essentials of Econometrics
Fourth Edition

Hilmer and Hilmer
Practical Econometrics
First Edition

MANAGERIAL ECONOMICS

Baye and Prince
Managerial Economics and Business
Strategy
Eighth Edition

Brickley, Smith, and Zimmerman
Managerial Economics and
Organizational Architecture
Sixth Edition

Thomas and Maurice
Managerial Economics
Eleventh Edition

INTERMEDIATE ECONOMICS

Bernheim and Whinston
Microeconomics
Second Edition

Dornbusch, Fischer, and Startz
Macroeconomics
Twelfth Edition

Frank
Microeconomics and Behavior
Ninth Edition

ADVANCED ECONOMICS

Romer
Advanced Macroeconomics
Fourth Edition

MONEY AND BANKING

Cecchetti and Schoenholtz
Money, Banking, and Financial
Markets
Fourth Edition

URBAN ECONOMICS

O'Sullivan
Urban Economics
Eighth Edition

LABOR ECONOMICS

Borjas
Labor Economics
Seventh Edition

**McConnell, Brue, and
Macpherson**
Contemporary Labor Economics
Tenth Edition

PUBLIC FINANCE

Rosen and Gayer
Public Finance
Tenth Edition

Seidman
Public Finance
First Edition

ENVIRONMENTAL ECONOMICS

Field and Field
Environmental Economics:
An Introduction
Sixth Edition

INTERNATIONAL ECONOMICS

Appleyard and Field
International Economics
Eighth Edition

King and King
International Economics,
Globalization, and Policy:
A Reader
Fifth Edition

Pugel
International Economics
Sixteenth Edition

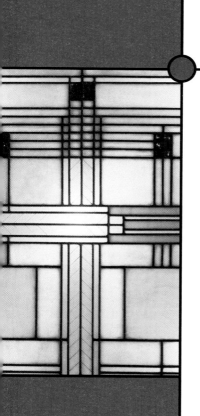

PRINCIPLES OF MACRO-ECONOMICS

Sixth Edition

ROBERT H. FRANK
Cornell University

BEN S. BERNANKE
Brookings Institution [affiliated]
Former Chairman, Board of Governors of the Federal Reserve System

KATE ANTONOVICS
University of California, San Diego

ORI HEFFETZ
Cornell University

with special contribution by
PER J. NORANDER
Missouri State University

PRINCIPLES OF MACROECONOMICS, SIXTH EDITION

Published by McGraw-Hill Education, 2 Penn Plaza, New York, NY 10121. Copyright © 2016 by McGraw-Hill Education. All rights reserved. Printed in the United States of America. Previous editions © 2013, 2009, and 2007. No part of this publication may be reproduced or distributed in any form or by any means, or stored in a database or retrieval system, without the prior written consent of McGraw-Hill Education, including, but not limited to, in any network or other electronic storage or transmission, or broadcast for distance learning.

Some ancillaries, including electronic and print components, may not be available to customers outside the United States.

This book is printed on acid-free paper.

1 2 3 4 5 6 7 8 9 0 DOW/DOW 1 0 9 8 7 6 5

ISBN   978-0-07-351899-2
MHID   0-07-351899-9

Senior Vice President, Products & Markets: *Kurt L. Strand*
Vice President, General Manager, Products & Markets: *Marty Lange*
Vice President, Content Design & Delivery: *Kimberly Meriwether David*
Managing Director: *James Heine*
Brand Manager: *Katie White Hoenicke*
Director, Product Development: *Rose Koos*
Product Developer: *Sarah Otterness*
Marketing Manager: *Katie White Hoenicke*
Director, Digital Content Development: *Douglas Ruby*
Digital Product Analyst: *Kevin Shanahan*
Director, Content Design & Delivery: *Linda Avenarius*
Program Manager: *Mark Christianson*
Content Project Managers: *Harvey Yep (Core), Kristin Bradley (Assessment)*
Buyer: *Laura M. Fuller*
Design: *Matt Diamond*
Content Licensing Specialists: *Shawntel Schmitt (Image), Rita Hingtgen (Text)*
Cover Image: © *Thomas A. Heinz/CORBIS*
Compositor: *Aptara®, Inc.*
Printer: *R. R. Donnelley*

Text Credits

Chapter 2, page 52: Bill Gates, *Business @ The Speed of Thought: Using a Digital Nervous System.* New York: Warner Books, USA, 1999. **Chapter 5, page 117:** Babe Ruth, Reported reply when a reporter objected that the salary Ruth was demanding ($80,000) was more than that of President Herbert Hoover's ($75,000), quoted in Benjamin G. Rader, *Baseball: A History of America's Game,* Chicago, IL: University of Illinois Press, 2002, p. 134; p. 434: Javier C. Hernandez, "Prices of Consumer Goods Hold Steady, Indicating That Inflation Is at Bay," *The New York Times,* March 18, 2010. **Chapter 10, page 279:** M. Douglas Ivester, *The New York Times,* October 28, 1999, p. C1; Constance L. Hays, "Variable-Price Coke Machine Being Tested," *The New York Times,* October 28, 1999. **Chapter 11, page 308:** The studies are "Did the 2008 Tax Rebates Stimulate Short-Term Growth?", "Estimated Impact of the American Recovery and Reinvestment Act on Employment and Economic Output as of September 2009," and "Estimated Impact of the American Recovery and Reinvestment Act on Employment and Economic Output from October 2009 through December 2009." All three studies are available at www.cbo.gov/publications/collections/collections.cfm?collect=12.

Library of Congress Control Number: 2014959483

The Internet addresses listed in the text were accurate at the time of publication. The inclusion of a website does not indicate an endorsement by the authors or McGraw-Hill Education, and McGraw-Hill Education does not guarantee the accuracy of the information presented at these sites.

DEDICATION

For Ellen
R. H. F.

For Anna
B. S. B.

For Fiona and Henry
K. A.

For Katrina, Eleanor, and Daniel
O. H.

ABOUT THE AUTHORS

ROBERT H. FRANK

Robert H. Frank is the H. J. Louis Professor of Management and Professor of Economics at Cornell's Johnson School of Management, where he has taught since 1972. His "Economic View" column appears regularly in *The New York Times*. He is a Distinguished Senior Fellow at Demos. After receiving his B.S. from Georgia Tech in 1966, he taught math and science for two years as a Peace Corps Volunteer in rural Nepal. He received his M.A. in statistics in 1971 and his Ph.D. in economics in 1972 from The University of California at Berkeley. During leaves of absence from Cornell, he has served as chief economist for the Civil Aeronautics Board (1978–1980), a Fellow at the Center for Advanced Study in the Behavioral Sciences (1992–93), Professor of American Civilization at l'École des Hautes Études en Sciences Sociales in Paris (2000–01), and the Peter and Charlotte Schoenfeld Visiting Faculty Fellow at the NYU Stern School of Business in 2008–09. His papers have appeared in the *American Economic Review, Econometrica,* the *Journal of Political Economy,* and other leading professional journals.

Professor Frank is the author of a best-selling intermediate economics textbook—*Microeconomics and Behavior,* Ninth Edition (Irwin/McGraw-Hill, 2015). His research has focused on rivalry and cooperation in economic and social behavior. His books on these themes include *Choosing the Right Pond* (Oxford, 1995), *Passions Within Reason* (W. W. Norton, 1988), *What Price the Moral High Ground?* (Princeton, 2004), *Falling Behind* (University of California Press, 2007), *The Economic Naturalist* (Basic Books, 2007), *The Economic Naturalist's Field Guide* (Basic Books, 2009), and *The Darwin Economy* (Princeton, 2011), which have been translated into 22 languages. *The Winner-Take-All Society* (The Free Press, 1995), co-authored with Philip Cook, received a Critic's Choice Award, was named a Notable Book of the Year by *The New York Times,* and was included in *BusinessWeek*'s list of the 10 best books of 1995. *Luxury Fever* (The Free Press, 1999) was named to the *Knight-Ridder* Best Books list for 1999.

Professor Frank has been awarded an Andrew W. Mellon Professorship (1987–1990), a Kenan Enterprise Award (1993), and a Merrill Scholars Program Outstanding Educator Citation (1991). He is a co-recipient of the 2004 Leontief Prize for Advancing the Frontiers of Economic Thought. He was awarded the Johnson School's Stephen Russell Distinguished Teaching Award in 2004, 2010, and 2012, and the School's Apple Distinguished Teaching Award in 2005. His introductory microeconomics course has graduated more than 7,000 enthusiastic economic naturalists over the years.

BEN S. BERNANKE

Professor Bernanke received his B.A. in economics from Harvard University in 1975 and his Ph.D. in economics from MIT in 1979. He taught at the Stanford Graduate School of Business from 1979 to 1985 and moved to Princeton University in 1985, where he was named the Howard Harrison and Gabrielle Snyder Beck Professor of Economics and Public Affairs, and where he served as Chairman of the Economics Department.

Professor Bernanke was sworn in on February 1, 2006, as Chairman and a member of the Board of Governors of the Federal Reserve System—his second term expired January 31, 2014. Professor Bernanke also serves as Chairman of the Federal Open Market Committee, the Fed's principal monetary policymaking body. He was appointed as a member of the Board to a full 14-year term, which expires January 31, 2020. Before his appointment as Chairman, Professor Bernanke was Chairman of the President's Council of Economic Advisers, from June 2005 to January 2006.

Professor Bernanke's intermediate textbook, with Andrew Abel and Dean Croushore, *Macroeconomics,* Eighth Edition (Addison-Wesley, 2011), is a best seller in its field. He has authored more than 50 scholarly publications in macroeconomics, macroeconomic history, and finance. He has done significant research on the causes of the Great Depression, the role of financial markets and institutions in the business cycle, and measurement of the effects of monetary policy on the economy.

Professor Bernanke has held a Guggenheim Fellowship and a Sloan Fellowship, and he is a Fellow of the Econometric Society and of the American Academy of Arts and Sciences. He served as the Director of the Monetary Economics Program of the National Bureau of Economic Research (NBER) and as a member of the NBER's Business Cycle Dating Committee. In July 2001, he was appointed editor of the *American Economic Review.* Professor Bernanke's work with civic and professional groups includes having served two terms as a member of the Montgomery Township (N.J.) Board of Education.

KATE ANTONOVICS

Professor Antonovics received her B.A. from Brown University in 1993 and her Ph.D. in economics from the University of Wisconsin in 2000. Shortly thereafter, she joined the faculty in the Economics Department at the University of California, San Diego, where she has been ever since.

Professor Antonovics is known for her superb teaching and her innovative use of technology in the classroom. Her highly popular introductory-level microeconomics course regularly enrolls over 450 students each fall. She also teaches labor economics at both the undergraduate and graduate level. In 2012, she received the UCSD Department of Economics award for best undergraduate teaching.

Professor Antonovics's research has focused on racial discrimination, gender discrimination, affirmative action, intergenerational income mobility, learning, and wage dynamics. Her papers have appeared in the *American Economic Review,* the *Review of Economics and Statistics,* the *Journal of Labor Economics,* and the *Journal of Human Resources.* She is a member of both the American Economic Association and the Society of Labor Economists.

ORI HEFFETZ

Professor Heffetz received his B.A. in physics and philosophy from Tel Aviv University in 1999 and his Ph.D. in economics from Princeton University in 2005. He is an Associate Professor of Economics at the Samuel Curtis Johnson Graduate School of Management at Cornell University, where he has taught since 2005.

Bringing the real world into the classroom, Professor Heffetz has created a unique macroeconomics course that introduces basic concepts and tools from economic theory and applies them to current news and global events. His popular classes are taken by hundreds of students every year, on the Cornell Ithaca campus and, via live videoconferencing, in dozens of cities across the U.S., Canada, and beyond.

Professor Heffetz's research studies the social and cultural aspects of economic behavior, focusing on the mechanisms that drive consumers' choices and on the links between economic choices, individual well-being, and policymaking. He has published scholarly work on household consumption patterns, individual economic decision making, and survey methodology and measurement. He was a visiting researcher at the Bank of Israel during 2011, is currently a Faculty Research Fellow at the National Bureau of Economic Research (NBER), and serves on the editorial board of *Social Choice and Welfare.*

Although many millions of dollars are spent each year on introductory economics instruction in American colleges and universities, the return on this investment has been disturbingly low. Studies have shown, for example, that several months after having taken a principles of economics course, former students are no better able to answer simple economic questions than others who never even took the course. Most students, it seems, leave our introductory courses without having learned even the most important basic economic principles.

The problem, in our view, is that these courses almost always try to teach students far too much. In the process, really important ideas get little more coverage than minor ones, and everything ends up going by in a blur. Many instructors ask themselves, "How much can I cover today?" when instead they should be asking, "How much can my students absorb?"

Our textbook grew out of our conviction that students will learn far more if we attempt to cover much less. Our basic premise is that a small number of basic principles do most of the heavy lifting in economics, and that if we focus narrowly and repeatedly on those principles, students can actually master them in just a single semester.

The enthusiastic reactions of users of previous editions of our textbook affirm the validity of this premise. Avoiding excessive reliance on formal mathematical derivations, we present concepts intuitively through examples drawn from familiar contexts. We rely throughout on a well-articulated list of seven Core Principles, which we reinforce repeatedly by illustrating and applying each principle in numerous contexts. We ask students periodically to apply these principles themselves to answer related questions, exercises, and problems.

Throughout this process, we encourage students to become "economic naturalists," people who employ basic economic principles to understand and explain what they observe in the world around them. An economic naturalist understands, for example, that infant safety seats are required in cars but not in airplanes because the marginal cost of space to accommodate these seats is typically zero in cars but often hundreds of dollars in airplanes. Scores of such examples are sprinkled throughout the book. Each one, we believe, poses a question that should make any curious person eager to learn the answer. These examples stimulate interest while teaching students to see each feature of their economic landscape as the reflection of one or more of the Core Principles. Students talk about these examples with their friends and families. Learning economics is like learning a language. In each case, there is no substitute for actually speaking. By inducing students to speak economics, the Economic Naturalist examples serve this purpose.

For those who would like to learn more about the role of examples in learning economics, Bob Frank's lecture on this topic is posted on YouTube's "Authors@Google" series (**www.youtube.com/watch?v=QalNVxeIKEE** or search "Authors@Google: Robert Frank").

KEY THEMES AND FEATURES

An Emphasis on Seven Core Principles

As noted, a few Core Principles do most of the work in economics. By focusing almost exclusively on these principles, the text ensures that students leave the course with a deep mastery of them. In contrast, traditional encyclopedic texts so overwhelm students with detail that they often leave the course with little useful working knowledge at all.

- **The Scarcity Principle:** Having more of one good thing usually means having less of another.

- **The Cost-Benefit Principle:** Take no action unless its marginal benefit is at least as great as its marginal cost.

- **The Incentive Principle:** Cost-benefit comparisons are relevant not only for identifying the decisions that rational people should make, but also for predicting the actual decisions they do make.

- **The Principle of Comparative Advantage:** Everyone does best when each concentrates on the activity for which he or she is relatively most productive.

- **The Principle of Increasing Opportunity Cost:** Use the resources with the lowest opportunity cost before turning to those with higher opportunity costs.

- **The Efficiency Principle:** Efficiency is an important social goal because when the economic pie grows larger, everyone can have a larger slice.

- **The Equilibrium Principle:** A market in equilibrium leaves no unexploited opportunities for individuals but may not exploit all gains achievable through collective action.

Economic Naturalism

Our ultimate goal is to produce economic naturalists—people who see each human action as the result of an implicit or explicit cost-benefit calculation. The economic naturalist sees mundane details of ordinary existence in a new light and becomes actively engaged in the attempt to understand them. Some representative examples:

- Why has investment in computers increased so much in recent decades?

- Why does news of inflation hurt the stock market?

- Why do almost all countries provide free public education?

Active Learning Stressed

The only way to learn to hit an overhead smash in tennis is through repeated practice. The same is true for learning economics. Accordingly, we consistently introduce new ideas in the context of simple examples and then follow them with applications showing how they work in familiar settings. At frequent intervals, we pose concept checks that both test and reinforce the understanding of these ideas. The end-of-chapter questions and problems are carefully crafted to help students internalize and extend core concepts. Experience with earlier editions confirms that this approach really does prepare students to apply basic economic principles to solve economic puzzles drawn from the real world.

Modern Macroeconomics

The *severe economic downturn* that began in late 2007 has renewed interest in cyclical fluctuations without challenging the importance of such long-run issues as growth, productivity, the evolution of real wages, and capital formation. Our treatment of these issues is organized as follows:

- A three-chapter treatment of *long-run issues,* followed by a modern treatment of *short-term fluctuations and stabilization policy,* emphasizes the important distinction between short- and long-run behavior of the economy.

- *Designed to allow for flexible treatment of topics,* these chapters are written so that short-run material (Chapters 10–14) can be used before long-run material (Chapters 7–9) with no loss of continuity.

- This book places a heavy emphasis on *globalization,* starting with an analysis of its effects on real wage inequality and progressing to such issues as the benefits of trade, the role of capital flows in domestic capital formation, and the links between exchange rates and monetary policy.

ORGANIZATION OF THE SIXTH EDITION

- **Flexible presentation:** Chapters 4–6 are a self-contained group of chapters that cover measurement issues. This allows instructors to proceed to a discussion of either long-run concepts as discussed in Chapters 7–9 or short-run concepts as covered in Chapters 10–14 with no loss of continuity.

- **Thorough discussion of labor markets:** Trends in employment, wages, and unemployment are covered together in Chapter 6 to help students understand and distinguish between long-term trends and short-term fluctuations in the labor market.

- **Capital formation through financial markets:** Chapter 8 now presents a complete discussion of financial markets, focusing on the part these markets play in capital formation. This will help students better understand the important distinction between financial investment and physical investment in economics.

- **The simple Keynesian model:** We present the simple Keynesian model through examples that are developed both graphically and numerically.

- **Modular presentation of money and monetary policy:** Chapter 9 introduces students to the concepts of money and financial intermediaries, which can be covered separately or in direct conjunction with the discussion of monetary policy in Chapter 12.

- **The presentation of aggregate demand and aggregate supply:** Chapters 13 and 14 work together to give students a thorough understanding of the *AD-AS* model.

  - In Chapter 13, we focus on the nuts and bolts of the *AD-AS* model itself. Coherent, intuitive derivations of the *AD* curve and *AS* curve are presented, with an emphasis on connecting each side of the model to concepts the students learned in previous chapters. The model is then applied to business cycles, with an emphasis on the 2007–2009 recession.

  - In Chapter 14, we apply the *AD-AS* model to macroeconomic policy. First, we focus on how fiscal and monetary policy should be conducted in the face of shocks to aggregate demand and aggregate supply. We then examine the role of inflation expectations and credibility in policymaking, and link this to a discussion of inflation targeting. Finally, we analyze the effects of fiscal policy on long-run growth with an emphasis on how changes in marginal tax rates can affect labor supply and hence potential output.

- **Flexible coverage of international economics:** Chapter 15 is a self-contained discussion of exchange rates that can be used whenever an instructor thinks it best to introduce this important subject. This chapter also integrates the discussion of trade and capital flows so that students see that the balance of trade and net capital inflows are two sides of the same issue.

CHANGES IN THE SIXTH EDITION

Changes Common to all Chapters

In all chapters, the narrative has been tightened and shortened slightly. Many of the examples have been updated, with a focus on examples that connect to current events such as the financial crisis of 2008 and the Great Recession of 2007–2009. The examples and exercises from the previous edition have been redesigned to provide more clarity and ease of use. Data have been updated throughout.

Chapter-by-Chapter Changes

- **Chapters 1–5:** Content and data updates have been made as needed.

- **Chapter 6:** Improved and timely coverage on the falling labor participation rate in the United States since 2000 has been added. The discussion on unemployment data has been updated to account for the contentious reduction in the official unemployment rate seen since the end of the last recession.

- **Chapter 7:** Content and data updates have been added as needed.

- **Chapter 8:** The discussion on how financial markets connect savers and borrowers, thereby allocating funds to the most productive uses, has been augmented to include a discussion on the most commonly used types of financial investments, such as bonds and stocks. This section was previously covered in Chapter 9.

- **Chapter 9:** This chapter is now solely focused on money and commercial banks, allowing it to be covered independently or in direct conjunction with Chapter 12. It is now titled *Money, Prices, and Financial Intermediaries.*

- **Chapters 10–11:** Content and data updates have been added as needed.

- **Chapter 12:** Payment of interest on reserves has been added as a separate monetary policy tool; this is important since this is a tool author Ben Bernanke has identified as crucial to keeping inflation in check. A section on unconventional monetary policy (such as quantitative easing) has also been added to this section of the chapter.

- **Chapters 13–14:** Content and data updates have been added as needed.

- **Chapter 15:** The section on international capital flows and the balance of trade has been reworked to more clearly present the relationships between national savings, private investment, and net capital flows. The connections between Chapter 8 and Chapter 15 have also been tightened through this reorganization.

ORGANIZED LEARNING IN THE SIXTH EDITION

Chapter Learning Objectives

Students and professors can be confident that the organization of each chapter surrounds common themes outlined by four to seven learning objectives listed on the first page of each chapter. These objectives, along with AACSB and Bloom's Taxonomy Learning Categories, are connected to all test bank questions and end-of-chapter material to offer a comprehensive, thorough teaching and learning experience.

Assurance of Learning Ready

Many educational institutions today are focused on the notion of assurance of learning, an important element of some accreditation standards. *Principles of Macroeconomics, 6/e,* is designed specifically to support your assurance of learning initiatives with a simple, yet powerful, solution.

You can use our test bank software, EZ Test, to easily query for learning objectives that directly relate to the objectives for your course. You can then use the reporting features of EZ Test to aggregate student results in a similar fashion, making the collection and presentation of assurance of learning data simple and easy.

AACSB Statement

The McGraw-Hill Companies is a proud corporate member of AACSB International. Recognizing the importance and value of AACSB accreditation, the authors of *Principles of Macroeconomics, 6/e,* have sought to recognize the curricula guidelines detailed in AACSB standards for business accreditation by connecting questions in the test bank and end-of-chapter material to the general knowledge and skill guidelines found in AACSB standards. It is important to note that the statements contained in *Principles of Macroeconomics, 6/e,* are provided only as a guide for the users of this text.

AN EXPANDED TEAM OF AUTHORS

Also, starting with this sixth edition, we are pleased to announce the we have expanded the list of authors, in addition to Robert Frank and Ben Bernanke, to include Kate Antonovics and Ori Heffetz. These two younger-generation authors bring with them a fresh touch, side by side with many years of classroom experience using previous editions of *Principles of Economics* in their microeconomics (Kate) and macroeconomics (Ori) classes. Our expanded team of authors has enabled us to increase the quality and range of digital materials that accompany the textbook, keeping us at the forefront of the latest developments in educational technology.

A NOTE ON THE WRITING OF THIS EDITION

Ben Bernanke was sworn in on February 1, 2006, as Chairman and a member of the Board of Governors of the Federal Reserve System, a position to which he was reappointed in January 2010. From June 2005 until January 2006, he served as chairman of the President's Council of Economic Advisers. These positions have allowed him to play an active role in making U.S. economic policy, but the rules of government service have restricted his ability to participate in the preparation of the sixth edition.

Fortunately, we were able to enlist the aid of Per J. Norander of Missouri State University to take the lead in creating the macro portion of the sixth edition. The authors express their deep gratitude to Per for the energy and creativity he has brought to his work on the book. He has created a great tool for students and professors.

ACKNOWLEDGMENTS

Our thanks first and foremost go to our brand manager, Scott Smith, and our product developer, Sarah Otterness. Scott encouraged us to think deeply about how to improve the book and helped us transform our ideas into concrete changes. Sarah shepherded us through the revision process in person, on the telephone, through the mail, and via e-mail with intelligence, sound advice, and good humor. We are grateful as well to the production team, whose professionalism (and patience) was outstanding: Harvey Yep, content project manager; Kristin Bradley, assessment project manager; Matt Diamond, lead designer; and all of those who worked on the production team to turn our manuscript into the book you see now. Finally, we also thank Katie Hoenicke, marketing manager, and Jennifer Jelinski, marketing specialist, for getting our message into the wider world.

Finally, our sincere thanks to the following teachers and colleagues, whose thorough reviews and thoughtful suggestions led to innumerable substantive improvements to *Principles of Macroeconomics, 6/e.*

Mark Abajian, *San Diego Mesa College*

Michael Adams, *SUNY College at Old Westbury*

Richard Agesa, *Marshall University*

Seemi Ahmad, *Dutchess Community College*

Justine Alessandroni, *Fordham University*

Ashraf Almurdaah, *Los Angeles City College*

Anna Antus, *Normandale Community College* and *University of Wisconsin–River Falls*

Robert B. Archibald, *College of William and Mary*

Nisha Aroskar, *Baton Rouge Community College*

Chris Azevedo, *University of Central Missouri*

Narine Badasyan, *Murray State University*

Rebecca Tuttle Baldwin, *Bellevue Community College*

Timothy Bastian, *Creighton University*

Klaus Becker, *Texas Tech University*

Christian Walter Beer, *Cape Fear Community College*

Valerie R. Bencivenga, *University of Texas–Austin*

Sigridur Benediktsdottir, *Yale University*

Thomas Beveridge, *Durham Technical Community College*

Joerg Bibow, *Skidmore College*

Okmyung Bin, *East Carolina University*

John Bishop, *East Carolina University*

Benjamin F. Blair, *Mississippi State University*

Elizabeth Brainerd, *Williams College*

William J. Brennan, *Minnesota State University–Mankato*

Brian C. Brush, *Marquette University*

Christopher Burkart, *University of West Florida*

Aslihan Cakmak, *Lehman College*

Joseph Calhoun, *Florida State University*

Giuliana Campanelli Andreopoulos, *William Paterson University*

J. Lon Carlson, *Illinois State University*

Anoshua Chaudhuri, *San Francisco State University*

Chiuping Chen, *American River College*

Nan-Ting Chou, *University of Louisville*

Buford Cordle Jr., *Southwest Virginia Community College*

Attila Cseh, *Valdosta State University*

Lawrence Paul DeBoer, Jr., *Purdue University*

Faruk Eray Düzenli, *Denison University*

Dennis S. Edwards, *Coastal Carolina University*

Harry Ellis, Jr., *University of North Texas*

Fred Englander, *Fairleigh Dickinson University*

Martha F. Evans, *Florida State University*

Christopher B. Fant, *Spartanburg Community College*

Johanna Francis, *Fordham University*

Roger Frantz, *San Diego State University*

Mark Frascatore, *Clarkson University*

Lydia L. Gan, *University of North Carolina–Pembroke*

John Gardino, *Front Range Community College*

Frank Garland, *Tricounty Tech College*

Greg George, *Macon State College*

Seth Gershenson, *Michigan State University*

Amy D. Gibson, *Christopher Newport University*

Harley Leroy Gill, *Ohio State University*

Michael Gootzeit, *University of Memphis*

Alan F. Gummerson, *Florida International University*

Barnali Gupta, *Miami University*

Gail Heyne Hafer, *St. Louis Community College–Meramec*

Moonsu Han, *North Shore Community College* and *Lasell College*

Richard Lloyd Hannah, *Middle Tennessee State University*

Michael J. Haupert, *University of Wisconsin–La Crosse*

Glenn S. Haynes IV, *Western Illinois University*

Susan He, *Washington State University*

John Hejkal, *University of Iowa*

Andrew Helms, *Washington College*

Ryan Herzog, *University of Oregon*

Lora Holcombe, *Florida State University*

Jack W. Hou, *California State University–Long Beach*

Kuang-Chung Hsu, *Kishwaukee College*

Greg Hunter, *California State University–Pomona*

Robert Jerome, *James Madison University*

Nancy Jo Ammon Jianakoplos, *Colorado State University*

Prathibha V. Joshi, *Gordon College*

David E. Kalist, *Shippensburg University*

Brian Kench, *University of Tampa*

David A. Kennett, *Vassar College*

Farida Chowdhury Khan, *University of Wisconsin–Parkside*

Lori G. Kletzer, *University of California–Santa Cruz*

Mary Kay Knudson, *University of Iowa*

Fredric R. Kolb, *University of Wisconsin–Eau Claire*

Janet Koscianski, *Shippensburg University*

Fritz Laux, *Northeastern State University*

Jaclyn Lindo, *University of Hawaii–Manoa*

Clifford Allen Lipscomb, *Valdosta State University*

Donald J. Liu, *University of Minnesota–Twin Cities*

Svitlana Maksymenko, *University of Pittsburgh*

Timothy Mathews, *Kennesaw State University*

Thomas S. McCaleb, *Florida State University*

Michael A. McPherson, *University of North Texas*

Ida Mirzaie, *The Ohio State University*

David F. Mitch, *University of Maryland–Baltimore County*

David M. Mitchell, *Missouri State University*

Shalah Maryam Mostashari, *Texas A&M University*

Steven Nafziger, *Williams College*

Michael A. Nelson, *Texas A&M University*

Diego Nocetti, *Clarkson University*

Thomas A. Odegaard, *Baylor University*

Farley Ordovensky Staniec, *University of the Pacific*

Stephanie Owings, *Fort Lewis College*

Robert L. Pennington, *University of Central Florida*

Claudiney Pereira, *Tulane University*

Martin Pereyra, *University of Missouri*

J.M. Pogodzinski, *San Jose State University*

Ed Price, *Oklahoma State University*

Steve Price, *Butte College*

Ratha Ramoo, *Diablo Valley College*

Bill Robinson, *University of Nevada–Las Vegas*

Christina Robinson, *North Carolina State University*

Brian Rosario, *University of California–Davis*

Marina V. Rosser, *James Madison University*

Elyce Rotella, *Indiana University*

Elham M. Rouhani, *Georgia State University*

Jeffrey Rubin, *Rutgers University*

Peter Rupert, *University of California–Santa Barbara*

Mark Ryan, *University of Oregon*

Caroliniana M. Sandifer, *University of Georgia*

Naveen Sarna, *Northern Virginia Community College*

Supriya Sarnikar, *Westfield State College*

Ousmane Seck, *California State University–Fullerton*

Atindra Sen, *Miami University*

John Shea, *University of Maryland–College Park*

Richard Sicotte, *University of Vermont*

Patricia K. Smith, *University of Michigan–Dearborn*

Sumati Srinivas, *Radford University*

Rebecca Stein, *University of Pennsylvania*

Thomas Stevens, *University of Massachusetts*

Carolyn Fabian Stumph, *Indiana University* and *Purdue University–Fort Wayne*

Chetan Subramanian, *SUNY–Buffalo*

Peggy Sueppel, *South Florida Community College*

Albert J. Sumell, *Youngstown State University*

Vera Alexandrova Tabakova, *East Carolina University*

James A. Tallant, *Cape Fear Community College*

Henry S. Terrell, *University of Maryland–College Park*

Steve Trost, *Virginia Tech University*

Philip Trostel, *University of Maine*

Markland Tuttle, *Sam Houston State University*

Nora Underwood, *University of Central Florida*

Jesus M. Valencia, *Slippery Rock University*

Jennifer A. Vincent, *Champlain College*

Nancy Virts, *California State University–Northridge*

Joseph P. Wesson, *Normandale Community College*

Elizabeth Wheaton, *Southern Methodist University*

Mark Wilson, *St. Bonaventure University*

William C. Wood, *James Madison University*

Ruhai Wu, *Florida Atlantic University*

Selin Yalcindag, *Mercyhurst College*

Bill Yang, *Georgia Southern University*

PEDAGOGICAL FEATURES

CHAPTER OPENER

Each chapter begins with a brief narrative of a realistic scenario illustrating the concepts to be learned in that chapter.

LEARNING OBJECTIVES

Approximately four to seven learning objectives are presented at the beginning of each chapter and are referenced again in the summary, the end-of-chapter review questions, and problems to which they relate. The learning objectives (LOs) serve as a quick introduction to the material and concepts to be mastered before moving to the next chapter.

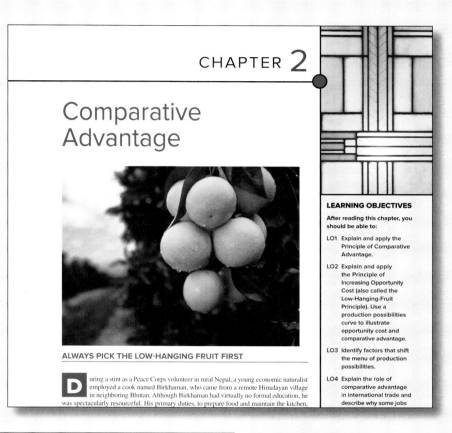

CHAPTER 2

Comparative Advantage

ALWAYS PICK THE LOW-HANGING FRUIT FIRST

D uring a stint as a Peace Corps volunteer in rural Nepal, a young economic naturalist employed a cook named Birkhaman, who came from a remote Himalayan village in neighboring Bhutan. Although Birkhaman had virtually no formal education, he was spectacularly resourceful. His primary duties, to prepare food and maintain the kitchen,

LEARNING OBJECTIVES

After reading this chapter, you should be able to:

LO1 Explain and apply the Principle of Comparative Advantage.

LO2 Explain and apply the Principle of Increasing Opportunity Cost (also called the Low-Hanging-Fruit Principle). Use a production possibilities curve to illustrate opportunity cost and comparative advantage.

LO3 Identify factors that shift the menu of production possibilities.

LO4 Explain the role of comparative advantage in international trade and describe why some jobs

---

average cost the total cost of undertaking *n* units of an activity divided by *n*

average benefit the total benefit of undertaking *n* units of an activity divided by *n*

To discover whether the advice makes economic sense, we must compare the marginal cost of a launch to its marginal benefit. The professor's estimates, however, tell us only the **average cost** and **average benefit** of the program. These are, respectively, the total cost of the program divided by the number of launches and the total benefit divided by the number of launches. Knowing the average benefit and average cost per launch for all shuttles launched thus far is simply not useful for deciding whether to expand the program. Of course, the average cost of the launches undertaken so far *might* be the same as the cost of adding another launch. But it also might be either higher or lower than the marginal cost of a launch. The same holds true regarding average and marginal benefits.

KEY TERMS

Key terms are indicated in bold and defined in the margin the first time each term is used. They are also listed among the end-of-chapter material. A glossary is available at the back of the book for quick reference.

CONCEPT CHECKS

These self-test questions in the body of the chapter enable students to determine whether the preceding material has been understood and reinforce understanding before reading further. Detailed Answers to Concept Checks are found at the end of each chapter.

CONCEPT CHECK 1.5

Should a basketball team's best player take all the team's shots?

A professional basketball team has a new assistant coach. The assistant notices that one player scores on a higher percentage of his shots than other players. Based on this information, the assistant suggests to the head coach that the star player should take *all* the shots. That way, the assistant reasons, the team will score more points and win more games.

On hearing this suggestion, the head coach fires his assistant for incompetence. What was wrong with the assistant's idea?

SEVEN CORE PRINCIPLES REFERENCES

There are seven Core Principles that this text focuses on almost exclusively to ensure student mastery. Throughout the text, these principles are called out and are denoted by an icon in the margin. Again, the seven Core Principles are: Scarcity, Cost-Benefit, Incentive, Comparative Advantage, Increasing Opportunity Cost, Efficiency, and Equilibrium.

If the housing market were completely unregulated, the immediate response to such a high level of excess demand would be for rents to rise sharply. But here the law prevents them from rising above $800. Many other ways exist, however, in which market participants can respond to the pressures of excess demand. For instance, owners will quickly learn that they are free to spend less on maintaining their rental units. After all, if there are scores of renters knocking at the door of each vacant apartment, a landlord has considerable room to maneuver. Leaking pipes, peeling paint, broken furnaces, and other problems are less likely to receive prompt attention—or, indeed, any attention at all—when rents are set well below market-clearing levels.

Nor are reduced availability of apartments and poorer maintenance of existing apartments the only difficulties. With an offering of only 1 million apartments per month, we see in Figure 3.8 that there are renters who'd be willing to pay as much as $2,400 per month for an apartment. As the Incentive Principle suggests, this pressure will almost always find ways, legal or illegal, of expressing itself. In New York City, for example, it is not uncommon to see "finder's fees" or "key deposits" as high as several thousand dollars. Owners who cannot charge a market-clearing rent for their apartments also have the option of converting them to condominiums or co-ops, which enables them to sell their assets for prices much closer to their true economic value.

Incentive

ECONOMIC NATURALIST EXAMPLES

Each Economic Naturalist example starts with a question to spark interest in learning an answer. These examples fuel interest while teaching students to see each feature of their economic landscape as the reflection of one or more of the Core Principles.

The Economic Naturalist 1.1

Why do many hardware manufacturers include more than $1,000 worth of "free" software with a computer selling for only slightly more than that?

The software industry is different from many others in the sense that its customers care a great deal about product compatibility. When you and your classmates are working on a project together, for example, your task will be much simpler if you all use the same word-processing program. Likewise, an executive's life will be easier at tax time if her financial software is the same as her accountant's.

The implication is that the benefit of owning and using any given software program increases with the number of other people who use that same product. This unusual relationship gives the producers of the most popular programs an enormous advantage and often makes it hard for new programs to break into the market.

NUMBERED EXAMPLES

Throughout the text, numbered and titled examples are referenced and called out to further illustrate concepts. With our use of engaging questions and examples from everyday life to apply economic concepts, the ultimate goal is to see that each human action is a result of an implicit or explicit cost-benefit calculation.

Specialization   EXAMPLE 2.5

How costly is failure to specialize?

Suppose that in Example 2.4 Susan and Tom had divided their time so that each person's output consisted of half nuts and half coffee. How much of each good would Tom and Susan have been able to consume? How much could they have consumed if each had specialized in the activity for which he or she enjoyed a comparative advantage?

RECAP

Sprinkled throughout each chapter are Recap boxes that underscore and summarize the importance of the preceding material and key concept takeaways.

RECAP	MARKET EQUILIBRIUM

Market equilibrium, the situation in which all buyers and sellers are satisfied with their respective quantities at the market price, occurs at the intersection of the supply and demand curves. The corresponding price and quantity are called the *equilibrium price* and the *equilibrium quantity.*

Unless prevented by regulation, prices and quantities are driven toward their equilibrium values by the actions of buyers and sellers. If the price is initially too high, so that there is excess supply, frustrated sellers will cut their price in order to sell more. If the price is initially too low, so that there is excess demand, competition among buyers drives the price upward. This process continues until equilibrium is reached.

END-OF-CHAPTER FEATURES

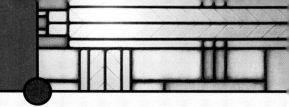

SUMMARY

Each chapter ends with a summary that reviews the key points and learning objectives to provide closure to the chapter.

○ SUMMARY ○

- The demand curve is a downward-sloping line that tells what quantity buyers will demand at any given price. The supply curve is an upward-sloping line that tells what quantity sellers will offer at any given price. *(LO1)*

- Alfred Marshall's model of supply and demand explains why neither cost of production nor value to the purchaser (as measured by willingness to pay) is, by itself, sufficient to explain why some goods are cheap and others are expensive. To explain variations in price, we must examine the interaction of cost and willingness to pay. As we've seen in this chapter, goods differ in price because of differences in their respective supply and demand curves. *(LO2)*

- Market equilibrium occurs when the quantity buyers demand at the market price is exactly the same as the quantity that sellers offer. The equilibrium price–quantity pair is the one at which the demand and supply curves intersect. In equilibrium, market price measures both the value of the last unit sold to buyers and the cost of the resources required to produce it. *(LO2)*

- When the price of a good lies above its equilibrium value, there is an excess supply of that good. Excess

3. An increase in supply will lead to a reduction in equilibrium price and an increase in equilibrium quantity.

4. A decrease in supply will lead to an increase in equilibrium price and a reduction in equilibrium quantity. *(LO3)*

- Incomes, tastes, population, expectations, and the prices of substitutes and complements are among the factors that shift demand schedules. Supply schedules, in turn, are primarily governed by such factors as technology, input prices, expectations, the number of sellers, and, especially for agricultural products, the weather. *(LO3)*

- The efficiency of markets in allocating resources does not eliminate social concerns about how goods and services are distributed among different people. For example, we often lament the fact many buyers enter the market with too little income to buy even the most basic goods and services. Concern for the well-being of the poor has motivated many governments to intervene in a variety of ways to alter the outcomes of market forces. Sometimes these interventions take the form of laws that peg prices below their equilibrium levels. Such laws almost invariably generate harmful, if unintended, consequences. Pro-

REVIEW QUESTIONS AND PROBLEMS

Approximately five review questions appear at the end of each chapter to test understanding of the logic behind economic concepts. The problems are crafted to help students internalize and extend core concepts. Learning objectives are also referenced at the end of each question and problem to reiterate the particular learning goal that is being examined.

○ REVIEW QUESTIONS ○

1. Explain the distinction between the horizontal and vertical interpretations of the demand curve. *(LO1)*

2. Why isn't knowing the cost of producing a good sufficient to predict its market price? *(LO2)*

3. In recent years, a government official proposed that gasoline price controls be imposed to protect the poor from rising gasoline prices. What evidence could you consult to discover whether this proposal was enacted? *(LO2)*

4. Distinguish between the meaning of the expressions "change in demand" and "change in the quantity demanded." *(LO3)*

5. Give an example of behavior you have observed that could be described as "smart for one but dumb for all." *(LO4)*

○ PROBLEMS ○

1. How would each of the following affect the U.S. market supply curve for corn? *(LO1)*
   a. A new and improved crop rotation technique is discovered.
   b. The price of fertilizer falls.
   c. The government offers new tax breaks to farmers.
   d. A tornado sweeps through Iowa.

McGraw Hill Education **connect** |ECONOMICS

SUPPLEMENTS FOR THE INSTRUCTOR

The following ancillaries are available for quick download and convenient access via the Instructor Resource material available through McGraw-Hill *Connect Plus®*.

Solutions Manual

Prepared by author Kate Antonovics, this manual provides detailed answers to the end-of-chapter questions.

Test Banks

Prepared by Richard Hansen of Hillsborough Community College (micro) and Mark Wilson of West Virginia University (macro), and carefully reviewed by author Kate Antonovics, each manual contains nearly 4,000 questions categorized by chapter learning objectives, AACSB learning categories, Bloom's Taxonomy objectives, and level of difficulty.

Computerized Test Bank

McGraw-Hill's EZ Test is a flexible and easy-to-use electronic testing program that allows you to create tests from book-specific items. It accommodates a wide range of question types and you can add your own questions. Multiple versions of the test can be created and any test can be exported for use with course management systems. EZ Test Online gives you a place to administer your EZ Test–created exams and quizzes online. Additionally, you can access the test bank through McGraw-Hill *Connect Plus*.

PowerPoints

Prepared by Per Norander, these slides contain a detailed, chapter-by-chapter review of the important ideas presented in the textbook, accompanied by animated graphs and slide notes. You can edit, print, or rearrange the slides to fit the needs of your course.

SUPPLEMENTS FOR THE STUDENT

Study Econ Mobile App

McGraw-Hill is proud to offer a mobile study app for students learning economics from Frank and Bernanke's *Principles of Macroeconomics,* sixth edition. The features of the Study Econ app include flashcards for all key terms, a basic math review, customizable self-quizzes, common mistakes, and games. For additional information please refer to the back inside cover of this book. Visit your mobile app store and download a trial version of the Frank Study Econ app today!

MCGRAW-HILL *CONNECT® ECONOMICS*

 **Less Managing. More Teaching. Greater Learning.** McGraw-Hill's *Connect® Economics* is an online assessment solution that connects students with the tools and resources they'll need to achieve success.

McGraw-Hill's *Connect Plus Economics* Features

Connect Economics offers a number of powerful tools and features to make managing assignments easier, so faculty can spend more time teaching. With *Connect Economics,* students can engage with their coursework anytime and anywhere, making the learning process more accessible and efficient. *Connect Economics* offers the features described here.

Simple Assignment Management

With *Connect Economics,* creating assignments is easier than ever, so you can spend more time teaching and less time managing. The assignment management function enables you to:

- Create and deliver assignments easily with selectable end-of-chapter questions and test bank items.

- Streamline lesson planning, student progress reporting, and assignment grading to make classroom management more efficient than ever.

- Go paperless with the eBook and online submission and grading of student assignments.

Smart Grading

Connect Economics helps students learn more efficiently by providing feedback and practice material when they need it, where they need it. The grading function enables you to:

- Have assignments scored automatically, giving students immediate feedback on their work and side-by-side comparisons with correct answers.

- Access and review each response; manually change grades or leave comments for students to review.

- Reinforce classroom concepts with practice tests and instant quizzes.

Instructor Library

The *Connect Economics* Instructor Library is your repository for additional resources to improve student engagement in and out of class. You can select and use any asset that enhances your lecture. The *Connect Economics* Instructor Library includes all of the instructor supplements for this text.

Student Resources

Any supplemental resources that align with the text for student use will be available through *Connect.*

Student Progress Tracking

Connect Economics keeps instructors informed about how each student, section, and class are performing, allowing for more productive use of lecture and office hours. The progress-tracking function enables you to:

- View scored work immediately and track individual or group performance with assignment and grade reports.

- Access an instant view of student or class performance relative to learning objectives.

- Collect data and generate reports required by many accreditation organizations, such as AACSB and AICPA.

Lecture Capture

Increase the attention paid to lecture discussion by decreasing the attention paid to note taking. Lecture Capture offers new ways for students to focus on the in-class discussion, knowing they can revisit important topics later. Lecture Capture enables you to:

- Record and distribute your lecture with the click of a button.

- Record and index PowerPoint presentations and anything shown on your computer so it is easily searchable, frame by frame.

- Offer access to lectures anytime and anywhere by computer, iPod, or mobile device.

- Increase intent listening and class participation by easing students' concerns about note taking. Lecture Capture will make it more likely you will see students' faces, not the tops of their heads.

Diagnostic and Adaptive Learning of Concepts: LearnSmart

LEARNSMART® Students want to make the best use of their study time. The LearnSmart adaptive self-study technology within *Connect Economics* provides students with a seamless combination of practice, assessment, and remediation for every concept in the textbook. LearnSmart's intelligent software adapts to every student response and automatically delivers concepts that advance students' understanding while reducing time devoted to the concepts already mastered. The result for every student is the fastest path to mastery of the chapter concepts. LearnSmart:

- Applies an intelligent concept engine to identify the relationships between concepts and to serve new concepts to each student only when he or she is ready.

- Adapts automatically to each student, so students spend less time on the topics they understand and practice more those they have yet to master.

- Provides continual reinforcement and remediation, but gives only as much guidance as students need.

- Integrates diagnostics as part of the learning experience.

- Enables you to assess which concepts students have efficiently learned on their own, thus freeing class time for more applications and discussion.

Smartbook

 Smartbook is an extension of Learn-Smart—an adaptive eBook that helps students focus their study time more effectively. As students read, Smartbook assesses comprehension and dynamically highlights where they need to study more.

For more information about *Connect Plus,* go to **connect .mheducation.com**, or contact your local McGraw-Hill sales representative.

MCGRAW-HILL'S CUSTOMER EXPERIENCE GROUP

We understand that getting the most from your new technology can be challenging. That's why our services don't stop after you purchase our products. You can e-mail our Product Specialists 24 hours a day to get product training online. Or you can search our knowledge bank of Frequently Asked Questions on our support website. For Customer Support, call **800-331-5094**, or visit **www.mhhe.com/support.**

TEGRITY CAMPUS

Tegrity Campus is a fully automated lecture capture solution used in traditional, hybrid, "flipped classes" and online courses to record lessons, lectures, and skills. Its personalized learning features make study time incredibly efficient and its ability to affordably scale brings this benefit to every student on campus. Patented search technology and real-time LMS integrations make Tegrity the market-leading solution and service.

MCGRAW-HILL CREATE

McGraw-Hill Create™ is a self-service website that allows you to create customized course materials using McGraw-Hill's comprehensive, cross-disciplinary content and digital products. You can even access third-party content such as readings, articles, cases, videos, and more. Arrange the content you've selected to match the scope and sequence of your course. Personalize your book with a cover design and choose the best format for your students— eBook, color print, or black-and-white print. And, when you are done, you'll receive a PDF review copy in just minutes!

COURSESMART

 Go paperless with eTextbooks from CourseSmart and move light years beyond traditional print textbooks. Read online or offline anytime, anywhere. Access your eTextbook on multiple devices with or without an Internet connection. CourseSmart eBooks include convenient, built-in tools that let you search topics quickly, add notes and highlights, copy/paste passages, and print any page.

BRIEF CONTENTS

CONTENTS

CORE PRINCIPLE 1
The Scarcity Principle
(also called the "No-Free-Lunch Principle")
Although we have boundless needs and wants, the resources available to us are limited. So having more of one good thing usually means having less of another.

Scarcity

CORE PRINCIPLE 2
The Cost-Benefit Principle
An individual (or a firm or a society) should take an action if, and only if, the extra benefits from taking the action are at least as great as the extra costs.

Cost-Benefit

CORE PRINCIPLE 3
The Incentive Principle
A person (or a firm or a society) is more likely to take an action if its benefit rises, and less likely to take it if its cost rises. In short, incentives matter.

Incentive

CORE PRINCIPLE 4
The Principle of Comparative Advantage
Everyone does best when each person (or each country) concentrates on the activities for which his or her opportunity cost is lowest.

Comparative Advantage

CORE PRINCIPLE 5
The Principle of Increasing Opportunity Cost
(also called the "Low-Hanging-Fruit Principle")
In expanding the production of any good, first employ those resources with the lowest opportunity cost, and only afterward turn to resources with higher opportunity costs.

Increasing Opportunity Cost

CORE PRINCIPLE 6
The Efficiency Principle
Efficiency is an important social goal because when the economic pie grows larger, everyone can have a larger slice.

Efficiency

CORE PRINCIPLE 7
The Equilibrium Principle
(also called the "No-Cash-on-the-Table Principle")
A market in equilibrium leaves no unexploited opportunities for individuals but may not exploit all gains achievable through collective action.

Equilibrium

ECONOMIC NATURALIST EXAMPLES

CHAPTER 1

Thinking Like an Economist

Nick Dolding/cultura/Corbis

PEOPLE OFTEN MAKE BAD DECISIONS BECAUSE THEY FAIL TO COMPARE THE RELEVANT COSTS AND BENEFITS

How many students are in your introductory economics class? Some classes have just 20 or so. Others average 35, 100, or 200 students. At some schools, introductory economics classes may have as many as 2,000 students. What size is best?

If cost were no object, the best size might be a single student. Think about it: the whole course, all term long, with just you and your professor! Everything could be custom-tailored to your own background and ability. You could cover the material at just the right pace. The tutorial format also would promote close communication and personal trust between you and your professor. And your grade would depend more heavily on what you actually learned than on your luck when taking multiple-choice exams. Let's suppose, for the sake of discussion, that students have been shown to learn best in the tutorial format.

Why, then, do so many introductory classes still have hundreds of students? The simple reason is that costs *do* matter. They matter not just to the university administrators who must build classrooms and pay faculty salaries, but also to *you*. The direct cost of providing you with your own personal introductory economics course might easily top $50,000. *Someone* has to pay these costs. In private universities, a large share of the cost would be recovered directly from higher tuition payments. In state universities, the

Are small classes "better" than large ones?

economics the study of how people make choices under conditions of scarcity and of the results of those choices for society

burden would be split between higher tuition payments and higher tax payments. But, in either case, the course would be unaffordable for most students.

With larger classes, of course, the cost per student goes down. For example, an introductory economics course with 300 students might cost as little as $200 per student. But a class that large would surely compromise the quality of the learning environment. Compared to the custom tutorial format, however, it would be dramatically more affordable.

In choosing what size introductory economics course to offer, then, university administrators confront a classic economic trade-off. In making the class larger, they lower the quality of instruction—a bad thing. At the same time, they reduce costs and hence the tuition students must pay—a good thing.

In this chapter, we'll introduce three simple principles that will help you understand and explain patterns of behavior you observe in the world around you. These principles also will help you avoid three pitfalls that plague decision makers in everyday life.

ECONOMICS: STUDYING CHOICE IN A WORLD OF SCARCITY

Even in rich societies like the United States, *scarcity* is a fundamental fact of life. There is never enough time, money, or energy to do everything we want to do or have everything we'd like to have. **Economics** is the study of how people make choices under conditions of scarcity and of the results of those choices for society.

In the class-size example just discussed, a motivated economics student might definitely prefer to be in a class of 20 rather than a class of 100, everything else being equal. But other things, of course, are not equal. Students can enjoy the benefits of having smaller classes, but only at the price of having less money for other activities. The student's choice inevitably will come down to the relative importance of competing activities.

That such trade-offs are widespread and important is one of the Core Principles of economics. We call it the *Scarcity Principle* because the simple fact of scarcity makes trade-offs necessary. Another name for the Scarcity Principle is the *No-Free-Lunch Principle* (which comes from the observation that even lunches that are given to you are never really free—somebody, somehow, always has to pay for them).

> **The Scarcity Principle (also called the No-Free-Lunch Principle):** Although we have boundless needs and wants, the resources available to us are limited. So having more of one good thing usually means having less of another.

Inherent in the idea of a trade-off is the fact that choice involves compromise between competing interests. Economists resolve such trade-offs by using cost-benefit analysis, which is based on the disarmingly simple principle that an action should be taken if, and only if, its benefits exceed its costs. We call this statement the *Cost-Benefit Principle*, and it, too, is one of the Core Principles of economics:

> **The Cost-Benefit Principle:** An individual (or a firm or a society) should take an action if, and only if, the extra benefits from taking the action are at least as great as the extra costs.

With the Cost-Benefit Principle in mind, let's think about our class-size question again. Imagine that classrooms come in only two sizes—100-seat lecture halls and 20-seat classrooms—and that your university currently offers introductory economics courses to classes of 100 students. Question: Should administrators reduce the class size to 20 students? Answer: Reduce if, and only if, the value of the improvement in instruction outweighs its additional cost.

This rule sounds simple. But to apply it we need some way to measure the relevant costs and benefits, a task that's often difficult in practice. If we make a few

Scarcity ⬤

Cost-Benefit ⬤

simplifying assumptions, however, we can see how the analysis might work. On the cost side, the primary expense of reducing class size from 100 to 20 is that we'll now need five professors instead of just one. We'll also need five smaller classrooms rather than a single big one, and this too may add slightly to the expense of the move. Let's suppose that classes with 20 cost $1,000 per student more than those with 100. Should administrators switch to the smaller class size? If they apply the Cost-Benefit Principle, they will realize that *doing so makes sense only if the value of attending the smaller class is at least $1,000 per student greater than the value of attending the larger class.*

Cost-Benefit

Would you (or your family) be willing to pay an extra $1,000 for a smaller class? If not, and if other students feel the same way, then sticking with the larger class size makes sense. But if you and others would be willing to pay the extra tuition, then reducing the class size makes good economic sense.

Notice that the "best" class size, from an economic point of view, will generally not be the same as the "best" size from the point of view of an educational psychologist. That's because the economic definition of "best" takes into account both the benefits *and* the costs of different class sizes. The psychologist ignores costs and looks only at the learning benefits of different class sizes.

In practice, of course, different people feel differently about the value of smaller classes. People with high incomes, for example, tend to be willing to pay more for the advantage. That helps to explain why average class size is smaller, and tuition higher, at private schools whose students come predominantly from high-income families.

The cost-benefit framework for thinking about the class-size problem also suggests a possible reason for the gradual increase in average class size that has been taking place in American colleges and universities. During the last 30 years, professors' salaries have risen sharply, making smaller classes more costly. During the same period, median family income—and hence the willingness to pay for smaller classes—has remained roughly constant. When the cost of offering smaller classes goes up but willingness to pay for smaller classes does not, universities shift to larger class sizes.

If Bill Gates saw a $100 bill lying on the sidewalk, would it be worth his time to pick it up?

Scarcity and the trade-offs that result also apply to resources other than money. Bill Gates is one of the richest men on Earth. His wealth was once estimated at over $100 billion. That's more than the combined wealth of the poorest 40 percent of Americans. Gates could buy more houses, cars, vacations, and other consumer goods than he could possibly use. Yet he, like the rest of us, has only 24 hours each day and a limited amount of energy. So even he confronts trade-offs. Any activity he pursues—whether it be building his business empire or redecorating his mansion or tending to his charitable foundation—uses up time and energy that he could otherwise spend on other things. Indeed, someone once calculated that the value of Gates's time is so great that pausing to pick up a $100 bill from the sidewalk simply wouldn't be worth his while.

APPLYING THE COST-BENEFIT PRINCIPLE

In studying choice under scarcity, we'll usually begin with the premise that people are **rational,** which means they have well-defined goals and try to fulfill them as best they can. The Cost-Benefit Principle is a fundamental tool for the study of how rational people make choices.

As in the class-size example, often the only real difficulty in applying the cost-benefit rule is to come up with reasonable measures of the relevant benefits and costs. Only in rare instances will exact dollar measures be conveniently available. But the cost-benefit framework can lend structure to your thinking even when no relevant market data are available.

To illustrate how we proceed in such cases, the following example asks you to decide whether to perform an action whose cost is described only in vague, qualitative terms.

rational person someone with well-defined goals who tries to fulfill those goals as best he or she can

Comparing Costs and Benefits	**EXAMPLE 1.1**

Should you walk downtown to save $10 on a $25 computer game?

Imagine you are about to buy a $25 computer game at the nearby campus store when a friend tells you that the same game is on sale at a downtown store for only $15. If the downtown store is a 30-minute walk away, where should you buy the game?

<table><tr><td>Cost-Benefit ⊖</td></tr></table>

The Cost-Benefit Principle tells us that you should buy it downtown if the benefit of doing so exceeds the cost. The benefit of taking any action is the dollar value of everything you gain by taking it. Here, the benefit of buying downtown is exactly $10, since that's the amount you'll save on the price of the game. The cost of taking any action is the dollar value of everything you give up by taking it. Here, the cost of buying downtown is the dollar value you assign to the time and trouble it takes to make the trip. But how do we estimate that value?

One way is to perform the following hypothetical auction. Imagine that a stranger has offered to pay you to do an errand that involves the same walk downtown (perhaps to drop off a letter for her at the post office). If she offered you a payment of, say, $1,000, would you accept? If so, we know that your cost of walking downtown and back must be less than $1,000. Now imagine her offer being reduced in small increments until you finally refuse the last offer. For example, if you'd agree to walk downtown and back for $9.00 but not for $8.99, then your cost of making the trip is $9.00. In this case, you should buy the game downtown because the $10 you'll save (your benefit) is greater than your $9.00 cost of making the trip.

But suppose your cost of making the trip had been greater than $10. In that case, your best bet would have been to buy the game from the nearby campus store. Confronted with this choice, different people may choose differently, depending on how costly they think it is to make the trip downtown. But although there is no uniquely correct choice, most people who are asked what they would do in this situation say they would buy the game downtown.

ECONOMIC SURPLUS

economic surplus the benefit of taking an action minus its cost

Suppose that in Example 1.1 your "cost" of making the trip downtown was $9. Compared to the alternative of buying the game at the campus store, buying it downtown resulted in an **economic surplus** of $1, the difference between the benefit of making the trip and its cost. In general, your goal as an economic decision maker is to choose those actions that generate the largest possible economic surplus. This means taking all actions that yield a positive total economic surplus, which is just another way of restating the Cost-Benefit Principle.

<table><tr><td>Cost-Benefit ⊖</td></tr></table>

Note that the fact that your best choice was to buy the game downtown doesn't imply that you *enjoy* making the trip, any more than choosing a large class means that you prefer large classes to small ones. It simply means that the trip is less unpleasant than the prospect of paying $10 extra for the game. Once again, you've faced a trade-off. In this case, the choice was between a cheaper game and the free time gained by avoiding the trip.

OPPORTUNITY COST

opportunity cost the value of what must be forgone to undertake an activity

Of course, your mental auction could have produced a different outcome. Suppose, for example, that the time required for the trip is the only time you have left to study for a difficult test the next day. Or suppose you are watching one of your favorite movies on cable, or that you are tired and would love a short nap. In such cases, we say that the **opportunity cost** of making the trip—that is, the value of what you must sacrifice to walk downtown and back—is high and you are more likely to decide against making the trip.

Strictly speaking, your opportunity cost of engaging in an activity is the value of everything you must sacrifice to engage in it. For instance, if seeing a movie requires not only that you buy a $10 ticket but also that you give up a $20 babysitting job that you would have been willing to do for free, then the opportunity cost of seeing the film is $30.

Under this definition, *all* costs—both implicit and explicit—are opportunity costs. Unless otherwise stated, we will adhere to this strict definition.

We must warn you, however, that some economists use the term *opportunity cost* to refer only to the implicit value of opportunities forgone. Thus, in the example just discussed, these economists wouldn't include the $10 ticket price when calculating the opportunity cost of seeing the film. But virtually all economists would agree that your opportunity cost of not doing the babysitting job is $20.

In the previous example, if watching the last hour of the cable TV movie is the most valuable opportunity that conflicts with the trip downtown, the opportunity cost of making the trip is the dollar value you place on pursuing that opportunity. It is the largest amount you'd be willing to pay to avoid missing the end of the movie. Note that the opportunity cost of making the trip is not the combined value of *all* possible activities you could have pursued, but only the value of your *best* alternative—the one you would have chosen had you not made the trip.

Throughout the text we'll pose concept checks like the one that follows. You'll find that pausing to answer them will help you to master key concepts in economics. Because doing these concept checks isn't very costly (indeed, many students report that they're actually fun), the Cost-Benefit Principle indicates that it's well worth your while to do them.

| Cost-Benefit |

CONCEPT CHECK 1.1

You would again save $10 by buying the game downtown rather than at the campus store, but your cost of making the trip is now $12, not $9. By how much would your economic surplus be smaller if you bought the game downtown rather than at the campus store?

THE ROLE OF ECONOMIC MODELS

Economists use the Cost-Benefit Principle as an abstract model of how an idealized rational individual would choose among competing alternatives. (By "abstract model" we mean a simplified description that captures the essential elements of a situation and allows us to analyze them in a logical way.) A computer model of a complex phenomenon like climate change, which must ignore many details and includes only the major forces at work, is an example of an abstract model.

Noneconomists are sometimes harshly critical of the economist's cost-benefit model on the grounds that people in the real world never conduct hypothetical mental auctions before deciding whether to make trips downtown. But this criticism betrays a fundamental misunderstanding of how abstract models can help to explain and predict human behavior. Economists know perfectly well that people don't conduct hypothetical mental auctions when they make simple decisions. All the Cost-Benefit Principle really says is that a rational decision is one that is explicitly or implicitly based on a weighing of costs and benefits.

Most of us make sensible decisions most of the time, without being consciously aware that we are weighing costs and benefits, just as most people ride a bike without being consciously aware of what keeps them from falling. Through trial and error, we gradually learn what kinds of choices tend to work best in different contexts, just as bicycle riders internalize the relevant laws of physics, usually without being conscious of them.

Even so, learning the explicit principles of cost-benefit analysis can help us make better decisions, just as knowing about physics can help in learning to ride a bicycle.

For instance, when a young economist was teaching his oldest son to ride a bike, he followed the time-honored tradition of running alongside the bike and holding onto his son, then giving him a push and hoping for the best. After several hours and painfully skinned elbows and knees, his son finally got it. A year later, someone pointed out that the trick to riding a bike is to turn slightly in whichever direction the bike is leaning. Of course! The economist passed this information along to his second son, who learned to ride almost instantly. Just as knowing a little physics can help you learn to ride a bike, knowing a little economics can help you make better decisions.

RECAP	COST-BENEFIT ANALYSIS

Scarcity is a basic fact of economic life. Because of it, having more of one good thing almost always means having less of another (the Scarcity Principle). The Cost-Benefit Principle holds that an individual (or a firm or a society) should take an action if, and only if, the extra benefit from taking the action is at least as great as the extra cost. The benefit of taking any action minus the cost of taking the action is called the *economic surplus* from that action. Hence, the Cost-Benefit Principle suggests that we take only those actions that create additional economic surplus.

THREE IMPORTANT DECISION PITFALLS[1]

Rational people will apply the Cost-Benefit Principle most of the time, although probably in an intuitive and approximate way, rather than through explicit and precise calculation. Knowing that rational people tend to compare costs and benefits enables economists to predict their likely behavior. As noted earlier, for example, we can predict that students from wealthy families are more likely than others to attend colleges that offer small classes. (Again, while the cost of small classes is the same for all families, their benefit, as measured by what people are willing to pay for them, tends to be higher for wealthier families.)

Yet researchers have identified situations in which people tend to apply the Cost-Benefit Principle inconsistently. In these situations, the Cost-Benefit Principle may not predict behavior accurately. But it proves helpful in another way, by identifying specific strategies for avoiding bad decisions.

PITFALL 1: MEASURING COSTS AND BENEFITS AS PROPORTIONS RATHER THAN ABSOLUTE DOLLAR AMOUNTS

As the next example makes clear, even people who seem to know they should weigh the pros and cons of the actions they are contemplating sometimes don't have a clear sense of how to measure the relevant costs and benefits.

Comparing Costs and Benefits   **EXAMPLE 1.2**

Should you walk downtown to save $10 on a $2,020 laptop computer?

You are about to buy a $2,020 laptop computer at the nearby campus store when a friend tells you that the same computer is on sale at a downtown store for only $2,010. If the downtown store is half an hour's walk away, where should you buy the computer?

---

[1]The examples in this section are inspired by the pioneering research of Daniel Kahneman and the late Amos Tversky. Kahneman was awarded the 2002 Nobel Prize in economics for his efforts to integrate insights from psychology into economics. You can read more about this work in Kahneman's brilliant 2011 book, *Thinking Fast and Slow* (New York: Macmillan).

Assuming that the laptop is light enough to carry without effort, the structure of this example is exactly the same as that of Example 1.1. The only difference is that the price of the laptop is dramatically higher than the price of the computer game. As before, the benefit of buying downtown is the dollar amount you'll save, namely, $10. And since it's exactly the same trip, its cost also must be the same as before. So if you are perfectly rational, you should make the same decision in both cases. Yet when people are asked what they would do in these situations, the overwhelming majority say they'd walk downtown to buy the game but would buy the laptop at the campus store. When asked to explain, most of them say something like "The trip was worth it for the game because you save 40 percent, but not worth it for the laptop because you save only $10 out of $2,020."

This is faulty reasoning. The benefit of the trip downtown is not the *proportion* you save on the original price. Rather, it is the *absolute dollar amount* you save. The benefit of walking downtown to buy the laptop is $10, exactly the same as for the computer game. And since the cost of the trip must also be the same in both cases, the economic surplus from making both trips must be exactly the same. That means that a rational decision maker would make the same decision in both cases. Yet, as noted, most people choose differently.

The pattern of faulty reasoning in the decision just discussed is one of several decision pitfalls to which people are often prone. In the discussion that follows, we will identify two additional decision pitfalls. In some cases, people ignore costs or benefits that they ought to take into account. On other occasions they are influenced by costs or benefits that are irrelevant.

CONCEPT CHECK 1.2

Which is more valuable: saving $100 on a $2,000 plane ticket to Tokyo or saving $90 on a $200 plane ticket to Chicago?

PITFALL 2: IGNORING IMPLICIT COSTS

Sherlock Holmes, Arthur Conan Doyle's legendary detective, was successful because he saw details that most others overlooked. In *Silver Blaze,* Holmes is called on to investigate the theft of an expensive racehorse from its stable. A Scotland Yard inspector assigned to the case asks Holmes whether some particular aspect of the crime requires further study. "Yes," Holmes replies, and describes "the curious incident of the dog in the nighttime." "The dog did nothing in the nighttime," responds the puzzled inspector. But, as Holmes realized, that was precisely the problem! The watchdog's failure to bark when Silver Blaze was stolen meant that the watchdog knew the thief. This clue ultimately proved the key to unraveling the mystery.

Just as we often don't notice when a dog fails to bark, many of us tend to overlook the implicit value of activities that fail to happen. As discussed earlier, however, intelligent decisions require taking the value of forgone opportunities properly into account.

The opportunity cost of an activity, once again, is the value of all that must be forgone in order to engage in that activity. If buying a computer game downtown means not watching the last hour of a movie, then the value to you of watching the end of that movie is an implicit cost of the trip. Many people make bad decisions because they tend to ignore the value of such forgone opportunities. To avoid overlooking implicit costs, economists often translate questions like "Should I walk downtown?" into ones like "Should I walk downtown or watch the end of the movie?"

Implicit costs are like dogs that fail to bark in the night.

| **Implicit Cost** | **EXAMPLE 1.3** |

Should you use your frequent-flyer coupon to fly to Fort Lauderdale for spring break?

With spring break only a week away, you are still undecided about whether to go to Fort Lauderdale with a group of classmates at the University of Iowa. The round-trip airfare from Cedar Rapids is $500, but you have a frequent-flyer coupon you could use for the trip. All other relevant costs for the vacation week at the beach total exactly $1,000. The most you would be willing to pay for the Fort Lauderdale vacation is $1,350. That amount is your benefit of taking the vacation. Your only alternative use for your frequent-flyer coupon is for your trip to Boston the weekend after spring break to attend your brother's wedding. (Your coupon expires shortly thereafter.) If the Cedar Rapids–Boston round-trip airfare is $400, should you use your frequent-flyer coupon to fly to Fort Lauderdale for spring break?

| Cost-Benefit ◯ |

Is your flight to Fort Lauderdale "free" if you travel on a frequent-flyer coupon?

The Cost-Benefit Principle tells us that you should go to Fort Lauderdale if the benefits of the trip exceed its costs. If not for the complication of the frequent-flyer coupon, solving this problem would be a straightforward matter of comparing your benefit from the week at the beach to the sum of all relevant costs. And since your airfare and other costs would add up to $1,500, or $150 more than your benefit from the trip, you would not go to Fort Lauderdale.

But what about the possibility of using your frequent-flyer coupon to make the trip? Using it for that purpose might make the flight to Fort Lauderdale seem free, suggesting you'd reap an economic surplus of $350 by making the trip. But doing so also would mean you'd have to fork over $400 for your airfare to Boston. So the implicit cost of using your coupon to go to Fort Lauderdale is really $400. If you use it for that purpose, the trip still ends up being a loser because the cost of the vacation, $1,400, exceeds the benefit by $50. In cases like these, you're much more likely to decide sensibly if you ask yourself, "Should I use my frequent-flyer coupon for this trip or save it for an upcoming trip?"

We cannot emphasize strongly enough that the key to using the Cost-Benefit Principle correctly lies in recognizing precisely what taking a given action prevents us from doing. Concept Check 1.3 illustrates this point by modifying the details of Example 1.3 slightly.

CONCEPT CHECK 1.3

Refer to given information in Example 1.3, but this time your frequent-flyer coupon expires in a week, so your only chance to use it will be for the Fort Lauderdale trip. Should you use your coupon?

PITFALL 3: FAILURE TO THINK AT THE MARGIN

When deciding whether to take an action, the only relevant costs and benefits are those that would occur as a result of taking the action. Sometimes people are influenced by costs they ought to ignore. Other times they compare the wrong costs and benefits. *The only costs that should influence a decision about whether to take an action are those we can avoid by not taking the action. Similarly, the only benefits we should consider are those that would not occur unless the action were taken.* As a practical matter, however, many decision makers appear to be influenced by costs or benefits that would have occurred no matter what. Thus, people are often influenced by **sunk costs**—costs that are

sunk cost a cost that is beyond recovery at the moment a decision must be made

beyond recovery at the moment a decision is made. For example, money spent on a nontransferable, nonrefundable airline ticket is a sunk cost.

As the following example illustrates, sunk costs must be borne *whether or not an action is taken,* so they are irrelevant to the decision of whether to take the action.

Sunk Cost   **EXAMPLE 1.4**

How much should you eat at an all-you-can-eat restaurant?

Sangam, an Indian restaurant in Philadelphia, offers an all-you-can-eat lunch buffet for $10. Customers pay $10 at the door, and no matter how many times they refill their plates, there is no additional charge. One day, as a goodwill gesture, the owner of the restaurant tells 20 randomly selected guests that their lunch is on the house. The remaining guests pay the usual price. If all diners are rational, will there be any difference in the average quantity of food consumed by people in these two groups?

Having eaten their first helping, diners in each group confront the following question: "Should I go back for another helping?" For rational diners, if the benefit of doing so exceeds the cost, the answer is yes; otherwise it is no. Note that at the moment of decision, the $10 charge for the lunch is a sunk cost. Those who paid it have no way to recover it. Thus, for both groups, the (extra) cost of another helping is exactly zero. And since the people who received the free lunch were chosen at random, there's no reason their appetites or incomes should be any different from those of other diners. The benefit of another helping thus should be the same, on average, for people in both groups. And since their respective costs and benefits are the same, the two groups should eat the same number of helpings, on average.

Psychologists and economists have experimental evidence, however, that people in such groups do *not* eat similar amounts.[2] In particular, those for whom the luncheon charge is not waived tend to eat substantially more than those for whom the charge is waived. People in the former group seem somehow determined to "get their money's worth." Their implicit goal is apparently to minimize the average cost per bite of the food they eat. Yet minimizing average cost is not a particularly sensible objective. It brings to mind the man who drove his car on the highway at night, even though he had nowhere to go, because he wanted to boost his average fuel economy. The irony is that diners who are determined to get their money's worth usually end up eating too much.

The fact that the cost-benefit criterion failed the test of prediction in Example 1.4 does nothing to invalidate its advice about what people *should* do. If you are letting sunk costs influence your decisions, you can do better by changing your behavior.

In addition to paying attention to costs and benefits that should be ignored, people often use incorrect measures of the relevant costs and benefits. This error often occurs when we must choose the *extent* to which an activity should be pursued (as opposed to choosing whether to pursue it at all). We can apply the Cost-Benefit Principle in such situations by repeatedly asking the question "Should I increase the level at which I am currently pursuing the activity?"

In attempting to answer this question, the focus should always be on the benefit and cost of an *additional* unit of activity. To emphasize this focus, economists refer to the cost of an additional unit of activity as its **marginal cost.** Similarly, the benefit of an additional unit of the activity is its **marginal benefit.**

marginal cost the increase in total cost that results from carrying out one additional unit of an activity

marginal benefit the increase in total benefit that results from carrying out one additional unit of an activity

[2]See, for example, Richard Thaler, "Toward a Positive Theory of Consumer Choice," *Journal of Economic Behavior and Organization* 1, no. 1 (1980).

When the problem is to discover the proper level for an activity, the cost-benefit rule is to keep increasing the level as long as the marginal benefit of the activity exceeds its marginal cost. As the following example illustrates, however, people often fail to apply this rule correctly.

Focusing on Marginal Costs and Benefits   EXAMPLE 1.5

Should NASA expand the space shuttle program from four launches per year to five?

Professor Kösten Banifoot, a prominent supporter of the National Aeronautics and Space Administration's (NASA) space shuttle program, estimated that the gains from the program are currently $24 billion per year (an average of $6 billion per launch) and that its costs are currently $20 billion per year (an average of $5 billion per launch). On the basis of these estimates, Professor Banifoot testified before Congress that NASA should definitely expand the space shuttle program. Should Congress follow his advice?

average cost the total cost of undertaking *n* units of an activity divided by *n*

average benefit the total benefit of undertaking *n* units of an activity divided by *n*

To discover whether the advice makes economic sense, we must compare the marginal cost of a launch to its marginal benefit. The professor's estimates, however, tell us only the **average cost** and **average benefit** of the program. These are, respectively, the total cost of the program divided by the number of launches and the total benefit divided by the number of launches. Knowing the average benefit and average cost per launch for all shuttles launched thus far is simply not useful for deciding whether to expand the program. Of course, the average cost of the launches undertaken so far *might* be the same as the cost of adding another launch. But it also might be either higher or lower than the marginal cost of a launch. The same holds true regarding average and marginal benefits.

Suppose, for the sake of discussion, that the benefit of an additional launch is in fact the same as the average benefit per launch thus far, $6 billion. Should NASA add another launch? Not if the cost of adding the fifth launch would be more than $6 billion. And the fact that the average cost per launch is only $5 billion simply does not tell us anything about the marginal cost of the fifth launch.

Suppose, for example, that the relationship between the number of shuttles launched and the total cost of the program is as described in Table 1.1. The average cost per launch (third column) when there are four launches would then be $20 billion/4 = $5 billion per launch, just as Professor Banifoot testified. But note in the second column of the table that adding a fifth launch would raise costs from $20 billion to $32 billion, making the marginal cost of the fifth launch $12 billion. So if the benefit of an additional launch is $6 billion, increasing the number of launches from four to five would make absolutely no economic sense.

TABLE 1.1
How Total Cost Varies with the Number of Launches

Number of launches	Total cost ($ billions)	Average cost ($ billion/launch)
0	0	0
1	3	3
2	7	3.5
3	12	4
4	20	5
5	32	6.4

The following example illustrates how to apply the Cost-Benefit Principle correctly in this case.

Focusing on Marginal Costs and Benefits   EXAMPLE 1.6

How many space shuttles should NASA launch?

NASA must decide how many space shuttles to launch. The benefit of each launch is estimated to be $6 billion, and the total cost of the program again depends on the number of launches as shown in Table 1.1. How many shuttles should NASA launch?

NASA should continue to launch shuttles as long as the marginal benefit of the program exceeds its marginal cost. In this example, the marginal benefit is constant at $6 billion per launch, regardless of the number of shuttles launched. NASA should thus keep launching shuttles as long as the marginal cost per launch is less than or equal to $6 billion.

Applying the definition of marginal cost to the total cost entries in the second column of Table 1.1 yields the marginal cost values in the third column of Table 1.2. (Because marginal cost is the change in total cost that results when we change the number of launches by one, we place each marginal cost entry midway between the rows showing the corresponding total cost entries.) Thus, for example, the marginal cost of increasing the number of launches from one to two is $4 billion, the difference between the $7 billion total cost of two launches and the $3 billion total cost of one launch.

TABLE 1.2
How Marginal Cost Varies with the Number of Launches

Number of launches	Total cost ($ billions)	Marginal cost ($ billion/launch)
0	0	
		3
1	3	
		4
2	7	
		5
3	12	
		8
4	20	
		12
5	32	

As we see from a comparison of the $6 billion marginal benefit per launch with the marginal cost entries in the third column of Table 1.2, the first three launches satisfy the cost-benefit test, but the fourth and fifth launches do not. NASA should thus launch three space shuttles.

CONCEPT CHECK 1.4

If the marginal benefit of each launch had been not $6 billion but $9 billion, how many shuttles should NASA have launched?

The cost-benefit framework emphasizes that the only relevant costs and benefits in deciding whether to pursue an activity further are *marginal* costs and benefits— measures that correspond to the *increment* of activity under consideration. In many contexts, however, people seem more inclined to compare the *average* cost and benefit of the activity. As Example 1.5 made clear, increasing the level of an activity may not be justified, even though its average benefit at the current level is significantly greater than its average cost.

CONCEPT CHECK 1.5

Should a basketball team's best player take all the team's shots?

A professional basketball team has a new assistant coach. The assistant notices that one player scores on a higher percentage of his shots than other players. Based on this information, the assistant suggests to the head coach that the star player should take *all* the shots. That way, the assistant reasons, the team will score more points and win more games.

On hearing this suggestion, the head coach fires his assistant for incompetence. What was wrong with the assistant's idea?

RECAP	THREE IMPORTANT DECISION PITFALLS

1. **The pitfall of measuring costs or benefits proportionally.** Many decision makers treat a change in cost or benefit as insignificant if it constitutes only a small proportion of the original amount. Absolute dollar amounts, not proportions, should be employed to measure costs and benefits.

2. **The pitfall of ignoring implicit costs.** When performing a cost-benefit analysis of an action, it is important to account for all relevant costs, including the implicit value of alternatives that must be forgone in order to carry out the action. A resource (such as a frequent-flyer coupon) may have a high implicit cost, even if you originally got it "for free," if its best alternative use has high value. The identical resource may have a low implicit cost, however, if it has no good alternative uses.

3. **The pitfall of failing to think at the margin.** When deciding whether to perform an action, the only costs and benefits that are relevant are those that would result from taking the action. It is important to ignore sunk costs—those costs that cannot be avoided even if the action isn't taken. Even though a ticket to a concert may have cost you $100, if you've already bought it and cannot sell it to anyone else, the $100 is a sunk cost and shouldn't influence your decision about whether to go to the concert. It's also important not to confuse average costs and benefits with marginal costs and benefits. Decision makers often have ready information about the total cost and benefit of an activity, and from these it's simple to compute the activity's average cost and benefit. A common mistake is to conclude that an activity should be increased if its average benefit exceeds its average cost. The Cost-Benefit Principle tells us that the level of an activity should be increased if, and only if, its *marginal* benefit exceeds its *marginal* cost.

Some costs and benefits, especially marginal costs and benefits and implicit costs, are important for decision making, while others, like sunk costs and average costs and benefits, are essentially irrelevant. This conclusion is implicit in our original statement of the Cost-Benefit Principle (an action should be taken if, and only if, the extra benefits of taking it exceed the extra costs). When we encounter additional examples of decision pitfalls, we will flag them by inserting the icon for the Cost-Benefit Principle in the margin.

Cost-Benefit

NORMATIVE ECONOMICS VERSUS POSITIVE ECONOMICS

The examples discussed in the preceding section make the point that people *sometimes* choose irrationally. We must stress that our purpose in discussing these examples was not to suggest that people *generally* make irrational choices. On the contrary, most people appear to choose sensibly most of the time, especially when their decisions are important or familiar ones. The economist's focus on rational choice thus offers not only useful advice about making better decisions, but also a basis for predicting and explaining human behavior. We used the cost-benefit approach in this way when discussing how rising faculty salaries have led to larger class sizes. And as we will see, similar reasoning helps to explain human behavior in virtually every other domain.

The Cost-Benefit Principle is an example of a **normative economic principle,** one that provides guidance about how we *should* behave. For example, according to the Cost-Benefit Principle, we should ignore sunk costs when making decisions about the future. As our discussion of the various decision pitfalls makes clear, however, the Cost-Benefit Principle is not always a **positive,** or descriptive, **economic principle,** one that describes how we actually *will* behave. As we saw, the Cost-Benefit Principle can be tricky to implement, and people sometimes fail to heed its prescriptions.

That said, we stress that knowing the relevant costs and benefits surely does enable us to predict how people will behave much of the time. If the benefit of an action goes up, it is generally reasonable to predict that people will be more likely to take that action. And conversely, if the cost of an action goes up, the safest prediction will be that people will be less likely to take that action. This point is so important that we designate it as the *Incentive Principle.*

The Incentive Principle: A person (or a firm or a society) is more likely to take an action if its benefit rises, and less likely to take it if its cost rises. In short, incentives matter.

The Incentive Principle is a positive economic principle. It stresses that the relevant costs and benefits usually help us predict behavior, but at the same time does not insist that people behave rationally in each instance. For example, if the price of heating oil were to rise sharply, we would invoke the Cost-Benefit Principle to say that people *should* turn their thermostats down, and invoke the Incentive Principle to predict that average thermostat settings *will* in fact go down.

normative economic principle one that says how people should behave

positive economic principle one that predicts how people will behave

⊘ Incentive

ECONOMICS: MICRO AND MACRO

By convention, we use the term **microeconomics** to describe the study of individual choices and of group behavior in individual markets. **Macroeconomics,** by contrast, is the study of the performance of national economies and of the policies that governments use to try to improve that performance. Macroeconomics tries to understand the determinants of such things as the national unemployment rate, the overall price level, and the total value of national output.

Our focus in this chapter is on issues that confront the individual decision maker, whether that individual confronts a personal decision, a family decision, a business decision, a government policy decision, or indeed any other type of decision. Further on, we'll consider economic models of groups of individuals such as all buyers or all sellers in a specific market. Later still we'll turn to broader economic issues and measures.

No matter which of these levels is our focus, however, our thinking will be shaped by the fact that, although economic needs and wants are effectively unlimited, the material and human resources that can be used to satisfy them are finite. Clear thinking about economic problems must therefore always take into account the idea of

microeconomics the study of individual choice under scarcity and its implications for the behavior of prices and quantities in individual markets

macroeconomics the study of the performance of national economies and the policies that governments use to try to improve that performance

trade-offs—the idea that having more of one good thing usually means having less of another. Our economy and our society are shaped to a substantial degree by the choices people have made when faced with trade-offs.

THE APPROACH OF THIS TEXT

Choosing the number of students to register in each class is just one of many important decisions in planning an introductory economics course. Another, to which the Scarcity Principle applies just as strongly, concerns which topics to include on the course syllabus. There's a virtually inexhaustible set of issues that might be covered in an introductory course, but only limited time in which to cover them. There's no free lunch. Covering some inevitably means omitting others.

All textbook authors are forced to pick and choose. A textbook that covered *all* the issues would take up more than a whole floor of your campus library. It is our firm view that most introductory textbooks try to cover far too much. One reason that each of us was drawn to the study of economics is that a relatively short list of the discipline's core ideas can explain a great deal of the behavior and events we see in the world around us. So rather than cover a large number of ideas at a superficial level, our strategy is to focus on this short list of core ideas, returning to each entry again and again, in many different contexts. This strategy will enable you to internalize these ideas remarkably well in the brief span of a single course. And the benefit of learning a small number of important ideas well will far outweigh the cost of having to ignore a host of other, less important ones.

So far, we've already encountered three core ideas: the Scarcity Principle, the Cost-Benefit Principle, and the Incentive Principle. As these core ideas reemerge in the course of our discussions, we'll call your attention to them. And shortly after a *new* core idea appears, we'll highlight it by formally restating it.

A second important element in our philosophy is a belief in the importance of active learning. In the same way that you can learn Spanish only by speaking and writing it, or tennis only by playing the game, you can learn economics only by *doing* economics. And because we want you to learn how to do economics, rather than just to read or listen passively as the authors or your instructor does economics, we'll make every effort to encourage you to stay actively involved.

For example, instead of just telling you about an idea, we'll usually first motivate the idea by showing you how it works in the context of a specific example. Often, these examples will be followed by concept checks for you to try, as well as applications that show the relevance of the idea to real life. Try working the concept checks *before* looking up the answers (which are at the back of the corresponding chapter).

Think critically about the applications: Do you see how they illustrate the point being made? Do they give you new insight into the issue? Work the problems at the end of the chapters and take extra care with those relating to points that you don't fully understand. Apply economic principles to the world around you. (We'll say more about this when we discuss economic naturalism below.) Finally, when you come across an idea or example that you find interesting, tell a friend about it. You'll be surprised to discover how much the mere act of explaining it helps you understand and remember the underlying principle. The more actively you can become engaged in the learning process, the more effective your learning will be.

ECONOMIC NATURALISM

With the rudiments of the cost-benefit framework under your belt, you are now in a position to become an "economic naturalist," someone who uses insights from economics to help make sense of observations from everyday life. People who have studied biology are able to observe and marvel at many details of nature that would otherwise have

Scarcity

escaped their notice. For example, on a walk in the woods in early April, the novice may see only trees. In contrast, the biology student notices many different species of trees and understands why some are already in leaf while others still lie dormant. Likewise, the novice may notice that in some animal species males are much larger than females, but the biology student knows that pattern occurs only in species in which males take several mates. Natural selection favors larger males in those species because their greater size helps them prevail in the often bloody contests among males for access to females. In contrast, males tend to be roughly the same size as females in monogamous species, in which there is much less fighting for mates.

Learning a few simple economic principles broadens our vision in a similar way. It enables us to see the mundane details of ordinary human existence in a new light. Whereas the uninitiated often fail even to notice these details, the economic naturalist not only sees them, but becomes actively engaged in the attempt to understand them. Let's consider a few examples of questions economic naturalists might pose for themselves.

The Economic Naturalist 1.1

Why do many hardware manufacturers include more than $1,000 worth of "free" software with a computer selling for only slightly more than that?

The software industry is different from many others in the sense that its customers care a great deal about product compatibility. When you and your classmates are working on a project together, for example, your task will be much simpler if you all use the same word-processing program. Likewise, an executive's life will be easier at tax time if her financial software is the same as her accountant's.

The implication is that the benefit of owning and using any given software program increases with the number of other people who use that same product. This unusual relationship gives the producers of the most popular programs an enormous advantage and often makes it hard for new programs to break into the market.

Recognizing this pattern, Intuit Corp. offered computer makers free copies of *Quicken*, its personal financial-management software. Computer makers, for their part, were only too happy to include the program, since it made their new computers more attractive to buyers. *Quicken* soon became the standard for personal financial-management programs. By giving away free copies of the program, Intuit "primed the pump," creating an enormous demand for upgrades of *Quicken* and for more advanced versions of related software. Thus, *TurboTax,* Intuit's personal income-tax software, has become the standard for tax-preparation programs.

Inspired by this success story, other software developers have jumped onto the bandwagon. Most hardware now comes bundled with a host of free software programs. Some software developers are even rumored to *pay* computer makers to include their programs!

The Economic Naturalist 1.1 illustrates a case in which the *benefit* of a product depends on the number of other people who own that product. As the next Economic Naturalist demonstrates, the *cost* of a product may also depend on the number of others who own it.

The Economic Naturalist 1.2

Why don't auto manufacturers make cars without heaters?

Virtually every new car sold in the United States today has a heater. But not every car has a satellite navigation system. Why this difference?

One might be tempted to answer that, although everyone *needs* a heater, people can get along without navigation systems. Yet heaters are of little use in places like Hawaii and southern California. What is more, cars produced as recently as the 1950s did *not* all have heaters. (The classified ad that led one young economic naturalist to his first car, a 1955 Pontiac, boasted that the vehicle had a radio, heater, and whitewall tires.)

Although heaters cost extra money to manufacture and are not useful in all parts of the country, they do not cost *much* money and are useful on at least a few days each year in most parts of the country. As time passed and people's incomes grew, manufacturers found that people were ordering fewer and fewer cars without heaters. At some point it actually became cheaper to put heaters in *all* cars, rather than bear the administrative expense of making some cars with heaters and others without. No doubt a few buyers would still order a car without a heater if they could save some money in the process, but catering to these customers is just no longer worth it.

Similar reasoning explains why certain cars today cannot be purchased without a satellite navigation system. Buyers of the 2015 BMW 750i, for example, got one whether they wanted it or not. Most buyers of this car, which sells for more than $75,000, have high incomes, so the overwhelming majority of them would have chosen to order a navigation system had it been sold as an option. Because of the savings made possible when all cars are produced with the same equipment, it would have actually cost BMW more to supply cars for the few who would want them without navigation systems.

Buyers of the least-expensive makes of car have much lower incomes on average than BMW 750i buyers. Accordingly, most of them have more pressing alternative uses for their money than to buy navigation systems for their cars, and this explains why some inexpensive makes continue to offer navigation systems only as options. But as incomes continue to grow, new cars without navigation systems will eventually disappear.

The insights afforded by The Economic Naturalist 1.2 suggest an answer to the following strange question:

The Economic Naturalist 1.3

Why do the keypad buttons on drive-up automated teller machines have Braille dots?

Braille dots on elevator buttons and on the keypads of walk-up automated teller machines enable blind people to participate more fully in the normal flow of daily activity. But even though blind people can do many remarkable things, they cannot drive automobiles on public roads. Why, then, do the manufacturers of automated teller machines install Braille dots on the machines at drive-up locations?

The answer to this riddle is that once the keypad molds have been manufactured, the cost of producing buttons with Braille dots is no higher than the cost of producing

Why do the keypad buttons on drive-up automated teller machines have Braille dots?

smooth buttons. Making both would require separate sets of molds and two different types of inventory. If the patrons of drive-up machines found buttons with Braille dots harder to use, there might be a reason to incur these extra costs. But since the dots pose no difficulty for sighted users, the best and cheapest solution is to produce only keypads with dots.

The preceding example was suggested by Cornell student Bill Tjoa, in response to the following assignment:

CONCEPT CHECK 1.6

In 500 words or less, use cost-benefit analysis to explain some pattern of events or behavior you have observed in your own environment.

There is probably no more useful step you can take in your study of economics than to perform several versions of the assignment in Concept Check 1.6. Students who do so almost invariably become lifelong economic naturalists. Their mastery of economic concepts not only does not decay with the passage of time, but it actually grows stronger. We urge you, in the strongest possible terms, to make this investment!

○ SUMMARY ○

- Economics is the study of how people make choices under conditions of scarcity and of the results of those choices for society. Economic analysis of human behavior begins with the assumption that people are rational—that they have well-defined goals and try to achieve them as best they can. In trying to achieve their goals, people normally face trade-offs: Because material and human resources are limited, having more of one good thing means making do with less of some other good thing. *(LO1)*

- Our focus in this chapter has been on how rational people make choices among alternative courses of action. Our basic tool for analyzing these decisions is cost-benefit analysis. The Cost-Benefit Principle says that a person should take an action if, and only if, the benefit of that action is at least as great as its cost. The benefit of an action is defined as the largest dollar amount the person would be willing to pay in order to take the action. The cost of an action is defined as the dollar value of everything the person must give up in order to take the action. *(LO2)*

- In using the cost-benefit framework, we need not presume that people choose rationally all the time. Indeed, we identified three common pitfalls that plague decision makers in all walks of life: a tendency to treat small proportional changes as insignificant, a tendency to ignore implicit costs, and a tendency to fail to think at the margin—for example, by failing to ignore sunk costs or by failing to compare marginal costs and benefits. *(LO3)*

- Often the question is not whether to pursue an activity but rather how many units of it to pursue. In these cases, the rational person pursues additional units as long as the marginal benefit of the activity (the benefit from pursuing an additional unit of it) exceeds its marginal cost (the cost of pursuing an additional unit of it). *(LO4)*

- Microeconomics is the study of individual choices and of group behavior in individual markets, while macroeconomics is the study of the performance of national economics and of the policies that governments use to try to improve economic performance.

○ CORE PRINCIPLES ○

Scarcity	**The Scarcity Principle (also called the No-Free-Lunch Principle)**
	Although we have boundless needs and wants, the resources available to us are limited. So having more of one good thing usually means having less of another.

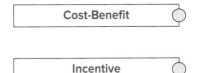

The Cost-Benefit Principle
An individual (or a firm or a society) should take an action if, and only if, the extra benefits from taking the action are at least as great as the extra costs.

The Incentive Principle
A person (or a firm or a society) is more likely to take an action if its benefit rises, and less likely to take it if its cost rises. In short, incentives matter.

○   KEY TERMS   ○

average benefit
average cost
economic surplus
economics
macroeconomics

marginal benefit
marginal cost
microeconomics
normative economic
 principle

opportunity cost
positive economic
 principle
rational person
sunk cost

○   REVIEW QUESTIONS   ○

1. A friend of yours on the tennis team says, "Private tennis lessons are definitely better than group lessons." Explain what you think he means by this statement. Then use the Cost-Benefit Principle to explain why private lessons are not necessarily the best choice for everyone. *(LO2)*

2. True or false: Your willingness to drive downtown to save $30 on a new appliance should depend on what fraction of the total selling price $30 is. Explain. *(LO3)*

3. Why might someone who is trying to decide whether to see a movie be more likely to focus on the $10 ticket price than on the $20 she would fail to earn by not babysitting? *(LO3)*

4. Many people think of their air travel as being free when they use frequent-flyer coupons. Explain why these people are likely to make wasteful travel decisions. *(LO3)*

5. Is the nonrefundable tuition payment you made to your university this semester a sunk cost? How would your answer differ if your university were to offer a full tuition refund to any student who dropped out of school during the first two months of the semester? *(LO3)*

○   PROBLEMS   ○

Visit your mobile app store and download the Frank: Study Econ app *today!*

1. Suppose the most you would be willing to pay to have a freshly washed car before going out on a date is $6. The smallest amount for which you would be willing to wash someone else's car is $3.50. You are going out this evening and your car is dirty. How much economic surplus would you receive from washing it? *(LO2)*

2. To earn extra money in the summer, you grow tomatoes and sell them at a local farmers' market for 30 cents per pound. By adding compost to your garden, you can increase your yield as shown in the table on the next page. If compost costs 50 cents per pound and your goal is to make as much profit as possible, how many pounds of compost should you add? *(LO2)*

3.* You and your friend Joe have identical tastes. At 2 p.m., you go to the local Ticketmaster outlet and buy a $30 ticket to a basketball game to be played that night in

*Denotes more difficult problem.

Pounds of compost	Pounds of tomatoes
	100
1	120
2	125
3	128
4	130
5	131
6	131.5

Syracuse, 50 miles north of your home in Ithaca. Joe plans to attend the same game, but because he cannot get to the Ticketmaster outlet, he plans to buy his ticket at the game. Tickets sold at the game cost only $25 because they carry no Ticketmaster surcharge. (Many people nonetheless pay the higher price at Ticketmaster, to be sure of getting good seats.) At 4 p.m., an unexpected snowstorm begins, making the prospect of the drive to Syracuse much less attractive than before (but ensuring the availability of good seats). If both you and Joe are rational, is one of you more likely to attend the game than the other? *(LO2)*

4. Tom is a mushroom farmer. He invests all his spare cash in additional mushrooms, which grow on otherwise useless land behind his barn. The mushrooms double in weight during their first year, after which time they are harvested and sold at a constant price per pound. Tom's friend Dick asks Tom for a loan of $200, which he promises to repay after one year. How much interest will Dick have to pay Tom in order for Tom to recover his opportunity cost of making the loan? Explain briefly. *(LO3)*

5. Suppose that in the last few seconds you devoted to question 1 on your physics exam you earned 4 extra points, while in the last few seconds you devoted to question 2 you earned 10 extra points. You earned a total of 48 and 12 points, respectively, on the two questions, and the total time you spent on each was the same. If you could take the exam again, how—if at all—should you reallocate your time between these questions? *(LO3)*

6. Martha and Sarah have the same preferences and incomes. Just as Martha arrived at the theater to see a play, she discovered that she had lost the $10 ticket she had purchased earlier. Sarah also just arrived at the theater planning to buy a ticket to see the same play when she discovered that she had lost a $10 bill from her wallet. If both Martha and Sarah are rational and both still have enough money to pay for a ticket, is one of them more likely than the other to go ahead and see the play anyway? *(LO3)*

7. Residents of your city are charged a fixed weekly fee of $6 for garbage collection. They are allowed to put out as many cans as they wish. The average household disposes of three cans of garbage per week under this plan. Now suppose that your city changes to a "tag" system. Each can of garbage to be collected must have a tag affixed to it. The tags cost $2 each and are not reusable. What effect do you think the introduction of the tag system will have on the total quantity of garbage collected in your city? Explain briefly. *(LO4)*

8. Once a week, Smith purchases a six-pack of cola and puts it in his refrigerator for his two children. He invariably discovers that all six cans are gone on the first day. Jones also purchases a six-pack of cola once a week for his two children, but unlike Smith, he tells them that each may drink no more than three cans per week. If the children use cost-benefit analysis each time they decide whether to drink a can of cola, explain why the cola lasts much longer at Jones's house than at Smith's. *(LO4)*

9.* For each long-distance call anywhere in the continental United States, a new phone service will charge users 30 cents per minute for the first 2 minutes and 2 cents per minute for additional minutes in each call. Tom's current phone service charges 10 cents per minute for all calls, and his calls are never shorter than 7 minutes. If Tom's dorm switches to the new phone service, what will happen to the average length of his calls? *(LO4)*

10.* The meal plan at university A lets students eat as much as they like for a fixed fee of $500 per semester. The average student there eats 250 pounds of food per semester. University B charges $500 for a book of meal tickets that entitles the student to eat 250 pounds of food per semester. If the student eats more than 250 pounds, he or she pays $2 for each additional pound; if the student eats less, he or she gets a $2 per pound refund. If students are rational, at which university will average food consumption be higher? Explain briefly. *(LO4)*

○ ANSWERS TO CONCEPT CHECKS ○

1.1 The benefit of buying the game downtown is again $10 but the cost is now $12, so your economic surplus would be $2 smaller than if you'd bought it at the campus store. *(LO2)*

1.2 Saving $100 is $10 more valuable than saving $90, even though the percentage saved is much greater in the case of the Chicago ticket. *(LO3)*

1.3 Since you now have no alternative use for your coupon, the opportunity cost of using it to pay for the Fort Lauderdale trip is zero. That means your economic surplus from the trip will be $1,350 − $1,000 = $350 > 0, so you should use your coupon and go to Fort Lauderdale. *(LO3)*

1.4 The marginal benefit of the fourth launch is $9 billion, which exceeds its marginal cost of $8 billion, so the fourth launch should be added. But the fifth launch should not, since its marginal cost ($12 billion) exceeds its marginal benefit ($9 billion). *(LO3)*

1.5 If the star player takes one more shot, some other player must take one less. The fact that the star player's *average* success rate is higher than the other players' does not mean that the probability of making his *next* shot (the marginal benefit of having him shoot once more) is higher than the probability of another player making his next shot. Indeed, if the best player took all his team's shots, the other team would focus its defensive effort entirely on him, in which case letting others shoot would definitely pay. *(LO3)*

*Denotes more difficult problem.

Working with Equations, Graphs, and Tables

Although many of the examples and most of the end-of-chapter problems in this book are quantitative, none requires mathematical skills beyond rudimentary high school algebra and geometry. In this brief appendix, we review some of the skills you'll need for dealing with these examples and problems.

One important skill is to be able to read simple verbal descriptions and translate the information they provide into the relevant equations or graphs. You'll also need to be able to translate information given in tabular form into an equation or graph, and sometimes you'll need to translate graphical information into a table or equation. Finally, you'll need to be able to solve simple systems with two equations and two unknowns. The following examples illustrate all the tools you'll need.

USING A VERBAL DESCRIPTION TO CONSTRUCT AN EQUATION

We begin with an example that shows how to construct a long-distance telephone billing equation from a verbal description of the billing plan.

| **A Verbal Description** | **EXAMPLE 1A.1** |

Your long-distance telephone plan charges you $5 per month plus 10 cents per minute for long-distance calls. Write an equation that describes your monthly telephone bill.

An **equation** is a simple mathematical expression that describes the relationship between two or more **variables,** or quantities that are free to assume different values in some range. The most common type of equation we'll work with contains two types of variables: **dependent variables** and **independent variables.** In this example, the dependent variable is the dollar amount of your monthly telephone bill and the independent variable is the variable on which your bill depends, namely, the volume of long-distance calls you make during the month. Your bill also depends on the $5 monthly fee and the 10 cents per minute charge. But, in this example, those amounts are **constants,** not variables. A constant, also called a **parameter,** is a quantity in an equation that is fixed in value, not free to vary. As the terms suggest, the dependent variable describes an outcome that depends on the value taken by the independent variable.

Once you've identified the dependent variable and the independent variable, choose simple symbols to represent them. In algebra courses, X is typically used to

equation a mathematical expression that describes the relationship between two or more variables

variable a quantity that is free to take a range of different values

dependent variable a variable in an equation whose value is determined by the value taken by another variable in the equation

independent variable a variable in an equation whose value determines the value taken by another variable in the equation

constant (or **parameter**) a quantity that is fixed in value

represent the independent variable and Y the dependent variable. Many people find it easier to remember what the variables stand for, however, if they choose symbols that are linked in some straightforward way to the quantities that the variables represent. Thus, in this example, we might use B to represent your monthly *bill* in dollars and T to represent the total *time* in minutes you spent during the month on long-distance calls.

Having identified the relevant variables and chosen symbols to represent them, you are now in a position to write the equation that links them:

$$B = 5 + 0.10T, \tag{1A.1}$$

where B is your monthly long-distance bill in dollars and T is your monthly total long-distance calling time in minutes. The fixed monthly fee (5) and the charge per minute (0.10) are parameters in this equation. Note the importance of being clear about the units of measure. Because B represents the monthly bill in dollars, we must also express the fixed monthly fee and the per-minute charge in dollars, which is why the latter number appears in Equation 1A.1 as 0.10 rather than 10. Equation 1A.1 follows the normal convention in which the dependent variable appears by itself on the left-hand side while the independent variable or variables and constants appear on the right-hand side.

Once we have the equation for the monthly bill, we can use it to calculate how much you'll owe as a function of your monthly volume of long-distance calls. For example, if you make 32 minutes of calls, you can calculate your monthly bill by simply substituting 32 minutes for T in Equation 1A.1:

$$B = 5 + 0.10(32) = 8.20. \tag{1A.2}$$

Your monthly bill when you make 32 minutes of calls is thus equal to $8.20.

CONCEPT CHECK 1A.1

Under the monthly billing plan described in Example 1A.1, how much would you owe for a month during which you made 45 minutes of long-distance calls?

GRAPHING THE EQUATION OF A STRAIGHT LINE

The next example shows how to portray the billing plan described in Example 1A.1 as a graph.

Graphing an Equation   **EXAMPLE 1A.2**

Construct a graph that portrays the monthly long-distance telephone billing plan described in Example 1A.1, putting your telephone charges, in dollars per month, on the vertical axis and your total volume of calls, in minutes per month, on the horizontal axis.

The first step in responding to this instruction is the one we just took, namely, to translate the verbal description of the billing plan into an equation. When graphing an equation, the normal convention is to use the vertical axis to represent the dependent variable and the horizontal axis to represent the independent variable. In Figure 1A.1, we therefore

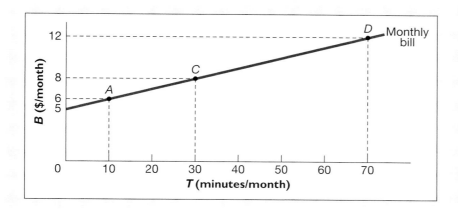

The Monthly Telephone Bill in Example 1A.1.

The graph of the equation $B = 5 + 0.10T$ is the straight line shown. Its vertical intercept is 5 and its slope is 0.10.

put B on the vertical axis and T on the horizontal axis. One way to construct the graph shown in the figure is to begin by plotting the monthly bill values that correspond to several different total amounts of long-distance calls. For example, someone who makes 10 minutes of calls during the month would have a bill of $B = 5 + 0.10(10) = \$6$. Thus, in Figure 1A.1 the value of 10 minutes per month on the horizontal axis corresponds to a bill of \$6 per month on the vertical axis (point A). Someone who makes 30 minutes of long-distance calls during the month will have a monthly bill of $B = 5 + 0.10(30) = \$8$, so the value of 30 minutes per month on the horizontal axis corresponds to \$8 per month on the vertical axis (point C). Similarly, someone who makes 70 minutes of long-distance calls during the month will have a monthly bill of $B = 5 + 0.10(70) = \$12$, so the value of 70 minutes on the horizontal axis corresponds to \$12 on the vertical axis (point D). The line joining these points is the graph of the monthly billing Equation 1A.1.

As shown in Figure 1A.1, the graph of the equation $B = 5 + 0.10T$ is a straight line. The parameter 5 is the **vertical intercept** of the line—the value of B when $T = 0$, or the point at which the line intersects the vertical axis. The parameter 0.10 is the **slope** of the line, which is the ratio of the **rise** of the line to the corresponding **run**. The ratio rise/run is simply the vertical distance between any two points on the line divided by the horizontal distance between those points. For example, if we choose points A and C in Figure 1A.1, the rise is $8 - 6 = 2$ and the corresponding run is $30 - 10 = 20$, so rise/run $= 2/20 = 0.10$. More generally, for the graph of any equation $Y = a + bX$, the parameter a is the vertical intercept and the parameter b is the slope.

vertical intercept in a straight line, the value taken by the dependent variable when the independent variable equals zero

slope in a straight line, the ratio of the vertical distance the straight line travels between any two points *(rise)* to the corresponding horizontal distance *(run)*

DERIVING THE EQUATION OF A STRAIGHT LINE FROM ITS GRAPH

The next example shows how to derive the equation for a straight line from a graph of the line.

Deriving an Equation from a Graph   EXAMPLE 1A.3

Figure 1A.2 shows the graph of the monthly billing plan for a new long-distance plan. What is the equation for this graph? How much is the fixed monthly fee under this plan? How much is the charge per minute?

FIGURE 1A.2

Another Monthly Long-Distance Plan.

The vertical distance between points A and C is $12 - 8 = 4$ units, and the horizontal distance between points A and C is $40 - 20 = 20$, so the slope of the line is $4/20 = 1/5 = 0.20$. The vertical intercept (the value of B when $T = 0$) is 4. So the equation for the billing plan shown is $B = 4 + 0.20T$.

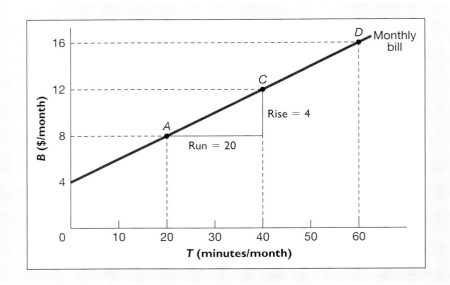

The slope of the line shown is the rise between any two points divided by the corresponding run. For points A and C, rise $= 12 - 8 = 4$ and run $= 40 - 20 = 20$, so the slope equals rise/run $= 4/20 = 1/5 = 0.20$. And since the horizontal intercept of the line is 4, its equation must be given by

$$B = 4 + 0.20T. \qquad (1A.3)$$

Under this plan, the fixed monthly fee is the value of the bill when $T = 0$, which is \$4. The charge per minute is the slope of the billing line, 0.20, or 20 cents per minute.

CONCEPT CHECK 1A.2

Write the equation for the billing plan shown in the accompanying graph. How much is its fixed monthly fee? Its charge per minute?

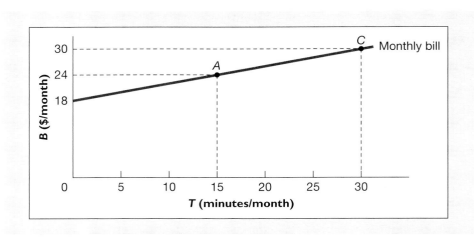

CHANGES IN THE VERTICAL INTERCEPT AND SLOPE

The next two examples and concept checks provide practice in seeing how a line shifts with a change in its vertical intercept or slope.

Change in Vertical Intercept

EXAMPLE 1A.4

Show how the billing plan whose graph is in Figure 1A.2 would change if the monthly fixed fee were increased from $4 to $8.

An increase in the monthly fixed fee from $4 to $8 would increase the vertical intercept of the billing plan by $4 but would leave its slope unchanged. An increase in the fixed fee thus leads to a parallel upward shift in the billing plan by $4, as shown in Figure 1A.3. For any given number of minutes of long-distance calls, the monthly charge

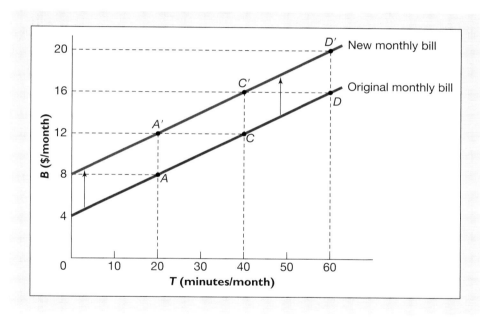

FIGURE 1A.3

The Effect of an Increase in the Vertical Intercept.

An increase in the vertical intercept of a straight line produces an upward parallel shift in the line.

on the new bill will be $4 higher than on the old bill. Thus 20 minutes of calls per month cost $8 under the original plan (point *A*) but $12 under the new plan (point *A′*). And 40 minutes cost $12 under the original plan (point *C*), $16 under the new plan (point *C′*); and 60 minutes cost $16 under the original plan (point *D*), $20 under the new plan (point *D′*).

CONCEPT CHECK 1A.3

Show how the billing plan whose graph is in Figure 1A.2 would change if the monthly fixed fee were reduced from $4 to $2.

Change in Slope

Show how the billing plan whose graph is in Figure 1A.2 would change if the charge per minute were increased from 20 cents to 40 cents.

Because the monthly fixed fee is unchanged, the vertical intercept of the new billing plan continues to be 4. But the slope of the new plan, shown in Figure 1A.4, is 0.40, or twice the slope of the original plan. More generally, in the equation $Y = a + bX$, an increase in b makes the slope of the graph of the equation steeper.

FIGURE 1A.4

The Effect of an Increase in the Charge per Minute.

Because the fixed monthly fee continues to be $4, the vertical intercept of the new plan is the same as that of the original plan. With the new charge per minute of 40 cents, the slope of the billing plan rises from 0.20 to 0.40.

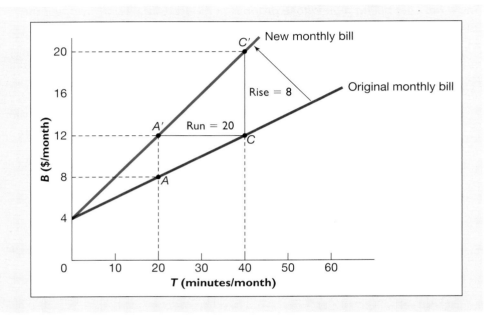

CONCEPT CHECK 1A.4

Show how the billing plan whose graph is in Figure 1A.2 would change if the charge per minute were reduced from 20 cents to 10 cents.

Concept Check 1A.4 illustrates the general rule that in an equation $Y = a + bX$, a reduction in b makes the slope of the graph of the equation less steep.

CONSTRUCTING EQUATIONS AND GRAPHS FROM TABLES

The next example and concept check show how to transform tabular information into an equation or graph.

Transforming a Table to a Graph

Table 1A.1 shows four points from a monthly long-distance telephone billing equation. If all points on this billing equation lie on a straight line, find the vertical intercept of the equation and graph it. What is the monthly fixed fee? What is the charge per minute? Calculate the total bill for a month with 1 hour of long-distance calls.

TABLE 1A.1
Points on a Long-Distance Billing Plan

Long-distance bill ($/month)	Total long-distance calls (minutes/month)
10.50	10
11.00	20
11.50	30
12.00	40

One approach to this problem is simply to plot any two points from the table on a graph. Since we are told that the billing equation is a straight line, that line must be the one that passes through any two of its points. Thus, in Figure 1A.5 we use A to denote the point from Table 1A.1 for which a monthly bill of $11 corresponds to 20 minutes per month of calls (second row) and C to denote the point for which a monthly bill of $12 corresponds to 40 minutes per month of calls (fourth row). The straight line passing through these points is the graph of the billing equation.

Unless you have a steady hand, however, or use extremely large graph paper, the method of extending a line between two points on the billing plan is unlikely to be very accurate. An alternative approach is to calculate the equation for the billing plan directly. Since the equation is a straight line, we know that it takes the general form $B = f + sT$, where f is the fixed monthly fee and s is the slope. Our goal is to calculate the vertical intercept f and the slope s. From the same two points we plotted earlier, A and C, we can calculate the slope of the billing plan as s = rise/run = $1/20$ = 0.05.

So all that remains is to calculate f, the fixed monthly fee. At point C on the billing plan, the total monthly bill is $12 for 40 minutes, so we can substitute $B = 12$, $s = 0.05$, and $T = 40$ into the general equation $B = f + sT$ to obtain

$$12 = f + 0.05(40), \tag{1A.4}$$

or

$$12 = f + 2, \tag{1A.5}$$

which solves for $f = 10$. So the monthly billing equation must be

$$B = 10 + 0.05T. \tag{1A.6}$$

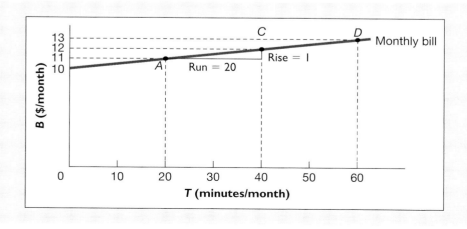

FIGURE 1A.5

Plotting the Monthly Billing Equation from a Sample of Points.

Point A is taken from row 2, Table 1A.1, and point C from row 4. The monthly billing plan is the straight line that passes through these points.

For this billing equation, the fixed fee is $10 per month, the calling charge is 5 cents per minute ($0.05/minute), and the total bill for a month with 1 hour of long-distance calls is $B = 10 + 0.05(60) = \$13$, just as shown in Figure 1A.5.

CONCEPT CHECK 1A.5

The following table shows four points from a monthly long-distance telephone billing plan.

Long-distance bill ($/month)	Total long-distance calls (minutes/month)
20.00	10
30.00	20
40.00	30
50.00	40

If all points on this billing plan lie on a straight line, find the vertical intercept of the corresponding equation without graphing it. What is the monthly fixed fee? What is the charge per minute? How much would the charges be for 1 hour of long-distance calls per month?

SOLVING SIMULTANEOUS EQUATIONS

The next example and concept check demonstrate how to proceed when you need to solve two equations with two unknowns.

Solving Simultaneous Equations   **EXAMPLE 1A.7**

Suppose you are trying to choose between two rate plans for your long-distance telephone service. If you choose Plan 1, your charges will be computed according to the equation

$$B = 10 + 0.04T, \tag{1A.7}$$

where B is again your monthly bill in dollars and T is your monthly volume of long-distance calls in minutes. If you choose Plan 2, your monthly bill will be computed according to the equation

$$B = 20 + 0.02T. \tag{1A.8}$$

How many minutes of long-distance calls would you have to make each month, on average, to make Plan 2 cheaper?

Plan 1 has the attractive feature of a relatively low monthly fixed fee, but also the unattractive feature of a relatively high rate per minute. In contrast, Plan 2 has a relatively high fixed fee but a relatively low rate per minute. Someone who made an extremely low volume of calls (for example, 10 minutes per month) would do better under Plan 1 (monthly bill = $10.40) than under Plan 2 (monthly bill = $20.20) because the low fixed fee of Plan 1 would more than compensate for its higher rate per minute. Conversely, someone who made an extremely high volume of calls (say, 10,000 minutes per month) would do better under Plan 2 (monthly bill = $220) than under Plan 1 (monthly bill = $410) because Plan 2's lower rate per minute would more than compensate for its higher fixed fee.

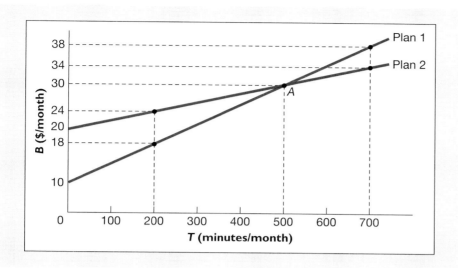

The Break-Even Volume of Long-Distance Calls.

When your volume of long-distance calls is 500 minutes per month, your monthly bill will be the same under both plans. For higher calling volumes, Plan 2 is cheaper; Plan 1 is cheaper for lower volumes.

Our task here is to find the *break-even calling volume,* which is the monthly calling volume for which the monthly bill is the same under the two plans. One way to answer this question is to graph the two billing plans and see where they cross. At that crossing point, the two equations are satisfied simultaneously, which means that the monthly call volumes will be the same under both plans, as will the monthly bills.

In Figure 1A.6, we see that the graphs of the two plans cross at A, where both yield a monthly bill of $30 for 500 minutes of calls per month. The break-even calling volume for these plans is thus 500 minutes per month. If your calling volume is higher than that, on average, you will save money by choosing Plan 2. For example, if you average 700 minutes, your monthly bill under Plan 2 ($34) will be $4 cheaper than under Plan 1 ($38). Conversely, if you average fewer than 500 minutes each month, you will do better under Plan 1. For example, if you average only 200 minutes, your monthly bill under Plan 1 ($18) will be $6 cheaper than under Plan 2 ($24). At 500 minutes per month, the two plans cost exactly the same ($30).

The question posed here also may be answered algebraically. As in the graphical approach just discussed, our goal is to find the point (T, B) that satisfies both billing equations simultaneously. As a first step, we rewrite the two billing equations, one on top of the other, as follows:

$$B = 10 + 0.04T. \quad \text{(Plan 1)}$$
$$B = 20 + 0.02T. \quad \text{(Plan 2)}$$

As you'll recall from high school algebra, if we subtract the terms from each side of one equation from the corresponding terms of the other equation, the resulting differences must be equal. So if we subtract the terms on each side of the Plan 2 equation from the corresponding terms in the Plan 1 equation, we get

$$
\begin{array}{ll}
B = & 10 + 0.04T \quad \text{(Plan 1)} \\
-B = & -20 - 0.02T \quad \text{(−Plan 2)} \\
\hline
0 = & -10 + 0.02T \quad \text{(Plan 1 − Plan 2).}
\end{array}
$$

Finally, we solve the last equation (Plan 1 − Plan 2) to get $T = 500$.

Plugging $T = 500$ into either plan's equation, we then find $B = 30$. For example, Plan 1's equation yields $10 + 0.04(500) = 30$, as does Plan 2's: $20 + 0.2(500) = 30$.

Because the point $(T, B) = (500, 30)$ lies on the equations for both plans simultaneously, the algebraic approach just described is often called *the method of simultaneous equations.*

CONCEPT CHECK 1A.6

Suppose you are trying to choose between two rate plans for your long-distance telephone service. If you choose Plan 1, your monthly bill will be computed according to the equation

$$B = 10 + 0.10T \qquad \text{(Plan 1)},$$

where B is again your monthly bill in dollars and T is your monthly volume of long-distance calls in minutes. If you choose Plan 2, your monthly bill will be computed according to the equation

$$B = 100 + 0.01T \qquad \text{(Plan 2)}.$$

Use the algebraic approach described in the preceding example to find the break-even level of monthly call volume for these plans.

○ KEY TERMS ○

constant	parameter	variable
dependent variable	rise	vertical intercept
equation	run	
independent variable	slope	

○ ANSWERS TO APPENDIX CONCEPT CHECKS ○

1A.1 To calculate your monthly bill for 45 minutes of calls, substitute 45 minutes for T in equation 1A.1 to get $B = 5 + 0.10(45) = \$9.50$.

1A.2 Calculating the slope using points A and C, we have rise $= 30 - 24 = 6$ and run $= 30 - 15 = 15$, so rise/run $= 6/15 = 2/5 = 0.40$. And since the horizontal intercept of the line is 18, its equation is $B = 18 + 0.40T$. Under this plan, the fixed monthly fee is \$18 and the charge per minute is the slope of the billing line, 0.40, or 40 cents per minute.

1A.3 A \$2 reduction in the monthly fixed fee would produce a downward parallel shift in the billing plan by \$2.

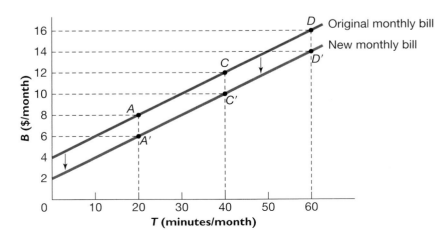

1A.4 With an unchanged monthly fixed fee, the vertical intercept of the new billing plan continues to be 4. The slope of the new plan is 0.10, half the slope of the original plan.

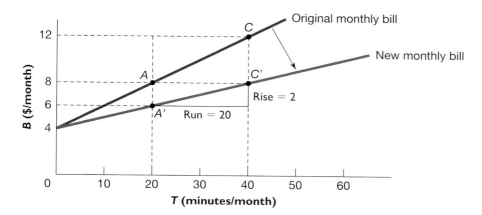

1A.5 Let the billing equation be $B = f + sT$, where f is the fixed monthly fee and s is the slope. From the first two points in the table, calculate the slope $s = $ rise/run $= 10/10 = 1.0$. To calculate f, we can use the information in row 1 of the table to write the billing equation as $20 = f + 1.0(10)$ and solve for $f = 10$. So the monthly billing equation must be $B = 10 + 1.0T$. For this billing equation, the fixed fee is \$10 per month, the calling charge is \$1 per minute, and the total bill for a month with 1 hour of long-distance calls is $B = 10 + 1.0(60) = \$70$.

1A.6 Subtracting the Plan 2 equation from the Plan 1 equation yields the equation

$$0 = -90 + 0.09T \qquad \text{(Plan 1} - \text{Plan 2)},$$

which solves for $T = 1,000$. So if you average more than 1,000 minutes of long-distance calls each month, you'll do better on Plan 2.

CHAPTER 2

Comparative Advantage

Kirk Weddle/Photodisc/Getty Images

ALWAYS PICK THE LOW-HANGING FRUIT FIRST

During a stint as a Peace Corps volunteer in rural Nepal, a young economic naturalist employed a cook named Birkhaman, who came from a remote Himalayan village in neighboring Bhutan. Although Birkhaman had virtually no formal education, he was spectacularly resourceful. His primary duties, to prepare food and maintain the kitchen, he performed extremely well. But he also had other skills. He could thatch a roof, butcher a goat, and repair shoes. An able tinsmith and a good carpenter, he could sew and fix a broken alarm clock, as well as plaster walls. And he was a local authority on home remedies.

Birkhaman's range of skills was broad even in Nepal, where the least-skilled villager could perform a wide range of services that most Americans hire others to perform. Why this difference in skills and employment?

One might be tempted to answer that the Nepalese are simply too poor to hire others to perform these services. Nepal is indeed a poor country, whose income per person is less than one one-fortieth that of the United States. Few Nepalese have spare cash to spend on outside services. But as reasonable as this poverty explanation may seem, the reverse is actually the case. The Nepalese do not perform their own services because they are poor; rather, they are poor largely *because* they perform their own services.

The alternative to a system in which everyone is a jack-of-all-trades is one in which people *specialize* in particular goods and services and then satisfy their needs by trading among

LEARNING OBJECTIVES

After reading this chapter, you should be able to:

LO1 Explain and apply the Principle of Comparative Advantage.

LO2 Explain and apply the Principle of Increasing Opportunity Cost (also called the Low-Hanging-Fruit Principle). Use a production possibilities curve to illustrate opportunity cost and comparative advantage.

LO3 Identify factors that shift the menu of production possibilities.

LO4 Explain the role of comparative advantage in international trade and describe why some jobs are more vulnerable to outsourcing than others.

themselves. Economic systems based on specialization and the exchange of goods and services are generally far more productive than those with little specialization. Our task in this chapter is to investigate why this is so.

As this chapter will show, the reason that specialization is so productive is *comparative advantage*. Roughly, a person has a comparative advantage at producing a particular good or service (say, haircuts) if that person is *relatively* more efficient at producing haircuts than at producing other goods or services. We will see that we can all have more of *every* good and service if each of us specializes in the activities at which we have a comparative advantage.

This chapter also will introduce the *production possibilities curve,* which is a graphical method of describing the combinations of goods and services that an economy can produce. This tool will allow us to see more clearly how specialization enhances the productive capacity of even the simplest economy.

Did this man perform most of his own services because he was poor, or was he poor because he performed most of his own services?

EXCHANGE AND OPPORTUNITY COST

Scarcity

The Scarcity Principle (see the chapter *Thinking Like an Economist*) reminds us that the opportunity cost of spending more time on any one activity is having less time available to spend on others. As the following example makes clear, this principle helps explain why everyone can do better by concentrating on those activities at which he or she performs best relative to others.

Should Joe Jamail prepare his own will?

absolute advantage one person has an absolute advantage over another if he or she takes fewer hours to perform a task than the other person

comparative advantage one person has a comparative advantage over another if his or her opportunity cost of performing a task is lower than the other person's opportunity cost

Scarcity Principle	**EXAMPLE 2.1**

Should Joe Jamail write his own will?

Joe Jamail, known in the legal profession as "The King of Torts," is the most renowned trial lawyer in American history. And at number 342 on the Forbes list of the 400 richest Americans, he is also one of the wealthiest, with net assets totaling more than $1.5 billion.

But although Jamail devotes virtually all of his working hours to high-profile litigation, he is also competent to perform a much broader range of legal services. Suppose, for example, that he could prepare his own will in two hours, only half as long as it would take any other attorney. Does that mean that Jamail should prepare his own will?

On the strength of his talent as a litigator, Jamail earns many millions of dollars a year, which means that the opportunity cost of any time he spends preparing his will would be several thousand dollars per hour. Attorneys who specialize in property law typically earn far less than that amount. Jamail would have little difficulty engaging a competent property lawyer who could prepare his will for him for less than $800. So even though Jamail's considerable skills would enable him to perform this task more quickly than another attorney, it would not be in his interest to prepare his own will.

In Example 2.1, economists would say that Jamail has an **absolute advantage** at preparing his will but a **comparative advantage** at trial work. He has an absolute advantage at preparing his will because he can perform that task in less time than a property lawyer could. Even so, the property lawyer has a comparative advantage at preparing wills because her opportunity cost of performing that task is lower than Jamail's.

Example 2.1 made the implicit assumption that Jamail would have been equally happy to spend an hour preparing his will or preparing for a trial. But suppose he was tired of trial preparation and felt it might be enjoyable to refresh his knowledge of property law. Preparing his own will might then have made perfect sense! But unless he expected to gain extra satisfaction from performing that task, he'd almost certainly do better to hire a property lawyer. The property lawyer would also benefit, or else she wouldn't have offered to prepare wills for the stated price.

THE PRINCIPLE OF COMPARATIVE ADVANTAGE

One of the most important insights of modern economics is that when two people (or two nations) have different opportunity costs of performing various tasks, they can always increase the total value of available goods and services by trading with one another. The following example captures the logic behind this insight.

Comparative Advantage   **EXAMPLE 2.2**

Should Mary update her own web page?

Consider a small community in which Mary is the only professional bicycle mechanic and Paula is the only professional HTML programmer. Mary also happens to be an even better HTML programmer than Paula. If the amount of time each of them takes to perform these tasks is as shown in Table 2.1, and if each regards the two tasks as equally pleasant (or unpleasant), does the fact that Mary can program faster than Paula imply that Mary should update her own web page?

The entries in the table show that Mary has an absolute advantage over Paula in both activities. While Mary, the mechanic, needs only 20 minutes to update a web page, Paula, the programmer, needs 30 minutes. Mary's advantage over Paula is even greater when the task is fixing bikes: She can complete a repair in only 10 minutes, compared to Paula's 30 minutes.

TABLE 2.1
Productivity Information for Paula and Mary

	Time to update a web page	Time to complete a bicycle repair
Mary	20 minutes	10 minutes
Paula	30 minutes	30 minutes

But the fact that Mary is a better programmer than Paula does *not* imply that Mary should update her own web page. As with the lawyer who litigates instead of preparing his own will, Paula has a comparative advantage over Mary at programming: She is *relatively* more productive at programming than Mary. Similarly, Mary has a comparative advantage in bicycle repair. (Remember that a person has a comparative advantage at a given task if his or her opportunity cost of performing that task is lower than another person's.)

What is Paula's opportunity cost of updating a web page? Since she takes 30 minutes to update each page—the same amount of time she takes to fix a bicycle—her opportunity cost of updating a web page is one bicycle repair. In other words, by taking the time to update a web page, Paula is effectively giving up the opportunity to do one bicycle repair. Mary, in contrast, can complete two bicycle repairs in the time she takes to update a single web page. For her, the opportunity cost of updating a web page is two bicycle repairs. Mary's opportunity cost of programming, measured in terms of bicycle repairs forgone, is twice as high as Paula's. Thus, Paula has a comparative advantage at programming.

The interesting and important implication of the opportunity cost comparison summarized in Table 2.2 is that the total number of bicycle repairs and web updates accomplished if Paula and Mary both spend part of their time at each activity will always be smaller than the number accomplished if each specializes in the activity in which she has a comparative advantage. Suppose, for example, that people in their community demand

TABLE 2.2
Opportunity Costs for Paula and Mary

	Opportunity cost of updating a web page	Opportunity cost of a bicycle repair
Mary	2 bicycle repairs	0.5 web page update
Paula	1 bicycle repair	1 web page update

a total of 16 web page updates per day. If Mary spent half her time updating web pages and the other half repairing bicycles, an eight-hour workday would yield 12 web page updates and 24 bicycle repairs. To complete the remaining 4 updates, Paula would have to spend two hours programming, which would leave her six hours to repair bicycles. And since she takes 30 minutes to do each repair, she would have time to complete 12 of them. So when the two women try to be jacks-of-all-trades, they end up completing a total of 16 web page updates and 36 bicycle repairs.

Consider what would have happened had each woman specialized in her activity of comparative advantage. Paula could have updated 16 web pages on her own and Mary could have performed 48 bicycle repairs. Specialization would have created an additional 12 bicycle repairs out of thin air.

"We're a natural, Rachel. I handle intellectual property, and you're a content-provider."

When computing the opportunity cost of one good in terms of another, we must pay close attention to the form in which the productivity information is presented. In Example 2.2, we were told how many minutes each person needed to perform each task. Alternatively, we might be told how many units of each task each person can perform in an hour. Work through the following concept check to see how to proceed when information is presented in this alternative format.

CONCEPT CHECK 2.1

Should Meg update her own web page?

Consider a small community in which Meg is the only professional bicycle mechanic and Pat is the only professional HTML programmer. If their productivity rates at the two tasks are as shown in the table, and if each regards the two tasks as equally pleasant (or unpleasant), does the fact that Meg can program faster than Pat imply that Meg should update her own web page?

	Productivity in programming	Productivity in bicycle repair
Pat	2 web page updates per hour	1 repair per hour
Meg	3 web page updates per hour	3 repairs per hour

The principle illustrated by the preceding examples is so important that we state it formally as one of the core principles of the course:

The Principle of Comparative Advantage: Everyone does best when each person (or each country) concentrates on the activities for which his or her opportunity cost is lowest.

> **Comparative Advantage**

Indeed, the gains made possible from specialization based on comparative advantage constitute the rationale for market exchange. They explain why each person does not devote 10 percent of his or her time to producing cars, 5 percent to growing food, 25 percent to building housing, 0.0001 percent to performing brain surgery, and so on. By concentrating on those tasks at which we are relatively most productive, together we can produce vastly more than if we all tried to be self-sufficient.

This insight brings us back to Birkhaman the cook. Though Birkhaman's versatility was marvelous, he was neither as good a doctor as someone who has been trained in medical school, nor as good a repairman as someone who spends each day fixing things. If a number of people with Birkhaman's native talents had joined together, each of them specializing in one or two tasks, together they would have enjoyed more and better goods and services than each could possibly have produced independently. Although there is much to admire in the resourcefulness of people who have learned through necessity to rely on their own skills, that path is no route to economic prosperity.

Specialization and its effects provide ample grist for the economic naturalist. Here's an example from the world of sports.

The Economic Naturalist 2.1

Where have all the .400 hitters gone?

In baseball, a .400 hitter is a player who averages at least four hits every 10 times he comes to bat. Though never common in professional baseball, .400 hitters used to appear relatively frequently. Early in the twentieth century, for example, a player known as Wee Willie Keeler batted .432, meaning that he got a hit in over 43 percent of his times at bat. But since Ted Williams of the Boston Red Sox batted .406 in 1941, there hasn't been a single .400 hitter in the major leagues. Why not?

Some baseball buffs argue that the disappearance of the .400 hitter means today's baseball players are not as good as yesterday's. But that claim does not withstand close examination. For example, today's players are bigger, stronger, and faster than

Why has no major league baseball player batted .400 since Ted Williams did it more than half a century ago?

© Bettmann/CORBIS

those of Willie Keeler's day. (Wee Willie himself was just a little over 5 feet 4 inches and weighed only 140 pounds.)

Bill James, a leading analyst of baseball history, argues that the .400 hitter has disappeared because the quality of play in the major leagues has *improved,* not declined. In particular, pitching and fielding standards are higher, which makes batting .400 more difficult.

Why has the quality of play in baseball improved? Although there are many reasons, including better nutrition, training, and equipment, specialization also has played an important role.[1] At one time, pitchers were expected to pitch for the entire game. Now pitching staffs include pitchers who specialize in starting the game ("starters"), others who specialize in pitching two or three innings in the middle of the game ("middle relievers"), and still others who specialize in pitching only the last inning ("closers"). Each of these roles requires different skills and tactics. Pitchers also may specialize in facing left-handed or right-handed batters, in striking batters out, or in getting batters to hit balls on the ground. Similarly, few fielders today play multiple defensive positions; most specialize in only one. Some players specialize in defense (to the detriment of their hitting skills); these "defensive specialists" can be brought in late in the game to protect a lead. Even in managing and coaching, specialization has increased markedly. Relief pitchers now have their own coaches, and statistical specialists use computers to discover the weaknesses of opposing hitters. The net result of these increases in specialization is that even the weakest of today's teams play highly competent defensive baseball. With no "weaklings" to pick on, hitting .400 over an entire season has become a near-impossible task.

SOURCES OF COMPARATIVE ADVANTAGE

At the individual level, comparative advantage often appears to be the result of inborn talent. For instance, some people seem to be naturally gifted at programming computers while others seem to have a special knack for fixing bikes. But comparative advantage is more often the result of education, training, or experience. Thus, we usually leave the design of kitchens to people with architectural training, the drafting of contracts to people who have studied law, and the teaching of physics to people with advanced degrees in that field.

At the national level, comparative advantage may derive from differences in natural resources or from differences in society or culture. The United States, which has a disproportionate share of the world's leading research universities, has a comparative advantage in the design of electronic computing hardware and software. Canada, which has one of the world's highest per-capita endowments of farm and forest land, has a comparative advantage in the production of agricultural products. Topography and climate explain why Colorado specializes in the skiing industry while Hawaii specializes as an ocean resort.

Seemingly noneconomic factors also can give rise to comparative advantage. For instance, the emergence of English as the de facto world language gives English-speaking countries a comparative advantage over non–English-speaking nations in the production of books, movies, and popular music. Even a country's institutions may affect the likelihood that it will achieve comparative advantage in a particular pursuit. For example, cultures that encourage entrepreneurship will tend to have a comparative advantage in the introduction of new products, whereas those that promote high standards of care and craftsmanship will tend to have a comparative advantage in the production of high-quality variants of established products.

[1]For an interesting discussion of specialization and the decline of the .400 hitter from the perspective of an evolutionary biologist, see Stephen Jay Gould, *Full House* (New York: Three Rivers Press, 1996), part 3.

The Economic Naturalist 2.2

What happened to the U.S. lead in the TV and digital video markets?

Televisions and digital video recorders (DVRs) were developed and first produced in the United States, but today the U.S. accounts for only a minuscule share of the total world production of these products. The early lead is explained in part by this country's comparative advantage in technological research, which in turn was supported by the country's outstanding system of higher education. Other contributing factors were high expenditures on the development of electronic components for the military and a culture that actively encourages entrepreneurship. As for the production of these products, the United States enjoyed an early advantage partly because the product designs were themselves evolving rapidly at first, which favored production facilities located in close proximity to the product designers. Early production techniques also relied intensively on skilled labor, which is abundant in the United States. In time, however, product designs stabilized and many of the more complex manufacturing operations were automated. Both of these changes gradually led to greater reliance on relatively less-skilled production workers. And at that point, factories located in high-wage countries like the United States could no longer compete with those located in low-wage areas overseas.

Why was the United States unable to remain competitive as a manufacturer of televisions and other electronic equipment?

RECAP	EXCHANGE AND OPPORTUNITY COST

Gains from exchange are possible if trading partners have comparative advantages in producing different goods and services. You have a comparative advantage in producing, say, web pages if your opportunity cost of producing a web page—measured in terms of other production opportunities forgone—is smaller than the corresponding opportunity costs of your trading partners. Maximum production is achieved if each person specializes in producing the good or service in which he or she has the lowest opportunity cost (the Principle of Comparative Advantage). Comparative advantage makes specialization worthwhile even if one trading partner is more productive than others, in absolute terms, in every activity.

COMPARATIVE ADVANTAGE AND PRODUCTION POSSIBILITIES

Comparative advantage and specialization allow an economy to produce more than if each person tries to produce a little of everything. In this section, we gain further insight into the advantages of specialization by introducing a graph that can be used to describe the various combinations of goods and services that an economy can produce.

THE PRODUCTION POSSIBILITIES CURVE

We begin with a hypothetical economy in which only two goods are produced: coffee and pine nuts. It's a small island economy and "production" consists either of picking coffee beans that grow on small bushes on the island's central valley floor or of gathering pine nuts that fall from trees on the steep hillsides overlooking the valley. The more time workers spend picking coffee, the less time they have available for gathering nuts. So if people want to drink more coffee, they must make do with a smaller amount of nuts.

production possibilities curve a graph that describes the maximum amount of one good that can be produced for every possible level of production of the other good

If we know how productive workers are at each activity, we can summarize the various combinations of coffee and nuts they can produce each day. This menu of possibilities is known as the **production possibilities curve.**

To keep matters simple, we begin with an example in which the economy has only a single worker, who can divide her time between the two activities.

Production Possibilities Curve   EXAMPLE 2.3

What is the production possibilities curve for an economy in which Susan is the only worker?

Consider a society consisting only of Susan, who allocates her production time between coffee and nuts. She has nimble fingers, a quality that makes her more productive at picking coffee than at gathering nuts. She can gather 2 pounds of nuts or pick 4 pounds of coffee in an hour. If she works a total of 6 hours per day, describe her production possibilities curve—the graph that displays, for each level of nut production, the maximum amount of coffee that she can pick.

The vertical axis in Figure 2.1 shows Susan's daily production of coffee and the horizontal axis shows her daily production of nuts. Let's begin by looking at two extreme allocations of her time. First, suppose she employs her entire workday (6 hours) picking coffee. In that case, since she can pick 4 pounds of coffee per hour, she would pick 24 pounds per day of coffee and gather zero pounds of nuts. That combination of coffee and nut production is represented by point A in Figure 2.1. It is the vertical intercept of Susan's production possibilities curve.

Now suppose, instead, that Susan devotes all her time to gathering nuts. Since she can gather 2 pounds of nuts per hour, her total daily production would be 12 pounds of nuts. That combination is represented by point D in Figure 2.1, the horizontal intercept of Susan's production possibilities curve. Because Susan's production of each good is exactly proportional to the amount of time she devotes to that good, the remaining points along her production possibilities curve will lie on the straight line that joins A and D.

FIGURE 2.1

Susan's Production Possibilities.

For the production relationships given, the production possibilities curve is a straight line.

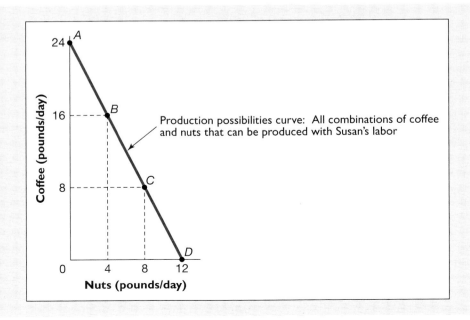

Production possibilities curve: All combinations of coffee and nuts that can be produced with Susan's labor

For example, suppose that Susan devotes 4 hours each day to picking coffee and 2 hours to gathering nuts. She will then end up with (4 hours/day) × (4 pounds/hour) = 16 pounds of coffee per day and (2 hours/day) × (2 pounds/hour) = 4 pounds of nuts. This is the point labeled *B* in Figure 2.1. Alternatively, if she devotes 2 hours to coffee and 4 to nuts, she will get (2 hours/day) × (4 pounds/ hour) = 8 pounds of coffee per day and (4 hours/day) × (2 pounds/hour) = 8 pounds of nuts. This alternative combination is represented by point *C* in Figure 2.1.

Since Susan's production possibilities curve (PPC) is a straight line, its slope is constant. The absolute value of the slope of Susan's PPC is the ratio of its vertical intercept to its horizontal intercept: (24 pounds of coffee/day)/(12 pounds of nuts/day) = (2 pounds of coffee)/(1 pound of nuts). (Be sure to keep track of the units of measure on each axis when computing this ratio.) *This ratio means that Susan's opportunity cost of an additional pound of nuts is 2 pounds of coffee.*

Note that Susan's opportunity cost (*OC*) of nuts can also be expressed as the following simple formula:

$$OC_{nuts} = \frac{\text{loss in coffee}}{\text{gain in nuts}},\qquad(2.1)$$

where "loss in coffee" means the amount of coffee given up and "gain in nuts" means the corresponding increase in nuts. Likewise, Susan's opportunity cost of coffee is expressed by this formula:

$$OC_{coffee} = \frac{\text{loss in nuts}}{\text{gain in coffee}}.\qquad(2.2)$$

To say that Susan's opportunity cost of an additional pound of nuts is 2 pounds of coffee is thus equivalent to saying that her opportunity cost of a pound of coffee is ½ pound of nuts.

The downward slope of the production possibilities curve shown in Figure 2.1 illustrates the Scarcity Principle—the idea that because our resources are limited, having more of one good thing generally means having to settle for less of another (see the chapter *Thinking Like an Economist*). Susan can have an additional pound of coffee if she wishes, but only if she is willing to give up half a pound of nuts. If Susan is the only person in the economy, her opportunity cost of producing a good becomes, in effect, its price. Thus, the price she has to pay for an additional pound of coffee is half a pound of nuts, or the price she has to pay for an additional pound of nuts is 2 pounds of coffee.

Any point that lies either along the production possibilities curve or within it is said to be an **attainable point,** meaning that it can be produced with currently available resources. In Figure 2.2, for example, points *A, B, C, D,* and *E* are attainable points. Points that lie outside the production possibilities curve are said to be **unattainable,** meaning that they cannot be produced using currently available resources. In Figure 2.2, *F* is an unattainable point because Susan cannot pick 16 pounds of coffee per day *and* gather 8 pounds of nuts. Points that lie within the curve are said to be **inefficient,** in the sense that existing resources would allow for production of more of at least one good without sacrificing the production of any other good. At *E,* for example, Susan is picking only 8 pounds of coffee per day and gathering 4 pounds of nuts. This means that she could increase her coffee harvest by 8 pounds per day without giving up any nuts (by moving from *E* to *B*). Alternatively, Susan could gather as many as 4 additional pounds of nuts each day without giving up any coffee (by moving from *E* to *C*). An **efficient point** is one that lies along the production possibilities curve. At any such point, more of one good can be produced only by producing less of the other.

Scarcity

attainable point any combination of goods that can be produced using currently available resources

unattainable point any combination of goods that cannot be produced using currently available resources

inefficient point any combination of goods for which currently available resources enable an increase in the production of one good without a reduction in the production of the other

efficient point any combination of goods for which currently available resources do not allow an increase in the production of one good without a reduction in the production of the other

FIGURE 2.2

Attainable and Efficient Points on Susan's Production Possibilities Curve.

Points that lie either along the production possibilities curve (for example, *A*, *B*, *C*, and *D*) or within it (for example, *E*) are said to be attainable. Points that lie outside the production possibilities curve (for example, *F*) are unattainable. Points that lie along the curve are said to be efficient, while those that lie within the curve are said to be inefficient.

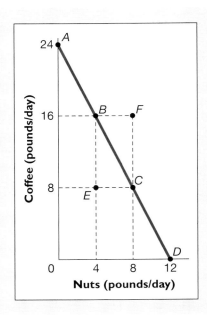

CONCEPT CHECK 2.2

For the PPC shown in Figure 2.2, state whether the following points are attainable and/or efficient:

a.   20 pounds per day of coffee, 4 pounds per day of nuts.

b.   12 pounds per day of coffee, 6 pounds per day of nuts.

c.   4 pounds per day of coffee, 8 pounds per day of nuts.

HOW INDIVIDUAL PRODUCTIVITY AFFECTS THE SLOPE AND POSITION OF THE PPC

To see how the slope and position of the production possibilities curve depend on an individual's productivity, let's compare Susan's PPC to that of Tom, who is less productive at picking coffee but more productive at gathering nuts.

Productivity Changes   **EXAMPLE 2.4**

How do changes in productivity affect the opportunity cost of nuts?

Tom is short and has keen eyesight, qualities that make him especially well-suited for gathering nuts that fall beneath trees on the hillsides. He can gather 4 pounds of nuts or pick 2 pounds of coffee per hour. If Tom were the only person in the economy, describe the economy's production possibilities curve.

We can construct Tom's PPC the same way we did Susan's. Note first that if Tom devotes an entire workday (6 hours) to coffee picking, he ends up with (6 hours/day) × (2 pounds/hour) = 12 pounds of coffee per day and zero pounds of nuts. So the vertical intercept of Tom's PPC is *A* in Figure 2.3. If instead he devotes all his time to gathering nuts, he gets (6 hours/day) × (4 pounds/hour) = 24 pounds of nuts per day and no coffee. That means the horizontal intercept of his PPC is *D* in Figure 2.3. Because Tom's production of each good is proportional to the amount of time he devotes to it, the remaining points on his PPC will lie along the straight line that joins these two extreme points.

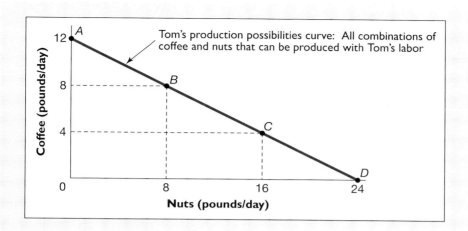

FIGURE 2.3

Tom's Production Possibilities Curve.

Tom's opportunity cost of producing 1 pound of nuts is only ½ pound of coffee.

For example, if he devotes 4 hours each day to picking coffee and 2 hours to gathering nuts, he'll end up with (4 hours/day) × (2 pounds/hour) = 8 pounds of coffee per day and (2 hours/day) × (4 pounds/hour) = 8 pounds of nuts per day. This is the point labeled *B* in Figure 2.3. Alternatively, if he devotes 2 hours to coffee and 4 to nuts, he'll get (2 hours/day) × (2 pounds/hour) = 4 pounds of coffee per day and (4 hours/day) × (4 pounds/hour) = 16 pounds of nuts. This alternative combination is represented by point *C* in Figure 2.3.

How does Tom's PPC compare with Susan's? Note in Figure 2.4 that because Tom is absolutely less productive than Susan at picking coffee, the vertical intercept of his PPC lies closer to the origin than Susan's. By the same token, because Susan is absolutely less productive than Tom at gathering nuts, the horizontal intercept of her PPC lies closer to the origin than Tom's. For Tom, the opportunity cost of an additional pound of nuts is ½ pound of coffee, which is one-fourth Susan's opportunity cost of nuts. This difference in opportunity costs shows up as a difference in the slopes of their PPCs: The absolute value of the slope of Tom's PPC is ½, whereas Susan's is 2.

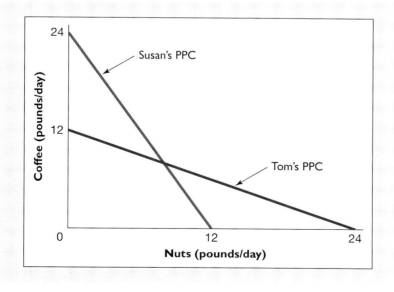

FIGURE 2.4

Individual Production Possibilities Curves Compared.

Tom is less productive in coffee than Susan, but more productive in nuts.

In this example, Tom has both an absolute advantage and a comparative advantage over Susan in gathering nuts. Susan, for her part, has both an absolute advantage and a comparative advantage over Tom in picking coffee.

We cannot emphasize strongly enough that the Principle of Comparative Advantage is a relative concept—one that makes sense only when the productivities of two or more people (or countries) are being compared.

CONCEPT CHECK 2.3

Suppose Susan can pick 2 pounds of coffee per hour or gather 4 pounds of nuts per hour; Tom can pick 1 pound of coffee per hour and gather 1 pound of nuts per hour. What is Susan's opportunity cost of gathering a pound of nuts? What is Tom's opportunity cost of gathering a pound of nuts? Where does Susan's comparative advantage now lie?

THE GAINS FROM SPECIALIZATION AND EXCHANGE

Earlier we saw that a comparative advantage arising from disparities in individual opportunity costs creates gains for everyone (see Examples 2.1 and 2.2). The following example shows how the same point can be illustrated using production possibility curves.

Specialization	EXAMPLE 2.5

How costly is failure to specialize?

Suppose that in Example 2.4 Susan and Tom had divided their time so that each person's output consisted of half nuts and half coffee. How much of each good would Tom and Susan have been able to consume? How much could they have consumed if each had specialized in the activity for which he or she enjoyed a comparative advantage?

Since Tom can produce twice as many pounds of nuts in an hour as pounds of coffee, to produce equal quantities of each, he must spend 2 hours picking coffee for every hour he devotes to gathering nuts. And since he works a 6-hour day, that means spending 2 hours gathering nuts and 4 hours picking coffee. Dividing his time in this way, he'll end up with 8 pounds of coffee per day and 8 pounds of nuts. Similarly, since Susan can produce twice as many pounds of coffee in an hour as pounds of nuts, to pick equal quantities of each, she must spend 2 hours gathering nuts for every hour she devotes to picking coffee. And since she too works a 6-hour day, that means spending 2 hours picking coffee and 4 hours gathering nuts. So, like Tom, she'll end up with 8 pounds of coffee per day and 8 pounds of nuts. (See Figure 2.5.) Their combined daily production will thus be 16 pounds of each good. By contrast, had they each specialized in their respective activities of comparative advantage, their combined daily production would have been 24 pounds of each good.

If they exchange coffee and nuts with one another, each can consume a combination of the two goods that would have been unattainable if exchange had not been possible. For example, Susan can give Tom 12 pounds of coffee in exchange for 12 pounds of nuts, enabling each to consume 4 pounds per day more of each good than when each produced and consumed alone. Note that point E in Figure 2.5, which has 12 pounds per day of each good, lies beyond each person's PPC, yet is easily attainable with specialization and exchange.

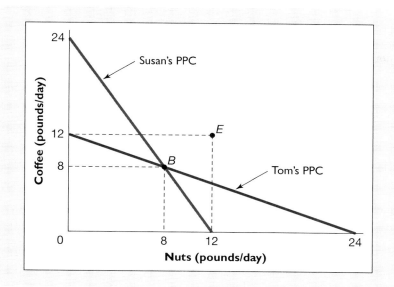

FIGURE 2.5

Production without Specialization.

When Tom and Susan divide their time so that each produces the same number of pounds of coffee and nuts, they can consume a total of 16 pounds of coffee and 16 pounds of nuts each day.

As the following concept check illustrates, the gains from specialization grow larger as the difference in opportunity costs increases.

CONCEPT CHECK 2.4

How do differences in opportunity cost affect the gains from specialization?

Susan can pick 5 pounds of coffee or gather 1 pound of nuts in an hour. Tom can pick 1 pound of coffee or gather 5 pounds of nuts in an hour. Assuming they again work 6-hour days and want to consume coffee and nuts in equal quantities, by how much will specialization increase their consumption compared to the alternative in which each produced only for his or her own consumption?

Although the gains from specialization and exchange grow with increases in the differences in opportunity costs among trading partners, these differences alone still seem insufficient to account for the enormous differences in living standards between rich and poor countries. Average income in the 20 richest countries in the year 2012, for example, was over $47,000 per person, compared to less than $1,000 per person in the 20 poorest countries.[2] Although we will say more later about specialization's role in explaining these differences, we first discuss how to construct the PPC for an entire economy and examine how factors other than specialization might cause it to shift outward over time.

A PRODUCTION POSSIBILITIES CURVE FOR A MANY-PERSON ECONOMY

Although most actual economies consist of millions of workers, the process of constructing a production possibilities curve for an economy of that size is really no different from the process for a one-person economy. Consider again an economy in which the only two goods are coffee and nuts, with coffee again on the vertical axis and nuts on the horizontal axis. The vertical intercept of the economy's PPC is the total amount of coffee that

[2]The 20 richest countries tracked by the International Monetary Fund: Australia, Austria, Belgium, Brunei, Canada, Denmark, Germany, Hong Kong, Iceland, Ireland, Kuwait, Luxembourg, Netherlands, Norway, Qatar, San Marino, Singapore, Sweden, Switzerland, Taiwan, and United States. The 20 poorest countries tracked by the International Monetary Fund: Afghanistan, Burundi, Central African Republic, Congo, Eritrea, Ethiopia, Guinea, Guinea-Bassau, Haiti, Liberia, Madagascar, Malawi, Mali, Mozambique, Niger, Sierra Leone, South Sudan, Togo, and Zimbabwe. (Source: IMF World Economic Outlook Database, October 2013, www.imf.org/external/pubs/ft/weo/2013/02/weodata/index.aspx.)

FIGURE 2.6

Production Possibilities Curve for a Large Economy.

For an economy with millions of workers, the PPC typically has a gentle outward bow shape.

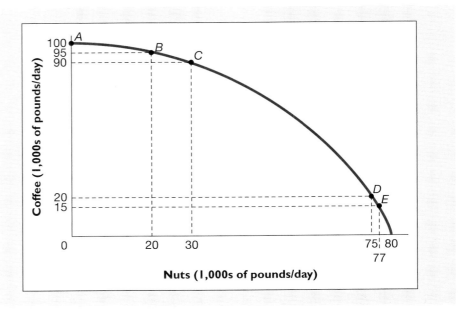

could be picked if all available workers worked full time picking coffee. Thus, the maximum attainable amount of coffee production is shown for the hypothetical economy in Figure 2.6 as 100,000 pounds per day (an amount chosen arbitrarily, for illustrative purposes). The horizontal intercept of the PPC is the amount of nuts that could be gathered if all available workers worked full time gathering nuts, shown for this same economy as 80,000 pounds per day (also an amount chosen arbitrarily). But note that the PPC shown in the diagram is not a straight line—as in the earlier examples involving only a single worker—but rather a curve that is bowed out from the origin.

We'll say more in a moment about the reasons for this shape. But first note that a bow-shaped PPC means that the opportunity cost of producing nuts increases as the economy produces more of them. Notice, for example, that when the economy moves from *A,* where it is producing only coffee, to *B,* it gets 20,000 pounds of nuts per day by giving up only 5,000 pounds per day of coffee. When nut production is increased still further, however—for example, by moving from *B* to *C*—the economy again gives up 5,000 pounds per day of coffee, yet this time gets only 10,000 additional pounds of nuts. This pattern of increasing opportunity cost persists over the entire length of the PPC. For example, note that in moving from *D* to *E,* the economy again gives up 5,000 pounds per day of coffee but now gains only 2,000 pounds a day of nuts. Note, finally, that the same pattern of increasing opportunity cost applies to coffee. Thus, as more coffee is produced, the opportunity cost of producing additional coffee—as measured by the amount of nuts that must be sacrificed—also rises.

Why is the PPC for the multiperson economy bow-shaped? The answer lies in the fact that some resources are relatively well-suited for gathering nuts while others are relatively well-suited for picking coffee. If the economy is initially producing only coffee and wants to begin producing some nuts, which workers will it reassign? Recall Susan and Tom, the two workers discussed in the preceding example, in which Tom's comparative advantage was gathering nuts and Susan's comparative advantage was picking coffee. If both workers were currently picking coffee and you wanted to reassign one of them to gather nuts instead, whom would you send? Tom would be the clear choice, because his departure would cost the economy only half as much coffee as Susan's and would augment nut production by twice as much.

The principle is the same in any large multiperson economy, except that the range of opportunity cost differences across workers is even greater than in the earlier two-worker example. As we keep reassigning workers from coffee production to nut production, sooner or later we must withdraw even coffee specialists like Susan from coffee production. Indeed, we must eventually reassign others whose opportunity cost of producing nuts is far higher than hers.

The shape of the production possibilities curve shown in Figure 2.6 illustrates the general principle that when resources have different opportunity costs, we should always exploit the resource with the lowest opportunity cost first. We call this the *Low-Hanging-Fruit Principle,* in honor of the fruit picker's rule of picking the most accessible fruit first:

The Principle of Increasing Opportunity Cost (also called the "Low-Hanging-Fruit Principle"): In expanding the production of any good, first employ those resources with the lowest opportunity cost, and only afterward turn to resources with higher opportunity costs.

Increasing
Opportunity Cost

A Note on the Logic of the Fruit Picker's Rule

Why should a fruit picker harvest the low-hanging fruit first? This rule makes sense for several reasons. For one, the low-hanging fruit is easier (and hence cheaper) to pick, and if he planned on picking only a limited amount of fruit to begin with, he would clearly come out ahead by avoiding the less-accessible fruit on the higher branches. But even if he planned on picking all the fruit on the tree, he would do better to start with the lower branches first because this would enable him to enjoy the revenue from the sale of the fruit sooner.

The fruit picker's job can be likened to the task confronting a new CEO who has been hired to reform an inefficient, ailing company. The CEO has limited time and attention, so it makes sense to focus first on problems that are relatively easy to correct and whose elimination will provide the biggest improvements in performance—the low-hanging fruit. Later on, the CEO can worry about the many smaller improvements needed to raise the company from very good to excellent.

Again, the important message of the Low-Hanging-Fruit Principle is to be sure to take advantage of your most favorable opportunities first.

RECAP	COMPARATIVE ADVANTAGE AND PRODUCTION POSSIBILITIES

For an economy that produces two goods, the production possibilities curve describes the maximum amount of one good that can be produced for every possible level of production of the other good. Attainable points are those that lie on or within the curve and efficient points are those that lie along the curve. The slope of the production possibilities curve tells us the opportunity cost of producing an additional unit of the good measured along the horizontal axis. The Principle of Increasing Opportunity Cost, or the Low-Hanging-Fruit Principle, tells us that the slope of the production possibilities curve becomes steeper as we move downward to the right. The greater the differences among individual opportunity costs, the more bow-shaped the production possibilities curve will be; and the more bow-shaped the production possibilities curve, the greater the potential gains from specialization will be.

FACTORS THAT SHIFT THE ECONOMY'S PRODUCTION POSSIBILITIES CURVE

As its name implies, the production possibilities curve provides a summary of the production options open to any society. At any given moment, the PPC confronts society with a trade-off. The only way people can produce and consume more nuts is to produce and consume less coffee. In the long run, however, it is often possible to

FIGURE 2.7

Economic Growth: An Outward Shift in the Economy's PPC.

Increases in productive resources (such as labor and capital equipment) or improvements in knowledge and technology cause the PPC to shift outward. They are the main factors that drive economic growth.

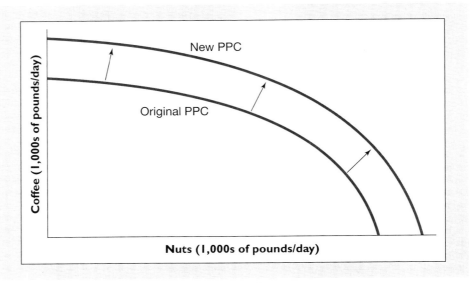

increase production of all goods. This is what is meant when people speak of economic growth. As shown in Figure 2.7, economic growth is an outward shift in the economy's production possibilities curve. It can result from increases in the amount of productive resources available or from improvements in knowledge or technology that render existing resources more productive.

What causes the quantity of productive resources to grow in an economy? One factor is investment in new factories and equipment. When workers have more and better equipment to work with, their productivity increases, often dramatically. This is surely an important factor behind the differences in living standards between rich and poor countries. According to one study, for example, the value of capital investment per worker in the United States is about 30 times as great as in Nepal.[3]

Such large differences in capital per worker don't occur all at once. They are a consequence of decades, even centuries, of differences in rates of savings and investment. Over time, even small differences in rates of investment can translate into extremely large differences in the amount of capital equipment available to each worker. Differences of this sort are often self-reinforcing: Not only do higher rates of saving and investment cause incomes to grow, but the resulting higher income levels also make it easier to devote additional resources to savings and investment. Over time, then, even small initial productivity advantages from specialization can translate into very large income gaps.

Population growth also causes an economy's PPC curve to shift outward and thus is often listed as one of the sources of economic growth. But because population growth also generates more mouths to feed, it cannot by itself raise a country's standard of living. Indeed it may even cause a decline in the standard of living if existing population densities have already begun to put pressure on available land, water, and other resources.

Perhaps the most important sources of economic growth are improvements in knowledge and technology. As economists have long recognized, such improvements often lead to higher output through increased specialization. Improvements in technology often occur spontaneously. More frequently they are directly or indirectly the result of increases in education.

Earlier we discussed a two-person example in which individual differences in opportunity cost led to a tripling of output from specialization (Concept Check 2.4).

---

[3]Alan Heston and Robert Summers, "The Penn World Table (Mark 5): An Expanded Set of International Comparisons, 1950–1988," *Quarterly Journal of Economics,* May 1991, pp. 327–68.

Real-world gains from specialization often are far more spectacular than those in the example. One reason is that specialization not only capitalizes on preexisting differences in individual skills but also deepens those skills through practice and experience. Moreover, it eliminates many of the switching and start-up costs people incur when they move back and forth among numerous tasks. These gains apply not only to people but also to the tools and equipment they use. Breaking a task down into simple steps, each of which can be performed by a different machine, greatly multiplies the productivity of individual workers.

Even in simple settings, these factors can combine to increase productivity hundreds- or even thousands-fold. Adam Smith, the Scottish philosopher who is remembered today as the founder of modern economics, was the first to recognize the enormity of the gains made possible by the division and specialization of labor. Consider, for instance, his description of work in an eighteenth-century Scottish pin factory:

> One man draws out the wire, another straightens it, a third cuts it, a fourth points it, a fifth grinds it at the top for receiving the head; to make the head requires two or three distinct operations . . . I have seen a small manufactory of this kind where only ten men were employed . . . [who] could, when they exerted themselves, make among them about twelve pounds of pins in a day. There are in a pound upwards of four thousand pins of middling size. Those ten persons, therefore, could make among them upwards of forty-eight thousand pins in a day. Each person, therefore, making a tenth part of forty-eight thousand pins, might be considered as making four thousand eight hundred pins in a day. But if they had all wrought separately and independently, and without any of them having been educated to this peculiar business, they certainly could not each of them have made twenty, perhaps not one pin in a day.[4]

The gains in productivity that result from specialization are indeed often prodigious. They constitute the single most important explanation for why societies that don't rely heavily on specialization and exchange have failed to keep pace.

WHY HAVE SOME COUNTRIES BEEN SLOW TO SPECIALIZE?

You may be asking yourself, "If specialization is such a great thing, why don't people in poor countries like Nepal just specialize?" If so, you're in good company. Adam Smith spent many years attempting to answer precisely the same question. In the end, his explanation was that population density is an important precondition for specialization. Smith, ever the economic naturalist, observed that work tended to be far more specialized in the large cities of England in the eighteenth century than in the rural Highlands of Scotland:

> In the lone houses and very small villages which are scattered about in so desert a country as the Highlands of Scotland, every farmer must be butcher, baker, and brewer for his own family. . . . A country carpenter . . . is not only a carpenter, but a joiner, a cabinet maker, and even a carver in wood, as well as a wheelwright, a ploughwright, a cart and waggon maker.[5]

In contrast, each of these same tasks was performed by a different specialist in the large English and Scottish cities of Smith's day. Scottish Highlanders also would have specialized had they been able to, but the markets in which they participated were simply too small and fragmented. Of course, high population density by itself provides no guarantee that specialization will result in rapid economic growth. But especially before the

---

[4]Adam Smith, *The Wealth of Nations* (New York: Everyman's Library, 1910 [1776]), book 1.
[5]Ibid., chapter 3.

Can specialization proceed too far?

arrival of modern shipping and electronic communications technology, low population density was a definite obstacle to gains from specialization.

Nepal remains one of the most remote and isolated countries on the planet. As recently as the mid-1960s, its average population density was less than 30 people per square mile (as compared, for example, to more than 1,000 people per square mile in New Jersey). Specialization was further limited by Nepal's rugged terrain. Exchanging goods and services with residents of other villages was difficult, because the nearest village in most cases could be reached only after trekking several hours, or even days, over treacherous Himalayan trails. More than any other factor, this extreme isolation accounts for Nepal's long-standing failure to benefit from widespread specialization.

Population density is by no means the only important factor that influences the degree of specialization. Specialization may be severely impeded, for example, by laws and customs that limit people's freedom to transact freely with one another. The communist governments of North Korea and the former East Germany restricted exchange severely, which helps explain why those countries achieved far less specialization than South Korea and the former West Germany, whose governments were far more supportive of exchange.

CAN WE HAVE TOO MUCH SPECIALIZATION?

Of course, the mere fact that specialization boosts productivity does not mean that more specialization is always better than less, for specialization also entails costs. For example, most people appear to enjoy variety in the work they do, yet variety tends to be one of the first casualties as workplace tasks become ever more narrowly specialized.

Indeed, one of Karl Marx's central themes was that the fragmentation of workplace tasks often exacts a heavy psychological toll on workers. Thus, he wrote,

> All means for the development of production . . . mutilate the laborer into a fragment of a man, degrade him to the level of an appendage of a machine, destroy every remnant of charm in his work and turn it into hated toil.[6]

Charlie Chaplin's 1936 film *Modern Times* paints a vivid portrait of the psychological costs of repetitive factory work. As an assembly worker, Chaplin's only task, all day

[6]Karl Marx, *Das Kapital* (New York: Modern Library), pp. 708, 709.

every day, is to tighten the nuts on two bolts as they pass before him on the assembly line. Finally, he snaps and staggers from the factory, wrenches in hand, tightening every nut-like protuberance he encounters.

Do the extra goods made possible by specialization simply come at too high a price? We must certainly acknowledge at least the *potential* for specialization to proceed too far. Yet specialization need not entail rigidly segmented, mind-numbingly repetitive work. And it is important to recognize that *failure* to specialize entails costs as well. Those who don't specialize must accept low wages or work extremely long hours.

When all is said and done, we can expect to meet life's financial obligations in the shortest time—thereby freeing up more time to do whatever else we wish—if we concentrate at least a significant proportion of our efforts on those tasks for which we have a comparative advantage.

COMPARATIVE ADVANTAGE AND INTERNATIONAL TRADE

The same logic that leads the individuals in an economy to specialize and exchange goods with one another also leads nations to specialize and trade among themselves. As with individuals, each nation can benefit from exchange, even though one may be generally more productive than the other in absolute terms.

The Economic Naturalist 2.3

If trade between nations is so beneficial, why are free-trade agreements so controversial?

One of the most heated issues in the 1996 presidential campaign was President Clinton's support for the North American Free Trade Agreement (NAFTA), a treaty to sharply reduce trade barriers between the United States and its immediate neighbors north and south. The treaty attracted fierce opposition from third-party candidate Ross Perot, who insisted that it would mean unemployment for millions of American workers. If exchange is so beneficial, why does anyone oppose it?

The answer is that, while reducing barriers to international trade increases the total value of all goods and services produced in each nation, it does not guarantee that each individual citizen will do better. One specific concern regarding NAFTA was that it would help Mexico to exploit a comparative advantage in the production of goods made by unskilled labor. Although U.S. consumers would benefit from reduced prices for such goods, many Americans feared that unskilled workers in the United States would lose their jobs to workers in Mexico.

In the end, NAFTA was enacted over the vociferous opposition of American labor unions. So far, however, studies have failed to detect significant overall job losses among unskilled workers in the United States, although there have been some losses in specific industries.

If free trade is so great, why do so many people oppose it?

OUTSOURCING

An issue very much in the news in recent years has been the **outsourcing** of U.S. service jobs. Although the term once primarily meant having services performed by subcontractors anywhere outside the confines of the firm, increasingly it connotes the act of replacing relatively expensive American service workers with much cheaper service workers in overseas locations.

A case in point is the transcription of medical records. In an effort to maintain accurate records, many physicians dictate their case notes for later transcription after examining

outsourcing a term increasingly used to connote having services performed by low-wage workers overseas

their patients. In the past, transcription was often performed by the physician's secretary in spare moments. But secretaries also must attend to a variety of other tasks that disrupt concentration. They must answer phones, serve as receptionists, prepare correspondence, and so on. As insurance disputes and malpractice litigation became more frequent during the 1980s and 1990s, errors in medical records became much more costly to physicians. In response, many turned to independent companies that offered transcription services by full-time, dedicated specialists.

These companies typically served physicians whose practices were located in the same community. But while many of the companies that manage transcription services are still located in the United States, an increasing fraction of the actual work itself is now performed outside the United States. For example, Eight Crossings, a company headquartered in northern California, enables physicians to upload voice dictation files securely to the Internet, whereupon they are transmitted to transcribers who perform the work in India. The finished documents are then transmitted back, in electronic form, to physicians, who may edit and even sign them online. The advantage for physicians, of course, is that the fee for this service is much lower than for the same service performed domestically because wage rates in India are much lower than in the United States.

In China, Korea, Indonesia, India, and elsewhere, even highly skilled professionals still earn just a small fraction of what their counterparts in the United States are paid. Accordingly, companies face powerful competitive pressure to import not just low-cost goods from overseas suppliers, but also a growing array of professional services.

As Microsoft Chairman Bill Gates put it in a 1999 interview,

> As a business manager, you need to take a hard look at your core competencies. Revisit the areas of your company that aren't directly involved in those competencies, and consider whether Web technologies can enable you to spin off those tasks. Let another company take over the management responsibilities for that work, and use modern communication technology to work closely with the people—now partners instead of employees are doing the work. In the Web work style, employees can push the freedom the Web provides to its limits.

In economic terms, the outsourcing of services to low-wage foreign workers is exactly analogous to the importation of goods manufactured by low-wage foreign workers. In both cases, the resulting cost savings benefit consumers in the United States. And in both cases, jobs in the United States may be put in jeopardy, at least temporarily. An American manufacturing worker's job is at risk if it is possible to import the good he produces from another country at lower cost. By the same token, an American service worker's job is at risk if a lower-paid worker can perform that same service somewhere else.

The Economic Naturalist 2.4

Is PBS economics reporter Paul Solman's job a likely candidate for outsourcing?

Paul Solman and his associate Lee Koromvokis produce video segments that provide in-depth analysis of current economic issues for the PBS evening news program *The NewsHour with Jim Lehrer.* Is it likely that his job will someday be outsourced to a low-wage reporter from Hyderabad?

In the book *The New Division of Labor,* economists Frank Levy and Richard Murnane attempt to identify the characteristics of a job that make it a likely candidate for outsourcing.[7] In their view, any job that is amenable to computerization is also vulnerable to

---

[7]Frank Levy and Richard Murnane, *The New Division of Labor: How Computers Are Creating the Next Job Market* (Princeton, NJ: Princeton University Press, 2004).

outsourcing. To computerize a task means to break it down into units that can be managed with simple rules. ATM machines, for example, were able to replace many of the tasks that bank tellers once performed because it was straightforward to reduce these tasks to a simple series of questions that a machine could answer. By the same token, the workers in offshore call centers who increasingly book our airline and hotel reservations are basically following simple scripts much like computer programs.

So the less rules-based a job is, the less vulnerable to outsourcing it is. Safest of all are those that Levy and Murnane describe as "face-to-face" jobs. Unlike most rules-based jobs, these jobs tend to involve complex face-to-face communication with other people, precisely the kind of communication that dominates Solman's economics reporting.

In an interview for the *NewsHour*, Solman asked Levy what he meant, exactly, by "complex communication."

Is a low-wage foreign economics reporter likely to replace Paul Solman?

> "Suppose I say the word *bill*," Levy responded, "and you hear that. And the question is what does that mean? . . . Am I talking about a piece of currency? Am I talking about a piece of legislation, the front end of a duck? The only way you're going to answer that is to think about the whole context of the conversation. But that's very complicated work to break down into some kind of software."[8]

Levy and Murnane describe a second category of tasks that are less vulnerable to outsourcing—namely, those that for one reason or another require the worker to be physically present. For example, it is difficult to see how someone in China or India could build an addition to someone's house in a Chicago suburb or repair a blown head gasket on someone's Chevrolet Corvette in Atlanta or fill a cavity in someone's tooth in Los Angeles.

So on both counts, Paul Solman's job appears safe for the time being. Because it involves face-to-face, complex communication, and because many of his interviews can be conducted only in the United States, it is difficult to see how a reporter from Hyderabad could displace him.

Of course, the fact that a job is relatively safe does not mean that it is completely sheltered. For example, although most dentists continue to think themselves immune from outsourcing, it is now possible for someone requiring extensive dental work to have the work done in New Delhi and still save enough to cover his airfare and a two-week vacation in India.

There are more than 135 million Americans in the labor force. Every three months or so, approximately 7 million of them lose their jobs and 7 million find new ones. At various points in your life, you are likely to be among this group in transition. In the long run, the greatest security available to you or any other worker is the ability to adapt quickly to new circumstances. Having a good education provides no guarantee against losing your job, but it should enable you to develop a comparative advantage at the kinds of tasks that require more than just executing a simple set of rules.

RECAP	COMPARATIVE ADVANTAGE AND INTERNATIONAL TRADE

Nations, like individuals, can benefit from exchange, even though one trading partner may be more productive than the other in absolute terms. The greater the difference between domestic opportunity costs and world opportunity costs, the more a nation benefits from exchange with other nations. But expansions of exchange do not guarantee that each individual citizen will do better. In particular, unskilled workers in high-wage countries may be hurt in the short run by the reduction of barriers to trade with low-wage nations.

[8]http://www.pbs.org/newshour/bb/business-july-dec04-jobs_8-16/

○ S U M M A R Y ○

- One person has an *absolute* advantage over another in the production of a good if she can produce more of that good than the other person. One person has a *comparative* advantage over another in the production of a good if she is relatively more efficient than the other person at producing that good, meaning that her opportunity cost of producing it is lower than her counterpart's. Specialization based on comparative advantage is the basis for economic exchange. When each person specializes in the task at which he or she is relatively most efficient, the economic pie is maximized, making possible the largest slice for everyone. *(LO1)*

- At the individual level, comparative advantage may spring from differences in talent or ability or from differences in education, training, and experience. At the national level, sources of comparative advantage include those innate and learned differences, as well as differences in language, culture, institutions, climate, natural resources, and a host of other factors. *(LO1)*

- The production possibilities curve is a simple device for summarizing the possible combinations of output that a society can produce if it employs its resources efficiently. In a simple economy that produces only coffee and nuts, the PPC shows the maximum quantity of coffee production (vertical axis) possible at each level of nut production (horizontal axis). The slope of the PPC at any point represents the opportunity cost of nuts at that point, expressed in pounds of coffee. *(LO2)*

- All production possibilities curves slope downward because of the Scarcity Principle, which states that the only way a consumer can get more of one good is to settle for less of another. In economies whose workers have different opportunity costs of producing each good, the slope of the PPC becomes steeper as consumers move downward along the curve. This change in slope illustrates the Principle of Increasing Opportunity Cost (or the Low-Hanging-Fruit Principle), which states that in expanding the production of any good, a society should first employ those resources that are relatively efficient at producing that good, only afterward turning to those that are less efficient. *(LO2)*

- Factors that cause a country's PPC to shift outward over time include investment in new factories and equipment, population growth, and improvements in knowledge and technology. *(LO3)*

- The same logic that prompts individuals to specialize in their production and exchange goods with one another also leads nations to specialize and trade with one another. On both levels, each trading partner can benefit from an exchange, even though one may be more productive than the other, in absolute terms, for each good. For both individuals and nations, the benefits of exchange tend to be larger the larger the differences are between the trading partners' opportunity costs. *(LO4)*

○ C O R E   P R I N C I P L E S ○

Comparative Advantage	**The Principle of Comparative Advantage**
	Everyone does best when each person (or each country) concentrates on the activities for which his or her opportunity cost is lowest.
Increasing Opportunity Cost	**The Principle of Increasing Opportunity Cost (also called the "Low-Hanging-Fruit Principle")**
	In expanding the production of any good, first employ those resources with the lowest opportunity cost, and only afterward turn to resources with higher opportunity costs.

○ K E Y   T E R M S ○

absolute advantage	efficient point	production possibilities curve
attainable point	inefficient point	unattainable point
comparative advantage	outsourcing	

○ REVIEW QUESTIONS ○

1. Explain what "having a comparative advantage" at producing a particular good or service means. What does "having an absolute advantage" at producing a good or service mean? *(LO1)*

2. How will a reduction in the number of hours worked each day affect an economy's production possibilities curve? *(LO3)*

3. How will technological innovations that boost labor productivity affect an economy's production possibilities curve? *(LO3)*

4. Why does saying that people are poor because they do not specialize make more sense than saying that people perform their own services because they are poor? *(LO2)*

5. What factors have helped the United States to become the world's leading exporter of movies, books, and popular music? *(LO3)*

○ PROBLEMS ○

1. Ted can wax a car in 20 minutes or wash a car in 60 minutes. Tom can wax a car in 15 minutes or wash a car in 30 minutes. What is each man's opportunity cost of washing a car? Who has a comparative advantage in washing cars? *(LO1)*

2. Nancy and Bill are auto mechanics. Nancy takes 4 hours to replace a clutch and 2 hours to replace a set of brakes. Bill takes 6 hours to replace a clutch and 2 hours to replace a set of brakes. State whether anyone has an absolute advantage at either task and, for each task, identify who has a comparative advantage. *(LO1)*

3. Consider a society consisting only of Helen, who allocates her time between sewing dresses and baking bread. Each hour she devotes to sewing dresses yields 4 dresses and each hour she devotes to baking bread yields 8 loaves of bread. *(LO2)*
   a. If Helen works a total of 8 hours per day, graph her production possibilities curve.
   b. Using your graph, which of the points listed below are attainable and/or efficient?
      28 dresses per day, 16 loaves per day.
      16 dresses per day, 32 loaves per day.
      18 dresses per day, 24 loaves per day.

4. Suppose that in Problem 3 a sewing machine is introduced that enables Helen to sew 8 dresses per hour rather than only 4. *(LO3)*
   a. Show how this development shifts her production possibilities curve.
   b. Indicate if the following points are attainable and/or efficient before and after the introduction of the sewing machine.
      16 dresses per day, 48 loaves per day.
      24 dresses per day, 16 loaves per day.
   c. Explain what is meant by the following statement: "An increase in productivity with respect to any one good increases our options for producing and consuming all other goods."

5. Susan can pick 4 pounds of coffee in an hour or gather 2 pounds of nuts. Tom can pick 2 pounds of coffee in an hour or gather 4 pounds of nuts. Each works 6 hours per day. *(LO2, LO3)*
   a. What is the maximum number of pounds of coffee the two can pick in a day?
   b. What is the maximum number of pounds of nuts the two can gather in a day?
   c. If Susan and Tom were picking the maximum number of pounds of coffee when they decided that they would like to begin gathering 4 pounds of nuts per day, who would gather the nuts, and how many pounds of coffee would they still be able to pick?

|ECONOMICS

Visit your mobile app store and download the Frank: Study Econ app *today*!

    d. Now suppose Susan and Tom were gathering the maximum number of pounds of nuts when they decided that they would like to begin picking 8 pounds of coffee per day. Who would pick the coffee, and how many pounds of nuts would they still be able to gather?

    e. Would it be possible for Susan and Tom in total to gather 26 pounds of nuts and pick 20 pounds of coffee each day? If so, how much of each good should each person pick?

    f. Is the point at 30 pounds of coffee per day, 12 pounds of nuts per day an attainable point? Is it an efficient point?

    g. Is the point at 24 pounds of coffee per day, 24 pounds of nuts per day an attainable point? Is it an efficient point?

    h. On a graph with pounds of coffee per day on the vertical axis and pounds of nuts per day on the horizontal axis, show all the points you identified in parts a–g.

6.* Refer to the two-person economy described in Problem 5. *(LO4)*

    a. Suppose that Susan and Tom could buy or sell coffee and nuts in the world market at a price of $2 per pound for coffee and $2 per pound for nuts. If each person specialized completely in the good for which he or she had a comparative advantage, how much could they earn by selling all they produce?

    b. At the prices just described, what is the maximum amount of coffee Susan and Tom could buy in the world market with the income they earned? What is the maximum amount of nuts? Would it be possible for them to consume 40 pounds of nuts and 8 pounds of coffee each day?

    c. In light of their ability to buy and sell in world markets at the stated prices, show on the same graph all combinations of the two goods it would be possible for them to consume.

○ ANSWERS TO CONCEPT CHECKS ○

2.1

	Productivity in programming	Productivity in bicycle repair
Pat	2 web page updates per hour	1 repair per hour
Meg	3 web page updates per hour	3 repairs per hour

The entries in the table tell us that Meg has an absolute advantage over Pat in both activities. While Meg, the mechanic, can update 3 web pages per hour, Pat, the programmer, can update only 2. Meg's absolute advantage over Pat is even greater in the task of fixing bikes—3 repairs per hour versus Pat's 1.

But as in the second example in this chapter, the fact that Meg is a better programmer than Pat does not imply that Meg should update her own web page. Meg's opportunity cost of updating a web page is 1 bicycle repair, whereas Pat must give up only half a repair to update a web page. Pat has a comparative advantage over Meg at programming and Meg has a comparative advantage over Pat at bicycle repair. *(LO1)*

2.2 In the accompanying graph, *A* (20 pounds per day of coffee, 4 pounds per day of nuts) is unattainable; *B* (12 pounds per day of coffee, 6 pounds per day of nuts) is

---

*Denotes more difficult problem.

both attainable and efficient; and *C* (4 pounds per day of coffee, 8 pounds per day of nuts) is attainable and inefficient. *(LO2)*

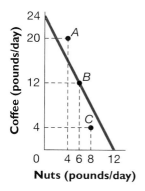

2.3 Susan's opportunity cost of gathering a pound of nuts is now ½ pound of coffee and Tom's opportunity cost of gathering a pound of nuts is now only 1 pound of coffee. So Tom has a comparative advantage at picking coffee and Susan has a comparative advantage at gathering nuts. *(LO2)*

2.4 Since Tom can produce five times as many pounds of nuts in an hour as pounds of coffee, to produce equal quantities of each, he must spend 5 hours picking coffee for every hour he devotes to gathering nuts. And since he works a 6-hour day, that means spending 5 hours picking coffee and 1 hour gathering nuts. Dividing his time in this way, he will end up with 5 pounds of each good. Similarly, if she is to produce equal quantities of each good, Susan must spend 5 hours gathering nuts and 1 hour picking coffee. So she too produces 5 pounds of each good if she divides her 6-hour day in this way. Their combined daily production will thus be 10 pounds of each good. By working together and specializing, however, they can produce and consume a total of 30 pounds per day of each good. *(LO2)*

CHAPTER 3

Supply and Demand

Christopher Kerrigan/The McGraw-Hill Companies

WHEN THERE'S EXCESS DEMAND FOR A PRODUCT, ITS PRICE TENDS TO RISE

LEARNING OBJECTIVES

After reading this chapter, you should be able to:

LO1 Describe how the demand and supply curves summarize the behavior of buyers and sellers in the marketplace.

LO2 Discuss how the supply and demand curves interact to determine equilibrium price and quantity.

LO3 Illustrate how shifts in supply and demand curves cause prices and quantities to change.

LO4 Explain and apply the Efficiency Principle and the Equilibrium Principle (also called "The No-Cash-on-the-Table Principle").

T he stock of foodstuffs on hand at any moment in New York City's grocery stores, restaurants, and private kitchens is sufficient to feed the area's 10 million residents for at most a week or so. Since most of these residents have nutritionally adequate and highly varied diets, and since almost no food is produced within the city proper, provisioning New York requires that millions of pounds of food and drink be delivered to locations throughout the city each day.

No doubt many New Yorkers, buying groceries at their favorite local markets or eating at their favorite Italian restaurants, give little or no thought to the nearly miraculous coordination of people and resources required to feed city residents on a daily basis. But near-miraculous it is, nevertheless. Even if the supplying of New York City consisted only of transporting a fixed collection of foods to a given list of destinations each day, it would be quite an impressive operation, requiring at least a small (and well-managed) army to carry out.

Yet the entire process is astonishingly more complex than that. For example, the system must somehow ensure that not only *enough* food is delivered to satisfy New Yorkers' discriminating palates, but also the *right kinds* of food. There can't be too much pheasant and not enough smoked eel; or too much bacon and not enough eggs; or too much caviar and not enough canned tuna; and so on. Similar judgments must be made *within* each category of food and drink: There must be the right amount of Swiss cheese and the right amounts of provolone, gorgonzola, and feta.

But even this doesn't begin to describe the complexity of the decisions and actions required to provide our nation's largest city with its daily bread. Someone has to decide where each particular type of food gets produced, and how, and by whom. Someone must decide how much of each type of food gets delivered to *each* of the tens of thousands of restaurants and grocery stores in the city. Someone must determine whether the deliveries should be made in big trucks or small ones, arrange that the trucks be in the right place at the right time, and ensure that gasoline and qualified drivers be available.

Thousands of individuals must decide what role, if any, they will play in this collective effort. Some people—just the right number—must choose to drive food delivery trucks rather than trucks that deliver lumber. Others—again, just the right number—must become the mechanics who fix these trucks rather than carpenters who build houses. Others must become farmers rather than architects or bricklayers. Still others must become chefs in upscale restaurants, or flip burgers at McDonald's, instead of becoming plumbers or electricians.

Yet despite the almost incomprehensible number and complexity of the tasks involved, somehow the supplying of New York City manages to get done remarkably smoothly. Oh, a grocery store will occasionally run out of flank steak or a diner will sometimes be told that someone else has just ordered the last serving of roast duck. But if episodes like these stick in memory, it is only because they are rare. For the most part, New York's food delivery system—like that of every other city in the country—functions so seamlessly that it attracts virtually no notice.

The situation is strikingly different in New York City's rental housing market. According to one estimate, the city needs between 20,000 and 40,000 new housing units each year merely to keep up with population growth and to replace existing housing that is deteriorated beyond repair. The actual rate of new construction in the city, however, is only 6,000 units per year. As a result, America's most densely populated city has been experiencing a protracted housing shortage. Yet, paradoxically, in the midst of this shortage, apartment houses are being demolished; and in the vacant lots left behind, people from the neighborhoods are planting flower gardens!

New York City is experiencing not only a growing shortage of rental housing, but also chronically strained relations between landlords and tenants. In one all-too-typical case, for example, a photographer living in a loft on the Lower East Side waged an eight-year court battle with his landlord that generated literally thousands of pages of legal documents. "Once we put up a doorbell for ourselves," the photographer recalled, "and [the landlord] pulled it out, so we pulled out the wires to his doorbell."[1] The landlord, for his part, accused the photographer of obstructing his efforts to renovate the apartment. According to the landlord, the tenant preferred for the apartment to remain in substandard condition since that gave him an excuse to withhold rent payments.

Same city, two strikingly different patterns: In the food industry, goods and services are available in wide variety and people (at least those with adequate income) are generally satisfied with what they receive and the choices available to them. In contrast, in the rental housing industry, chronic shortages and chronic dissatisfaction are rife among both buyers and sellers. Why this difference?

The brief answer is that New York City relies on a complex system of administrative rent regulations to allocate housing units but leaves the allocation of food essentially in the hands of market forces—the forces of supply and demand. Although intuition might suggest otherwise, both theory and experience suggest that the seemingly chaotic and unplanned outcomes of market forces, in most cases, can

age fotostock/SuperStock

Julius Lando/Imagestate Media Partners Limited - Impact Photos / Alamy

Why does New York City's food distribution system work so much better than its housing market?

---

[1] Quoted by John Tierney, "The Rentocracy: At the Intersection of Supply and Demand," *New York Times Magazine,* May 4, 1997, p. 39.

do a better job of allocating economic resources than can (for example) a government agency, even if the agency has the best of intentions.

In this chapter we'll explore how markets allocate food, housing, and other goods and services, usually with remarkable efficiency despite the complexity of the tasks. To be sure, markets are by no means perfect, and our stress on their virtues is to some extent an attempt to counteract what most economists view as an underappreciation by the general public of their remarkable strengths. But, in the course of our discussion, we'll see why markets function so smoothly most of the time and why bureaucratic rules and regulations rarely work as well in solving complex economic problems.

To convey an understanding of how markets work is a major goal of this course, and in this chapter we provide only a brief introduction and overview. As the course proceeds, we'll discuss the economic role of markets in considerably more detail, paying attention to some of the problems of markets as well as their strengths.

WHAT, HOW, AND FOR WHOM? CENTRAL PLANNING VERSUS THE MARKET

No city, state, or society—regardless of how it is organized—can escape the need to answer certain basic economic questions. For example, how much of our limited time and other resources should we devote to building housing, how much to the production of food, and how much to providing other goods and services? What techniques should we use to produce each good? Who should be assigned to each specific task? And how should the resulting goods and services be distributed among people?

In the thousands of different societies for which records are available, issues like these have been decided in essentially one of two ways. One approach is for all economic decisions to be made centrally, by an individual or small number of individuals on behalf of a larger group. For example, in many agrarian societies throughout history, families or other small groups consumed only those goods and services that they produced for themselves, and a single clan or family leader made most important production and distribution decisions. On an immensely larger scale, the economic organization of the former Soviet Union (and other communist countries) was also largely centralized. In so-called centrally planned communist nations, a central bureaucratic committee established production targets for the country's farms and factories, developed a master plan for how to achieve the targets (including detailed instructions concerning who was to produce what), and set up guidelines for the distribution and use of the goods and services produced.

Communist

Neither form of centralized economic organization is much in evidence today. When implemented on a small scale, as in a self-sufficient family enterprise, centralized decision making is certainly feasible. For the reasons discussed in the preceding chapter, however, the jack-of-all-trades approach was doomed once it became clear how dramatically people could improve their living standards by specialization—that is, by having each individual focus his or her efforts on a relatively narrow range of tasks. And with the fall of the Soviet Union and its satellite nations in the late 1980s, there are now only three communist economies left in the world: Cuba, North Korea, and China. The first two of these appear to be on their last legs, economically speaking, and China has largely abandoned any attempt to control production and distribution decisions from the center. The major remaining examples of centralized allocation and control now reside in the bureaucratic agencies that administer programs like New York City's rent controls—programs that are themselves becoming increasingly rare.

At the beginning of the twenty-first century, we are therefore left, for the most part, with the second major form of economic system, one in which production and distribution decisions are left to individuals interacting in private markets. In the so-called capitalist, or free-market, economies, people decide for themselves which careers to pursue and which products to produce or buy. In fact, there are no *pure* free-market economies today. Modern industrial countries are more properly described as "mixed economies." Their goods and services are allocated by a combination of free markets, regulation, and other forms of collective control. Still, it makes sense to refer to such systems as free-market economies because people are for the most part free to start businesses, shut them down, or sell them. And within broad limits, the distribution of goods and services is determined by individual preferences backed by individual purchasing power, which in most cases comes from the income people earn in the labor market.

In country after country, markets have replaced centralized control for the simple reason that they tend to assign production tasks and consumption benefits much more effectively. The popular press and conventional wisdom often assert that economists disagree about important issues. (As someone once quipped, "If you lay all the economists in the world end to end, they still wouldn't reach a conclusion.") The fact is, however, that there is overwhelming agreement among economists about a broad range of issues. A substantial majority believes that markets are the most effective means for allocating society's scarce resources. For example, a recent survey found that more than 90 percent of American professional economists believe that rent regulations like the ones implemented by New York City do more harm than good. That the stated aim of these regulations—to make rental housing more afford-able for middle- and low-income families—is clearly benign was not enough to prevent them from wreaking havoc on New York City's housing market. To see why, we must explore how goods and services are allocated in private markets, and why nonmarket means of allocating goods and services often do not produce the expected results.

BUYERS AND SELLERS IN MARKETS

market the market for any good consists of all buyers and sellers of that good

Beginning with some simple concepts and definitions, we will explore how the inter-actions among buyers and sellers in markets determine the prices and quantities of the various goods and services traded. We begin by defining a market: The market for any good consists of all the buyers and sellers of that good. So, for example, the market for pizza on a given day in a given place is just the set of people (or other economic actors such as firms) potentially able to buy or sell pizza at that time and location.

In the market for pizza, sellers comprise the individuals and companies that either do sell—or might, under the right circumstances, sell—pizza. Similarly, buyers in this market include all individuals who buy—or might buy—pizza.

In most parts of the country, a decent pizza can still be had for less than $10. Where does the market price of pizza come from? Looking beyond pizza to the vast array of other goods that are bought and sold every day, we may ask, "Why are some goods cheap and others expensive?" Aristotle had no idea. Nor did Plato, or Copernicus, or Newton. On reflection, it is astonishing that, for almost the entire span of human history, not even the most intelligent and creative minds on Earth had any real inkling of how to answer that seemingly simple question. Even Adam Smith, the Scottish moral philosopher whose *Wealth of Nations* launched the discipline of economics in 1776, suffered confusion on this issue.

Smith and other early economists (including Karl Marx) thought that the market price of a good was determined by its cost of produc-tion. But although costs surely do affect prices, they cannot explain why one of Pablo Picasso's paintings sells for so much more than one of Jackson Pollock's.

Why do Pablo Picasso's paintings sell for so much more than Jackson Pollock's?

Wu Ching-teng/Corbis Wire/Corbis

Stanley Jevons and other nineteenth-century economists tried to explain price by focusing on the value people derived from consuming different goods and services. It certainly seems plausible that people will pay a lot for a good they value highly. Yet willingness to pay cannot be the whole story, either. Deprive a person in the desert of water, for example, and he will be dead in a matter of hours, and yet water sells for less than a penny a gallon. By contrast, human beings can get along perfectly well without gold, and yet gold sells for more than $1,000 an ounce.

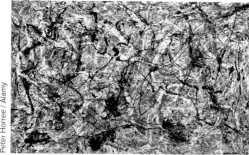

A Jackson Pollock painting.

Cost of production? Value to the user? Which is it? The answer, which seems obvious to today's economists, is that both matter. Writing in the late nineteenth century, the British economist Alfred Marshall was among the first to show clearly how costs and value interact to determine both the prevailing market price for a good and the amount of it that is bought and sold. Our task in the pages ahead will be to explore Marshall's insights and gain some practice in applying them. As a first step, we introduce the two main components of Marshall's pathbreaking analysis: the demand curve and the supply curve.

THE DEMAND CURVE

Marshall's analysis

In the market for pizza, the **demand curve** for pizza is a simple schedule or graph that tells us how many slices people would be willing to buy at different prices. By convention, economists usually put price on the vertical axis of the demand curve and quantity on the horizontal axis.

A fundamental property of the demand curve is that it is downward-sloping with respect to price. For example, the demand curve for pizza tells us that as the price of pizza falls, buyers will buy more slices. Thus, the daily demand curve for pizza in Chicago on a given day might look like the curve seen in Figure 3.1. (Although economists usually refer to demand and supply "curves," we often draw them as straight lines in examples.)

The demand curve in Figure 3.1 tells us that when the price of pizza is low—say $2 per slice—buyers will want to buy 16,000 slices per day, whereas they will want to buy only 12,000 slices at a price of $3 and only 8,000 at a price of $4. The demand curve for pizza—as for any other good—slopes downward for multiple reasons. Some have to do with the individual consumer's reactions to price changes. Thus, as pizza becomes more expensive, a consumer may switch to chicken sandwiches, hamburgers, or other foods that substitute for pizza. This is called the **substitution effect** of a price change. In addition, a price increase reduces the quantity demanded because it reduces purchasing power: A consumer simply can't afford to buy as many slices of pizza at higher prices as at lower prices. This is called the **income effect** of a price change.

demand curve a schedule or graph showing the quantity of a good that buyers wish to buy at each price

substitution effect the change in the quantity demanded of a good that results because buyers switch to or from substitutes when the price of the good changes

income effect the change in the quantity demanded of a good that results because a change in the price of a good changes the buyer's purchasing power

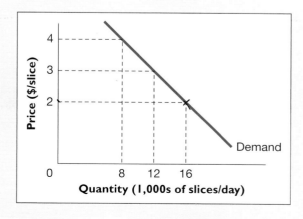

FIGURE 3.1

The Daily Demand Curve for Pizza in Chicago.

The demand curve for any good is a downward-sloping function of its price.

buyer's reservation price the largest dollar amount the buyer would be willing to pay for a good

Another reason the demand curve slopes downward is that consumers differ in terms of how much they're willing to pay for the good. The Cost-Benefit Principle tells us that a given person will buy the good if the benefit he expects to receive from it exceeds its cost. The benefit is the **buyer's reservation price,** the highest dollar amount he'd be willing to pay for the good. The cost of the good is the actual amount that the buyer actually must pay for it, which is the market price of the good. In most markets, different buyers have different reservation prices. So, when the good sells for a high price, it will satisfy the cost-benefit test for fewer buyers than when it sells for a lower price.

To put this same point another way, the fact that the demand curve for a good is downward-sloping reflects the fact that the reservation price of the marginal buyer declines as the quantity of the good bought increases. Here the marginal buyer is the person who purchases the last unit of the good sold. If buyers are currently purchasing 12,000 slices of pizza a day in Figure 3.1, for example, the reservation price for the buyer of the 12,000th slice must be $3. (If someone had been willing to pay more than that, the quantity demanded at a price of $3 would have been more than 12,000 to begin with.) By similar reasoning, when the quantity sold is 16,000 slices per day, the marginal buyer's reservation price must be only $2.

We defined the demand curve for any good as a schedule telling how much of it consumers wish to purchase at various prices. This is called the *horizontal interpretation* of the demand curve. Using the horizontal interpretation, we start with price on the vertical axis and read the corresponding quantity demanded on the horizontal axis. Thus, at a price of $4 per slice, the demand curve in Figure 3.1 tells us that the quantity of pizza demanded will be 8,000 slices per day.

The demand curve also can be interpreted in a second way, which is to start with quantity on the horizontal axis and then read the marginal buyer's reservation price on the vertical axis. Thus, when the quantity of pizza sold is 8,000 slices per day, the demand curve in Figure 3.1 tells us that the marginal buyer's reservation price is $4 per slice. This second way of reading the demand curve is called the *vertical interpretation.*

CONCEPT CHECK 3.1

In Figure 3.1, what is the marginal buyer's reservation price when the quantity of pizza sold is 10,000 slices per day? For the same demand curve, what will be the quantity of pizza demanded at a price of $2.50 per slice?

THE SUPPLY CURVE

supply curve a graph or schedule showing the quantity of a good that sellers wish to sell at each price

In the market for pizza, the **supply curve** is a simple schedule or graph that tells us, for each possible price, the total number of slices that all pizza vendors would be willing to sell at that price. What does the supply curve of pizza look like? The answer to this question is based on the logical assumption that suppliers should be willing to sell additional slices as long as the price they receive is sufficient to cover their opportunity cost of supplying them. Thus, if what someone could earn by selling a slice of pizza is insufficient to compensate her for what she could have earned if she had spent her time and invested her money in some other way, she will not sell that slice. Otherwise, she will.

Just as buyers differ with respect to the amounts they are willing to pay for pizza, sellers also differ with respect to their opportunity cost of supplying pizza. For those with limited education and work experience, the opportunity cost of selling pizza is relatively low (because such individuals typically do not have a lot of high-paying alternatives). For others, the opportunity cost of selling pizza is of moderate value, and for still others—like rock stars and professional athletes—it is prohibitively high. In part because of these differences in opportunity cost among people, the daily supply curve of pizza will be *upward-sloping* with respect to price. As an illustration, see Figure 3.2, which shows a hypothetical supply curve for pizza in the Chicago market on a given day.

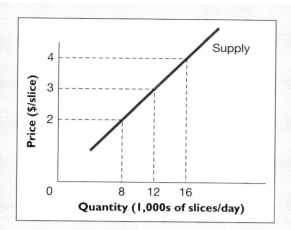

FIGURE 3.2

The Daily Supply Curve of Pizza in Chicago.

At higher prices, sellers generally offer more units for sale.

The fact that the supply curve slopes upward may be seen as a consequence of the Low-Hanging-Fruit Principle, discussed in the chapter on comparative advantage. This principle tells us that as we expand the production of pizza, we turn first to those whose opportunity cost of producing pizza is lowest, and only then to others with a higher opportunity cost.

Like the demand curve, the supply curve can be interpreted either horizontally or vertically. Under the horizontal interpretation, we begin with a price and then go over to the supply curve to read the quantity that sellers wish to sell at that price on the horizontal axis. For instance, at a price of $2 per slice, sellers in Figure 3.2 wish to sell 8,000 slices per day.

Under the vertical interpretation, we begin with a quantity and then go up to the supply curve to read the corresponding marginal cost on the vertical axis. Thus, if sellers in Figure 3.2 are currently supplying 12,000 slices per day, the opportunity cost of the marginal seller is $3 per slice. In other words, the supply curve tells us that the marginal cost of producing the 12,000th slice of pizza is $3. (If someone could produce a 12,001st slice for less than $3, she would have an incentive to supply it, so the quantity of pizza supplied at $3 per slice would not have been 12,000 slices per day to begin with.) By similar reasoning, when the quantity of pizza supplied is 16,000 slices per day, the marginal cost of producing another slice must be $4. The **seller's reservation price** for selling an additional unit of a good is her marginal cost of producing that good. It is the smallest dollar amount for which she would not be worse off if she sold an additional unit.

Increasing Opportunity Cost

seller's reservation price the smallest dollar amount for which a seller would be willing to sell an additional unit, generally equal to marginal cost

CONCEPT CHECK 3.2

In Figure 3.2, what is the marginal cost of a slice of pizza when the quantity of pizza sold is 10,000 slices per day? For the same supply curve, what will be the quantity of pizza supplied at a price of $3.50 per slice?

RECAP	DEMAND AND SUPPLY CURVES

The *market* for a good consists of the actual and potential buyers and sellers of that good. For any given price, the *demand curve* shows the quantity that demanders would be willing to buy and the *supply curve* shows the quantity that suppliers of the good would be willing to sell. Suppliers are willing to sell more at higher prices (supply curves slope upward) and demanders are willing to buy less at higher prices (demand curves slope downward).

MARKET EQUILIBRIUM

equilibrium a balanced or unchanging situation in which all forces at work within a system are canceled by others

The concept of **equilibrium** is employed in both the physical and social sciences, and it is of central importance in economic analysis. In general, a system is in equilibrium when all forces at work within the system are canceled by others, resulting in a balanced or unchanging situation. In physics, for example, a ball hanging from a spring is said to be in equilibrium when the spring has stretched sufficiently that the upward force it exerts on the ball is exactly counterbalanced by the downward force of gravity. In economics, a market is said to be in equilibrium when no participant in the market has any reason to alter his or her behavior, so that there is no tendency for production or prices in that market to change.

If we want to determine the final position of a ball hanging from a spring, we need to find the point at which the forces of gravity and spring tension are balanced and the system is in equilibrium. Similarly, if we want to find the price at which a good will sell (which we will call the **equilibrium price**) and the quantity of it that will be sold (the **equilibrium quantity**), we need to find the equilibrium in the market for that good. The basic tools for finding the equilibrium in a market for a good are the supply and demand curves for that good. For reasons we will explain, the equilibrium price and equilibrium quantity of a good are the price and quantity at which the supply and demand curves for the good intersect. For the hypothetical supply and demand curves shown earlier for the pizza market in Chicago, the equilibrium price will therefore be $3 per slice, and the equilibrium quantity of pizza sold will be 12,000 slices per day, as shown in Figure 3.3.

equilibrium price and **equilibrium quantity** the price and quantity at the intersection of the supply and demand curves for the good

Note that at the equilibrium price of $3 per slice, both sellers and buyers are "satisfied" in the following sense: Buyers are buying exactly the quantity of pizza they wish to buy at that price (12,000 slices per day) and sellers are selling exactly the quantity of pizza they wish to sell (also 12,000 slices per day). And since they are satisfied in this sense, neither buyers nor sellers face any incentives to change their behavior.

market equilibrium occurs in a market when all buyers and sellers are satisfied with their respective quantities at the market price

Note the limited sense of the term "satisfied" in the definition of **market equilibrium.** It doesn't mean that sellers wouldn't be pleased to receive a price higher than the equilibrium price. Rather, it means only that they're able to sell all they wish to sell at that price. Similarly, to say that buyers are satisfied at the equilibrium price doesn't mean that they wouldn't be happy to pay less than that price. Rather, it means only that they're able to buy exactly as many units of the good as they wish to at the equilibrium price.

Note also that if the price of pizza in our Chicago market were anything other than $3 per slice, either buyers or sellers would be frustrated. Suppose, for example, that the price of pizza were $4 per slice, as shown in Figure 3.4. At that price, buyers wish to buy only 8,000 slices per day, but sellers wish to sell 16,000. And since no one can force someone to buy a slice of pizza against her wishes, this means that buyers will buy only

FIGURE 3.3

The Equilibrium Price and Quantity of Pizza in Chicago.

The equilibrium quantity and price of a product are the values that correspond to the intersection of the supply and demand curves for that product.

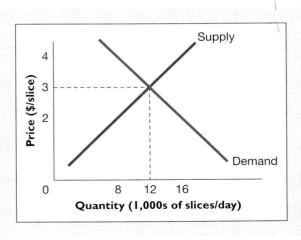

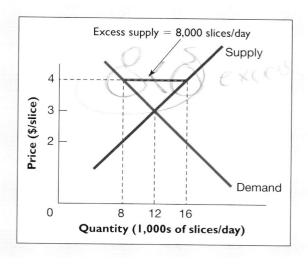

FIGURE 3.4

Excess Supply.

When price exceeds equilibrium price, there is excess supply, or surplus, the difference between quantity supplied and quantity demanded.

the 8,000 slices they wish to buy. So when price exceeds the equilibrium price, it is sellers who end up being frustrated. At a price of $4 in this example, they are left with an **excess supply** of 8,000 slices per day.

Conversely, suppose that the price of pizza in our Chicago market were less than the equilibrium price—say, $2 per slice. As shown in Figure 3.5, buyers want to buy 16,000 slices per day at that price, whereas sellers want to sell only 8,000. And since sellers cannot be forced to sell pizza against their wishes, this time it is the buyers who end up being frustrated. At a price of $2 per slice in this example, they experience an **excess demand** of 8,000 slices per day.

An extraordinary feature of private markets for goods and services is their automatic tendency to gravitate toward their respective equilibrium prices and quantities. This tendency is a simple consequence of the Incentive Principle. The mechanisms by which the adjustment happens are implicit in our definitions of excess supply and excess demand. Suppose, for example, that the price of pizza in our hypothetical market was $4 per slice, leading to excess supply as shown in Figure 3.4. Because sellers are frustrated in the sense of wanting to sell more pizza than buyers wish to buy, sellers have an incentive to take whatever steps they can to increase their sales. The simplest strategy available to them is to cut their price slightly. Thus, if one seller reduced his price from $4 to, say, $3.95 per slice, he would attract many of the buyers who had been paying $4 per slice for pizza supplied by other sellers. Those sellers, in order to recover their lost business, would then have an incentive to match the price cut. But

excess supply the amount by which quantity supplied exceeds quantity demanded when the price of a good exceeds the equilibrium price

excess demand the amount by which quantity demanded exceeds quantity supplied when the price of a good lies below the equilibrium price

Incentive

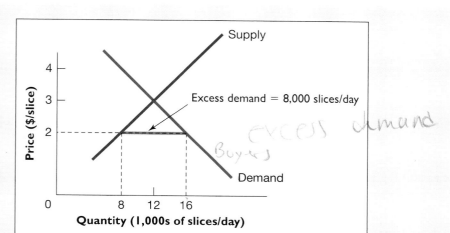

FIGURE 3.5

Excess Demand.

When price lies below equilibrium price, there is excess demand, the difference between quantity demanded and quantity supplied.

notice that if all sellers lowered their prices to $3.95 per slice, there would still be considerable excess supply. So sellers would face continuing incentives to cut their prices. This pressure to cut prices won't go away until prices fall all the way to $3 per slice.

Conversely, suppose that price starts out less than the equilibrium price—say, $2 per slice. This time it is buyers who are frustrated. A person who can't get all the pizza he wants at a price of $2 per slice has an incentive to offer a higher price, hoping to obtain pizza that would otherwise have been sold to other buyers. And sellers, for their part, will be only too happy to post higher prices as long as queues of frustrated buyers remain.

The upshot is that price has a tendency to gravitate to its equilibrium level under conditions of either excess supply or excess demand. And when price reaches its equilibrium level, both buyers and sellers are satisfied in the technical sense of being able to buy or sell precisely the amounts of their choosing.

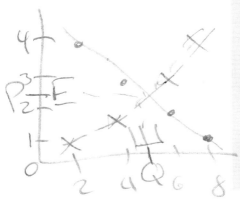

| Market Equilibrium | EXAMPLE 3.1 |

Samples of points on the demand and supply curves of a pizza market are provided in Table 3.1. Graph the demand and supply curves for this market and find its equilibrium price and quantity.

TABLE 3.1
Points along the Demand and Supply Curves of a Pizza Market

Demand for Pizza		Supply of Pizza	
Price ($/slice)	Quantity demanded (1,000s of slices/day)	Price ($/slice)	Quantity supplied (1,000s of slices/day)
1	8	1	2
2	6	2	4
3	4	3	6
4	2	4	8

The points in the table are plotted in Figure 3.6 and then joined to indicate the supply and demand curves for this market. These curves intersect to yield an equilibrium price of $2.50 per slice and an equilibrium quantity of 5,000 slices per day.

FIGURE 3.6

Graphing Supply and Demand and Finding Equilibrium Price and Quantity.

To graph the demand and supply curves, plot the relevant points given in the table and then join them with a line. Equilibrium price and quantity occur at the intersection of these curves.

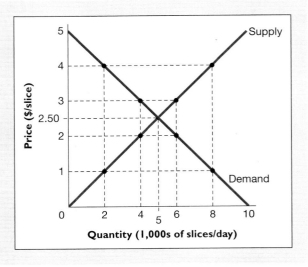

We emphasize that market equilibrium doesn't necessarily produce an ideal outcome for all market participants. Thus, in Example 3.1, market participants are satisfied with the amount of pizza they buy and sell at a price of $2.50 per slice, but for a poor buyer this may signify little more than that he *can't* buy additional pizza without sacrificing other more highly valued purchases.

Indeed, buyers with extremely low incomes often have difficulty purchasing even basic goods and services, which has prompted governments in almost every society to attempt to ease the burdens of the poor. Yet the laws of supply and demand cannot simply be repealed by an act of the legislature. In the next section, we'll see that when legislators attempt to prevent markets from reaching their equilibrium prices and quantities, they often do more harm than good. Fortunately, there are other, more effective, ways of providing assistance to needy families.

RENT CONTROLS RECONSIDERED

Consider again the market for rental housing units in New York City and suppose that the demand and supply curves for one-bedroom apartments are as shown in Figure 3.7. This market, left alone, would reach an equilibrium monthly rent of $1,600, at which 2 million one-bedroom apartments would be rented. Both landlords and tenants would be satisfied, in the sense that they would not wish to rent either more or fewer units at that price.

This wouldn't necessarily mean, of course, that all is well and good. Many potential tenants, for example, might simply be unable to afford a rent of $1,600 per month and thus be forced to remain homeless (or to move out of the city to a cheaper location). Suppose that, acting purely out of benign motives, legislators made it unlawful for landlords to charge more than $800 per month for one-bedroom apartments. Their stated aim in enacting this law was that no person should have to remain homeless because decent housing was unaffordable.

But note in Figure 3.8 that when rents for one-bedroom apartments are prevented from rising above $800 per month, landlords are willing to supply only 1 million apartments per month, 1 million fewer than at the equilibrium monthly rent of $1,600. Note also that at the controlled rent of $800 per month, tenants want to rent 3 million one-bedroom apartments per month. (For example, many people who would have decided to live in New Jersey rather than pay $1,600 a month in New York will now choose to live in the city.) So when rents are prevented from rising above $800 per month, we see an excess demand for one-bedroom apartments of 2 million units each month. Put another way, the rent controls result in a housing shortage of 2 million units each month. What is more, the number of apartments actually available *declines* by 1 million units per month.

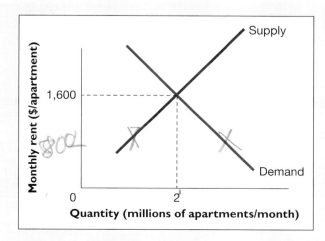

FIGURE 3.7

An Unregulated Housing Market.

For the supply and demand curves shown, the equilibrium monthly rent is $1,600 and 2 million apartments will be rented at that price.

FIGURE 3.8

Rent Controls.

When rents are prohibited from rising to the equilibrium level, the result is excess demand in the housing market.

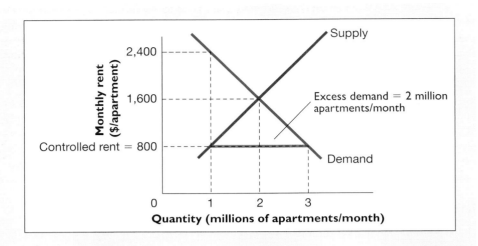

Incentive

If the housing market were completely unregulated, the immediate response to such a high level of excess demand would be for rents to rise sharply. But here the law prevents them from rising above $800. Many other ways exist, however, in which market participants can respond to the pressures of excess demand. For instance, owners will quickly learn that they are free to spend less on maintaining their rental units. After all, if there are scores of renters knocking at the door of each vacant apartment, a landlord has considerable room to maneuver. Leaking pipes, peeling paint, broken furnaces, and other problems are less likely to receive prompt attention—or, indeed, any attention at all—when rents are set well below market-clearing levels.

Nor are reduced availability of apartments and poorer maintenance of existing apartments the only difficulties. With an offering of only 1 million apartments per month, we see in Figure 3.8 that there are renters who'd be willing to pay as much as $2,400 per month for an apartment. As the Incentive Principle suggests, this pressure will almost always find ways, legal or illegal, of expressing itself. In New York City, for example, it is not uncommon to see "finder's fees" or "key deposits" as high as several thousand dollars. Owners who cannot charge a market-clearing rent for their apartments also have the option of converting them to condominiums or co-ops, which enables them to sell their assets for prices much closer to their true economic value.

Even when rent-controlled apartment owners don't hike their prices in these various ways, serious misallocations result. For instance, ill-suited roommates often remain together despite their constant bickering because each is reluctant to reenter the housing market. Or a widow might steadfastly remain in her seven-room apartment even after her children have left home because it is much cheaper than alternative dwellings not covered by rent control. It would be much better for all concerned if she relinquished that space to a larger family that valued it more highly. But under rent controls, she has no economic incentive to do so.

There's also another more insidious cost of rent controls. In markets without rent controls, landlords cannot discriminate against potential tenants on the basis of race, religion, sexual orientation, physical disability, or national origin without suffering an economic penalty. Refusal to rent to members of specific groups would reduce the demand for their apartments, which would mean having to accept lower rents. When rents are artificially pegged below their equilibrium level, however, the resulting excess demand for apartments enables landlords to engage in discrimination with no further economic penalty.

Rent controls are not the only instance in which governments have attempted to repeal the law of supply and demand in the interest of helping the poor. During the late 1970s, for example, the federal government tried to hold the price of gasoline below its equilibrium level out of concern that high gasoline prices imposed unacceptable hardships on low-income drivers. As with controls in the rental housing market, unintended consequences of price controls in the gasoline market made the policy an extremely costly way of trying to aid the poor. For example, gasoline shortages resulted in long lines at the pumps, a waste not only of valuable time, but also of gasoline as cars sat idling for extended periods.

In their opposition to rent controls and similar measures, are economists revealing a total lack of concern for the poor? Although this claim is sometimes made by those who don't understand the issues, or who stand to benefit in some way from government regulations, there is little justification for it. *Economists simply realize that there are much more effective ways to help poor people than to try to give them apartments and other goods at artificially low prices.*

One straightforward approach would be to give the poor additional income and let them decide for themselves how to spend it. True, there are also practical difficulties involved in transferring additional purchasing power into the hands of the poor—most importantly, the difficulty of targeting cash to the genuinely needy without weakening others' incentives to fend for themselves. But there are practical ways to overcome this difficulty. For example, for far less than the waste caused by price controls, the government could afford generous subsidies to the wages of the working poor and could sponsor public-service employment for those who are unable to find jobs in the private sector.

[handwritten: weakening incentive to fend for self]

Regulations that peg prices below equilibrium levels have far-reaching effects on market outcomes. The following concept check asks you to consider what happens when a price control is established at a level above the equilibrium price.

CONCEPT CHECK 3.3

In the rental housing market whose demand and supply curves are shown below, what will be the effect of a law that prevents rents from rising above $1,200 per month?

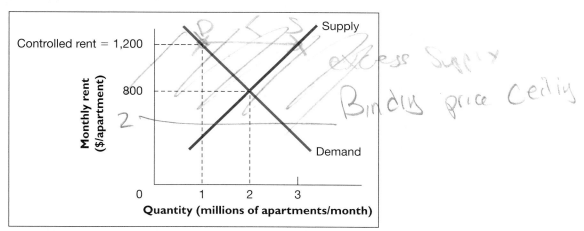

[handwritten annotations: excess supply; Binding price ceiling]

PIZZA PRICE CONTROLS?

The sources of the contrast between the rent-controlled housing market and the largely unregulated food markets in New York City can be seen more vividly by trying to imagine what would happen if concern for the poor led the city's leaders to implement price controls on pizza. Suppose, for example, that the supply and demand curves for pizza are as shown in Figure 3.9 and that the city imposes a **price ceiling** of $2 per slice, making it unlawful to charge more than that amount. At $2 per slice, buyers want to buy 16,000 slices per day, but sellers want to sell only 8,000.

price ceiling a maximum allowable price, specified by law

FIGURE 3.9

Price Controls in the Pizza Market.

A price ceiling below the equilibrium price of pizza would result in excess demand for pizza.

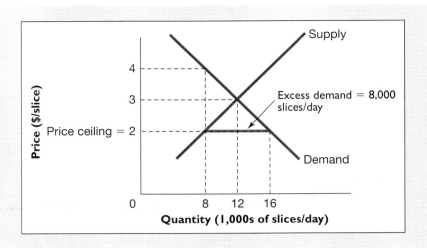

At a price of $2 per slice, every pizza restaurant in the city will have long queues of buyers trying unsuccessfully to purchase pizza. Frustrated buyers will behave rudely to clerks, who will respond in kind. Friends of restaurant managers will begin to get preferential treatment. Devious pricing strategies will begin to emerge (such as the $2 slice of pizza sold in combination with a $5 cup of Coke). Pizza will be made from poorer-quality ingredients. Rumors will begin to circulate about sources of black-market pizza. And so on.

The very idea of not being able to buy a pizza seems absurd, yet precisely such things happen routinely in markets in which prices are held below the equilibrium levels. For example, prior to the collapse of communist governments, it was considered normal in those countries for people to stand in line for hours to buy bread and other basic goods, while the politically connected had first choice of those goods that were available.

RECAP	MARKET EQUILIBRIUM

Market equilibrium, the situation in which all buyers and sellers are satisfied with their respective quantities at the market price, occurs at the intersection of the supply and demand curves. The corresponding price and quantity are called the *equilibrium price* and the *equilibrium quantity.*

Unless prevented by regulation, prices and quantities are driven toward their equilibrium values by the actions of buyers and sellers. If the price is initially too high, so that there is excess supply, frustrated sellers will cut their price in order to sell more. If the price is initially too low, so that there is excess demand, competition among buyers drives the price upward. This process continues until equilibrium is reached.

PREDICTING AND EXPLAINING CHANGES IN PRICES AND QUANTITIES

change in the quantity demanded a movement along the demand curve that occurs in response to a change in price

change in demand a shift of the entire demand curve

If we know how the factors that govern supply and demand curves are changing, we can make informed predictions about how prices and the corresponding quantities will change. But when describing changing circumstances in the marketplace, we must take care to recognize some important terminological distinctions. For example, we must distinguish between the meanings of the seemingly similar expressions **change in the quantity demanded** and **change in demand.** When we speak of a "change in the

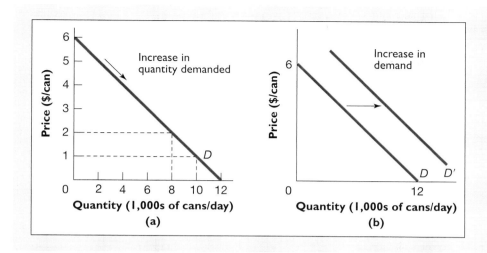

FIGURE 3.10

An Increase in the Quantity Demanded versus an Increase in Demand.

(a) An increase in quantity demanded describes a downward movement along the demand curve as price falls. (b) An increase in demand describes an outward shift of the demand curve.

quantity demanded," this means the change in the quantity that people wish to buy that occurs in response to a change in price. For instance, Figure 3.10(a) depicts an increase in the quantity demanded that occurs in response to a reduction in the price of tuna. When the price falls from $2 to $1 per can, the quantity demanded rises from 8,000 to 10,000 cans per day. By contrast, when we speak of a "change in demand," this means a *shift in the entire demand curve*. For example, Figure 3.10(b) depicts an increase in demand, meaning that at every price the quantity demanded is higher than before. In summary, a "change in the quantity demanded" refers to a movement *along* the demand curve and a "change in demand" means a *shift* of the entire curve.

A similar terminological distinction applies on the supply side of the market. A **change in supply** means a shift in the entire supply curve, whereas a **change in the quantity supplied** refers to a movement along the supply curve.

Alfred Marshall's supply and demand model is one of the most useful tools of the economic naturalist. Once we understand the forces that govern the placements of supply and demand curves, we're suddenly in a position to make sense of a host of interesting observations in the world around us.

change in supply a shift of the entire supply curve

change in the quantity supplied a movement along the supply curve that occurs in response to a change in price

SHIFTS IN DEMAND

To get a better feel for how the supply and demand model enables us to predict and explain price and quantity movements, it's helpful to begin with a few simple examples. The first one illustrates a shift in demand that results from events outside the particular market itself.

Complements   **EXAMPLE 3.2**

What will happen to the equilibrium price and quantity of tennis balls if court rental fees decline?

Let the initial supply and demand curves for tennis balls be as shown by the curves *S* and *D* in Figure 3.11, where the resulting equilibrium price and quantity are $1 per ball and 40 million balls per month, respectively. Tennis courts and tennis balls are what economists call **complements,** goods that are more valuable when used in combination than when used alone. Tennis balls, for example, would be of little value if there were no tennis courts on which to play. (Tennis balls would still have *some* value even without courts—for example, to the parents who pitch them to their children for batting practice.) As tennis courts become cheaper to use, people will respond by playing more tennis, and this will increase their demand for tennis balls. A decline in court-rental fees will thus shift the demand curve for tennis balls rightward to *D'*. (A "rightward shift" of a demand curve

complements two goods are complements in consumption if an increase in the price of one causes a leftward shift in the demand curve for the other (or if a decrease causes a rightward shift)

FIGURE 3.11

The Effect on the Market for Tennis Balls of a Decline in Court-Rental Fees.

When the price of a complement falls, demand shifts right, causing equilibrium price and quantity to rise.

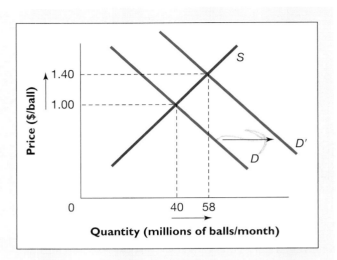

also can be described as an "upward shift." These distinctions correspond, respectively, to the horizontal and vertical interpretations of the demand curve.)

Note in Figure 3.11 that, for the illustrative demand shift shown, the new equilibrium price of tennis balls, $1.40, is higher than the original price and the new equilibrium quantity, 58 million balls per month, is higher than the original quantity.

Substitutes   EXAMPLE 3.3

What will happen to the equilibrium price and quantity of overnight letter delivery service as the price of Internet access falls?

substitutes two goods are substitutes in consumption if an increase in the price of one causes a rightward shift in the demand curve for the other (or if a decrease causes a leftward shift)

Suppose the initial supply and demand curves for overnight letter deliveries are as shown by the curves S and D in Figure 3.12 and that the resulting equilibrium price and quantity are denoted P and Q. E-mail messages and overnight letters are examples of what economists call **substitutes,** meaning that, in many applications at least, the two serve similar functions for people. (Many noneconomists would call them substitutes, too. Economists don't *always* choose obscure terms for important concepts!) When two goods or services are substitutes, a decrease in the price of one will cause a leftward shift in the demand curve for the other. (A "leftward shift" in a demand curve can also be described as a "downward shift.") Diagrammatically, the demand curve for overnight delivery service shifts from D to D' in Figure 3.12.

FIGURE 3.12

The Effect on the Market for Overnight Letter Delivery of a Decline in the Price of Internet Access.

When the price of a substitute falls, demand shifts left, causing equilibrium price and quantity to fall.

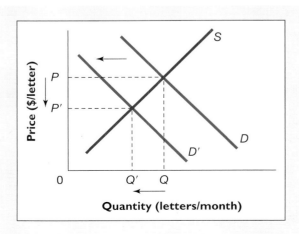

As the figure shows, both the new equilibrium price, P', and the new equilibrium quantity, Q', are lower than the initial values, P and Q. Cheaper Internet access probably won't put Federal Express and UPS out of business, but it will definitely cost them many customers.

To summarize, economists define goods as substitutes if an increase in the price of one causes a rightward shift in the demand curve for the other. By contrast, goods are complements if an increase in the price of one causes a leftward shift in the demand curve for the other.

The concepts of substitutes and complements enable you to answer questions like the one posed in the following concept check.

CONCEPT CHECK 3.4

How will a decline in airfares affect intercity bus fares and the price of hotel rooms in resort communities?

Demand curves are shifted not just by changes in the prices of substitutes and complements but also by other factors that change the amounts people are willing to pay for a given good or service. One of the most important such factors is income.

The Economic Naturalist 3.1

When the federal government implements a large pay increase for its employees, why do rents for apartments located near Washington Metro stations go up relative to rents for apartments located far away from Metro stations?

For the citizens of Washington, D.C., a substantial proportion of whom are government employees, it's more convenient to live in an apartment located one block from the nearest subway station than to live in one that is 20 blocks away. Conveniently located apartments thus command relatively high rents. Suppose the initial demand and supply curves for such apartments are as shown in Figure 3.13. Following a federal pay raise, some government employees who live in less convenient apartments will be willing and able to use part of their extra income to bid for more conveniently located apartments, and those who already live in such apartments will be willing and able to pay more to keep them. The effect of the pay raise is thus to shift the demand curve for conveniently located apartments to the right, as indicated by the demand curve labeled D'. As a result, both the equilibrium price and quantity of such apartments, P' and Q', will be higher than before.

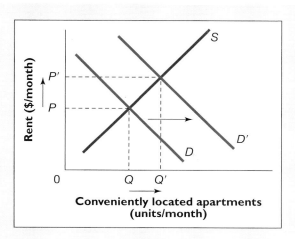

Who gets to live in the most conveniently located apartments?

FIGURE 3.13

The Effect of a Federal Pay Raise on the Rent for Conveniently Located Apartments in Washington, D.C.

An increase in income shifts demand for a normal good to the right, causing equilibrium price and quantity to rise.

Incentive

It might seem natural to ask how there could be an increase in the number of conveniently located apartments, which might appear to be fixed by the constraints of geography. But the Incentive Principle reminds us never to underestimate the ingenuity of sellers when they confront an opportunity to make money by supplying more of something that people want. For example, if rents rose sufficiently, some landlords might respond by converting warehouse space to residential use. Or perhaps people with cars who do not place high value on living near a subway station might sell their co-op apartments to landlords, thereby freeing them for people eager to rent them. (Note that these responses constitute movements along the supply curve of conveniently located apartments, as opposed to shifts in that supply curve.)

When incomes increase, the demand curves for most goods will behave like the demand curve for conveniently located apartments, and in recognition of that fact, economists have chosen to call such goods **normal goods.**

normal good a good whose demand curve shifts rightward when the incomes of buyers increase and leftward when the incomes of buyers decrease

Not all goods are normal goods, however. In fact, the demand curves for some goods actually shift leftward when income goes up. Such goods are called **inferior goods.**

When would having more money tend to make you want to buy less of something? In general, this happens with goods for which there exist attractive substitutes that sell for only slightly higher prices. Apartments in unsafe, inconveniently located neighborhoods are an example. Most residents would choose to move out of such neighborhoods as soon as they could afford to, which means that an increase in income would cause the demand for such apartments to shift leftward.

inferior good a good whose demand curve shifts leftward when the incomes of buyers increase and rightward when the incomes of buyers decrease

CONCEPT CHECK 3.5

How will a large pay increase for federal employees affect the rents for apartments located far away from Washington Metro stations?

Ground beef with high fat content is another example of an inferior good. For health reasons, most people prefer grades of meat with low fat content, and when they do buy high-fat meats it's usually a sign of budgetary pressure. When people in this situation receive higher incomes, they usually switch quickly to leaner grades of meat.

Cost-Benefit

Preferences, or tastes, are another important factor that determines whether the purchase of a given good will satisfy the Cost-Benefit Principle. Steven Spielberg's film *Jurassic Park* appeared to kindle a powerful, if previously latent, preference among children for toy dinosaurs. When this film was first released, the demand for such toys shifted sharply to the right. And the same children who couldn't find enough dinosaur toys suddenly seemed to lose interest in toy designs involving horses and other present-day animals, whose respective demand curves shifted sharply to the left.

Expectations about the future are another factor that may cause demand curves to shift. If Apple Macintosh users hear a credible rumor, for example, that a cheaper or significantly upgraded model will be introduced next month, the demand curve for the current model is likely to shift leftward.

SHIFTS IN THE SUPPLY CURVE

The preceding examples involved changes that gave rise to shifts in demand curves. Next, we'll look at what happens when supply curves shift. Because the supply curve is based on costs of production, anything that changes production costs will shift the supply curve, resulting in a new equilibrium quantity and price.

Increasing Opportunity Cost

EXAMPLE 3.4

What will happen to the equilibrium price and quantity of skateboards if the price of fiberglass, a substance used for making skateboards, rises?

Suppose the initial supply and demand curves for skateboards are as shown by the curves *S* and *D* in Figure 3.14, resulting in an equilibrium price and quantity of

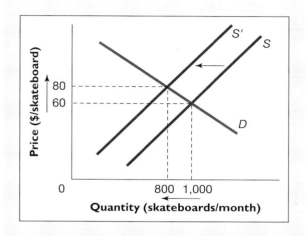

FIGURE 3.14

The Effect on the Skateboard Market of an Increase in the Price of Fiberglass.

When input prices rise, supply shifts left, causing equilibrium price to rise and equilibrium quantity to fall.

$60 per skateboard and 1,000 skateboards per month, respectively. Since fiberglass is one of the materials used to produce skateboards, the effect of an increase in its price is to raise the marginal cost of producing skateboards. How will this affect the supply curve of skateboards? Recall that the supply curve is upward-sloping because when the price of skateboards is low, only those potential sellers whose marginal cost of making skateboards is low can sell boards profitably, whereas at higher prices, those with higher marginal costs also can enter the market profitably (again, the Low-Hanging-Fruit Principle). So if the cost of one of the materials used to produce skateboards rises, the number of potential sellers who can profitably sell skateboards at any given price will fall. And this, in turn, implies a leftward shift in the supply curve for skateboards. Note that a "leftward shift" in a supply curve also can be viewed as an "upward shift" in the same curve. The first corresponds to the horizontal interpretation of the supply curve, while the second corresponds to the vertical interpretation. We will use these expressions to mean exactly the same thing. The new supply curve (after the price of fiberglass rises) is the curve labeled *S'* in Figure 3.14.

Does an increase in the cost of fiberglass have any effect on the demand curve for skateboards? The demand curve tells us how many skateboards buyers wish to purchase at each price. Any given buyer is willing to purchase a skateboard if his reservation price for it exceeds its market price. And since each buyer's reservation price, which is based on the benefits of owning a skateboard, does not depend on the price of fiberglass, there should be no shift in the demand curve for skateboards.

In Figure 3.14, we can now see what happens when the supply curve shifts leftward and the demand curve remains unchanged. For the illustrative supply curve shown, the new equilibrium price of skateboards, $80, is higher than the original price, and the new equilibrium quantity, 800 per month, is lower than the original quantity. (These new equilibrium values are merely illustrative. There is insufficient information provided in the example to determine their exact values.) People who don't place a value of at least $80 on owning a skateboard will choose to spend their money on something else.

Increasing
Opportunity Cost

The effects on equilibrium price and quantity run in the opposite direction whenever marginal costs of production decline, as illustrated in the next example.

Reduction of Marginal Cost   **EXAMPLE 3.5**

What will happen to the equilibrium price and quantity of new houses if the wage rate of carpenters falls?

Suppose the initial supply and demand curves for new houses are as shown by the curves S and D in Figure 3.15, resulting in an equilibrium price of $120,000 per house

FIGURE 3.15

The Effect on the Market for New Houses of a Decline in Carpenters' Wage Rates.

When input prices fall, supply shifts right, causing equilibrium price to fall and equilibrium quantity to rise.

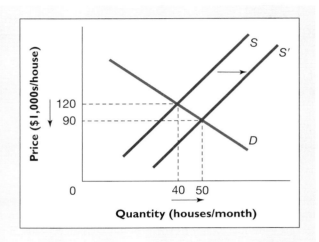

and an equilibrium quantity of 40 houses per month, respectively. A decline in the wage rate of carpenters reduces the marginal cost of making new houses, and this means that, for any given price of houses, more builders can profitably serve the market than before. Diagrammatically, this means a rightward shift in the supply curve of houses, from S to S'. (A "rightward shift" in the supply curve also can be described as a "downward shift.")

Does a decrease in the wage rate of carpenters have any effect on the demand curve for houses? The demand curve tells us how many houses buyers wish to purchase at each price. Because carpenters are now earning less than before, the maximum amount that they are willing to pay for houses may fall, which would imply a leftward shift in the demand curve for houses. But because carpenters make up only a tiny fraction of all potential home buyers, we may assume that this shift is negligible. Thus, a reduction in carpenters' wages produces a significant rightward shift in the supply curve of houses, but no appreciable shift in the demand curve.

We see from Figure 3.15 that the new equilibrium price, $90,000 per house, is lower than the original price and the new equilibrium quantity, 50 houses per month, is higher than the original quantity.

Examples 3.4 and 3.5 involved changes in the cost of a material, or input, in the production of the good in question—fiberglass in the production of skateboards and carpenters' labor in the production of houses. As the following example illustrates, supply curves also shift when technology changes.

The Economic Naturalist 3.2

Why do major term papers go through so many more revisions today than in the 1970s?

Students in the dark days before word processors were in widespread use could not make even minor revisions in their term papers without having to retype their entire manuscript from scratch. The availability of word-processing technology has, of course, radically changed the picture. Instead of having to retype the entire draft, now only the changes need be entered.

In Figure 3.16, the curves labeled S and D depict the supply and demand curves for revisions in the days before word processing, and the curve S' depicts the supply curve for revisions today. As the diagram shows, the result is not only a sharp decline in the price per revision, but also a corresponding increase in the equilibrium number of revisions.

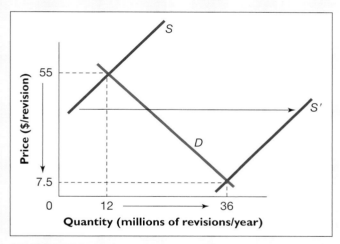

Why does written work go through so many more revisions now than in the 1970s?

FIGURE 3.16

The Effect of Technical Change on the Market for Term-Paper Revisions.

When a new technology reduces the cost of production, supply shifts right, causing equilibrium price to fall and equilibrium quantity to rise.

Note that in The Economic Naturalist 3.2 we implicitly assumed that students purchased typing services in a market. In fact, however, many students type their own term papers. Does that make a difference? Even if no money actually changes hands, students pay a price when they revise their term papers—namely, the opportunity cost of the time it takes to perform that task. Because technology has radically reduced that cost, we would expect to see a large increase in the number of term-paper revisions even if most students type their own work.

Changes in input prices and technology are two of the most important factors that give rise to shifts in supply curves. In the case of agricultural commodities, weather may be another important factor, with favorable conditions shifting the supply curves of such products to the right and unfavorable conditions shifting them to the left. (Weather also may affect the supply curves of nonagricultural products through its effects on the national transportation system.) Expectations of future price changes also may shift current supply curves, as when the expectation of poor crops from a current drought causes suppliers to withhold supplies from existing stocks in the hope of selling at higher prices in the future. Changes in the number of sellers in the market also can cause supply curves to shift.

FOUR SIMPLE RULES

For supply and demand curves that have the conventional slopes (upward-sloping for supply curves, downward-sloping for demand curves), the preceding examples illustrate the four basic rules that govern how shifts in supply and demand affect equilibrium prices and quantities. These rules are summarized in Figure 3.17.

FIGURE 3.17

Four Rules Governing the Effects of Supply and Demand Shifts.

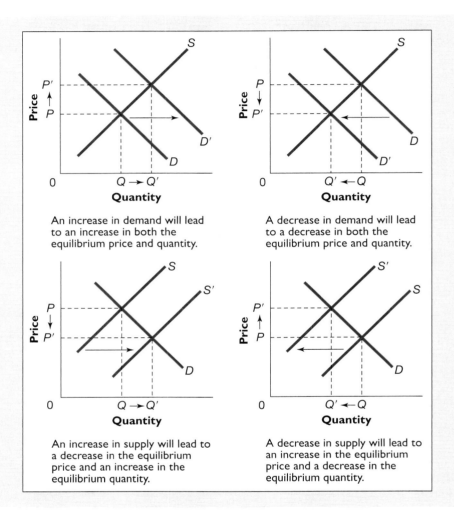

An increase in demand will lead to an increase in both the equilibrium price and quantity.

A decrease in demand will lead to a decrease in both the equilibrium price and quantity.

An increase in supply will lead to a decrease in the equilibrium price and an increase in the equilibrium quantity.

A decrease in supply will lead to an increase in the equilibrium price and a decrease in the equilibrium quantity.

RECAP	FACTORS THAT SHIFT SUPPLY AND DEMAND

Factors that cause an increase (rightward or upward shift) in demand:

1. A decrease in the price of complements to the good or service.

2. An increase in the price of substitutes for the good or service.

3. An increase in income (for a normal good).

4. An increased preference by demanders for the good or service.

5. An increase in the population of potential buyers.

6. An expectation of higher prices in the future.

When these factors move in the opposite direction, demand will shift left.

Factors that cause an increase (rightward or downward shift) in supply:

1. A decrease in the cost of materials, labor, or other inputs used in the production of the good or service.

2. An improvement in technology that reduces the cost of producing the good or service.

3. An improvement in the weather (especially for agricultural products).

4. An increase in the number of suppliers.

5. An expectation of lower prices in the future.

When these factors move in the opposite direction, supply will shift left.

The qualitative rules summarized in Figure 3.17 hold for supply or demand shifts of any magnitude, provided the curves have their conventional slopes. But as the next example demonstrates, when both supply and demand curves shift at the same time, the direction in which equilibrium price or quantity changes will depend on the relative magnitudes of the shifts.

Shifts in Supply and Demand   EXAMPLE 3.6

How do shifts in both demand and supply affect equilibrium quantities and prices?

What will happen to the equilibrium price and quantity in the corn tortilla chip market if both of the following events occur: (1) researchers prove that the oils in which tortilla chips are fried are harmful to human health and (2) the price of corn harvesting equipment falls?

The conclusion regarding the health effects of the oils will shift the demand for tortilla chips to the left because many people who once bought chips in the belief that they were healthful will now switch to other foods. The decline in the price of harvesting equipment will shift the supply of chips to the right because additional farmers will now find it profitable to enter the corn market. In Figures 3.18(a) and 3.18(b), the original supply and demand curves are denoted by S and D, while the new curves are denoted by S' and D'. Note that in both panels the shifts lead to a decline in the equilibrium price of chips.

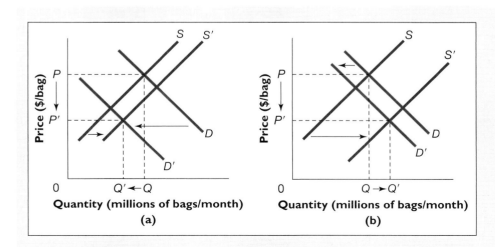

FIGURE 3.18

The Effects of Simultaneous Shifts in Supply and Demand.

When demand shifts left and supply shifts right, equilibrium price falls, but equilibrium quantity may either rise (b) or fall (a).

But note also that the effect of the shifts on equilibrium quantity cannot be determined without knowing their relative magnitudes. Taken separately, the demand shift causes a decline in equilibrium quantity, whereas the supply shift causes an increase in equilibrium quantity. The net effect of the two shifts thus depends on which of the individual effects is larger. In Figure 3.18(a), the demand shift dominates, so equilibrium quantity declines. In Figure 3.18(b), the supply shift dominates, so equilibrium quantity goes up.

The following concept check asks you to consider a simple variation on the problem posed in the previous example.

CONCEPT CHECK 3.6

What will happen to the equilibrium price and quantity in the corn tortilla chip market if both of the following events occur: (1) researchers discover that a vitamin found in corn helps protect against cancer and heart disease and (2) a swarm of locusts destroys part of the corn crop?

The Economic Naturalist 3.3

Why do the prices of some goods, like airline tickets to Europe, go up during the months of heaviest consumption, while others, like sweet corn, go down?

Seasonal price movements for airline tickets are primarily the result of seasonal variations in demand. Thus, ticket prices to Europe are highest during the summer months because the demand for tickets is highest during those months, as shown in Figure 3.19(a), where the w and s subscripts denote winter and summer values, respectively.

Why are some goods cheapest during the months of heaviest consumption, while others are most expensive during those months?

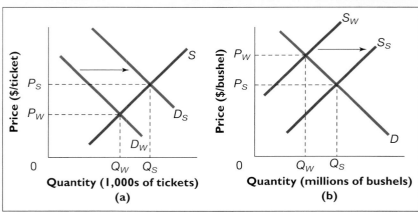

FIGURE 3.19

Seasonal Variation in the Air Travel and Corn Markets.

(a) Prices are highest during the period of heaviest consumption when heavy consumption is the result of high demand. (b) Prices are lowest during the period of heaviest consumption when heavy consumption is the result of high supply.

By contrast, seasonal price movements for sweet corn are primarily the result of seasonal variations in supply. The price of sweet corn is lowest in the summer months because its supply is highest during those months, as seen in Figure 3.19(b).

EFFICIENCY AND EQUILIBRIUM

Markets represent a highly effective system of allocating resources. When a market for a good is in equilibrium, the equilibrium price conveys important information to potential suppliers about the value that potential demanders place on that good. At the same time, the equilibrium price informs potential demanders about the opportunity cost of supplying the good. This rapid, two-way transmission of information is the reason that markets can coordinate an activity as complex as supplying New York City with food and drink, even though no one person or organization oversees the process.

But are the prices and quantities determined in market equilibrium socially optimal, in the sense of maximizing total economic surplus? That is, does equilibrium in unregulated markets always maximize the difference between the total benefits and total costs experienced by market participants? As we'll see, the answer is "it depends": A market that is out of equilibrium, such as the rent-controlled New York housing market, always creates opportunities for individuals to arrange transactions that will increase their individual economic surplus. As we'll also see, however, a market for a good that is in equilibrium makes the largest possible contribution to total economic surplus only when its supply and demand curves fully reflect all costs and benefits associated with the production and consumption of that good.

CASH ON THE TABLE

In economics we assume that all exchange is purely voluntary. This means that a transaction cannot take place unless the buyer's reservation price for the good exceeds the seller's reservation price. When that condition is met and a transaction takes place, both parties receive an economic surplus. The **buyer's surplus** from the transaction is the difference between his reservation price and the price he actually pays. The **seller's surplus** is the difference between the price she receives and her reservation price. The **total surplus** from the transaction is the sum of the buyer's surplus and the seller's surplus. It is also equal to the difference between the buyer's reservation price and the seller's reservation price.

Suppose there is a potential buyer whose reservation price for an additional slice of pizza is $4 and a potential seller whose reservation price is only $2. If this buyer purchases a slice of pizza from this seller for $3, the total surplus generated by this exchange is $4 − $2 = $2, of which $4 − $3 = $1 is the buyer's surplus and $3 − $2 = $1 is the seller's surplus.

A regulation that prevents the price of a good from reaching its equilibrium level unnecessarily prevents exchanges of this sort from taking place, and in the process reduces total economic surplus. Consider again the effect of price controls imposed in the market for pizza. The demand curve in Figure 3.20 tells us that if a price ceiling of $2 per slice were imposed, only 8,000 slices of pizza per day would be sold. At that quantity, the vertical interpretations of the supply and demand curves tell us that a buyer would be willing to pay as much as $4 for an additional slice and that a seller would be willing to sell one for as little as $2. The difference—$2 per slice—is the additional economic surplus that would result if an additional slice were produced and sold. As noted earlier, an extra slice sold at a price of $3 would result in an additional $1 of economic surplus for both buyer and seller.

When a market is out of equilibrium, it's always possible to identify mutually beneficial exchanges of this sort. When people have failed to take advantage of all mutually beneficial exchanges, we often say that there's **"cash on the table"**—the economist's metaphor for unexploited opportunities. When the price in a market is below the equilibrium price, there's cash on the table because the reservation price of sellers (marginal cost) will always be lower than the reservation price of buyers. In the absence of a law preventing buyers from paying more than $2 per slice, restaurant owners would quickly raise their prices and expand their production until the equilibrium price of $3 per slice were reached. At that price, buyers would be able to

buyer's surplus the difference between the buyer's reservation price and the price he or she actually pays

seller's surplus the difference between the price received by the seller and his or her reservation price

total surplus the difference between the buyer's reservation price and the seller's reservation price

cash on the table an economic metaphor for unexploited gains from exchange

FIGURE 3.20

Price Controls in the Pizza Market.

A price ceiling below the equilibrium price of pizza would result in excess demand for pizza.

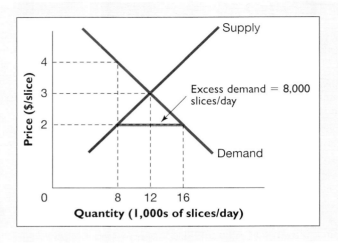

get precisely the 12,000 slices of pizza they want to buy each day. All mutually beneficial opportunities for exchange would have been exploited, leaving no more cash on the table.

<table>
<tr><td>Incentive</td></tr>
</table>

With the Incentive Principle in mind, it should be no surprise that buyers and sellers in the marketplace have an uncanny ability to detect the presence of cash on the table. It is almost as if unexploited opportunities give off some exotic scent triggering neuro-chemical explosions in the olfactory centers of their brains. The desire to scrape cash off the table and into their pockets is what drives sellers in each of New York City's thousands of individual food markets to work diligently to meet their customers' demands. That they succeed to a far higher degree than participants in the city's rent-controlled housing market is plainly evident. Whatever flaws it might have, the market system moves with considerably greater speed and agility than any centralized allocation mechanisms yet devised. But as we emphasize in the following section, this does not mean that markets *always* lead to the greatest good for all.

SMART FOR ONE, DUMB FOR ALL

<table>
<tr><td>Cost-Benefit</td></tr>
</table>

socially optimal quantity the quantity of a good that results in the maximum possible economic surplus from producing and consuming the good

efficiency (or **economic efficiency**) a condition that occurs when all goods and services are produced and consumed at their respective socially optimal levels

The **socially optimal quantity** of any good is the quantity that maximizes the total economic surplus that results from producing and consuming the good. From the Cost-Benefit Principle, we know that we should keep expanding production of the good as long as its marginal benefit is at least as great as its marginal cost. This means that the socially optimal quantity is that level for which the marginal cost and marginal benefit of the good are the same.

When the quantity of a good is less than the socially optimal quantity, boosting its production will increase total economic surplus. By the same token, when the quantity of a good exceeds the socially optimal quantity, reducing its production will increase total economic surplus. **Economic efficiency, or efficiency,** occurs when all goods and services in the economy are produced and consumed at their respective socially optimal levels.

Efficiency is an important social goal. Failure to achieve efficiency means that total economic surplus is smaller than it could have been. Movements toward efficiency make the total economic pie larger, making it possible for everyone to have a larger slice. The importance of efficiency will be a recurring theme as we move forward, and we state it here as one of the core principles:

<table>
<tr><td>Efficiency</td></tr>
</table>

The Efficiency Principle: Efficiency is an important social goal because when the economic pie grows larger, everyone can have a larger slice.

Is the market equilibrium quantity of a good efficient? That is, does it maxi the total economic surplus received by participants in the market for that good? W the private market for a given good is in equilibrium, we can say that the cost *to seller* of producing an additional unit of the good is the same as the benefit *to the bu* of having an additional unit. If all costs of producing the good are borne directly sellers, and if all benefits from the good accrue directly to buyers, it follows that market equilibrium quantity of the good will equate the marginal cost and margi benefit of the good. And this means that the equilibrium quantity also maximizes to economic surplus.

But sometimes the production of a good entails costs that fall on people other th those who sell the good. This will be true, for instance, for goods whose producti generates significant levels of environmental pollution. As extra units of these goods are produced, the extra pollution harms other people besides sellers. In the market equilibrium for such goods, the benefit *to buyers* of the last good produced is, as before, equal to the cost incurred by sellers to produce that good. But since producing that good also imposes pollution costs on others, we know that the *full* marginal cost of the last unit produced—the seller's private marginal cost plus the marginal pollution cost borne by others—must be higher than the benefit of the last unit produced. So in this case the market equilibrium quantity of the good will be larger than the socially optimal quantity. Total economic surplus would be higher if output of the good were lower. Yet neither sellers nor buyers have any incentive to alter their behavior.

Another possibility is that people other than those who buy a good may receive significant benefits from it. For instance, when someone purchases a vaccination against measles from her doctor, she not only protects herself, but also makes it less likely that others will catch this disease. From the perspective of society as a whole, we should keep increasing the number of vaccinations until their marginal cost equals their marginal benefit. The marginal benefit of a vaccination is the value of the protection it provides the person vaccinated *plus* the value of the protection it provides all others. Private consumers, however, will choose to be vaccinated only if the marginal benefit *to them* exceeds the price of the vaccination. In this case, then, the market equilibrium quantity of vaccinations will be smaller than the quantity that maximizes total economic surplus. Again, however, individuals would have no incentive to alter their behavior.

Situations like the ones just discussed provide examples of behaviors that we may call "smart for one but dumb for all." In each case, the individual actors are behaving rationally. They are pursuing their goals as best they can, and yet there remain unexploited opportunities for gain from the point of view of the whole society. The difficulty is that these opportunities cannot be exploited by individuals acting alone. In subsequent chapters, we will see how people can often organize collectively to exploit such opportunities. For now, we simply summarize this discussion in the form of the following core principle:

The Equilibrium Principle (also called the "No-Cash-on-the-Table Principle"): A market in equilibrium leaves no unexploited opportunities for individuals but may not exploit all gains achievable through collective action.

Equilibrium

RECAP	MARKETS AND SOCIAL WELFARE

When the supply and demand curves for a good reflect all significant costs and benefits associated with the production and consumption of that good, the market equilibrium will result in the largest possible economic surplus. But if people other than buyers benefit from the good, or if people other than sellers bear costs because of it, market equilibrium need not result in the largest possible economic surplus.

○ SUMMARY ○

...and curve is a downward-sloping line that ...what quantity buyers will demand at any given ...ce. The supply curve is an upward-sloping line that tells what quantity sellers will offer at any given price. *(LO1)*

- Alfred Marshall's model of supply and demand explains why neither cost of production nor value to the purchaser (as measured by willingness to pay) is, by itself, sufficient to explain why some goods are cheap and others are expensive. To explain variations in price, we must examine the interaction of cost and willingness to pay. As we've seen in this chapter, goods differ in price because of differences in their respective supply and demand curves. *(LO2)*

- Market equilibrium occurs when the quantity buyers demand at the market price is exactly the same as the quantity that sellers offer. The equilibrium price–quantity pair is the one at which the demand and supply curves intersect. In equilibrium, market price measures both the value of the last unit sold to buyers and the cost of the resources required to produce it. *(LO2)*

- When the price of a good lies above its equilibrium value, there is an excess supply of that good. Excess supply motivates sellers to cut their prices and price continues to fall until equilibrium price is reached. When price lies below its equilibrium value, there is excess demand. With excess demand, frustrated buyers are motivated to offer higher prices and the upward pressure on prices persists until equilibrium is reached. A remarkable feature of the market system is that, relying only on the tendency of people to respond in self-interested ways to market price signals, it somehow manages to coordinate the actions of literally billions of buyers and sellers worldwide. When excess demand or excess supply occurs, it tends to be small and brief, except in markets where regulations prevent full adjustment of prices. *(LO2)*

- The basic supply and demand model is a primary tool of the economic naturalist. Changes in the equilibrium price of a good, and in the amount of it traded in the marketplace, can be predicted on the basis of shifts in its supply or demand curves. The following four rules hold for any good with a downward-sloping demand curve and an upward-sloping supply curve:
  1. An increase in demand will lead to an increase in equilibrium price and quantity.
  2. A reduction in demand will lead to a reduction in equilibrium price and quantity.
  3. An increase in supply will lead to a reduction in equilibrium price and an increase in equilibrium quantity.
  4. A decrease in supply will lead to an increase in equilibrium price and a reduction in equilibrium quantity. *(LO3)*

- Incomes, tastes, population, expectations, and the prices of substitutes and complements are among the factors that shift demand schedules. Supply schedules, in turn, are primarily governed by such factors as technology, input prices, expectations, the number of sellers, and, especially for agricultural products, the weather. *(LO3)*

- The efficiency of markets in allocating resources does not eliminate social concerns about how goods and services are distributed among different people. For example, we often lament the fact many buyers enter the market with too little income to buy even the most basic goods and services. Concern for the well-being of the poor has motivated many governments to intervene in a variety of ways to alter the outcomes of market forces. Sometimes these interventions take the form of laws that peg prices below their equilibrium levels. Such laws almost invariably generate harmful, if unintended, consequences. Programs like rent-control laws, for example, lead to severe housing shortages, black marketeering, and a rapid deterioration of the relationship between landlords and tenants. *(LO4)*

- If the difficulty is that the poor have too little money, the best solution is to discover ways of boosting their incomes directly. The law of supply and demand cannot be repealed by the legislature. But legislatures do have the capacity to alter the underlying forces that govern the shape and position of supply and demand schedules. *(LO4)*

- When the supply and demand curves for a good reflect all significant costs and benefits associated with the production and consumption of that good, the market equilibrium price will guide people to produce and consume the quantity of the good that results in the largest possible economic surplus. This conclusion, however, does not apply if others, besides buyers, benefit from the good (as when someone benefits from his neighbor's purchase of a vaccination against measles) or if others besides sellers bear costs because of the good (as when its production generates pollution). In such cases, market equilibrium does not result in the greatest gain for all. *(LO4)*

○ CORE PRINCIPLES ○

| Efficiency | **The Efficiency Principle**
Efficiency is an important social goal because when the economic pie grows larger, everyone can have a larger slice. |

| Equilibrium | **The Equilibrium Principle (also called the "No-Cash-on-the-Table Principle")**
A market in equilibrium leaves no unexploited opportunities for individuals but may not exploit all gains achievable through collective action. |

○ KEY TERMS ○

buyer's reservation price	economic efficiency	normal good
buyer's surplus	efficiency	price ceiling
cash on the table	equilibrium	seller's reservation price
change in demand	equilibrium price	seller's surplus
change in the quantity demanded	equilibrium quantity	socially optimal quantity
change in the quantity supplied	excess demand	substitutes
change in supply	excess supply	substitution effect
complements	income effect	supply curve
demand curve	inferior good	total surplus
	market	
	market equilibrium	

○ REVIEW QUESTIONS ○

1. Explain the distinction between the horizontal and vertical interpretations of the demand curve. *(LO1)*

2. Why isn't knowing the cost of producing a good sufficient to predict its market price? *(LO2)*

3. In recent years, a government official proposed that gasoline price controls be imposed to protect the poor from rising gasoline prices. What evidence could you consult to discover whether this proposal was enacted? *(LO2)*

4. Distinguish between the meaning of the expressions "change in demand" and "change in the quantity demanded." *(LO3)*

5. Give an example of behavior you have observed that could be described as "smart for one but dumb for all." *(LO4)*

○ PROBLEMS ○

1. How would each of the following affect the U.S. market supply curve for corn? *(LO1)*
   a. A new and improved crop rotation technique is discovered.
   b. The price of fertilizer falls.
   c. The government offers new tax breaks to farmers.
   d. A tornado sweeps through Iowa.

2. Indicate how you think each of the following would shift demand in the indicated market: *(LO1)*
    a. The incomes of buyers in the market for Adirondack vacations increases.
    b. Buyers in the market for pizza read a study linking pepperoni consumption to heart disease.
    c. Buyers in the market for CDs learn of an increase in the price of downloadable MP3s (a substitute for CDs).
    d. Buyers in the market for CDs learn of an increase in the price of CDs.

3. An Arizona student claims to have spotted a UFO over the desert outside of Tucson. How will his claim affect the *supply* (not the quantity supplied) of binoculars in Tucson stores? *(LO1)*

4. State whether the following pairs of goods are complements, or substitutes, or both. *(LO3)*
    a. Washing machines and dryers.
    b. Tennis rackets and tennis balls.
    c. Ice cream and chocolate.
    d. Cloth diapers and disposable diapers.

5. How will an increase in the birth rate affect the equilibrium price of land? *(LO3)*

6. What will happen to the equilibrium price and quantity of beef if the price of chickenfeed increases? *(LO3)*

7. How will a new law mandating an increase in required levels of automobile insurance affect the equilibrium price and quantity in the market for new automobiles? *(LO3)*

8. Predict what will happen to the equilibrium price and quantity of oranges if the following events take place. *(LO3)*
    a. A study finds that a daily glass of orange juice reduces the risk of heart disease.
    b. The price of grapefruit falls drastically.
    c. The wage paid to orange pickers rises.
    d. Exceptionally good weather provides a much greater than expected harvest.

9. Suppose the current issue of *The New York Times* reports an outbreak of mad cow disease in Nebraska, as well as the discovery of a new breed of chicken that gains more weight than existing breeds that consume the same amount of food. How will these developments affect the equilibrium price and quantity of chickens sold in the United States? *(LO3)*

10. Twenty-five years ago, tofu was available only from small businesses operating in predominantly Asian sections of large cities. Today tofu has become popular as a high-protein health food and is widely available in supermarkets throughout the United States. At the same time, tofu production has evolved to become factory-based using modern food-processing technologies. Draw a diagram with demand and supply curves depicting the market for tofu 25 years ago and the market for tofu today. Given the information above, what does the demand–supply model predict about changes in the volume of tofu sold in the United States between then and now? What does it predict about changes in the price of tofu? *(LO3)*

⊙ ANSWERS TO CONCEPT CHECKS ⊙

3.1 At a quantity of 10,000 slices per day, the marginal buyer's reservation price is $3.50 per slice. At a price of $2.50 per slice, the quantity demanded will be 14,000 slices per day. *(LO1)*

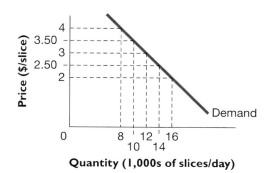

3.2 At a quantity of 10,000 slices per day, the marginal cost of pizza is $2.50 per slice. At a price of $3.50 per slice, the quantity supplied will be 14,000 slices per day. *(LO1)*

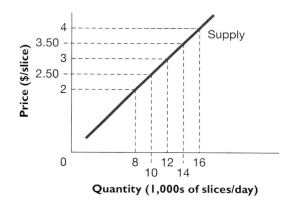

3.3 Since landlords are permitted to charge less than the maximum rent established by rent-control laws, a law that sets the maximum rent at $1,200 will have no effect on the rents actually charged in this market, which will settle at the equilibrium value of $800 per month. *(LO2)*

3.4 Travel by air and travel by intercity bus are substitutes, so a decline in airfares will shift the demand for bus travel to the left, resulting in lower bus fares and fewer bus trips taken. Travel by air and the use of resort hotels are complements, so a decline in airfares will shift the demand for resort hotel rooms to the right, resulting in higher hotel rates and an increase in the number of rooms rented. *(LO3)*

3.5 Apartments located far from Washington Metro stations are an inferior good. A pay increase for federal workers will thus shift the demand curve for such apartments downward, which will lead to a reduction in their equilibrium rent. *(LO3)*

3.6 The vitamin discovery shifts the demand for chips to the right and the crop losses shift the supply of chips to the left. Both shifts result in an increase in the equilibrium price of chips. But depending on the relative magnitude of the shifts, the equilibrium quantity of chips may either rise (left panel) or fall (right panel). *(LO3)*

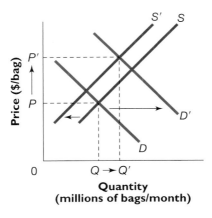
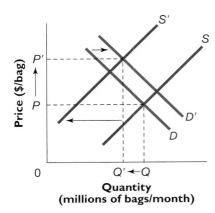

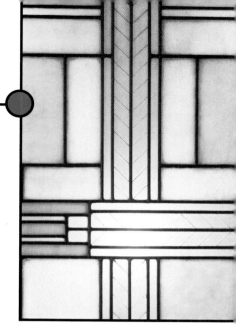

APPENDIX

The Algebra of Supply and Demand

I n the text of this chapter, we developed supply and demand analysis in a geometric framework. The advantage of this framework is that many find it an easier one within which to visualize how shifts in either curve affect equilibrium price and quantity.

It is a straightforward extension to translate supply and demand analysis into algebraic terms. In this brief appendix, we show how this is done. The advantage of the algebraic framework is that it greatly simplifies computing the numerical values of equilibrium prices and quantities.

Consider, for example, the supply and demand curves in Figure 3A.1, where P denotes the price of the good and Q denotes its quantity. What are the equations of these curves?

Recall from the appendix *Working with Equations, Graphs, and Tables* that the equation of a straight-line demand curve must take the general form $P = a + bQ^d$, where P is the price of the product (as measured on the vertical axis), Q^d is the quantity demanded at that price (as measured on the horizontal axis), a is the vertical intercept of the demand curve, and b is its slope. For the demand curve shown in Figure 3A.1, the vertical intercept is 16 and the slope is -2. So the equation for this demand curve is

$$P = 16 - 2Q^d. \tag{3A.1}$$

Similarly, the equation of a straight-line supply curve must take the general form $P = c + dQ^s$, where P is again the price of the product, Q^s is the quantity supplied at that price, c is the vertical intercept of the supply curve, and d is its slope. For the supply curve shown in Figure 3A.1, the vertical intercept is 4 and the slope is also 4. So the equation for this supply curve is

$$P = 4 + 4Q^s. \tag{3A.2}$$

If we know the equations for the supply and demand curves in any market, it is a simple matter to solve them for the equilibrium price and quantity using the method of simultaneous equations described in the appendix *Working with Equations, Graphs, and Tables*. The following example illustrates how to apply this method.

FIGURE 3A.1

Supply and Demand Curves.

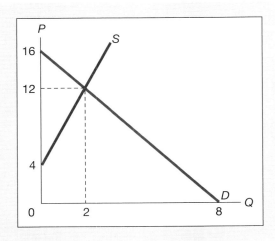

Simultaneous Equations   EXAMPLE 3A.1

If the supply and demand curves for a market are given by P = 4 + 4Q^s and P = 16 − 2Q^d, respectively, find the equilibrium price and quantity for this market.

In equilibrium, we know that $Q^s = Q^d$. Denoting this common value as Q^*, we may then equate the right-hand sides of Equations 3A.1 and 3A.2 and solve

$$4 + 4Q^* = 16 - 2Q^*, \tag{3A.3}$$

which yields $Q^* = 2$. Substituting $Q^* = 2$ back into either the supply or demand equation gives the equilibrium price $P^* = 12$.

Of course, having already begun with the graphs of Equations 3A.1 and 3A.2 in hand, we could have identified the equilibrium price and quantity by a simple glance at Figure 3A.1. (That is why it seems natural to say that the graphical approach helps us visualize the equilibrium outcome.) As the following concept check illustrates, the advantage of the algebraic approach to finding the equilibrium price and quantity is that it is much less painstaking than having to produce accurate drawings of the supply and demand schedules.

CONCEPT CHECK 3A.1

Find the equilibrium price and quantity in a market whose supply and demand curves are given by $P = 2Q^s$ and $P = 8 - 2Q^d$, respectively.

○   A N S W E R   T O   A P P E N D I X   C O N C E P T   C H E C K   ○

3A.1 Let Q^* denote the equilibrium quantity. Since the equilibrium price and quantity lie on both the supply and demand curves, we equate the right-hand sides of the supply and demand equations to obtain

$$2Q^* = 8 - 2Q^*,$$

which solves for $Q^* = 2$. Substituting $Q^* = 2$ back into either the supply or demand equation gives the equilibrium price $P^* = 4$.

CHAPTER 4

Spending, Income, and GDP

Michael Ventura/PhotoEdit

LEARNING OBJECTIVES

After reading this chapter, you should be able to:

LO1 Explain how economists define and measure an economy's output.

LO2 Apply the expenditure method for measuring GDP to analyze economic activity.

LO3 Define and compute nominal GDP and real GDP.

LO4 Discuss the relationships between real GDP and economic well-being.

HOW DO ECONOMISTS MEASURE THE ECONOMY'S OVERALL HEALTH?

Nonfarm payrolls grew at a 2 percent rate in the third quarter . . . "

"The Dow Jones Industrial Average closed up 93 points yesterday in moderate trading . . . "

"Inflation appears subdued as the consumer price index registered an increase of only 0.2 percent last month . . . "

"The unemployment rate last month rose to 5.8 percent, its highest level since . . . "

News reports like these fill the airwaves—some TV and radio stations carry nothing else. In fact, all kinds of people are interested in economic data. The average person hopes to learn something that will be useful in a business decision, a financial investment, or a career move. The professional economist depends on economic data in much the same way that a doctor depends on a patient's vital signs—pulse, blood pressure, and temperature—to make an accurate diagnosis. To understand economic developments and to be able to give useful advice to policymakers, businesspeople, and financial investors, an economist simply must have up-to-date, accurate data. Political leaders and policymakers also need economic data to help them in their decisions and planning.

Interest in measuring the economy, and attempts to do so, date back as far as the mid-seventeenth century, when Sir William Petty (1623–1687) conducted a detailed survey of the land and wealth of Ireland. Not until the twentieth century, though, did economic measurement come into its own. World War II was an important catalyst for the development of accurate economic statistics since its very outcome was thought to depend on the mobilization of economic resources. Two economists—Simon Kuznets in the United States and Richard Stone in the United Kingdom—developed comprehensive systems for measuring a nation's output of goods and services, which were of great help to Allied leaders in their wartime planning. Kuznets and Stone each received a Nobel Prize in Economics for their work, which became the basis for the economic accounts used today by almost all the world's countries. The governments of the United States and many other countries now collect and publish a wealth of statistics covering all aspects of their economies, including three basic macroeconomic variables: *gross domestic product,* or *GDP;* the *rate of inflation;* and the *rate of unemployment.* The focus of this chapter is on GDP, which measures the overall level of economic activity in a country.

By the end of this chapter, you will understand how official measures of output are constructed and used and will gain some insight into the debates over their accuracy. Understanding the strengths and limitations of economic data is the first critical step toward becoming an intelligent user of economic statistics, as well as a necessary background for the economic analysis in the chapters to come.

GROSS DOMESTIC PRODUCT: MEASURING THE NATION'S OUTPUT

gross domestic product (GDP) the market value of the final goods and services produced in a country during a given period

The most frequently used measure of an economy's output is called the *gross domestic product,* or *GDP.* **Gross domestic product (GDP)** is the market value of the final goods and services produced in a country during a given period.

To understand this definition, let's take it apart and examine each of its parts separately. The first key phrase in the definition is "market value."

MARKET VALUE

market value the selling prices of goods and services in the open market.

A modern economy produces many different goods and services, from dental floss (a good) to acupuncture (a service). To be able to talk about concepts like the "total output" or "total production"—as opposed to the production of specific items like dental floss—economists need to *aggregate* the quantities of the many different goods and services into a single number. They do so by adding up the market values of the different goods and services the economy produces. **Market value** is the selling prices of goods and services in the open market. We use these prices since they are the prices at which buyers and sellers agree to make their transactions. Example 4.1 will illustrate the process.

Measuring a Nation's Output	EXAMPLE 4.1

What is Orchardia's GDP?

In the imaginary economy of Orchardia, total production is 4 apples and 6 bananas. To find the total output of Orchardia, we could add the number of apples to the number of bananas and conclude that total output is 10 pieces of fruit. But what if this economy also produced 3 pairs of shoes? There really is no sensible way to add apples and bananas to shoes.

Suppose, though, that we know that apples sell for $0.25 each, bananas for $0.50 each, and shoes for $20.00 a pair. Then the market value of this economy's production, or its GDP, is equal to

$$(4 \text{ apples} \times \$0.25/\text{apple}) + (6 \text{ bananas} \times \$0.50/\text{banana})$$
$$+ (3 \text{ pairs of shoes} \times \$20.00/\text{pair}) = \$64.00.$$

Notice that when we calculate total output this way, the more expensive items (the shoes) receive a higher weighting than the cheaper items (the apples and bananas). In general, the amount people are willing to pay for an item is an indication of the economic benefit they expect to receive from it. For this reason, higher-priced items should count for more in a measure of aggregate output.

CONCEPT CHECK 4.1

Suppose Orchardia produces the original quantities of the three goods at the same prices as in Example 4.1. In addition, it produces 5 oranges at $0.30 each. What is the GDP of Orchardia now?

Market values provide a convenient way to add together, or aggregate, the many different goods and services produced in a modern economy. A drawback of using market values, however, is that not all economically valuable goods and services are bought and sold in markets. For example, the unpaid work of a homemaker, although it is of economic value, is not sold in markets and so isn't counted in GDP. But paid housekeeping and child care services, which are sold in markets, do count.

Although homemaking activities are excluded from measured GDP, in a few cases goods and services that are not sold in markets are included in GDP. By far the most important are the goods and services provided by federal, state, and local governments. The protection provided by the army and navy, the transportation convenience of the interstate highway system, and the education provided by public school systems are examples of publicly provided goods and services that are not sold in markets.

As market prices for publicly provided goods and services do not exist, economic statisticians add to the GDP the *costs* of providing those goods and services as rough measures of their economic value. For instance, to include public education in the GDP, the statisticians add to GDP the salaries of teachers and administrators, the costs of textbooks and supplies, and the like. Similarly, the economic value of the national defense establishment is approximated, for the purposes of measuring GDP, by the *costs* of defense: the pay earned by soldiers and sailors, the costs of acquiring and maintaining weapons, and so on.

With a few exceptions, like publicly provided goods and services, GDP is calculated by adding up market values. However, not all goods and services that have a market value are counted in GDP. As we will see next, GDP includes only those goods and services that are the end products of the production process, called *final goods and services.*

FINAL GOODS AND SERVICES

Many goods are used in the production process. For instance, before a baker can produce a loaf of bread, grain must be grown and harvested and then ground into flour. The flour is then used along with other ingredients to make bread. Of the three major goods that are produced during this process—the grain, the flour, and the bread—only the bread is used by consumers. Because producing the bread is the ultimate purpose of the process, the bread is called a *final good*.

In general, a **final good or service** is the end product of a process, the product or service that consumers actually use. The goods or services produced on the way toward making the final product—here, the grain and the flour—are called **intermediate goods or services.** Economists are interested in measuring only those items that are of direct

final goods or services
goods or services consumed by the ultimate user; because they are the end products of the production process, they are counted as part of GDP

intermediate goods or services goods or services used up in the production of final goods and services and therefore not counted as part of GDP economic value. Thus, *only final goods and services are included in GDP.* Intermediate goods and services are *not* included.

To illustrate, suppose that the grain from the previous example has a market value of $0.50 (the price the milling company paid for the grain). The grain is then ground into flour, which has a market value of $1.20 (the price the baker paid for the flour). Finally, the flour is made into a loaf of fine French bread, worth $2.00 at the local store. In calculating the contribution of these activities to GDP, would we want to add together the values of the grain, the flour, and the bread? No. This would incorrectly measure GDP as $0.50 + $1.20 + $2.00 = $3.70. The value of the grain would then be counted three times: once as grain, then as part of the value of the flour, and finally as part of the value of the bread. The grain and flour are valuable only because they are intermediate goods that can be used to make bread. Since their value is included in the $2.00 value of the final product, the loaf of bread, the total contribution to GDP is $2.00.

Example 4.2 illustrates the same distinction but this time with a focus on services.

GDP for the Barber and His Assistant   EXAMPLE 4.2

How do we count a haircut in GDP?

Your barber charges $10 for a haircut. In turn, the barber pays his assistant $2 per haircut in return for sharpening the scissors, sweeping the floor, and other chores. For each haircut given, what is the total contribution of the barber and his assistant, taken together, to GDP?

The answer to this problem is $10, the price, or market value, of the haircut. The haircut is counted in GDP because it is the final service, the one that actually has value to the final user. The services provided by the assistant have value only because they contribute to the production of the haircut. Their $2 value is included in the $10 price of the haircut.

Our next example demonstrates that the same good can be either intermediate or final, depending on how it is used.

A Good That Can Be Either Intermediate or Final   EXAMPLE 4.3

What is an intermediate good?

Farmer Brown produces $100 worth of milk. He sells $40 worth of milk to his neighbors and uses the rest to feed his pigs, which he sells to his neighbors for $120. What is Farmer Brown's contribution to the GDP?

The final goods in this example are the $40 worth of milk and the $120 worth of pigs sold to the neighbors. Adding $40 and $120, we get $160, which is Farmer Brown's contribution to the GDP. Note that part of the milk Farmer Brown produced serves as an intermediate good and part as a final good. The $60 worth of milk that is fed to the pigs is an intermediate good, and so it is not counted in GDP. The $40 worth of milk sold to the neighbors is a final good, and so it is counted.

capital good a long-lived good that is used in the production of other goods and services

A special type of good that is difficult to classify as intermediate or final is a capital good. A **capital good** is a long-lived good that is used in the production of other goods or services. Factories and machines are examples of capital goods. Houses and apartment buildings, which produce dwelling services, are also a form of capital good. Capital goods do not fit the definition of final goods since their purpose is to produce other goods. On the other hand, they are not used up during the production process, except over a very long period, so they are not exactly intermediate goods either.

For purposes of measuring GDP, economists have agreed to classify newly produced capital goods as final goods even though they are not consumed by the ultimate user. Otherwise, a country that invested in its future by building modern factories and buying new machines would be counted as having a lower GDP than a country that devoted all its resources to producing consumer goods.

We have established the rule that only final goods and services (including newly produced capital goods) are counted in GDP. Intermediate goods and services, which are used up in the production of final goods and services, are not counted. In practice, however, this rule is not easy to apply because the production process often stretches over several periods.

For example, recall the earlier example of the grain that was milled into flour, which in turn was baked into a loaf of French bread. The contribution of the whole process to GDP is $2, the value of the bread (the final product). Suppose, though, that the grain and the flour were produced near the end of the year 2013 and the bread was baked early the next year in 2014. In this case, should we attribute the $2 value of the bread to the GDP for the year 2013 or to the GDP for the year 2014?

Neither choice seems quite right since part of the bread's production process occurred in each year. Part of the value of the bread should probably be counted in the year 2013 GDP and part in the year 2014 GDP. But how should we make the split?

To deal with this problem, economists determine the market value of final goods and services indirectly, by adding up the *value added* by each firm in the production process. The **value added** by any firm equals the market value of its product or service minus the cost of inputs purchased from other firms. As we'll see, summing the value added by all firms (including producers of both intermediate and final goods and services) gives the same answer as simply adding together the value of final goods and services. The value-added method thus eliminates the problem of dividing the value of a final good or service between two periods.

value added for any firm, the market value of its product or service minus the cost of inputs purchased from other firms

To illustrate this method, let's revisit the example of the French bread, which is the result of multiple stages of production. We have already determined that the total contribution of this production process to GDP is $2, the value of the bread. Let's show now that we can get the same answer by summing value added. Suppose that the bread is the ultimate product of three corporations: ABC Grain Company, Inc., produces grain; General Flour produces flour; and Hot'n'Fresh Baking produces the bread. If we make the same assumptions as before about the market value of the grain, the flour, and the bread, what is the value added by each of these three companies?

ABC Grain Company produces $0.50 worth of grain, with no inputs from other companies, so ABC's value added is $0.50. General Flour uses $0.50 worth of grain from ABC to produce $1.20 worth of flour. The value added by General Flour is thus the value of its product ($1.20) less the cost of purchased inputs ($0.50), or $0.70. Finally, Hot'n'Fresh Baking buys $1.20 worth of flour from General Flour and uses it to produce $2.00 worth of bread. So the value added by Hot'n'Fresh is $0.80.

Table 4.1 shows that the value added by each company gives the same contribution to GDP, $2.00, as the method based on counting final goods and services

TABLE 4.1
Value Added in Bread Production

Company	Revenues	− Cost of purchased inputs	= Value added
ABC Grain	$0.50	$0.00	$0.50
General Flour	$ 1.20	$0.50	$0.70
Hot'n'Fresh	$2.00	$ 1.20	$0.80
Total			$2.00

only. Basically, the value added by each firm represents the portion of the value of the final good or service that the firm creates in its stage of production. Summing the value added by all firms in the economy yields the total value of final goods and services, or GDP.

This example also illustrates how the value-added method solves the problem of production processes that bridge two or more periods. Suppose that the grain and flour are produced during the year 2013, but the bread is not baked until 2014. Using the value-added method, the contribution of this production process to the year 2013 GDP is the value added by the grain company plus the value added by the flour company, or $1.20. The contribution of the production process to the year 2014 GDP is the value added by the baker, which is $0.80. Thus, part of the value of the final product, the bread, is counted in the GDP for each year, reflecting the fact that part of the production of the bread took place in each year.

CONCEPT CHECK 4.2

Amy's card shop receives a shipment of Valentine's Day cards in December 2014. Amy pays the wholesale distributor of the cards a total of $500. In February 2013 she sells the cards for a total of $700. What are the contributions of these transactions to GDP in the years 2012 and 2013?

PRODUCED WITHIN A COUNTRY DURING A GIVEN PERIOD

The word *domestic* in the term *gross domestic product* tells us that GDP is a measure of economic activity within a given country. Thus, only production that takes place within the country's borders is counted. For example, the GDP of the United States includes the market value of *all* cars produced within U.S. borders, even if they are made in foreign-owned plants. However, cars produced in Mexico by a U.S.-based company like General Motors are *not* counted.

We have seen that GDP is intended to measure the amount of production that occurs during a given period such as the calendar year. For this reason, only goods and services that are actually produced during a particular year are included in the GDP for that year. The following example and concept check demonstrate this point.

The Sale of a House and GDP	**EXAMPLE 4.4**

Does the sale of an existing home count in GDP?

A 20-year-old house is sold to a young family for $200,000. The family pays the real estate agent a 6 percent commission, or $12,000. What is the contribution of this transaction to GDP?

Because the house was not produced during the current year, its value is *not* counted in this year's GDP. (The value of the house was included in the GDP 20 years earlier, when the house was built.) In general, purchases and sales of existing assets such as old houses or used cars do not contribute to the current year's GDP. However, the $12,000 fee paid to the real estate agent represents the market value of the agent's services in helping the family find the house and make the purchase. Since those services were provided during the current year, the agent's fee *is* counted in current-year GDP.

CONCEPT CHECK 4.3

Lotta Doe sells 100 shares of stock in Benson Buggywhip for $50 per share. She pays her broker a 2 percent commission for executing the sale. How does Lotta's transaction affect the current-year GDP?

RECAP	MEASURING GDP

Gross domestic product (GDP) equals the *market* **value of final goods and services produced within a country during** *a given period.*

- GDP is an aggregate of the market values of the many goods and services produced in the economy.

- Goods and services that are not sold in markets, such as unpaid housework, are not counted in GDP. An important exception is goods and services provided by the government, which are included in GDP at the government's cost of providing them.

- Final goods and services—goods and services consumed by the ultimate user—are counted in GDP. By convention, newly produced capital goods, such as factories and machines, also are treated as final goods and are counted in GDP. Intermediate goods and services, which are used up in the production of final goods and services, are not counted.

- In practice, the value of final goods and services is determined by the value-added method. The value added by any firm equals the firm's revenue from selling its product minus the cost of inputs purchased from other firms. Summing the value added by all firms in the production process yields the value of the final good or service.

- Only goods and services produced within a nation's borders are included in GDP.

- Only goods and services produced during the current year (or the portion of the value produced during the current year) are counted as part of the current-year GDP.

THE EXPENDITURE METHOD FOR MEASURING GDP

GDP is a measure of the quantity of goods and services *produced* by an economy. But any good or service that is produced also will be *purchased* and used by some economic agent—a consumer buying Christmas gifts or a firm investing in new machinery, for example. For many purposes, knowing not only how much is produced but who uses it and how is important.

Economists divide the users of the final goods and services that make up the GDP for any given year into four categories: *households, firms, governments,* and the *foreign sector* (that is, foreign purchasers of domestic products). They assume that all the final goods and services that are produced in a country in a given year will be purchased and used by members of one or more of these four groups. Furthermore, the amounts that purchasers spend on various goods and services should be equal to the market values of those goods and services.

GDP can thus be measured by either of two methods: (1) adding up the market values of all the final goods and services that are produced domestically or (2) adding up the total amount spent by each of the four groups on final goods and services and subtracting spending on imported goods and services. The values obtained by the two methods will be the same.

Corresponding to the four groups of final users are four components of expenditure: consumption, investment, government purchases, and net exports. That is, households consume, firms invest, governments make government purchases, and the foreign sector buys the nation's exports. Table 4.2 gives the dollar values for each of these components for the U.S. economy in 2013. As the table shows, GDP for the United States in 2013 was about $16.8 trillion, roughly $54,000 per person. Let's examine each type of expenditure individually, as well as some of the important subcomponents. As we walk through each one, refer to Table 4.2 to get a sense of the relative importance of each type of spending.

TABLE 4.2
Expenditure Components of U.S. GDP, 2013 (billions of dollars and % of total GDP)

Consumptions		**11,484.4**	**68.5%**
Durable Goods	1249.3		
Nondurable Goods	2601.9		
Services	7633.2		
Investment		**2,648.0**	**15.8%**
Business fixed investment	2054.0		
Residential investment	519.9		
Inventory investment	74.1		
Government Purchases		**3,143.9**	**18.7%**
Net Exports		**−508.2**	**−3.0%**
Exports	2262.9		
Imports	2770.2		
Total: Gross domestic product		**16,768.1**	

SOURCE: U.S. Bureau of Economic Analysis, www.bea.gov.

consumption expenditure (or consumption) spending by households on goods and services such as food, clothing, and entertainment

Consumption expenditure, or simply **consumption,** is spending by households on goods and services such as food, clothing, and entertainment. Consumption expenditure is subdivided into three subcategories:

- *Consumer durable goods* are long-lived consumer goods such as cars and furniture. Note that new houses are not treated as consumer durables but as part of investment.

- *Consumer nondurable goods* are shorter-lived goods like food and clothing.

- *Services* is the largest single component of consumer spending and includes everything from haircuts and taxi rides to legal, financial, and educational services.

investment spending by firms on final goods and services, primarily capital goods

Investment is spending by firms on final goods and services, primarily capital goods. Investment is divided into three subcategories:

- *Business fixed investment* is the purchase by firms of new capital goods such as machinery, factories, and office buildings. (Remember that for the purposes of calculating GDP, long-lived capital goods are treated as final goods rather than as intermediate goods.) Firms buy capital goods to increase their capacity to produce.

- *Residential investment* is construction of new homes and apartment buildings. Recall that homes and apartment buildings, sometimes called residential capital, are also capital goods. For GDP accounting purposes, residential investment is treated as an investment by the business sector, which then sells the homes to households.

- *Inventory investment* is the addition of unsold goods to company inventories. In other words, the goods that a firm produces but doesn't sell during the current period are treated, for accounting purposes, as if the firm had bought those goods from itself. (This convention guarantees that production equals expenditure.) Inventory investment can be positive or negative, depending on whether the value of inventories rises or falls over the course of the year.

People often refer to purchases of financial assets, such as stocks or bonds, as "investments." That use of the term is different from the definition we give here. A person who buys a share of a company's stock acquires partial ownership of the *existing* physical and financial assets controlled by the company. A stock purchase does not usually correspond to the creation of *new* physical capital, however, and so is not investment in the sense we are using the term in this chapter. We will generally refer to purchases of financial assets, such as stocks and bonds, as "financial investments," to distinguish them from a firm's investment in new capital goods such as factories and machines.

Government purchases are final goods and services bought by federal, state, and local governments. These expenditures run the gamut from buying fighter planes to paying public school teachers. Government purchases do *not* include transfer payments, which are payments made by the government in return for which no current goods or services are received. Examples of transfer payments are Social Security benefits, unemployment benefits, pensions paid to government workers, and welfare payments. Interest paid on the government debt is also excluded from government purchases.

Net exports equals exports minus imports.

- *Exports* are domestically produced final goods and services that are sold abroad.

- *Imports* are purchases by domestic buyers of goods and services that were produced abroad. Since imports are included in consumption, investment, and government purchases but do not represent spending on domestic production, they must be subtracted. A shorthand way of adding exports and subtracting imports is to add net exports, which equals exports minus imports.

government purchases purchases by federal, state, and local governments of final goods and services; government purchases do *not* include *transfer payments,* which are payments made by the government in return for which no current goods or services are received, nor do they include interest paid on the government debt

net exports exports minus imports

"My parents sent back all my stuff that came from China."

A country's net exports reflects the net demand by the rest of the world for its goods and services. Net exports can be negative, since imports can exceed exports in any given year. As Table 4.2 shows, the United States had greater imports than exports in 2013. It is a large $ amount but pretty insignificant in terms of % of GDP.

The relationship between GDP and expenditures on goods and services can be summarized by an equation. Let

$$Y \equiv \text{gross domestic product, or output}$$
$$C \equiv \text{consumption expenditure}$$
$$I \equiv \text{investment}$$
$$G \equiv \text{government purchases}$$
$$NX \equiv \text{net exports.}$$

The equation for GDP is thus

$$Y = C + I + G + NX.$$

Measuring GDP by Production and Expenditure   EXAMPLE 4.5

Do we get the same GDP using two different methods?

An economy produces 1,000,000 automobiles valued at $15,000 each. Of these, 700,000 are sold to consumers, 200,000 are sold to businesses, 50,000 are sold to the government, and 25,000 are sold abroad. No automobiles are imported. The automobiles left unsold at the end of the year are held in inventory by the auto producers. The market value of the production of final goods and services in this economy is 1,000,000 autos times $15,000 per auto, or $15 billion.

To measure GDP in terms of expenditure, we must add spending on consumption, investment, government purchases, and net exports. Consumption is 700,000 autos times $15,000, or $10.5 billion. Government purchases are 50,000 autos times $15,000, or $0.75 billion. Net exports is equal to exports (25,000 autos at $15,000, or $0.375 billion) minus imports (zero), so net exports is $0.375 billion.

What about investment? Here we must be careful. The 200,000 autos that are sold to businesses, worth $3 billion, count as investment. But notice too that the auto companies produced 1,000,000 automobiles but sold only 975,000 (700,000 + 200,000 + 50,000 + 25,000). Hence, 25,000 autos were unsold at the end of the year and were added to the automobile producers' inventories. This addition to producer inventories (25,000 autos at $15,000, or $0.375 billion) counts as inventory investment, which is part of total investment. Thus, total investment spending equals the $3 billion worth of autos sold to businesses plus the $0.375 billion in inventory investment, or $3.375 billion.

Recapitulating, in this economy, consumption is $10.5 billion, investment (including inventory investment) is $3.375 billion, government purchases equal $0.75 billion, and net exports is $0.375 billion. Summing these four components of expenditure yields $15 billion—the same value for GDP that we got by calculating the market value of production.

CONCEPT CHECK 4.4

Extending Example 4.5, suppose that 25,000 of the automobiles purchased by households are imported rather than domestically produced. Domestic production remains at 1,000,000 autos valued at $15,000 each. Once again, find GDP in terms of (a) the market value of production and (b) the components of expenditure.

GDP AND THE INCOMES OF CAPITAL AND LABOR

GDP can be thought of as a measure of total production or as a measure of total expenditure—either method gives the same final answer. There is, however, a third way to think of GDP, which is as the *incomes of capital and labor.*

Whenever a good or service is produced and sold, the revenue from the sale is distributed to the workers and the owners of the capital involved in the production of the good or service. Thus, except for some technical adjustments that we will ignore, GDP also equals labor income plus capital income.

- *Labor income* (equal to about two-thirds of GDP) comprises wages, salaries, and the incomes of the self-employed.

- *Capital income* (about one-third of GDP) is made up of payments to owners of physical capital (such as factories, machines, and office buildings) and intangible capital (such as copyrights and patents). The components of capital income include items such as profits earned by businessowners, the rents paid to owners of land or buildings, interest received by bondholders, and the royalties received by the holders of copyrights or patents.

Both labor income and capital income are to be understood as measured prior to payment of taxes; ultimately, of course, a portion of both types of income is captured by the government in the form of tax collections.

Figure 4.1 may help you visualize the three equivalent ways of thinking about GDP: the market value of production, the total value of expenditure, and the sum of labor income and capital income. The figure also roughly captures the relative importance of the expenditure and income components. About 70 percent of expenditure is consumption spending, about 20 percent is government purchases, and the rest is investment spending and net exports. (Actually, as Table 4.2 shows, net exports has been negative in recent years, reflecting the U.S. trade deficit.) As we mentioned, labor income is about two-thirds of total income, with capital income making up the rest.

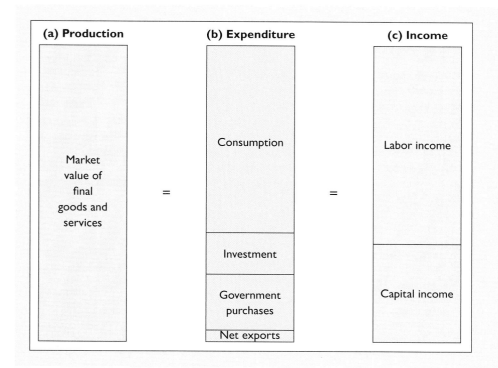

FIGURE 4.1

The Three Faces of GDP.

The GDP can be expressed equally well as (a) the market value of production, (b) total expenditure (consumption, investment, government purchases, net exports), or (c) total income (labor income and capital income).

RECAP	EXPENDITURE COMPONENTS OF GDP

GDP can be expressed as the sum of expenditures on domestically produced final goods and services. The four types of expenditures that are counted in the GDP, and the economic groups that make up each type of expenditure, are as follows:

Type of expenditure?	Who makes the expenditure?	Examples
Consumption	Households	Food, clothes, haircuts, new cars
Investment	Business firms	New factories and equipment, new houses, increases in inventory stocks
Government purchases	Government	New school buildings, new military hardware, salaries of soldiers and government officials
Net exports, or exports minus imports	Foreign sector	Exported manufactured goods, legal or financial services provided by domestic residents to foreigners

NOMINAL GDP VERSUS REAL GDP

GDP in a given year is useful in comparisons of economic activity in different places. For example, GDP data for the year 2013, broken down state by state, could be used to compare aggregate production in New York and California during that year. However, economists are interested in comparing levels of economic activity not only in different *locations* but *over time* as well. For instance, a president who is running for reelection on the basis of successful economic policies might want to know how much output in the U.S. economy increased during his term.

Using GDP to compare economic activity at two different points in time may give misleading answers, however, as the following example shows. Suppose, for the sake of illustration, that the economy produces only pizzas and calzones. The prices and quantities of the two goods in the years 2009 and 2013, the beginning and end of the president's term, are shown in Table 4.3. If we calculate GDP in each year as the market value of production, we find that the GDP for 2009 is (10 pizzas × $10/pizza) + (15 calzones × $5/calzone) = $175. The GDP for 2013 is (20 pizzas × $12/pizza) + (30 calzones × $6/calzone) = $420. Comparing the GDP for the year 2009 to the GDP for the year 2013, we might conclude that it is 2.4 times greater ($420/$175).

Can you see what is wrong with this conclusion? The quantities of both pizzas and calzones produced in the year 2013 are exactly twice the quantities produced in the

TABLE 4.3
Prices and Quantities in 2009 and 2013

	Quantity of pizzas	Price of pizzas	Quantity of calzones	Price of calzones
2009	10	$10	15	$5
2013	20	$12	30	$6

year 2009. If economic activity, as measured by actual production of both goods, exactly doubled over the four years, why do the calculated values of GDP show a greater increase?

The answer, as you also can see from the table, is that prices as well as quantities rose between 2009 and 2013. Because of the increase in prices, the *market value* of production grew more over those four years than the *physical volume* of production. So in this case, GDP is a misleading gauge of economic growth during the president's term, since the physical quantities of the goods and services produced in any given year, not the dollar values, are what determine people's economic well-being. Indeed, if the prices of pizzas and calzones had risen 2.4 times between 2009 and 2013 with no changes in the quantities of pizzas and calzones produced, GDP would have risen 2.4 times as well, with no increase in physical production! In that case, the claim that the economy's (physical) output had more than doubled during the president's term would obviously be wrong.

Economists often need to measure GDP at different points in time. We therefore need a method for calculating GDP that excludes the effects of price changes. Put another way, we need a way of adjusting GDP for inflation. Economists make this adjustment by using a common set of prices to value quantities produced in different years.

The standard approach is to pick a particular year, called the *base year,* and use the prices from that year to calculate the market value of output. There is no particular rule about which year to choose as the base year, but it is usually some recent year. When GDP is calculated using the prices from a base year, rather than the current year's prices, it is called **real GDP,** to indicate that it is a measure of real physical production. Real GDP is GDP adjusted for inflation. To distinguish real GDP, in which quantities produced are valued at base-year prices, from GDP valued at current-year prices, economists refer to the latter measure as **nominal GDP.**

real GDP a measure of GDP in which the quantities produced are valued at the prices in a base year rather than at current prices; real GDP measures the actual *physical volume* of production

nominal GDP a measure of GDP in which the quantities produced are valued at current-year prices; nominal GDP measures the *current dollar value* of production

---

Calculating the Change in Real GDP over the President's Term   **EXAMPLE 4.6**

How much did real GDP grow during the president's term?

Using data from Table 4.3 and assuming that 2009 is the base year, find real GDP for the years 2013 and 2009. By how much did real output grow between 2009 and 2013?

To find real GDP for the year 2013, we must value the quantities produced that year using the prices in the base year, 2009. Using the data in Table 4.3,

Year 2013 real GDP = (year 2013 quantity of pizzas × year 2009 price of pizzas) + (year 2013 quantity of calzones × year 2009 price of calzones)

= (20 × $10) + (30 × $5)

= $350.

The real GDP of this economy in the year 2013 is $350.

What is the real GDP for 2009? By definition, the real GDP for 2009 equals 2009 quantities valued at base-year prices. The base year in this example happens to be 2009, so real GDP for 2009 equals 2009 quantities valued at 2009 prices, which is the same as nominal GDP for 2009. In general, in the base year, real GDP and nominal GDP are the same. We already found nominal GDP for 2009, $175, so that is also the real GDP for 2009.

We can now determine how much real production has actually grown over the four-year period. Since real GDP was $175 in 2009 and $350 in 2013, the physical volume of production doubled between 2009 and 2013. This conclusion makes sense, since Table 4.3 shows that the production of both pizzas and calzones exactly doubled over the period. By using real GDP, we have eliminated the effects of price changes and obtained a reasonable measure of the actual change in physical production over the four-year span.

Of course, the production of all goods will not necessarily grow in equal proportion, as in the previous example. Concept Check 4.5 asks you to find real GDP when pizza and calzone production grow at different rates.

CONCEPT CHECK 4.5

Suppose production and prices of pizzas and calzones in 2009 and 2013 are as follows:

	Quantity of pizzas	Price of pizzas	Quantity of calzones	Price of calzones
2009	10	$10	15	$5
2013	30	$12	30	$6

These data are the same as those in Table 4.3, except that pizza production has tripled rather than doubled between 2009 and 2013. Find real GDP in 2013 and 2009, and calculate the growth in real output over the four-year period. (Continue to assume that 2009 is the base year.)

After you complete Concept Check 4.5, you will find that the growth in real GDP between 2009 and 2013 reflects a sort of average of the growth in physical production of pizzas and calzones. Real GDP therefore remains a useful measure of overall physical production, even when the production of different goods and services grows at different rates.[1]

The Economic Naturalist 4.1

Can nominal and real GDP ever move in different directions?

In most countries, both nominal and real GDP increase in almost every year. It is possible, however, for them to move in opposite directions. The last time this happened in the United States was 1990–1991. Using 2005 as a base year, real GDP fell by 0.2 percent, from $8.03 trillion to $8.02 trillion. This reflected an overall reduction in the physical quantities of goods and services produced. Nominal GDP, however, rose by 3.3 percent, from $5.00 trillion to $5.99 trillion, over the same period because prices rose by more than quantities fell.

The preceding example also illustrates the fact that nominal GDP will be *less* than real GDP if prices during the current year are less than prices during the base year. This will generally be the case when the current year is earlier than the base year.

Could real GDP ever rise during a year in which nominal GDP fell? Once again, the answer is yes. For example, this could happen when a country experiences economic growth and falling prices (deflation) at the same time. This actually happened in Japan during several years in the 1990s.

---

[1]The method of calculating real GDP just described was followed for many decades by the Bureau of Economic Analysis (BEA), the U.S. government agency responsible for GDP statistics. However, in recent years the BEA has adopted a more complicated procedure of determining real GDP, called *chain weighting*. The new procedure makes the official real GDP data less sensitive to the particular base year chosen. However, the chain-weighting and traditional approaches share the basic idea of valuing output in terms of base-year prices, and the results obtained by the two methods are generally similar.

RECAP	NOMINAL GDP VERSUS REAL GDP

Real GDP is calculated using the prices of goods and services that prevailed in a base year rather than in the current year. Nominal GDP is calculated using current-year prices. Real GDP is GDP adjusted for inflation; it may be thought of as measuring the physical volume of production. Comparisons of economic activity at different times should always be done using real GDP, not nominal GDP.

REAL GDP AND ECONOMIC WELL-BEING

Figure 4.2 shows the level of real GDP in the United States from 1929 to 2013. Government policymakers pay close attention to these data, often behaving as if the higher the real GDP, the better. At best, it is an imperfect measure of economic well-being because, for the most part, it captures only those goods and services that are priced and sold in markets. Many factors that contribute to people's economic well-being are not priced and sold in markets and thus are largely or even entirely omitted from GDP. Maximizing real GDP is not, therefore, always the right goal for government policymakers. Whether or not policies that increase GDP will also make people better off has to be determined on a case-by-case basis.

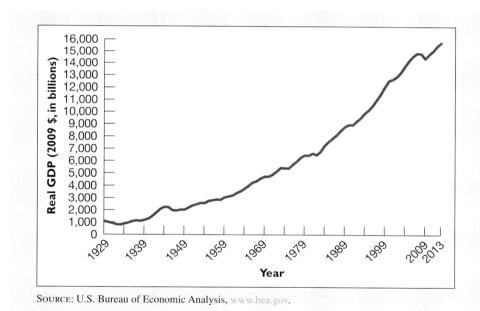

FIGURE.4.2

Output of the U.S. Economy, 1929–2013.

Real GDP in 2013 is roughly 15 times its level in 1929 and about 5 times as large as it was in 1960.

SOURCE: U.S. Bureau of Economic Analysis, www.bea.gov.

WHY REAL GDP ISN'T THE SAME AS ECONOMIC WELL-BEING

To understand why an increase in real GDP does not always promote economic well-being, let's look at some factors that are not included in GDP but do affect whether people are better off.

Leisure Time

Most Americans (and most people in other industrialized countries as well) work many fewer hours than their great-grandparents did 100 years ago. Early in the twentieth century, some industrial workers—steelworkers, for example—worked as many as 12 hours a day, 7 days a week. Today, the 40-hour workweek is typical. Also, Americans tend to start working later in life (after college or graduate school), and, in many cases, they are able to retire earlier. The increased leisure time available to workers in the United States and other industrialized countries—which allows them to pursue many worthwhile activities, including being with family and friends, participating in sports and hobbies, and pursuing cultural and educational activities—is a major benefit of living in a wealthy society. These extra hours of leisure are not priced in markets, however, and therefore are not reflected in GDP.

The Economic Naturalist 4.2

Why do people work fewer hours today than their great-grandparents did?

Americans start work later in life, retire earlier, and in many cases work fewer hours per week than people of 50 or 100 years ago. The *opportunity cost* of working less—retiring earlier, for example, or working fewer hours per week—is the earnings you forgo by not working. If you can, say, make $400 per week at a summer job in a department store, then leaving the job two weeks early to take a trip with some friends has an opportunity cost of $800. The fact that people are working fewer hours today suggests that their opportunity cost of forgone earnings is lower than their grandparents' and great-grandparents' opportunity cost. Why this difference?

> **Cost-Benefit**

We can use the Cost-Benefit Principle to help us understand this phenomenon. Over the past century, rapid economic growth in the United States and other industrialized countries has greatly increased the purchasing power of the average worker's wages. In other words, the typical worker today can buy more goods and services with his or her hourly earnings than ever before. This fact would seem to suggest that the opportunity cost of forgone earnings (measured in terms of what those earnings can buy) is greater, not smaller, today than in earlier times. But because the buying power of wages is so much higher today than in the past, Americans can achieve a reasonable standard of living by working fewer hours than they did in the past. Thus, while your grandparents may have had to work long hours to pay the rent or put food on the table, today the extra income from working long hours is more likely to buy relative luxuries, like nicer clothes or a fancier car. Because such discretionary purchases are easier to give up than basic food and shelter, the true opportunity cost of forgone earnings is lower today than it was 50 years ago. As the opportunity cost of leisure has fallen, Americans have chosen to enjoy more of it.

Nonmarket Economic Activities

Not all economically important activities are bought and sold in markets; with a few exceptions, such as government services, nonmarket economic activities are omitted from GDP. We mentioned earlier the example of unpaid housekeeping services. Another example is volunteer services, such as the volunteer fire and rescue squads that serve many small towns. The fact that these unpaid services are left out of GDP does *not* mean that they are unimportant. The problem is that, because there are no market prices and quantities for unpaid services, estimating their market values is very difficult.

How far do economists go wrong by leaving nonmarket economic activities out of GDP? The answer depends on the type of economy being studied. Although nonmarket economic activities exist in all economies, they are particularly important in poor economies. For example, in rural villages of developing countries, people commonly trade services with each other or cooperate on various tasks without exchanging any money. Families in these communities also tend to be relatively self-sufficient, growing their own food and providing many of their own basic services. Because such nonmarket economic activities are not counted in official statistics, GDP data may substantially understate the true amount of economic activity in the poorest countries.

Closely related to nonmarket activities is the *underground economy*, which includes transactions that are never reported to government officials and data collectors. The underground economy encompasses both legal and illegal activities, from informal babysitting jobs to organized crime. For instance, some people pay temporary or part-time workers like housecleaners and painters in cash, which allows these workers to avoid paying taxes on their income. Economists who have tried to estimate the value of such services by studying how much cash the public holds have concluded that these sorts of transactions make up an important share of overall economic activity, even in advanced industrial economies.

Environmental Quality and Resource Depletion

China has recently experienced tremendous growth in real GDP. But in expanding its manufacturing base, it also has suffered a severe decline in air and water quality. Increased pollution certainly detracts from the quality of life, but because air and water quality are not bought and sold in markets, the Chinese GDP does not reflect this downside of its economic growth.

The exploitation of finite natural resources also tends to be overlooked in GDP. When an oil company pumps and sells a barrel of oil, GDP increases by the value of the oil. But the fact that there is one less barrel of oil in the ground, waiting to be pumped sometime in the future, is not reflected in GDP.

A number of efforts have been made to incorporate factors like air quality and resource depletion into a comprehensive measure of GDP. Doing so is difficult, since it often involves placing a dollar value on intangibles, like having a clean river to swim in instead of a dirty one. But the fact that the benefits of environmental quality and resource conservation are hard to measure in dollars and cents does not mean that they are unimportant.

Quality of Life

What makes a particular town or city an attractive place to live? Some desirable features you might think of are reflected in GDP: spacious, well-constructed homes, good restaurants and stores; a variety of entertainment; and high-quality medical services. However, other indicators of the good life are not sold in markets and so may be omitted from GDP. Examples include a low crime rate, minimal traffic congestion, active civic organizations, and open space. Thus, while some citizens of a community may oppose the construction of a new Walmart because they believe it may have a negative effect on the quality of life, others may support it because Walmart sells goods at lower prices and may increase local GDP.

Poverty and Economic Inequality

GDP measures the *total* quantity of goods and services produced and sold in an economy, but it conveys no information about who gets to enjoy those goods and services. Two countries may have identical GDPs but differ radically in the distribution of economic welfare across the population. Suppose, for example, that in one country—call it Equalia—most people have a comfortable middle-class existence; both extreme poverty and extreme wealth are rare. But in another country, Inequalia—which has the same real GDP as Equalia—a few wealthy families control the economy, and the majority of the population lives in poverty. While most people would say that Equalia has a better economic situation overall, that judgment would not be reflected in the GDPs of the two countries, which are the same.

In the United States, absolute poverty has been declining. Today, many families whose income is below today's official "poverty line" (in 2014, $23,850 for a family of four) own a television, a car, and in some cases their own home. Some economists have argued that people who are considered poor today live as well as many middle-class people did in the 1950s.

But, though absolute poverty seems to be decreasing in the United States, inequality of income has generally been rising. The chief executive officer of a large U.S. corporation may earn hundreds of times what the typical worker in the same firm receives. Psychologists tell us that people's economic satisfaction depends not only on their absolute economic position—the quantity and quality of food, clothing, and shelter they have—but on what they have compared to what others have. If you own an old, beat-up car but are the only person in your neighborhood to have a car, you may feel privileged. But if everyone else in the neighborhood owns a luxury car, you are likely to be less satisfied. To the extent that such comparisons affect people's well-being, inequality matters as well as absolute poverty. Again, because GDP focuses on total production rather than on the distribution of output, it does not capture the effects of inequality.

BUT GDP IS RELATED TO ECONOMIC WELL-BEING

You might conclude from the list of important factors omitted from the official figures that GDP is useless as a measure of economic welfare. Indeed, numerous critics have made that claim. Clearly, in evaluating the effects of a proposed economic policy, considering only the likely effects on GDP is not sufficient. Planners must also ask whether the policy will affect aspects of economic well-being that are not captured in GDP. Environmental regulations may reduce production of steel, for example, which reduces the GDP. But that fact is not a sufficient basis on which to decide whether such regulations are good or bad. The right way to decide such questions is to apply the Cost-Benefit Principle: Are the benefits of cleaner air worth more to people than the costs the regulations impose in terms of lost output and lost jobs? If so, then the regulations should be adopted; otherwise, they should not.

Although looking at the effects of a proposed policy on real GDP is not the only basis on which to evaluate a policy, real GDP per person *does* tend to be positively associated with many things people value, including a high material standard of living, better health and life expectancies, and better education. We discuss next some of the ways in which a higher real GDP implies greater economic well-being.

> **Cost-Benefit**

Availability of Goods and Services

Obviously, citizens of a country with a high GDP are likely to possess more and better goods and services (after all, that is what GDP measures). On average, people in high-GDP countries enjoy larger, better-constructed, and more comfortable homes; higher-quality food and clothing; a greater variety of entertainment and cultural opportunities; better access to transportation and travel; better communications and sanitation; and other advantages. While social commentators may question the value of material consumption—and we agree that riches do not necessarily bring happiness or peace of mind—the majority of people in the world place great importance on achieving material prosperity. Throughout history people have made tremendous sacrifices and taken great risks to secure a higher standard of living for themselves and their families. In fact, to a great extent the United States was built by people who were willing to leave their native lands, often at great personal hardship, in hopes of bettering their economic condition.

Health and Education

Beyond an abundance of consumer goods, a high GDP brings other more basic advantages. Table 4.4 shows the differences between rich and poor countries with regard to some important indicators of well-being. The data are drawn from the United Nations *Human Development Report,* which measures economic development using a variety of education and health indicators in addition to GDP. The first row of Table 4.4 shows four groups of countries with radically different levels of GDP per

TABLE 4.4
GDP and Basic Indicators of Well-Being

Indicator and year	Very high human development	High human development	Medium human development	Low human development
GDP per person (U.S. dollars), 2011	32,931	11,572	5,203	1,621
Total population in group of countries (millions), 2012	1,134,305	1,039,178	3,520,535	1,280,676
Life expectancy at birth (years), 2012	80.1	73.4	69.9	59.1
Under-5 mortality rate (per 1,000 live births), 2010	6	18	42	110
Expected years of schooling (of children), 2012	16.3	13.9	11.4	8.5

SOURCE: United Nations, *Human Development Report 2013,* http://hdr.undp.org/en/data.

person. Most noticeably, GDP per person in the countries with very high human development is roughly 20 times that of the countries with low human development.[2]

How do these large differences in GDP relate to other measures of well-being? Table 4.4 shows that on some of the most basic measures of human welfare, the low human development countries fare much worse than the high human development countries. A child born in one of the countries with low human development has roughly an 11 percent chance of dying before his or her fifth birthday. Compare this with a 0.6 percent chance of dying before the fifth birthday in the countries with very high human development. A child born in a country with very high human development has a life expectancy of about 80 years, compared to about 59 years in the low human development countries.

Table 4.4 shows that citizens of very high human development countries attend school for twice as many years as those in the low human development countries. Furthermore, data on years of schooling do not capture important differences in the quality of education available in rich and poor countries, as measured by indicators such as the educational backgrounds of teachers and student–teacher ratios.

A child born in one of the low human development countries has a 11 percent chance of dying before her or his fifth birthday.

The Economic Naturalist 4.3

Why do far fewer children complete high school in poor countries than in rich countries?

One possible explanation is that people in poor countries place a lower priority on getting an education than people in rich countries. This seems unlikely since immigrants from poor countries often put a heavy emphasis on education—though it may be that people who emigrate from poor countries are unrepresentative of the population as a whole.

[2]The GDP data in Table 4.4 use U.S. prices to value goods and services in low human development nations. Since basic goods and services tend to be cheaper in poor countries, this adjustment significantly increases measured GDP in those countries.

An economic naturalist's explanation for the lower schooling rates in poor countries would rely not on cultural differences but on differences in opportunity costs. In poor societies, most of which are heavily agricultural, children are an important source of labor. Sending children to school beyond a certain age imposes a high opportunity cost on the family. Children who are in school are not available to help with planting, harvesting, and other tasks that must be done if the family is to survive. In addition, the cost of books and school supplies imposes a major hardship on poor families. The Cost-Benefit Principle thus implies that children will stay at home rather than go to school. In rich, nonagricultural countries, school-age children have few work opportunities, and their potential earnings are small relative to other sources of family income. The low opportunity cost of sending children to school in rich countries is an important reason for the higher enrollment rates in those countries. It is probably also true that the benefits or returns from receiving an education are higher in rich countries, as there are more employment opportunities for people with education than in poor countries.

Cost-Benefit

RECAP	REAL GDP AND ECONOMIC WELL-BEING

Real GDP is an imperfect measure of economic well-being. Among the factors affecting well-being omitted from real GDP are the availability of leisure time, nonmarket services such as unpaid homemaking and volunteer services, environmental quality and resource conservation, and quality-of-life indicators such as a low crime rate. The GDP also does not reflect the degree of economic inequality in a country. Because real GDP is not the same as economic well-being, proposed policies should not be evaluated strictly in terms of whether or not they increase the GDP.

Although GDP is not the same as economic well-being, it is positively associated with many things that people value, including a higher material standard of living, better health, longer life expectancies, and higher rates of literacy and educational attainment. This relationship between real GDP and economic well-being has led many people to emigrate from poor nations in search of a better life and has motivated policymakers in low human development countries to try to increase their nations' rates of economic growth.

○ SUMMARY ○

- The basic measure of an economy's output is *gross domestic product (GDP)*, the market value of the final goods and services produced in a country during a given period. Expressing output in terms of market values allows economists to aggregate the millions of goods and services produced in a modern economy. *(LO1)*

- Only *final goods and services* (which include *capital goods*) are counted in GDP, since they are the only goods and services that directly benefit final users. *Intermediate goods and services,* which are used up in the production of final goods and services, are not counted in GDP, nor are sales of existing assets. Summing the value added by each firm in the production process is a useful method of determining the value of final goods and services. *(LO1)*

- GDP also can be expressed as the sum of four types of expenditure: *consumption, investment, government purchases,* and *net exports.* These four types of expenditures correspond to the spending of households, firms, the government, and the foreign sector, respectively. *(LO2)*

- To compare levels of GDP over time, economists must eliminate the effects of inflation. They do so by measuring the market value of goods and services in terms of the prices in a base year. GDP measured in this way is called *real GDP,* while GDP measured in terms of current-year prices is called *nominal GDP.* Real GDP should always be used in making comparisons of economic activity over time. *(LO3)*

- Real GDP per person is an imperfect measure of economic well-being. With a few exceptions, notably government purchases of goods and services (which are included in GDP at their cost of production), GDP includes only those goods and services sold in markets. It excludes important factors that affect people's well-being, such as the amount of leisure time available to them, the value of unpaid or volunteer services, the quality of the environment, the quality-of-life indicators such as the crime rate, and the degree of economic inequality. *(LO4)*

- Real GDP is still a useful indicator of economic well-being, however. Countries with a high real GDP per person not only enjoy high average standards of living; they also tend to have higher life expectancies, low rates of infant and child mortality, and high rates of school enrollment and literacy. *(LO4)*

○ KEY TERMS ○

capital good
consumption
consumption expenditure
final goods or
   services

government purchases
gross domestic product
  (GDP)
intermediate goods or services
investment

market value
net exports
nominal GDP
real GDP
value added

○ REVIEW QUESTIONS ○

1. Why do economists use market values when calculating GDP? What is the economic rationale for giving high-value items more weight in GDP than low-value items? *(LO1)*

2. A large part of the agricultural sector in developing countries is subsistence farming, in which much of the food that is produced is consumed by the farmer and the farmer's family. Discuss the implications of this fact for the measurement of GDP in poor countries. *(LO1)*

3. Give examples of each of the four types of aggregate expenditure. Which of the four represents the largest share of GDP in the United States? Can an expenditure component be negative? Explain. *(LO2)*

4. Al's Shoeshine Stand shined 1,000 pairs of shoes last year and 1,200 pairs this year. He charged $4 for a shine last year and $5 this year. If last year is taken as the base year, find Al's contribution to both nominal GDP and real GDP in both years. Which measure would be better to use if you were trying to measure the change in Al's productivity over the past year? Why? *(LO3)*

5. Would you say that real GDP per person is a useful measure of economic well-being? Defend your answer. *(LO4)*

○ PROBLEMS ○

1. George and John, stranded on an island, use clamshells for money. Last year George caught 300 fish and 5 wild boars. John grew 200 bunches of bananas. In the two-person economy that George and John set up, fish sell for 1 clamshell each, boars sell for 10 clamshells each, and bananas go for 5 clamshells a bunch. George paid John a total of 30 clamshells for helping him to dig bait for fishing, and he also purchased five of John's mature banana trees for 30 clamshells each. What is the GDP of George's and John's island in terms of clamshells? *(LO1)*

2. How would each of the following transactions affect the GDP of the United States? *(LO1)*
   a. The U.S. government pays $1 billion in salaries for government workers.
   b. The U.S. government pays $1 billion to Social Security recipients.
   c. The U.S. government pays a U.S. firm $1 billion for newly produced airplane parts.

Visit your mobile app store and download the Frank: Study Econ app *today*!

d. The U.S. government pays $1 billion in interest to holders of U.S. government bonds.

e. The U.S. government pays $1 billion to Saudi Arabia for crude oil to add to U.S. government-owned oil reserves.

3. Intelligence Incorporated produces 100 computer chips and sells them for $200 each to Bell Computers. Using the chips and other labor and materials, Bell produces 100 personal computers. Bell sells the computers, bundled with software that Bell licenses from Macrosoft at $50 per computer, to PC Charlie's for $800 each. PC Charlie's sells the computers to the public for $1,000 each. Calculate the total contribution to GDP using the value-added method. Do you get the same answer by summing up the market values of final goods and services? *(LO1)*

4. MNLogs harvested logs (with no inputs from other companies) from its property in northern Minnesota. It sold these logs to MNLumber for $1,500 and MNLumber cut and planed the logs into lumber. MNLumber then sold the lumber for $4,000 to MNFurniture. MNFurniture used the lumber to produce 100 tables that it sold to customers for $70 each. *(LO1)*

a. Complete the table below to calculate the value added by each firm.

Company	Revenues	Cost of purchased inputs	Value added
MNLogs			
MNLumber			
MNFurniture			

b. Suppose that all of these transactions took place in 2014. By how much did GDP increase because of these transactions?

c. Suppose that MNLogs harvested the logs in October 2014 and sold them to MNLumber in December 2014. MNLumber then sold the finished lumber to MNFurniture in April 2015 and MNFurniture sold all 100 tables during the rest of 2015. By how much did GDP increase in 2014 and 2015 because of these transactions?

5. For each of the following transactions, state the effect both on U.S. GDP and on the four components of aggregate expenditure. *(LO2)*

a. Your mother buys a new car from a U.S. producer.

b. Your mother buys a new car imported from Sweden.

c. Your mother's car rental business buys a new car from a U.S. producer.

d. Your mother's car rental business buys a new car imported from Sweden.

e. The U.S. government buys a new, domestically produced car to be used by your mother, who has been appointed the ambassador to Sweden.

6. Calculate GDP for an economy that features the following data. *(LO2)*

Consumption expenditures	$600
Exports	75
Government purchases of goods and services	200
Construction of new homes and apartments	100
Sales of existing homes and apartments	200
Imports	50
Beginning-of-year inventory stocks	100
End-of-year inventory stocks	125
Business fixed investment	100
Government payments to retirees	100
Household purchases of durable goods	150

7. The nation of Potchatoonie produces hockey pucks, cases of root beer, and sandals. The following table provides prices and quantities of the three goods in the years 2011 and 2014.

	Pucks		Root Beer		Sandals	
Year	Quantity	Price	Quantity	Price	Quantity	Price
2011	100	$5	300	$20	100	$20
2014	125	$7	250	$20	110	$25

Assume that 2011 is the base year. Find nominal GDP and real GDP for both years. *(LO3)*

8. The government is considering a policy to reduce air pollution by restricting the use of "dirty" fuels by factories. In deciding whether to implement the policy, how, if at all, should the likely effects of the policy on real GDP be taken into account? Discuss. *(LO4)*

9. We discussed how the opportunity cost of sending children to school affects the level of school enrollment across countries. The United Nations *Human Development Report 2013* reports the following data for per capita income in 2012 (in the equivalent of 2011 U.S. dollars): *(LO4)*

Canada	$40,588
Denmark	$ 41,524
Greece	$ 25,391
Lesotho	$ 2,368
Ethiopia	$ 1,218

a. Which country would you expect to have the highest school enrollment rate? The lowest rate?
b. Discuss what other factors besides GDP per capita a family might consider when applying the Cost-Benefit Principle to the decision of whether or not to send a child to school.

○ ANSWERS TO CONCEPT CHECKS ○

4.1 In the text, GDP was calculated to be $64.00. If, in addition, Orchardia produces 5 oranges at $0.30 each, GDP is increased by $1.50 to $65.50. *(LO1)*

4.2 The value added of the wholesale distributor together with the ultimate producers of the cards is $500. Amy's value added—her revenue less her payments to other firms—is $200. Since the cards were produced and purchased by Amy during the year 2012 (we assume), the $500 counts toward year 2012 GDP. The $200 in value added originating in Amy's card shop counts in year 2013 GDP since Amy actually sold the cards in that year. *(LO1)*

4.3 The sale of stock represents a transfer of ownership of part of the assets of Benson Buggywhip, not the production of new goods or services. Hence, the stock sale itself does not contribute to GDP. However, the broker's commission of $100 (2 percent of the stock sale proceeds) represents payment for a current service and is counted in GDP. *(LO1)*

4.4 As in the original example, the market value of domestic production is 1,000,000 autos times $15,000 per auto, or $15 billion.

Also as in the original example, consumption is $10.5 billion and government purchases are $0.75 billion. However, because 25,000 of the autos that are purchased are imported rather than domestic, the domestic producers have unsold inventories at the end of the year of 50,000 (rather than 25,000 as in the original example). Thus, inventory investment is 50,000 autos times $15,000, or $0.75 billion, and total investment (autos purchased by businesses plus inventory investment) is $3.75 billion. Since exports and imports are equal (both are 25,000 autos), net exports (equal to exports minus imports) is zero. Notice that since we subtract imports to get net exports, it is unnecessary also to subtract imports from consumption. Consumption is defined as total purchases by households, not just purchases of domestically produced goods.

Total expenditure is $C + I + G + NX$ = $10.5 billion + $3.75 billion + $0.75 billion + 0 = $15 billion, the same as the market value of production. *(LO2)*

4.5 Real GDP in the year 2013 equals the quantities of pizzas and calzones produced in the year 2013, valued at the market prices that prevailed in the base year 2009. So real GDP in 2013 = (30 pizzas × $10/pizza) + (30 calzones × $5/calzone) = $450.

Real GDP in 2009 equals the quantities of pizzas and calzones produced in 2009, valued at 2009 prices, which is $175. Notice that since 2009 is the base year, real GDP and nominal GDP are the same for that year.

The real GDP in the year 2013 is $450/$175, or about 2.6 times what it was in 2009. Hence the expansion of real GDP lies between the threefold increase in pizza production and the doubling in calzone production that occurred between 2009 and 2013. *(LO3)*

CHAPTER 5

Inflation and the Price Level

HOW DO WE MEASURE INFLATION?

In 1930 the great baseball player Babe Ruth earned a salary of $80,000. When it was pointed out to him that he had earned more than President Hoover, Ruth replied, with some justification, "I had a better year than he did." In 2001 Barry Bonds broke the major league home run record by hitting 73 home runs and earned $10.3 million. Which baseball player was better off? Was Barry Bonds able to buy more goods and services in 2001 with his $10.3 million or was Babe Ruth better off with his $80,000 in 1930? The answer is not obvious because the price of just about everything increased dramatically between 1930 and 2001, reflecting the inflation that occurred in the United States over that time period.

Inflation can make a comparison of economic conditions at different points in time quite difficult. Your grandparents remember being able to buy both a comic book and a chocolate sundae for a quarter. Today the same two items might cost $4 or $5. You might conclude from this fact that kids were much better off in "the good old days," but were they really? Without more information, we can't tell, for though the prices of comic books and sundaes have gone up, so have allowances. The real question is whether young people's spending money has increased as much as or more than the prices of the things they want to buy. If so, then they are no worse off today than their grandparents were when they were young and candy bars cost a nickel.

Quantities that are measured in dollars (or other currency units) and then adjusted for inflation are called *real* quantities (for example, real GDP is gross domestic product adjusted for inflation). By working with real quantities, economists can

LEARNING OBJECTIVES

After reading this chapter, you should be able to:

LO1 Explain how the consumer price index (CPI) is constructed and use it to calculate the inflation rate.

LO2 Show how the CPI is used to adjust dollar amounts to eliminate the effects of inflation.

LO3 Discuss the two most important biases in the CPI.

LO4 Distinguish between inflation and relative price changes in order to find the true costs of inflation.

LO5 Summarize the connections among inflation, nominal interest rates, and real interest rates.

compare the real incomes of Babe Ruth and Barry Bonds, as well as any economic measurement that is expressed in dollars. In this chapter, we'll discuss how economists measure inflation and you will learn how dollar amounts can be adjusted for the effects of inflation.

Inflation also makes it difficult to compare interest rates across time. The interest rate on a 30-year mortgage was 18.5 percent in October 1981, while the interest rate on the same type of mortgage in May 2014 was 4.2 percent. Which one was higher in *real* terms; that is, which mortgage cost more in terms of purchasing power? We will discuss the answer to this question, and in the process you'll discover how to calculate the real interest rate, the interest rate adjusted for the effects of inflation.

An important benefit of studying macroeconomics is learning how to avoid the confusion inflation creates when we compare economic conditions over time. It is equally important to understand the true costs of inflation. Economic policymakers usually claim that a low and stable rate of inflation is one of their chief objectives. We'll see why this is an important goal and show how the costs of inflation might be very different than what you think they are.

THE CONSUMER PRICE INDEX AND INFLATION

consumer price index (CPI) for any period, a measure of the cost in that period of a standard basket of goods and services relative to the cost of the same basket of goods and services in a fixed year, called the *base year*

The basic tool economists use to measure the price level in the U.S. economy is the *consumer price index,* or CPI for short. The CPI is a measure of the "cost of living" during a particular period. Specifically, the **consumer price index (CPI)** for any period measures the cost in that period of a standard set, or basket, of goods and services *relative* to the cost of the same basket of goods and services in a fixed year, called the *base year.*

To illustrate how the CPI is constructed, suppose the government has designated 2010 as the base year. Assume for the sake of simplicity that in 2010 a typical American family's monthly household budget consisted of spending on just three items: rent on a two-bedroom apartment, hamburgers, and movie tickets. In reality, of course, families purchase hundreds of different items each month, but the basic principles of constructing the CPI are the same no matter how many items are included. Suppose too that the family's average monthly expenditures in 2010, the base year, were as shown in Table 5.1.

TABLE 5.1
Monthly Household Budget of the Typical Family in 2010 (Base Year)

Item	Cost (in 2010)
Rent, two-bedroom apartment	$500
Hamburgers (60 at $2.00 each)	120
Movie tickets (10 at $6.00 each)	60
Total expenditure	$680

Now let's fast-forward to the year 2015. Over that period, the prices of various goods and services are likely to have changed; some will have risen and some fallen. Let's suppose that by the year 2015 the rent that our family pays for their two-bedroom apartment has risen to $630. Hamburgers now cost $2.50 each, and the price of movie tickets has risen to $7.00 each. So, in general, prices have been rising.

By how much did the family's cost of living increase between 2010 and 2015? Table 5.2 shows that if the typical family wanted to consume the *same basket of goods and services* in the year 2015 as they did in the year 2010, they would have to spend $850 per month, or $170 more than the $680 per month they spent in 2010. In

TABLE 5.2
Cost of Reproducing the 2010 (Base-Year) Basket of Goods and Services in Year 2015

Item	Cost (in 2015)	Cost (in 2010)
Rent, two-bedroom apartment	$630	$500
Hamburgers (60 at $2.50 each)	150	120
Movie tickets (10 at $7.00 each)	70	60
Total expenditure	$850	$680

other words, to live the same way in the year 2015 as they did in the year 2010, the family would have to spend 25 percent more ($170/$680) each month. So, in this example, the cost of living for the typical family rose 25 percent between 2010 and 2015.

The Bureau of Labor Statistics (BLS) calculates the official consumer price index (CPI) using essentially the same method. The first step in deriving the CPI is to pick a base year and determine the basket of goods and services that were consumed by the typical family during that year. In practice, the government learns how consumers allocate their spending through a detailed survey, called the Consumer Expenditure Survey, in which randomly selected families record every purchase they make and the price they paid over a given month. Let's call the basket of goods and services that results the *base-year basket*. Then, each month BLS employees visit thousands of stores and conduct numerous interviews to determine the current prices of the goods and services in the base-year basket.[1]

The CPI in any given year is computed using this formula:

$$\text{CPI} = \frac{\text{Cost of base-year basket of goods and services in current year}}{\text{Cost of base-year basket of goods and services in base year}}.$$

Returning to the example of the typical family that consumes three goods, we can calculate the CPI in the year 2015 as

$$\text{CPI in year 2015} = \frac{\$850}{\$680} = 1.25.$$

In other words, in this example, the cost of living in the year 2015 is 25 percent higher than it was in 2010, the base year. Notice that the base-year CPI is always equal to 1.00, since in that year the numerator and the denominator of the CPI formula are the same. The CPI for a given period (such as a month or year) measures the cost of living in that period *relative* to what it was in the base year.

The BLS multiplies the CPI by 100 to get rid of the decimal point. If we were to do that here, the year 2015 CPI would be expressed as 125 rather than 1.25, and the base-year CPI would be expressed as 100 rather than 1.00. However, many calculations are simplified if the CPI is stated in decimal form, so we will not adopt the convention of multiplying it by 100.

Calculating the CPI   **EXAMPLE 5.1**

How do we measure the typical family's cost of living?

Suppose that in addition to the three goods and services the typical family consumed in 2010, they also bought four sweaters at $30 each. In the year 2015, the same sweaters cost $50 each. The prices of the other goods and services in 2010 and 2015 were the same

[1]More details on how the Bureau of Labor Statistics constructs the CPI are available at www.bls.gov/cpi/cpifaq.htm.

as in Table 5.2. With this additional item, what was the change in the family's cost of living between 2010 and 2015?

In the example in the text, the cost of the base-year (2010) basket was $680. Adding four sweaters at $30 each raises the cost of the base-year basket to $800. What does this same basket (including the four sweaters) cost in 2015? The cost of the apartment, the hamburgers, and the movie tickets is $850, as before. Adding the cost of the four sweaters at $50 each raises the total cost of the basket to $1,050. The CPI equals the cost of the basket in 2015 divided by the cost of the basket in 2010 (the base year), or $1,050/$800 = 1.31. We conclude that the family's cost of living rose 31 percent between 2010 and 2015.

CONCEPT CHECK 5.1

Returning to the three-good example in Tables 5.1 and 5.2, find the year 2015 CPI if the rent on the apartment falls from $500 in 2010 to $400 in 2015. The prices for hamburgers and movie tickets in the two years remain the same as in the two tables.

price index a measure of the average price of a given quality of goods or services relative to the price of the same goods or services in a base year

The CPI does not measure the price of a specific good or service. Indeed, it has no units of measurement at all since the dollars in the numerator of the fraction cancel with the dollars in the denominator. Rather, the CPI is an *index*. The *value* of an index in a particular year has meaning only in comparison with the value of that index in another year. Thus, a **price index** measures the average price of a quality of goods or services relative to the price of those same goods or services in a base year. The CPI is an especially well-known price index, one of many economists use to assess economic trends. For example, because manufacturers tend to pass on increases in the prices of raw materials to their customers, economists use indexes of raw materials' prices to forecast changes in the prices of manufactured goods. Other indexes are used to study the rate of price change in energy, food, health care, and other major sectors.

CONCEPT CHECK 5.2

The consumer price index captures the cost of living for the "typical" or average family. Suppose you were to construct a personal price index to measure changes in your own cost of living over time. In general, how would you go about constructing such an index? Why might changes in your personal price index differ from changes in the CPI?

INFLATION

rate of inflation the annual percentage rate of change in the price level, as measured, for example, by the CPI

The CPI provides a measure of the average *level* of prices relative to prices in the base year. *Inflation*, in contrast, is a measure of how fast the average price level is *changing* over time. The **rate of inflation** is the annual percentage rate of change in the price level, as measured, for example, by the CPI. The price level (0.05) divided by the initial price level (1.25), which is equal to 4 percent.

| Calculating Inflation Rates: 2009–2013 | **EXAMPLE 5.2** |

How do we calculate the inflation rate using the CPI?

CPI values for the years 2009 to 2013 are shown on the next page.

Year	CPI
2009	2.15
2010	2.18
2011	2.25
2012	2.30
2013	2.33

The inflation rate between 2009 and 2010 is the percentage increase in the price level between those years: $(2.18 - 2.15)/2.15 = 1.4$ percent. On your own, calculate the inflation rate for the remaining years.

CONCEPT CHECK 5.3

Below are CPI values for the years 1929 through 1933. Find the rates of inflation between 1929 and 1930, 1930 and 1931, 1931 and 1932, and 1932 and 1933.

Year	CPI
1929	0.171
1930	0.167
1931	0.152
1932	0.137
1933	0.130

How did inflation rates in the 1930s differ from those since 2009?

The results of the calculations for Concept Check 5.3 include some examples of *negative* inflation rates. A situation in which the prices of most goods and services are falling over time so that inflation is negative is called **deflation.** The early 1930s was the last time the United States experienced significant deflation. Japan experienced relatively mild deflation during the 1990s.

Figure 5.1 puts the previous examples in context by showing the inflation rate in the United States for 1956 to 2013.

deflation a situation in which the prices of most goods and services are falling over time so that inflation is negative

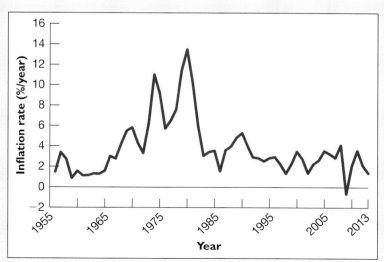

FIGURE 5.1

The U.S. Inflation Rate, 1956–2013.

The U.S. Inflation rate has fluctuated over time. Inflation was high in the 1970s but has been quite low recently.

SOURCE: FRED, Federal Reserve Economic Data, from the Federal Reserve Bank of St. Louis, http://research.stlouisfed.org/fred2/.

The Economic Naturalist 5.1

What is core inflation?

An article in *The New York Times* from March 18, 2010, began, "Prices showed no movement overall last month, the Labor Department said, but when volatile food and fuel costs were excluded, costs as measured by the consumer price index rose 0.1 percent." Why would we exclude food and energy costs when measuring inflation? Food and fuel are two of the most important things households buy, so isn't that messing up our inflation measure?

core rate of inflation the rate of increase of all prices except energy and food

We defined inflation as a measure of how fast the average price level is changing over time. Over the course of a month or so, this rate can fluctuate greatly, making it difficult to sort out short-run movements in prices from the long-run trend in the inflation rate. The **core rate of inflation** is defined as the rate of increase of all prices except energy and food, the two items most frequently responsible for short-run fluctuations in the inflation rate. Because core inflation excludes the sources of the most volatile price changes, it is considered to be a useful short-term measure of the underlying inflation trend.

For example, Table 5.3 presents the general and core rates of inflation for 2008–2012. The CPI inflation fell to a negative value in 2009, turned positive in 2010, and was higher in 2011 than in 2012. The core rate showed the same trend over these years, but with smaller changes from year to year. Notice how these values support the notion that the core inflation rate is less susceptible to short-term fluctuations than the CPI inflation rate is.

TABLE 5.3
U.S. Annualized Inflation Rates, 2008–2012

Year	CPI Inflation	Core Inflation
2008	3.84	2.30
2009	−.36	1.70
2010	1.64	.96
2011	3.16	1.66
2012	2.07	2.11

SOURCE: Calculated using data from *Economic Report of the President,* March 2013, Table B-62, www.gpo.gov/erp.

Thus, a focus on core inflation does not mean increases in oil and food prices are unimportant. Rather, the core inflation rate allows us to monitor what is happening to inflation over the long run, and whether or not policies need to be instituted to keep inflation in check. We can use both measures together: the inflation rate to see what is going on from month to month, and the core inflation rate to monitor long-run inflation.

ADJUSTING FOR INFLATION

The CPI is an extremely useful tool. Not only does it allow us to measure changes in the cost of living; it also can be used to adjust economic data to eliminate the effects of inflation. In this section we will see how the CPI can be used to convert quantities measured at current dollar values into real terms, a process called *deflating*. We also will see that the CPI can be used to convert real quantities into current-dollar terms, a procedure called *indexing*. Both procedures are useful not only to economists but to anyone who needs to adjust payments, accounting measures, or other economic quantities for the effects of inflation.

DEFLATING A NOMINAL QUANTITY

An important use of the CPI is to adjust **nominal quantities**—quantities measured at their current dollar values—for the effects of inflation. To illustrate, suppose we know that the typical family in a certain metropolitan area had a total income of $40,000 in 2010 and $44,000 in 2015. Was this family economically better off in the year 2015 than in 2010?

> **nominal quantity** a quantity that is measured in terms of its current dollar value

Without any more information than this, we might be tempted to say yes. After all, their income rose by 10 percent over the five-year period. But prices also might have been rising, as fast as or faster than the family's income. Suppose the prices of the goods and services the family consumes rose 25 percent over the same period. Since the family's income rose only 10 percent, we would have to conclude that the family is worse off, in terms of the goods and services they can afford to buy, despite the increase in their *nominal,* or current-dollar, income.

We can make a more precise comparison of the family's purchasing power in 2010 and 2015 by calculating their incomes in those years in *real* terms. In general, a **real quantity** is one that is measured in physical terms—for example, in terms of quantities of goods and services. To convert a nominal quantity into a real quantity, we must divide the nominal quantity by a price index for the period, as shown in Table 5.4. The calculations in the table show that in *real* or purchasing power terms, the family's income actually *decreased* by $4,800, or 12 percent of their initial real income of $40,000, between 2010 and 2015.

> **real quantity** a quantity that is measured in physical terms—for example, in terms of quantities of goods and services

TABLE 5.4
Comparing the Real Values of a Family's Income in 2010 and 2015

Year	Nominal family income	CPI	Real family income = Nominal family income/CPI
2010	$40,000	1.00	$40,000/1.00 = $40,000
2015	$44,000	1.25	$44,000/1.25 = $35,200

$$40 \quad \frac{44- 40}{40} =$$

The problem for this family is that though their income has been rising in nominal (dollar) terms, it has not kept up with inflation. Dividing a nominal quantity by a price index to express the quantity in real terms is called **deflating the nominal quantity.** (Be careful not to confuse the idea of deflating a nominal quantity with deflation, or negative inflation. The two concepts are different.)

> **deflating (a nominal quantity)** the process of dividing a nominal quantity by a price index (such as the CPI) to express the quantity in real terms

Deflating a nominal quantity is a very useful tool. It can be used to eliminate the effects of inflation from comparisons of any nominal quantity—workers' wages, health care expenditures, the components of the federal budget—over time. Why does this method work? In general, if you know both how many dollars you have spent on a given item and the item's price, you can figure out how many of the item you bought (by dividing your expenditures by the price). For example, if you spent $100 on hamburgers last month and hamburgers cost $2.50 each, you can determine that you purchased 40 hamburgers. Similarly, if you divide a family's dollar income or expenditures by a price index, which is a measure of the average price of the goods and services they buy, you will obtain a measure of the real quantity of goods and services they purchased. Such real quantities are sometimes referred to as *inflation-adjusted* quantities.

| **Babe Ruth versus Barry Bonds** | EXAMPLE 5.3 |

Who earned more, Babe Ruth or Barry Bonds?

Let's return to the question posed at the beginning of this chapter. When Barry Bonds earned $10.3 million in 2001, was he better or worse off than Babe Ruth was in 1930 earning $80,000?

To answer this question, we need to convert both men's earnings into real terms. The CPI (using the average of 1982–1984 as the base year since an extensive survey of consumer purchases was made in this period) was 0.167 in 1930 and 1.78 in 2001. Dividing Babe Ruth's salary by 0.167, we obtain approximately $479,000, which is Ruth's salary "in 1982–1984 dollars." In other words someone would need $479,000 in the 1982–1984 period to buy the same amount of goods and services as Babe Ruth could in 1930 with his $80,000 salary. Dividing Barry Bonds' 2001 salary by the 2001 CPI, 1.78, yields a salary of $5.79 million in 1982–1984 dollars. Thus, someone would need $5.79 million in the 1982–1984 period to buy the same amount of goods and services as Barry Bonds could in 2001 with his $10.3 million salary. We can now compare the real earnings of the two power hitters in 1982–1984 dollars: $479,000 and $5.79 million. Although adjusting for inflation brings the two figures closer together, in real terms Bonds still earned more than 12 times Ruth's salary. Incidentally, Bonds also earned about 25 times what President Bush earned in 2001.

real wage the wage paid to workers measured in terms of purchasing power; the real wage for any given period is calculated by dividing the nominal (dollar) wage by the CPI for that period

Clearly, in comparing wages or earnings at two different points in time, we must adjust for changes in the price level. Doing so yields the **real wage**—the wage measured in terms of real purchasing power. The real wage for any given period is calculated by dividing the nominal (dollar) wage by the CPI for that period.

CONCEPT CHECK 5.4

In 2009 Alex Rodriguez of the New York Yankees earned $27.5 million. In that year the CPI was 2.15. How did Rodriguez's 2009 real earnings compare to Bond's 2001 real earnings, as stated in Example 5.3?

| **Real Wages of U.S. Production Workers** | EXAMPLE 5.4 |

How do you compare workers' real wages?

Production workers are nonsupervisory workers, such as those who work on factory assembly lines. The average U.S. production worker earned $3.40 per hour in 1970 and $20.14 in 2013. Compare the real wages for this group of workers in these years.

To find the real wage in 1970 and 2013, we need to know the CPI in both years and then divide the wage in each year by the CPI for that year. For 1970, the nominal wage was $3.40 and the CPI was 0.39 (using the 1982–1984 average as the base period), so the real wage in 1970 was $8.72. Similarly, in 2013 the nominal wage was $20.14, and the CPI was 2.29, so the real wage in 2013 was $8.79. Thus, we find that, in real terms, production workers' wages actually stayed roughly the same between 1970 and 2013, despite the fact that the nominal wage in 2013 was almost six times the nominal wage in 1970.

Figure 5.2 shows nominal wages and real wages for U.S. production workers for the period 1970–2013. Notice the dramatic difference between the two trends. Looking only at nominal wages, one might conclude that production-line workers were much better paid in 2013 than in 1970. But once wages are adjusted for inflation, we see that, in terms of buying power, production-line workers' wages have stagnated since the early 1970s. Example 5.4 illustrates the crucial importance of adjusting for inflation when comparing dollar values over time.

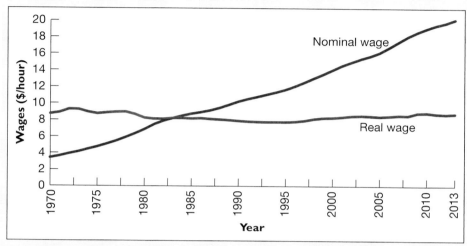

FIGURE 5.2

Nominal and Real Wages for Production Workers, 1970–2013.

Though nominal wages of production workers have risen dramatically since 1970, real wages have stagnated.

SOURCE: FRED, Federal Reserve Economic Data, from the Federal Reserve Bank of St. Louis, http://research.stlouisfed.org/fred2/.

CONCEPT CHECK 5.5

In 1950 the minimum wage prescribed by federal law was $0.75 per hour. In 2013 it was $7.25 per hour. How does the real minimum wage in 2013 compare to that of 1950? The CPI was 0.24 in 1950 and 2.29 in 2013.

INDEXING TO MAINTAIN BUYING POWER

The consumer price index also can be used to convert real quantities to nominal quantities. Suppose, for example, that in the year 2010 the government paid certain Social Security recipients $1,000 per month in benefits. Let's assume that Congress would like the buying power of these benefits to remain constant over time so that the recipients' standard of living is unaffected by inflation. To achieve that goal, at what level should Congress set the monthly Social Security benefit in the year 2015?

The nominal, or dollar, benefit Congress should pay in the year 2015 to maintain the purchasing power of retired people depends on how much inflation has taken place between 2010 and 2015. Suppose that the CPI has risen 20 percent between 2010 and 2015. That is, on average the prices of the goods and services consumers buy have risen 20 percent over that period. For Social Security recipients to "keep up" with inflation, their benefit in the year 2015 must be $1,000 + .20($1,000) = $1,200 per month, or 20 percent more than it was in 2010. In general, to keep purchasing power constant, the dollar benefit must be increased each year by the percentage increase in the CPI.

The practice of increasing a nominal quantity according to changes in a price index to prevent inflation from eroding purchasing power is called **indexing.** In the case of Social Security, federal law provides for the automatic indexing of benefits. Each year,

indexing the practice of increasing a nominal quantity each period by an amount equal to the percentage increase in a specified price index. Indexing prevents the purchasing power of the nominal quantity from being eroded by inflation without any action by Congress, benefits increase by an amount equal to the percentage increase in the CPI. Some labor contracts are indexed as well so that wages are adjusted fully or partially for changes in inflation.

An Indexed Labor Contract   EXAMPLE 5.5

How much do workers get paid when they have an indexed contract?

A labor contract provides for a first-year wage of $12.00 per hour and specifies that the real wage will rise by 2 percent in the second year of the contract and by another 2 percent in the third year. The CPI is 1.00 in the first year, 1.05 in the second year, and 1.10 in the third year. What are the dollar wages that must be paid in the second and third years of the contract?

Because the CPI is 1.00 in the first year, both the nominal wage and the real wage are $12.00. Let W_2 stand for the nominal wage in the second year. Deflating by the CPI in the second year, we can express the real wage in the second year as $W_2/1.05$. The contract says that the second-year real wage must be 2 percent higher than the real wage in the first year, so $W_2/1.05 = \$12.00 \times 1.02 = \$12.24$. Multiplying through by 1.05 to solve for W_2, we get $W_2 = \$12.85$, the nominal wage required by the contract in the second year. In the third year the nominal wage W_3 must satisfy the equation $W_3/1.10 = \$12.24 \times 1.02 = \$12.48$. (Why?) Solving this equation for W_3 yields $13.73 as the nominal wage that must be paid in the third year.

CONCEPT CHECK 5.6

The minimum wage is not indexed to inflation, but suppose it had been starting in 1950. What would the nominal minimum wage have been in 2015? See Concept Check 5.5 for the data necessary to answer this question.

Because the minimum wage is not indexed to inflation, its purchasing power falls as prices rise. Congress must therefore raise the nominal minimum wage periodically to keep the real value of the minimum wage from eroding.

RECAP	METHODS TO ADJUST FOR INFLATION

Deflating. To correct a nominal quantity, such as a family's dollar income, for changes in the price level, divide it by a price index such as the CPI. This process expresses the nominal quantity in terms of real purchasing power. If nominal quantities from two different years are deflated by a price index with the same base year, the purchasing power of the two deflated quantities can be compared.

Indexing. To ensure that a nominal payment, such as a Social Security benefit, represents a constant level of real purchasing power, increase the nominal quantity each year by a percentage equal to the rate of inflation for that year.

DOES THE CPI MEASURE "TRUE" INFLATION? ——

Policymakers pay close attention to the latest inflation numbers when deciding what actions to take. Furthermore, because of the widespread use of indexing, changes in the CPI directly impact the government's budget. For example, if the CPI rises by

3 percent during a given year, by law Social Security benefits—which are a significant part of the federal budget—increase automatically by 3 percent. Many other government payments and private contracts, such as union labor contracts, are indexed to the CPI as well.

However, what if the CPI is a poor measure of "true" inflation? First, the indexing of Social Security and other government benefits to the CPI could be costing the federal government billions of dollars more than necessary every year. Second, an overstated rate of inflation could lead us to underestimate the true improvement in living standards over time. For instance, if the typical family's nominal income increases by 3 percent per year, and inflation is reported to be 3 percent per year, economists would conclude that American families are experiencing no increase in their real income. But if the "true" inflation rate is really 2 percent per year, then the family's real income is actually rising by 1 percent per year (the 3 percent increase in nominal income minus 2 percent inflation).

A 1996 report, known as the Boskin Commission Report, concluded that the official CPI inflation rate overstates the true inflation rate by as much as 1 to 2 percentage points a year. It gave a number of reasons why this might be the case; two are particularly important. First, in practice, government statisticians cannot always adjust adequately for changes in the *quality* of goods and services. Suppose a new personal computer has 20 percent more memory, computational speed, and data storage capacity than last year's model. Suppose too for the sake of illustration that its price is 20 percent higher. Has there been inflation in computer prices? Economists would say no; although consumers are paying 20 percent more for a computer, they are getting a 20 percent better machine. The situation is really no different from paying 20 percent more for a pizza that is 20 percent bigger. However, because quality change is difficult to measure precisely and because they have many thousands of goods and services to consider, government statisticians often miss or understate changes in quality. In general, whenever statisticians fail to adjust adequately for improvements in the quality of goods or services, they will tend to overstate inflation. This type of overstatement is called *quality adjustment bias.*[2]

An extreme example of quality adjustment bias can occur whenever a totally new good becomes available. For instance, the introduction of the first effective AIDS drugs significantly increased the quality of medical care received by AIDS patients. In practice, however, quality improvements that arise from totally new products are likely to be poorly captured by the CPI, if at all. The problem is that since the new good was not produced in the base year, there is no base-year price with which to compare the current price of the good. Government statisticians use various approaches to correct for this problem, such as comparing the cost of the new drug to the cost of the next-best therapies. But such methods are necessarily imprecise and open to criticism.

The second problem emphasized by the Boskin Commission arises from the fact that the CPI is calculated for a fixed basket of goods and services. This procedure does not allow for the possibility that consumers can switch from products whose prices are rising to those whose prices are stable or falling. Ignoring the fact that consumers can switch from more expensive to less expensive goods leads statisticians to overestimate the true increase in the cost of living.

Suppose, for instance, that people like coffee and tea equally well and in the base year consumed equal amounts of each. But then a frost hits a major coffee-producing nation, causing the price of coffee to double. The increase in coffee prices encourages consumers to forgo coffee and drink tea instead—a switch that doesn't make them worse off, since they like coffee and tea equally well. However, the CPI, which

---

[2]There are many hardworking employees at the Bureau of Labor Statistics trying to measure quality changes. Some improvements, such as increases in computer speeds and memory, are relatively easy to measure. But many others are much harder to quantify.

measures the cost of buying the base-year basket of goods and services, will rise significantly when the price of coffee doubles. This rise in the CPI, which ignores the fact that people can substitute tea for coffee without being made worse off, exaggerates the true increase in the cost of living. This type of overstatement of inflation is called *substitution bias.*

Substitution bias   EXAMPLE 5.6

Why does substitution bias matter?

Suppose the CPI basket for 2010, the base year, is as follows:

Item	Expenditure
Coffee (50 cups at $1/cup)	$ 50.00
Tea (50 cups at $1/cup)	50.00
Scones (100 at $1 each)	100.00
Total	$200.00

Assume that consumers are equally happy to drink coffee or tea with their scones. In 2010, coffee and tea cost the same, and the average person drinks equal amounts of coffee and tea.

In the year 2015, coffee has doubled in price to $2 per cup. Tea remains at $1 per cup, and scones are $1.50 each. What has happened to the cost of living as measured by the CPI? How does this result compare to the true cost of living?

To calculate the value of the CPI for the year 2015, we must first find the cost of consuming the 2010 basket of goods in that year. At year 2015 prices, 50 cups each of coffee and tea and 100 scones cost (50 × $2) + (50 × $1) + (100 × $1.50) = $300. Since consuming the same basket of goods cost $200 in 2010, the base year, the CPI in 2015 is $300/$200, or 1.50. This calculation leads us to conclude that the cost of living has increased 50 percent between 2010 and 2015.

However, we have overlooked the possibility that consumers can substitute a cheaper good (tea) for the more expensive one (coffee). Indeed, since consumers like coffee and tea equally well, when the price of coffee doubles they will shift entirely to tea. Their new consumption basket—100 cups of tea and 100 scones—is just as enjoyable to them as their original basket. If we allow for the substitution of less expensive goods, how much has the cost of living really increased? The cost of 100 cups of tea and 100 scones in the year 2015 is only $250, not $300. From the consumer's point of view, the true cost of living has risen by only $50, or 25 percent. The 50 percent increase in the CPI therefore overstates the increase in the cost of living as the result of substitution bias.

The Boskin Commission's findings have been controversial. While quality adjustment bias and substitution bias undoubtedly distort the measurement of inflation, estimating precisely how much of an overstatement they create is difficult. (If economists knew exactly how big these biases were, they could simply correct the data.) But the Bureau of Labor Statistics has recently made significant efforts to improve the quality of its data as a result of the commission's report.

THE COSTS OF INFLATION: NOT WHAT YOU THINK

In the late 1970s, when inflation was considerably higher than it is now, the public told poll takers that they viewed it as "public enemy number one"—that is, as the nation's most serious problem.

Although U.S. inflation rates have not been very high in recent years, today many Americans remain concerned about inflation or the threat of inflation. Why do people worry so much about inflation? Detailed opinion surveys often find that many people are confused about the meaning of inflation and its economic effects. When people complain about inflation, they are often concerned primarily about relative price changes.

Before describing the true economic costs of inflation, which are real and serious, let's examine this confusion people experience about inflation and its costs.

We need first to distinguish between the *price level* and the *relative price* of a good or service. The **price level** is a measure of the overall level of prices at a particular point in time as measured by a price index such as the CPI. Recall that the inflation rate is the percentage change in the price level from year to year. In contrast, a **relative price** is the price of a specific good or service *in comparison to* the prices of other goods and services. For example, if the price of oil were to rise by 10 percent while the prices of other goods and services were rising on average by 3 percent, the relative price of oil would increase. But if oil prices rise by 3 percent while other prices rise by 10 percent, the relative price of oil would decrease. That is, oil would become cheaper relative to other goods and services, even though it has not become cheaper in absolute terms.

Public opinion surveys suggest that many people are confused about the distinction between inflation, which is an increase in the overall *price level,* and an increase in a specific *relative price.* Suppose that supply disruptions in the Middle East were to double the price of gas at the pump, leaving other prices unaffected. Appalled by the increase in gasoline prices, people might demand that the government do something about "this inflation." But while the increase in gas prices hurts consumers, is it an example of inflation? Gasoline is only one item in a consumer's budget, one of the thousands of goods and services that people buy every day. Thus, the increase in the price of gasoline might affect the overall price level, and hence the inflation rate, only slightly. In this example, inflation is not the real problem. What upsets consumers is the change in the *relative price* of gasoline, particularly compared to the price of labor (wages). By increasing the cost of using a car, the increase in the relative price of gasoline reduces the income people have left over to spend on other things.

Again, changes in relative prices do *not* necessarily imply a significant amount of inflation. For example, increases in the prices of some goods could well be counterbalanced by decreases in the prices of other goods, in which case the price level and the inflation rate would be largely unaffected. Conversely, inflation can be high without affecting relative prices. Imagine, for instance, that all prices in the economy, including wages and salaries, go up exactly 10 percent each year. The inflation rate is 10 percent, but relative prices are not changing. Indeed, because wages (the price of labor) are increasing by 10 percent per year, people's ability to buy goods and services is unaffected by the inflation.

These examples show that changes in the price level and changes in the relative prices of specific goods are two quite different issues. The public's tendency to confuse the two is important because the remedies for the two problems are different. To counteract changes in relative prices, the government would need to implement policies that affect the supply and demand for specific goods. In the case of an increase in oil prices, for example, the government could try to encourage the development of alternative sources of energy. To counteract inflation, however, the government must resort (as we will see) to changes in macroeconomic policies such as monetary or fiscal policies. If, in

price level a measure of the overall level of prices at a particular point in time as measured by a price index such as the CPI

relative price the price of a specific good or service *in comparison to* the prices of other goods and services

confusion, the public forces the government to adopt anti-inflationary policies when the real problem is a relative price change, the economy could actually be hurt by the effort. This is an important example of why economic literacy is important, to both policymakers and the general public.

| **The Price Level, Relative Prices, and Inflation** | **EXAMPLE 5.7** |

How are the price level, relative prices, and inflation related?

Suppose the value of the CPI is 1.20 in the year 2013, 1.32 in 2014, and 1.40 in 2015. Assume also that the price of oil increases 8 percent between 2013 and 2014 and another 8 percent between 2014 and 2015. What is happening to the price level, the inflation rate, and the relative price of oil?

The price level can be measured by the CPI. Since the CPI is higher in 2014 than in 2013 and higher still in 2015 than in 2014, the price level is rising throughout the period. Since the CPI increases by 10 percent between 2013 and 2014, the inflation rate between those years is 10 percent. However, the CPI increases only about 6 percent between 2014 and 2015 ($1.40/1.32 \approx 1.06$), so the inflation rate decreases to about 6 percent between those years. The decline in the inflation rate implies that although the price level is still rising, it is doing so at a slower pace than the year before.

The price of oil rises 8 percent between 2013 and 2014. But because the general inflation over that period is 10 percent, the relative price of oil—that is, its price *relative to all other goods and services*—falls by about 2 percent ($8\% - 10\% = -2\%$). Between 2014 and 2015 the price of oil rises by another 8 percent, while the general inflation rate is about 6 percent. Hence the relative price of oil rises between 2014 and 2015 by about 2 percent ($8\% - 6\%$).

THE TRUE COSTS OF INFLATION

Having dispelled the common confusion between inflation and relative price changes, we are now free to address the true economic costs of inflation. There are a variety of such costs, each of which tends to reduce the efficiency of the economy. Five of the most important are discussed here.

"Noise" in the Price System

Consider the remarkable economic coordination that is necessary to provide the right amount and the right kinds of food to New Yorkers every day. This feat is not orchestrated by some Food Distribution Ministry staffed by bureaucrats. It is done much better by the workings of free markets, operating without central guidance, than a ministry ever could.

How do free markets transmit the enormous amounts of information necessary to accomplish complex tasks like the provisioning of New York City? The answer is through the price system. When the owners of French restaurants in Manhattan cannot find sufficient quantities of chanterelles, a particularly rare and desirable mushroom, they bid up its market price. Specialty food suppliers notice the higher price for chanterelles and realize that they can make a profit by supplying more chanterelles to the market. At the same time, price-conscious diners will shift to cheaper, more available mushrooms. The market for chanterelles will reach equilibrium only when there are no more unexploited opportunities for profit, and both suppliers and demanders are satisfied at the market price (the Equilibrium Principle). Multiply this example a million times, and you will gain a sense of how the price system achieves a truly remarkable degree of economic coordination.

Equilibrium

When inflation is high, however, the subtle signals that are transmitted through the price system become more difficult to interpret, much in the way that static, or "noise," makes a radio message harder to interpret. In an economy with little or no inflation, the supplier of specialty foodstuffs will immediately recognize the increase in chanterelle prices as a signal to bring more to market. If inflation is high, however, the supplier must ask whether a price increase represents a true increase in the demand for chanterelles or is just a result of the general inflation, which causes all food prices to rise. If the price rise reflects only inflation, the price of chanterelles *relative to other goods and services* has not really changed. The supplier therefore should not change the quantity of mushrooms he brings to market.

In an inflationary environment, to discern whether the increase in chanterelle prices is a true signal of increased demand, the supplier needs to know not only the price of chanterelles but also what is happening to the prices of other goods and services. Since this information takes time and effort to collect, the supplier's response to the change in chanterelle prices is likely to be slower and more tentative.

In summary, price changes are the market's way of communicating information to suppliers and demanders. An increase in the price of a good or service, for example, tells demanders to economize on their use of the good or service and suppliers to bring more of it to market. But in the presence of inflation, prices are affected not only by changes in the supply and demand for a product but by changes in the general price level. Inflation creates static, or "noise," in the price system, obscuring the information transmitted by prices and reducing the efficiency of the market system. This reduction in efficiency imposes real economic costs.

Distortions of the Tax System

Just as some government expenditures, such as Social Security benefits, are indexed to inflation, many taxes are also indexed. In the United States, people with higher incomes pay a higher *percentage* of their income in taxes. Without indexing, an inflation that raises people's nominal incomes would force them to pay an increasing percentage of their income in taxes, even though their *real* incomes may not have increased. To avoid this phenomenon, which is known as *bracket creep,* Congress has indexed income tax brackets to the CPI. The effect of this indexation is that a family whose nominal income is rising at the same rate as inflation does not have to pay a higher percentage of income in taxes.

Although indexing has solved the problem of bracket creep, many provisions of the tax code have not been indexed, either because of lack of political support or because of the complexity of the task. As a result, inflation can produce unintended changes in the taxes people pay, which in turn may cause them to change their behavior in economically undesirable ways.

To illustrate, an important provision in the business tax code for which inflation poses problems is the *capital depreciation allowance,* which works as follows. Suppose a firm buys a machine for $1,000, expecting it to last for 10 years. Under U.S. tax law, the firm can take one-tenth of the purchase price, or $100, as a deduction from its taxable profits in each of the 10 years. By deducting a fraction of the purchase price from its taxable profits, the firm reduces its taxes. The exact amount of the yearly tax reduction is the tax rate on corporate profits times $100.

The idea behind this provision of the tax code is that the wearing out of the machine is a cost of doing business that should be deducted from the firm's profit. Also, in giving firms a tax break for investing in new machinery, Congress intended to encourage firms to modernize their plants. Yet capital depreciation allowances are not indexed to inflation. Suppose that, at a time when the inflation rate is high, a firm is considering purchasing a $1,000 machine. The managers know that the purchase will allow them to deduct

$100 per year from taxable profits for the next 10 years. But that $100 is a fixed amount that is not indexed to inflation. Looking forward, managers will recognize that 5, 6, or 10 years into the future, the real value of the $100 tax deduction will be much lower than at present because of inflation. They will have less incentive to buy the machine and may decide not to make the investment at all. Indeed, many studies have found that a high rate of inflation can significantly reduce the rate at which firms invest in new factories and equipment.

Because the U.S. tax code contains hundreds of provisions and tax rates that are not indexed, inflation can seriously distort the incentives provided by the tax system for people to work, save, and invest. The resulting effects on economic efficiency and economic growth represent a real cost of inflation.

"Shoe-Leather" Costs

As all shoppers know, cash is convenient. Unlike checks, which are not accepted everywhere, and credit cards, for which a minimum purchase is sometimes required, cash can be used in almost any routine transaction. Businesses, too, find cash convenient to hold. Having plenty of cash on hand facilitates transactions with customers and reduces the need for frequent deposits and withdrawals from the bank.

Inflation raises the cost of holding cash to consumers and businesses. Consider a with $10,000 in $20 bills under his mattress. What happens to the buying power of his hoard over time? If inflation is zero so that on average the prices of goods and services are not changing, the buying power of the $10,000 does not change over time. At the end of a year, the miser's purchasing power is the same as it was at the beginning of the year. But suppose the inflation rate is 10 percent. In that case, the purchasing power of the miser's hoard will fall by 10 percent each year. After a year, he will have only $9,000 in purchasing power. In general, the higher the rate of inflation, the less people will want to hold cash because of the loss of purchasing power that they will suffer.

Technically, currency is a debt owed by the government to the currency holder. So when currency loses value, the losses to holders of cash are offset by gains to the government, which now owes less in real terms to currency holders. Thus, from the point of view of society as a whole, the loss of purchasing power is not in itself a cost of inflation because it does not involve wasted resources. (Indeed, no real goods or services were used up when the miser's currency hoard lost part of its value.)

However, when faced with inflation, people are not likely to accept a loss in purchasing power but instead will take actions to try to "economize" on their cash holdings. For example, instead of drawing out enough cash for a month the next time they visit the bank, they will draw out only enough to last a week. The inconvenience of visiting the bank more often to minimize one's cash holdings is a real cost of inflation. Similarly, businesses will reduce their cash holdings by sending employees to the bank more frequently, or by installing computerized systems to monitor cash usage. To deal with the increase in bank transactions required by consumers and businesses trying to use less cash, banks will need to hire more employees and expand their operations.

The costs of more frequent trips to the bank, new cash management systems, and expanded employment in banks are real costs. They use up resources, including time and effort, that could be used for other purposes. Traditionally, the costs of economizing on cash have been called *shoe-leather costs*—the idea being that shoe leather is worn out during extra trips to the bank. Shoe-leather costs probably are not a significant problem in the United States today, where inflation is only 2 to 3 percent per year. But in economies with high rates of inflation, they can become quite significant.

Unexpected Redistributions of Wealth

When inflation is unexpected, it may arbitrarily redistribute wealth from one group to another. Consider a group of union workers who signed a contract setting their wages for the next three years. If those wages are not indexed to inflation, then the workers will be vulnerable to upsurges in the price level. Suppose, for example, that inflation is much higher than expected over the three years of the contract. In that case, the buying power of the workers' wages—their real wages—will be less than anticipated when they signed the contract.

From society's point of view, is the buying power that workers lose to inflation really "lost"? The answer is no; the loss in their buying power is exactly matched by an unanticipated gain in the employer's buying power because the real cost of paying the workers is less than anticipated. In other words, the effect of the inflation is not to *destroy* purchasing power but to *redistribute* it, in this case from the workers to the employer. If inflation had been *lower* than expected, the workers would have enjoyed greater purchasing power than they anticipated and the employer would have been the loser.

Another example of the redistribution caused by inflation takes place between borrowers (debtors) and lenders (creditors). Suppose one of the authors of this book wants to buy a house on a lake and borrows $150,000 from the bank to pay for it. Shortly after signing the mortgage agreement, he learns that inflation is likely to be much higher than expected. How should he react to the news? Perhaps as a public-spirited macroeconomist, the author should be saddened to hear that inflation is rising, but as a consumer he should be pleased. In real terms, the dollars with which he will repay his loan in the future will be worth much less than expected. The loan officer should be distraught because the dollars the bank will receive from the author will be worth less, in purchasing power terms, than expected at contract signing. Once again, no real wealth is "lost" to the inflation; rather, the borrower's gain is just offset by the lender's loss. *In general, unexpectedly high inflation rates help borrowers at the expense of lenders* because borrowers are able to repay their loans in less-valuable dollars. Unexpectedly low inflation rates, in contrast, help lenders and hurt borrowers by forcing borrowers to repay in dollars that are worth more than expected when the loan was made.

Although redistributions caused by inflation do not directly destroy wealth, but only transfer it from one group to another, they are still bad for the economy. Our economic system is based on incentives. For it to work well, people must know that if they work hard, save some of their income, and make wise financial investments, they will be rewarded in the long run with greater real wealth and a better standard of living. Some observers have compared a high-inflation economy to a casino, in which wealth is distributed largely by luck—that is, by random fluctuations in the inflation rate. In the long run, a "casino economy" is likely to perform poorly, as its unpredictability discourages people from working and saving. A high-inflation economy encourages people to use up resources in trying to anticipate inflation and protect themselves against it.

Interference with Long-Term Planning

The fifth and final cost of inflation we will examine is its tendency to interfere with the long-term planning of households and firms. Many economic decisions take place within a long time horizon. Planning for retirement, for example, may begin when workers are in their twenties or thirties. And firms develop long-term investment and business strategies that look decades into the future.

Clearly, high and erratic inflation can make long-term planning difficult. Suppose, for example, that you want to enjoy a certain standard of living when you retire. How much of your income do you need to save to make your dreams a reality? That depends on what the goods and services you plan to buy will cost 30 or 40 years from now. With high and erratic inflation, even guessing what your chosen lifestyle will cost by the time you retire is extremely difficult. You may end up saving too little and having to compromise on your retirement plans; or you may save too much, sacrificing more than you need to during your working years. Either way, inflation will have proved costly.

In summary, inflation damages the economy in a variety of ways. Some of its effects are difficult to quantify and affect different segments of the population in different ways. But most economists agree that a low and stable inflation rate is instrumental in maintaining a healthy economy.

HYPERINFLATION

hyperinflation a situation in which the inflation rate is extremely high

Although there is some disagreement about whether an inflation rate of, say, 5 percent per year imposes important costs on an economy, few economists would question the fact that an inflation rate of 500 percent or 1,000 percent per year disrupts economic performance. A situation in which the inflation rate is extremely high is called **hyperinflation.** Although there is no official threshold above which inflation becomes hyperinflation, inflation rates in the range of 500 to 1,000 percent per year would surely qualify.

In the past few decades, episodes of hyperinflation have occurred in Israel (400 percent inflation in 1985), several South American countries (including Bolivia, Argentina, and Brazil), Nicaragua (33,000 percent inflation in 1988), Zimbabwe (officially 24,470 percent inflation in 2007, unofficially 150,000 percent), and several countries attempting to make the transition from communism to capitalism, including Russia. Perhaps the most well-known episode occurred in Germany in 1923 when inflation was 102,000,000 percent. In the German hyperinflation, prices rose so rapidly that for a time workers were paid twice each day so their families could buy food before the afternoon price increases, and many people's life savings became worthless. But the most extreme hyperinflation ever recorded was in Hungary in 1945, at the end of the Second World War, when inflation peaked at 3.8×10^{27} percent. The United States has never experienced hyperinflation, although the short-lived Confederate States of America suffered severe inflation during the Civil War. Between 1861 and 1865, prices in the Confederacy rose to 92 times their prewar levels.

Hyperinflation greatly magnifies the costs of inflation. For example, shoe-leather costs—a relatively minor consideration in times of low inflation—become quite important during hyperinflation. In this type of environment, people may visit the bank two or three times per day to hold money for as short a time as possible. With prices changing daily or even hourly, markets work quite poorly, slowing economic growth. Massive redistributions of wealth take place, impoverishing many and enriching only a few. Not surprisingly, episodes of hyperinflation rarely last more than a few years; they are so disruptive that they quickly lead to public outcry for relief.

RECAP	THE TRUE COSTS OF INFLATION

The public sometimes confuses changes in relative prices (such as the price of oil) with inflation, which is a change in the overall level of prices. This confusion can cause problems because the remedies for undesired changes in relative prices and for inflation are different.

There are a number of true costs of inflation, which together tend to reduce economic growth and efficiency. These include:

- "Noise" in the price system, which occurs when general inflation makes it difficult for market participants to interpret the information conveyed by prices.

- Distortions of the tax system, for example, when provisions of the tax code are not indexed.

- "Shoe-leather" costs, or the costs of economizing on cash (for example, by making more frequent trips to the bank or installing a computerized cash management system).

- Unexpected redistributions of wealth, as when higher-than-expected inflation hurts wage earners to the benefit of employers or hurts creditors to the benefit of debtors.

- Interference with long-term planning, arising because people find it difficult to forecast prices over long periods.

INFLATION AND INTEREST RATES

So far we have focused on the measurement and economic costs of inflation. Another important aspect of inflation is its close relationship to other key macroeconomic variables. For example, economists have long realized that during periods of high inflation, interest rates tend to be high as well. We will close this chapter with a look at the relationship between inflation and interest rates. No real reason for this if we allow for instructors to use a modular approach.

INFLATION AND THE REAL INTEREST RATE

In our discussion of the ways in which inflation redistributes wealth, we saw that inflation tends to hurt creditors and help debtors by reducing the value of the dollars with which debts are repaid. The effect of inflation on debtors and creditors can be explained more precisely using an economic concept called the *real interest rate.* An example will illustrate.

Suppose that there are two neighboring countries, Alpha and Beta. In Alpha, whose currency is called the alphan, the inflation rate is zero and is expected to remain at zero. In Beta, where the currency is the betan, the inflation rate is 10 percent and is expected to remain at that level. Bank deposits pay 2 percent annual interest in Alpha and 10 percent annual interest in Beta. In which countries are bank depositors getting a better deal?

You may answer "Beta," since interest rates on deposits are higher in that country. But if you think about the effects of inflation, you will recognize that Alpha, not Beta, offers the better deal to depositors. To see why, think about the change over a year in the real purchasing power of deposits in the two countries. In Alpha, someone who deposits 100 alphans in the bank on January 1 will have 102 alphans on December 31. Because there is no inflation in Alpha, on average prices are the same at the end of the year as they were at the beginning. Thus, the 102 alphans the depositor can withdraw represent a 2 percent increase in buying power.

In Beta, the depositor who deposits 100 betans on January 1 will have 110 betans by the end of the year—10 percent more than she started with. But the prices of goods and services in Beta, we have assumed, also will rise by 10 percent. Thus, the Beta depositor can afford to buy precisely the same amount of goods and services at the end of the year as she could at the beginning; she gets no increase in buying power. So the Alpha depositor has the better deal, after all.

Economists refer to the annual percentage increase in the *real* purchasing power of a financial asset as the **real interest rate,** or the *real rate of return,* on that asset. In our example, the real purchasing power of deposits rises by 2 percent per year in Alpha and by 0 percent per year in Beta. So the real interest rate on deposits is 2 percent in Alpha and 0 percent in Beta. The real interest rate should be distinguished from the more familiar market interest rate, also called the *nominal interest rate.* The **nominal interest rate** is the annual percentage increase in the nominal, or dollar, value of an asset.

As the example of Alpha and Beta illustrates, we can calculate the real interest rate for any financial asset by subtracting the rate of inflation from the market or nominal interest rate on that asset. So in Alpha, the real interest rate on deposits equals the nominal interest rate (2 percent) minus the inflation rate (0 percent), or 2 percent. Likewise in Beta, the real interest rate equals the nominal interest rate (10 percent) minus the inflation rate (10 percent), or 0 percent.

We can write this definition of the real interest rate in mathematical terms:

$$r = i - \pi,$$

where,

r = the real interest rate,

i = the nominal, or market, interest rate,

π = the current inflation rate.

Most economists think that the real interest rate should be measured by the nominal interest rate minus expected inflation. However, it is sometimes difficult to interpret what the expected inflation rate is exactly. Therefore, we assume here that the current inflation rate is a relatively good predictor of future inflation, or at least a relatively good indicator of the expected inflation rate.

real interest rate the annual percentage increase in the purchasing power of a financial asset; the real interest rate on any asset equals the nominal interest rate on that asset minus the inflation rate

nominal interest rate (or market interest rate) the annual percentage increase in the nominal value of a financial asset

Real Interest Rates, 1975 to 2010   EXAMPLE 5.8

Why is the real interest rate important?

Following are interest rates on 10-year government bonds for selected years since 1975. In which of these years did the financial investors who bought government bonds get the best deal? The worst deal?

Year	Interest rate (%)	Inflation rate (%)	Real interest rate (%)
1975	8.0	9.1	−1.1
1980	11.4	13.5	−2.1
1985	10.6	3.6	7.0
1990	8.6	5.4	3.2
1995	6.6	2.8	3.8
2000	6.0	3.4	2.6
2005	4.3	3.4	0.9
2010	3.2	1.6	1.6

Financial investors and lenders do best when the real (not the nominal) interest rate is high since the real interest rate measures the increase in their purchasing power. We can calculate the real interest rate for each year by subtracting the inflation rate from the nominal interest rate. The results are shown in the third column of the table above. For purchasers of government bonds, the best of these years was 1985, when they enjoyed a real return of 7 percent. The worst year was 1980, when their real return was negative 2.1 percent. In other words, despite receiving 11.4 percent nominal interest, financial investors ended up losing buying power in 1980, as the inflation rate exceeded the interest rate earned by their investments.

Figure 5.3 shows the real interest rate in the United States since 1970 as measured by the nominal interest rate paid on the federal government's debt minus the inflation rate. Note that the real interest rate was sometimes negative during this period, and reached historically high levels in the mid-1980s.

FIGURE 5.3

The Real Interest Rate in the United States, 1970–2013.

The real interest rate is the nominal interest rate—here the interest rate on funds borrowed by the federal government for a term of three months—minus the rate of inflation.

SOURCE: *The Economic Report of the President,* February 2013, Tables B-17 and B-10, www.gpo.gov/erp, and authors' calculations.

The concept of the real interest rate helps to explain more precisely why an unexpected surge in inflation is bad for lenders and good for borrowers. For any given nominal interest rate that the lender charges the borrower, the higher the inflation rate, the lower the real interest rate the lender actually receives. So unexpectedly high inflation leaves the lender worse off. Borrowers, on the other hand, are better off when inflation is unexpectedly high because their real interest rate is lower than anticipated.

Although unexpectedly high inflation hurts lenders and helps borrowers, a high rate of inflation that is *expected* may not redistribute wealth at all because expected inflation can be built into the nominal interest rate. Suppose, for example, that the lender requires a real interest rate of 2 percent on new loans. If the inflation rate is confidently expected to be zero, the lender can get a 2 percent real interest rate by charging a nominal interest rate of 2 percent. But if the inflation rate is expected to be 10 percent, the lender can still ensure a real interest rate of 2 percent by charging a nominal interest rate of 12 percent. Thus, high inflation, if it is *expected,* need not hurt lenders—as long as the lenders can adjust the nominal interest they charge to reflect the expected inflation rate.

In response to people's concerns about unexpected inflation, in 1997 the United States Treasury introduced **inflation-protected bonds,** which pay a fixed real interest rate. People who buy these bonds receive a nominal interest rate each year equal to a fixed real rate plus the actual rate of inflation during that year. Owners of inflation-protected bonds suffer no loss in real wealth even if inflation is unexpectedly high.

inflation-protected bonds bonds that pay a nominal interest rate each year equal to a fixed real rate plus the actual rate of inflation during that year

THE FISHER EFFECT

Earlier we made the observation that interest rates tend to be high when inflation is high and low when inflation is low. This relationship can be seen in Figure 5.4, which shows both the U.S. inflation rate and a nominal interest rate (the rate at which the government borrows for short periods) from 1970 to 2013. Notice that nominal interest rates have tended to be high in periods of high inflation, such as the early 1980s, and relatively low in periods of low inflation, such as the late 1990s and early 2000s.

FIGURE 5.4

Inflation and Interest Rates in the United States, 1970–2013.

Nominal interest rates tend to be high when inflation is high and low when inflation is low, a phenomenon called the Fisher effect.

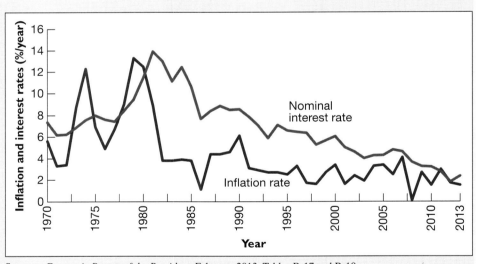

SOURCE: *Economic Report of the President,* February 2013, Tables B-17 and B-10, www.gpo.gov/erp.

Why do interest rates tend to be high when inflation is high? Our discussion of real interest rates provides the answer. Suppose inflation has recently been high, so borrowers and lenders anticipate that it will be high in the near future. We would expect lenders to raise their nominal interest rate so that their real rate of return will be unaffected. For their part, borrowers are willing to pay higher nominal interest rates when inflation is high because they understand that the higher nominal interest rate only serves to compensate the lender for the fact that the loan will be repaid in dollars of reduced real value—in real terms, their cost of borrowing is unaffected by an equal increase in the nominal interest rate and the inflation rate. Conversely, when inflation is low, lenders do not need to charge so high a nominal interest rate to ensure a given real return. Thus, nominal interest rates will be high when inflation is high and low when inflation is low.

This tendency for nominal interest rates to follow inflation rates is called the **Fisher effect,** after the early twentieth-century American economist Irving Fisher, who first pointed out the relationship.

Fisher effect the tendency for nominal interest rates to be high when inflation is high and low when inflation is low

---

○ SUMMARY ○

- The basic tool for measuring inflation is the consumer price index (CPI). The CPI measures the cost of purchasing a fixed basket of goods and services in any period relative to the cost of the same basket of goods and services in a base year. The inflation rate is the annual percentage rate of change in the price level as measured by a price index such as the CPI. (LO1)

- A nominal quantity is a quantity that is measured in terms of its current dollar value. Dividing a nominal quantity such as a family's income or a worker's wage in dollars by a price index such as the CPI expresses that quantity in terms of real purchasing power. This procedure is called deflating the nominal quantity. If nominal quantities from two different years are deflated by a common price index, the purchasing power of the two quantities can be compared. To ensure that a nominal payment such as a Social Security benefit represents a constant level of real purchasing power, the nominal payment should be increased each year by a percentage equal to the inflation rate. This method of adjusting nominal payments to maintain their purchasing power is called indexing. (LO2)

- The official U.S. inflation rate, based on the CPI, may overstate the true inflation rate for two reasons: First, it may not adequately reflect improvements in the quality of goods and services. Second, the method of calculating the CPI ignores the fact that consumers can substitute cheaper goods and services for more expensive ones. (LO3)

- The public sometimes confuses increases in the relative prices for specific goods or services with inflation, which is an increase in the general price level. Since the remedies for a change in relative prices are different from the remedies for inflation, this confusion can cause problems. (LO4)

- Inflation imposes a number of true costs on the economy, including "noise" in the price system; distortions of the tax system; "shoe-leather" costs, which are the real resources that are wasted as people try to economize on cash holdings; unexpected redistributions of wealth; and interference with long-term planning. Because of these costs, most economists agree that sustained economic growth is more likely if inflation is low and stable. Hyperinflation, a situation in which the inflation rate is extremely high, greatly magnifies the costs of inflation and is highly disruptive to the economy. (LO4)

- The real interest rate is the annual percentage increase in the purchasing power of a financial asset. It is equal to the nominal, or market, interest rate minus the inflation rate. When inflation is unexpectedly high, the real interest rate is lower than anticipated, which hurts lenders but benefits borrowers. When inflation is unexpectedly low, lenders benefit and borrowers are hurt. To obtain a given real rate of return, lenders must charge a high nominal interest rate when inflation is high and a low nominal interest rate when inflation is low. The tendency for nominal interest rates to be high when inflation is high and low when inflation is low is called the Fisher effect. (LO5)

○ KEY TERMS ○

consumer price index (CPI)	indexing	price level
core rate of inflation	inflation-protected bonds	rate of inflation
deflating (a nominal quantity)	market interest rate	real interest rate
deflation	nominal interest rate	real quantity
Fisher effect	nominal quantity	real wage
hyperinflation	price index	relative price

○ REVIEW QUESTIONS ○

1. Explain why changes in the cost of living for any particular individual or family may differ from changes in the official cost-of-living index, the CPI. *(LO1)*

2. What is the difference between the *price level* and the *rate of inflation* in an economy? *(LO1)*

3. Why is it important to adjust for inflation when comparing nominal quantities (for example, workers' average wages) at different points in time? What is the basic method for adjusting for inflation? *(LO2)*

4. Describe how indexation might be used to guarantee that the purchasing power of the wage agreed to in a multiyear labor contract will not be eroded by inflation. *(LO2)*

5. Give two reasons why the official inflation rate may understate the "true" rate of inflation. Illustrate by examples. *(LO3)*

6. "It's true that unexpected inflation redistributes wealth, from creditors to debtors, for example. But what one side of the bargain loses, the other side gains. So from the perspective of the society as a whole, there is no real cost." Do you agree? Discuss. *(LO4)*

7. How does inflation affect the real return on holding cash? *(LO5)*

8. True or false: If both the potential lender and the potential borrower correctly anticipate the rate of inflation, inflation will not redistribute wealth from the creditor to the debtor. Explain. *(LO5)*

○ PROBLEMS ○

Visit your mobile app store and download the Frank: Study Econ app *today!*

1. Government survey takers determine that typical family expenditures each month in the year designated as the base year are as follows:

   20 pizzas at $10 each
   Rent of apartment, $600 per month
   Gasoline and car maintenance, $100
   Phone service (basic service plus 10 long-distance calls), $50

   In the year following the base year, the survey takers determine that pizzas have risen to $11 each, apartment rent is $640, gasoline and maintenance have risen to $120, and phone service has dropped in price to $40. *(LO1)*
   a. Find the CPI in the subsequent year and the rate of inflation between the base year and the subsequent year.
   b. The family's nominal income rose by 5 percent between the base year and the subsequent year. Are they worse off or better off in terms of what their income is able to buy?

2. Here are values of the CPI (multiplied by 100) for each year from 1990 to 2000. For each year beginning with 1991, calculate the rate of inflation from the previous year. What happened to inflation rates over the 1990s? *(LO1)*

1990	130.7
1991	136.2
1992	140.3
1993	144.5
1994	148.2
1995	152.4
1996	156.9
1997	160.5
1998	163.0
1999	166.6
2000	172.2

3. Refer to the CPI data given in Problem 2. A report found that the real entry-level wage for college graduates declined by 8 percent between 1990 and 1997. The nominal entry-level wage in 1997 was $13.65 per hour. *(LO2)*
   a. What was the real entry-level wage in 1997?
   b. What was the real entry-level wage in 1990?
   c. What was the nominal entry-level wage in 1990?

4. Consider the table below. It shows a hypothetical income tax schedule, expressed in nominal terms, for the year 2014:

Family income	Taxes due (percent of income)
≤ $20,000	10
$20,001–$30,000	12
$30,001–$50,000	15
$50,001–$80,000	20
> $80,000	25

The legislature wants to ensure that families with a given real income are not pushed up into higher tax brackets by inflation. The CPI (times 100) is 175 in 2014 and 185 in 2016. How should the income tax schedule above be adjusted for the year 2016 to meet the legislature's goal? *(LO2)*

5. According to the U.S. Census Bureau (www.census.gov), nominal income for the typical family of four in the United States (median income) was $23,618 in 1985, $34,076 in 1995, $46,326 in 2005, and $49,276 in 2010. In purchasing power terms, how did family income compare in each of those four years? You will need to know that the CPI (multiplied by 100, 1982–1984 = 100) was 107.6 in 1985, 152.4 in 1995, 195.3 in 2005, and 218.1 in 2010. In general terms, how would your answer be affected if the Boskin Commission's conclusions about the CPI were confirmed? *(LO2, LO3)*

6. The typical consumer's food basket in the base year 2015 is as follows:

   30 chickens at $3.00 each
   10 hams at $6.00 each
   10 steaks at $8.00 each

   A chicken feed shortage causes the price of chickens to rise to $5.00 each in the year 2016. Hams rise to $7.00 each, and the price of steaks is unchanged. *(LO1, LO3)*
   a. Calculate the change in the "cost-of-eating" index between 2015 and 2016.
   b. Suppose that consumers are completely indifferent between two chickens and one ham. For this example, how large is the substitution bias in the official "cost-of-eating" index?

7. The following table lists the actual per-gallon prices for unleaded regular gasoline for June of each year between 1978 and 1986, together with the values of the CPIs for those years. For each year from 1979 to 1986, find the CPI inflation rate and the change in the real price of gasoline, both from the previous year. Would it be fair to say that most of the changes in gas prices during this period were due to general inflation, or were factors specific to the oil market playing a role as well? *(LO1, LO4)*

Year	Gasoline price ($/gallon)	CPI (1982–1984 = 1.00)
1978	0.663	0.652
1979	0.901	0.726
1980	1.269	0.824
1981	1.391	0.909
1982	1.309	0.965
1983	1.277	0.996
1984	1.229	1.039
1985	1.241	1.076
1986	0.955	1.136

8. On January 1, 2012, Albert invested $1,000 at 6 percent interest per year for three years. The CPI on January 1, 2012, stood at 100. On January 1, 2013, the CPI (times 100) was 105; on January 1, 2014, it was 110; and on January 1, 2015, the day Albert's investment matured, the CPI was 118. Find the real rate of interest earned by Albert in each of the three years and his total real return over the three-year period. Assume that interest earnings are reinvested each year and themselves earn interest. *(LO5)*

9. Frank is lending $1,000 to Sarah for two years. Frank and Sarah agree that Frank should earn a 2 percent real return per year. *(LO5)*
   a. The CPI (times 100) is 100 at the time that Frank makes the loan. It is expected to be 110 in one year and 121 in two years. What nominal rate of interest should Frank charge Sarah?
   b. Suppose Frank and Sarah are unsure about what the CPI will be in two years. Show how Frank and Sarah could index Sarah's annual repayments to ensure that Frank gets an annual 2 percent real rate of return.

○ ANSWERS TO CONCEPT CHECKS ○

5.1 The cost of the family's basket in 2010 remains at $680, as in Table 5.1. If the rent on their apartment falls to $400 in 2015, the cost of reproducing the 2010 basket of goods and services in 2015 is $620 ($400 for rent + $150 for hamburgers + $70 for movie tickets). The CPI for 2015 is accordingly $620/$680, or 0.912. So in this example, the cost of living fell nearly 9 percent between 2010 and 2015. *(LO1)*

5.2 To construct your own personal price index, you would need to determine the basket of goods and services that you personally purchased in the base year. Your personal price index in each period would then be defined as the cost of your personal basket in that period relative to its cost in the base year. To the extent that your mix of purchases differs from that of the typical American consumer, your cost-of-living index will differ from the official CPI. For example, if in the base year you spent a higher share of your budget than the typical American on goods and services that have risen relatively rapidly in price, your personal inflation rate will be higher than the CPI inflation rate. *(LO1)*

5.3 The percentage changes in the CPI in each year from the previous year are as follows:

1930	$-2.3\% = (0.167 - 0.171)/0.171$
1931	-9.0%
1932	-9.9%
1933	-5.1%

Negative inflation is called deflation. The experience of the 1930s, when prices were falling, contrasts sharply with inflation since 2009. *(LO1)*

5.4 Rodriguez's real earnings, in 1982–1984 dollars, were $27.5 million/2.15, or $12.8 million. Barry Bonds earned $5.79 million (in 1982–1984 dollars), so Rodriguez earned about 121 percent more in 2009 than Bonds did in 2001. *(LO2)*

5.5 The real minimum wage in 1950 is $0.75/0.24, or $3.12 in 1982–1984 dollars. The real minimum wage in 2013 is $7.25/2.29, or $3.17 in 1982–1984 dollars. So the real minimum wage in 2013 was only 1.6 percent higher than what it was in 1950. *(LO2)*

5.6 The increase in the cost of living between 1950 and 2013 is reflected in the ratio of the 2013 CPI to the 1950 CPI, or 2.29/0.24 = 9.54. That is, the cost of living in 2013 was more than nine times what it was in 1950. If the minimum wage were indexed to preserve its purchasing power, it would have been 9.54 times higher in 2013 than in 1950, or 9.54 × $0.75 = $7.15. *(LO2)*

CHAPTER 6

Wages and Unemployment

Rob Crandall/The Image Works

HOW DO GLOBALIZATION AND TECHNOLOGICAL CHANGE AFFECT WAGES AND EMPLOYMENT?

■ n 1999, *New York Times* columnist Thomas L. Friedman published a best-selling book about the changing global economy, *The Lexus and the Olive Tree.*[1] The theme of Friedman's book is that one of the most striking features of the modern world is the juxtaposition of rapid economic and technological change (represented by the Lexus automobile) with traditional values and customs (represented by the olive tree, a tree with deep roots that cannot be easily transplanted). Friedman notes that, in many countries, the conflicting pulls of modernization and traditional ways of life have created enormous social conflicts. Further, the powerful forces of modernization have widened the gap between the "haves"—those who can take advantage of rapid technological and economic change—and the "have-nots"—those who are unable or unwilling to do so.

To understand how economic growth and change affect different groups, we must turn to the labor market. Except for retirees and others receiving government support, most people rely almost entirely on wages and salaries to pay their bills and put something away for the future. Hence, it is in the labor market that most people will see the benefits of economic growth.

[1] New York: Farrar, Straus, & Giroux, 1999.

This chapter describes and explains some important trends in the labor markets of industrial countries. We will see that two key factors contributing to recent trends in wages, employment, and unemployment are the *globalization* of the economy, as reflected in the increasing importance of international trade, and ongoing *technological change*. To see this, we focus first on several important trends in real wages and employment and then develop and apply a supply and demand model of the labor market. We then turn to the problem of unemployment and explain how the unemployment rate and some related statistics are defined and measured. We close with a discussion of different types of unemployment and the costs of unemployment, both to the unemployed and to the economy as a whole.

THREE IMPORTANT LABOR MARKET TRENDS

To understand labor markets at a macroeconomic level, it is helpful to keep in mind three important trends involving real wages. We discuss each of them in turn.

1. Over the twentieth century, all industrial countries have enjoyed substantial growth in real wages.

In the United States in 2010, the average worker's yearly earnings could command twice as many goods and services as in 1960 and nearly five times as much as in 1929, just prior to the Great Depression. Similar trends have prevailed in other industrialized countries.

2. Since the early 1970s, however, the rate of real wage growth has stagnated, while both the number of people with jobs and the percentage of the population employed have grown substantially.

Though the post–World War II period has seen impressive increases in real wages, the fastest rates of increase occurred during the 1960s and early 1970s. In the 13 years between 1960 and 1973, the buying power of workers' incomes rose at a rate of 2.5 percent per year, a strong rate of increase. But from 1973 to 1995, real hourly wages fell by almost 11 percent or an average of .75 percent per year. The good news is that from 1996 to 2010, real hourly wages grew at an average of about 1 percent per year, despite two recessions in the 2000s. *Real hourly wages, however, were exactly the same in 2012 as they were in 1970.* Since its peak in 2000, the share of the working-age population that is either employed or actively looking for work has dramatically decreased, thereby eradicating some of the previous gains in employment.

3. Furthermore, recent decades have brought a pronounced increase in wage inequality in the United States.

A growing gap in real wages between skilled and unskilled workers has been of particular concern. Although real GDP per capita doubled between 1960 and 2010, average real weekly earnings among production workers actually fell, and the real wages of the least-skilled, least-educated workers have declined by as much as 25 to 30 percent, according to some studies. At the same time, the best-educated, highest-skilled workers have enjoyed continuing gains in real wages. Data for a recent year showed that, in the United States, the typical worker with an advanced degree beyond college earned almost three times the income of a high school graduate, and four times the income of a worker with less than a high school degree. Many observers worry that the United States is developing a "two-tier" labor market: plenty of good jobs at good wages for the well-educated and highly skilled, but less and less opportunity for those without schooling or skills.

What explains these trends in employment and wages? In the next two sections, we will show that a supply and demand analysis of the labor market can help to explain these important developments.

RECAP	THREE IMPORTANT LABOR MARKET TRENDS

- Over a long period, average real wages have risen substantially both in the United States and in other industrialized countries.

- Despite the long-term upward trend in real wages, real wage growth has been stagnant in the United States since the early 1970s. Employment also grew substantially from the 1970s through the 1990s. However, over the last decade the share of the working-age population either employed or actively looking for work has dramatically decreased from its peak in 2000.

- In the United States, wage inequality has increased dramatically in recent decades. The real wages of most unskilled workers have actually declined, while the real wages of skilled and educated workers have continued to rise.

SUPPLY AND DEMAND IN THE LABOR MARKET

In the chapter *Supply and Demand* we saw how supply and demand analysis can be used to determine equilibrium prices and quantities for individual goods and services. The same approach is useful for studying labor market conditions. In the market for labor, the "price" is the real wage paid to workers in exchange for their services. The wage is expressed per unit of time, for example, per hour or per year. The "quantity" is the amount of labor firms use, which in this book we will generally measure by number of workers employed. Alternatively, we could state the quantity of labor in terms of the number of hours worked; the choice of units is a matter of convenience.

Who are the demanders and suppliers in the labor market? Firms and other employers demand labor in order to produce goods and services. Virtually all of us supply labor during some phase of our lives. Whenever people work for pay, they are supplying labor services at a price equal to the wage they receive. In this chapter, we'll discuss both the supply of and demand for labor, with an emphasis on the demand side of the labor market. Changes in the demand for labor turn out to be key in explaining the aggregate trends in wages and employment described in the preceding section.

The labor market is studied by microeconomists as well as macroeconomists, and both use the tools of supply and demand. However, microeconomists focus on issues such as the determination of wages for specific types of jobs or workers. In this chapter, we take the macroeconomic approach and examine factors that affect aggregate, or economywide, trends in employment and wages.

WAGES AND THE DEMAND FOR LABOR

Let's start by thinking about what determines the number of workers employers want to hire at any given wage, that is, the demand for labor. As we will see, the demand for labor depends on both the productivity of labor and the price that the market sets on workers' output. The more productive workers are, or the more valuable the goods and services they produce, the greater the number of workers an employer will want to hire at any given wage.

Table 6.1 shows the relationship between output and the number of workers employed at Banana Computer Company (BCC), which builds and sells computers. Column 1 of the table shows some different possibilities for the number of technicians BCC could employ in its plant. Column 2 shows how many computers the company can produce each year, depending on the number of workers employed. The more workers, the greater the number of computers BCC can produce. For the sake of simplicity, we will assume that the plant, equipment, and materials the workers use to build computers are fixed quantities.

TABLE 6.1
Production and Marginal Product for Banana Computers

(1) Number of workers	(2) Computers produced per year	(3) Marginal product	(4) Value of marginal product (at $3,000/computer)
0	0		
		25	$75,000
1	25		
		23	69,000
2	48		
		21	63,000
3	69		
		19	57,000
4	88		
		17	51,000
5	105		
		15	45,000
6	120		
		13	39,000
7	133		
		11	33,000
8	144		

diminishing returns to labor if the amount of capital and other inputs in use is held constant, then the greater the quantity of labor already employed, the less each additional worker adds to production

Increasing
Opportunity Cost

Column 3 of Table 6.1 shows the *marginal product* of each worker, the extra production that is gained by adding one more worker. Note that each additional worker adds less to total production than the previous worker did. The tendency for marginal product to decline as more and more workers are added is called **diminishing returns to labor.** Specifically, if the amount of capital and other inputs in use is held constant, then the greater the quantity of labor already employed, the less each additional worker adds to production.

The economic basis of diminishing returns to labor is the Principle of Increasing Opportunity Cost, also known as the Low-Hanging-Fruit Principle. A firm's managers want to use their available inputs in the most productive way possible. Hence, an employer who has one worker will assign that worker to the most productive job. If she hires a second worker, she'll assign that worker to the second-most productive job. The third worker will be given the third-most productive job available, and so on. The greater the number of workers already employed, the lower the marginal product of adding another worker, as shown in Table 6.1.

If BCC computers sell for $3,000 each, then column 4 of Table 6.1 shows the *value of the marginal product* of each worker. The value of a worker's marginal product is the amount of extra revenue that the worker generates for the firm. Specifically, the value of the marginal product of each BCC worker is that worker's marginal product, stated in terms of the number of additional computers produced, multiplied by the price of output, here $3,000 per computer. We now have all the information necessary to find BCC's demand for workers.

BCC's Demand for Labor	**EXAMPLE 6.1**

How many workers should BCC hire?

Suppose that the going wage for computer technicians is $60,000 per year. BCC managers know that this is the wage being offered by all their competitors, so they cannot hire qualified workers for less. How many technicians will BCC hire? What would the answer be if the wage were $50,000 per year?

BCC will hire an extra worker if and only if the value of that worker's marginal product (which equals the extra revenue the worker creates for the firm) exceeds the wage BCC must pay. The going wage for computer technicians, which BCC takes as given, is $60,000 per year. Table 6.1 shows that the value of the marginal product of the first, second, and third workers each exceeds $60,000. Hiring these workers will be profitable for BCC because the extra revenue each generates exceeds the wage that BCC must pay. However, the fourth worker's marginal product is worth only $57,000. If BCC's managers hired a fourth worker, they would be paying $60,000 in extra wages for additional output that is worth only $57,000. Since hiring the fourth worker is a money-losing proposition, BCC will hire only three workers. Thus, the quantity of labor BCC demands when the going wage is $60,000 per year is three technicians.

If the market wage for computer technicians were $50,000 per year instead of $60,000, the fourth technician would be worth hiring, since the value of his marginal product, $57,000, would be $7,000 more than his wages. The fifth technician also would be worth hiring, since the fifth worker's marginal product is worth $51,000—$1,000 more than the going wage. The value of the marginal product of a sixth technician, however, is only $45,000, so hiring a sixth worker would not be profitable. When wages are $50,000 per year, then BCC's labor demand is five technicians.

CONCEPT CHECK 6.1

Continuing with Example 6.1, how many workers will BCC hire if the going wage for technicians is $35,000 per year?

The lower the wage a firm must pay, the more workers it will hire. Thus, the demand for labor is like the demand for other goods or services in that the quantity demanded rises as the price (in this case, the wage) falls. Figure 6.1 shows a hypothetical labor demand curve for a firm or industry, with the wage on the vertical axis and employment on the horizontal axis. All else being equal, the higher the wage, the fewer workers a firm or industry will demand.

In our example thus far, we have discussed how labor demand depends on the *nominal,* or dollar, wage. As we explained in the chapter *Inflation and the Price Level,* it is generally more illuminating to examine the real wage, which is the wage expressed in terms of its purchasing power. We shall temporarily hold the general price level constant so that changes in the nominal wage also reflect changes in the real wage.

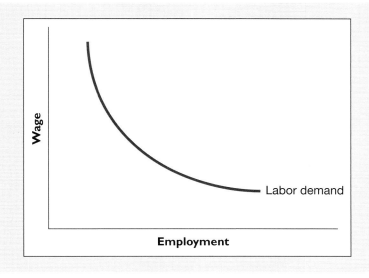

FIGURE 6.1

The Demand Curve for Labor.

The demand curve for labor is downward-sloping. The higher the wage, the fewer workers employers will hire.

SHIFTS IN THE DEMAND FOR LABOR

The number of workers that BCC will employ at any given real wage depends on the value of their marginal product, as shown in column 4 of Table 6.1. Changes in the economy that increase the value of workers' marginal product will increase the value of extra workers to BCC, and thus BCC's demand for labor at any given real wage. In other words, any factor that raises the value of the marginal product of BCC's workers will shift BCC's labor demand curve to the right.

Two main factors could increase BCC's labor demand:

1. An increase in the price of the company's output (computers).

2. An increase in the productivity of BCC's workers.

The next two examples illustrate both of these possibilities.

Real Wage and an Increase in Demand	**EXAMPLE 6.2**

Will BCC hire more workers if the price of computers rises?

Suppose an increase in the demand for BCC's computers raises the price of its computers to $5,000 each. How many technicians will BCC hire now if the real wage is $60,000 per year? If the real wage is $50,000?

The effect of the increase in computer prices is shown in Table 6.2. Columns 1 to 3 of the table are the same as in Table 6.1. The number of computers a given number of technicians can build (column 2) has not changed; hence, the marginal product of particular technicians (column 3) is the same. But because computers can now be sold for $5,000 each instead of $3,000, the *value* of each worker's marginal product has increased by two-thirds (compare column 4 of Table 6.2 with column 4 of Table 6.1).

TABLE 6.2
Production and Marginal Product for Banana Computers after an Increase in Computer Prices

(1) Number of workers	(2) Computers produced per year	(3) Marginal product	(4) Value of marginal product (at $5,000/computer)
0	0		
		25	$125,000
1	25		
		23	115,000
2	48		
		21	105,000
3	69		
		19	95,000
4	88		
		17	85,000
5	105		
		15	75,000
6	120		
		13	65,000
7	133		
		11	55,000
8	144		

How does the increase in the price of computers affect BCC's demand for labor? Recall from our first example that when the price of computers was $3,000 and the going wage for technicians was $60,000, BCC's demand for labor was three workers. But now, with computers selling for $5,000 each, the value of the marginal product of each of the first seven workers exceeds $60,000 (Table 6.2). So, if the real wage of computer technicians is still $60,000, BCC would increase its demand from three workers to seven.

Suppose instead that the going real wage for technicians is $50,000. In the example above, when the price of computers was $3,000 and the wage was $50,000, BCC demanded five workers. But if computers sell for $5,000, we can see from column 4 of Table 6.2 that the value of the marginal product of even the eighth worker exceeds the wage of $50,000. So if the real wage is $50,000, the increase in computer prices raises BCC's demand for labor from five workers to eight.

CONCEPT CHECK 6.2

Refer to Example 6.2. How many workers will BCC hire if the going wage for technicians is $100,000 per year and the price of computers is $5,000? Compare your answer to the demand for technicians at a wage of $100,000 when the price of computers is $3,000.

The general conclusion to be drawn from Example 6.2 is that *an increase in the price of workers' output increases the demand for labor,* shifting the labor demand curve to the right, as shown in Figure 6.2. A higher price for workers' output makes workers more valuable, leading employers to demand more workers at any given real wage.

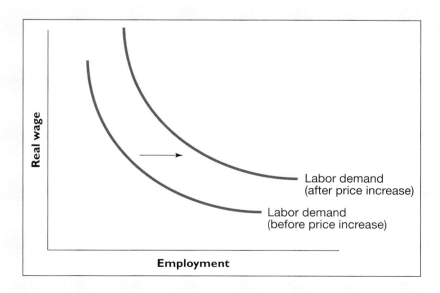

FIGURE 6.2

A Higher Price of Output Increases the Demand for Labor.

An increase in the price of workers' output increases the value of their marginal product, shifting the labor demand curve to the right.

The second factor that affects the demand for labor is worker productivity. Since an increase in productivity increases the value of a worker's marginal product, it also increases the demand for labor, as Example 6.3 shows.

Worker Productivity and Demand for Labor   **EXAMPLE 6.3**

Do productivity improvements hurt workers?

Suppose BCC adopts a new technology that reduces the number of components to be assembled, permitting each technician to build 50 percent more machines per year. Assume that the price of computers is $3,000 per machine. How many technicians will BCC hire if the real wage is $60,000 per year?

Table 6.3 shows workers' marginal products and the value of their marginal products after the 50 percent increase in productivity, assuming that computers sell for $3,000 each.

Before the productivity increase, BCC would have demanded three workers at a wage of $60,000 (see Table 6.1). After the productivity increase, however, the

TABLE 6.3
Production and Marginal Product for Banana Computers after an Increase in Worker Productivity

(1) Number of workers	(2) Computers produced per year	(3) Marginal product	(4) Value of marginal product ($3,000/computer)
0	0		
		37.5	$112,500
1	37.5		
		34.5	103,500
2	72		
		31.5	94,500
3	103.5		
		28.5	85,500
4	132		
		25.5	76,500
5	157.5		
		22.5	67,500
6	180		
		19.5	58,500
7	199.5		
		16.5	49,500
8	216		

value of the marginal product of the first six workers exceeds $60,000 (see Table 6.3, column 4). So at a wage of $60,000, BCC's demand for labor increases from three workers to six.

CONCEPT CHECK 6.3

Refer back to Example 6.3. How many workers will BCC hire after the 50 percent increase in productivity if the going wage for technicians is $50,000 per year? Compare this figure to the demand for workers at a $50,000 wage before the increase in productivity.

In general, *an increase in worker productivity increases the demand for labor,* shifting the labor demand curve to the right, as in Figure 6.3.

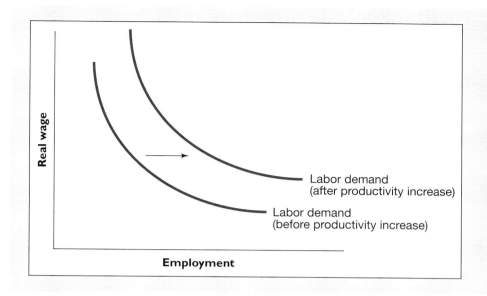

FIGURE 6.3

Higher Productivity Increases the Demand for Labor.

An increase in productivity raises workers' marginal product and—assuming no change in the price of output—the value of their marginal product. Since a productivity increase raises the value of marginal product, employers will hire more workers at any given real wage, shifting the labor demand curve to the right.

THE SUPPLY OF LABOR

We've discussed the demand for labor by employers; to complete the story, we need to consider the supply of labor. The suppliers of labor are workers and potential workers. At any given real wage, potential suppliers of labor must decide if they're willing to work. The total number of people who are willing to work at each real wage is the supply of labor.[2]

Reservation Price for Labor   **EXAMPLE 6.4**

Will you clean your neighbor's basement or go to the beach?

You were planning to go to the beach today, but your neighbor asks you to clean out his basement. You like the beach a lot more than fighting cobwebs. Do you take the job?

Unless you are motivated primarily by neighborliness, your answer to this job offer would probably be, "It depends on how much my neighbor will pay." You probably would not be willing to take the job for $10 or $20, unless you have a severe and immediate need for cash. But if your neighbor were wealthy and eccentric enough to offer you $500 (to take an extreme example), you would very likely say yes. Somewhere between $20 and the unrealistic figure of $500 is the minimum payment you would be willing to accept to tackle the dirty basement. This minimum payment, the *reservation price* you set for your labor, is the compensation level that leaves you just indifferent between working and not working.

In economic terms, deciding whether to work at any given wage is a straightforward application of the Cost-Benefit Principle. The cost to you of cleaning out the basement is the opportunity cost of your time (you would rather be surfing) plus the cost you place on having to work in unpleasant conditions. You can measure this total cost in dollars simply by asking yourself, "What is the minimum amount of money I would take to clean out the basement instead of going to the beach?" The minimum payment that you would accept is the same as your reservation price. The benefit of taking the job is measured by the pay you receive, which will go toward that new smartphone you want. You should take the job only if the promised pay (the benefit of working) exceeds your reservation price (the cost of working).

Cost-Benefit

---

[2]We are still holding the general price level constant, so any increase in the nominal wage also represents an increase in the real wage.

FIGURE 6.4

The Supply of Labor.
The labor supply curve is upward-sloping because, in general, the higher the wage, the more people are willing to work.

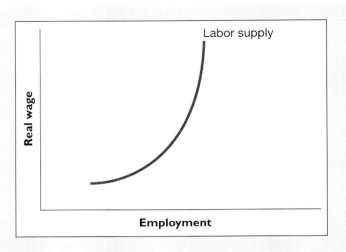

In Example 6.4, your willingness to supply labor is greater, the higher the wage. In general, the same is true for the population as a whole. Certainly people work for many reasons, including personal satisfaction, the opportunity to develop skills and talents, and the chance to socialize with co-workers. Still, for most people, income is one of the principal benefits of working, so the higher the real wage, the more willing they are to sacrifice other possible uses of their time. The fact that people are more willing to work when the wage they are offered is higher is captured in the upward slope of the supply curve of labor (see Figure 6.4).

CONCEPT CHECK 6.4

You want a career in broadcasting. The local radio station is offering an unpaid summer internship that would give you valuable experience. Your alternative to the internship is to earn $3,000 working in a car wash. How would you decide which job to take? Would a decision to take the internship contradict the conclusion that the labor supply curve is upward-sloping?

SHIFTS IN THE SUPPLY OF LABOR

Any factor that affects the quantity of labor offered at a given real wage will shift the labor supply curve. At the macroeconomic level, the most important factor affecting the supply of labor is the size of the working-age population, which is influenced by factors such as the domestic birthrate, immigration and emigration rates, and the ages at which people normally first enter the workforce and retire. All else being equal, an increase in the working-age population raises the quantity of labor supplied at each real wage, shifting the labor supply curve to the right. Changes in the percentage of people of working age who seek employment—for example, as a result of social changes that encourage women to work outside the home—also can affect the supply of labor.

Now that we've discussed both the demand for and supply of labor, we're ready to apply supply and demand analysis to real-world labor markets. But first, try your hand at using supply and demand analysis to answer the following question.

CONCEPT CHECK 6.5

Labor unions typically favor tough restrictions on immigration, while employers tend to favor more liberal rules. Why? (*Hint:* How is an influx of potential workers likely to affect real wages?)

RECAP	SUPPLY AND DEMAND IN THE LABOR MARKET

The demand for labor

The extra production gained by adding one more worker is the *marginal product* of that worker. The *value of the marginal product* of a worker is that worker's marginal product times the price of the firm's output. A firm will employ a worker only if the worker's value of marginal product, which is the same as the extra revenue the worker generates for the firm, exceeds the real wage that the firm must pay. The lower the real wage, the more workers the firm will find it profitable to employ. Thus, the labor demand curve, like most demand curves, is downward-sloping.

For a given real wage, any change that increases the value of workers' marginal products will increase the demand for labor and shift the labor demand curve to the right. Examples of factors that increase labor demand are an increase in the price of workers' output and an increase in productivity.

The supply of labor

An individual is willing to supply labor if the real wage that is offered is greater than the opportunity cost of the individual's time. Generally, the higher the real wage, the more people are willing to work. Thus, the labor supply curve, like most supply curves, is upward-sloping.

For a given real wage, any factor that increases the number of people available and willing to work increases the supply of labor and shifts the labor supply curve to the right. Examples of factors that increase labor supply include an increase in the working-age population or an increase in the share of the working-age population seeking employment.

EXPLAINING THE TRENDS IN REAL WAGES AND EMPLOYMENT

We are now ready to analyze the important trends in real wages and employment discussed earlier in the chapter.

WHY HAVE REAL WAGES INCREASED BY SO MUCH IN THE INDUSTRIALIZED COUNTRIES?

As we discussed, real annual earnings in the United States have quintupled since 1929, and other industrialized countries have experienced similar gains. These increases have greatly improved the standard of living of workers in these countries. Why have real wages increased by so much in the United States and other industrialized countries?

The large increase in real wages results from the sustained growth in productivity experienced by the industrialized countries during the twentieth century. (We discuss the sources of this growth in productivity in the next chapter, *Economic Growth.*) As illustrated by Figure 6.5, increased productivity raises the demand for labor, increasing employment and the real wage.

Of the factors contributing to productivity growth in the industrialized countries, two of the most important were (1) the dramatic technological progress that occurred during the twentieth century and (2) large increases in capital, which provided workers with more and better tools with which to work. Labor supply increased during the century as well, of course (not shown in the diagram). However, the increases in labor demand, driven by rapidly expanding productivity, have been so great as to overwhelm the depressing effect on real wages of increased labor supply.

FIGURE 6.5

An Increase in Productivity Raises the Real Wage.

An increase in productivity raises the demand for labor, shifting the labor demand curve from D to D'. The real wage rises from w to w' and employment rises from N to N'.

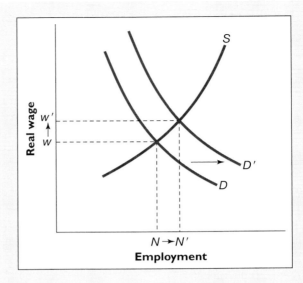

SINCE THE 1970s, REAL WAGE GROWTH IN THE UNITED STATES HAS STAGNATED, WHILE EMPLOYMENT GROWTH HAS BEEN RAPID

With the exception of the late 1990s, rates of real wage growth after 1973 in the United States have been significantly lower than in previous decades prior to 1973. But during most of this time period, the economy created new jobs at a record rate. What accounts for these trends?

Let's begin with the slowdown in real wage growth since the early 1970s. Supply and demand analysis tells us that a slowdown in real wage growth must result from slower growth in the demand for labor, more rapid growth in the supply of labor, or both. On the demand side, since the early 1970s the United States and other industrialized nations have experienced a slowdown in productivity growth. Thus, one possible explanation for the slowdown in the growth of real wages since the early 1970s is the decline in the pace of productivity gains.

Some evidence for a relationship between productivity and real wages is given in Table 6.4, which shows the average annual growth rates in labor productivity and real

TABLE 6.4
Growth Rates in Productivity and Real Earnings

	Average Annual Growth Rate (%)	
	Productivity	**Real earnings**
1970–1979	1.92	0
1980–1989	1.47	−0.81%
1990–1999	2.03	0.34
2000–2009	2.57	0.72

SOURCE: Real wage: *FRED, Federal Reserve Economic Data*, from the Federal Reserve Bank of St. Louis, https://research.stlouisfed.org/fred2/. Labor productivity: Bureau of Labor Statistics (www.bls.gov). Productivity is output per hour in the nonfarm business sector; real earnings equal real compensation per hour in the nonfarm business sector.

wages for each decade since 1970. You can see the growth in productivity corresponds closely to the growth in real earnings. Particularly striking is the very low growth in productivity and actual decline in real wages during the 1980s. However, more recent improvements in productivity have corresponds to growth in real wages again.

While the effects of the slowdown in productivity on the demand for labor are an important reason for declining real wage growth, they can't be the whole story. We know this because, with labor supply held constant, slower growth in labor demand would lead to reduced rates of employment growth, as well as reduced growth in real wages. But until the recent downturn, job growth in the United States in recent decades had been rapid. Large increases in employment in the face of slow growth of labor demand can be explained only by simultaneous increases in the supply of labor (see Concept Check 6.6).

Labor supply in the United States does appear to have grown rapidly in recent decades. In particular, increased participation in the labor market by women has increased the U.S. supply of labor since the mid-1970s. Other factors, including the coming of age of the baby boomers and high rates of immigration, also help to explain the increase in the supply of labor. The combination of slower growth in labor demand (the result of the productivity slowdown) and accelerated growth in labor supply (the result of increased participation by women in the workforce, together with other factors) helps to explain why real wage growth has been sluggish for many years in the United States, even during periods of rapid employment growth.

What about the future? Labor supply is likely to diminish in the coming decades. We already see the share of the working-age population that is either employed or actively looking for work decreasing since its peak in 2000. This is at least in part due to baby boomers retiring and the percentage of women in the labor force stabilizing. Productivity did increase during the 1990s and 2000s, reflecting the benefits of new technologies, among other factors. However, since 2010, productivity growth in the United States has again slowed. It remains to be seen if this is a temporary slowdown or a new long-term trend in productivity growth. If the productivity trend from the 1990s and 2000s returns, there seems to be a good chance that workers will see healthy gains in real wages in the year to come.

CONCEPT CHECK 6.6

As we just discussed, relatively weak growth in productivity and relatively strong growth in labor supply after about 1973 can explain (1) the slowdown in real wage growth and (2) the more rapid expansion in employment after about 1973. Show this point graphically by drawing two supply and demand diagrams of the labor market, one corresponding to the period 1960–1972 and the other to 1973–2000 (the period ending just before the 2001 recession). Assuming that productivity growth was strong but labor supply growth was modest during 1960–1972, show that we would expect to see rapid real wage growth but only moderate growth in employment in that period. Now apply the same analysis to 1973–2000, assuming that productivity growth is weaker but labor supply growth stronger than in 1960–1972. What do you predict for growth in the real wage and employment in 1973–2000 relative to the earlier period?

INCREASING WAGE INEQUALITY: THE EFFECTS OF GLOBALIZATION

Another important trend in U.S. labor markets is increasing inequality in wages. Specifically, many commentators have blamed the increasing divergence between the wages of skilled and unskilled workers on the phenomenon of "globalization." This popular term refers to the fact that, to an increasing extent, the markets for many goods and services are becoming international, rather than national or local in scope.

The main economic benefit of globalization is increased specialization and the efficiency that it brings. Instead of each country trying to produce everything its citizens consume, each can concentrate on producing those goods and services at which it is relatively most efficient. As implied by the Principle of Comparative Advantage, the result is that consumers of all countries enjoy a greater variety of goods and services, of better quality and at lower prices, than they would without international trade.

The effects of globalization on the *labor* market are mixed, however, which explains why many politicians oppose free trade agreements. Expanded trade means that consumers stop buying certain goods and services from domestic producers and switch to foreign-made products. Consumers would not make this switch unless the foreign products were better, cheaper, or both, so expanded trade clearly makes them better off. But the workers and firm owners in the domestic industries that lose business may well suffer from the increase in foreign competition.

The effects of increasing trade on the labor market can be analyzed using Figure 6.6. The figure contrasts the supply and demand for labor in two different industries: (a) textiles and (b) computer software. Imagine that, initially, there is little or no international trade in these two goods. Without trade, the demand for workers in each industry is indicated by the curves marked D_{textiles} and D_{software}, respectively. Wages and employment in each industry are determined by the intersection of the demand curves and the labor supply curves in each industry. As we have drawn the figure, initially, the real wage is the same in both industries, equal to w. Employment is N_{textiles} in textiles and N_{software} in software.

Comparative Advantage

FIGURE 6.6

The Effect of Globalization on the Demand for Workers in Two Industries.

Initially, real wages in the two industries are equal at *w*. After an increase in trade, (a) demand for workers in the importing industry (textiles) declines, lowering real wages and employment, while (b) demand for workers in the exporting industry (software) increases, raising real wages and employment in that industry.

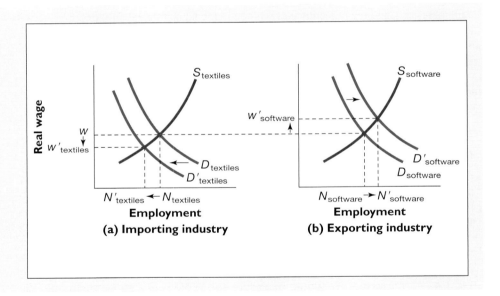

When countries open themselves to trade, they will begin to produce for export those goods or services at which they are relatively more efficient and to import goods or services that they are relatively less efficient at producing. Suppose the country in this example is relatively more efficient at producing software than manufacturing textiles. With the opening of trade, the country gains new foreign markets for its software and begins to produce for export as well as for domestic use. Meanwhile, because the country is relatively less efficient at producing textiles, consumers begin to purchase foreign-made textiles, which are cheaper or of higher quality, instead of the domestic product. In short, software becomes an exporting industry and textiles an importing industry.

These changes in the demand for domestic products are translated into changes in the demand for labor. The opening of export markets increases the demand for domestic software, raising its price. The higher price for domestic software, in turn, raises the value of the marginal products of software workers, shifting the labor demand curve in the software industry to the right, from $D_{software}$ to $D'_{software}$ in Figure 6.6(b). Wages in the software industry rise, from w to $w'_{software}$, and employment in the industry rises as well. In the textile industry the opposite happens. Demand for domestic textiles falls as consumers switch to imports. The price of domestic textiles falls with demand, reducing the value of the marginal product of textile workers and hence the demand for their labor, to $D'_{textiles}$ in Figure 6.6(a). Employment in the textile industry falls, and the real wage falls as well, from w to $w'_{textiles}$.

In sum, Figure 6.6 shows how globalization can contribute to increasing wage inequality. Initially, we assumed that software workers and textile workers received the same wage. However, the opening up of trade raised the wages of workers in the "winning" industry (software) and lowered the wages of workers in the "losing" industry (textiles), increasing inequality.

In practice, the tendency of trade to increase wage inequality may be even worse than depicted in the example because the great majority of the world's workers, particularly those in developing countries, have relatively low skill levels. Thus, when industrialized countries like the United States open up trade with developing countries, the domestic industries that are likely to face the toughest international competition are those that use mostly low-skilled labor. Conversely, the industries that are likely to do the best in international competition are those that employ mostly skilled workers. Thus, increased trade may lower the wages of those workers who are already poorly paid and increase the wages of those who are well paid.

The fact that increasing trade may exacerbate wage inequality explains some of the political resistance to globalization, but in general it does not justify attempts to reverse the trend. Increasing trade and specialization is a major source of improvement in living standards, both in the United States and abroad, so trying to stop the process is counterproductive. Indeed, the economic forces behind globalization—primarily, the desire of consumers for better and cheaper products and of producers for new markets—are so powerful that the process would be hard to stop even if government officials were determined to do so.

Rather than trying to stop globalization, helping the labor market to adjust to the effects of globalization is probably a better course. To a certain extent, indeed, the economy will adjust on its own. Figure 6.6 showed that, following the opening to trade, real wages and employment fall in (a) textiles and rise in (b) software. At that point, wages and job opportunities are much more attractive in the software industry than in textiles. Will this situation persist? Clearly, there is a strong incentive for workers who are able to do so to leave the textile industry and seek employment in the software industry.

The movement of workers between jobs, firms, and industries is called **worker mobility.** In our example, worker mobility will tend to reduce labor supply in textiles and increase it in software, as workers move from the contracting industry to the growing one. This process will reverse some of the increase in wage inequality by raising wages in textiles and lowering them in software. It also will shift workers from a less competitive sector to a more competitive sector. To some extent, then, the labor market can adjust on its own to the effects of globalization.

worker mobility the movement of workers between jobs, firms, and industries

Of course, there are many barriers to a textile worker becoming a software engineer. So there also may be a need for *transition aid* to workers in the affected sectors. Ideally, such aid helps workers train for and find new jobs. If that is not possible or desirable—say, because a worker is nearing retirement—transition aid can take the form of government payments to help the worker maintain his or her standard of living. The Efficiency Principle reminds us that transition aid and similar programs are useful because trade and specialization increase the total economic pie. The "winners" from globalization can afford the taxes necessary to finance aid and still enjoy a net benefit from increased trade.

Efficiency

INCREASING WAGE INEQUALITY: TECHNOLOGICAL CHANGE

A second source of increasing wage inequality is ongoing technological change that favors more highly skilled or educated workers. New scientific knowledge and the technological advances associated with it are a major source of improved productivity and economic growth. Increases in worker productivity are in turn a driving force behind wage increases and higher average living standards. In the long run and on average, technological progress is undoubtedly the worker's friend.

This sweeping statement is not true at all times and in all places, however. Whether a particular technological development is good for a particular worker depends on the effect of that innovation on the worker's value of marginal product and, hence, on his or her wage. For example, at one time the ability to add numbers rapidly and accurately was a valuable skill; a clerk with that skill could expect advancement and higher wages. However, the invention and mass production of the electronic calculator has rendered human calculating skills less valuable, to the detriment of those who have that skill.

History is replete with examples of workers who opposed new technologies out of fear that their skills would become less valuable. In England in the early nineteenth century, rioting workmen destroyed newly introduced labor-saving machinery. The name of the workers' reputed leader, Ned Ludd, has been preserved in the term *Luddite,* meaning a person who is opposed to the introduction of new technologies. The same theme appears in American folk history in the tale of John Henry, the mighty pile-driving man who died in an attempt to show that a human could tunnel into a rock face more quickly than a steam-powered machine.

How do these observations bear on wage inequality? According to some economists, many recent technological advances have taken the form of **skill-biased technological change,** that is, technological change that affects the marginal product of higher-skilled workers differently from that of lower-skilled workers. Specifically, technological developments in recent decades appear to have favored more-skilled and -educated workers.

Developments in automobile production are a case in point. The advent of mass production techniques in the 1920s provided highly paid work for several generations of relatively low-skilled autoworkers. But in recent years automobile production, like the automobiles themselves, has become considerably more sophisticated. The simplest production jobs have been taken over by robots and computer-controlled machinery, which require skilled operatives who know how to use and maintain the new equipment. Consumer demands for luxury features and customized options also have raised the automakers' demand for highly skilled craftspeople. Thus, in general, the skill requirements for jobs in automobile production have risen.

Figure 6.7 illustrates the effects of technological change that favors skilled workers. Figure 6.7(a) shows the market for unskilled workers; Figure 6.7(b) shows the market for skilled workers. The demand curves labeled $D_{\text{unskilled}}$ and D_{skilled} show the demand for each

skill-biased technological change technological change that affects the marginal products of higher-skilled workers differently from those of lower-skilled workers

FIGURE 6.7

The Effect of Skill-Biased Technological Change on Wage Inequality.

The figure shows the effects of a skill-biased technological change that increases the marginal product of skilled workers and reduces the marginal product of unskilled workers. The resulting increase in the demand for skilled workers raises their wages (b), while the decline in demand for unskilled workers reduces their wages (a). Wage inequality increases.

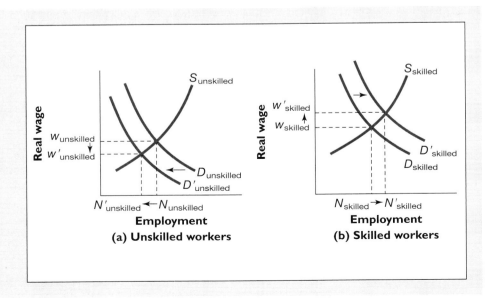

type of worker before a skill-biased technological change. Wages and employment for each type of worker are determined by the intersection of the demand and supply curves in each market. Figure 6.7 shows that, even before the technological change, unskilled workers received lower real wages than skilled workers ($w_{unskilled} < w_{skilled}$), reflecting the lower marginal products of the unskilled.

Now suppose that a new technology—computer-controlled machinery, for example—is introduced. This technological change is biased toward skilled workers, which means that it raises their marginal productivity relative to unskilled workers. We will assume in this example that the new technology also lowers the marginal productivity of unskilled workers, perhaps because they are unable to use the new technology, but all that is necessary for our conclusions is that they benefit less than skilled workers. Figure 6.7 shows the effect of this change in marginal products. In part (b) the increase in the marginal productivity of skilled workers raises the demand for those workers; the demand curve shifts rightward to $D'_{skilled}$. Accordingly, the real wages and employment of skilled workers also rise. In contrast, because they have been made less productive by the technological change, the demand for unskilled workers shifts leftward to $D'_{unskilled}$ [Figure 6.7(a)]. Lower demand for unskilled workers reduces their real wages and employment.

In summary, this analysis supports the conclusion that technological change that is biased in favor of skilled workers will tend to increase the wage gap between the skilled and unskilled. Empirical studies have confirmed the role of skill-biased technological change in recent increases in wage inequality.

Because new technologies that favor skilled workers increase wage inequality, should government regulators act to block them? As in the case of globalization, most economists would argue against trying to block new technologies since technological advances are necessary for economic growth and improved living standards. If the Luddites had somehow succeeded in preventing the introduction of labor-saving machinery in Great Britain, economic growth and development over the past few centuries might have been greatly reduced.

The remedies for the problem of wage inequalities caused by technological change are similar to those for wage inequalities caused by globalization. First among them is worker mobility. As the pay differential between skilled and unskilled work increases, unskilled workers will have a stronger incentive to acquire education and skills, to everyone's benefit. A second remedy is transition aid. Government policymakers should consider programs that will help workers to retrain if they are able, or provide income support if they are not.

RECAP	EXPLAINING THE TRENDS IN REAL WAGES AND EMPLOYMENT

- The long-term increase in real wages enjoyed by workers in industrial countries results primarily from large productivity gains, which have raised the demand for labor. Technological progress and an expanded and modernized capital stock are two important reasons for these long-term increases in productivity.

- The stagnation in real wage growth that began in the 1970s resulted in part from the slowdown in productivity growth (and, hence, the slower growth in labor demand) that occurred at about the same time. Increased labor supply, arising from such factors as the increased participation of women and the coming of age of the baby-boom generation, depressed real wages further while also expanding employment. In the latter part of the 1990s, resurgence in productivity growth was accompanied by an increase in real wage growth. However, real wages remained exactly the same in 2012 as in 1970.

- Both globalization and skill-biased technological change contribute to wage inequality. Globalization raises the wages of workers in exporting industries by raising the demand for those workers, while reducing the wages of workers in importing industries. Technological change that favors more-skilled workers increases the demand for such workers, and hence their wages, relative to the wages of less-skilled workers.

  Attempting to block either globalization or technological change is not the best response to the problem of wage inequality. To some extent, worker mobility (movement of workers from low-wage to high-wage industries) will offset the inequality created by these forces. Where mobility is not practical, transition aid—government assistance to workers whose employment prospects have worsened—may be the best solution.

UNEMPLOYMENT AND THE UNEMPLOYMENT RATE

Economists analyze a variety of statistics to assess the level of economic activity in a country. In the last two chapters, *Spending, Income, and GDP* and *Inflation and the Price Level,* we discussed how economists use measures such as GDP and inflation to carry out this assessment. Here, we turn our attention to measures of employment and unemployment. In particular, the unemployment rate is a sensitive indicator of conditions in the labor market. When the unemployment rate is low, jobs are secure and relatively easier to find. Low unemployment is often associated with improving wages and working conditions as well, as employers compete to attract and retain workers.

MEASURING UNEMPLOYMENT

In the United States, defining and measuring unemployment is the responsibility of the Bureau of Labor Statistics, or BLS. Each month the BLS surveys about 60,000 randomly selected households. Each person in those households who is 16 years or older is placed in one of three categories:

1. *Employed.* A person is employed if he or she worked full-time or part-time (even for a few hours) during the past week or is on vacation or sick leave from a regular job.

2. *Unemployed.* A person is unemployed if he or she did not work during the preceding week but made some effort to find work (for example, by going to a job interview) in the past four weeks.

3. *Out of the labor force.* A person is considered to be out of the labor force if he or she did not work in the past week and did not look for work in the past four weeks. In other words, people who are neither employed nor unemployed (in the sense of looking for work but not being able to find it) are "out of the labor force." Full-time students, unpaid homemakers, retirees, and people unable to work because of disabilities are examples of people who are out of the labor force.

Based on the results of the survey, the BLS estimates how many people in the whole country fit into each of the three categories. The working-age population is the sum of these three categories, and consists of the population age 16 and over.[3]

  To find the unemployment rate, the BLS must first calculate the size of the *labor force.* The **labor force** is defined as the total number of employed and unemployed people in the economy (the first two categories of respondents to the BLS survey).

labor force the total number of employed and unemployed people in the economy

---

[3]See www.bls.gov/cps/cps_htgm.htm for complete details on how the government collects and categorizes these data.

The **unemployment rate** is then defined as the number of unemployed people divided by the labor force. Notice that people who are out of the labor force (because they are in school, have retired, or are disabled, for example) are not counted as unemployed and thus do not affect the unemployment rate. In general, a high rate of unemployment indicates that the economy is performing poorly.

> **unemployment rate** the number of unemployed people divided by the labor force

Table 6.5 illustrates the calculation of key labor market statistics, using data based on the BLS survey for August 2014. In that month unemployment was 6.1 percent of the labor force. Figure 6.8 shows the U.S. unemployment rate since 1960. Unemployment rates were exceptionally low—just above 4 percent—in the late 1960s and the late 1990s. By this measure, the latter part of the 1990s was an exceptionally good time for American workers. However, unemployment rose in 2001–2003 and even more so in 2007–2010 following the recessions in those years. Note how the unemployment rate moves in cycles up and down, as the economy moves through short-term fluctuations. We will discuss these economic upswings (or expansions) and downswings (or recessions) and their relationship with unemployment in greater detail in the chapter *Short-Term Economic Fluctuations.*

Another useful statistic is the **participation rate,** or the percentage of the working-age population in the labor force (that is, the percentage that is either employed or actively looking for work). The participation rate is calculated by dividing the labor force by the working-age (16 years and older) population. The participation rate in August 2014 was about

> **participation rate** the percentage of the working-age population in the labor force (that is, the percentage that is either employed or looking for work)

TABLE 6.5
U.S. Employment Data, August 2014 (in millions)

Employed	146.37
Unemployed	9.59
Labor force	155.96
Not in labor force	92.27
Working-age (over 16) population	248.23
Unemployment rate = 9.59/155.96 = 6.1%	
Participation rate = 155.96/248.23 = 62.8%	

SOURCE: Bureau of Labor Statistics, www.bls.gov.

$$UR = \frac{9.59}{155.96}$$

$$P\,rate = \frac{155.96}{248.23}$$

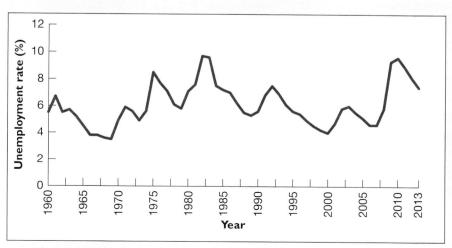

FIGURE 6.8

The U.S. Unemployment Rate, 1960–2013.

The unemployment rate—the fraction of the U.S. labor force that is unemployed—was just above 4 percent in the late 1990s, the lowest recorded rate since the latter part of the 1960s. Unemployment rose above 9 percent in 2009 during the recession that began in December 2007, and it began falling again in 2010.

SOURCE: Bureau of Labor Statistics, www.bls.gov.

FIGURE 6.9

The U.S. Participation Rate, 1960–2013.

The participation rate—the percentage of the working-age population in the labor force—has gone from below 60 percent in 1960 to above 67 percent in 2000 and then back down to around 63 percent in 2013. Unlike the unemployment rate in Figure 6.8, the participation rate displays clear historical trends.

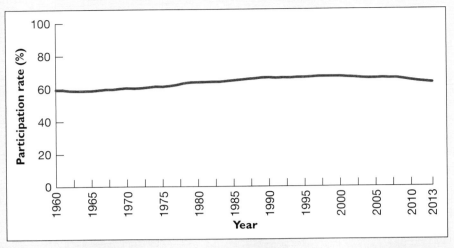

SOURCE: Bureau of Labor Statistics, www.bls.gov.

63 percent; that is, less than two out of every three adults had a job or were looking for work. Figure 6.9 shows that in 1970, about 60 percent of the over-16 population in the United States was either employed or actively looking for work. In the next three decades, that number increased to a high of 67 percent by the year 2000. This was in large part due to the baby-boomer generation and women entering the workforce, as discussed earlier. However, over the last decade, the U.S. participation rate has dramatically diminished, reaching levels not seen since the late 1970s. There are several possible reasons for this recent decline including the aging of the baby-boomer generation, who have started to retire, the effects of skill-biased technology changes on unskilled workers (both discussed in the section on labor market trends), and the severity and duration of the unemployment caused by the most recent recession (see Figure 6.8). Others argue that a substantial increase in the number of workers qualifying for and receiving disability insurance is one of the contributing factors, as well as changes in U.S. immigration policies over the last decade, which have made it harder for foreign workers to become part of the U.S. labor force. Unlike the short-term cyclical variations seen in the unemployment rate shown in Figure 6.8, the participation rate displays clear historical long-term trends over the last five decades.

CONCEPT CHECK 6.7

Following are August 2014 Bureau of Labor Statistics U.S. employment data for African Americans.

Employed	16.69 million
Unemployed	2.16 million
Not in the labor force	12.04 million

Find the labor force, the working-age population, the unemployment rate, and the participation rate for African Americans and compare your results to those in Table 6.5.

THE COSTS OF UNEMPLOYMENT

Unemployment imposes *economic, psychological,* and *social* costs on a nation. From an economic perspective, the main cost of unemployment is the output that is lost because the workforce is not fully utilized. Much of the burden of the reduced output is borne by the unemployed themselves, whose incomes fall when they are not working and whose skills may deteriorate from lack of use. However, society at large also bears part of the economic cost of unemployment. For example, workers who become unemployed are liable to stop paying taxes and start receiving government support payments such as unemployment benefits. This net drain on the government's budget is a cost to all taxpayers.

The *psychological* costs of unemployment are felt primarily by unemployed workers and their families. Studies show that lengthy periods of unemployment can lead to a loss of self-esteem, feelings of loss of control over one's life, depression, and even suicidal behavior.[4] The unemployed worker's family is likely to feel increased psychological stress, compounded by the economic difficulties created by the loss of income.

The *social* costs of unemployment are a result of the economic and psychological effects. People who have been unemployed for a while tend not only to face severe financial difficulties but also to feel anger, frustration, and despair. Not surprisingly, increases in unemployment tend to be associated with increases in crime, domestic violence, alcoholism, drug abuse, and other social problems. The costs created by these problems are borne not only by the unemployed but by society in general, as more public resources must be spent to counteract these problems—for example, by hiring more police to control crime or increasing spending on social services.

THE DURATION OF UNEMPLOYMENT

In assessing the impact of unemployment on jobless people, economists must know how long individual workers have been without work. Generally, the longer a person has been out of work, the more severe are the economic and psychological costs that person will face. People who are unemployed for only a few weeks, for example, are not likely to suffer a serious reduction in their standard of living, since for a short period they can draw upon their savings and perhaps on government benefits. Nor would we expect someone who is unemployed for only a short time to experience psychological problems such as depression or loss of self-esteem, at least not to the same extent as someone who has been out of work for months or years.

In its surveys, therefore, the BLS asks respondents how long they have been unemployed. A period during which an individual is continuously unemployed is called an **unemployment spell;** it begins when the worker becomes unemployed and ends when the worker either finds a job or leaves the labor force. (Remember, people outside the labor force are not counted as unemployed.) The length of an unemployment spell is called its **duration.** The duration of unemployment rises during recessions, reflecting the greater difficulty of finding work during those periods.

unemployment spell a period during which an individual is continuously unemployed

duration the length of an unemployment spell

At any given time, a substantial fraction of unemployed workers have been unemployed for six months or more; we will refer to this group as the *long-term unemployed.* Long-term unemployment creates the highest economic, psychological, and social costs, both for the unemployed themselves and for society as a whole.

When the economy is not in a recession, most unemployment spells are relatively short. For example, in January 2008, 35 percent of the unemployed had been out of work for just 5 weeks or less, another 32 percent had been unemployed for 5 to 14 weeks, and about 33 percent of the unemployed had been without a job for more than 14 weeks (about three months). However, during the latest recession, unemployment spells grew longer. For example, in April 2011, 20 percent of the unemployed had been out of work for 5 weeks or less, 22 percent had been unemployed for 5 to 14 weeks, and 58 percent of the unemployed had been searching for work without any success for more than 14 weeks.

Even these statistics are a bit deceptive, however, because short unemployment spells can arise from two very different patterns of labor market experience. For instance, some people have short unemployment spells that end in their finding a stable long-term job. These workers, whom we will refer to as the *short-term unemployed,* do not typically

[4]For a survey of the literature on the psychological effects of unemployment, see William Darity Jr. and Arthur H. Goldsmith, "Social Psychology, Unemployment and Macroeconomics," *Journal of Economic Perspectives* 10 (Winter 1996), pp. 121–40.

bear a high cost of unemployment. By contrast, other workers have short unemployment spells that typically end either in their withdrawal from the labor force or in a short-term or temporary job that soon leaves the worker unemployed again. Workers whose unemployment spells are broken up by brief periods of employment or withdrawals from the labor force are referred to as the *chronically unemployed.* In terms of the costs of unemployment, the experience of these workers is similar to that of the long-term unemployed.

THE UNEMPLOYMENT RATE VERSUS "TRUE" UNEMPLOYMENT

Like GDP measurement, unemployment measurement has its critics. Most of them argue that the official unemployment rate understates the true extent of unemployment. They point in particular to two groups of people who are not counted among the unemployed: so-called *discouraged workers* and *involuntary part-time workers.*

discouraged workers people who say they would like to have a job but have not made an effort to find one in the past four weeks because they believe there are no jobs available for them

Discouraged workers are people who say they would like to have a job but have not made an effort to find one in the past four weeks, specifically because they believed no jobs were available for them or there were none for which they would qualify. Because they have not sought work in the past four weeks, discouraged workers are counted as being out of the labor force rather than unemployed. Some observers have suggested that treating discouraged workers as unemployed would provide a more accurate picture of the labor market.

Involuntary part-time workers are people who say they would like to work full-time but are able to find only part-time work. Because they do have jobs, involuntary part-time workers are counted as employed rather than unemployed. These workers are sometimes also referred to as *underemployed* or part-time workers for economic reasons. Some economists have suggested that these workers should be counted as partially unemployed.

In response to these criticisms, in recent years the BLS has released special unemployment rates that include estimates of the number of discouraged workers and involuntary part-time workers. In August 2014, when the official unemployment rate was 6.1 percent (see Table 6.5), the BLS calculated that if both discouraged workers and involuntary part-time workers were counted as unemployed, the unemployment rate would have been 12.0 percent.[5] Thus, the problem of discouraged and underemployed workers appears to be fairly significant.

TYPES OF UNEMPLOYMENT AND THEIR COSTS

Economists have found it useful to think of unemployment as being of three broad types: *frictional* unemployment, *structural* unemployment, and *cyclical* unemployment. Each type of unemployment has different causes and imposes different economic and social costs.

FRICTIONAL UNEMPLOYMENT

The function of the labor market is to match available jobs with available workers. If all jobs and workers were the same, or if the set of jobs and workers were static and unchanging, this matching process would be quick and easy. But the real world is more complicated. In practice, both jobs and workers are highly *heterogeneous.* Jobs differ in their location, in the skills they require, in their working conditions and hours, and in many other ways. Workers differ in their career aspirations, their skills and experience, their preferred working hours, their willingness to travel, and so on.

The real labor market is also *dynamic,* or constantly changing and evolving. On the demand side of the labor market, technological advances, globalization, and changing consumer tastes spur the creation of new products, new firms, and even new industries, while outmoded products, firms, and industries disappear. As a result of this upheaval, new jobs are constantly being created, while some old jobs cease to be viable. The workforce

[5]This measure is known as the U-6 unemployment rate and is available at www.bls.gov.

in a modern economy is equally dynamic. People move, gain new skills, leave the labor force for a time to rear children or go back to school, and even change careers.

Because the labor market is heterogeneous and dynamic, the process of matching jobs with workers often takes time. For example, a software engineer who loses or quits her job in Silicon Valley may take weeks or even months to find an appropriate new job. In her search she will probably consider alternative areas of software development or even totally new challenges. She also may want to think about different regions of the country in which software companies are located, such as North Carolina's Research Triangle Park or New York City's Silicon Alley. During the period in which she is searching for a new job, she is counted as unemployed.

Short-term unemployment that is associated with the process of matching workers with jobs is called **frictional unemployment.** The *costs* of frictional unemployment are low and may even be negative; that is, frictional unemployment may be economically beneficial. First, frictional unemployment is short-term, so its psychological effects and direct economic losses are minimal. Second, to the extent that the search process leads to a better match between worker and job, a period of frictional unemployment is actually productive, in the sense that it leads to higher output over the long run. Indeed, a certain amount of frictional unemployment seems essential to the smooth functioning of a rapidly changing, dynamic economy.

STRUCTURAL UNEMPLOYMENT

A second major type of unemployment is **structural unemployment,** or the long-term and chronic unemployment that exists even when the economy is producing at a normal rate. Several factors contribute to structural unemployment. First, a *lack of skills, language barriers,* or *discrimination* keeps some workers from finding stable, long-term jobs. Migrant farmworkers and unskilled construction workers who find short-term or temporary jobs from time to time, but never stay in one job for very long, fit the definition of chronically unemployed.

Second, economic changes sometimes create a *long-term mismatch* between the skills some workers have and the available jobs. The U.S. steel industry, for example, has declined over the years, while the computer software industry has grown rapidly. Ideally, steelworkers who lose their jobs would be able to find new jobs in software firms (worker mobility), so their unemployment would only be frictional in nature. In practice, of course, many ex-steelworkers lack the education, ability, or interest necessary to work in the computer industry. Since their skills are no longer in demand, these workers may drift into chronic or long-term unemployment. The recent decline in labor force participation can also be seen as a sign of an increase in the number of U.S. workers facing this type of long-term mismatch between skills and the jobs available.

Finally, structural unemployment can result from *structural features of the labor market* that act as barriers to employment. Examples of such barriers include unions and minimum wage laws, both of which may keep wages above their market-clearing level, creating unemployment. We will discuss some of these structural features shortly.

The *costs* of structural unemployment are much higher than those of frictional unemployment. Because structurally unemployed workers do little productive work over long periods, their idleness causes substantial economic losses both to the unemployed workers and to society. Structurally unemployed workers also lose out on the opportunity to develop new skills on the job, and their existing skills wither from disuse. Long spells

Frictional = looking for a job

frictional unemployment the short-term unemployment associated with the process of matching workers with jobs

Structural = long term unemployment

structural unemployment the long-term and chronic unemployment that exists even when the economy is producing at a normal rate

"The one single thought that sustains me is that the fundamentals are good."

of unemployment are also much more difficult for workers to handle psychologically than the relatively brief spells associated with frictional unemployment.

CYCLICAL UNEMPLOYMENT

cyclical unemployment the extra unemployment that occurs during periods of recession

The third type of unemployment occurs during periods of recession (that is, periods of unusually low production) and is called **cyclical unemployment.** The sharp peaks in unemployment shown in Figure 6.8 reflect the cyclical unemployment that occurs during recessions. Increases in cyclical unemployment, although they are relatively short-lived, are associated with significant declines in real GDP and are therefore quite costly economically. We will study cyclical unemployment in more detail later in the chapters dealing with expansions and recessions.

In principle, frictional, structural, and cyclical unemployment add up to the total unemployment rate. In practice, sharp distinctions often cannot be made between the different categories, so any breakdown of the total unemployment rate into the three types of unemployment is necessarily subjective and approximate.

IMPEDIMENTS TO FULL EMPLOYMENT

In discussing structural unemployment, we mentioned that structural features of the labor market may contribute to long-term and chronic unemployment. Let's discuss a few of those features.

Minimum Wage Laws

The federal government and most states have minimum wage laws, which prescribe the lowest hourly wage that employers may pay to workers. Basic supply and demand analysis shows that if the minimum wage law has any effect at all, it must raise the unemployment rate. Figure 6.10 shows why. The figure shows the demand and supply curves for low-skilled workers, to whom the minimum wage is most relevant. The market-clearing real wage, at which the quantity of labor demanded equals the quantity of labor supplied, is w, and the corresponding level of employment of low-skilled workers is N. Now suppose there is a legal minimum wage w_{min} that exceeds the market-clearing wage w, as shown in Figure 6.10. At the minimum wage, the number of people who want jobs, N_B, exceeds the number of workers that employers are willing to hire, N_A. The result is unemployment in the amount $N_B - N_A$, also equal to the length of the line segment AB in the

FIGURE 6.10

A Legal Minimum Wage May Create Unemployment.

If the minimum wage w_{min} exceeds the market-clearing wage w for low-skilled workers, it will create unemployment equal to the difference between the number of people who want to work at the minimum wage, N_B, and the number of people that employers are willing to hire, N_A.

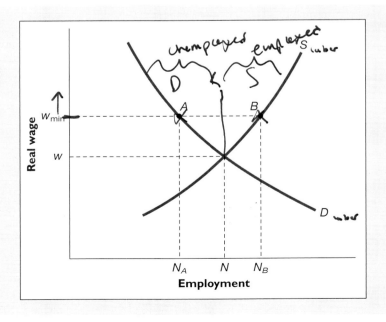

figure. If there were no minimum wage, this unemployment would not exist, since the labor market would clear at wage w.

If minimum wages create unemployment, why are they politically popular? A minimum wage creates two classes of workers: those who are lucky enough to find jobs at the minimum wage and those who are shut out because the minimum wage exceeds the market-clearing wage. Workers who do find jobs at the minimum wage will earn more than they would have otherwise because the minimum wage is higher than the market-clearing wage. If the minimum wage were put to a vote, the number of workers who benefit from the legislation, and who could thus be expected to support it, might well exceed the number of workers who are hurt by it. In creating groups of "winners" and "losers," minimum wage legislation resembles rent control legislation (see the chapter *Supply and Demand*). But like rent controls, minimum wages create economic inefficiency. Thus, other methods of attacking poverty, such as direct grants to the working poor, might prove more effective.

Labor Unions

Labor unions are organizations that negotiate with employers on behalf of workers. Among the issues that unions negotiate, which are embodied in the contracts they draw up with employers, are the wages workers earn, rules for hiring and firing, the duties of different types of workers, working hours and conditions, and procedures for resolving disputes between workers and employers. Unions gain negotiating power by their power to call a strike—that is, to refuse work until a contract agreement has been reached.

Through the threat of a strike, a union can usually get employers to agree to a wage that is higher than the market-clearing wage. Thus, Figure 6.10 could represent conditions in a unionized industry if w_{min} is interpreted as the union wage instead of the legal minimum wage. As in the case of a minimum wage, a union wage that is higher than the market-clearing wage leads to unemployment, in the amount $N_B - N_A$ in Figure 6.10. Furthermore, a high union wage creates a trade-off similar to the one created by a minimum wage. Those workers who are lucky enough to get jobs as union members will be paid more than they would be otherwise. Unfortunately, their gain comes at the expense of other workers who are unemployed as a result of the artificially high union wage.

Are labor unions good for the economy? That is a controversial, emotionally charged question. Early in the twentieth century, some employers who faced little local competition for workers—coal-mining companies in Appalachia, for example—exploited their advantage by forcing workers to toil long hours in dangerous conditions for low pay. Through bitter and sometimes bloody confrontations with these companies, labor organizations succeeded in eliminating many of the worst abuses. Unions also point with pride to their historic political role in supporting progressive labor legislation, such as laws that banned child labor. Finally, union leaders often claim to increase productivity and promote democracy in the workplace by giving workers some voice in the operations of the firm.

Opponents of unions, while acknowledging that these organizations may have played a positive role in the past, question their value in a modern economy. Today, more and more workers are professionals or semiprofessionals, rather than production workers, so they can move relatively easily from firm to firm. Indeed, many labor markets have become national or even international, so today's workers have numerous potential employers. Thus, the forces of competition—the fact that employers must persuade talented workers to work for them—should provide adequate protection for workers. Indeed, opponents would argue that unions are becoming increasingly self-defeating since firms that must pay artificially high union wages and abide by inflexible work rules will not be able to compete in a global economy. The ultimate effect of such handicaps will be the failure of unionized firms and the loss of union jobs. Indeed, unions are in decline in the United States and now represent 12.3 percent of the workforce—a large fraction of which are government workers such as public school teachers and the police.

Unemployment Insurance

Another structural feature of the labor market that may increase the unemployment rate is the availability of *unemployment insurance,* or government transfer payments to unemployed workers. Unemployment insurance provides an important social benefit in that it helps the unemployed to maintain a decent standard of living while they are looking for a job. But because its availability allows the unemployed to search longer or less intensively for a job, it may lengthen the average amount of time the typical unemployed worker is without a job.

Most economists would argue that unemployment insurance should be generous enough to provide basic support to the unemployed but not so generous as to remove the incentive to actively seek work. Thus, unemployment insurance should last for only a limited time, and its benefits should not be as high as the income a worker receives when working.

Other Government Regulations

Besides minimum wage legislation, many other government regulations bear on the labor market. They include *health and safety regulations,* which establish the safety standards employers must follow, and rules that prohibit racial or gender-based discrimination in hiring.

Cost-Benefit and Efficiency

Legislators and other policymakers need to keep in mind both the Cost-Benefit Principle and the Efficiency Principle when considering labor market regulation. Many regulations are beneficial; however, in some cases the costs of complying with them may exceed the benefits they provide. Further, to the extent that regulations increase employer costs and reduce productivity, they depress the demand for labor, lowering real wages and contributing to unemployment and reducing the size of the economic pie.

RECAP	UNEMPLOYMENT AND THE UNEMPLOYMENT RATE

Defining and measuring unemployment involves distinguishing among the employed, the unemployed, and those not in the labor force. We can then use these concepts to calculate measures such as the unemployment rate, which is the number of people unemployed divided by the labor force, and the participation rate, which is the labor force divided by the working-age population.

Economists distinguish among three broad types of unemployment. *Frictional unemployment* is the short-term unemployment that is associated with the process of matching workers with jobs. *Structural unemployment* is the long-term or chronic unemployment that occurs even when the economy is producing at a normal rate. *Cyclical unemployment* is the extra unemployment that occurs during periods of recession. Frictional unemployment may be economically beneficial, as improved matching of workers and jobs may increase output in the long run. Structural unemployment and cyclical unemployment impose heavy economic costs on workers and society, as well as psychological costs on workers and their families.

Structural features of the labor market may cause structural unemployment. Examples of such features are legal minimum wages or union contracts that set wages above market-clearing levels; unemployment insurance, which allows unemployed workers to search longer or less intensively for a job; and government regulations that impose extra costs on employers. Regulation of the labor market is not necessarily undesirable, but it should be subject to the cost-benefit criterion.

○ SUMMARY ○

- There are three important trends in wages, employment, and unemployment that we focused on in this chapter. First, over a long period, average real wages have risen substantially both in the United States and in other industrialized countries. Second, despite the long-term upward trend in real wages, real wage growth has been stagnant in the United States since the early 1970s while employment grew substantially from the 1970s through the 1990s. Third, in the United States, wage inequality has increased dramatically in recent decades. The real wages of most unskilled workers have actually declined, while the real wages of skilled and educated workers have continued to rise. *(LO1)*

- Trends in real wages and employment can be studied using a supply and demand model of the labor market. At a given price level, the productivity of labor and the price of workers' output determine the demand for labor. Employers will hire workers only as long as the value of the marginal product of the last worker hired equals or exceeds the wage the firm must pay. Because of diminishing returns to labor, the more workers a firm employs, the less additional product will be obtained by adding yet another worker. The lower the going wage, the more workers will be hired and thus the demand-for-labor curve slopes downward. Factors that increase the value of labor's marginal product, such as an increase in the price of workers' output or an increase in productivity, shift the labor demand curve to the right. Conversely, changes that reduce the value of labor's marginal product shift the labor demand curve to the left. *(LO2)*

- The supply curve for labor shows the number of people willing to work at any given real wage. The supply curve slopes downward since more people will generally work at a higher real wage. An increase in the working-age population or a social change that promotes labor market participation (such as the changing role of women in the labor force) will increase labor supply and shift the labor supply curve to the right. *(LO2)*

- Improvements in productivity, which raise the demand for labor, account for the bulk of the increase in U.S. real wages over the last century. The stagnation in real wage growth that has occurred in recent decades is the result of slower growth in labor demand, which was caused in turn by a slowdown in the rate of productivity improvement, and of more rapid growth in labor supply. Rapid growth in labor supply, caused by such factors as immigration and increased labor force participation by women, also has contributed to the continued expansion of employment. Recently, however, overall labor force participation, has dramatically decreased. *(LO3)*

- Two reasons for the increasing wage inequality in the United States are economic globalization and skill-biased technological change. Both have increased the demand for, and hence the real wages of, relatively skilled and educated workers. Attempting to block globalization and technological change is counterproductive, however, since both factors are important in promoting increased productivity. To some extent, the movement of workers from lower-paying to higher-paying jobs or industries will counteract the trend toward wage inequality. A policy of providing transition aid and training for workers with obsolete skills is a more useful response to the problem. *(LO3)*

- The unemployment rate is based on surveys conducted by the Bureau of Labor Statistics. The surveys classify all respondents over age 16 as employed, unemployed, or not in the labor force. The labor force is the sum of employed and unemployed workers—that is, people who have a job or are looking for one. The unemployment rate is calculated as the number of unemployed workers divided by the labor force. The participation rate is the percentage of the working-age population that is in the labor force. *(LO4)*

- The costs of unemployment include the economic cost of lost output, the psychological costs borne by unemployed workers and their families, and the social costs associated with problems like increased crime and violence. The greatest costs are imposed by long unemployment spells (periods of unemployment). Critics of the official unemployment rate argue that it understates "true" unemployment by excluding discouraged workers and involuntary part-time workers. *(LO5)*

- There are three broad types of unemployment: frictional, structural, and cyclical. Frictional unemployment is the short-term unemployment associated with the process of matching workers with jobs in a dynamic, heterogeneous labor market. Structural unemployment is the long-term and chronic unemployment that exists even when the economy is producing at a normal rate. It arises from a variety of factors, including language barriers, discrimination, structural features of the labor market, lack of skills, or long-term mismatches between the skills workers have and the available jobs. Cyclical unemployment is the extra unemployment that occurs during periods of recession. The costs of frictional unemployment are low, as it tends to be brief and to create more productive matches between workers and jobs. Structural unemployment, which is often long term, and cyclical unemployment, which is associated with significant reductions in real GDP, tend to be more costly. *(LO5)*

- Structural features of the labor market that may contribute to unemployment include minimum wage laws, which discourage firms from hiring low-skilled workers; labor unions, which can set wages above market-clearing levels; unemployment insurance, which reduces the incentives of the unemployed to find work quickly; and other government regulations, which—although possibly conferring benefits—increase the costs of employing workers. *(LO5)*

○ KEY TERMS ○

cyclical unemployment
diminishing returns to labor
discouraged workers
duration (of an unemployment
  spell)

frictional unemployment
labor force
participation rate
skill-biased technological
  change

structural unemployment
unemployment rate
unemployment spell
worker mobility

○ REVIEW QUESTIONS ○

1. List and discuss the three important labor market trends given in the first section of the chapter. *(LO1)*

2. Acme Corporation is considering hiring Jane Smith. Based on her other opportunities in the job market, Jane has told Acme that she will work for them for $40,000 per year. How should Acme determine whether to employ her? *(LO2)*

3. Why have real wages risen by so much in the United States in the past century? Why did real wage growth stagnate beginning in the early 1970s? *(LO3)*

4. What are two major factors contributing to increased inequality in wages? Briefly, why do these factors raise wage inequality? Contrast possible policy responses to increasing inequality in terms of their effects on economic efficiency. *(LO3)*

5. True or false: A high participation rate in an economy implies a low unemployment rate. Explain. *(LO4)*

6. What are the costs of a high unemployment rate? Do you think providing more generous government benefits to the unemployed would increase these costs, reduce these costs, or leave them unchanged? Discuss. *(LO5)*

7. List three types of unemployment and their causes. Which of these types is economically and socially the least costly? Explain. *(LO5)*

○ PROBLEMS ○

Visit your mobile app
store and download
the Frank: Study
Econ app *today*!

1. Production data for Bob's Bicycle Factory are as follows:

Number of workers	Bikes assembled per day
1	10
2	18
3	24
4	28
5	30

Other than wages, Bob has costs of $100 (for parts and so on) for each bike assembled. *(LO2)*

    a. Bikes sell for $130 each. Find the marginal product and the value of the marginal product for each worker (don't forget about Bob's cost for parts).

    b. Make a table showing Bob's demand curve for labor.

    c. Repeat part b for the case in which bikes sell for $140 each.

    d. Repeat part b for the case in which worker productivity increases by 50 percent. Bikes sell for $130 each.

2. How would each of the following factors be likely to affect the economywide supply of labor? *(LO2)*

    a. The age at which people are eligible for Medicare is increased.

    b. Increased productivity causes real wages to rise.

    c. War preparations lead to the institution of a national draft, and many young people are called up.

    d. More people decide to have children (consider both short-term and long-term effects).

    e. Social Security benefits are made more generous.

3. How would each of the following likely affect the real wage and employment of unskilled workers on an automobile plant assembly line? *(LO3)*

    a. Demand for the type of car made by the plant increases.

    b. A sharp increase in the price of gas causes many commuters to switch to mass transit.

    c. Because of alternative opportunities, people become less willing to do factory work.

4. Skilled or unskilled workers can be used to produce a small toy. Initially, assume that the wages paid to both types of workers are equal. *(LO3)*

    a. Suppose that electronic equipment is introduced that increases the marginal product of skilled workers (who can use the equipment to produce more toys per hour worked). The marginal products of unskilled workers are unaffected. Explain, using words and graphs, what happens to the equilibrium wages for the two groups.

    b. Suppose that unskilled workers find it worthwhile to acquire skills when the wage differential between skilled and unskilled workers reaches a certain point. Explain what will happen to the supply of unskilled workers, the supply of skilled workers, and the equilibrium wage for the two groups. In particular, what are equilibrium wages for skilled workers relative to unskilled workers after some unskilled workers acquire training?

5. The following is a report from a not-very-efficient BLS survey taker: "There were 65 people in the houses I visited, 10 of them children under 16; 25 people had full-time jobs, and 5 had part-time jobs. There were 10 retirees, 5 full-time homemakers, 5 full-time students over age 16, and 2 people who were disabled and couldn't work. The remaining people did not have jobs but all said they would like one. One of these people had not looked actively for work for three months, however." Find the labor force, the working-age population, the number of employed workers, and the number of unemployed workers. *(LO4)*

6. Ellen is downloading labor market data for the most recent month, but her connection is slow and so far this is all she has been able to get:

Unemployment rate	5.0%
Participation rate	62.5%
Not in the labor force	60 million

Find the labor force, the working-age population, the number of employed workers, and the number of unemployed workers. *(LO4)*

7. For each of the following scenarios, state whether the unemployment is frictional, structural, or cyclical. Justify your answer. *(LO5)*
   a. Ted lost his job when the steel mill closed down. He lacks the skills to work in another industry and so has been unemployed over a year.
   b. Alice was laid off from her job at the auto plant because the recession reduced the demand for cars. She expects to get her job back when the economy picks up.
   c. Gwen had a job as a clerk but quit when her husband was transferred to another state. She looked for a month before finding a new job that she liked.

8. The towns of Sawyer and Thatcher each have a labor force of 1,200 people. In Sawyer, 100 people were unemployed for the entire year, while the rest of the labor force was employed continuously. In Thatcher, every member of the labor force was unemployed for 1 month and employed for 11 months. *(LO4, LO5)*
   a. What is the average unemployment rate over the year in each of the two towns?
   b. What is the average duration of unemployment spells in each of the two towns?
   c. In which town do you think the costs of unemployment are higher? Explain.

○ ANSWERS TO CONCEPT CHECKS ○

6.1 The value of the marginal product of the seventh worker is $39,000, and the value of the marginal product of the eighth worker is $33,000. So the seventh but not the eighth worker is profitable to hire at a wage of $35,000. *(LO2)*

6.2 With the computer price at $5,000, it is profitable to hire three workers at a wage of $100,000, since the third worker's value of marginal product ($105,000) exceeds $100,000, but the fourth worker's value of marginal product ($95,000) is less than $100,000. At a computer price of $3,000, we can refer to Table 6.1 to find that not even the first worker has a value of marginal product as high as $100,000, so at that computer price, BCC will hire no workers. In short, at a wage of $100,000, the increase in the computer price raises the demand for technicians from zero to three. *(LO2)*

6.3 The seventh but not the eighth worker's value of marginal product exceeds $50,000 (Table 6.3), so it is profitable to hire seven workers if the going wage is $50,000. From Table 6.1, before the increase in productivity, the first five workers have values of marginal product greater than $50,000, so the demand for labor at a given wage of $50,000 is five workers. Thus, the increase in productivity raises the quantity of labor demanded at a wage of $50,000 from five workers to seven workers. *(LO2)*

6.4 Even though you are receiving no pay, the valuable experience you gain as an intern is likely to raise the pay you will be able to earn in the future, so it is an investment in human capital. You also find working in the radio station more enjoyable than working in a car wash, presumably. To decide which job to take, you should ask yourself, "Taking into account both the likely increase in my future earnings and my greater enjoyment from working in the radio station, would I be willing to pay $3,000 to work in the radio station rather than earn $3,000 working in the car wash?" If the answer is yes, then you should work in the radio station; otherwise, you should go to the car wash.

A decision to work in the radio station does not contradict the idea of an upward-sloping labor supply curve, if we are willing to think of the total compensation for that job as including not just cash wages but such factors as the value of the training that you receive. Your labor supply curve is still upward-sloping in the sense that the greater the value you place on the internship experience, the more likely you are to accept the job. *(LO2)*

6.5 Immigration to a country raises labor supply—indeed, the search for work is one of the most powerful factors drawing immigrants in the first place. As shown in the accompanying figure, an increase in labor supply will tend to lower the wages that employers have to pay (from *w* to *w′*), while raising overall employment (from *N* to *N′*). Because of the tendency of large-scale immigration to reduce real wages, labor unions generally oppose it, while employers support it.

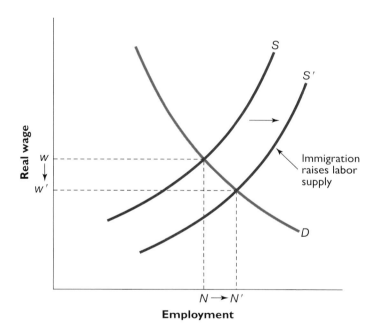

Although the figure shows the overall, or aggregate, supply of labor in the economy, the specific effects of immigration on wages depend on the skills and occupations of the immigrants. Current U.S. immigration policy makes the reunification of families the main reason for admitting immigrants, and for the most part immigrants are not screened by their education or skills. The United States also has a good deal of illegal immigration, made up largely of people looking for economic opportunity. These two factors create a tendency for new immigrants to the United States to be relatively low-skilled. Since immigration tends to increase the supply of unskilled labor by relatively more, it depresses wages of domestic low-skilled workers more than it does the wages of domestic high-skilled workers. Some economists, such as George Borjas of Harvard University, have argued that low-skilled immigration is another important factor reducing the wages of less-skilled workers relative to workers with greater skills and education. Borjas argues that the United States should adopt the approach used by Canada and give preference to potential immigrants with relatively higher levels of skills and education. *(LO2)*

6.6 Part (a) of the accompanying figure shows the labor market in 1960–1972; part (b) shows the labor market in 1973–2000. For comparability, we set the initial labor supply (*S*) and demand (*D*) curves the same in both parts, implying the same initial values of the real wage (*w*) and employment (*N*). In part (a) we show the effects of a large increase in labor demand (from *D* to *D'*), the result of rapid productivity growth, and a relatively small increase in labor supply (from *S* to *S'*). The real wage rises to *w'* and employment rises to *N'*. In part (b) we observe the effects of a somewhat smaller increase in labor demand (from *D* to *D''*) and a larger increase in labor supply (from *S* to *S''*). Part (b), corresponding to the 1973–2000 period, shows a smaller increase in the real wage and a larger increase in employment than part (a), corresponding to 1960–1972. These results are consistent with actual developments in the U.S. labor market over these two periods. *(LO3)*

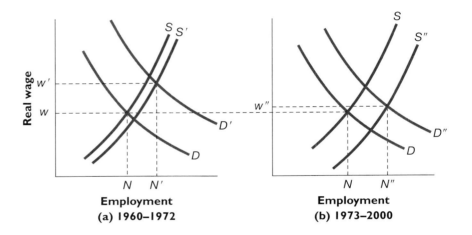

6.7 Labor force = Employed + Unemployed
$$= 16.69 \text{ million} + 2.16 \text{ million} = 18.85 \text{ million}$$

Working-age population = Labor force + Not in labor force
$$= 18.85 \text{ million} + 12.04 \text{ million}$$
$$= 30.89 \text{ million}$$

Unemployment rate $= \dfrac{\text{Unemployed}}{\text{Labor force}} = \dfrac{2.16 \text{ million}}{18.85 \text{ million}} = 11.46$ percent

Participation rate $= \dfrac{\text{Labor force}}{\text{Working-age population}} = \dfrac{18.85 \text{ million}}{30.89 \text{ million}}$
$= 61.0$ percent

In August 2014, African Americans represented 12.1 percent of the labor force and 12.4 percent of the working-age population. The participation rate for African Americans was slightly lower than that of the population as a whole while the unemployment rate was close to twice (88 percent higher than) that of the population as a whole. *(LO4)*

CHAPTER 7

Economic Growth

Martin Ruegner/Photodisc/Getty Images

HOW DO ECONOMIES GROW AND FLOURISH?

One of us attended a conference on the effects of economic growth and development at which a speaker posed the following question: "Which would you rather be? An ordinary, middle-class American living today, or the richest person in America at the time of George Washington?"

A member of the audience spoke out immediately: "I can answer that question in one word. Dentistry."

The answer drew a laugh because it reminded people of George Washington's famous wooden teeth. But it was a good answer. Dentistry in early America—whether the patient was rich or poor—was a primitive affair. Most dentists simply pulled a patient's rotten teeth, with a shot of whiskey for anesthetic.

Other types of medical care were not much better than dentistry. Eighteenth-century doctors had no effective weapons against tuberculosis, typhoid fever, diphtheria, influenza, pneumonia, and other communicable diseases. Such illnesses, now quite treatable, were major killers in Washington's time. Infants and children were particularly susceptible to deadly infectious diseases, especially whooping cough and measles. Even a well-to-do family often lost two or three children to these illnesses. Washington, an unusually large and vigorous man, lived to the age of 67, but the average life expectancy during his era was probably not much more than 40 years.

Medical care is not the only aspect of ordinary life that has changed drastically over the past two centuries. Author Stephen Ambrose, in his account of the Lewis and Clark expedition, described the limitations of transportation and communication in early America:

> A critical fact in the world of 1801 was that nothing moved faster than the speed of a horse. No human being, no manufactured item, no bushel of

LEARNING OBJECTIVES

After reading this chapter, you should be able to:

LO1 Show how small differences in growth rates can lead to large differences in living standards.

LO2 Explain why GDP per capita is the product of average labor productivity and the proportion of the population that is employed and use this decomposition to discuss the sources of economic growth.

LO3 Discuss the determinants of average labor productivity within a particular country and use these concepts to analyze per capita GDP differences across countries.

LO4 Discuss and evaluate government policies that promote economic growth.

LO5 Compare and contrast the benefits of economic growth with its costs.

Would you rather be a rich person living in the eighteenth century or a middle-class person living in the twenty-first century?

wheat, no side of beef (or any beef on the hoof for that matter), no letter, no information, no idea, order, or instruction of any kind moved faster, and, as far as Jefferson's contemporaries were able to tell, nothing ever would.

And except on a racetrack, no horse moved very fast. Road conditions in the United States ranged from bad to abominable, and there weren't very many of them. The best highway in the country ran from Boston to New York; it took a light stagecoach . . . three full days to make the 175-mile journey. The hundred miles from New York to Philadelphia took two full days.[1]

Today New Yorkers can go to Philadelphia by train in an hour and a half. What would George Washington have thought of that? And how would nineteenth-century pioneers, who crossed the continent by wagon train, have reacted to the idea that their great-grandchildren would be able to have breakfast in New York and lunch the same day in San Francisco?

No doubt you can think of other enormous changes in the way average people live, even over the past few decades. Computer technologies and the Internet have changed the ways people work and study in just a few years, for example. Though these changes are due in large part to scientific advances, such discoveries *by themselves* usually have little effect on most people's lives. New scientific knowledge leads to widespread improvements in living standards only when it is commercially applied. Better understanding of the human immune system, for example, has little impact unless it leads to new therapies or drugs. And a new drug will do little to help unless it is affordable to those who need it.

A tragic illustration of this point is the AIDS epidemic in Africa. Although some new drugs will moderate the effects of the virus that causes AIDS, they are so expensive that they are of little practical value in poverty-stricken African nations grappling with the disease. But even if the drugs were affordable, they would have limited benefit without modern hospitals, trained health professionals, and adequate nutrition and sanitation. In short, most improvements in a nation's living standard are the result not just of scientific and technological advances but of an economic system that makes the benefits of those advances available to the average person.

In this chapter, we will explore the sources of economic growth and rising living standards in the modern world. We will begin by reviewing the remarkable economic growth in the industrialized countries, as measured by real GDP per person. Since the mid-nineteenth century (and earlier in some countries), a radical transformation in living standards has occurred in these countries. What explains this transformation? The key to rising living standards is a *continuing increase in average labor productivity,* which depends on several factors, from the skills and motivation workers bring to their jobs to the legal and social environment in which they work. We will analyze each of these factors and discuss its implications for government policies to promote growth. We also will discuss the costs of rapid economic growth and consider whether there may be limits to the amount of economic growth a society can achieve.

THE REMARKABLE RISE IN LIVING STANDARDS: THE RECORD

The advances in health care and transportation mentioned in the beginning of this chapter illustrate only a few of the impressive changes that have taken place in people's material well-being over the past two centuries, particularly in industrialized countries like the United States. To study the factors that affect living standards systematically, however, we must go beyond anecdotes and adopt a specific measure of economic well-being in a particular country and time.

In the chapter *Spending, Income, and GDP,* we introduced real GDP as a basic measure of the level of economic activity in a country. Recall that, in essence, real GDP measures the physical volume of goods and services produced within a country's borders during a specific period, such as a quarter or a year. Consequently, real GDP *per person*

[1]Stephen E. Ambrose, *Undaunted Courage: Meriwether Lewis, Thomas Jefferson, and the Opening of the American West* (New York: Touchstone [Simon & Schuster], 1996), p. 52.

provides a measure of the quantity of goods and services available to the typical resident of a country at a particular time. Although real GDP per person is certainly not a perfect indicator of economic well-being, as we saw in the chapter *Spending, Income, and GDP,* it is positively related to a number of pertinent variables, such as life expectancy, infant health, and literacy. Economists have, therefore, focused on real GDP per person as a key measure of a country's living standard and stage of economic development.

Figure 7.1 shows the remarkable growth in real GDP per person that occurred in the United States between 1929 and 2013. For comparison, Table 7.1 and Figure 7.2 show real GDP per person in eight countries in selected years from 1870 to 2010. These data tell a dramatic story, and you should take a moment to look at them closely. For example, in the United States (which was already a relatively wealthy industrialized country in 1870), real GDP per person in 2010 was more than 12 times its 1870 level. In Japan, real GDP per person was almost 30 (!) times its 1870 level. Underlying these statistics is an amazingly rapid process of economic growth and transformation. In just a few generations relatively poor agrarian societies became highly industrialized economies with average standards of living that could scarcely have been imagined in 1870. As Table 7.1 and

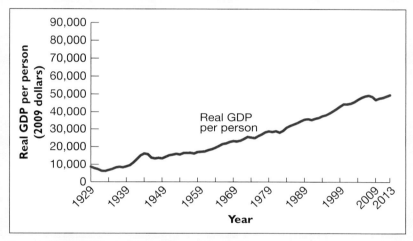

FIGURE 7.1

Real GDP per Person in the U.S., 1929–2013.

The red line shows the real GDP per person in the U.S. economy since 1929. Real GDP per person today is almost six times what it was 1929.

SOURCE: Bureau of Economic Analysis, www.bea.gov.

TABLE 7.1
Real GDP per Person in Selected Countries, 1870–2010

Country	1870	1913	1950	1980	1990	2010	Annual % change 1870–2010	Annual % change 1950–2010	Annual % change 1980–2010
United States	2,445	5,301	9,561	18,577	23,201	30,491	1.8	2.0	1.7
United Kingdom	3,190	4,921	6,939	12,931	16,430	23,777	1.4	2.1	2.1
Germany	1,839	3,648	3,881	14,114	15,929	20,661	1.7	2.8	1.3
Japan	737	1,387	1,921	13,428	18,789	21,935	2.5	4.1	1.6
China	530	552	448	1,061	1,871	8,032	2.0	4.9	7.0
Brazil	713	811	1,672	5,195	4,920	6,879	1.6	2.4	0.9
India	533	673	619	938	1,309	3,372	1.3	2.9	4.4
Ghana	439	781	1,122	1,157	1,062	1,922	1.1	0.9	1.7

SOURCE: Angus Maddison, *The Maddison Project,* www.ggdc.net/maddison. Real GDP per person is measured in 1990 international dollars. "Germany" refers to West Germany in 1950 and 1980.

FIGURE 7.2

Real GDP per Person in a Sample of Countries, 1870–2010.

The U.S., the U.K., and Germany began with high levels of GDP per person in 1870 and remained high-income countries throughout the period. Economic growth has been especially rapid since the 1950s in Japan and since 1980 in China and India. Ghana and the rest of sub-Saharan Africa experienced very low growth rates.

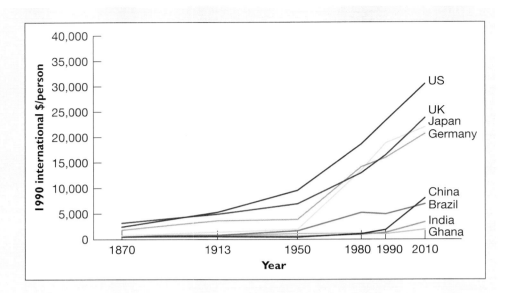

Figure 7.2 show, a significant part of this growth has occurred since 1950, particularly in Japan and China. Further, both China and India have grown significantly faster since 1990 than they did in earlier periods.

A note of caution is in order. The farther back in time we go, the less precise are historical estimates of real GDP. Most governments did not keep official GDP statistics until after World War II; production records from earlier periods are often incomplete or of questionable accuracy. Comparing economic output over a century or more is also problematic because many goods and services that are produced today were unavailable—indeed, inconceivable—in 1870. Despite the difficulty of making precise comparisons, however, we can say with certainty that the variety, quality, and quantity of available goods and services increased enormously in industrialized countries during the nineteenth and twentieth centuries, a fact reflected in the data on real GDP per capita.

WHY "SMALL" DIFFERENCES IN GROWTH RATES MATTER

The last three columns of Table 7.1 show annual growth rates of real GDP per person for both the entire 1870–2010 period and two more recent periods. At first glance, these growth rates don't seem to differ much from country to country. For example, for the period 1870–2010, the highest growth rate is 2.5 percent (Japan) and the lowest is 1.1 percent (Ghana).

But don't let small differences in growth rates fool you. For example, in 1870 China's output per person was roughly 120 percent that of Ghana, yet by 2010 China had more than four times the output per person of Ghana. This widening of the gap between these two countries is the result of the difference between China's 2.0 percent annual growth rate and Ghana's 1.1 percent annual growth rate, maintained for almost 140 years. Small differences in growth rates can have large long-run effects because of the power of growth rates that are compounded over time. A good illustration of this power is the effect of compound interest on a bank deposit.

Compound Interest: Part 1	**EXAMPLE 7.1**

What is compound interest?

In 1800 your great-great-grandfather deposited $10.00 in a checking account at 4 percent interest. Interest is compounded annually (so that interest paid at the end of each year receives interest itself in later years). Great-Great-Grandpa's will specified that the account be turned over to his most direct descendant (you) in the year 2015. When you withdrew the funds in that year, how much was the account worth?

The account was worth $10.00 in 1800; $10.00 × 1.04 = $10.40 in 1801; $10.00 × 1.04 × 1.04 = $10.00 × $(1.04)^2$ = $10.82 in 1802; and so on. Since 215 years elapsed between 1800, when the deposit was made, and the year 2015, when the account was closed, the value of the account in the year 2015 was $10.00 × $(1.04)^{215}$, or $10.00 × 1.04 to the 215th power. Using a calculator, you will find that $10.00 times 1.04 to the 215th power is $45,937.56—a good return for a $10.00 deposit!

Compound interest—an arrangement in which interest is paid not only on the original deposit but on all previously accumulated interest—is distinguished from *simple interest,* in which interest is paid only on the original deposit. If your great-great-grandfather's account had been deposited at 4 percent simple interest, it would have accumulated only 40 cents each year (4 percent of the original $10.00 deposit), for a total value of $10.00 + 215 × $0.40 = $96.00 after 215 years. The tremendous growth in the value of his account came from the compounding of the interest—hence the phrase "the power of compound interest."

compound interest the payment of interest not only on the original deposit but on all previously accumulated interest

Compound Interest: Part 2   EXAMPLE 7.2

What is the difference between 2% interest and 6% interest, compounded annually?

Continuing with Example 7.1, what would your great-great-grandfather's $10.00 deposit have been worth after 215 years if the annual interest rate had been 2 percent? 6 percent?

At 2 percent interest, the account would be worth $10.00 in 1800; $10.00 × 1.02 = $10.20 in 1801; $10.00 × $(1.02)^2$ = $10.40 in 1802; and so on. In the year 2015, the value of the account would be $10.00 × $(1.02)^{215}$, or $706.38. If the interest rate were 6 percent, after 215 years the account would be worth $10.00 × $(1.06)^{215}$, or $2,759,059.28. Let's summarize the results of these three examples:

Interest rate (%)	Value of $10 after 215 years
2	$706.38
4	$45,937.56
6	$2,759,059.28

Compound interest is so powerful that even at relatively low rates of interest, a small sum, compounded over a long enough period, can greatly increase in value. A more subtle point, illustrated by this example, is that small differences in interest rates matter a lot. The difference between a 2 percent and a 4 percent interest rate doesn't seem like much, but over a long period of time it implies large differences in the amount of interest accumulated in a bank account.

Just as the value of a bank deposit grows each year at a rate equal to the interest rate, so the size of a nation's economy expands each year at the rate of economic growth. This analogy suggests that even a relatively modest rate of growth in output per person—say, 1 to 2 percent per year—will produce tremendous increases in average living standards over a long period. And relatively small *differences* in growth rates, as in the case of China and Ghana, will ultimately produce very different living standards.

Economists employ a useful formula for approximating the number of years it will take for an initial amount to double at various growth or interest rates. The formula is 72 divided by the growth or interest rate. Thus, if the interest rate is 2 percent per year, it will take 72/2 = 36 years for the initial sum to double. If the interest rate is 4 percent, it will take $72/4 = 18$ years. This formula is a good approximation only for small and moderate interest rates.

Over the long run, then, the rate of economic growth is an extremely important variable. Hence, government policy changes or other factors that affect the long-term growth rate even by a small amount will have a major economic impact.

CONCEPT CHECK 7.1

Suppose that real GDP per capita in the United States had grown at 2.5 percent per year, as Japan's did, instead of the actual 1.8 percent per year, from 1870 to 2010. How much larger would real GDP per person have been in the United States in 2010?

WHY NATIONS BECOME RICH: THE CRUCIAL ROLE OF AVERAGE LABOR PRODUCTIVITY

What determines a nation's economic growth rate? To get some insight into this vital question, we will find it useful to express real GDP per person as the product of two terms: average labor productivity and the share of the population that is working.

To do this, let Y equal total real output (as measured by real GDP, for example), N equal the number of employed workers, and POP equal the total population. Then real GDP per person can be written as Y/POP; **average labor productivity,** or output per employed worker, equals Y/N; and the share of the population that is working is N/POP. The relationship between these three variables is

average labor productivity
output per employed worker

$$\frac{Y}{POP} = \frac{Y}{N} \times \frac{N}{POP},$$

which, as you can see by canceling out N on the right-hand side of the equation, always holds exactly. In words, this basic relationship is

Real GDP per person = Average labor productivity
× Share of population employed.

This expression for real GDP per person tells us something very basic and intuitive: The quantity of goods and services that each person can consume depends on (1) how much each worker can produce and (2) how many people (as a fraction of the total population) are working. Furthermore, because real GDP per person equals average labor productivity times the share of the population that is employed, real GDP per person can *grow* only to the extent that there is *growth* in worker productivity and/or the fraction of the population that is employed.

Figures 7.3 and 7.4 show the U.S. figures for the three key variables in the relationship above for the period 1960–2013. Figure 7.3 shows both real GDP per person and real GDP per worker (average labor productivity). Figure 7.4 shows the portion of the entire U.S. population (not just the working-age population) that was employed during that period. Once again, we see that the expansion in output per person in the United States has been impressive. Between 1960 and 2013, real GDP per person in the United States grew by 189 percent. Thus, in 2013, the average American enjoyed close to three times as many goods and services as in 1960. Figures 7.3 and 7.4 show that increases in both labor productivity and the share of the population holding a job contributed to this rise in living standard.

Let's look more closely at these two contributing factors, beginning with the share of the population that is employed. As Figure 7.4 shows, between 1960 and 2013, the number of people employed in the United States rose from about 36 to 46 percent of the entire population, a remarkable increase. The growing tendency of women to work outside the home was the most important reason for this rise in employment. Another factor leading to higher rates of employment was an increase in the share of the general population that is of working age

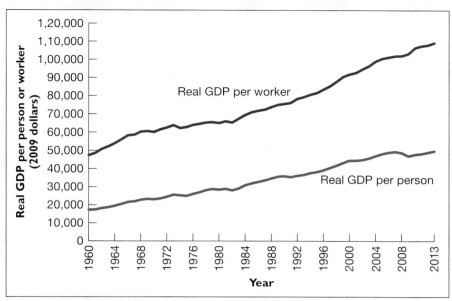

FIGURE 7.3

Annual Real GDP per Person and Average Labor Productivity in the United States, 1960–2013.

Real GDP per person in the United States grew 189 percent between 1960 and 2013, and real GDP per worker (average labor productivity) grew by 131 percent.

SOURCE: Bureau of Labor Statistics, www.bls.gov.

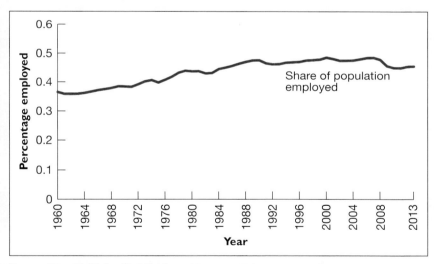

FIGURE 7.4

Share of the U.S. Population Employed, 1960–2013.

The share of the U.S. population holding a job increased from about 36 percent in 1960 to about 46 percent in 2013.

SOURCE: Bureau of Labor Statistics, www.bls.gov.

(ages 16 to 65). The coming of age of the "baby-boom" generation, born in the years after World War II, and to a lesser extent the immigration of young workers from other countries, helped cause this growth in the workforce.

Although the rising share of the U.S. population with jobs contributed significantly to the increase in real GDP per person during the past four decades, as discussed in the chapter *Wages and Unemployment,* this trend has already started to reverse itself. Women's participation in the labor force seems unlikely to continue rising at the same rate as in the past four decades. More important, the baby-boom generation began reaching retirement age in 2010. As more and more baby boomers retire, the fraction of the population that is employed will begin to drop, probably significantly. In the long run, then, the improvement in living standards brought about by the rising share of Americans with jobs will likely prove transitory.

What about the other factor that determines output per person, average labor productivity? As Figure 7.3 shows, between 1960 and 2013, average labor productivity in the United States increased by 131 percent, accounting for a sizable share of the overall increase in GDP per person. In other periods, the link between average labor productivity and output per person in the United States has often been even stronger, since in most earlier periods the share of the population holding jobs was more stable than it has been recently.

This quick look at recent data supports a more general conclusion. *In the long run, increases in output per person arise primarily from increases in average labor productivity.* Furthermore, the more people can produce, the more they can consume. To understand why economies grow, then, we must understand the reasons for increased labor productivity.

RECAP	ECONOMIC GROWTH AND PRODUCTIVITY

Real GDP per person, a basic indicator of living standards, has grown dramatically in the industrialized countries. This growth reflects the *power of compound interest:* Even a modest growth rate, if sustained over a long period of time, can lead to large increases in the size of the economy.

Output per person equals average labor productivity times the share of the population that is employed. Since 1960 the share of the U.S. population with jobs has risen significantly, but this variable has started to decline in recent years. In the long run, increases in output per person and hence living standards arise primarily from increases in average labor productivity.

THE DETERMINANTS OF AVERAGE LABOR PRODUCTIVITY

What determines the productivity of the average worker in a particular country at a particular time? Popular discussions of this issue often equate worker productivity with the willingness of workers of a given nationality to work hard. Everything else being equal, a culture that promotes hard work certainly tends to increase worker productivity. But intensity of effort alone cannot explain the huge differences in average labor productivity that we observe around the world. For example, average labor productivity in the United States is about 24 times what it is in Indonesia and 100 times what it is in Bangladesh, though there is little doubt that Indonesians and Bangladeshis work very hard.

In this section, we will examine six factors that appear to account for the major differences in average labor productivity, both between countries and between generations. Later in the chapter we will discuss how economic policies can influence these factors to spur productivity and growth.

HUMAN CAPITAL

To illustrate the factors that determine average labor productivity, we introduce two prototypical assembly-line workers, Lucy and Ethel.

Assembly-Line Productivity   **EXAMPLE 7.3**

Are Lucy and Ethel more productive as a team or by themselves?

Lucy and Ethel have jobs wrapping chocolate candies and placing them into boxes. Lucy, a novice wrapper, can wrap only 100 candies per hour. Ethel, who has had on-the-job training, can wrap 300 candies per hour. Each works 40 hours per week. What is average labor productivity, in terms of candies wrapped per week and candies wrapped per hour for (a) Lucy, (b) Ethel, and (c) Lucy and Ethel as a team?

In the previous section, we defined average labor productivity as output per worker. Note, though, that the measurement of average labor productivity depends on the time period that is specified. For example, the data presented in Figure 7.3 tell us how much the average worker produces *in a year*. In this example, we are concerned with how much Lucy and Ethel can produce *per hour* of work or *per week* of work. Any one of these ways of measuring labor productivity is equally valid, as long as we are clear about the time unit we are using.

Lucy and Ethel's hourly productivities are given in the problem: Lucy can wrap 100 candies per hour and Ethel can wrap 300. Lucy's weekly productivity is (40 hours/week) × (100 candies wrapped/hour) = 4,000 wrapped candies per week. Ethel's weekly productivity is (40 hours/week) × (300 candies wrapped/hour), or 12,000 candies per week.

Together, Lucy and Ethel can wrap 16,000 candies per week. As a team, their average weekly individual productivity is (16,000 candies wrapped)/(2 weeks of work), or 8,000 candies per week. Their average hourly individual productivity as a team is (16,000 candies wrapped)/(80 hours of work) = 200 candies per hour. Notice that, taken as a team, the two women's productivity lies midway between their individual productivities.

How productive are these workers?

Ethel is more productive than Lucy because she has had on-the-job training, which has allowed her to develop her candy-wrapping skills to a higher level than Lucy's. Because of her training, Ethel can produce more than Lucy can in a given number of hours.

CONCEPT CHECK 7.2

Refer back to Example 7.3. Suppose Ethel attends additional classes in candy wrapping and learns how to wrap 500 candies per hour. Find the output per week and output per hour for Lucy and Ethel, both individually and as a team.

Economists would explain the difference in the two women's performance by saying that Ethel has more human capital than Lucy. **Human capital** comprises the talents, education, training, and skills of workers. Workers with a large stock of human capital are more productive than workers with less training. For example, an administrative assistant who knows how to use a word-processing program will be able to type more letters than one who doesn't; an auto mechanic who is familiar with computerized diagnostic equipment will be able to fix engine problems that less-well-trained mechanics could not.

human capital an amalgam of factors such as education, training, experience, intelligence, energy, work habits, trustworthiness, and initiative that affects the value of a worker's marginal product

The Economic Recovery of West Germany and Japan

EXAMPLE 7.4

Why did West Germany and Japan recover so successfully from the devastation of World War II?

Germany and Japan sustained extensive destruction of their cities and industries during World War II and entered the postwar period impoverished. Yet within 30 years both countries not only had been rebuilt but had become worldwide industrial and economic leaders. What accounts for these "economic miracles"?

Many factors contributed to the economic recovery of West Germany and Japan from World War II, including the substantial aid provided by the United States to Europe under the Marshall Plan and to Japan during the U.S. occupation. Most economists agree, however, that high levels of human capital played a crucial role in both countries.

At the end of the war, Germany's population was exceptionally well educated, with a large number of highly qualified scientists and engineers. The country also had (and still does today) an extensive apprentice system that provided on-the-job training to young workers. As a result, Germany had a skilled industrial workforce. In addition, the area that became West Germany benefited substantially from an influx of skilled workers from East Germany and the rest of Soviet-controlled Europe, including 20,000 trained engineers and technicians. Beginning as early as 1949, this concentration of human capital contributed to a major expansion of Germany's technologically sophisticated, highly productive manufacturing sector. By 1960 West Germany was a leading exporter of high-quality manufactured goods, and its citizens enjoyed one of the highest standards of living in Europe.

Japan, which probably sustained greater physical destruction in the war than Germany, also began the postwar period with a skilled and educated labor force. In addition, occupying American forces restructured the Japanese school system and encouraged all Japanese to obtain a good education. Even more so than the Germans, however, the Japanese emphasized on-the-job training. As part of a lifetime employment system, under which workers were expected to stay with the same company their entire career, Japanese firms invested extensively in worker training. The payoff to these investments in human capital was a steady increase in average labor productivity, particularly in manufacturing. By the 1980s Japanese manufactured goods were among the most advanced in the world and Japan's workers among the most skilled.

Although high levels of human capital were instrumental in the rapid economic growth of West Germany and Japan, human capital alone cannot create a high living standard. A case in point is Soviet-dominated East Germany, which had a level of human capital similar to West Germany's after the war but did not enjoy the same economic growth. For reasons we'll discuss later in the chapter, the communist system imposed by the Soviets utilized East Germany's human capital far less effectively than the economic systems of Japan and West Germany.

Human capital is analogous to physical capital (such as machines and factories) in that it is acquired primarily through the investment of time, energy, and money. For example, to learn how to use a word-processing program, an administrative assistant might need to attend a technical school at night. The cost of going to school includes not only the tuition paid but also the *opportunity cost* of the administrative assistant's time spent attending class and studying. The benefit of the schooling is the increase in wages that can be earned when the course has been completed. We know by the Cost-Benefit Principle that the administrative assistant should learn word processing only if the benefits exceed the costs, including the opportunity costs. In general, then, we would expect to see people acquire additional education and skills when the difference in the wages paid to skilled and unskilled workers is significant.

| Cost-Benefit |

PHYSICAL CAPITAL

Workers' productivity depends not only on their skills and effort but on the tools they have to work with. Even the most skilled surgeon cannot perform open-heart surgery without sophisticated equipment, and an expert computer programmer is of limited value without a computer. These examples illustrate the importance of *physical capital* such as factories and machines. More and better capital allows workers to produce more efficiently, as the next example shows.

Physical Capital and Efficiency   **EXAMPLE 7.5**

Will a candy-wrapping machine make Lucy and Ethel more productive?

Continuing with Example 7.3, suppose that Lucy and Ethel's boss acquired an electric candy-wrapping machine, which is designed to be operated by one worker. Using this machine, an untrained worker can wrap 500 candies per hour. What are Lucy and Ethel's hourly and weekly outputs now? Will the answer change if the boss gets a second machine? A third?

Suppose for the sake of simplicity that a candy-wrapping machine must be assigned to one worker only. (This assumption rules out sharing arrangements, in which one worker uses the machine on the day shift and another on the night shift.) If the boss buys just one machine, she will assign it to Lucy. (Why? See Concept Check 7.3.) Now Lucy will be able to wrap 500 candies per hour, while Ethel can wrap only 300 per hour. Lucy's weekly output will be 20,000 wrapped candies (40 hours × 500 candies wrapped per hour). Ethel's weekly output is still 12,000 wrapped candies (40 hours × 300 candies wrapped per hour). Together they can now wrap 32,000 candies per week, or 16,000 candies per week each. On an hourly basis, average labor productivity for the two women taken together is 32,000 candies wrapped per 80 hours of work, or 400 candies wrapped per hour—twice their average labor productivity before the boss bought the machine.

With two candy-wrapping machines available, both Lucy and Ethel could use a machine. Each could wrap 500 candies per hour, for a total of 40,000 wrapped candies per week. Average labor productivity for both women taken together would be 20,000 wrapped candies per week, or 500 wrapped candies per hour.

What would happen if the boss purchased a third machine? With only two workers, a third machine would be useless: It would add nothing to either total output or average labor productivity.

CONCEPT CHECK 7.3

Using the assumptions made in Examples 7.3 and 7.5, explain why the boss should give the single available candy-wrapping machine to Lucy rather than Ethel. (*Hint:* Apply the Principle of Increasing Opportunity Cost.)

Increasing Opportunity Cost

The candy-wrapping machine is an example of a *capital good,* which was defined in the chapter *Spending, Income, and GDP* as a long-lived good, which is itself produced and used to produce other goods and services. Capital goods include machines and equipment (such as computers, earthmovers, or assembly lines) as well as buildings (such as factories or office buildings).

Capital goods like the candy-wrapping machine enhance workers' productivity. Table 7.2 summarizes the results of our Lucy and Ethel examples. For each number of machines the boss might acquire (column 1), Table 7.2 gives the total weekly output of Lucy and Ethel taken together (column 2), the total number of hours worked by the two women (column 3), and average output per hour (column 4), equal to total weekly output divided by total weekly hours.

Table 7.2 demonstrates two important points about the effect of additional capital on output. First, for a given number of workers, adding more capital generally increases both total output and average labor productivity. For example, adding the first candy-wrapping machine increases weekly output (column 2) by 16,000 candies and average labor productivity (column 4) by 200 candies wrapped per hour.

TABLE 7.2
Capital, Output, and Productivity in the Candy-Wrapping Factory

(1) Number of machines (capital)	(2) Total number of candies wrapped each week (output)	(3) Total hours worked per week	(4) Candies wrapped per hour worked (productivity)
0	16,000	80	200
1	32,000	80	400
2	40,000	80	500
3	40,000	80	500

The second point illustrated by Table 7.2 is that the more capital that is already in place, the smaller the benefits of adding extra capital. Notice that the first machine adds 16,000 candies to total output, but the second machine adds only 8,000. The third machine, which cannot be used since there are only two workers, does not increase output or productivity at all. This result illustrates a general principle of economics, called **diminishing returns to capital:** If the amount of labor and other inputs employed is held constant, then the greater the amount of capital already in use, the less an additional unit of capital adds to production. In the case of the candy-wrapping factory, diminishing returns to capital imply that the first candy-wrapping machine acquired adds more output than the second, which in turn adds more output than the third.

Diminishing returns to capital are a natural consequence of firms' incentive to use each piece of capital as productively as possible. To maximize output, managers will assign the first machine that a firm acquires to the most productive use available, the next machine to the next most productive use, and so on—an illustration of the Principle of Increasing Opportunity Cost. When many machines are available, all the highly productive ways of using them already have been exploited. Thus, adding yet another machine will not raise output or productivity by very much. If Lucy and Ethel are already operating two candy-wrapping machines, there is little point to buying a third machine, except perhaps as a replacement or spare.

The implications of Table 7.2 can be applied to the question of how to stimulate economic growth. First, increasing the amount of capital available to the workforce will tend to increase output and average labor productivity. The more adequately equipped workers are, the more productive they will be. Second, the degree to which productivity can be increased by an expanding stock of capital is limited. Because of diminishing returns to capital, an economy in which the quantity of capital available to each worker is already very high will not benefit much from further expansion of the capital stock.

Is there empirical evidence that giving workers more capital makes them more productive? Figure 7.5 shows the relationship between average labor productivity (real GDP per worker) in 1990 and the amount of capital per worker in 15 countries. The figure shows a strong relationship between the amounts of capital per worker and productivity, consistent with the theory. Note, though, that the relationship between capital and productivity is somewhat weaker for the richest countries. For example, Germany has more capital per worker than the United States, but German workers are less productive than American workers on average. Diminishing returns to capital may help to explain the weakening of the relationship between capital and productivity at high levels of capital. In addition, Figure 7.5 does not account for many other differences among countries, such as differences in economic systems or government policies. Thus, we should not expect to see a perfect relationship between the two variables.

diminishing returns to capital
if the amount of labor and other inputs employed is held constant, then the greater the amount of capital already in use, the less an additional unit of capital adds to production

Increasing Opportunity Cost

FIGURE 7.5

Average Labor Productivity and Capital per Worker in 15 Countries, 1990.

Countries with large amounts of capital per worker also tend to have high average labor productivity, as measured by real GDP per worker.

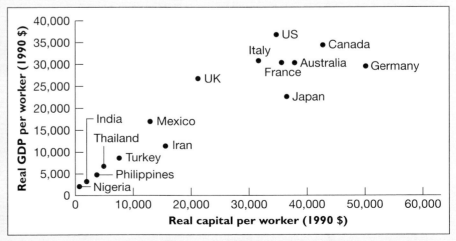

SOURCE: Penn World Tables, The National Bureau of Economic Research, www.nber.org.

LAND AND OTHER NATURAL RESOURCES

Besides capital goods, other inputs to production help to make workers more productive, among them land, energy, and raw materials. Fertile land is essential to agriculture, and modern manufacturing processes make intensive use of energy and raw materials.

In general, an abundance of natural resources increases the productivity of the workers who use them. For example, a farmer can produce a much larger crop in a land-rich country like the United States or Australia than in a country where the soil is poor or arable land is limited in supply. With the aid of modern farm machinery, a form of physical capital, and great expanses of land, today's American farmers are so productive that even though they constitute less than 3 percent of the population, they provide enough food not only to feed the country but to export to the rest of the world.

Although there are limits to a country's supply of arable land, many other natural resources, such as petroleum and metals, can be obtained through international markets. Because resources can be obtained through trade, countries need not possess large quantities of natural resources within their own borders to achieve economic growth. Indeed, a number of countries have become rich without substantial natural resources of their own, including Japan, Hong Kong, Singapore, and Switzerland. Just as important as possessing natural resources is the ability to use them productively—for example, by means of advanced technologies.

TECHNOLOGY

Besides human capital, physical capital, and natural resources, a country's ability to develop and apply new, more productive technologies will help to determine its productivity. Consider just one industry, transportation. Two centuries ago, as suggested by the quote from Stephen Ambrose in the beginning of the chapter, the horse and wagon were the primary means of transportation—a slow and costly method indeed. But in the nineteenth century, technological advances such as the steam engine supported the expansion of riverborne transportation and the development of a national rail network. In the twentieth century, the invention of the internal combustion engine and the development of aviation, supported by the construction of an extensive infrastructure of roads and airports, produced increasingly rapid, cheap, and reliable transport. Technological change has clearly been a driving force in the transportation revolution.

New technologies can improve productivity in industries other than the one in which they are introduced. For instance, in the late eighteenth century, American farmers could sell their produce only in local and regional markets. Now the availability of rapid shipping and refrigerated transport allows American farmers to sell their products virtually anywhere in the world. With a broader market in which to sell, farmers can specialize in those products best suited to local land and weather conditions. Similarly, factories can obtain their raw materials wherever they are cheapest and most abundant, produce the goods they are most efficient at manufacturing, and sell their products wherever they will fetch the best price. Both these examples illustrate the Principle of Comparative Advantage, that overall productivity increases when producers concentrate on those activities at which they are relatively most efficient.

Comparative Advantage

Numerous other technological developments have led to increased productivity, including advances in communication and medicine and the introduction of computer technology. All indications are that the Internet has had and will continue to have a major impact on the U.S. economy, not just in retailing but in many other sectors. In fact, *most economists would probably agree that new technologies are the single most important source of productivity improvement,* and hence of economic growth in general.

However, economic growth does not automatically follow from breakthroughs in basic science. To make the best use of new knowledge, an economy needs entrepreneurs who can exploit scientific advances commercially, as well as a legal and political environment that encourages the practical application of new knowledge.

CONCEPT CHECK 7.4

A new kind of wrapping paper has been invented that makes candy-wrapping quicker and easier. The use of this paper *increases* the number of candies a person can wrap by hand by 200 per hour, and the number of candies a person can wrap by machine by 300 per hour. Using the data from Examples 7.3 and 7.5, construct a table like Table 7.2 that shows how this technological advance affects average labor productivity. Do diminishing returns to capital still hold?

| Labor Productivity | EXAMPLE 7.6 |

Why has U.S. labor productivity grown so rapidly since 1995?

During the 1950s and 1960s, most industrialized countries experienced rapid growth in real GDP and average labor productivity. Between 1947 and 1973, for example, U.S. labor productivity grew by 2.8 percent per year.[2] Between 1973 and 1995, however, labor productivity growth in the United States fell by half, to 1.4 percent per year. Other countries experienced similar productivity slowdowns, and many articles and books were written trying to uncover the reasons. In recent years, however, there has been a rebound in productivity growth, particularly in the United States. Between 1995 and 2010, U.S. labor productivity growth averaged 2.6 percent per year. What caused this resurgence in productivity growth? Can it be sustained?

Economists agree that the pickup in productivity growth was the product of rapid technological progress and increased investment in new information and communication technologies (ICT). Research indicates that productivity has grown rapidly in both those industries that *produce* ICT, such as silicon chips and fiber optics, and those industries that *use* ICT. The application of these advances had ripple effects in areas ranging from automobile production to retail inventory management. The rapid growth of the Internet, for example, made it possible for consumers to shop and find information online. But it also helped companies improve their efficiency by improving coordination between manufacturers and their suppliers. On the other hand, there has been no acceleration in labor productivity growth in those industries that neither produce nor use much ICT.[3]

Optimists argue that advances in mobile computing, communications, biotechnology, and other ICT fields will allow productivity growth to continue at this elevated rate. Others are more cautious, arguing that the increases in productivity growth from these developments may be temporary rather than permanent. A great deal is riding on which view will turn out to be correct.

ENTREPRENEURSHIP AND MANAGEMENT

entrepreneurs people who create new economic enterprises

The productivity of workers depends in part on the people who help to decide what to produce and how to produce it: entrepreneurs and managers. **Entrepreneurs** are people who create new economic enterprises. Because of the new products, services, technological processes, and production methods they introduce, entrepreneurs are critical to a dynamic,

---

[2]Data refer to labor productivity growth in the nonfarm business sector and can be found at www.bls.gov.
[3]Kevin J. Stiroh, "Information Technology and the U.S. Productivity Revival: What Do the Industry Data Say?" *American Economic Review* 92 (December 2002), pp. 1559–76.

healthy economy. In the late nineteenth and early twentieth centuries, individuals like Henry Ford and Alfred Sloan (automobiles), Andrew Carnegie (steel), John D. Rockefeller (oil), and J. P. Morgan (finance) played central roles in the development of American industry—and, not incidentally, amassed huge personal fortunes in the process. These people and others like them (including contemporary entrepreneurs like Bill Gates) have been criticized for some of their business practices, in some cases with justification. Clearly, though, they and dozens of other prominent business leaders of the past century have contributed significantly to the growth of the U.S. economy. Henry Ford, for example, developed the idea of mass production, which lowered costs sufficiently to bring automobiles within reach of the average American family. Ford began his business in his garage, a tradition that has been maintained by thousands of innovators ever since. Larry Page and Sergey Brin, the cofounders of Google, revolutionized the way college students and many professionals conduct research by developing a method to prioritize the list of websites obtained in a search of the Internet.

Entrepreneurship, like any form of creativity, is difficult to teach, although some of the supporting skills, like financial analysis and marketing, can be learned in college or business school. How, then, does a society encourage entrepreneurship? History suggests that the entrepreneurial spirit will always exist; the challenge to society is to channel entrepreneurial energies in economically productive ways. For example, economic policymakers need to ensure that taxation is not so heavy, and regulation not so inflexible, that small businesses—some of which will eventually become big businesses—cannot get off the ground. Sociological factors may play a role as well. Societies in which business and commerce are considered to be beneath the dignity of refined, educated people are less likely to produce successful entrepreneurs. In the United States, for the most part, business has been viewed as a respectable activity. Overall, a social and economic milieu that allows entrepreneurship to flourish appears to promote economic growth and rising productivity, perhaps especially so in high-technology eras like our own.

Inventing the Personal Computer   EXAMPLE 7.7

Does entrepreneurship pay?

In 1975 Steve Jobs and Steve Wozniak were two 20-year-olds who designed computer games for Atari. They had an idea to make a computer that was smaller and cheaper than the closet-sized mainframes that were then in use. To set up shop in Steve Jobs's parents' garage and buy their supplies, they sold their two most valuable possessions, Jobs's used Volkswagen van and Wozniak's Hewlett-Packard scientific calculator, for a total of $1,300. The result was the first personal computer, which they named after their new company (and Jobs's favorite fruit): Apple. The rest is history. Clearly, Jobs's and Wozniak's average labor productivity as the inventors of the personal computer eventually became many times what it was when they designed computer games. Creative entrepreneurship can increase productivity just like additional capital or land.

The Economic Naturalist 7.1

Why did medieval China stagnate economically?

The Sung period in China (A.D. 960–1270) was one of considerable technological sophistication; its inventions included paper, waterwheels, water clocks, gunpowder, and possibly the compass. Yet no significant industrialization occurred, and in subsequent centuries Europe saw more economic growth and technological innovation than China. Why did medieval China stagnate economically?

According to research by economist William Baumol,[4] the main impediment to industrialization during the Sung period was a social system that inhibited entrepreneurship. Commerce and industry were considered low-status activities, not fit for an educated person. In addition, the emperor had the right to seize his subjects' property and to take control of their business enterprises—a right that greatly reduced his subjects' incentives to undertake business ventures. The most direct path to status and riches in medieval China was to go through a system of demanding civil service examinations given by the government every three years. The highest scorers on these national examinations were granted lifetime positions in the imperial bureaucracy, where they wielded much power and often became wealthy, in part through corruption. Not surprisingly, medieval China did not develop a dynamic entrepreneurial class, and consequently its scientific and technological advantages did not translate into sustained economic growth. China's experience shows why scientific advances alone cannot guarantee economic growth; to have economic benefits, scientific knowledge must be commercially applied through new products and new, more efficient means of producing goods and services.

Although entrepreneurship may be more glamorous, managers—the people who run businesses on a daily basis—also play an important role in determining average labor productivity. Managerial jobs span a wide range of positions, from the supervisor of the loading dock to the CEO (chief executive officer) at the helm of a *Fortune* 500 company. Managers work to satisfy customers, deal with suppliers, organize production, obtain financing, assign workers to jobs, and motivate them to work hard and effectively. Such activities enhance labor productivity. For example, in the 1970s and 1980s, Japanese managers introduced new production methods that greatly increased the efficiency of Japanese manufacturing plants. Among them was the *just-in-time* inventory system, in which suppliers deliver production components to the factory just when they are needed, eliminating the need for factories to stockpile components. Japanese managers also pioneered the idea of organizing workers into semi-independent production teams, which allowed workers more flexibility and responsibility than the traditional assembly line. Managers in the United States and other countries studied the Japanese managerial techniques closely and adopted many of them.

THE POLITICAL AND LEGAL ENVIRONMENT

So far we have emphasized the role of the private sector in increasing average labor productivity. But government too has a role to play in fostering improved productivity. One of the key contributions government can make is to provide a *political and legal environment* that encourages people to behave in economically productive ways—to work hard, save and invest wisely, acquire useful information and skills, and provide the goods and services that the public demands.

One specific function of government that appears to be crucial to economic success is the establishment of *well-defined property rights*. Property rights are well defined when the law provides clear rules for determining who owns what resources (through a system of deeds and titles, for example) and how those resources can be used. Imagine living in a society in which a dictator, backed by the military and the police, could take whatever he wanted, and regularly did so. In such a country, what incentive would you have to raise a large crop or to produce other valuable goods and services? Very little, since much of what you produced would likely be taken away from you. Unfortunately, in many countries of the world today, this situation is far from hypothetical.

Political and legal conditions affect the growth of productivity in other ways, as well. Political scientists and economists have documented the fact that *political*

---

[4]"Entrepreneurship: Productive, Unproductive, and Destructive," *Journal of Political Economy,* October 1990, pp. 893–921.

instability can be detrimental to economic growth. This finding is reasonable, since entrepreneurs and savers are unlikely to invest their resources in a country whose government is unstable, particularly if the struggle for power involves civil unrest, terrorism, or guerrilla warfare. On the other hand, a political system that promotes the *free and open exchange of ideas* will speed the development of new technologies and products. For example, some economic historians have suggested that the decline of Spain as an economic power was due in part to the advent of the Spanish Inquisition, which permitted no dissent from religious orthodoxy. Because of the Inquisition's persecution of those whose theories about the natural world contradicted Church doctrine, Spanish science and technology languished, and Spain fell behind more tolerant nations like the Netherlands.

CONCEPT CHECK 7.5

A Bangladeshi worker who immigrates to America is likely to find that his average labor productivity is much higher in the United States than it was at home. The worker is, of course, the same person he was when he lived in Bangladesh. How can the simple act of moving to the United States increase the worker's productivity? What does your answer say about the incentive to immigrate?

An Economic Look at Communism   EXAMPLE 7.8

Why did communism fail?

For more than 70 years, from the Russian revolution in 1917 until the collapse of the Soviet Union in 1991, communism was believed by many to pose a major challenge to market-based economic systems. Yet, by the time of the Soviet Union's breakup, the poor economic record of communism had become apparent. Indeed, low living standards in communist countries, compared to those achieved in the West, were a major reason for the popular discontent that brought down the communist system in Europe. Economically speaking, why did communism fail?

The poor growth records of the Soviet Union and other communist countries did not reflect a lack of resources or economic potential. The Soviet Union had a highly educated workforce; a large capital stock; a vast quantity of natural resources, including land and energy; and access to sophisticated technologies. Yet, at the time of its collapse, output per person in the Soviet Union was probably less than one-seventh what it was in the United States.

Most observers would agree that the political and legal environment that established the structure of the communist economic system was a major cause of its ultimate failure. The economic system of the Soviet Union and other communist countries had two main elements: First, the capital stock and other resources were owned by the government rather than by individuals or private corporations. Second, most decisions regarding production and distribution were made and implemented by a government planning agency rather than by individuals and firms interacting through markets. This system performed poorly, we now understand, for several reasons.

One major problem was *the absence of private property rights.* With no ability to acquire a significant amount of private property, Soviet citizens had little incentive to behave in economically productive ways. The owner of an American or Japanese firm is strongly motivated to cut costs and to produce goods that are highly valued by the public because the owner's income is determined by the firm's profitability. In contrast, the performance of a Soviet firm manager was judged on whether the manager produced the quantities of goods specified by the government's plan—irrespective of the quality of the goods produced or whether consumers wanted them. Soviet managers had little incentive to reduce costs or produce better, more highly valued products, as any extra profits would accrue to the government and not to the manager; nor were there any opportunities for entrepreneurs to start new businesses. Likewise, workers had little reason to work hard or effectively under the communist system, as pay rates were determined by the government planning agency rather than by the economic value of what the workers produced.

A second major weakness of the communist system was the *absence of free markets.* In centrally planned economies, markets are replaced by detailed government plans that specify what should be produced and how. But, as illustrated by the example of New York City's food supply (in the chapter *Supply and Demand*), the coordination of even relatively basic economic activities can be extremely complex and require a great deal of information, much of which is dispersed among many people. In a market system, changes in prices both convey information about the goods and services people want and provide suppliers the incentives to bring these goods and services to market. Indeed, as we know from the Equilibrium Principle, a market in equilibrium leaves individuals with no unexploited opportunities. Central planners in communist countries proved far less able to deal with this complexity than decentralized markets. As a result, under communism consumers suffered constant shortages and shoddy goods.

| Equilibrium |

After the collapse of communism, many formerly communist countries began the difficult transition to a market-oriented economic system. Changing an entire economic system (the most extreme example of a *structural policy*) is a slow and difficult task, and many countries saw economic conditions worsen at first rather than improve. *Political instability* and the absence of a modern *legal framework,* particularly laws applying to commercial transactions, have often hampered the progress of reforms. However, a number of formerly communist countries, including Poland, the Czech Republic, and the former East Germany, have succeeded in implementing Western-style market systems and have begun to achieve significant economic growth.

| **RECAP** | **DETERMINANTS OF AVERAGE LABOR PRODUCTIVITY** |

- Key factors determining average labor productivity in a country include:

    The skills and training of workers, called *human capital.*

    The quantity and quality of *physical capital*—machines, equipment, and buildings.

    The availability of land and other *natural resources.*

    The sophistication of the *technologies* applied in production.

    The effectiveness of *management* and *entrepreneurship.*

    The broad *social and legal environment.*

- Labor productivity growth slowed throughout the industrialized world in the 1970s and 1980s. Between 1995 and 2010, labor productivity rebounded (especially in the United States), largely because of advances in information and communication technology. Since 2010, labor productivity in the U.S. has again slowed, but it remains to be seen if this is a temporary effect of the last recession or the beginning of a new period of slowdown in labor productivity.

PROMOTING ECONOMIC GROWTH

If a society decides to try to raise its rate of economic growth, what are some of the measures that policymakers might take to achieve this objective? Here is a short list of suggestions, based on our discussion of the factors that contribute to growth in average labor productivity and, hence, output per person.

POLICIES TO INCREASE HUMAN CAPITAL

Because skilled and well-educated workers are more productive than unskilled labor, governments in most countries try to increase the human capital of their citizens by supporting education and training programs. In the United States, government provides public education through high school and grants extensive support to postsecondary schools, including technical schools, colleges, and universities. Publicly funded early intervention programs like Head Start also attempt to build human capital by helping disadvantaged children prepare for school. To a lesser degree than some other countries, the U.S. government also funds job training for unskilled youths and retraining for workers whose skills have become obsolete.

The Economic Naturalist 7.2

Why do almost all countries provide free public education?

All industrial countries provide their citizens free public education through high school, and most subsidize college and other postsecondary schools. Why?

Americans are so used to the idea of free public education that this question may seem odd. But why should the government provide free education when it does not provide even more essential goods and services such as food or medical care for free, except to the most needy? Furthermore, educational services can be, and indeed commonly are, supplied and demanded on the private market, without the aid of the government.

An important argument for free or at least subsidized education is that the private demand curve for educational services does not include all the social benefits of education. (Recall the Equilibrium Principle, which states in part that a market in equilibrium may not exploit all gains achievable from collective action.) For example, the democratic political system relies on an educated citizenry to operate effectively—a factor that an individual demander of educational services has little reason to consider. From a narrower economic perspective, we might argue that individuals do not capture the full economic returns from their schooling. For example, people with high human capital, and thus high earnings, pay more taxes—funds that can be used to finance government services and aid the less fortunate. Because of income taxation, the private benefit to acquiring human capital is less than the social benefit, and the demand for education on the private market may be less than optimal from society's viewpoint. Similarly, educated people are more likely than others to contribute to technological development, and hence to general productivity growth, which may benefit many other people besides themselves. Finally, another argument for public support of education is that poor people who would like to invest in human capital may not be able to do so because of insufficient income.

The Nobel laureate Milton Friedman, among many economists, suggested that these arguments may justify government grants, called educational *vouchers,* to help citizens purchase educational services in the private sector, but they do *not* justify the government providing education directly, as through the public school system. Defenders of public education, on the other hand, argue that the government should have some direct control over education in order to set standards and monitor quality. What do you think?

○━━ | **Equilibrium** |

Why do almost all countries provide free public education?

POLICIES THAT PROMOTE SAVING AND INVESTMENT

Average labor productivity increases when workers can utilize a sizable and modern capital stock. To support the creation of new capital, government can encourage high rates of saving and investment in the private sector.

Many provisions in the U.S. tax code are designed expressly to stimulate households to save and firms to invest. For example, a household that opens an Individual Retirement Account (IRA) is able to save for retirement without paying taxes on either the funds deposited in the IRA or the interest earned on the account. (However, taxes are due when the funds are withdrawn at retirement.) The intent of IRA legislation is to make saving more financially attractive to American households. Similarly, at various times Congress has instituted an investment tax credit, which reduces the tax bills of firms that invest in new capital. (Private-sector saving and investment are discussed in greater detail in the chapter *Saving, Capital Formation, and Financial Markets.*)

Government can contribute directly to capital formation through *public investment,* or the creation of government-owned capital. Public investment includes the building of roads, bridges, airports, dams, and, in some countries, energy and communications networks. The construction of the U.S. interstate highway system, begun during the administration of President Eisenhower, is often cited as an example of successful public investment. The interstate system substantially reduced long-haul transportation costs in the United States, improving productivity throughout the economy.

Today, the expansion of high-speed data connection through fiber optic cables is having a similar effect. This project, too, received crucial government funding in its early stages. Many research studies have confirmed that government investment in the *infrastructure,* the public capital that supports private-sector economic activities, can be a significant source of growth.

POLICIES THAT SUPPORT RESEARCH AND DEVELOPMENT

Productivity is enhanced by technological progress, which in turn requires investment in research and development (R&D). In many industries, private firms have adequate incentive to conduct research and development activities. There is no need, for example, for the government to finance research for developing a better underarm deodorant.

But some types of knowledge, particularly basic scientific knowledge, may have widespread economic benefits that cannot be captured by a single private firm. The developers of the silicon computer chip, for example, were instrumental in creating huge new industries, yet they received only a small portion of the profits flowing from their inventions.

Because society in general, rather than the individual inventors, may receive much of the benefit from basic research, government may need to support basic research, as it does through agencies such as the National Science Foundation. The federal government also sponsors a great deal of applied research, particularly in military and space applications. To the extent that national security allows, the government can increase growth by sharing the fruits of such research with the private sector. For example, the Global Positioning System (GPS), which was developed originally for military purposes, is now available in private passenger vehicles, helping drivers find their way.

THE LEGAL AND POLITICAL FRAMEWORK

Although economic growth comes primarily from activities in the private sector, the government plays an essential role in providing the framework within which the private sector can operate productively. We have discussed the importance of secure property rights and a well-functioning legal system, of an economic environment that encourages entrepreneurship, and of political stability and the free and open exchange of ideas. Government policymakers also should consider the potential effects of tax and regulatory policies on activities that increase productivity, such as investment, innovation, and risk taking.

THE POOREST COUNTRIES: A SPECIAL CASE?

Radical disparities in living standards exist between the richest and poorest countries of the world. Achieving economic growth in the poorest countries is thus particularly urgent. Are the policy prescriptions of this section relevant to those countries, or are very different types of measures necessary to spur growth in the poorest nations?

To a significant extent, the same factors and policies that promote growth in richer countries apply to the poorest countries as well. Increasing human capital by supporting education and training, increasing rates of saving and investment, investing in public capital and infrastructure, supporting research and development, and encouraging entrepreneurship are all measures that will enhance economic growth in poor countries.

However, to a much greater degree than in richer countries, most poor countries need to improve the legal and political environment that underpins their economies. For example, many developing countries have poorly developed or corrupt legal systems, which discourage entrepreneurship and investment by creating uncertainty about property rights.

Taxation and regulation in developing countries are often heavy-handed and administered by inefficient bureaucracies, to the extent that it may take months or years to obtain the approvals needed to start a small business or expand a factory. In many poor countries, excessive government regulation or government ownership of companies prevents markets from operating efficiently to achieve economic growth. For example, government regulation, rather than the market, may determine the allocation of bank credit or the prices for agricultural products.

Structural policies that aim to ameliorate these problems are important preconditions for generating growth in the poorest countries. But probably most important—and most difficult, for some countries—is establishing political stability and the rule of law. Without political stability, domestic and foreign savers will be reluctant to invest in the country, and economic growth will be difficult if not impossible to achieve.

Can rich countries help poor countries to develop? Historically, richer nations have tried to help by providing financial aid through loans or grants from individual countries (foreign aid) or by loans made by international agencies such as the World Bank. Experience has shown, however, that financial aid to countries that do not undertake structural reforms, such as reducing excessive regulation or improving the legal system, is of limited value. To make their foreign aid most effective, rich countries should help poor countries achieve political stability and undertake the necessary reforms to the structure of their economies.

THINKING ABOUT THE COSTS OF ECONOMIC GROWTH

In this chapter (and earlier, in the chapter *Spending, Income, and GDP*), we emphasized the positive effects of economic growth on the average person's living standard. But should societies always strive for the highest possible rate of economic growth? The answer is no. Even if we accept for the moment the idea that increased output per person is always desirable, attaining a higher rate of economic growth does impose costs on society.

What are the costs of increasing economic growth? The most straightforward is the cost of creating new capital. We know that by expanding the capital stock we can increase future productivity and output. But, to increase the capital stock, we must divert resources that could otherwise be used to increase the supply of consumer goods. For example, to add more robot-operated assembly lines, a society must employ more of its skilled technicians in building industrial robots and fewer in designing video games. To build new factories, more carpenters and lumber must be assigned to factory construction and less to finishing basements or renovating family rooms. In short, high rates of investment in new capital require people to tighten their belts, consume less, and save more—a real economic cost.

Should a country undertake a high rate of investment in capital goods at the sacrifice of consumer goods? The answer depends on the extent that people are willing and able to sacrifice consumption today to have a bigger economic pie tomorrow. In a country that is very poor, or is experiencing an economic crisis, people may prefer to keep consumption relatively high and savings and investment relatively low. The midst of a thunderstorm is not the time to be putting something aside for a rainy day! But in a society that is relatively well off, people may be more willing to make sacrifices to achieve higher economic growth in the future.

Consumption sacrificed to capital formation is not the only cost of achieving higher growth. In the United States in the nineteenth and early twentieth centuries, periods of rapid economic growth were often times in which many people worked extremely long hours at dangerous and unpleasant jobs. While those workers helped to build the economy that Americans enjoy today, the costs were great in terms of reduced leisure time and, in some cases, workers' health and safety. Today we continue to see these trade-offs between the costs and benefits of economic growth in many developing nations around the world.

Other costs of growth include the cost of the research and development that is required to improve technology and the costs of acquiring training and skill (human capital). The fact that a higher living standard tomorrow must be purchased at the cost of current sacrifices is an example of the Scarcity Principle, that having more of one good thing usually means having less of another. Because achieving higher economic growth imposes real economic costs, we know from the Cost-Benefit Principle that higher growth should be pursued only if the benefits outweigh the costs.

| Scarcity |
| Cost-Benefit |

ARE THERE LIMITS TO GROWTH?

Earlier in this chapter, we saw that even relatively low rates of economic growth, if sustained for a long period, will produce huge increases in the size of the economy. This fact raises the question of whether economic growth can continue indefinitely without depleting natural resources and causing massive damage to the global environment.

The concern that economic growth may not be sustainable is not a new one. An influential 1972 book, *The Limits to Growth*,[5] reported the results of computer simulations that suggested that unless population growth and economic expansion were halted, the world would soon be running out of natural resources, drinkable water, and breathable air. This book, and later works in the same vein, raise some fundamental questions that cannot be done full justice here. However, in some ways its conclusions are misleading.

One problem with the "limits to growth" thesis lies in its underlying concept of economic growth. Those who emphasize the environmental limits on growth assume implicitly that economic growth will always take the form of more of what we have now—more smoky factories, more polluting cars, more fast-food restaurants. If that were indeed the case, then surely there would be limits to the growth the planet can sustain.

But growth in real GDP does not necessarily take such a form. Increases in real GDP also can arise from new or higher-quality products. For example, not too long ago tennis rackets were relatively simple items made primarily of wood. Today they are made of newly invented synthetic materials and designed for optimum performance using sophisticated computer simulations. Because these new high-tech tennis rackets are more valued by consumers than the old wooden ones, their introduction increased real GDP. Likewise, the introduction of new pharmaceuticals has contributed to economic growth, as have the expanded number of TV channels, digital sound, and Internet-based sales. Thus, economic growth need not take the form of more and more of the same old stuff; it can mean newer, better, and perhaps cleaner and more efficient goods and services.

A second problem with the "limits to growth" conclusion is that it overlooks the fact that increased wealth and productivity expand society's capacity to take measures to safeguard the environment. In fact, the most polluted countries in the world are not the richest but those that are in a relatively early stage of industrialization. At this stage countries must devote the bulk of their resources to basic needs—food, shelter, health care—and continued industrial expansion. In these countries, clean air and water may be viewed as a luxury rather than a basic need. In more economically developed countries, where the most basic needs are more easily met, extra resources are available to keep the environment clean. Thus, continuing economic growth may lead to less, not more, pollution.

A third problem with the pessimistic view of economic growth is that it ignores the power of the market and other social mechanisms to deal with scarcity. During the

[5]Donella H. Meadows, Dennis L. Meadows, Jørgen Randers, and William W. Behrens III, *The Limits to Growth* (New York: New American Library, 1972).

oil-supply disruptions of the 1970s, newspapers were filled with headlines about the energy crisis and the imminent depletion of world oil supplies. Yet 30 years later, the world's known oil reserves are actually *greater* than they were in the 1970s.[6]

Today's energy situation is so much better than was expected 30 years ago because the market went to work. Reduced oil supplies led to an increase in prices that changed the behavior of both demanders and suppliers. Consumers insulated their homes, purchased more energy-efficient cars and appliances, and switched to alternative sources of energy. Suppliers engaged in a massive hunt for new reserves, opening up major new sources in Latin America, the North Sea, and more recently North America's large shale oil deposits. In short, market forces helped society respond effectively to the energy crisis.

In general, shortages in any resource will trigger price changes that induce suppliers and demanders to deal with the problem. Simply extrapolating current economic trends into the future ignores the power of the market system to recognize shortages and make the necessary corrections. Government actions spurred by political pressures, such as the allocation of public funds to preserve open space or reduce air pollution, can be expected to supplement market adjustments.

Despite the shortcomings of the "limits to growth" perspective, most economists would agree that not all the problems created by economic growth can be dealt with effectively through the market or the political process. Global environmental problems, such as global warming or the ongoing destruction of rain forests, are a particular challenge for existing economic and political institutions. Environmental quality is not bought and sold in markets and thus will not automatically reach its optimal level through market processes (recall the Equilibrium Principle). Nor can local or national governments effectively address problems that are global in scope. Unless international mechanisms are established for dealing with global environmental problems, these problems may become worse as economic growth continues.

> **Equilibrium**

Air Pollution in Mexico   `EXAMPLE 7.9`

Why is the air quality so poor in Mexico City?

Developing countries like Mexico, which are neither fully industrialized nor desperately poor, often have severe environmental problems. Why?

One concern about economic growth is that it will cause ever-increasing levels of environmental pollution. Empirical studies show, however, that the relationship between pollution and real GDP per person is more like an inverted U (see Figure 7.6). In other words, as countries move from very low levels of real GDP per person to "middle-income" levels, most measures of pollution tend to worsen, but environmental quality improves as real GDP per person rises even further. One study of the relationship between air quality and real GDP per person found that the level of real GDP per person at which air quality is the worst—indicated by point A in Figure 7.6—is roughly equal to the average income level in Mexico.[7] And indeed, the air quality in Mexico City is exceptionally poor, as any visitor to that sprawling metropolis can attest.

That pollution may worsen as a country industrializes is understandable, but why does environmental quality improve when real GDP per person climbs to very high levels? There are a variety of explanations for this phenomenon. Compared to middle-income economies, the richer economies are relatively more concentrated in "clean," high-value services like finance and software production as opposed to pollution-intensive industries like heavy manufacturing. Rich economies are also more likely to have the expertise to

---

[6]The U.S. is currently the world's largest oil producer, having overtaken Saudi Arabia and Russia.
[7]Gene M. Grossman and Alan B. Krueger, "Environmental Impacts of a North American Free Trade Agreement," in Peter Garber, ed., *The Mexico–U.S. Free Trade Agreement* (Cambridge, MA: MIT Press, 1993). See also Grossman and Krueger, "Economic Growth and the Environment," *Quarterly Journal of Economics,* May 1995, pp. 353–78; and World Bank, *World Development Report: Development and the Environment,* 1992.

FIGURE 7.6

The Relationship between Air Pollution and Real GDP per Person.

Empirically, air pollution increases with real GDP per person up to a point and then begins to decline. Maximum air pollution (point *A*) occurs at a level of real GDP per person roughly equal to that of Mexico.

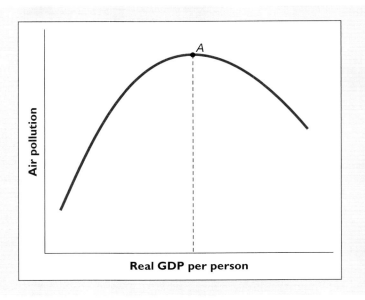

Scarcity

develop sophisticated and cost-effective antipollution technologies. The most important reason richer economies tend to be cleaner is the same reason that the homes of rich people are generally cleaner and in better condition than the homes of the poor. As income rises above the level necessary to fulfill basic needs, more resources remain to dedicate to "luxuries" like a clean environment (the Scarcity Principle). For the rich family, the extra resources will pay for a cleaning service; for the rich country, they will pay for pollution control devices in factories and on automobiles. Indeed, antipollution laws are generally tougher and more strictly enforced in rich countries than in middle-income and poor countries.

RECAP	ECONOMIC GROWTH: BENEFITS AND COSTS

- Policies for promoting economic growth include policies to increase human capital (education and training); policies that promote saving and capital formation; policies that support research and development; and the provision of a legal and political framework within which the private sector can operate productively. Deficiencies in the legal and political framework (for example, official corruption or poorly defined property rights) are a special problem for many developing countries.

- Economic growth has substantial costs, notably the sacrifice of current consumption that is required to free resources for creating new capital and new technologies. Higher rates of growth should be pursued only if the benefits outweigh the costs.

- Some have argued that finite resources imply ultimate limits to economic growth. This view overlooks the facts that growth can take the form of better, rather than more, goods and services; that increased wealth frees resources to safeguard the environment; and that political and economic mechanisms exist to address many of the problems associated with growth. However, these mechanisms may not work well when environmental or other problems arising from economic growth are global in scope.

○ SUMMARY ○

- Over the past two centuries, the industrialized nations saw enormous improvements in living standards, as reflected in large increases in real GDP per person. Because of the power of compound interest, relatively small differences in growth rates, if continued over long periods, can produce large differences in real GDP per person and average living standards. Thus, the rate of long-term economic growth is an economic variable of critical importance. *(LO1)*

- Real GDP per person is the product of average labor productivity (real GDP per employed worker) and the share of the population that is employed. Growth in real GDP per person can occur only through growth in average labor productivity, in the share of the population that is working, or both. In the period since 1960, increases in the share of the U.S. population holding a job contributed significantly to rising real GDP per person. But in the past four decades, as in most periods, the main source of the increase in real GDP per person was rising average labor productivity. *(LO2)*

- Among the factors that determine labor productivity are the talents, education, training, and skills of workers, or human capital; the quantity and quality of the physical capital that workers use; the availability of land and other natural resources; the application of technology to the production and distribution of goods and services; the effectiveness of entrepreneurs and managers; and the broad social and legal environment. Because of diminishing returns to capital, beyond a certain point expansion of the capital stock is not the most effective way to increase average labor productivity. Economists generally agree that new technologies are the most important single source of improvements in productivity. *(LO3)*

- In the 1970s and 1980s, the industrial world experienced a slowdown in productivity growth, but productivity growth rebounded between 1995 and 2010, largely as a result of advances in information and communication technology. *(LO3)*

- Among the ways in which government can stimulate economic growth are by adopting policies that encourage the creation of human capital; that promote saving and investment, including public investment in infrastructure; that support research and development, particularly in the basic sciences; and that provide a legal and political framework that supports private-sector activities. The poorest countries, with poorly developed legal, tax, and regulatory systems, are often in the greatest need of an improved legal and political framework and increased political stability. *(LO4)*

- Economic growth has costs as well as benefits. Prominent among them is the need to sacrifice current consumption to achieve a high rate of investment in new capital goods; other costs of growing more quickly include extra work effort and the costs of research and development. Thus, more economic growth is not necessarily better; whether increased economic growth is desirable depends on whether the benefits of growth outweigh the costs. *(LO5)*

- Are there limits to growth? Arguments that economic growth must be constrained by environmental problems and the limits of natural resources ignore the fact that economic growth can take the form of increasing quality as well as increasing quantity. Indeed, increases in output can provide additional resources for cleaning up the environment. Finally, the market system, together with political processes, can solve many of the problems associated with economic growth. On the other hand, global environmental problems, which can be handled neither by the market nor by individual national governments, have the potential to constrain economic growth. *(LO5)*

○ KEY TERMS ○

average labor productivity	diminishing returns to	entrepreneurs
compound interest	capital	human capital

○ REVIEW QUESTIONS ○

1. What has happened to real GDP per person over the past century? What implications does this have for the average person? Are the implications different for countries in different regions (e.g., Japan versus Ghana)? *(LO1)*

2. Why do economists consider growth in average labor productivity to be the key factor in determining long-run living standards? *(LO2)*

3. What is *human capital*? Why is it economically important? How is new human capital created? *(LO3)*

4. You have employed five workers of varying physical strength to dig a ditch. Workers without shovels have zero productivity in ditchdigging. How should you assign shovels to workers if you don't have enough shovels to go around? How should you assign any additional shovels that you obtain? Using this example, discuss (a) the relationship between the availability of physical capital and average labor productivity and (b) the concept of diminishing returns to capital. *(LO3)*

5. What was the cause of the resurgence in U.S. labor productivity growth since 1995? How do we know? *(LO3)*

6. Discuss how talented entrepreneurs and effective managers can enhance average labor productivity. *(LO3)*

7. What major contributions can the government make to the goal of increasing average labor productivity? *(LO4)*

8. Discuss the following statement: "Because the environment is fragile and natural resources are finite, ultimately economic growth must come to an end." *(LO5)*

○ PROBLEMS ○

Visit your mobile app store and download the Frank: Study Econ app *today*!

1. Richland's real GDP per person is $10,000, and Poorland's real GDP per person is $5,000. However, Richland's real GDP per person is growing at 1 percent per year and Poorland's is growing at 3 percent per year. Compare real GDP per person in the two countries after 10 years and after 20 years. Approximately how many years will it take Poorland to catch up to Richland? *(LO1)*

2. Calculate how much higher U.S. labor productivity will be in the year 2035 (relative to 2015) if: *(LO1)*
   a. Productivity continues to grow by 2.6 percent per year.
   b. Productivity growth falls to 2 percent per year, its average rate during the period 1970–2009. (*Note:* You do not need to know the actual values of average labor productivity in any year to solve this problem.)

3. The "graying of America" will substantially increase the fraction of the population that is retired in the decades to come. To illustrate the implications for U.S. living standards, suppose that over the 53 years following 2013 the share of the population that is working returns to its 1960 level, while average labor productivity increases by as much as it did during 1960–2013. Under this scenario, what would be the net change in real GDP per person between 2013 and 2066? The following data will be useful: *(LO2)*

	Average labor productivity	Share of population employed
1960	$47,256	36.4%
2013	$109,152	45.5%

4. Consider the table below containing data for Germany and Japan on the ratio of employment to population in 1980 and 2010.

	1980	2010
Germany	0.33	0.52
Japan	0.48	0.49

Using data from Table 7.1, find average labor productivity for each country in 1980 and 2010. How much of the increase in output per person in each country over the 1980 to 2010 period is due to increased labor productivity? To increased employment relative to population? *(LO2)*

5. Joanne has just completed high school and is trying to determine whether to go to junior college for two years or go directly to work. Her objective is to maximize the savings she will have in the bank five years from now. If she goes directly to work,

she will earn $20,000 per year for each of the next five years. If she goes to junior college, for each of the next two years she will earn nothing—indeed, she will have to borrow $6,000 each year to cover tuition and books. This loan must be repaid in full three years after graduation. If she graduates from junior college, in each of the subsequent three years, her wages will be $38,000 per year. Joanne's total living expenses and taxes, excluding tuition and books, equal $15,000 per year. *(LO3)*

    a. Suppose, for simplicity, that Joanne can borrow and lend at 0 percent interest. On purely economic grounds, should she go to junior college or work?

    b. Does your answer to part a change if she can earn $23,000 per year with only a high school degree?

    c. Does your answer to part a change if Joanne's tuition and books cost $8,000 per year?

    d.*Suppose that the interest rate at which Joanne can borrow and lend is 10 percent per year, but other data are as in part a. Savings are deposited at the end of the year they are earned and receive (compound) interest at the end of each subsequent year. Similarly, the loans are taken out at the end of the year in which they are needed, and interest does not accrue until the end of the subsequent year. Now that the interest rate has risen, should Joanne go to college or go to work?

6. The Good'n'Fresh Grocery Store has two checkout lanes and four employees. Employees are equally skilled, and all are able to either operate a register (checkers) or bag groceries (baggers). The store owner assigns one checker and one bagger to each lane. A lane with a checker and a bagger can check out 40 customers per hour. A lane with a checker only can check out 25 customers per hour. *(LO3)*

    a. In terms of customers checked out per hour, what are total output and average labor productivity for the Good'n'Fresh Grocery Store?

    b. The owner adds a third checkout lane and register. Assuming that no employees are added, what is the best way to reallocate the workers to tasks? What are total output and average labor productivity (in terms of customers checked out per hour) now?

    c. Repeat part b for the addition of a fourth checkout lane, and a fifth. Do you observe diminishing returns to capital in this example?

7. Harrison, Carla, and Fred are housepainters. Harrison and Carla can paint 100 square feet per hour using a standard paintbrush, and Fred can paint 80 square feet per hour. Any of the three can paint 200 square feet per hour using a roller. *(LO3)*

    a. Assume Harrison, Carla, and Fred have only paintbrushes at their disposal. What is the average labor productivity, in terms of square feet per painter-hour, for the three painters taken as a team? Assume that the three painters always work the same number of hours.

    b. Repeat part a for the cases in which the team has one, two, three, or four rollers available. Are there diminishing returns to capital?

    c. An improvement in paint quality increases the area that can be covered per hour (by either brushes or rollers) by 20 percent. How does this technological improvement affect your answers to part b? Are there diminishing returns to capital? Does the technological improvement increase or reduce the economic value of an additional roller?

8. Hester's Hatchery raises fish. At the end of the current season Hester has 1,000 fish in the hatchery. She can harvest any number of fish that she wishes, selling them to restaurants for $5 apiece. Because big fish make little fish, for every fish that she leaves in the hatchery this year, she will have two fish at the end of next year. The price of fish is expected to be $5 each next year as well. Hester relies entirely on income from current fish sales to support herself. *(LO3)*

    a. How many fish should Hester harvest if she wants to maximize the growth of her stock of fish from this season to next season?

    b. Do you think maximizing the growth of her fish stock is an economically sound strategy for Hester? Why or why not? Relate to the text discussion on the costs of economic growth.

*Denotes more difficult problem.

c. How many fish should Hester harvest if she wants to maximize her current income? Do you think this is a good strategy?

d. Explain why Hester is unlikely to harvest either all or none of her fish, but instead will harvest some and leave the rest to reproduce.

9. Discuss the following statement, using concrete examples where possible to illustrate your arguments: For advances in basic science to translate into improvements in standards of living, they must be supported by favorable economic conditions. *(LO3, LO4)*

10. Write a short essay evaluating the U.S. economy in terms of each of the six determinants of average labor productivity discussed in the text. Are there any areas in which the United States is exceptionally strong, relative to other countries? Areas where the United States is less strong than some other countries? Illustrate your arguments with numbers from the *Statistical Abstract of the United States* (available online at www.census.gov/compendia/statab) and other sources, as appropriate. *(LO3, LO4)*

○ ANSWERS TO CONCEPT CHECKS ○

7.1 If the United States had grown at the Japanese rate for the period 1870–2010, real GDP per person in 2010 would have been ($2,445) $\times$ $(1.025)^{140}$ = $77,556.82. Actual GDP per person in the United States in 2010 was $30,491, so at the higher rate of growth, output per person would have been 2.54 times higher. *(LO1)*

7.2 As before, Lucy can wrap 4,000 candies per week, or 100 candies per hour. Ethel can wrap 500 candies per hour, and working 40 hours weekly she can wrap 20,000 candies per week. Together Lucy and Ethel can wrap 24,000 candies per week. Since they work a total of 80 hours between them, their output per hour as a team is 24,000 candies wrapped per 80 hours = 300 candies wrapped per hour, midway between their hourly productivities as individuals. *(LO3)*

7.3 Because Ethel can wrap 300 candies per hour by hand, the benefit of giving Ethel the machine is 500 − 300 = 200 additional candies wrapped per hour. Because Lucy wraps only 100 candies per hour by hand, the benefit of giving Lucy the machine is 400 additional candies wrapped per hour. So the benefit of giving the machine to Lucy is greater than of giving it to Ethel. Equivalently, if the machine goes to Ethel, then Lucy and Ethel between them can wrap 500 + 100 = 600 candies per hour, but if Lucy uses the machine, the team can wrap 300 + 500 = 800 candies per hour. So output is increased by letting Lucy use the machine. *(LO3)*

7.4 Now, working by hand, Lucy can wrap 300 candies per hour and Ethel can wrap 500 candies per hour. With a machine, either Lucy or Ethel can wrap 800 candies per hour. As in Concept Check 7.3, the benefit of giving a machine to Lucy (500 additional candies per hour) exceeds the benefit of giving a machine to Ethel (300 additional candies per hour), so if only one machine is available, Lucy should use it.

The table analogous to Table 7.2 now looks like this:

Relationship of Capital, Output, and Productivity in the Candy-Wrapping Factory			
Number of machines (K)	Candies wrapped per week (Y)	Total hours worked (N)	Average hourly labor productivity (Y/N)
0	32,000	80	400
1	52,000	80	650
2	64,000	80	800
3	64,000	80	800

Comparing this table with Table 7.2, you can see that technological advance has increased labor productivity for any value of *K,* the number of machines available.

Adding one machine increases output by 20,000 candies wrapped per week, adding the second machine increases output by 12,000 candies wrapped per week, and adding the third machine does not increase output at all (because there is no worker available to use it). So diminishing returns to capital still hold after the technological improvement. *(LO3)*

7.5 Although the individual worker is the same person he was in Bangladesh, by coming to the United States he gains the benefit of factors that enhance average labor productivity in this country, relative to his homeland. These include more and better capital to work with, more natural resources per person, more advanced technologies, sophisticated entrepreneurs and managers, and a political-legal environment that is conducive to high productivity. It is not guaranteed that the value of the immigrant's human capital will rise (it may not, for example, if he speaks no English and has no skills applicable to the U.S. economy), but normally it will.

Since increased productivity leads to higher wages and living standards, on economic grounds the Bangladeshi worker has a strong incentive to immigrate to the United States if he is able to do so. *(LO3)*

CHAPTER 8

Saving, Capital Formation, and Financial Markets

Dave Bradley Photography/Getty Images

LEARNING OBJECTIVES

After reading this chapter, you should be able to:

LO1 Explain the relationship between saving and wealth.

LO2 Identify and apply the components of national saving.

LO3 Discuss the reasons why people save.

LO4 Discuss the reasons why firms choose to invest in capital rather than in financial assets.

LO5 Differentiate between bonds and stocks and show how the financial market improves the allocation of saving to productive uses.

LO6 Analyze financial markets using the tools of supply and demand.

WHAT IS SAVING AND WHY DOES IT MATTER?

You've probably heard Aesop's fable of the ant and the grasshopper. All summer the ant worked hard laying up food for the winter. The grasshopper mocked the ant's efforts and contented himself with basking in the sunshine, ignoring the ant's earnest warnings. When winter came the ant was well-fed, while the grasshopper starved. Moral: When times are good, the wise put aside something for the future.

Of course, there is also the modern ending to the fable, in which the grasshopper breaks his leg by tripping over the anthill, sues the ant for negligence, and ends up living comfortably on the ant's savings. (Nobody knows what happened to the ant.) Moral: Saving is risky; live for today.

The pitfalls of modern life notwithstanding, saving is important, both to individuals and to nations. People need to save to provide for their retirement and for other future needs, such as their children's education or a new home. An individual's or a family's savings also can provide a crucial buffer in the event of an economic emergency, such as the loss of a job or unexpected medical bills. At the national level, the production of new capital goods—factories, equipment, and housing—is an important factor promoting economic growth and higher living standards. As we will see in this chapter, the resources necessary to produce new capital come primarily from a nation's collective saving.

In this chapter, we will look at saving and its links to the formation of new capital. We begin by defining the concepts of saving and wealth and exploring the connection between them. We then turn to national saving—the collective saving of households, businesses, and government. Because national saving determines the capacity of an economy to create new capital, it is the most important measure of saving from a macroeconomic perspective.

We next discuss the economics of household saving and capital formation by firms. We first consider why people choose to save, rather than spending all their income. Then, we examine capital formation by firms; it turns out that a firm's decision to invest in capital is in many respects analogous to its decision about whether to increase employment. We also look at how financial markets such as bond and stock markets actually allocate saving to productive uses. We conclude the chapter by showing how national saving and capital formation are related using a supply and demand approach.

SAVING AND WEALTH

saving current income minus spending on current needs

saving rate saving divided by income

wealth the value of assets minus liabilities

assets anything of value that one *owns*

liabilities the debts one *owes*

balance sheet a list of an economic unit's assets and liabilities on a specific date

In general, the **saving** of an economic unit—whether a household, a business, a university, or a nation—is defined as its *current income* minus its *spending on current needs*. For example, if Consuelo earns $300 per week, spends $280 weekly on living expenses such as rent, food, clothes, and entertainment, and deposits the remaining $20 in the bank, her saving is $20 per week. The **saving rate** of any economic unit is its saving divided by its income. Since Consuelo saves $20 of her weekly income of $300, her saving rate is $20/$300, or 6.7 percent.

The saving of an economic unit is closely related to its **wealth,** which is the value of its assets minus its liabilities. **Assets** are anything of value that one *owns,* either *financial* or *real.* Examples of financial assets that you or your family might own include cash, a checking account, stocks, and bonds. Examples of real assets include a home or other real estate, jewelry, consumer durables like cars, and valuable collectibles. **Liabilities,** on the other hand, are the debts one *owes.* Examples of liabilities are credit card balances, student loans, and mortgages.

By comparing an economic unit's assets and liabilities, economists calculate that unit's wealth, also called its *net worth.* This comparison is done using a list of assets and liabilities on a particular date, called a **balance sheet.**

| **Constructing a Balance Sheet** | **EXAMPLE 8.1** |

What is Consuelo's wealth on January 1, 2015?

To answer this question, Consuelo must assemble her assets and liabilities as of January 1, 2015, in a balance sheet. The result is shown in Table 8.1.

Consuelo's financial assets are the cash in her wallet, the balance in her checking account, and the current value of some shares of stock. Together her financial assets are worth $2,280. She also lists $4,000 in real assets, the sum of the market values of her car and her furniture. Consuelo's total assets, both financial and real, come to $6,280. Her liabilities are the student loan she owes the bank and the balance due on her credit card, which total $3,250. Consuelo's wealth, or net worth, on January 1, 2015, is the value of her assets ($6,280) minus the value of her liabilities ($3,250), or $3,030.

TABLE 8.1
Consuelo's Balance Sheet on January 1, 2015

Assets		Liabilities	
Cash	$ 80	Student loan	$3,000
Checking account	1,200	Credit card balance	250
Shares of stock	1,000		
Car (market value)	3,500		
Furniture (market value)	500		
Total	$6,280		$3,250
		Net worth	$3,030

CONCEPT CHECK 8.1

Refer back to Example 8.1. What would Consuelo's net worth be if her student loan were for $6,500 rather than $3,000? Construct a new balance sheet for her.

Saving and wealth are related because saving contributes to wealth. To understand this relationship better, we must distinguish between *stocks* and *flows*.

STOCKS AND FLOWS

Saving is an example of a **flow,** a measure that is defined *per unit of time*. For example, Consuelo's saving is $20 *per week*. Wealth, in contrast, is a **stock,** a measure that is defined *at a point in time*. Consuelo's wealth of $3,030, for example, is her wealth on a particular date—January 1, 2015.

To visualize the difference between stocks and flows, think of water running into a bathtub. The amount of water in the bathtub at any specific moment—for example, 40 gallons at 7:15 p.m.—is a stock because it is measured at a specific point in time. The rate at which the water flows into the tub—for example, 2 gallons per minute—is a flow because it is measured per unit of time. In many cases, a flow is the *rate of change* in a stock: If we know that there are 40 gallons of water in the tub at 7:15 p.m., for example, and that water is flowing in at 2 gallons per minute, we can easily determine that the stock of water will be changing at the rate of 2 gallons per minute and will equal 42 gallons at 7:16 p.m., 44 gallons at 7:17 p.m., and so on, until the bathtub overflows.

flow a measure that is defined *per unit of time*

stock a measure that is defined *at a point in time*

CONCEPT CHECK 8.2

Continuing the example of the bathtub: If there are 40 gallons of water in the tub at 7:15 p.m. and water is being *drained* at the rate of 3 gallons per minute (and no more water is added to the tub), what will be the stock and flow at 7:16 p.m.? At 7:17 p.m.? Does the flow still equal the rate of change in the stock?

The relationship between saving (a flow) and wealth (a stock) is similar to the relationship between the flow of water into a bathtub and the stock of water in the tub in that the *flow* of saving causes the *stock* of wealth to change at the same rate. Indeed, as the following example illustrates, every dollar that a person saves adds a dollar to his or her wealth.

The Link between Saving and Wealth	EXAMPLE 8.2

What is the relationship between Consuelo's saving and her wealth?

Consuelo saves $20 per week. How does this saving affect her wealth on January 8, 2015? Does the change in her wealth depend on whether Consuelo uses her saving to accumulate assets or to pay down her liabilities?

Consuelo could use the $20 she saved during the first week in January to increase her assets—for example, by adding the $20 to her checking account—or to reduce her liabilities—for example, by paying down her credit card balance. Suppose she adds the $20 to her checking account, increasing her assets on January 8, 2015, by $20. Since her liabilities are unchanged, her wealth also increases by $20, to $3,050 (see Table 8.1).

If Consuelo decides to use the $20 she saved during the first week in January to pay down her credit card balance, she reduces it from $250 to $230. That action would reduce her liabilities by $20, leaving her assets unchanged. Since wealth equals assets minus liabilities, reducing her liabilities by $20 increases her wealth by $20, to $3,050. Thus, saving $20 per week raises Consuelo's stock of wealth on January 8, 2015, by $20, regardless of whether she uses her saving to increase her assets or reduce her liabilities.

The close relationship between saving and wealth explains why saving is so important to an economy. Higher rates of saving today lead to faster accumulation of wealth, and the wealthier a nation is, the higher its standard of living. Thus, a high rate of saving today contributes to an improved standard of living in the future.

CAPITAL GAINS AND LOSSES

Saving is not the only factor that determines wealth. Wealth also can change because of changes in the values of the real or financial assets one owns. Suppose, for example, that Consuelo's shares of stock rise in value during January, from $1,000 to $1,500. This increase in the value of Consuelo's stock raises her total assets by $500 without affecting her liabilities. As a result, Consuelo's wealth rises by $500, from $3,030 on January 1, 2015, to $3,530 on February 1, 2015 (see Table 8.2).

capital gains increases in the value of existing assets

capital losses decreases in the value of existing assets

Changes in the value of existing assets are called **capital gains** when an asset's value increases and **capital losses** when an asset's value decreases. Just as capital gains increase wealth, capital losses decrease wealth. Capital gains and losses are not counted as part of saving, however. Instead, the change in a person's wealth during any period equals the saving done during the period plus capital gains minus capital losses during that period. In terms of an equation,

$$\text{Change in wealth} = \text{Saving} + \text{Capital gains} - \text{Capital losses.}$$

TABLE 8.2
Consuelo's Balance Sheet on February 1, 2015, after an Increase in the Value of Her Stocks

Assets		Liabilities	
Cash	$ 80	Student loan	$3,000
Checking account	1,200	Credit card balance	250
Shares of stock	1,500		
Car (market value)	3,500		
Furniture (market value)	500		
Total	**$6,780**		**$3,250**
		Net worth	**$3,530**

CONCEPT CHECK 8.3

How would each of the following actions or events affect Consuelo's *saving* and her *wealth*?

a. Consuelo deposits $20 in the bank at the end of the week as usual. She also charges $50 on her credit card, raising her credit card balance to $300.

b. Consuelo uses $300 from her checking account to pay off her credit card bill.

c. Consuelo's old car is recognized as a classic. Its market value rises from $3,500 to $4,000.

d. Consuelo's furniture is damaged and as a result falls in value from $500 to $200.

Capital gains and losses can have a major effect on one's overall wealth, as our next example illustrates.

| **Bull Markets and Household Wealth** | **EXAMPLE 8.3** |

How did American households increase their wealth in the 1990s while saving very little?

On the whole, Americans felt very prosperous during the 1990s: Measures of household wealth during this period showed enormous gains. Yet saving by U.S. households was quite low throughout those years. How did American households increase their wealth in the 1990s while saving very little?

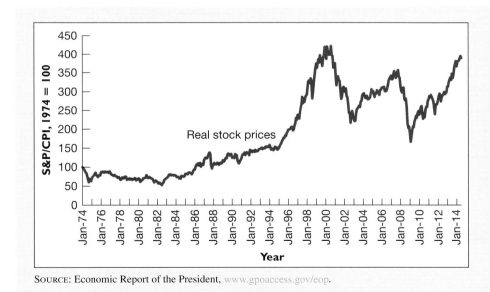

SOURCE: Economic Report of the President, www.gpoaccess.gov/eop.

FIGURE 8.1

Bull Markets.

This figure shows the Standard & Poor's 500 index of stock prices, divided by the CPI to correct for inflation, for the period 1974–2014. Real stock prices rose sharply during the 1990s, peaking in 2000, greatly increasing the wealth of households that held stocks. Since 2009, a new bull market has taken hold in the U.S. stock market.

During the 1990s an increasing number of Americans acquired stocks, either directly through purchases or indirectly through their pension and retirement funds. At the same time, stock prices rose at record rates (see Figure 8.1). The strongly rising "bull market," which increased the prices of most stocks, enabled many Americans to enjoy significant capital gains and increased wealth without saving much, if anything. Indeed, some economists argued that the low household saving rate of the 1990s is partially *explained* by the bull market; because capital gains increased household wealth by so much, many people saw no need to save.

The stock market peaked in early 2000 and stock prices fell quite sharply over the following two years. It is interesting that U.S. households did not choose to save more in 2000 and in subsequent years, despite the decline in their stock market wealth. One explanation is that an even larger component of household wealth—the value of privately owned homes—rose significantly in 2000–2006, partly offsetting the effect of the decline in stock values on household wealth. As the stock market enters another period of sustained growth in real stock prices after the 2007–2009 recession, some fear that household savings will once again decrease. The savings rate of households will be further discussed later in this chapter and can be seen in Figure 8.3.

RECAP	SAVING AND WEALTH

In general, *saving* is current income minus spending on current needs. *Wealth* is the value of assets—anything of value that one owns—minus liabilities—the debts one owes. Saving is measured per unit of time (for example, dollars per week) and thus is a *flow*. Wealth is measured at a point in time and thus is a *stock*. In the same way the flow of water through the faucet increases the stock of water in a bathtub, the flow of saving increases the stock of wealth. Wealth also can be increased by *capital gains* (increases in the value of existing assets) or reduced by *capital losses* (decreases in asset values).

NATIONAL SAVING AND ITS COMPONENTS

Thus far we have examined saving and wealth from the individual's perspective. But macroeconomists are interested primarily in saving and wealth for the country as a whole. In this section we will study *national saving,* or the aggregate saving of the economy. National saving includes the saving of business firms and the government as well as that of households. Later in the chapter we will examine the close link between national saving and the rate of capital formation in an economy.

THE MEASUREMENT OF NATIONAL SAVING

To define the saving rate of a country as a whole, we will start with a basic accounting identity introduced in the chapter *Spending, Income, and GDP*. According to this identity, for the economy as a whole, production (or income) must equal total expenditure. In symbols, the identity is

$$Y = C + I + G + NX,$$

where Y stands for either production or aggregate income (which must be equal), C equals consumption expenditure, I equals investment spending, G equals government purchases of goods and services, and NX equals net exports.

For now, let's assume that net exports (NX) are equal to zero, which would be the case if a country did not trade at all with other countries or if its exports and imports were always balanced. (We discuss the foreign sector in the chapter *Exchange Rates, International Trade, and Capital Flows*.) With net exports set at zero, the condition that output equals expenditure becomes

$$Y = C + I + G.$$

To determine how much saving is done by the nation as a whole, we can apply the general definition of saving. As for any other economic unit, a nation's saving equals its *current income* less its *spending on current needs*. The current income of the country as a whole is its GDP, or Y, that is, the value of the final goods and services produced within the country's borders during the year.

Identifying the part of total expenditure that corresponds to the nation's spending on current needs is more difficult than identifying the nation's income. The component of aggregate spending that is easiest to classify is investment spending *I*. We know that investment spending—the acquisition of new factories, equipment, and other capital goods, as well as residential construction—is done to expand the economy's future productive capacity or provide more housing for the future, not to satisfy current needs. So investment spending clearly is *not* part of spending on current needs.

Deciding how much of consumption spending by households, *C,* and government purchases of goods and services, *G,* should be counted as spending on current needs is less straightforward. Certainly most consumption spending by households—on food, clothing, utilities, entertainment, and so on—is for current needs. But consumption spending also includes purchases of long-lived *consumer durables* such as cars, furniture, and appliances. Consumer durables are only partially used up during the current year; they may continue to provide service, in fact, for years after their purchase. So household spending on consumer durables is a combination of spending on current needs and spending on future needs.

As with consumption spending, most government purchases of goods and services are intended to provide for current needs. However, like household purchases, a portion of government purchases is devoted to the acquisition or construction of long-lived capital goods such as roads, bridges, schools, government buildings, and military hardware. And like consumer durables, these forms of *public capital* are only partially used up during the current year; most will provide useful services far into the future. So, like consumption spending, government purchases are in fact a mixture of spending on current needs and spending on future needs.

In its official data, the government has begun to distinguish investment in public capital from the rest of government purchases. Nevertheless, this is a relatively small portion of the total, and determining precisely how much of spending is for current needs and how much is for future needs is extremely difficult. For simplicity's sake, in this book we will follow the traditional practice of treating *all* of both consumption expenditures (*C*) and government purchases (*G*) as spending on current needs. But keep in mind that because consumption spending and government purchases do in fact include some spending for future rather than current needs, treating all of *C* and *G* as spending on current needs will understate the true amount of national saving.

If we treat all consumption spending and government purchases as spending on current needs, then the nation's saving is its income *Y* less its spending on current needs, *C* + *G*. So we can define **national saving** *S* as

$$S = Y - C - G. \tag{8.1}$$

national saving the saving of the entire economy, equal to GDP less consumption expenditures and government purchases of goods and services, or $Y - C - G$

Figure 8.2 shows the U.S. national saving rate (national saving as a percentage of GDP) for the years 1960 through 2013. Since 1960 the U.S. national saving rate fell from 18 percent of GDP in 1960 to almost 13 percent in 2013.

PRIVATE AND PUBLIC COMPONENTS OF NATIONAL SAVING

To understand national saving better, let's examine its two major components: private saving and public saving. Private saving is the amount households and businesses save from private-sector income. Public saving is the amount governments save from public-sector income. Although the private sector's total income from the production of goods and services is *Y,* it must pay taxes from this income and it collects additional amounts from the government in the form of *transfer payments* and *interest* paid to individuals and institutions that hold government bonds. **Transfer payments** are payments the government makes to the public for which it receives no current goods or services in return. For instance, Social Security benefits, welfare payments, farm support payments, and pensions to government workers are transfer payments.

transfer payments payments the government makes to the public for which it receives no current goods or services in return

Subtracting transfers and government interest payments from total taxes yields the net amount paid by the private sector to the government—the amount it pays to the government

FIGURE 8.2

U.S. National Saving Rate, 1960–2013.

Since 1960, U.S. national saving has fallen from a high of around 19 percent of GDP to below 9 percent of GDP. The U.S. national saving rate has, however, increased from that low in the last couple of years.

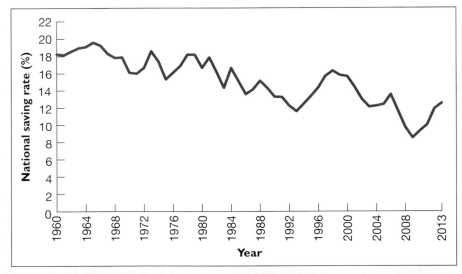

SOURCE: Bureau of Economic Analysis, www.bea.gov.

minus the amount it receives from the government. We call this amount *net taxes,* which we label *T*:

$$T = \text{Total taxes} - \text{Transfer payments} - \text{Government interest payments}.$$

private saving the saving of the private sector of the economy is equal to the after-tax income of the private sector minus consumption expenditures (*Y* − *T* − *C*); private saving can be further broken down into household saving and business saving

Private saving is the amount of the private sector's after-tax income that is not spent on current consumption expenditures. Private saving S_{private} is therefore equal to total private income from the production of goods and services minus net taxes minus consumption, or

$$S_{\text{private}} = Y - T - C.$$

Private saving can be further broken down into saving done by households and business firms. *Household saving,* also called *personal saving,* is saving done by families and individuals. Household saving corresponds to the familiar image of families putting aside part of their incomes each month, and it is the focus of much attention in the news media. But businesses are important savers as well—indeed business saving makes up the bulk of private saving in the United States. Businesses use the revenues from their sales to pay workers' salaries and other operating costs, to pay taxes, and to provide dividends to their shareholders. The funds remaining after these payments have been made are equal to *business saving.* A business firm's savings are available for the purchase of new capital equipment or the expansion of its operations. Alternatively, a business can put its savings in the bank for future use.

public saving the saving of the government sector is equal to net tax payments minus government purchases (*T* − *G*)

Public saving is the amount of the public sector's income that is not spent on current needs. The public sector includes state and local governments as well as the federal government. Public-sector income is merely net taxes *T*. Government spending on current needs is equal to government purchases *G* (remember that, for the sake of simplicity, we are ignoring the investment portion of government purchases). Thus, we calculate public saving S_{public} as

$$S_{\text{public}} = T - G.$$

If we add public and private saving together, we can derive the expression for total national saving that appears in Equation 8.1 in another way:

$$S_{\text{private}} + S_{\text{public}} = (Y - T - C) + (T - G) = Y - C - G = S \qquad (8.2)$$

This equation confirms that national saving S is the sum of private saving and public saving. Since private saving can be broken down in turn into household and business saving, we see that national saving is made up of the saving of three groups: households, businesses, and the government.

PUBLIC SAVING AND THE GOVERNMENT BUDGET

Although the idea that households and businesses can save is familiar to most people, the fact that the government also can save is less widely understood. Public saving is closely linked to the government's decisions about spending and taxing. Governments finance the bulk of their spending by taxing the private sector. If taxes and spending in a given year are equal, the government is said to have a *balanced budget*. If in any given year the amount that the government collects in taxes is greater than the amount it spends, the difference is called the **government budget surplus.** When a government has a surplus, it uses the extra funds to pay down its outstanding debt to the public. Algebraically, the government budget surplus may be written as $T - G$, or net tax collections minus government purchases.

If the algebraic expression for the government budget surplus, $T - G$, looks familiar, that is because it is also the definition of public saving. Thus, *public saving is identical to the government budget surplus.* In other words, when the government collects more in taxes than it spends, public saving will be positive. In the year 2000, for example, the federal government had the largest budget surplus in history. The following example illustrates the relationships among public saving, the government budget surplus, and national saving in that year.

government budget surplus
the excess of government tax collections over government spending $(T - G)$; the government budget surplus equals public saving

Government Saving	**EXAMPLE 8.4**

How do we calculate government saving?

Following are data on U.S. government revenues and expenditures for 2000, in billions of dollars.

Federal government:	
Receipts	2,057.1
Expenditures	1,871.9
State and local governments:	
Receipts	1,322.6
Expenditures	1,281.3

SOURCE: Bureau of Economic Analysis, www.bea.gov.

Government saving consists of the budget surpluses of all levels of government: federal, state, and local. In 2000, the federal government ran a budget surplus of $185.2 billion, and state and local governments ran a collective budget surplus of $41.3 billion. The budget surplus of the entire government sector was therefore $226.5 billion. So the contribution of the government sector to U.S. national saving in 2000 was $226.5 billion.

If, on the other hand, the government spends more than it collects in taxes, public saving will be negative. In this circumstance, we speak about the **government budget deficit,** which is the amount by which spending exceeds taxes and is calculated by $G - T$.[1] If the government runs a deficit, it must make up the difference by borrowing from the public by issuing new government bonds.

government budget deficit
the excess of government spending over tax collections $(G - T)$

[1]Note that a budget deficit of $100 billion is the same as a budget surplus of −$100 billion.

Although the government had a budget surplus of $226.5 billion in the year 2000, it subsequently ran budget deficits. By 2010, the budget deficit was −$1,300.6 billion. The table below provides details for 2010. (Again, all amounts are in billions of dollars.)

Federal government:	
Receipts	2,385.2
Expenditures	3,718.7
State and local governments:	
Receipts	2,128.1
Expenditures	2,095.2

SOURCE: Bureau of Economic Analysis, www.bea.gov.

In 2010, the federal government ran a record budget deficit of $1,333.5 billion. State and local governments typically keep balanced budgets or earn budget surpluses, and in 2010 they ran a collective budget *surplus* of $32.9 billion. Thus, the budget deficit for all levels of government was $1,300.6 billion. This means that government saving in 2010 was −$1,300.6 billion.

There were three main reasons for this dramatic turnaround in the government budget. First, government receipts fell because of the recessions in 2001 and even more so in 2007 to 2009. During a recession incomes fall. Since many taxes are based on income, during a recession tax receipts also fall or rise more slowly than expected. The second reason was the reduction in tax rates enacted by President Bush and Congress during the president's first term. Finally, government expenditures rose dramatically between 2000 and 2010, in large part as a result of the wars in Iraq and Afghanistan and expenditures by the Department of Homeland Security in response to the terrorist attack on September 11, 2001.

Figure 8.2 showed the U.S. national saving rate since 1960. Figure 8.3 shows the behavior since 1960 of the three components of national saving: household saving, business

FIGURE 8.3

The Three Components of National Saving, 1960–2013.

Of the three components of national saving, business saving is the most important. Household saving was steadily declining until the beginning of 2007. Government saving has generally been negative, except in the 1960s and for a brief period in the late 1990s.

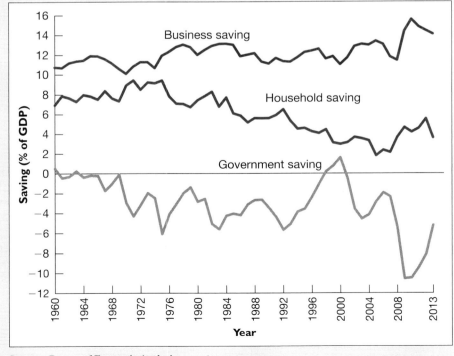

SOURCE: Bureau of Economic Analysis, www.bea.gov.

saving, and government saving, each measured as a percentage of GDP. Note that business saving played a major role in national saving during these years, while the role of household saving was relatively modest. As we see in Figure 8.3, U.S. households reversed the trend of declining savings rates in 2007, after reaching a low of less than 2 percent. However, it remains to be seen if this was only temporary or the beginning of a new long-term trend.

The contribution of public saving has varied considerably over time. Until about 1970, the federal, state, and local governments typically ran a combined surplus, making a positive contribution to national saving. But since then, public saving has been almost continuously negative, reflecting large budget deficits, particularly at the federal level. With the exception for a brief period in the late 1990s, the government has been a net drain on national savings ever since the 1960s.

RECAP	NATIONAL SAVING AND ITS COMPONENTS

- *National saving,* the saving of the nation as a whole, is defined by $S = Y - C - G$, where Y is GDP, C is consumption spending, and G is government purchases of goods and services. National saving is the sum of public saving and private saving: $S = S_{private} + S_{public}$.

- *Private saving,* the saving of the private sector, is defined by $S_{private} = Y - T - C$, where T is net tax payments. Private saving can be broken down further into household saving and business saving.

- *Public saving,* the saving of the government, is defined by $S_{public} = T - G$. Public saving equals the government budget surplus, $T - G$. When the government budget is in surplus, government saving is positive; when the government budget is in deficit, public saving is negative.

life-cycle saving saving to meet long-term objectives such as retirement, college attendance, or the purchase of a home

precautionary saving saving for protection against unexpected setbacks such as the loss of a job or a medical emergency

WHY DO PEOPLE SAVE?

Why do people save part of their income instead of spending everything they earn? Economists have identified three broad reasons for saving. First, people save to meet long-term objectives such as a comfortable retirement. By putting away part of their income during their working years, they can live better after retirement than they would if they had to rely solely on Social Security and their company pensions. Other long-term objectives might include college tuition for one's children and the purchase of a new home or car. Economists call this type of saving **life-cycle saving** since many of these needs occur at fairly predictable stages in a person's life.

A second reason to save is to protect oneself and family against unexpected setbacks—the loss of a job, for example, or a costly health problem. Personal financial advisors typically suggest that families maintain an emergency reserve (a "rainy-day fund") equal to three to six months' worth of income. Saving for protection against potential emergencies is called **precautionary saving.**

"Fortunately, you have the life savings of a man three times your age."

bequest saving saving done for the purpose of leaving an inheritance

A third reason to save is to accumulate an estate to leave to one's heirs, usually one's children but possibly a favorite charity or other worthy cause. Saving for the purpose of leaving an inheritance, or bequest, is called **bequest saving.** Bequest saving is done primarily by people at the higher end of the income ladder. But because these people control a large share of the nation's wealth, bequest saving is an important part of overall saving.

To be sure, people usually do not mentally separate their saving into these three categories; rather, all three reasons for saving motivate most savers to varying degrees. Our next example shows how the three reasons for saving can explain household saving behavior in Japan.

Household Saving in Japan   EXAMPLE 8.5

Why did Japanese saving rates rise until 1990 and then decline since then?

After World War II Japanese households increased their saving rates to 15–25 percent of their income, an unusually high rate. Although cultural factors often were cited as a reason for the high Japanese propensity to save, saving rates in Japan were much lower before World War II. Moreover, household saving rates in Japan have declined since 1990 (although they remain higher than those in the United States). Why did the Japanese save so much until about 1990, and why have Japanese saving rates declined somewhat since then?

Among the reasons for saving we discussed, *life-cycle* reasons are probably the most important determinants of saving in Japan. The Japanese have long life expectancies, and many retire relatively early. With a long period of retirement to finance, Japanese families must save a great deal during their working years. When the working-age population was a high percentage of the total population, the overall saving rate was high. As the baby-boom generation reached the age of retirement and the Japanese fertility rate declined, so too has the Japanese saving rate declined.[2]

Other factors also help to explain the changes in Japanese saving rates. Down payment requirements on houses are high in Japan compared to other countries. Before 1990, land and housing prices in Japan were extremely high, so that young people had to save a great deal or borrow their parents' savings to buy their first homes. After the Japanese real estate market crashed at the beginning of the 1990s, however, land and housing prices fell, so young people do not need to save as much as before.

Studies also have found that *bequest saving* is important in Japan. Many older people live with their children after retirement. In return for support and attention during their later years, parents feel they must provide substantial inheritances for their children.

Precautionary saving is probably lower in Japan than in some other countries, however. Although Japan's recent economic troubles have reduced the practice of *lifetime employment,* Japanese firms still make extensive use of the system, which essentially guarantees a job for life to workers who join a firm after graduating from college. This type of job security, coupled with Japan's traditionally low unemployment rate, reduces the need for precautionary saving.

Although most people are usually motivated to save for at least one of the three reasons we have discussed, the amount they choose to save may depend on the economic environment. One economic variable that is quite significant in saving decisions is the real interest rate.

[2]Maiko Koga, "The Decline of the Saving Rate and the Demographic Effects," Bank of Japan Research and Statistics Department, November 2004.

SAVING AND THE REAL INTEREST RATE

Most people don't save by putting cash in a mattress. Instead, they make financial investments that they hope will provide a good return on their saving. For example, a checking account may pay interest on the account balance. More sophisticated financial investments such as government bonds or shares of stock in a corporation, which we discuss later in this chapter, also pay returns in the form of interest payments, dividends, or capital gains. High returns are desirable, of course, because the higher the return, the faster one's savings will grow.

The rate of return that is most relevant to saving decisions is the *real interest rate,* denoted *r.* Recall from the chapter *Inflation and the Price Level* that the real interest rate is the rate at which the real purchasing power of a financial asset increases over time. The real interest rate equals the market, or nominal, interest rate (i) minus the inflation rate (π).

The real interest rate is relevant to savers because it is the "reward" for saving. Suppose you are thinking of increasing your saving by $1,000 this year. If the real interest rate is 5 percent, then in a year your extra saving will give you extra purchasing power of $1,050, measured in today's dollars. But if the real interest rate were 10 percent, your sacrifice of $1,000 this year would be rewarded by $1,100 in purchasing power next year. Obviously, all else being equal, you would be more willing to save today if you knew the reward next year would be greater. In either case the *cost* of the extra saving—giving up your weekly night out—is the same. But the *benefit* of the extra saving, in terms of increased purchasing power next year, is higher if the real interest rate is 10 percent rather than 5 percent.

> **Cost-Benefit**

Saving versus Consumption

> **EXAMPLE 8.6**

By how much does a high saving rate enhance a family's future living standard?

The Spends and the Thrifts are similar families, except that the Spends save 5 percent of their income each year and the Thrifts save 20 percent. The two families began to save in 1980 and plan to continue to save until their respective breadwinners retire in the year 2015. Both families earn $40,000 a year in real terms in the labor market, and both put their savings in a mutual fund that has yielded a real return of 8 percent per year, a return they expect to continue into the future. Compare the amount that the two families consume in each year from 1980 to 2015, and compare the families' wealth at retirement.

In the first year, 1980, the Spends saved $2,000 (5 percent of their $40,000 income) and consumed $38,000 (95 percent of $40,000). The Thrifts saved $8,000 in 1980 (20 percent of $40,000) and hence consumed only $32,000 in that year, $6,000 less than the Spends. In 1981, the Thrifts' income was $40,640, the extra $640 representing the 8 percent return on their $8,000 savings. The Spends saw their income grow by only $160 (8 percent of their savings of $2,000) in 1981. With an income of $40,640, the Thrifts consumed $32,512 in 1981 (80 percent of $40,640) compared to $38,152 (95 percent of $40,160) for the Spends. The consumption gap between the two families, which started out at $6,000, thus fell to $5,640 after one year.

Because of the more rapid increase in the Thrifts' wealth and hence interest income, each year the Thrifts' income grew faster than the Spends'; each year the Thrifts continued to save 20 percent of their higher incomes compared to only 5 percent for the Spends. Figure 8.4 shows the paths followed by the consumption spending of the two families. You can see that the Thrifts' consumption, though starting at a lower level, grows relatively more quickly. By 1995 the Thrifts had overtaken the Spends, and from that point onward, the amount by which the Thrifts outspent the Spends grew with each passing year. Even though the Spends continued to consume 95 percent of their income each year, their income grew so slowly that, by 2000, they were consuming nearly $3,000 a year less than the Thrifts ($41,158 a year versus $43,957). And as the two

FIGURE 8.4

Consumption Trajectories of the Thrifts and the Spends.

The figure shows consumption spending in each year by two families, the Thrifts and the Spends. By the time of retirement in the year 2015, the Thrifts are consuming significantly more each year than the Spends and also have a retirement nest egg that is five times as much.

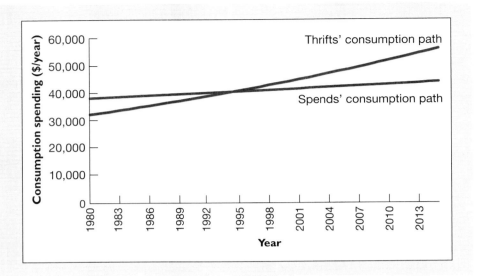

families retire in 2015, the Thrifts are consuming more than $12,000 per year more than the Spends ($55,774 versus $43,698). Even more striking is the difference between the retirement nest eggs of the two families. Whereas the Spends enter retirement with total accumulated savings of just over $77,000, the Thrifts have more than $385,000, five times as much.

These dramatic differences illustrated in Example 8.6 depend in part on the assumption that the real rate of return is 8 percent—lower than the actual return to mutual funds since 1980 but still a relatively high rate of return from a historical perspective. On the other hand, the Spend family in our example actually saves more than typical U.S. households, many of which carry $5,000 or more in credit card debt at high rates of interest and have no significant savings at all. The point of Example 8.6, which remains valid under alternative assumptions about the real interest rate and saving rates, is that, because of the power of compound interest, a high rate of saving pays off handsomely in the long run.

While a higher real interest rate increases the reward for saving, which tends to strengthen people's willingness to save, another force counteracts that extra incentive. Recall that a major reason for saving is to attain specific goals: a comfortable retirement, a college education, or a first home. If the goal is a specific amount—say, $25,000 for a down payment on a home—then a higher rate of return means that households can save *less* and still reach their goal because funds that are put aside will grow more quickly. For example, to accumulate $25,000 at the end of five years, at a 5 percent interest rate a person would have to save about $4,309 per year. At a 10 percent interest rate, reaching the $25,000 goal would require saving only about $3,723 per year. To the extent that people are *target savers* who save to reach a specific goal, higher interest rates actually decrease the amount they need to save.

In sum, a higher real interest rate has both positive and negative effects on saving—a positive effect because it increases the reward for saving and a negative effect because it reduces the amount people need to save each year to reach a given target. Empirical evidence suggests that, in practice, higher real interest rates lead to modest increases in saving.

SAVING, SELF-CONTROL, AND DEMONSTRATION EFFECTS

The reasons for saving we just discussed are based on the notion that people are rational decision makers who will choose their saving rates to maximize their welfare over the long run. Yet many psychologists, and some economists, have argued instead that people's saving behavior is based as much on psychological as on economic factors. For example, psychologists stress that many people lack the *self-control* to do what they know is in their own best interest. People smoke or eat greasy food, despite the known long-term health risks. Similarly, they may have good intentions about saving but lack the self-control to put aside as much as they ought to each month.

One way to strengthen self-control is to remove temptations from the immediate environment. A person who is trying to quit smoking will make a point of not having cigarettes in the house, and a person with a weight problem will avoid going to a bakery. Similarly, a person who is not saving enough might arrange to use a payroll savings plan, through which a predetermined amount is deducted from each paycheck and set aside in a special account from which withdrawals are not permitted until retirement. Making saving automatic and withdrawals difficult eliminates the temptation to spend all of current earnings or squander accumulated savings. Payroll savings plans have helped many people to increase the amount that they save for retirement or other purposes.

An implication of the self-control hypothesis is that consumer credit arrangements that make borrowing and spending easier may reduce the amount that people save. For example, in recent years banks have encouraged people to borrow against the *equity* in their homes, that is, the value of the home less the value of the outstanding mortgage. Such financial innovations, by increasing the temptation to spend, may have reduced the household saving rate. The increased availability of credit cards with high borrowing limits is another temptation.

Downward pressure on the saving rate also may occur when additional spending by some consumers stimulates additional spending by others. Such *demonstration effects* arise when people use the spending of others as a yardstick by which to measure the adequacy of their own living standards. For example, a family in an upper-middle-class American suburb in which the average house has 3,000 square feet of living space might regard a 1,500-square-foot house as being uncomfortably small—too cramped, for example, to entertain friends in the manner to which community members have become accustomed. In contrast, a similar family living in a low-income neighborhood might find the very same house luxuriously large.

The implication of demonstration effects for saving is that families who live among others who consume more than they do may be strongly motivated to increase their own consumption spending. When satisfaction depends in part on *relative* living standards, an upward spiral may result in which household spending is higher, and saving lower, than would be best for either the individual families involved or the economy as a whole.

Household Saving in the United States   **EXAMPLE 8.7**

Why is the U.S. household saving rate so low?

U.S. households decreased their saving rates from roughly 10 percent around 1970 to a low around 2 percent in 2005.

One possible reason for low saving is the availability of government assistance to the elderly. From a *life-cycle* perspective, an important motivation for saving is to provide for retirement. In general, the U.S. government provides a less comprehensive "social safety net" than other industrialized countries; that is, it offers relatively fewer programs to assist people in need. To the extent that the U.S. government does provide income support, however, it is heavily concentrated on the older segment of the population. Together the Social Security and Medicare programs, both of which are designed primarily to assist retired people, constitute a major share of the federal government's expenditures. These programs have been very successful; indeed, they have virtually wiped out poverty among the elderly. To the extent that Americans believe that the government will ensure them an adequate living standard in retirement, however, their incentive to save for the future is reduced.

Another important life-cycle objective is buying a home. We have seen that the Japanese must save a great deal to purchase a home because of high house prices and down payment requirements. The same is true in many other countries. But in the United States, with its highly developed financial system, people can buy homes with down payments of 20 percent or less of the purchase price.

What about *precautionary saving*? Unlike Japan and Europe, which had to rebuild after World War II, the United States has not known sustained economic hardship since the Great Depression of the 1930s (which fewer and fewer Americans are alive to remember). Perhaps the nation's prosperous past has led Americans to be more confident about the future and hence less inclined to save for economic emergencies than other people, even though the United States does not offer the level of employment security found in Japan or in Europe.

U.S. household saving is not only low by international standards, it has been declining. The good performance of the stock market in the 1990s along with increases in the prices of family homes probably helps to explain this savings decline. As long as Americans enjoy capital gains, they see their wealth increase almost without effort, and their incentive to save is reduced.

Psychological factors also may explain Americans' saving behavior. For example, unlike in most countries, U.S. homeowners can easily borrow against their home equity. This ability, made possible by the highly developed U.S. financial markets, may exacerbate *self-control* problems by increasing the temptation to spend. Finally, *demonstration effects* may have depressed saving in recent decades. The chapter *Wages and Unemployment,* discusses the phenomenon of increasing wage inequality, which has improved the relative position of more skilled and educated workers. Increased spending on houses, cars, and other consumption goods by households at the top of the earnings scale may have led those just below them to spend more as well, and so on. Middle-class families that were once content with medium-priced cars may now feel they need Volvos and BMWs to keep up with community standards. To the extent that demonstration effects lead families to spend beyond their means, they reduce their saving rate.

RECAP	WHY DO PEOPLE SAVE?

Motivations for saving include saving to meet long-term objectives such as retirement *(life-cycle saving),* saving for emergencies *(precautionary saving),* and saving to leave an inheritance or bequest *(bequest saving).* The amount that people save also depends on macroeconomic factors such as the real interest rate. A higher real interest rate stimulates saving by increasing the reward for saving, but it also can depress saving by making it easier for savers to reach a specific savings target. On net, a higher real interest rate appears to lead to modest increases in saving.

Psychological factors also may affect saving rates. If people have *self-control* problems, then financial arrangements (such as automatic payroll deductions) that make it more difficult to spend will increase their saving. People's saving decisions also may be influenced by *demonstration effects,* as when people feel compelled to spend at the same rate as their neighbors, even though they may not be able to afford to do so.

INVESTMENT AND CAPITAL FORMATION

From the point of view of the economy as a whole, the importance of national saving is that it provides the funds needed for investment. Investment—the creation of new capital goods and housing—is critical to increasing average labor productivity and improving standards of living.

What factors determine whether and how much firms choose to invest? Firms acquire new capital goods for the same reason they hire new workers: They expect that doing so will be profitable. The chapter *Wages and Unemployment* states that the profitability of employing an extra worker depends primarily on two factors: the cost of employing the worker and the value of the worker's marginal product. In the same way, firms' willingness to acquire new factories and machines depends on the expected *cost* of using them and the expected *benefit,* equal to the value of the marginal product that they will provide.

Cost-Benefit

Investing in a Capital Good: Part 1   EXAMPLE 8.8

Should Larry buy a riding lawn mower?

Larry is thinking of going into the lawn care business. He can buy a $4,000 riding mower by taking out a loan at 6 percent annual interest. With this mower and his own labor, Larry can net $6,000 per summer, after deduction of costs such as gasoline and maintenance. Of the $6,000 net revenues, 20 percent must be paid to the government in taxes. Assume that Larry could earn $4,400 after taxes by working in an alternative job. Assume also that the lawn mower can always be resold for its original purchase price of $4,000. Should Larry buy the lawn mower?

    To decide whether to invest in the capital good (the lawn mower), Larry should compare the financial benefits and costs. With the mower he can earn revenue of $6,000, net of gasoline and maintenance costs. However, 20 percent of that, or $1,200, must be paid in taxes, leaving Larry with $4,800. Larry could earn $4,400 after taxes by working at an alternative job, so the financial benefit to Larry of buying the mower is the difference between $4,800 and $4,400, or $400; $400 is the value of the marginal product of the lawn mower.

    Since the mower does not lose value over time and since gasoline and maintenance costs have already been deducted, the only remaining cost Larry should take into account is the interest on the loan for the mower. Larry must pay 6 percent interest on $4,000, or $240 per year. Since this financial cost is less than the financial benefit of $400, the value of the mower's marginal product, Larry should buy the mower.

    Larry's decision might change if the costs and benefits of his investment in the mower change, as Example 8.9 shows.

Investing in a Capital Good: Part 2   EXAMPLE 8.9

How do changes in the costs and benefits affect Larry's decision?

Begin with all the same assumptions as in Example 8.8; then consider how each of these changes (considered one-by-one) affect Larry's decision.

a. If the interest rate is 12 percent rather than 6 percent.

b. If the purchase price of the mower is $7,000 rather than $4,000.

c. If the tax rate on Larry's net revenues is 25 percent rather than 20 percent.

d. If the mower is less efficient than Larry originally thought so that his net revenues will be $5,500 rather than $6,000.

    In each case, Larry must compare the financial costs and benefits of buying the mower.

a. If the interest rate is 12 percent, then the interest cost will be 12 percent of $4,000, or $480, which exceeds the value of the mower's marginal product ($400). Larry should not buy the mower.

b. If the cost of the mower is $7,000, then Larry must borrow $7,000 instead of $4,000. At 6 percent interest, his interest cost will be $420—too high to justify the purchase since the value of the mower's marginal product is $400.

c. If the tax rate on net revenues is 25 percent, then Larry must pay 25 percent of his $6,000 net revenues, or $1,500, in taxes. After taxes, his revenues from mowing will be $4,500, which is only $100 more than he could make working at an alternative job. Furthermore, the $100 will not cover the $240 in interest that Larry would have to pay. So again, Larry should not buy the mower.

d. If the mower is less efficient than originally expected so that Larry can earn net revenues of only $5,500, Larry will be left with only $4,400 after taxes—the same amount he could earn by working at another job. So in this case, the value of the mower's marginal product is zero. At any interest rate greater than zero, Larry should not buy the mower.

CONCEPT CHECK 8.4

Repeat Example 8.9, but assume that, over the course of the year, wear and tear reduces the resale value of the lawn mower from $4,000 to $3,800. Should Larry buy the mower?

Examples 8.8 and 8.9 illustrate the main factors firms must consider when deciding whether to invest in new capital goods. On the cost side, two important factors are the *price of capital goods* and the *real interest rate*. Clearly, the more expensive new capital goods are, the more reluctant firms will be to invest in them. Buying the mower was profitable for Larry when its price was $4,000, but not when its price was $7,000.

Why is the real interest rate an important factor in investment decisions? The most straightforward case is when a firm has to borrow (as Larry did) to purchase its new capital. The real interest rate then determines the real cost to the firm of paying back its debt. Since financing costs are a major part of the total cost of owning and operating a piece of capital, much as mortgage payments are a major part of the cost of owning a home, increases in the real interest rate make the purchase of capital goods less attractive to firms, all else being equal.

Even if a firm does not need to borrow to buy new capital—say, because it has accumulated enough profits to buy the capital outright—the real interest rate remains an important determinant of the desirability of an investment. If a firm does not use its profits to acquire new capital, most likely it will use those profits to acquire financial assets such as bonds, which will earn the firm the real rate of interest (we will discuss financial assets such as stocks and bonds in greater detail in the next section of this chapter). If the firm uses its profits to buy capital rather than to purchase a bond, it forgoes the opportunity to earn the real rate of interest on its funds. Thus, the real rate of interest measures the *opportunity cost* of a capital investment. Since an increase in the real interest rate raises the opportunity cost of investing in new capital, it lowers the willingness of firms to invest, even if they do not literally need to borrow to finance new machines or equipment.

On the benefit side, the key factor in determining business investment is the *value of the marginal product* of the new capital, which should be calculated net of both operating and maintenance expenses and taxes paid on the revenues the capital generates. The value of the marginal product is affected by several factors. For example, a technological advance that allows a piece of capital to produce more goods and services would increase the value of its marginal product, as would lower taxes on the revenues produced by the new capital. An increase in the price of the good or service that the capital is used to produce will also increase the value of the marginal product and, hence, the desirability of the investment. For example, if the going price for lawn-mowing services were to rise, then all else being equal, investing in the mower would become more profitable for Larry.

> **Increasing Opportunity Cost**

The Economic Naturalist 8.1

Why has investment in computers increased so much in recent decades?

Since about 1980, investment in new computer systems by U.S. firms has risen sharply (see Figure 8.5). Purchases of new computers and software by firms now exceed 2.2 percent of GDP and amount to about 18 percent of all private nonresidential investment. Why has investment in computers increased so much?

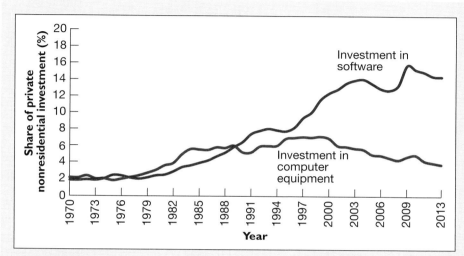

FIGURE 8.5

Investment in Computers and Software, 1970–2013.

Investment in computer equipment and software since 1970 shown as a percentage of private nonresidential investment. Note how computer investments by U.S. firms started rising significantly as a percentage of private investment in 1980, but have since started to decline.

SOURCE: Bureau of Economic Analysis, www.bea.gov.

Investment in computers has increased by much more than other types of investment. Hence, the factors that affect all types of investment (such as the real interest rate and the tax rate) are not likely to be responsible for the boom. The two main causes of increased investment in computers appear to be the declining price of computing power and the increase in the value of the marginal product of computers. In recent years, the price of computing power has fallen at a precipitous rate. An industry rule of thumb is that the amount of computing power that is obtainable at a given price doubles every 18 months. As the price of computing power falls, an investment in computers becomes more and more likely to pass the cost-benefit test.

On the benefit side, for some years after the beginning of the computer boom, economists were unable to associate the technology with significant productivity gains. Defenders of investment in computer systems argued that the improvements in goods and services computers create are particularly hard to measure. How does one quantify the value to consumers of 24-hour-a-day access to cash or of the ability to make airline reservations online? Critics responded that the expected benefits of the computer revolution may have proved illusory because of problems such as user-unfriendly software and poor technical training. However, U.S. productivity did increase noticeably in the years following the beginning of widespread use of the Internet.

Cost-Benefit

RECAP	INVESTMENT AND CAPITAL FORMATION

Any of the following factors will increase the willingness of firms to invest in new capital:

1. A decline in the price of new capital goods.

2. A decline in the real interest rate.

3. Technological improvement that raises the marginal product of capital.

4. Lower taxes on the revenues generated by capital.

5. A higher relative price for the firm's output.

BONDS, STOCKS, AND THE ALLOCATION OF SAVINGS

Large and well-established corporations that wish to obtain funds for investment—the creation of new capital goods—have several alternative options to do so. They will, just like smaller firms, sometimes go to banks to borrow the funds (a process that we discuss in greater detail in the chapter *Money, Prices, and Financial Intermediaries*). However, larger firms can also obtain funds more directly through the corporate bond market and the stock market. We first discuss some of the mechanics of bonds and stocks, then return to the role of bond and stock markets in allocating saving for capital formation.

BONDS

bond a legal promise to repay a debt, usually including both the principal amount and regular interest, or coupon, payments

principal amount the amount originally lent

maturation date the date at which the principal of a bond will be repaid

coupon payments regular interest payments made to the bondholder

coupon rate the interest rate promised when a bond is issued; the annual coupon payments are equal to the coupon rate times the principal amount of the bond

A **bond** is a legal promise to repay a debt. These repayments typically consist of two parts. First, the **principal amount,** which is the amount originally lent, is paid at some specific date in the future, called the **maturation date.** Second, the owner of the bond, called the *bondholder,* receives regular interest, or **coupon payments,** until the bond's maturation date. For example, a bond may have a principal amount of $1,000 payable on January 1, 2030, and annual coupon payments of $50. These coupon payments are also equal to the principal amount times the **coupon rate,** where the coupon rate is the interest rate promised when the bond is issued. (The coupon rate therefore is also equal to the annual coupon payment divided by the principal.) In the example above, the principal is $1,000 and the coupon rate is 5 percent, resulting in annual coupon payments of (.05) ($1,000), or $50.

Corporations and governments frequently raise funds by issuing bonds and selling them to savers. The coupon rate that a newly issued bond must promise in order to be attractive to savers depends on a number of factors, including the bond's term, its credit risk, and its tax treatment. The *term* of a bond is the length of time until the bond's maturation date, which can range from 30 days to 30 years or more. The annual coupon rates on long-term (30-year) bonds generally exceed those on short-term (1-year) bonds because lenders require higher coupon rates (and, hence, higher annual coupon payments) to lend for a long term.

Credit risk is the risk that the borrower will go bankrupt and thus not repay the loan. A borrower that is viewed as risky will have to pay a higher coupon rate to compensate lenders for taking the chance of losing all or part of their financial investment. For example, so-called high-yield bonds, less formally known as "junk bonds," are bonds issued by firms judged to be risky by credit-rating agencies; these bonds pay higher coupon rates than bonds issued by companies thought to be less risky.

Bonds also differ in their *tax treatment.* For example, interest paid on bonds issued by local governments, called *municipal bonds,* is exempt from federal taxes, whereas interest on other types of bonds is treated as taxable income. Because of this tax advantage, lenders are willing to accept a lower coupon rate on municipal bonds.

Bond owners are not required to hold their bonds until their maturation dates. They are always free to sell their bonds in the *bond market,* an organized market run by professional bond traders. The market value of a particular bond at any given point in time is called the *price* of the bond. The price of a bond can be greater than, less than, or equal to the principal amount of the bond, depending on how the current or prevailing interest rate in financial markets compares with the interest rate at the time the bond was issued. The close relationship between the price of a bond and the current interest rate is illustrated by the following example.

Bond Prices and Interest Rates   **EXAMPLE 8.10**

What is the relationship between bond prices and interest rates?

On January 1, 2015, Tanya purchases a newly issued, two-year government bond with a principal amount of $1,000 for a price of $1,000. The coupon rate on the bond is 5 percent, paid annually, reflecting the prevailing interest rates on January 1, 2015. Hence, Tanya, or whoever owns the bond at the time, will receive a coupon payment of $50 (5 percent of $1,000) on January 1, 2016. The owner of the bond will receive another coupon payment of $50 on January 1, 2017, at which time she also will receive repayment of the principal amount of $1,000.

On January 1, 2016, after receiving her first year's coupon payment, Tanya decides to sell her bond to raise the funds to take a vacation. She offers her bond for sale in the bond market. The buyer of the bond will receive $1,050 on January 1, 2017, representing the second coupon payment of $50, plus repayment of the $1,000 principal. How much can Tanya expect to get for her "used" bond? The answer depends on the prevailing interest rate in the bond market when she sells her bond on January 1, 2016.

Suppose first that, on January 1, 2016, when Tanya takes her bond to the bond market, the prevailing interest rate on newly issued one-year bonds has risen to 6 percent. Thus, someone who buys a new one-year bond on January 1, 2016, with a 6 percent coupon rate for $1,000 will receive $1,060 on January 1, 2017 ($1,000 principal repayment plus a $60 coupon payment). Would that person also be willing to pay Tanya the $1,000 Tanya paid for her bond? No. Note that the coupon payment on Tanya's "used" bond does not rise when interest rates rise but remains equal to $50. Consequently, the purchaser of Tanya's "used" bond will receive only $1,050 on January 1, 2017, when the bond matures. In order to sell her "used" bond, Tanya will have to reduce the price below $1,000.

This example illustrates the fact that *bond prices and interest rates are inversely related.* When the interest rate being paid on newly issued bonds rises, the price financial investors are willing to pay for existing bonds falls.

How much would the price for Tanya's "used" bond have to fall? Recall that the person who buys the newly issued one-year bond on January 1, 2016, for $1,000 will receive $1,060 on January 1, 2017. This $60 gain represents a 6 percent return on the price he paid. That person will buy Tanya's "used" bond only if Tanya's bond also will give him a 6 percent return. The price for Tanya's bond that allows the purchaser to earn a 6 percent return must satisfy the equation

$$\text{Bond price} \times 1.06 = \$1,050.$$

Solving the equation for the bond price, we find that Tanya's bond will sell for $1,050/1.06, or just under $991. To check this result, note that on January 1, 2017, the purchaser of the bond will receive $1,050, or $59 more than he paid on January 1, 2016. His rate of return is $59/$991, or 6 percent, as expected.

What if the prevailing interest rate had instead fallen to 4 percent? When prevailing interest rates fall, bond prices rise. The price of Tanya's "used" bond would rise until it, too, gave a return of 4 percent. At that point, the price of Tanya's bond would satisfy the relationship

$$\text{Bond price} \times 1.04 = \$1,050,$$

implying that the price of her bond would rise to $1,050/1.04, or almost $1,010.

Finally, what happens if the interest rate when Tanya wants to sell is 5 percent, the same as it was when she originally bought the bond? You should show that in this case the bond would sell at its original price of $1,000.

CONCEPT CHECK 8.5

Three-year government bonds are issued with a principal amount of $1,000 and an annual coupon rate of 7 percent. Thus, the owner will receive three coupon payments of (0.07)($1,000) = $70 at the end of each year. One year prior to the maturation date of these bonds, a newspaper headline reads, "Bad Economic News Causes Prices of Bonds to Plunge," and the story reveals that these three-year bonds have fallen in price to $960. What has happened to prevailing interest rates? What is the one-year interest rate at the time of the newspaper story?

Issuing bonds is one means by which a corporation or a government can obtain funds from savers. Another important way of raising funds, but one restricted to corporations, is by issuing stock to the public.

STOCKS

stock (or equity) a claim to partial ownership of a firm

A share of **stock** (or *equity*) is a claim to partial ownership of a firm. For example, if a corporation has 1 million shares of stock outstanding, ownership of one share is equivalent to ownership of one-millionth of the company. Stockholders receive returns on their financial investment in two forms.

dividend a regular payment received by stockholders for each share that they own

First, stockholders receive a regular payment called a **dividend** for each share of stock they own. Dividends are determined by the firm's management and usually depend on the firm's recent profits. Second, stockholders receive returns in the form of *capital gains* when the price of their stock increases.

Prices of stocks are determined through trading on a stock exchange such as the New York Stock Exchange. A stock's price rises and falls as the demand for the stock changes. Demand for stocks in turn depends on factors such as news about the prospects of the company. For example, the stock price of a pharmaceutical company that announces the discovery of an important new drug is likely to rise on the announcement, even if actual production and marketing of the drug are some time away, because financial investors expect the company to become more profitable in the future. Example 8.11 illustrates numerically some key factors that affect stock prices.

Buying Shares in a New Company   **EXAMPLE 8.11**

How much should you pay for a share of FortuneCookie.com?

You have the opportunity to buy shares in a new company called FortuneCookie.com, which plans to sell gourmet fortune cookies online. Your stockbroker estimates that the company will pay $1.00 per share in dividends a year from now, and that in a year the market price of the company will be $80.00 per share. Assuming that you accept your broker's estimates as accurate, what is the most that you should be willing to pay today per share of FortuneCookie.com? How does your answer change if you expect a $5.00 dividend? If you expect a $1.00 dividend but an $84.00 stock price in one year?

Based on your broker's estimates, you conclude that in one year each share of FortuneCookie.com you own will be worth $81.00 in your pocket—the $1.00 dividend plus the $80.00 you could get by reselling the stock. Finding the maximum price you would pay for the stock today, therefore, boils down to asking how much would you invest today to have $81.00 a year from today. Answering this question in turn requires one more piece of information, which is the expected rate of return that you require in order to be willing to buy stock in this company.

How would you determine your required rate of return to hold stock in FortuneCookie .com? For the moment, let's imagine that you are not too worried about the potential riskiness of the stock, either because you think that it is a "sure thing" or because you are a devil-may-care type who is not bothered by risk. In that case, you can apply the Cost-Benefit Principle. Your required rate of return to hold FortuneCookie.com should be about the same as you can get on other financial investments such as government bonds. The available return on other financial investments gives the opportunity cost of your funds.

Cost-Benefit

For example, if the interest rate currently being offered by government bonds is 6 percent, you should be willing to accept a 6 percent return to hold FortuneCookie.com as well. In that case, the maximum price you would pay today for a share of FortuneCookie .com satisfies the equation

$$\text{Stock price} \times 1.06 = \$81.00.$$

This equation defines the stock price you should be willing to pay if you are willing to accept a 6 percent return over the next year. Solving this equation yields stock price = $81.00/1.06 = $76.42. If you buy FortuneCookie.com for $76.42, then your return over the year will be ($81.00 − $76.42)/$76.42 = $4.58/$76.42 = 6 percent, which is the rate of return you required to buy the stock.

If, instead, the dividend is expected to be $5.00, then the total benefit of holding the stock in one year, equal to the expected dividend plus the expected price, is $5.00 + $80.00, or $85.00. Assuming again that you are willing to accept a 6 percent return to hold FortuneCookie.com, the price you are willing to pay for the stock today satisfies the relationship stock price × 1.06 = $85.00. Solving this equation for the stock price yields stock price = $85.00/1.06 = $80.19.

Comparing this price with that in the previous case, we see that a higher expected dividend in the future increases the value of the stock today. That's why good news about the future prospects of a company—such as the announcement by a pharmaceutical company that it has discovered a useful new drug—affects its stock price immediately.

If the expected future price of the stock is $84.00, with the dividend at $1.00, then the value of holding the stock in one year is once again $85.00, and the calculation is the same as the previous one. Again, the price you should be willing to pay for the stock is $80.19.

These examples show that an increase in the future dividend or in the future expected stock price raises the stock price today, whereas an increase in the return a saver requires to hold the stock lowers today's stock price. Since we expect required returns in the stock market to be closely tied to market interest rates, this last result implies that increases in interest rates tend to depress stock prices as well as bond prices.

Our examples also took the future stock price as given. But what determines the future stock price? Just as today's stock price depends on the dividend shareholders expect to receive this year and the stock price a year from now, the stock price a year from now depends on the dividend expected for next year and the stock price two years from now, and so on.

Ultimately, then, today's stock price is affected by not only the dividend expected this year but future dividends as well. A company's ability to pay dividends depends on its earnings. If a company's earnings are expected to increase rapidly in the future, its future dividends will probably grow too. Thus, as we noted in the example of the pharmaceutical company that announces the discovery of a new drug, news about future earnings—even earnings quite far in the future—is likely to affect a company's stock price immediately.

CONCEPT CHECK 8.6

Continuing with Example 8.11, you expect a share of FortuneCookie.com to be worth $80.00 per share in one year, and also to pay a dividend of $1.00 in one year. What should you be willing to pay for the stock today if the prevailing interest rate, equal to your required rate of return, is 4 percent? What if the interest rate is 8 percent? In general, how would you expect stock prices to react if economic news arrives that implies that interest rates will rise in the very near future?

risk premium the rate of return that financial investors require to hold risky assets minus the rate of return on safe assets

In the examples we have studied, we assumed that you were willing to accept a return of 6 percent to hold FortuneCookie.com, the same return that you could get on a government bond. However, financial investments in the stock market are quite risky in that returns to holding stocks can be highly variable and unpredictable. For example, although you expect a share of FortuneCookie.com to be worth $80.00 in one year, you also realize that there is a chance it might sell as low as $50.00 or as high as $110.00 per share. Most financial investors dislike risk and unpredictability and thus have a higher required rate of return for holding risky assets like stocks than for holding relatively safe assets like government bonds. The difference between the required rate of return to hold risky assets and the rate of return on safe assets, like government bonds, is called the **risk premium.**

Riskiness and Stock Prices	**EXAMPLE 8.12**

What is the relationship between stock prices and risk?

Let's build on our previous examples by introducing risk. Suppose that FortuneCookie.com is expected to pay a $1.00 dividend and have a market price of $80.00 per share in one year. The interest rate on government bonds is 6 percent per year. However, to be willing to hold a risky asset like a share of FortuneCookie.com, you require an expected return four percentage points higher than the rate paid by safe assets like government bonds (a risk premium of 4 percent). Hence, you require a 10 percent expected return to hold FortuneCookie.com. What is the most you would be willing to pay for the stock now? What do you conclude about the relationship between perceived riskiness and stock prices?

As a share of FortuneCookie.com is expected to pay $81.00 in one year and the required return is 10 percent, we have stock price × 1.10 = $81.00. Solving for the stock price, we find the price to be $81.00/1.10 = $73.64, less than the price of $76.42 we found when there was no risk premium and the required rate of return was 6 percent. We conclude that financial investors' dislike of risk, and the resulting risk premium, lowers the prices of risky assets like stocks.

THE INFORMATIONAL ROLE OF BOND AND STOCK MARKETS

Savers and their financial advisors know that, to get the highest possible returns on their financial investments, they must find the potential borrowers with the most profitable opportunities. This knowledge provides a powerful incentive to scrutinize potential borrowers carefully.

For example, companies considering a new issue of stocks or bonds know that their recent performance and plans for the future will be carefully studied by professional analysts on Wall Street and other financial investors. If the analysts and other potential purchasers have doubts about the future profitability of the firm, they will offer a relatively low price for the newly issued shares or they will demand a high interest rate on newly issued bonds. Knowing this, a company will be reluctant to go to the bond or stock market for financing unless its management is confident that it can convince financial investors that the firm's planned use of the funds will be profitable. *Thus, the ongoing search by savers and their financial advisors for high returns leads the bond and stock markets to direct funds to the uses that appear most likely to be productive.*

RISK SHARING AND DIVERSIFICATION

Many highly promising investment projects are also quite risky. The successful development of a new drug to lower cholesterol could create billions of dollars in profits for a drug company, for example; but if the drug turns out to be less effective than some others on the market, none of the development costs will be recouped. An individual who lent his or her life savings to help finance the development of the anticholesterol drug might enjoy a handsome return but also takes the chance of losing everything. Savers are generally reluctant to take large risks, so without some means of reducing the risk faced by each saver, it might be very hard for the company to find the funds to develop the new drug.

Bond and stock markets help reduce risk by giving savers a means to *diversify* their financial investments. **Diversification** is the practice of spreading one's wealth over a variety of different financial investments to reduce overall risk. The idea of diversification follows from the adage that "you shouldn't put all your eggs in one basket." Rather than putting all of his or her saving in one very risky project, a financial investor will find it much safer to allocate a small amount of saving to each of a large number of stocks and bonds. That way, if some financial assets fall in value, there is a good chance that others will rise in value, with gains offsetting losses. The following example illustrates the benefits of diversification.

diversification the practice of spreading one's wealth over a variety of different financial investments to reduce overall risk

The Benefits of Diversification   EXAMPLE 8.13

What are the benefits of diversification?

Vikram has $200 to invest and is considering two stocks, Smith Umbrella Co. and Jones Suntan Lotion Co. Suppose the price of one share of each stock is $100. The umbrella company will turn out to be the better investment if the weather is rainy, but the suntan lotion company will be the better investment if the weather is sunny. In Table 8.3, we illustrate the amounts by which the price of one share of each stock will change and how this depends on the weather.

TABLE 8.3
Changes in the Stock Price of Two Companies

Actual weather	Increase in Stock Price per Share	
	Smith Umbrella Co.	Jones Suntan Lotion Co.
Rainy	+$10	Unchanged
Sunny	Unchanged	+$10

According to Table 8.3, the price of one share of Smith Umbrella Co. stock will rise by $10 (from $100 to $110) if it rains but will remain unchanged if the weather is sunny.

The price of one share of Jones Suntan Lotion Co. stock, on the other hand, is expected to rise by $10 (from $100 to $110) if it is sunny but will remain unchanged if there is rain.

Suppose the chance of rain is 50 percent, and the chance of sunshine is 50 percent. How should Vikram invest his $200? If Vikram were to invest all his $200 in Smith Umbrella, he could buy two shares. Half of the time it will rain and each share will rise by $10, for a total gain of $20. Half of the time, however, it will be sunny, in which case the stock price will remain unchanged. Thus, his average gain will be 50 percent (or one-half) times $20 plus 50 percent times $0, which is equal to $10.

If, however, Vikram invested all of his $200 in Jones Suntan Lotion Co., he could again buy two shares for $100 each. Each share would rise by $10 if the weather is sunny (for a total gain of $20) and remain unchanged if the weather is rainy. Since it will be sunny half the time, the average gain will be 50 percent times $20 plus 50 percent times $0, or $10.

Although Vikram can earn an *average* gain of $10 if he puts all of his money into either stock, investing in only one stock is quite risky, since his actual gain varies widely depending on whether there is rain or shine. Can Vikram *guarantee* himself a gain of $10, avoiding the uncertainty and risk? Yes, all he has to do is buy one share of each of the two stocks. If it rains, he will earn $10 on his Smith Umbrella stock and nothing on his Jones Suntan stock. If it's sunny, he will earn nothing on Smith Umbrella but $10 on Jones Suntan. Rain or shine, he is guaranteed to earn $10—without risk.

The existence of bond markets and stock markets makes it easy for savers to diversify by putting a small amount of their saving into each of a wide variety of different financial assets, each of which represents a share of a particular company or investment project. From society's point of view, diversification makes it possible for risky but worthwhile projects to obtain funding, without individual savers having to bear too much risk.

For the typical person, a particularly convenient way to diversify is to buy bonds and stocks indirectly through mutual funds. A **mutual fund** is a financial intermediary that sells shares in itself to the public and then uses the funds raised to buy a wide variety of financial assets. Holding shares in a mutual fund thus amounts to owning a little bit of many different financial assets, which helps to achieve diversification. The advantage of mutual funds is that it is usually less costly and time-consuming to buy shares in one or two mutual funds than to buy many different stocks and bonds directly. Over the past 40 years, mutual funds have become increasingly popular in the United States.

mutual fund a financial intermediary that sells shares in itself to the public and then uses the funds raised to buy a wide variety of financial assets

A few words of caution before we end our discussion on bond and stock markets: There are millions of shares of stocks and bonds traded daily in U.S. financial markets. The vast majority of these represent what is often called the *secondary market,* which refers to trades between savers rather than between savers and borrowers—you can think of this as the market for used bonds and stocks. However, these transactions between savers, where only the ownership of the bonds or stocks changes hands, do not meet the definition of investment in economics. Since no new funds are allocated from savers to borrowers, no new capital formation is taking place.

SAVING, INVESTMENT, AND FINANCIAL MARKETS

In a market economy like that of the United States, savings are allocated by means of a decentralized, market-oriented financial system. The U.S. financial system consists both of financial institutions, like banks, and financial markets such as bond markets and stock markets. In the last section of this chapter, we examine the basic workings of financial markets without regard to the particular assets (bonds or stocks) that are being traded. In particular, we focus on the role that the real interest rate plays in allocating resources from savers to borrowers. In the *Money, Prices, and Financial Intermediaries* chapter, we will examine financial institutions and relate this discussion to the role of money in a market economy.

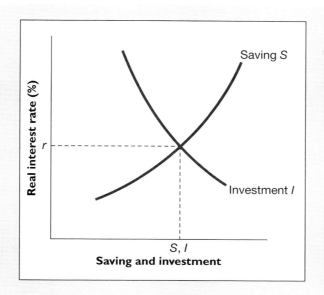

FIGURE 8.6

The Supply of and Demand for Saving.

Saving is supplied by households, firms, and the government and demanded by borrowers wishing to invest in new capital goods. In financial market equilibrium, the real interest rate takes the value that equates the quantity of saving supplied and demanded.

Figure 8.6 shows the supply of saving and the demand for investment in a financial market. Quantities of national saving and investment are measured on the horizontal axis; the real interest rate is shown on the vertical axis. As we will see, in the market for saving, the real interest rate functions as the "price."

In the figure the supply of saving is shown by the upward-sloping curve marked S. This curve shows the quantity of national saving that households, firms, and the government are willing to supply at each value of the real interest rate. The saving curve is upward-sloping because empirical evidence suggests that increases in the real interest rate stimulate saving. The demand for saving is given by the downward-sloping curve marked I for investment. This curve shows the quantity of investment in new capital that firms would choose and hence the amount they would need to borrow in financial markets, at each value of the real interest rate. Because higher real interest rates raise the cost of borrowing and reduce firms' willingness to invest, the demand for saving curve is downward-sloping.

Putting aside the possibility of borrowing from foreigners (which we discuss in the chapter *Exchange Rates, International Trade, and Capital Flows*), a country can invest only those resources that its savers make available. In equilibrium, then, desired investment (the demand for saving) and desired national saving (the supply of saving) must be equal. As Figure 8.6 suggests, desired saving is equated with desired investment through adjustments in the real interest rate, which functions as the "price" of saving. The movements of the real interest rate clear the market for saving in much the same way that the price of apples clears the market for apples. In Figure 8.6, the real interest rate that clears the market for saving is r, the real interest rate that corresponds to the intersection of the supply and demand curves.

The forces that push the real interest rate toward its equilibrium level are similar to the forces that lead to equilibrium in any other market, as we first saw in the chapter covering supply and demand. Suppose, for example, that the real interest rate exceeded r. At a higher real interest rate, savers would provide more funds than firms would want to invest. As lenders (savers) competed among themselves to attract borrowers (investors), the real interest rate would be bid down. The real interest rate would fall until it equaled r, the only interest rate at which both borrowers and lenders are satisfied, and no opportunities are left unexploited in the financial market. The Equilibrium Principle thus holds in this market as it does in others that we have studied through this book.

Equilibrium

Changes in factors *other than the real interest rate* that affect the supply of or demand for saving will shift the curves, leading to a new equilibrium in the financial market. Changes in the real interest rate cannot shift the curves, just as a change in the price of apples cannot shift the supply or demand for apples, because the effects of the real interest rate on saving are already incorporated in the slopes of the curves. The following examples will illustrate the use of the supply and demand model of financial markets.

| **The Effects of New Technology** | **EXAMPLE 8.14** |

How does the introduction of new technologies affect saving, investment, and the real interest rate?

Exciting new technologies have been introduced in recent years, ranging from the Internet to new applications of genetics. A number of these technologies appear to have great commercial potential. How does the introduction of new technologies affect saving, investment, and the real interest rate?

The introduction of any new technology with the potential for commercial application creates profit opportunities for those who can bring the fruits of the technology to the public. In economists' language, the technical breakthrough raises the marginal product of new capital. Figure 8.7 shows the effects of a technological breakthrough, with a resulting increase in the marginal product of capital. At any given real interest rate, an increase in the marginal product of capital makes firms more eager to invest. Thus, the advent of the new technology causes the demand for saving to shift upward and to the right, from I to I'.

FIGURE 8.7

The Effects of a New Technology on National Saving and Investment.

A technological breakthrough raises the marginal product of new capital goods, increasing desired investment and the demand for saving. The real interest rate rises, as do national saving and investment.

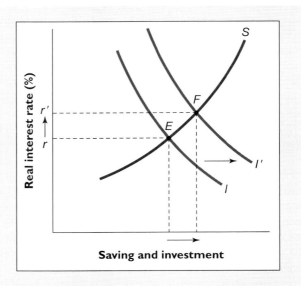

At the new equilibrium point F, investment and national saving are higher than before, as is the real interest rate, which rises from r to r'. The rise in the real interest rate reflects the increased demand for funds by investors as they race to apply the new technologies. Because of the incentive of higher real returns, saving increases as well. Indeed, the real interest rate in the United States was relatively high in the late 1990s (Figure 5.3), as was the rate of investment, reflecting the opportunities created by new technologies.

Next, let's examine how a change in the supply of saving affects the financial markets.

An Increase in the Government Budget Deficit   EXAMPLE 8.15

How does an increase in the government budget deficit affect saving, investment, and the real interest rate?

Suppose the government increases its spending without raising taxes, thereby increasing its budget deficit (or reducing its budget surplus). How will this decision affect national saving, investment, and the real interest rate?

National saving includes both private saving (saving by households and businesses) and public saving, which is equivalent to the government budget surplus. An increase in the government budget deficit (or a decline in the surplus) reduces public saving. Assuming that private saving does not change, the reduction in public saving will reduce national saving as well.

Figure 8.8 shows the effect of the increased government budget deficit on the market for saving and investment. At any real interest rate, a larger deficit reduces national saving, causing the saving curve to shift to the left, from S to S'. At the new equilibrium point F, the real interest rate is higher at r' and both national saving and investment are lower. In economic terms, the government has dipped further into the pool of private savings to borrow the funds to finance its budget deficit. The government's extra borrowing forces investors to compete for a smaller quantity of available saving, driving up the real interest rate. The higher real interest rate makes investment less attractive, ensuring the investment will decrease along with national saving.

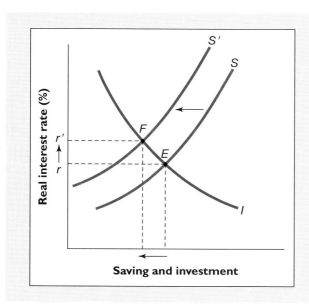

FIGURE 8.8

The Effects of an Increase in the Government Budget Deficit on National Saving and Investment.

An increase in the government budget deficit reduces the supply of saving, raising the real interest rate and lowering investment. The tendency of increased government deficits to reduce investment in new capital is called *crowding out*.

The tendency of government budget deficits to reduce investment spending is called **crowding out.** Reduced investment spending implies lower capital formation, and thus lower economic growth, as we saw in the chapter *Economic Growth*. This adverse effect of budget deficits on economic growth is a key reason that economists advise governments to minimize their deficits. Note that this analysis keeps the level of national income constant. As we will discuss in other chapters, an increase in government spending may increase the level of GDP; thus, an increase in government spending might lead to only a small decrease in national saving.

crowding out the tendency of increased government deficits to reduce investment spending

CONCEPT CHECK 8.7

Suppose the general public becomes more "grasshopper-like" and less "ant-like" in their saving decisions, becoming less concerned about saving for the future. How will the change in public attitudes affect the country's rate of capital formation and economic growth?

Increasing National Saving	EXAMPLE 8.16

Are there government policies that would increase national saving?

Most policymakers recognize that the United States would eventually benefit from higher national saving rates. The government could increase public saving by reducing budget deficits. However, this will be difficult to accomplish in the coming years. Earlier, we pointed out that budget deficits grew primarily because of the tax-rate reductions in the early 2000s, the increased defense spending needed to fight wars in Iraq and Afghanistan, and the reductions in tax revenue and increases in government spending associated with the most recent recession. All of these factors will have to be addressed in order to decrease future budget deficits, yet each has a powerful constituency in favor or need of each one. Thus, the political climate is not conducive to reducing budget deficits in the near future.

Alternatively, increasing the incentives for households and firms to save would increase private saving. Some economists, for example, believe that the federal income tax should be scrapped in favor of a federal consumption tax. A consumption tax would be similar to the sales tax collected in most states, wherein people are taxed only when they spend. Taxing the portion of income that is consumed but not the portion that is saved would increase the incentive to save.

Other economists favor further reductions in the tax rates on dividends and capital gains beyond those passed during George W. Bush's first term as president. These tax cuts would increase the after-tax rate of return to saving and thereby promote additional private saving. If private saving rises by more than the immediate loss in tax revenues, national saving also will rise.

At the national level, high saving rates lead to greater investment in new capital goods and thus higher standards of living. At the individual or family level, a high saving rate promotes the accumulation of wealth and the achievement of economic security.

RECAP	SAVING, INVESTMENT, AND FINANCIAL MARKETS

Any of the following factors will shift the demand for savings (I) to the right.

1. A decline in the price of new capital goods.
2. Technological improvement that raises the marginal product of capital.
3. Lower taxes on the revenues generated by capital.
4. A higher relative price for the firm's output.

The supply of savings will shift right if national saving, private and/or public saving, is increased.

○ SUMMARY ○

- In general, saving equals current income minus spending on current needs; the saving rate is the percentage of income that is saved. Wealth, or net worth, equals the market value of assets (real or financial items of value) minus liabilities (debts). Saving is a flow, being measured in dollars per unit of time; wealth is a stock, measured in dollars at a point in time. Just as the amount of water in a bathtub changes according to the rate at which water flows in, the stock of wealth increases at the saving rate. Wealth also increases if the value of existing assets rises (capital gains) and decreases if the value of existing assets falls (capital losses). *(LO1)*

- The saving of an entire country is *national saving S*. National saving is defined by $S = Y - C - G$, where Y represents total output or income, C equals consumption spending, and G equals government purchases of goods and services. National saving can be broken up into private saving, or $Y - T - C$, and public saving, or $T - G$, where T stands for taxes paid to the government less transfer payments and interest paid by the government to the private sector. Private saving can be further broken down into household saving and business saving. In the United States, the bulk of private saving is done by businesses. *(LO2)*

- Public saving is equivalent to the government budget surplus, $T - G$; if the government runs a budget deficit, then public saving is negative. The U.S. national saving rate is low relative to other industrialized countries, but it is higher and more stable than U.S. household saving. *(LO2)*

- Individuals and households save for a variety of reasons, including life-cycle objectives, such as saving for retirement or a new home; the need to be prepared for an emergency (precautionary saving); and the desire to leave an inheritance (bequest saving). The amount people save also is affected by the real interest rate, which is the "reward" for saving. Evidence suggests that higher real interest rates lead to modest increases in saving. Saving also can be affected by psychological factors such as the degree of self-control and the desire to consume at the level of one's neighbors (demonstration effects). *(LO3)*

- Investment is the purchase or construction of new capital goods, including housing. Firms will invest in new capital goods if the benefits of doing so outweigh the costs.

Two factors that determine the cost of investment are the price of new capital goods and the real interest rate. The higher the real interest rate, the more expensive it is to borrow, and the less likely firms are to invest. The benefit of investment is the value of the marginal product of new capital, which depends on factors such as the productivity of new capital goods, the taxes levied on the revenues they generate, and the relative price of the firm's output. *(LO4)*

- Businesses can obtain financing by issuing bonds or stocks. A bond is a legal promise to repay a debt, including both the principal amount and regular interest or coupon payments. The prices of existing bonds decline when interest rates rise. A share of stock is a claim to partial ownership of a firm. The price of a stock depends positively on the dividend the stock is expected to pay and on the expected future price of the stock and negatively on the rate of return required by financial investors to hold the stock. The required rate of return in turn is the sum of the return on safe assets and the additional return required to compensate financial investors for the riskiness of stocks, called the risk premium. *(LO5)*

- Financial markets, such as bond markets and stock markets, improve the allocation of saving in two ways. First, they provide information to savers about which possible uses of their funds are likely to prove most productive and hence pay the highest return. Second, financial markets help savers share the risks of lending by permitting them to diversify their financial investments. *(LO5)*

- In the absence of international borrowing or lending, the supply of and demand for national saving must be equal. The supply of national saving depends on the saving decisions of households and businesses and the fiscal policies of the government (which determine public saving). The demand for saving is the amount business firms want to invest in new capital. The real interest rate, which is the "price" of borrowed funds, changes to equate the supply of and demand for national saving. Factors that affect the supply of or demand for saving will change saving, investment, and the equilibrium real interest rate. For example, an increase in the government budget deficit will reduce national saving and investment and raise the equilibrium real interest rate. The tendency of government budget deficits to reduce investment is called crowding out. *(LO6)*

○ KEY TERMS ○

assets
balance sheet
bequest saving
bond
capital gains
capital losses
coupon payments
coupon rate
crowding out
diversification

dividend
flow
government budget deficit
government budget surplus
liabilities
life-cycle saving
maturation date
mutual fund
national saving
precautionary saving

principal amount
private saving
public saving
risk premium
saving
saving rate
stock
stock (or equity)
transfer payments
wealth

○ REVIEW QUESTIONS ○

1. Explain the relationship between saving and wealth, using the concepts of flows and stocks. Is saving the only means by which wealth can increase? Explain. *(LO1)*

2. Define *national saving,* relating your definition to the general concept of saving. Why does the standard U.S. definition of national saving potentially understate the true amount of saving being done in the economy? *(LO2)*

3. Household saving rates in the United States are very low. Is this fact a problem for the U.S. economy? Why or why not? *(LO2)*

4. Give three basic motivations for saving. Illustrate each with an example. What other factors would psychologists cite as being possibly important for saving? *(LO3)*

5. Why do increases in real interest rates reduce the quantity of saving demanded? (*Hint:* Who are the "demanders" of saving?) *(LO4)*

6. Arjay plans to sell a bond that matures in one year and has a principal value of $1,000. Can he expect to receive $1,000 in the bond market for the bond? Explain. *(LO5)*

7. Stock prices surge, but the prices of government bonds remain stable. What can you infer from the behavior of bond prices about the possible causes of the increase in stock values? *(LO5)*

8. Name one factor that could increase the supply of saving and one that could increase the demand for saving. Show the effects of each on saving, investment, and the real interest rate. *(LO6)*

○ PROBLEMS ○

Visit your mobile app
store and download
the Frank: Study
Econ app *today!*

1. a. Corey has a mountain bike worth $300, a credit card debt of $150, $200 in cash, a Harmon Killebrew baseball card worth $400, $1,200 in a checking account, and an electric bill due for $250. Construct Corey's balance sheet and calculate his net worth. For each remaining part, explain how the event affects Corey's assets, liabilities, and wealth.

   b. Corey goes to a baseball card convention and finds out that his baseball card is a worthless forgery.

   c. Corey uses $150 from his paycheck to pay off his credit card balance. The remainder of his earnings is spent.

   d. Corey writes a $150 check on his checking account to pay off his credit card balance. Of the events in the previous three parts, which, if any, corresponds to saving on Corey's part? *(LO1)*

2. State whether each of the following is a stock or a flow, and explain. *(LO1)*

   a. The gross domestic product.

   b. National saving.

   c. The value of the U.S. housing stock on January 1, 2015.

   d. The amount of U.S. currency in circulation as of this morning.

e. The government budget deficit.

f. The quantity of outstanding government debt on January 1, 2015.

3. In each part that follows, use the economic data given to find national saving, private saving, public saving, and the national saving rate. *(LO2)*

a. Household saving = 200   Business saving = 400
Government purchases of goods and services = 100
Government transfers and interest payments = 100
Tax collections =150   GDP = 2,200

b. GDP = 6,000   Tax collections = 1,200
Government transfers and interest payments = 400
Consumption expenditures = 4,500
Government budget surplus = 100

c. Consumption expenditures = 4,000   Investment = 1,000
Government purchases = 1,000   Net exports = 0
Tax collections = 1,500
Government transfers and interest payments = 500

4. Ellie and Vince are a married couple, both with college degrees and jobs. How would you expect each of the following events to affect the amount they save each month? Explain your answers in terms of the basic motivations for saving. *(LO3)*

a. Ellie learns she is pregnant.

b. Vince reads in the paper about possible layoffs in his industry.

c. Vince had hoped that his parents would lend financial assistance toward the couple's planned purchase of a house, but he learns that they can't afford it.

d. Ellie announces that she would like to go to law school in the next few years.

e. A boom in the stock market greatly increases the value of the couple's retirement funds.

f. Vince and Ellie agree that they would like to leave a substantial amount to local charities in their wills.

5. Individual retirement accounts (IRAs) were established by the U.S. government to encourage saving. An individual who deposits part of current earnings in an IRA does not have to pay income taxes on the earnings deposited, nor are any income taxes charged on the interest earned by the funds in the IRA. However, when the funds are withdrawn from the IRA, the full amount withdrawn is treated as income and is taxed at the individual's current income tax rate. In contrast, an individual depositing in a non-IRA account has to pay income taxes on the funds deposited and on interest earned in each year but does not have to pay taxes on withdrawals from the account. Another feature of IRAs that is different from a standard savings account is that funds deposited in an IRA cannot be withdrawn prior to retirement, except upon payment of a substantial penalty. *(LO3)*

a. Greg, who is five years from retirement, receives a $10,000 bonus at work. He is trying to decide whether to save this extra income in an IRA or in a regular savings account. Both accounts earn 5 percent nominal interest, and Greg is in the 30 percent tax bracket in every year (including his retirement year). Compare the amounts that Greg will have in five years under each of the two saving strategies, net of all taxes. Is the IRA a good deal for Greg?

b. Would you expect the availability of IRAs to increase the amount that households save? Discuss in light of (1) the response of saving to changes in the real interest rate and (2) psychological theories of saving.

6. Ellie and Vince are trying to decide whether to purchase a new home. The house they want is priced at $200,000. Annual expenses such as maintenance, taxes, and insurance equal 4 percent of the home's value. If properly maintained, the house's real value is not expected to change. The real interest rate in the economy is 6 percent, and Ellie and Vince can qualify to borrow the full amount of the purchase price (for simplicity, assume no down payment) at that

rate. Ignore the fact that mortgage interest payments are tax-deductible in the United States. *(LO4)*

a. Ellie and Vince would be willing to pay $1,500 monthly rent to live in a house of the same quality as the one they are thinking about purchasing. Should they buy the house?

b. Does the answer to part a change if they are willing to pay $2,000 monthly rent?

c. Does the answer to part a change if the real interest rate is 4 percent instead of 6 percent?

d. Does the answer to part a change if the developer offers to sell Ellie and Vince the house for $150,000?

e. Why do home-building companies dislike high interest rates?

7. The builder of a new movie theater complex is trying to decide how many screens she wants. Below are her estimates of the number of patrons the complex will attract each year, depending on the number of screens available.

Number of screens	Total number of patrons
1	40,000
2	75,000
3	105,000
4	130,000
5	150,000

After paying the movie distributors and meeting all other noninterest expenses, the owner expects to net $2.00 per ticket sold. Construction costs are $1,000,000 per screen. *(LO4)*

a. Make a table showing the value of marginal product for each screen from the first through the fifth. What property is illustrated by the behavior of marginal products?

How many screens will be built if the real interest rate is:

b. 5.5 percent?

c. 7.5 percent?

d. 10 percent?

e. If the real interest rate is 5.5 percent, how far would construction costs have to fall before the builder would be willing to build a five-screen complex?

8. Simon purchases a bond, newly issued by Amalgamated Corporation, for $1,000. The bond pays $60 to its holder at the end of the first and second years and pays $1,060 upon its maturity at the end of the third year. *(LO5)*

a. What are the principal amount, the term, the coupon rate, and the coupon payment for Simon's bond?

b. After receiving the second coupon payment (at the end of the second year), Simon decides to sell his bond in the bond market. What price can he expect for his bond if the one-year interest rate at that time is 3 percent? 8 percent? 10 percent?

c. Can you think of a reason that the price of Simon's bond after two years might fall below $1,000, even though the market interest rate equals the coupon rate?

9. Shares in Brothers Grimm, Inc., manufacturers of gingerbread houses, are expected to pay a dividend of $5 in one year and to sell for $100 per share at that time. How much should you be willing to pay today per share of Grimm: *(LO5)*

a. If the safe rate of interest is 5 percent and you believe that investing in Grimm carries no risk?

b. If the safe rate of interest is 10 percent and you believe that investing in Grimm carries no risk?

c. If the safe rate of interest is 5 percent, but your risk premium is 3 percent?

d. Repeat parts a to c, assuming that Grimm is not expected to pay a dividend, but the expected price is unchanged.

10. Your financial investments consist of U.S. government bonds maturing in 10 years and shares in a start-up company doing research in pharmaceuticals. How would you expect each of the following news items to affect the value of your assets? Explain your reasoning. *(LO5)*

a. Interest rates of newly issued government bonds rise.

b. Inflation is forecasted to be much lower than previously expected *(Hint:* Recall the Fisher effect from the chapter *Inflation and the Price Level.)* Assume for simplicity that this information does *not* affect your forecast of the dollar value of the pharmaceutical company's future dividends and stock price.

In parts c to f, interest rates on newly issued government bonds are assumed to remain unchanged.

c. Large swings in the stock market increase financial investors' concerns about market risk.

d. The start-up company whose stock you own announces the development of a valuable new drug. However, the drug will not come to market for at least five years.

e. The pharmaceutical company announces that it will not pay a dividend next year.

f. The federal government announces a system of price controls on prescription drugs.

11. You have $1,000 to invest and are considering buying some combination of the shares of two companies, DonkeyInc and ElephantInc. Shares of DonkeyInc will pay a 10 percent return if the Democrats are elected, an event you believe to have a 40 percent probability; otherwise the shares pay a zero return. Shares of ElephantInc will pay 8 percent if the Republicans are elected (a 60 percent probability), zero otherwise. Either the Democrats or the Republicans will be elected. *(LO5)*

a. If your only concern is maximizing your average expected return, with no regard for risk, how should you invest your $1,000?

b. What is your expected return if you invest $500 in each stock? *(Hint:* Consider what your return will be if the Democrats win and if the Republicans win; then weight each outcome by the probability that event occurs.)

c. The strategy of investing $500 in each stock does *not* give the highest possible average expected return. Why might you choose it anyway?

d. Devise an investment strategy that guarantees at least a 4.4 percent return, no matter which party wins.

e. Devise an investment strategy that is riskless, that is, one in which the return on your $1,000 does not depend at all on which party wins.

12. For each of the following scenarios, use supply and demand analysis to predict the resulting changes in the real interest rate, national saving, and investment. Show all your diagrams. *(LO6)*

a. The legislature passes a 10 percent investment tax credit. Under this program, for every $100 that a firm spends on new capital equipment, it receives an extra $10 in tax refunds from the government.

b. A reduction in military spending moves the government's budget from deficit into surplus.

c. A new generation of computer-controlled machines becomes available. These machines produce manufactured goods much more quickly and with fewer defects.

d. The government raises its tax on corporate profits. Other tax changes also are made, such that the government's deficit remains unchanged.

e. Concerns about job security raise precautionary saving.

f. New environmental regulations increase firms' costs of operating capital.

⊙ ANSWERS TO CONCEPT CHECKS ⊙

8.1 If Consuelo's student loan were for $6,500 instead of $3,000, her liabilities would be $6,750 (the student loan plus the credit card balance) instead of $3,250. The value of her assets, $6,280, is unchanged. In this case, Consuelo's wealth is negative, since assets of $6,280 less liabilities of $6,750 equals −$470. Negative wealth or net worth means one owes more than one owns. *(LO1)*

8.2 If water is being drained from the tub, the flow is negative, equal to −3 gallons per minute. There are 37 gallons in the tub at 7:16 p.m. and 34 gallons at 7:17 p.m. The rate of change of the stock is −3 gallons per minute, which is the same as the flow. *(LO1)*

8.3 a. Consuelo has set aside her usual $20, but she has also incurred a new liability of $50. So her net saving for the week is *minus* $30. Since her assets (her checking account) have increased by $20 but her liabilities (her credit card balance) have increased by $50, her wealth also has declined by $30. *(LO1)*
   b. In paying off her credit card bill, Consuelo reduces her assets by $300 by drawing down her checking account and reduces her liabilities by the same amount by reducing her credit card balance to zero. Thus, there is no change in her wealth. There is also no change in her saving (note that Consuelo's income and spending on current needs have not changed).
   c. The increase in the value of Consuelo's car raises her assets by $500. So her wealth also rises by $500. Changes in the value of existing assets are not treated as part of saving, however, so her saving is unchanged.
   d. The decline in the value of Consuelo's furniture is a capital loss of $300. Her assets and wealth fall by $300. Her saving is unchanged.

8.4 The loss of value of $200 over the year is another financial cost of owning the mower, which Larry should take into account in making his decision. His total cost is now $240 in interest costs plus $200 in anticipated loss of value of the mower (known as depreciation), or $440. This exceeds the value of marginal product, $400, and so now Larry should not buy the mower. *(LO4)*

8.5 Since bond prices fell, interest rates must have risen. To find the interest rate, note that bond investors are willing to pay only $960 today for a bond that will pay back $1,070 (a coupon payment of $70 plus the principal amount of $1,000) in one year. To find the one-year return, divide $1,070 by $960 to get 1.115. Thus, the interest rate must have risen to 11.5 percent. *(LO5)*

8.6 The share of stock will be worth $81.00 in one year—the sum of its expected future price and the expected dividend. At an interest rate of 4 percent, its value today is $81.00/1.04 = $77.88. At an interest rate of 8 percent, the stock's current value is $81.00/1.08 = 75.00. Recall from Example 8.11 that, when the interest rate is 6 percent, the value of a share of FortuneCookie.com is $76.42. Since higher interest rates imply lower stock values, news that interest rates are about to rise should cause the stock market to fall. *(LO5)*

8.7 Household saving is part of national saving. A decline in household saving, and hence national saving, at any given real interest rate shifts the saving supply curve to the left. The results are as in Figure 8.8. The real interest rate rises and the equilibrium values of national saving and investment fall. Lower investment is the same as a lower rate of capital formation, which would be expected to slow economic growth. *(LO6)*

CHAPTER 9

Money, Prices, and Financial Intermediaries

HOW DOES THE FINANCIAL SYSTEM WORK IN A MODERN ECONOMY?

LEARNING OBJECTIVES

After reading this chapter, you should be able to:

LO1 Describe the role of financial intermediaries such as commercial banks in the financial system.

LO2 Discuss the three functions of money and how the money supply is measured.

LO3 Analyze how the lending behavior of commercial banks affects the money supply.

LO4 Explain how a central bank controls the money supply and how control of the money supply is related to inflation in the long run.

> 'We're in the money, come on, my honey,
> Let's lend it, spend it, send it rolling along!'
>   "We're in the Money," lyrics by Al Dubin,
>   music by Harry Warren (from the film *Gold Diggers of 1933*)

When people use the word "money," they often mean something different than what economists mean when they use the word. For an economist, when you get a paycheck, you are receiving income, and any amount that you do not spend is saving. Or think about someone who has done well in the stock market: Most people would say that they "made money" in the market. No, an economist would answer, their wealth increased. These terms don't make for a catchy song, but a good economic naturalist must use words like *income, saving, wealth,* and *money* carefully because each plays a different role in the financial system.

We stated in the chapter *Saving, Capital Formation, and Financial Markets* that the U.S. financial system consists of financial institutions, like banks, and financial markets such as bond markets and stock markets. We then developed a supply and demand model of financial markets that showed how the real interest rate acts to allocate resources from savers to borrowers. In this chapter, we build on this foundation and examine some important institutional details of the financial system. First, we study how institutions such as banks actually allocate saving to productive uses. Second, we examine what economists mean by the term "money" and discuss how economists measure its supply and how it's created by the lending behavior of banks. Third, we analyze how central banks, like the Federal Reserve System in the United States, can affect the supply of money and determine the long-run rate of inflation in a market economy. By the end of this chapter, you may not be able to write a classic song, but you will have a better understanding of what money means in economic terms.

THE BANKING SYSTEM AND THE ALLOCATION OF SAVING TO PRODUCTIVE USES

We have emphasized the importance of high rates of saving and capital formation for economic growth and increased productivity. High rates of saving and investment by themselves are not sufficient, however. A successful economy not only saves but also uses its saving wisely by applying these limited funds to the investment projects that seem likely to be the most productive.

The banking system of a country like the United States improves the allocation of saving in two distinct ways. First, it provides *information* to savers about which of the many possible uses of their funds are likely to prove most productive and hence pay the highest return. By evaluating the potential productivity of alternative capital investments, the banking system helps to direct saving to its best uses. Second, the banking system helps savers to *share the risks* of individual investment projects. In the chapter *Saving, Capital Formation, and Financial Markets,* we defined *diversification* as the practice of spreading one's wealth over a variety of different financial investments to reduce overall risk. Note that the banking system also helps diversification by spreading the wealth of an individual saver on many borrowers and consequently the risk of a specific borrowing over many savers. This sharing of risks protects individual savers from bearing excessive risk, while at the same time making it possible to direct saving to projects such as the development of new technologies and capital that are potentially very productive.

The U.S. banking system consists of thousands of commercial banks that accept deposits from individuals and businesses and use those deposits to make loans. Banks are the most important example of a class of institutions called **financial intermediaries,** firms that extend credit to borrowers using funds raised from savers. Other examples of financial intermediaries are savings and loan associations and credit unions.

financial intermediaries
firms that extend credit to borrowers using funds raised from savers

Comparative Advantage

Why are financial intermediaries such as banks, which "stand between" savers and investors, necessary? The main reason is that, through specialization, banks and other intermediaries develop a comparative advantage in evaluating the quality of borrowers—the information-gathering function that we referred to a moment ago. Most savers, particularly small savers, do not have the time or the knowledge to determine for themselves which borrowers are likely to use the funds they receive most productively. In contrast, banks and other intermediaries have gained expertise in performing the information-gathering activities necessary for profitable lending, including checking out the borrower's background, determining whether the borrower's business plans make sense, and monitoring the borrower's activities during the life of the loan. Because banks specialize in evaluating potential borrowers, they can perform this function at a much lower cost, and with better results, than individual savers could on their own.

Banks also reduce the costs of gathering information about potential borrowers by pooling the saving of many individuals to make large loans. Each large loan needs to be evaluated only once, by the bank, rather than separately by each of the hundreds of individuals whose saving may be pooled to make the loan.

Banks help savers by eliminating their need to gather information about potential borrowers and by directing their saving toward higher-return, more-productive investments. Banks help borrowers as well, by providing access to credit that might otherwise not be available. Unlike a *Fortune* 500 corporation, which typically has many ways to raise funds, a small business that wants to buy a copier or remodel its offices will have few options other than going to a bank. Because the bank's lending officer has developed expertise in evaluating small-business loans, and even may have an ongoing business relationship with the small-business owner, the bank will be able to gather the information it needs to make the loan at a reasonable cost. Likewise, consumers who want to borrow to finish a basement or add a room to a house will find few good alternatives to a bank.

In sum, banks' expertise at gathering information about alternative lending opportunities allows them to bring together small savers looking for good uses for their funds and small borrowers with worthwhile investment projects.

"O.K., folks, let's move along. I'm sure you've all seen someone qualify for a loan before."

In addition to being able to earn a return on their saving, a second reason that people hold bank deposits is to make it easier to make payments. Most bank deposits allow the holder to write a check against them or draw on them using a debit card or ATM card. For many transactions, paying by check or debit card is more convenient than using cash. For example, unlike paying with cash, paying by check gives you a record of the transaction. Also, debit cards allow bank depositors to buy goods and services over the Internet.

The Japanese Banking Crisis	EXAMPLE 9.1

How did the banking crisis of the 1990s in Japan affect the Japanese economy?

During the 1980s, real estate and stock prices soared in Japan. Japanese banks made many loans to real estate developers, and the banks themselves acquired stock in corporations. (Unlike in the United States, in Japan it is legal for commercial banks to own stock.) However, in the early 1990s, land prices plummeted in Japan, leading many bank borrowers to default on their loans. Stock prices also came down sharply, reducing the value of banks' shareholdings. The net result was that most Japanese banks fell into severe financial trouble, with many large banks near bankruptcy. What was the effect of this crisis, which lasted more than a decade, on the Japanese economy?

Relative to the United States, which has more developed stock and bond markets, Japan has traditionally relied very heavily on banks to allocate its saving. Thus, when the severe financial problems of the banks prevented them from operating normally, many borrowers found it unusually difficult to obtain credit—a situation known as a "credit crunch." Smaller borrowers such as small- and medium-sized businesses had been particularly dependent on banks for credit and thus suffered disproportionately.

The Japanese economy, after many years of robust growth, suffered a severe recession throughout the 1990s. Many factors contributed to this sharp slowdown. However, the virtual breakdown of the banking system certainly did not help the situation, as credit shortages interfered with smaller firms' ability to make capital investments and, in some cases, to purchase raw materials and pay workers.

The Japanese government recognized these problems but responded very slowly, in large part out of reluctance to bear the high costs of returning the banks to a healthy financial condition. In recent years, the health of the Japanese banking system appears to have improved significantly, although problems remain and the Japanese economy has not returned to its earlier high rate of growth.

The commercial banking system also plays a central role in determining the quantity of money in the economy. We will return to this point shortly, but first we need to look at money and its uses.

MONEY AND ITS USES

money any asset that can be used in making purchases

What exactly is money? To the economist, **money** is any asset that can be used in making purchases. Common examples of money in the modern world are currency and coins. A checking account balance represents another asset that can be used in making payments (as when you write a check to pay for your weekly groceries) and so is also counted as money. In contrast, shares of stock, for example, cannot be used directly in most transactions. Stock must first be sold—that is, converted into cash or a checking account deposit—before further transactions, such as buying your groceries, can be made.

Historically, a wide variety of objects have been used as money, including gold and silver coins, shells, beads, feathers, and, on the Island of Yap, large, immovable boulders. Prior to the use of metallic coins, by far the most common form of money was the cowrie, a type of shell found in the South Pacific. Cowries were used as money in some parts of Africa until very recently, being officially accepted for payment of taxes in Uganda until the beginning of the twentieth century. Today money can be virtually intangible, as in the case of your checking account.

Why do people use money? Money has three principal uses: a *medium of exchange,* a *unit of account,* and a *store of value.*

medium of exchange an asset used in purchasing goods and services

Money serves as a **medium of exchange** when it is used to purchase goods and services, as when you pay cash for a newspaper or write a check to cover your utilities bill.

This is perhaps money's most crucial function. Think about how complicated daily life would become if there were no money. Without money, all economic transactions would have to be in the form of **barter,** which is the direct trade of goods or services for other goods or services.

barter the direct trade of goods or services for other goods or services

Barter is highly inefficient because it requires that each party to a trade has something that the other party wants, a so-called double coincidence of wants. For example, under a barter system, a musician could get her dinner only by finding someone willing to trade food for a musical performance. Finding such a match of needs, where each party happens to want exactly what the other person has to offer, would be difficult to do on a regular basis. In a world with money, the musician's problem is considerably simpler. First, she must find someone who is willing to pay money for her musical performance. Then, with the money received, she can purchase the food and other goods and services that she needs. In a society that uses money, it is not necessary that the person who wants to hear music and the person willing to provide food to the musician be one and the same. In other words, there need not be a double coincidence of wants for trades of goods and services to take place.

In a world without money, she could eat only by finding someone willing to trade food for a musical performance.

By eliminating the problem of having to find a double coincidence of wants in order to trade, the use of money in a society permits individuals to specialize in producing particular goods or services, as opposed to having every family or village produce most of what it needs. Specialization greatly increases economic efficiency and material standards of living, as we discussed in the chapter *Comparative Advantage* when we developed the Principle of Comparative Advantage. This usefulness of money in making transactions explains why savers hold money, even though money generally pays a low rate of return. Cash, for example, pays no interest at all, and the balances in checking accounts usually pay a lower rate of interest than could be obtained in alternative financial investments.

Comparative Advantage

Money's second function is as a *unit of account.* As a **unit of account,** money is the basic yardstick for measuring economic value. In the United States virtually all prices—including the price of labor (wages) and the prices of financial assets such as shares of stock—are expressed in dollars. Expressing economic values in a common unit of account allows for easy comparisons. For example, grain can be measured in bushels and coal in tons, but to judge whether 20 bushels of grain are economically more or less valuable than a ton of coal, we express both values in dollar terms. The use of money as a unit of account is closely related to its use as a medium of exchange; because money is used to buy and sell things, it makes sense to express prices of all kinds in money terms.

unit of account a basic measure of economic value

As a **store of value,** its third function, money is a way of holding wealth. For example, the miser who stuffs cash in his mattress or buries gold coins under the old oak tree at midnight is holding wealth in money form. Likewise, if you regularly keep a balance in your checking account, you are holding part of your wealth in the form of money. Although money is usually the primary medium of exchange or unit of account in an economy, it is not the only store of value. There are numerous other ways of holding wealth, such as owning stocks, bonds, or real estate.

store of value an asset that serves as a means of holding wealth

For most people, money is not a particularly good way to hold wealth, apart from its usefulness as a medium of exchange. Unlike government bonds and other types of financial assets, most forms of money pay no interest, and there is always the risk of cash being lost or stolen. However, cash has the advantage of being anonymous and difficult to trace, making it an attractive store of value for smugglers, drug dealers, and others who want their assets to stay out of the view of the Internal Revenue Service.

Private Money: Ithaca Hours, LETS, and Bitcoin   EXAMPLE 9.2

Is there such a thing as private money?

Money is usually issued by the government, not private individuals, but in part this reflects legal restrictions on private money issuance. Where the law allows, private moneys do sometimes emerge.[1] For example, privately issued currencies circulate in more than 30 U.S. communities. In Ithaca, New York, a private currency known as "Ithaca Hours" has circulated since 1991. Instituted by town resident Paul Glover, each Ithaca Hour is equivalent to $10, the average hourly wage of workers in the county. The bills, printed with specially developed inks to prevent counterfeiting, honor local people and the environment. An estimated 1,600 individuals and businesses have earned and spent Hours. Founder Paul Glover argues that the use of Hours, which can't be spent elsewhere, induces people to do more of their shopping in the local economy.

A more high-tech form of private money is associated with computerized trading systems called LETS, for local electronic trading system. These are quite popular in Australia, New Zealand, and Great Britain. Participants in a LETS post a list of goods and services they would like to buy or sell. When transactions are made, the appropriate number of "computer credits" is subtracted from the buyer's account and added to the seller's account. People are allowed to have negative balances in their accounts, so participants have to trust other members not to abuse the system by buying many goods and services and then quitting. LETS credits exist online only and are never in the form of paper or metal. In this respect, LETS may foreshadow the electronic monetary systems of the future.

A more recent development in private money was the emergence of the virtual currency known as Bitcoin in 2009. This is a peer-to-peer online payment system without a central administrator where payments are recorded in a public ledger using Bitcoin as the unit of account. New Bitcoins are created as a reward for payment processing work, known as mining, in which users offer their computing power to verify and record payments into the public ledger. Besides mining, Bitcoins can also be obtained in exchange for other currencies, products, and services, which means that the supply of Bitcoins is constantly increasing. Users can then send and receive Bitcoins electronically using special wallet software on a personal computer, mobile device, or web application. As of August 2014 the value of one Bitcoin was around US$580 with over 13 million Bitcoins in circulation. However, the commercial use of Bitcoin is still relatively small compared to its use by speculators, which has contributed to significant price volatility. This volatility in the Bitcoin market also limits Bitcoin's ability to act as a stable store of value, which we earlier described as one of the three principle uses of money.

What do Ithaca Hours, LETS credits, and Bitcoin have in common? By functioning as a medium of exchange, each facilitates trade within a community.

MEASURING MONEY

How much money, defined as financial assets usable for making purchases, is there in the U.S. economy at any given time? This question is not simple to answer because in practice it is not easy to draw a clear distinction between those assets that should be counted as money and those that should not. Dollar bills are certainly a form of money, and a van Gogh painting certainly is not. However, brokerage firms now offer accounts that allow their owners to combine financial investments in stocks and bonds with check-writing and credit card privileges. Should the balances in these accounts, or some part of them, be counted as money? It is difficult to tell.

M1 the sum of currency outstanding and balances held in checking accounts

M2 All the assets in M1 plus some additional assets that are usable in making payments but at greater cost or inconvenience than currency or checks

Economists skirt the problem of deciding what is and isn't money by using several alternative definitions of money, which vary in how broadly the concept of money is defined. A relatively "narrow" definition of the amount of money in the U.S. economy is called M1. **M1** is the sum of currency outstanding and balances held in checking accounts. A broader measure of money, called **M2,** includes all the assets in M1 plus some additional assets that are usable in making payments, but at greater cost or

[1]Barbara A. Good, "Private Money: Everything Old Is New Again," Federal Reserve Bank of Cleveland, *Economic Commentary,* April 1, 1998.

inconvenience than currency or checks. Table 9.1 lists the components of M1 and M2 and also gives the amount of each type of asset outstanding as of July 2014. For most purposes, however, it is sufficient to think of money as the sum of currency outstanding and balances in checking accounts, or M1.

TABLE 9.1
Components of M1 and M2, July 2014

M1		2,856.5
Currency	1,218.4	
Demand deposits	1,148.1	
Other checkable deposits	486.8	
Travelers' checks	3.2	
M2		11,422.4
M1	2,856.5	
Savings deposits	7,405.3	
Small-denomination time deposits	529.8	
Money market mutual funds	630.7	

NOTES: Billions of dollars, adjusted for seasonal variations. In M1, currency refers to cash and coin. Demand deposits are noninterest-bearing checking accounts, and "other checkable deposits" includes checking accounts that bear interest. M2 includes all the components of M1, balances in savings accounts, "small-denomination" (under $100,000) deposits held at banks for a fixed term, and money market mutual funds (MMMFs). MMMFs are organizations that sell shares, use the proceeds to buy safe assets (like government bonds), and often allow their shareholders some check-writing privileges.

SOURCE: Federal Reserve, release www.federalreserve.gov/releases/h6/current.

Note that credit card balances are not included in either M1 or M2 even though people increasingly use credit cards to pay for many of their purchases, including food, clothing, cars, and even college tuition. The main reason credit card balances are not included in the money supply is that they do not represent part of people's wealth. Indeed, a credit card charge of $1,000 represents an obligation to pay someone else $1,000.

RECAP	MONEY AND ITS USES

Money is any asset that can be used in making purchases, such as currency or a checking account. Money serves as a *medium of exchange* when it is used to purchase goods and services. The use of money as a medium of exchange eliminates the need for *barter* and the difficulties of finding a "double coincidence of wants." Money also serves as a *unit of account* and a *store of value*.

In practice, two basic measures of money are M1 and M2. M1, a more narrow measure, is made up primarily of currency and balances held in checking accounts. The broader measure, M2, includes all the assets in M1 plus some additional assets usable in making payments.

Credit card balances are never counted as or even considered money, as credit card balances are merely obligations to pay others.

COMMERCIAL BANKS AND THE CREATION OF MONEY

What determines the amount of money in the economy? If the economy's supply of money consisted entirely of currency, the answer would be simple: The supply of money would just be equal to the value of the currency created and circulated by the government. However, as we have seen, in modern economies the money supply consists not only of currency but also of deposit balances held by the public in commercial banks.

Earlier in this chapter, we discussed the role commercial banks play as financial intermediaries. Here, we will examine how commercial banks and their depositors affect an economy's money supply. To see how, we will use the example of a fictional country, the Republic of Gorgonzola. Initially, we assume, Gorgonzola has no commercial banking system. To make trading easier and eliminate the need for barter, the government directs the central bank of Gorgonzola to put into circulation a million identical paper notes, called guilders. The central bank prints the guilders and distributes them to the populace. At this point the Gorgonzolan money supply is a million guilders.

However, the citizens of Gorgonzola are unhappy with a money supply made up entirely of paper guilders since the notes may be lost or stolen. In response to the demand for safekeeping of money, some Gorgonzolan entrepreneurs set up a system of commercial banks. At first, these banks are only storage vaults where people can deposit their guilders. When people need to make a payment, they can either physically withdraw their guilders or, more conveniently, write a check on their account.

Checks give the banks permission to transfer guilders from the account of the person paying by check to the account of the person to whom the check is made out. With a system of payments based on checks, the paper guilders need never leave the banking system, although they flow from one bank to another as a depositor of one bank makes a payment to a depositor in another bank. Deposits do not pay interest in this economy; indeed, the banks can make a profit only by charging depositors fees in exchange for safeguarding their cash.

Let's suppose for now that people prefer bank deposits to cash and so deposit all of their guilders with the commercial banks. With all guilders in the vaults of banks, the balance sheet of all of Gorgonzola's commercial banks taken together is as shown in Table 9.2.

TABLE 9.2
Consolidated Balance Sheet of Gorgonzolan Commercial Banks (Initial)

Assets		Liabilities	
Currency	1,000,000 guilders	Deposits	1,000,000 guilders

The *assets* of the commercial banking system in Gorgonzola are the paper guilders sitting in the vaults of all the individual banks. The banking system's *liabilities* are the deposits of the banks' customers since checking account balances represent money owed by the banks to the depositors.

bank reserves cash or similar assets held by commercial banks for the purpose of meeting depositor withdrawals and payments

Cash or similar assets held by banks are called **bank reserves.** In this example, bank reserves, for all the banks taken together, equal 1,000,000 guilders—the currency listed on the asset side of the consolidated balance sheet. Banks hold reserves to meet depositors' demands for cash withdrawals or to pay checks drawn on their depositors' accounts. In this example, the bank reserves of 1,000,000 guilders equal 100 percent of banks' deposits, which are also 1,000,000 guilders. A situation in which bank reserves equal 100 percent of bank deposits is called **100 percent reserve banking.**

100 percent reserve banking a situation in which banks' reserves equal 100 percent of their deposits

Bank reserves are held by banks in their vaults, rather than circulated among the public, and thus are *not* counted as part of the money supply. However, bank deposit balances, which can be used in making transactions, *are* counted as money. So, after the introduction of "safekeeper" banks in Gorgonzola, the money supply, equal to the value of bank deposits, is 1,000,000 guilders, which is the same as it was prior to the introduction of banks.

To continue the story, the commercial bankers of Gorgonzola eventually realize that keeping 100 percent reserves against deposits is not necessary. True, a few guilders flow in and out of the typical bank as depositors receive payments or write checks, but for the most part the stacks of paper guilders just sit in the bank vaults. It occurs to the bankers that they can meet the random inflow and outflow of guilders to their banks with reserves that are less than 100 percent of their deposits. After some observation, the bankers conclude that keeping reserves equal to only 10 percent of deposits is enough to meet the random ebb and flow of withdrawals and payments from their individual banks. The remaining 90 percent of reserves, which covers the remaining deposits, the bankers realize, can be lent out to borrowers to earn interest.

So the bankers decide to keep reserves equal to 100,000 guilders, or 10 percent of their deposits. The banks' **reserve-deposit ratio,** which is bank reserves divided by deposits, is now equal to 100,000/1,000,000, or 10 percent. The other 900,000 guilders they lend out at interest to Gorgonzolan cheese producers who want to use the money to make improvements to their farms. After the loans are made, the balance sheet of all of Gorgonzola's commercial banks taken together has changed, as shown in Table 9.3.

reserve-deposit ratio bank reserves divided by deposits

TABLE 9.3
Consolidated Balance Sheet of Gorgonzolan Commercial Banks after One Round of Loans

Assets		Liabilities	
Currency (= reserves)	100,000 guilders	Deposits	1,000,000 guilders
Loans to farmers	900,000 guilders		

After the loans are made, the banks' reserves of 100,000 guilders no longer equal 100 percent of the banks' deposits of 1,000,000 guilders. A banking system in which banks hold fewer reserves than deposits so that the reserve-deposit ratio is less than 100 percent is called a **fractional-reserve banking system.**

Notice that 900,000 guilders have flowed out of the banking system (as loans to farmers) and are now in the hands of the public. But we have assumed that private citizens prefer bank deposits to cash for making transactions. So ultimately people will redeposit the 900,000 guilders in the banking system. After these deposits are made, the consolidated balance sheet of the commercial banks is as in Table 9.4.

Notice that bank deposits, and hence the economy's money supply, now equal 1,900,000 guilders. These deposits, which are liabilities of the banks, are balanced by assets of 1,000,000 guilders in reserves and 900,000 guilders in loans owed to the banks.

fractional-reserve banking system a banking system in which bank reserves are less than deposits so that the reserve-deposit ratio is less than 100 percent

TABLE 9.4
Consolidated Balance Sheet of Gorgonzolan Commercial Banks after Guilders Are Redeposited

Assets		Liabilities	
Currency (= reserves)	1,000,000 guilders	Deposits	1,900,000 guilders
Loans to farmers	900,000 guilders		

The fractional-reserve commercial banking system has thus led to the creation of additional money over and above the initial 1,000,000 guilders in currency.

However, the story does not end here. On examining their balance sheets the bankers are surprised to see that they once again have "too many," or excess, reserves. With deposits of 1,900,000 guilders and a 10 percent reserve-deposit ratio they require only 190,000 guilders in reserves. These reserves are sometimes referred to as *required reserves* for this very reason. But they have 1,000,000 guilders in reserves—810,000 too many. Since lending out their excess guilders is always more profitable than leaving them in the vault, the bankers proceed to make another 810,000 guilders in loans. Eventually these loaned-out guilders are redeposited in the banking system, after which the consolidated balance sheet of the banks is as shown in Table 9.5.

TABLE 9.5
Consolidated Balance Sheet of Gorgonzolan Commercial Banks after Two Rounds of Loans and Redeposits

Assets		Liabilities	
Currency (= reserves)	1,000,000 guilders	Deposits	2,710,000 guilders
Loans to farmers	1,710,000 guilders		

Now the money supply has increased to 2,710,000 guilders, equal to the value of bank deposits. Despite the expansion of loans and deposits, however, the bankers find that their reserves of 1,000,000 guilders *still* exceed the desired level of 10 percent of deposits, which are 2,710,000 guilders. In other words, there are still excess or lendable reserves on hand, and so yet another round of lending will take place.

CONCEPT CHECK 9.1

Determine what the balance sheet of the Gorgonzolan banking system will look like after a third round of lending to farmers and redeposits of guilders into the commercial banking system. What is the money supply at that point?

The process of expansion of loans and deposits will only end when reserves equal 10 percent of bank deposits because as long as reserves exceed 10 percent of deposits, the banks will find it profitable to lend out the extra reserves. Since reserves at the end of every round equal 1,000,000 guilders, for the reserve-deposit ratio to equal 10 percent, total deposits must equal 10,000,000 guilders. Further, since the balance sheet must balance, with assets equal to liabilities, we know as well that at the end of the process, loans to cheese producers must equal 9,000,000 guilders. If loans equal 9,000,000 guilders, then bank assets, the sum of loans and reserves (1,000,000 guilders), will equal 10,000,000 guilders, which is the same as bank liabilities (bank deposits). The final consolidated balance sheet is as shown in Table 9.6.

TABLE 9.6
Final Consolidated Balance Sheet of Gorgonzolan Commercial Banks

Assets		Liabilities	
Currency (= reserves)	1,000,000 guilders	Deposits	10,000,000 guilders
Loans to farmers	9,000,000 guilders		

The money supply, which is equal to total deposits, is 10,000,000 guilders at the end of the process. We see that the existence of a fractional-reserve banking system has multiplied the money supply by a factor of 10, relative to the economy with no banks or the economy with 100 percent reserve banking. Put another way, with a 10 percent reserve-deposit ratio, each guilder deposited in the banking system can "support" 10 guilders worth of deposits.

To find the money supply in this example more directly, notice that deposits will expand through additional rounds of lending as long as the ratio of bank reserves to bank deposits exceeds the reserve-deposit ratio desired by banks. The expansion stops when the actual ratio of bank reserves to deposits equals the desired reserve-deposit ratio. So ultimately, deposits in the banking system satisfy the following relationship:

$$\frac{\text{Bank reserves}}{\text{Bank deposits}} = \text{Desired reserve-deposit ratio.}$$

This equation can be rewritten to solve for bank deposits:

$$\text{Bank deposits} = \frac{\text{Bank reserves}}{\text{Desired reserve-deposit ratio}}. \qquad (9.1)$$

In Gorgonzola, since all the currency in the economy flows into the banking system, bank reserves equal 1,000,000 guilders. The reserve-deposit ratio desired by banks is 0.10. Therefore, using Equation 9.1, we find that bank deposits equal (1,000,000 guilders)/0.10, or 10 million guilders, the same answer we found in the consolidated balance sheet of the banks, Table 9.6.

CONCEPT CHECK 9.2

Find deposits and the money supply in Gorgonzola if the banks' desired reserve-deposit ratio is 5 percent rather than 10 percent. What if the total amount of currency circulated by the central bank is 2,000,000 guilders and the desired reserve-deposit ratio remains at 10 percent?

THE MONEY SUPPLY WITH BOTH CURRENCY AND DEPOSITS

In the Gorgonzola example, we assumed that all money is held in the form of deposits in banks. In reality, of course, people keep only part of their money holdings in the form of bank accounts and hold the rest in the form of currency. Fortunately, allowing for the fact that people hold both currency and bank deposits does not greatly complicate the determination of the money supply, as Example 9.3 shows.

The Money Supply with Both Currency and Deposits   **EXAMPLE 9.3**

What is the money supply in Gorgonzola when there is both currency and bank deposits?

Suppose that the citizens of Gorgonzola choose to hold a total of 500,000 guilders in the form of currency and to deposit the rest of their money in banks. Banks keep reserves equal to 10 percent of deposits. What is the money supply in Gorgonzola?

The money supply is the sum of currency in the hands of the public and bank deposits. Currency in the hands of the public is given as 500,000 guilders. What is the quantity of bank deposits? Since 500,000 of the 1,000,000 guilders issued by the central bank are being used by the public in the form of currency, only the remaining 500,000 guilders is available to serve as bank reserves. We know that deposits equal bank reserves divided by the reserve-deposit ratio, so deposits are 500,000 guilders/0.10 = 5,000,000 guilders. The total money supply is the sum of currency in the hands of the public (500,000 guilders) and bank deposits (5,000,000 guilders), or 5,500,000 guilders.

We can write a general relationship that captures the reasoning of this example. First, let's write out the fact that the money supply equals currency plus bank deposits:

$$\text{Money supply} = \text{Currency held by the public} + \text{Bank deposits.}$$

We also know that bank deposits equal bank reserves divided by the reserve-deposit ratio that is desired by commercial banks (Equation 9.1). Using that relationship to substitute for bank deposits in the expression for the money supply, we get

$$\text{Money supply} = \text{Currency held by public} + \frac{\text{Bank reserves}}{\text{Desired reserve-deposit ratio}}. \qquad (9.2)$$

We can use Equation 9.2 to confirm our reasoning in the previous example. In that example, currency held by the public is 500,000 guilders, bank reserves are 500,000 guilders, and the desired reserve-deposit ratio is 0.10. Plugging these values into Equation 9.2, we get that the money supply equals $500,000 + 500,000/0.10 = 5,500,000$, the same answer we found before.

The Money Supply at Christmas	**EXAMPLE 9.4**

How does Christmas shopping affect the money supply?

During the Christmas season, people choose to hold unusually large amounts of currency for shopping. With no action by the central bank, how would this change in currency holding affect the national money supply?

To illustrate with a numerical example, suppose that initially bank reserves are 500, the amount of currency held by the public is 500, and the desired reserve-deposit ratio in the banking system is 0.2. Inserting these values into Equation 9.2, we find that the money supply equals $500 + 500/0.2 = 3,000$.

Now suppose that because of Christmas shopping needs, the public increases its currency holdings to 600 by withdrawing 100 from commercial banks. These withdrawals reduce bank reserves to 400. Using Equation 9.2, we find now that the money supply is $600 + 400/0.2 = 2,600$. So the public's increased holdings of currency have caused the money supply to drop, from 3,000 to 2,600. The reason for the drop is that, with a reserve-deposit ratio of 20 percent, every dollar in the vaults of banks can "support" $5 of deposits and hence $5 of money supply. However, the same dollar in the hands of the public becomes $1 of currency, contributing only $1 to the total money supply. So when the public withdraws cash from the banks, the overall money supply declines. (We will see in the next section, however, that in practice the central bank has means to offset the impact of the public's actions on the money supply.)

RECAP	COMMERCIAL BANKS AND THE CREATION OF MONEY

- Part of the money supply consists of deposits in private commercial banks. Hence, the behavior of commercial banks and their depositors helps to determine the money supply.

- Cash or similar assets held by banks are called *bank reserves.* In modern economies, banks' reserves are less than their deposits, a situation called *fractional-reserve banking.* The ratio of bank reserves to deposits is called the *reserve-deposit ratio;* in a fractional-reserve banking system, this ratio is less than 1.

- The portion of bank reserves that is in excess of what is desired to support the banks' deposits can be lent out by the banks to earn interest. Banks will continue to make loans and accept deposits as long as the reserve-deposit ratio exceeds its desired level. This process stops only when the actual and desired reserve-deposit ratios are equal. At that point, total bank deposits equal bank reserves divided by the desired reserve-deposit ratio, and the money supply equals the currency held by the public plus bank deposits.

CENTRAL BANKS, THE MONEY SUPPLY, AND PRICES

The **Federal Reserve System** is one of the most important agencies of the federal government. The Fed, as it is referred to in the press, is the central bank of the United States. Central banks in general have two main responsibilities. First, they are responsible for **monetary policy,** which means that a country's central bank determines how much money circulates in the economy. Second, along with other government agencies, the central bank has important responsibilities for the oversight and regulation of financial markets. In particular, central banks play important roles during periods of crisis in financial markets.

In the chapter *Monetary Policy and the Federal Reserve,* we will review the history and structure of the Fed and analyze how the Fed's actions affect the U.S. economy during financial crises and recessions. In this chapter, we focus on how a central bank can control the money supply and how changes in the money supply affect the price level and the rate of inflation in the long run.

CONTROLLING THE MONEY SUPPLY WITH OPEN-MARKET OPERATIONS

A central bank's primary responsibility is making monetary policy, which involves decisions about the appropriate size of the nation's money supply. As we saw in the previous section, central banks in general, and the Fed in particular, do not control the money supply directly. Nevertheless, they can control the money supply indirectly in several ways. In this chapter we limit our discussion to the most important of these, called *open-market operations.* In the chapter *Monetary Policy and the Federal Reserve,* we discuss other methods the Fed can use to change the money supply, such as lending at the discount window, changing reserve requirements, and paying interest on reserves.

Suppose that the Fed wants to increase bank reserves, with the ultimate goal of increasing bank deposits and the money supply. To accomplish this, the Fed buys financial assets, usually government bonds, from the public. To simplify the actual procedure a bit, think of the Fed as buying bonds that the public had originally purchased from the government and paying the public for these bonds with newly printed money.

Assuming that the public is already holding all the currency that it wants, they will deposit the cash they receive as payment for their bonds in commercial banks. Thus, the reserves of the commercial banking system will increase by an amount equal to the value of the bonds purchased by the Fed. The increase in bank reserves will lead in turn, through the process of lending and redeposit of funds described in the previous section, to an expansion of bank deposits and the money supply, as summarized by Equation 9.2. The Fed's purchase of government bonds from the public, with the result that bank reserves and the money supply are increased, is called an **open-market purchase.**

To reduce bank reserves and hence the money supply, the Fed reverses the procedure. It sells some of the government bonds that it holds (acquired in previous open-market purchases) to the public. Assume that the public pays for the bonds by writing checks on their accounts in commercial banks. Then, when the Fed presents the checks to

Federal Reserve System (or **the Fed)** the central bank of the United States

monetary policy determination of the nation's money supply

open-market purchase the purchase of government bonds from the public by the Fed for the purpose of increasing the supply of bank reserves and the money supply

open-market sale the sale by the Fed of government bonds to the public for the purpose of reducing bank reserves and the money supply

open-market operations open-market purchases and open-market sales

the commercial banks for payment, reserves equal in value to the government bonds sold by the Fed are transferred from the commercial banks to the Fed. The Fed retires these reserves from circulation, lowering the supply of bank reserves and, hence, the overall money supply. The sale of government bonds by the Fed to the public for the purpose of reducing bank reserves and hence the money supply is called an **open-market sale.**

Open-market purchases and sales together are called **open-market operations.** Open-market operations are the most convenient and flexible tool that the Federal Reserve has for affecting the money supply and are employed on a regular basis.

Open-Market Operations   EXAMPLE 9.5

How do open-market operations affect the money supply?

In a particular economy, currency held by the public is 1,000 shekels, bank reserves are 200 shekels, and the desired reserve-deposit ratio is 0.2. What is the money supply? How is the money supply affected if the central bank prints 100 shekels and uses this new currency to buy government bonds from the public? Assume that the public does not wish to change the amount of currency it holds.

As bank reserves are 200 shekels and the reserve-deposit ratio is 0.2, bank deposits must equal 200 shekels/0.2, or 1,000 shekels. The money supply, equal to the sum of currency held by the public and bank deposits, is therefore 2,000 shekels, a result you can confirm using Equation 9.2.

The open-market purchase puts 100 more shekels into the hands of the public. We assume that the public continues to want to hold 1,000 shekels in currency, so they will deposit the additional 100 shekels in the commercial banking system, raising bank reserves from 200 to 300 shekels. As the desired reserve-deposit ratio is 0.2, multiple rounds of lending and redeposit will eventually raise the level of bank deposits to 300 shekels/0.2, or 1,500 shekels. The money supply, equal to 1,000 shekels held by the public plus bank deposits of 1,500 shekels, equals 2,500 shekels. So the open-market purchase of 100 shekels, by raising bank reserves by 100 shekels, has increased the money supply by 500 shekels. Again, you can confirm this result using Equation 9.2.

CONCEPT CHECK 9.3

Continuing Example 9.5, suppose that instead of an open-market purchase of 100 shekels, the central bank conducts an open-market sale of 50 shekels' worth of government bonds. What happens to bank reserves, bank deposits, and the money supply?

MONEY AND PRICES

From a macroeconomic perspective, a major reason that control of the supply of money is important is that, *in the long run, the amount of money circulating in an economy and the general level of prices are closely linked.* Indeed, it is virtually unheard of for a country to experience high, sustained inflation without a comparably rapid growth in the amount of money held by its citizens. For instance, the link between money growth and inflation for nine countries in Latin America during the period 1995–2007 is illustrated in Figure 9.1. Although the relationship is somewhat loose, countries with higher rates of money growth clearly tend to have higher rates of inflation, and this relationship has been found in other countries and in other periods.

The economist Milton Friedman summarized the inflation–money relationship by saying, "Inflation is always and everywhere a monetary phenomenon." We will see later

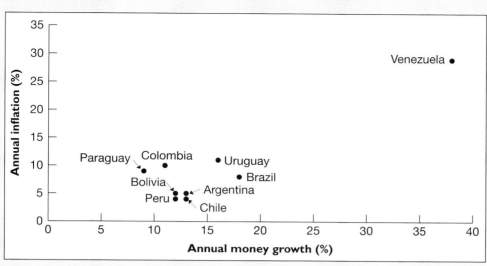

FIGURE 9.1

Inflation and Money Growth in Latin America, 1995–2007.

Latin American countries with higher rates of growth in their money supplies also tended to have higher rates of inflation between 1995 and 2007.

SOURCE: WorldBank, World Development Indicators.

that, over short periods, inflation can arise from sources other than an increase in the supply of money. But over a longer period, and particularly for more severe inflations, Friedman's dictum is certainly correct: The rate of inflation and the rate of growth of the money supply are closely related.

The existence of a close link between money supply and prices should make intuitive sense. Imagine a situation in which the available supply of goods and services is approximately fixed. Then the more cash (say, dollars) that people hold, the more they will be able to bid up the prices of the fixed supply of goods and services. Thus, a large money supply relative to the supply of goods and services (too much money chasing too few goods) tends to result in high prices. Likewise, a rapidly *growing* supply of money will lead to quickly *rising* prices—that is, inflation.

VELOCITY

To explore the relationship of money growth and inflation in a bit more detail, it is useful to introduce the concept of *velocity*. In economics, **velocity** is a measure of the speed at which money changes hands in transactions involving final goods and services. For example, a given dollar bill might pass from your hand to the grocer's when you buy a quart of milk. The same dollar may then pass from the grocer to a new car dealer when your grocer buys a car, and then from the car dealer to her doctor in exchange for medical services. The more quickly money circulates from one person to the next, the higher its velocity.

More formally, velocity is defined as the number of times per year the typical dollar in the money supply is used to buy final goods or services, according to the following formula:

$$\text{Velocity} = \frac{\text{Nominal GDP}}{\text{Money stock}}.$$

Let V stand for velocity and let M stand for the particular money stock being considered (for example, M1 or M2). Nominal GDP (a measure of the total value of transactions) equals the price level P times real GDP (Y). Using this notation, we can write the definition of velocity as

$$V = \frac{P \times Y}{M}. \tag{9.3}$$

The higher this ratio, the faster the "typical" dollar is circulating.

velocity a measure of the speed at which money changes hands in transactions involving final goods and services, or, equivalently, nominal GDP divided by the stock of money.

| **The Velocity of Money in the U.S. Economy** | **EXAMPLE 9.6** |

What is the velocity of the U.S. money supply?

In 2013, M1 was $2,638.8 billion, M2 was $10,968.3 billion, and nominal GDP was $16,768.1 billion. We can use these data along with Equation 9.3 to find velocity for both definitions of the money supply. For M1, we have

$$V = \frac{\$16,768.1 \text{ billion}}{\$2,638.8 \text{ billion}} = 6.35.$$

Similarly, velocity for M2 was

$$V = \frac{\$16,768.1 \text{ billion}}{\$10,968.3 \text{ billion}} = 1.53.$$

You can see that the velocity of M1 is higher than that of M2. This makes sense: Because the components of M1, such as cash and checking accounts, are used more frequently for transactions, each dollar of M1 "turns over" more often than the average dollar of M2.

A variety of factors determine velocity. A leading example is advances in payment technologies such as the introduction of credit cards and debit cards or the creation of networks of automated teller machines (ATMs). These technologies and payment methods have allowed people to carry out their daily business while holding less cash, and thus have tended to increase velocity over time.

MONEY AND INFLATION IN THE LONG RUN

We can use the definition of velocity to see how money and prices are related in the long run. First, rewrite the definition of velocity, Equation 9.3, by multiplying both sides of the equation by the money stock M. This yields

$$M \times V = P \times Y. \tag{9.4}$$

quantity equation money times velocity equals nominal GDP.

Equation 9.4 is called the *quantity equation*. The **quantity equation** states that money times velocity equals nominal GDP. Because the quantity equation is simply a rewriting of the definition of velocity, Equation 9.3, it always holds exactly.

The quantity equation is historically important because late nineteenth- and early twentieth-century monetary economists used this relationship to theorize about the relationship between money and prices. We can do the same thing here. To keep things simple, imagine that velocity V is determined by current payment technologies and thus is approximately constant over the period we are considering. Likewise, suppose that real output Y is approximately constant. If we use a bar over a variable to indicate that the variable is constant, we can rewrite the quantity equation as

$$M \times \overline{V} = P \times \overline{Y}, \tag{9.5}$$

where we are treating $\overline{V}$ and $\overline{Y}$ as fixed numbers.

Now look at Equation 9.5 and imagine that for some reason the Federal Reserve increases the money supply M by 10 percent. Because $\overline{V}$ and $\overline{Y}$ are assumed to be fixed, Equation 9.5 can continue to hold only if the price level P also rises by 10 percent. That is, according to the quantity equation, a 10 percent increase in the money supply M should cause a 10 percent increase in the price level P, that is, an inflation of 10 percent.

The intuition behind this conclusion is the one we mentioned at the beginning of this section. If the quantity of goods and services Y is approximately constant (and assuming that velocity V also is constant), an increase in the supply of money will lead people to bid up the prices of the available goods and services. Thus, high rates of money growth will tend to be associated with high rates of inflation, which is exactly what we observed in Figure 9.1.

If high rates of money growth lead to inflation, why do countries allow their money supplies to rise quickly? Usually, rapid rates of money growth are the result of large government budget deficits. Particularly in developing countries or countries suffering from war or political instability, governments sometimes find that they cannot raise sufficient taxes or borrow enough from the public to cover their expenditures. In this situation, the government's only recourse may be to print new money and use this money to pay its bills. If the resulting increase in the amount of money in circulation is large enough, the result will be inflation.

Sometimes, a country's budget deficit becomes so large that the only way to finance it is to print money. We can use Equation 9.5 to analyze the consequences of this policy. In this case, M grows at an extremely high rate leading P to rise at an equally rapid rate. The result is *hyperinflation,* which we discussed in the chapter *Inflation and the Price Level*. The Confederate States of America during the Civil War and Germany after World War I were in exactly this situation: They could not raise sufficient taxes to cover government spending needs, so they printed large quantities of paper money to pay for government expenditures. As Equation 9.5 predicts, this resulted in hyperinflations both in the Confederacy and in the Weimar Republic in Germany.

Equation 9.5 also provides a way to stop hyperinflations: Reduce the growth rate of the money supply. This is, of course, easier said than done. To accomplish this, the government must somehow cut spending and/or raise taxes so that the budget deficit can be financed through borrowing rather than money issue. The German government, for example, enacted reforms in late 1923 that made it difficult for the government to print money to cover its budget deficits. Inflation slowed dramatically in the months after the reform. The Confederacy, on the other hand, was unable to stop its hyperinflation. After the battles of Gettysburg and Vicksburg in 1863, it was clear that the Confederacy would ultimately lose the war. It could only sell bonds at exorbitant interest rates, and could not collect taxes since the individual states controlled tax collections. Hyperinflation ended only with the Confederacy's defeat in April 1865.

RECAP	CENTRAL BANKS, THE MONEY SUPPLY, AND PRICES

- Central banks control the money supply through open-market operations. Open-market purchases increase the money supply while open-market sales decrease the money supply.

- A high rate of money growth generally leads to inflation. The larger the amount of money in circulation, the higher the public will bid up the prices of available goods and services.

- *Velocity* measures the speed at which money circulates in payments for final goods and services; equivalently it is equal to nominal GDP divided by the stock of money. A numerical value for velocity can be obtained from the equation $V = (P \times Y)/M$, where V is velocity, $P \times Y$ is nominal GDP, and M is the money supply.

- The *quantity equation* states that money times velocity equals nominal GDP, or, in symbols, $M \times V = P \times Y$. The quantity equation is a restatement of the definition of velocity and thus always holds. If velocity and output are approximately constant, the quantity equation implies that a given percentage increase in the money supply leads to the same percentage increase in the price level. In other words, the rate of growth of the money supply equals the rate of inflation.

○ SUMMARY ○

- The U.S. banking system consists of thousands of commercial banks that accept deposits from individuals and businesses and use those deposits to make loans. Banks are the most important example of a class of institutions called financial intermediaries. Financial intermediaries develop expertise in evaluating prospective borrowers, making it unnecessary for small savers to do that on their own. *(LO1)*

- The banking system improves the allocation of saving in two ways. First, it provides information to savers about which of the many possible uses of their funds are likely to prove most productive and hence pay the highest return. Second, it helps savers share the risks of lending by permitting them to diversify their financial investments. *(LO1)*

- Money is any asset that can be used in making purchases. Money has three main functions: as a medium of exchange, as a unit of account, and as a store of value. In practice, it is difficult to measure the money supply since many assets have some money-like features. A relatively narrow measure of money is M1, which includes currency and checking accounts. A broader measure of money, M2, includes all the assets in M1 plus additional assets that are somewhat less convenient to use in transactions than those included in M1. *(LO2)*

- Because bank deposits are part of the money supply, the behavior of commercial banks and of bank depositors affects the amount of money in the economy. Specifically, commercial banks create money through multiple rounds of lending and accepting deposits. The money supply equals currency held by the public plus deposits in the banking system. *(LO3)*

- The central bank of the United States is called the Federal Reserve System, or the Fed for short. The Fed can affect the money supply indirectly in several ways. In the most important of these, called open-market operations, the Fed buys or sells government securities in exchange for currency held by banks or the public. *(LO4)*

- Control of the money supply is important in the long run because the rate of growth of the money supply and the rate of inflation are closely linked. In particular, the quantity equation can be used to show that, under certain conditions, a given percentage increase in the money supply will lead to the same percentage increase in the price level. *(LO4)*

○ KEY TERMS ○

bank reserves
barter
Federal Reserve System (the Fed)
financial intermediaries
fractional-reserve banking system
M1
M2

medium of exchange
monetary policy
money
100 percent reserve banking
open-market operations
open-market purchase
open-market sale

quantity equation
reserve-deposit ratio
store of value
unit of account
velocity

○ REVIEW QUESTIONS ○

1. Give two ways that the banking system helps to improve the allocation of saving. Illustrate with examples. *(LO1)*

2. What is money? Why do people hold money even though it pays a lower return than other financial assets? *(LO2)*

3. Suppose that the public switches from doing most of its shopping with currency to using checks instead. If the Fed takes no action, what will happen to the national money supply? Explain. *(LO1, LO3)*

4. The Fed wants to reduce the U.S. money supply using open-market operations. Describe what it would do, and explain how this action would accomplish the Fed's objective. *(LO4)*

5. Use the quantity equation to explain why money growth and inflation tend to be closely linked. *(LO4)*

○ PROBLEMS ○

1. During World War II, an Allied soldier named Robert Radford spent several years in a large German prisoner-of-war camp. At times more than 50,000 prisoners were held in the camp, with some freedom to move about within the compound. Radford later wrote an account of his experiences. He described how an economy developed in the camp, in which prisoners traded food, clothing, and other items. Services such as barbering also were exchanged. Lacking paper money, the prisoners began to use cigarettes (provided monthly by the Red Cross) as money. Prices were quoted, and payments made, using cigarettes. *(LO2)*

   a. In Radford's POW camp, how did cigarettes fulfill the three functions of money?

   b. Why do you think the prisoners used cigarettes as money, as opposed to other items of value such as squares of chocolate or pairs of boots?

   c. Do you think a nonsmoking prisoner would have been willing to accept cigarettes in exchange for a good or service in Radford's camp? Why or why not?

Visit your mobile app store and download the Frank: Study Econ app *today*!

2. Redo the example of Gorgonzola in the text (refer to Tables 9.2 to 9.6), assuming that (1) initially, the Gorgonzolan central bank puts 5,000,000 guilders into circulation (instead of the 1,000,000 guilders used in the example) and (2) commercial banks desire to hold reserves of 20 percent of deposits (instead of the 10 percent used in the original example). As in the text, assume that the public holds no currency. Show the consolidated balance sheets of Gorgonzolan commercial banks for each of the following instances. *(LO3)*

   a. After the initial deposits (compare to Table 9.2).

   b. After one round of loans (compare to Table 9.3).

   c. After the first redeposit of guilders (compare to Table 9.4).

   d. After two rounds of loans and redeposits (compare to Table 9.5).

   e. What are the final values of bank reserves, loans, deposits, and the money supply (compare to Table 9.6)?

3. Answer each of the following questions. *(LO3)*

   a. Bank reserves are 100, the public holds 200 in currency, and the desired reserve-deposit ratio is 0.25. Find deposits and the money supply.

   b. The money supply is 500 and currency held by the public equals bank reserves. The desired reserve-deposit ratio is 0.25. Find currency held by the public and bank reserves.

   c. The money supply is 1,250, of which 250 is currency held by the public. Bank reserves are 100. Find the desired reserve-deposit ratio.

4. When a central bank increases bank reserves by $1, the money supply rises by more than $1. The amount of extra money created when the central bank increases bank reserves by $1 is called the *money multiplier. (LO3)*

   a. Explain why the money multiplier is generally greater than 1. In what special case would it equal 1?

   b. The initial money supply is $1,000, of which $500 is currency held by the public. The desired reserve-deposit ratio is 0.2. Find the increase in money supply associated with increases in bank reserves of $1, $5, and $10. What is the money multiplier in this economy?

   c. Find a general rule for calculating the money multiplier.

   d. Suppose the Fed wanted to reduce the money multiplier, perhaps because it believes that change would give it more precise control over the money supply. What action could the Fed take to achieve its goal?

5. Consider a country in which real GDP is $8 trillion, nominal GDP is $10 trillion, M1 is $2 trillion, and M2 is $5 trillion. *(LO4)*

   a. Find velocity for M1 and for M2.

   b. Show that the quantity equation holds for both M1 and M2.

6. Consider the following hypothetical data for 2015 and 2016: *(LO4)*

	2015	**2016**
Money supply	1,000	1,050
Velocity	8	8
Real GDP	12,000	12,000

a. Find the price level for 2015 and 2016. What is the rate of inflation between the two years?
b. What is the rate of inflation between 2015 and 2016 if the money supply in 2016 is 1,100 instead of 1,050?
c. What is the rate of inflation between 2015 and 2016 if the money supply in 2016 is 1,100 and output in 2016 is 12,600?

○ ANSWERS TO CONCEPT CHECKS ○

9.1 Table 9.5 shows the balance sheet of banks after two rounds of lending and rede-posits. At that point, deposits are 2,710,000 guilders and reserves are 1,000,000 guilders. Since banks have a desired reserve-deposit ratio of 10 percent, they will keep 271,000 guilders (10 percent of deposits) as reserves and lend out the remaining 729,000 guilders. Loans to farmers are now 2,439,000 guilders. Eventually the 729,000 guilders lent to the farmers will be redeposited into the banks, giving the banks deposits of 3,439,000 guilders and reserves of 1,000,000 guilders. The balance sheet is as shown in the accompanying table.

Assets		**Liabilities**	
Currency (= reserves)	1,000,000 guilders	Deposits	3,439,000 guilders
Loans to farmers	2,439,000 guilders		

Notice that assets equal liabilities. The money supply equals deposits, or 3,439,000 guilders. Currency held in the banks as reserves does not count in the money supply. *(LO3)*

9.2 Because the public holds no currency, the money supply equals bank deposits, which in turn equal bank reserves divided by the reserve-deposit ratio (Equation 9.1). If bank reserves are 1,000,000 and the reserve-deposit ratio is 0.05, then deposits equal 20,000,000 guilders, which is also the money supply. If bank reserves are 2,000,000 guilders and the reserve-deposit ratio is 0.10, then the money supply and deposits are again equal to 20,000,000 guilders, or 2,000,000/0.10. *(LO3)*

9.3 If the central bank sells 50 shekels of government bonds in exchange for currency, the immediate effect is to reduce the amount of currency in the hands of the public by 50 shekels. To restore their currency holding to the desired level of 1,000 shekels, the public will withdraw 50 shekels from commercial banks, reducing bank reserves from 200 shekels to 150 shekels. The desired reserve-deposit ratio is 0.2, so ultimately deposits must equal 150 shekels in reserves divided by 0.2, or 750 shekels. (Note that, to reduce their deposits, the commercial banks will have to "call in" loans, reducing their loans outstanding.) The money supply equals 1,000 shekels in currency held by the public plus 750 shekels in deposits, or 1,750 shekels. Thus, the open-market purchase has reduced the money supply from 2,000 to 1,750 shekels. *(LO4)*

CHAPTER 10

Short-Term Economic Fluctuations

Ingram Publishing

UNEMPLOYMENT AMONG CONSTRUCTION WORKERS RISES SUBSTANTIALLY DURING RECESSIONS

"Home Sales and Prices Continue to Plummet."
"As Jobs Vanish, Motel Rooms Become Home."
"Global Stock Markets Plummet."
"Energy Prices Surge, and Stocks Fall Again."
"Steep Slide in Economy as Unsold Goods Pile Up."
"Fed Plans to Inject Another $1 Trillion to Aid the Economy."
"World Bank Says Global Economy Will Shrink in '09."

These headlines from *The New York Times* tell the story: From 2007 to 2009, the U.S. economy passed through its worst economic downturn since the Great Depression of the 1930s. Average incomes fell; thousands of Americans lost their jobs, their health insurance, and even their homes; and governments at all levels struggled to deal with falling tax collections colliding with increased demands for public services like unemployment benefits and health care.

In the preceding chapters of the book, we discussed the factors that determine long-run economic growth. Over the broad sweep of history, those factors determine the economic success of a society. Indeed, over a span of 30, 50, or 100 years, relatively small differences in the rate of economic growth can have an enormous effect on the average person's standard of living. But even though the economic "climate" (long-run economic conditions) is the ultimate determinant of living standards, changes in the economic

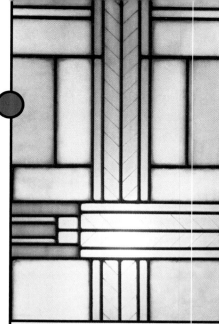

LEARNING OBJECTIVES

After reading this chapter, you should be able to:

LO1 Identify the four phases of the business cycle and explain the primary characteristics of recessions and expansions.

LO2 Use potential output and the output gap to analyze an economy's position in the business cycle.

LO3 Define the natural rate of unemployment and show how it is related to cyclical unemployment.

LO4 Apply Okun's law to analyze the relationship between the output gap and cyclical unemployment.

LO5 Discuss the basic differences between how the economy operates in the short run versus the long run.

"weather" (short-run fluctuations in economic conditions) are also important. A good long-run growth record is not much consolation to a worker who has lost her job, her health insurance, or even her home.

This chapter begins our study of short-term fluctuations in economic activity, commonly known as business cycles. We will start with some background on the history and characteristics of these economic ups and downs. We next develop concepts that allow us to measure the severity of business cycles. These concepts allow us to analyze short-run economic activity from different perspectives, and to link fluctuations in output to changes in unemployment. Finally, we introduce a verbal description of a basic model of booms and recessions. Throughout this chapter, we will connect the data we examine and the theories we develop to the recession that began in late 2007 and officially ended in 2009, which has since become known as the *Great Recession.*

RECESSIONS AND EXPANSIONS

Figure 10.1 shows the path of real GDP in the United States since 1929. As you can see, the growth path of real GDP is not always smooth; the bumps and wiggles correspond to short periods of faster or slower growth. These fluctuations in GDP, along with similar fluctuations in other variables such as unemployment, are known as **business cycles.**

business cycles short-term fluctuations in GDP and other variables

A period in which the economy is growing at a rate significantly below normal is called a **recession** or a *contraction.* An extremely severe or protracted recession is called a **depression.** You should be able to pick out the Great Depression in Figure 10.1, particularly the sharp initial decline between 1929 and 1933. But you also can see that the U.S. economy was volatile in the mid-1970s and the early 1980s, with serious recessions in 1973–1975 and 1981–1982. A moderate recession occurred in 1990–1991. The next recession did not begin for another 10 years, the longest period without a recession in U.S. history. It, too, was short and relatively mild, beginning in March 2001 and ending eight months later. The beginning of the latest recession in 2007 and its end in 2009 are clearly visible in Figure 10.1.

recession (or **contraction)** a period in which the economy is growing at a rate significantly below normal

depression a particularly severe or protracted recession

FIGURE 10.1

Fluctuations in U.S. Real GDP, 1929–2013.

Real GDP does not grow smoothly but has speedups (expansions or booms) and slowdowns (recessions or depressions).

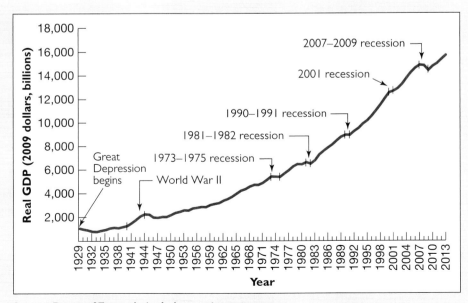

SOURCE: Bureau of Economic Analysis, www.bea.gov.

TABLE 10.1
U.S. Recessions since 1929

Peak date (beginning)	Trough date (end)	Duration (months)	Highest unemployment rate (%)	Change in real GDP (%)	Duration of subsequent expansion (months)
Aug. 1929	Mar. 1933	43	24.9	−28.8	50
May 1937	June 1938	13	19.0	−5.5	80
Feb. 1945	Oct. 1945	8	3.9	−8.5	37
Nov. 1948	Oct. 1949	11	5.9	−1.4	45
July 1953	May 1954	10	5.5	−1.2	39
Aug. 1957	Apr. 1958	8	6.8	−1.7	24
Apr. 1960	Feb. 1961	10	6.7	2.3	106
Dec. 1969	Nov. 1970	11	5.9	0.1	36
Nov. 1973	Mar. 1975	16	8.5	−1.1	58
Jan. 1980	July 1980	6	7.6	−0.3	12
July 1981	Nov. 1982	16	9.7	−2.1	92
July 1990	Mar. 1991	8	7.5	−0.9	120
Mar. 2001	Nov. 2001	8	5.8	0.8	73
Dec. 2007	June 2009	18	10.0	−4.1	

NOTES: Unemployment rate is the annual rate. Peak and trough dates from the National Bureau of Economic Research. Unemployment and real GDP data from *Historical Statistics of the United States* and the *Economic Report of the President*. Unemployment rate is the annual rate for the trough year or the subsequent year, whichever is higher. Change in annual real GDP is measured from the peak year to the trough year, except that the entry for the 1945 recession is the 1945–1946 change in real GDP, the entry for the 1980 recession is the 1979–1980 change, the entry for 2001 is the 2000–2001 change, and the 2007 entry is for 2007–2009.

SOURCES: Peak and trough dates, National Bureau of Economic Research; unemployment and real GDP, *Historical Statistics of the United States* and *Economic Report of the President*.

An informal definition of a recession, often cited by reporters, is a period during which real GDP falls for at least two consecutive quarters. This definition is not a bad rule of thumb, as real GDP usually does fall during recessions. However, many economists would argue that periods in which real GDP growth is well below normal, though not actually negative, should be counted as recessions. Indeed, real GDP fell in only one quarter during the 2001 recession. Another problem with relying on GDP figures for dating recessions is that GDP data can be substantially revised, sometimes years after the fact. In practice, when trying to determine whether a recession is in progress, economists look at a variety of economic data, not just GDP.

Table 10.1 lists the beginning and ending dates of U.S. recessions since 1929, as well as the *duration* (length, in months) of each. The table also gives the highest unemployment rate recorded during each recession and the percentage change in real GDP. (Ignore the last column of the table for now.) The beginning of a recession is called the **peak** because it represents the high point of economic activity prior to a downturn. The end of a recession, which marks the low point of economic activity prior to a recovery, is called the **trough.** The dates of peaks and troughs reported in Table 10.1 were determined by the National Bureau of Economic Research (NBER), a nonprofit organization that has been a major source of research on short-term economic fluctuations since its founding in 1920. The NBER is not a government agency, but it is usually treated by the news media and the government as the "official" arbiter of the dates of peaks and troughs.

Table 10.1 shows that, since 1929, by far the longest and most severe recession in the United States was the Great Depression. According to the NBER, the Depression began

peak the beginning of a recession; the high point of economic activity prior to a downturn

trough the end of a recession; the low point of economic activity prior to a recovery

"Please stand by for a series of tones. The first indicates the official end of the recession, the second indicates prosperity, and the third the return of the recession."

in August 1929, two months before the famous stock market crash in October 1929, and lasted until March 1933. Between 1933 and 1937, the economy grew fairly rapidly, so technically the period was not a recession, although unemployment remained very high at close to 20 percent of the workforce. In 1937–1938, the nation was hit by another significant recession. Full economic recovery from the Depression did not come until U.S. entry into World War II at the end of 1941. The economy boomed from 1941 to 1945 (see Figure 10.1), reflecting the enormous wartime production of military equipment and supplies.

In sharp contrast to the 1930s, U.S. recessions from the 1940s through the early 2000s were relatively short, between 6 and 16 months from peak to trough. As Table 10.1 shows, the two most severe recessions prior to 2007, those of 1973–1975 and 1981–1982, lasted 16 months as opposed to the 43-month duration of the Great Depression. The 2007–2009 recession was the longest since World War II, lasting 18 months with GDP falling 4.1 percent from peak to trough. Unemployment rates during these three recessions were quite high by today's standards, but they were low compared to the 25 percent unemployment rate recorded during the Great Depression.

expansion a period in which the economy is growing at a rate significantly above normal

boom a particularly strong and protracted expansion

The opposite of a recession is an **expansion**—a period in which the economy is growing at a rate that is significantly *above* normal. A particularly strong and protracted expansion is called a **boom.** In the United States, strong expansions occurred during 1933–1937, 1961–1969, 1982–1990, and 1991–2001, with exceptionally strong growth during 1995–2000 (see Figure 10.1). On average, expansions have been much longer than recessions. The final column of Table 10.1 shows the duration, in months, of U.S. expansions since 1929. As you can see in the table, the 1961–1969 expansion lasted 106 months; the 1982–1990 expansion, 92 months. The longest expansion of all began in March 1991, at the trough of the 1990–1991 recession. This expansion lasted 120 months, a full 10 years, until a new recession began in March 2001.

Calling the 2007 Recession　　　　　　　　　　**EXAMPLE 10.1**

How do we know that a recession began in December 2007?

The Business Cycle Dating Committee of the National Bureau of Economic Research determined that a recession began in December 2007. What led the committee to choose that date?

The Business Cycle Dating Committee is the group within the National Bureau of Economic Research that determines recession dates. The determination of whether and when a recession has begun involves intensive statistical analysis, mixed in with a significant amount of human judgment. The committee typically relies heavily on a small set of statistical indicators that measure the overall strength of the economy. It prefers indicators that are available monthly because they are available quickly and may provide relatively precise information about the timing of peaks and troughs. Four of the most important indicators used by the committee are:

- Industrial production, which measures the output of factories and mines.

- Total sales in manufacturing, wholesale trade, and retail trade.

- Nonfarm employment (the number of people at work outside of agriculture).

- Real after-tax income received by households, excluding transfers like Social Security payments.

Each of these indicators measures a different aspect of the economy. Because their movements tend to coincide with the overall movements in the economy, they are called *coincident indicators.*

Normally the coincident indicators move more or less together. During this latest recession, two of the indicators showed the same pattern: employment and after-tax income. Both of these measures peaked in December 2007. Industrial production was the next to peak, in January 2008. Real manufacturing and wholesale/retail sales peaked last, in June 2008. Thus the business cycle peak was relatively easy to identify.

SOME FACTS ABOUT SHORT-TERM ECONOMIC FLUCTUATIONS

Figure 10.1 and Table 10.1 show only twentieth-century data, but periods of expansion and recession have been a feature of industrial economies since at least the late eighteenth century. Karl Marx and Friedrich Engels referred to these fluctuations, which they called "commercial crises," in their *Communist Manifesto* of 1848. In the United States, economists have been studying short-term fluctuations for more than a century.

Expansions and recessions usually are not limited to a few industries or regions but are *felt throughout the economy.* Indeed, the largest fluctuations may have a *global impact.* For instance, the Great Depression of the 1930s affected nearly all the world's economies, and the 1973–1975 and 1981–1982 recessions also were widely felt outside the United States. The 2007–2009 recession was worldwide in scope, and some of its effects are still being felt around the world today.

Figure 10.2, which shows growth rates of real GDP over the period 2002–2013 for Canada, Germany, Japan, the United Kingdom, and the United States, illustrates this point. You can see that all five countries in the sample plunged into a recession in 2008 and sunk deeper there in 2009. The 2010 data suggest that the recession ended for all of these economies sometime in 2009. Figure 10.2 also makes it clear that many nations have continued to experience weak or even negative growth in the years following the end of this recession in 2009.

Unemployment is a key indicator of short-term economic fluctuations. The unemployment rate typically rises sharply during recessions and recovers (although more slowly) during expansions. Figure 6.8 (in the chapter *Wages and Unemployment*) shows the U.S. unemployment rate since 1960. You should be able to identify the recessions by noting the sharp peaks in the unemployment rate in those years. Note that the part of unemployment that is associated with recessions is called *cyclical unemployment.* Beyond this increase in unemployment, labor market conditions generally worsen during recessions. For example, during recessions, real wages grow more slowly, workers are less likely to receive promotions or bonuses, and new entrants to the labor force (such as college graduates) have a much tougher time finding attractive jobs.

FIGURE 10.2

Real GDP Growth in Five Major Countries, 2002–2013.

Annual growth rates for five major industrialized countries show that all of these countries fell into recession in 2008 and remained there into 2009.

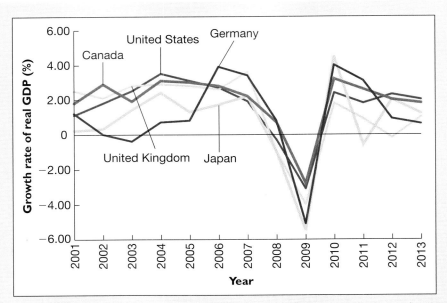

SOURCE: *Economic Report of the President,* March 2013, Table B112, www.gpoaccess.gov/eop.

Generally, industries that produce *durable goods* such as cars, houses, and capital equipment are more affected than others by recessions and booms. In contrast, industries that provide *services* and *nondurable goods* like food are much less sensitive to short-term fluctuations. Thus, an automobile worker or a construction worker is far more likely to lose his or her job in a recession than is a barber or a baker.

Like unemployment, *inflation* follows a typical pattern in recessions and expansions, though it is not so sharply defined. Figure 10.3 shows the U.S. inflation rate since 1960; in the figure, periods of recession are indicated by shaded vertical bars. As you can see, recessions tend to be followed soon after by a decline in the rate of inflation. For example, the recession of 1981–1982 was followed by a sharp reduction in inflation. Furthermore, many—though not all—postwar recessions have been preceded by increases in inflation, as Figure 10.3 shows. The behavior of inflation during expansions and recessions will be discussed more fully in other chapters.

FIGURE 10.3

U.S. Inflation, 1960–2012.

U.S. inflation since 1960 is measured by the change in the CPI, and periods of recession are indicated by the shaded vertical bars. Note that inflation declined following the recessions of 1960–1961, 1969–1970, 1973–1975, 1980, 1981–1982, 1990–1991, 2001, and 2007–2009, and rose prior to many of those recessions.

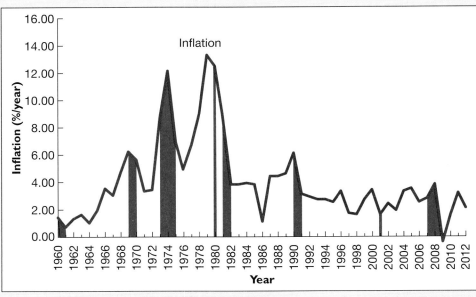

SOURCE: *Economic Report of the President,* March 2013, Table B-64, www.gpoaccess.gov/eop/.

RECAP	SOME FACTS ABOUT SHORT-TERM ECONOMIC FLUCTUATIONS

- A recession is a period in which output is growing more slowly than normal. An expansion, or boom, is a period in which output is growing more quickly than normal.

- The beginning of a recession is called the peak, and its end (which corresponds to the beginning of the subsequent expansion) is called the trough.

- The sharpest recession in the history of the United States was the initial phase of the Great Depression in 1929–1933. Severe recessions also occurred in 1973–1975, 1981–1982, and 2007–2009. Two relatively mild recessions occurred in 1990–1991 and 2001.

- Short-term economic fluctuations (recessions and expansions) are irregular in length and severity, and thus are difficult to predict.

- Expansions and recessions have widespread (and sometimes global) impacts, affecting most regions and industries.

- Unemployment rises sharply during a recession and falls, usually more slowly, during an expansion.

- Durable goods industries are more affected by expansions and recessions than other industries. Services and nondurable goods industries are less sensitive to ups and downs in the economy.

- Recessions tend to be followed by a decline in inflation and are often preceded by an increase in inflation.

OUTPUT GAPS AND CYCLICAL UNEMPLOYMENT

How can we tell whether a particular recession or boom is "big" or "small"? The answer to this question is important to both economists who study business cycles and policymakers who must formulate responses to economic fluctuations. Intuitively, a "big" recession or expansion is one in which output and the unemployment rate deviate significantly from their normal or trend levels. In this section we will attempt to be more precise about this idea by introducing the concept of the *output gap,* which measures how far output is from its normal level at a particular time. We also will revisit the idea of *cyclical unemployment,* or the deviation of unemployment from its normal level. Finally, we will examine how these two concepts are related.

POTENTIAL OUTPUT

The concept of potential output is a useful starting point for thinking about expansions and recessions. **Potential output,** also called *potential GDP* or *full-employment output,* is the maximum sustainable amount of output (real GDP) that an economy can produce. Note that *potential output* is not simply the maximum amount of output. Because capital and labor can be utilized at greater-than-normal rates for limited periods of time, a country's actual output can temporarily exceed its potential output. These greater-than-normal utilization rates, however, cannot be sustained indefinitely, partly because workers cannot work overtime every week and machinery occasionally must be shut down for maintenance and repairs.

potential output, Y^* **(or potential GDP** or **full-employment output)** the maximum sustainable amount of output (real GDP) that an economy can produce

FIGURE 10.4

U.S. Potential Output, 1949–2013.

Potential output grows more smoothly than real GDP. Compare these data with Figure 10.1.

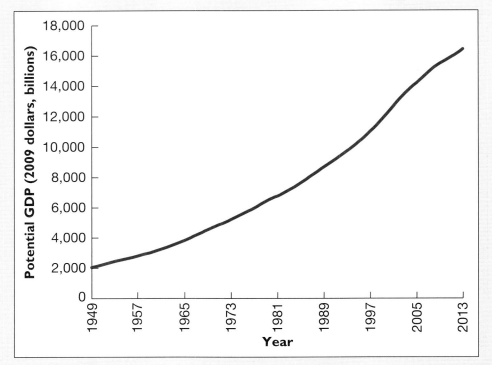

SOURCE: Federal Reserve Bank of St. Louis FRED database, http://research.stlouisfed.org/fred2.

Potential output is not a fixed number but grows over time, reflecting increases in both the amounts of available capital and labor and their productivity. Figure 10.4 presents potential output for the United States from 1949 to 2013. Compare this graph with the data on actual real GDP shown in Figure 10.1. Notice that potential output is much smoother than actual output; this reflects the fact that increases in the economy's productive capacity are due to factors (such as human capital) that grow relatively smoothly over time. Potential output therefore grows relatively smoothly as well.

Why does a nation's actual output sometimes grow quickly and sometimes slowly, as shown for the United States in Figure 10.1? Logically, there are two possibilities: First, changes in the rate of output growth may reflect *changes in the rate at which the country's potential output is increasing.* For example, unfavorable weather conditions, such as a severe drought, would reduce the rate of potential output growth in an agricultural economy, and a decline in the rate of technological innovation might reduce the rate of potential output growth in an industrial economy. Under the assumption that the country is using its resources at normal rates, so that actual output equals potential output, a significant slowdown in potential output growth would tend to result in recession. Similarly, new technologies, increased capital investment, or a surge in immigration that swells the labor force could produce unusually brisk growth in potential output, and hence an economic boom.

Undoubtedly, changes in the rate of growth of potential output are part of the explanation for expansions and recessions. In the United States, for example, the economic boom of the second half of the 1990s was propelled in part by new information technologies such as the Internet. And the severe slowdown in Japan during the decade of the 1990s reflected in part a reduction in the growth of potential output, arising from factors such as slower growth in the Japanese labor force and capital stock. When changes in the rate of GDP growth reflect changes in the growth rate of potential output, the appropriate policy responses are those discussed in the chapter *Economic Growth.* In particular, when a recession results from slowing growth in potential output, the government's best response is to try to promote saving, investment, technological innovation, human capital formation, and other activities that support growth.

THE OUTPUT GAP

A second possible explanation for short-term economic fluctuations is that *actual output does not always equal potential output.* For example, potential output may be growing normally, but for some reason the economy's capital and labor resources may not be fully utilized, so that actual output is significantly below the level of potential output. This low level of output, resulting from underutilization of economic resources, would generally be interpreted as a recession. Alternatively, capital and labor may be working much harder than normal—firms may put workers on overtime, for example—so that actual output expands beyond potential output, creating a boom.

At any point in time, the difference between potential output and actual output is called the **output gap.** Unfortunately, we cannot measure the output gap by simply taking the difference between real GDP and potential output at a point in time since both are growing over time. For instance, a difference of $100 billion between actual and potential output is large compared to potential GDP of $2 trillion (roughly the size of potential output in the early 1950s), but small compared to $15 trillion of potential output (about the level of potential output in 2009).

output gap the difference between the economy's actual output and its potential output, relative to potential output, at a point in time

To accurately measure the output gap for a particular year, we need to compare the difference between actual and potential GDP with the economy's potential GDP in that year. We therefore calculate the output gap as a percentage of potential output. Specifically, let Y^* be the symbol for potential output at a point in time, and Y will continue to stand for real GDP at a point in time. We can express the output gap as follows:

$$\text{Output gap (in percent)} = \frac{Y - Y^*}{Y^*} \times 100.$$

Figure 10.5 shows the output gap for the U.S. from 1949 to 2013. You'll notice that sometimes the output gap is negative; for example, the output gap is quite large in the early 1980s and in the late 2000s. This reflects the severe recessions the U.S. economy experienced from 1981 to 1983 and from 2007 to 2010. A negative output gap is a situation in which actual output is below potential and resources are not being fully utilized, so it is called a **recessionary gap.** Similarly, when actual output is above

recessionary gap a negative output gap, which occurs when potential output exceeds actual output ($Y < Y^*$)

FIGURE 10.5

The Output Gap in the U.S., 1949–2013.

SOURCE: Authors' calculations using data from Figures 10.1 and 10.4.

expansionary gap a positive output gap, which occurs when actual output is higher than potential output ($Y > Y^*$)

potential, resources are being utilized at above normal rates and the economy is expanding rapidly. Thus, a positive output gap is referred to as an **expansionary gap.**

Policymakers generally view both recessionary gaps and expansionary gaps as problems. It is not difficult to see why a recessionary gap is bad news for the economy: When there is a recessionary gap, capital and labor resources are not being fully utilized, and output and employment are below maximum sustainable levels.

In addition to the fact that it is unsustainable, an expansionary gap is considered a problem by policymakers for a more subtle reason: What's wrong, after all, with having higher output and employment, even if it is temporary? A prolonged expansionary gap is problematic because, when faced with a demand for their products that significantly exceeds their sustainable capacity, firms tend to raise prices. Thus, an expansionary gap typically results in increased inflation, which reduces the efficiency of the economy in the longer run.

Thus, whenever an output gap exists, whether it is recessionary or expansionary, policymakers have an incentive to try to eliminate the gap by returning actual output to potential. In other chapters we will discuss both how output gaps arise and the tools that policymakers have for *stabilizing* the economy—that is, bringing actual output into line with potential output.

THE NATURAL RATE OF UNEMPLOYMENT AND CYCLICAL UNEMPLOYMENT

Whether recessions arise because of slower growth in potential output or because actual output falls below potential, they bring bad times. In either case, output falls (or at least grows more slowly), implying reduced living standards. Recessionary output gaps are particularly frustrating for policymakers, however, because they imply that the economy has the *capacity* to produce more, but for some reason available resources are not being

Efficiency

fully utilized. Recessionary gaps violate the Efficiency Principle in that they unnecessarily reduce the total economic pie, making the typical person worse off.

An important indicator of the low utilization of resources during recessions is the unemployment rate. In general, a *high* unemployment rate means that labor resources are not being fully utilized, so that output has fallen below potential (a recessionary gap). By the same logic, an unusually *low* unemployment rate suggests that labor is being utilized at an unsustainably high rate, so that actual output exceeds potential output (an expansionary gap).

To better understand the relationship between the output gap and unemployment, recall from the chapter *Wages and Unemployment* the three broad types of unemployment: frictional unemployment, structural unemployment, and cyclical unemployment. *Frictional unemployment* is the short-term unemployment that is associated with the matching of workers and jobs. Some amount of frictional unemployment is necessary for the labor market to function efficiently in a dynamic, changing economy. *Structural unemployment* is the long-term and chronic unemployment that occurs even when the economy is producing at its normal rate. Structural unemployment often results when workers' skills are outmoded and do not meet the needs of employers—so, for example, steelworkers may become structurally unemployed as the steel industry goes into a long-term decline, unless those workers can retrain to find jobs in growing industries. Finally, *cyclical unemployment* is the extra unemployment that occurs during periods of recession.

natural rate of unemployment, u^* the part of the total unemployment rate that is attributable to frictional and structural unemployment; equivalently, the unemployment rate that prevails when cyclical unemployment is zero, so that the economy has neither a recessionary nor an expansionary output gap

Unlike cyclical unemployment, which is present only during recessions, frictional unemployment and structural unemployment are always present in the labor market, even when the economy is operating normally. Economists call the part of the total unemployment rate that is attributable to frictional and structural unemployment the **natural rate of unemployment.** Put another way, the natural rate of unemployment is the unemployment rate that prevails when cyclical unemployment is zero, so that the economy has neither a recessionary nor an expansionary output gap. We will denote the natural rate of unemployment as u^*.

Cyclical unemployment, which is the difference between the total unemployment rate and the natural rate, can thus be expressed as $u - u^*$, where u is the actual unemployment rate and u^* denotes the natural rate of unemployment. In a recession, the actual unemployment rate u exceeds the natural unemployment rate u^*, so cyclical unemployment, $u - u^*$, is positive. When the economy experiences an expansionary gap, in contrast, the actual unemployment rate is lower than the natural rate, so that cyclical unemployment is negative. Negative cyclical unemployment corresponds to a situation in which labor is being used at an unsustainably high level, so that actual unemployment has dipped below its usual frictional and structural levels.

The Natural Rate of Unemployment   **EXAMPLE 10.2**

Why was the natural rate of unemployment so much lower in the U.S. during the late 2000s than in the late 1970s?

According to the Congressional Budget Office, which regularly estimates the natural rate of unemployment in the United States, the natural rate fell steadily from 6.3 percent of the labor force in 1979 to about 4.8 percent in 2007.[1] Some economists, noting that unemployment remained close to 4 percent for several years around the turn of the millennium, have argued for an even lower natural rate, perhaps as low as 4.5 percent. Why was the U.S. natural rate of unemployment so much lower in the late 2000s than in the late 1970s?

The natural rate of unemployment may have fallen because of reduced frictional unemployment, reduced structural unemployment, or both. A variety of ideas have been advanced to explain declines in both types of unemployment. One promising suggestion is based on the changing age structure of the U.S. labor force.[2] The average age of U.S. workers is rising, reflecting the aging of the baby-boom generation. Indeed, over the past 25 years, the share of the labor force aged 16–24 has fallen from about 25 percent to about 15 percent. Since younger workers are more prone to unemployment than older workers, the aging of the labor force may help to explain the overall decline in unemployment.

Why are young workers more likely to be unemployed? Compared to teenagers and workers in their twenties, older workers are much more likely to hold long-term, stable jobs. In contrast, younger workers tend to hold short-term jobs, perhaps because they are not ready to commit to a particular career, or because their time in the labor market is interrupted by schooling or military service. Because they change jobs more often, younger workers are more prone than others to frictional unemployment. They also have fewer skills, on average, than older workers, so they may experience more structural unemployment. As workers age and gain experience, however, their risk of unemployment declines.

Another possible explanation for the declining natural rate of unemployment is that labor markets have become more efficient at matching workers with jobs, thereby reducing both frictional and structural unemployment. For example, agencies that arrange temporary help have become much more commonplace in the United States in recent years. Although the placements these agencies make are intended to be temporary, they often become permanent when an employer and worker discover that a particularly good match has been made. Online job services, which allow workers to search for jobs nationally and even internationally, also are becoming increasingly important. By reducing the time people must spend in unemployment and by creating more lasting matches between workers and jobs, temporary help agencies, online job services, and similar innovations may have reduced the natural rate of unemployment.[3]

[1]Congressional Budget Office, *The Budget and Outlook: Fiscal Years 2008 to 2017*, January 2008, available online at www.cbo.gov.
[2]See Robert Shimer, "Why Is the U.S. Unemployment Rate So Much Lower?" in B. Bernanke and J. Rotemberg, eds., *NBER Macroeconomics Annual*, 1998.
[3]For a detailed analysis of factors affecting the natural rate, see Lawrence Katz and Alan Krueger, "The High-Pressure U.S. Labor Market of the 1990s," *Brookings Papers on Economic Activity* 1 (1999), pp. 1–88.

In the years following the 2007–2009 recession, the natural rate of unemployment has again started to increase. Economists have cited several possible reasons for this rise in recent years. One such reason could be the extension of eligibility for unemployment benefits from 26 weeks to as many as 99 weeks in 2009.[4] While reducing the hardship on unemployed workers and their families, this extension of benefits may also reduce the incentive of the unemployed to seek and accept less desirable jobs. A second explanation is that the degree of mismatch between job seekers and potential employers has increased, thereby increasing structural unemployment, which is counted as part of the natural unemployment rate. It remains to be seen how much of this increase in natural unemployment is strictly temporary; in particular this depends on how much of the increase was caused by the extension of unemployment benefits. As the labor market continues to recover after the 2007–2009 recession, we should develop a clearer picture of the new normal rate of unemployment.

OKUN'S LAW

Okun's law each extra percentage point of cyclical unemployment is associated with about a 2 percent widening of a negative output gap, measured in relation to potential output

We have already observed that by definition, cyclical unemployment is positive when the economy has a recessionary gap, negative when there is an expansionary gap, and zero when there is no output gap. A more quantitative relationship between cyclical unemployment and the output gap is given by a rule of thumb called *Okun's law,* after Arthur Okun, one of President Kennedy's chief economic advisors. According to **Okun's law,** each 1 percent increase in cyclical unemployment is associated with about a 2 percent widening of a negative output gap, measured in relation to potential output. So, for example, if cyclical unemployment increases from 1 percent to 2 percent of the labor force, the recessionary gap will increase from -2 percent to -4 percent of potential GDP.

We can also express Okun's law as an equation. Using our expression for the output gap, we have

$$\frac{Y - Y^*}{Y^*} \times 100 = -2 \times (u - u^*).$$

The following example further illustrates Okun's law.

| Okun's Law and the Output Gap in the U.S. Economy | EXAMPLE 10.3 |

How is Okun's law applied to real-world data?

The table below presents data on the actual unemployment rate, the natural unemployment rate, and potential GDP (in billions of 2005 dollars) for the U.S. economy in four selected years.

Year	*u*	*u**	*Y**
1995	5.6%	5.3%	9,216.4
2000	4.0	5.0	10,880.7
2005	5.1	5.0	12,576.3
2010	9.6	5.2	14,017.1

In 1995, cyclical unemployment, $u - u^*$, was 0.3 percent of the labor force (5.6% $-$ 5.3%). Applying Okun's law, the output gap for 1995 was -2 times that

[4]Justin Weidner and John C. Williams, "What Is the New Normal Unemployment Rate?" *FRBSF Economic Letter 2011-5,* February 14, 2011, www.frbsf.org/publications/economics/letter/2011/el201105.html.

percentage, or −0.6 percent of potential output. Potential output was estimated to be $9,216.4 billion, so the value of the output gap for that year was $55.3 billion.

2000 was near the end of an expansion and the actual unemployment rate was below the natural rate. Specifically, cyclical unemployment was −1.0 percent; using Okun's law this means that the output gap was 2.0 percent and the U.S. economy's output was $217.6 billion more than it typically would have been in 2000.

The data for 2010 give a sense of the depth of the most recent recession. Cyclical unemployment rose to 4.4 percent, implying an output gap of −8.8 percent. Thus, according to Okun's law, the U.S. economy was producing about $1,233.5 (.088 × 14,017.1) billion *less* than it would produce had all resources been fully employed. There were about 309 million people in the United States in 2010, so Okun's law implies that average incomes (i.e., per capita GDP) could have been almost $4,000 higher in 2010—about $16,000 for a family of four—had the economy not been operating below potential. Thus output gaps and cyclical unemployment have significant costs, a conclusion that justifies the concern that the public and policymakers have about recessions.

CONCEPT CHECK 10.1

In the first quarter of 2011, the U.S. unemployment rate was 9.8 percent. The Congressional Budget Office estimated that the natural rate of unemployment was 5.2 percent. By what percentage did actual GDP differ from potential GDP in the first quarter of 2011?

The Federal Reserve's Slowing of the U.S. Economy   EXAMPLE 10.4

Why did the Federal Reserve act to slow down the economy in 1999 and 2000?

As noted in the chapter *Money, Prices, and Financial Intermediaries,* monetary policy decisions of the Federal Reserve—actions that change the level of the nation's money supply—affect the performance of the U.S. economy. Why did the Federal Reserve take measures to slow down the economy in 1999 and 2000?

Throughout the 1990s, cyclical unemployment in the United States fell dramatically, becoming negative sometime in 1997, according to Congressional Budget Office estimates. Okun's law indicates that growing negative cyclical unemployment rates signal an increasing expansionary gap, and with it an increased risk of future inflation.

In 1997 and 1998 the Federal Reserve argued that the inflationary pressures typically caused by rapidly expanding output and falling unemployment rates were being offset by productivity gains and international competition, leaving inflation rates lower than expected. Because inflation remained low during this period—despite a small but growing expansionary gap—the Federal Reserve did little to eliminate the gap.

However, as the actual unemployment rate continued to fall throughout 1999 and early 2000, the expansionary gap continued to widen, causing the Federal Reserve to grow increasingly concerned about the growing imbalance between actual and potential GDP and the threat of increasing inflation. In response, the Federal Reserve took actions in 1999 and 2000 to slow the growth of output and bring actual and potential output closer into alignment (we will give more details in the chapter *Monetary Policy and the Federal Reserve* about how the Fed can do this). The Fed's actions helped to "promote overall balance in the economy"[5] and restrain inflation throughout 2000. By early 2001, however, the U.S. economy stalled and fell into recession, leading the Federal Reserve to reverse course and take policy measures aimed at eliminating the growing *recessionary* gap.

[5]Testimony of Chairman Alan Greenspan, *The Federal Reserve's semiannual report on the economy and monetary policy,* Committee on Banking and Financial Services, U.S. House of Representatives, February 17, 2000. Available online at www.federalreserve.gov/boarddocs/hh/2000/February/Testimony.htm.

RECAP	OUTPUT GAPS AND CYCLICAL UNEMPLOYMENT

- Potential output is the maximum sustainable amount of output (real GDP) that an economy can produce. The output gap is the difference between the economy's actual output and its potential output, relative to potential output, at a point in time. When actual output is below potential, the resulting output gap is called a recessionary gap. When actual output is above potential, the difference is called an expansionary gap. A recessionary gap reflects a waste of resources, while an expansionary gap threatens to ignite inflation; hence, policymakers have an incentive to try to eliminate both types of output gaps.

- The natural rate of unemployment u^* is the sum of the frictional and structural unemployment rates. It is the rate of unemployment that is observed when the economy is operating at a normal level, with no output gap.

- Cyclical unemployment, $u - u^*$, is the difference between the actual unemployment rate u and the natural rate of unemployment u^*. Cyclical unemployment is positive when there is a recessionary gap, negative when there is an expansionary gap, and zero when there is no output gap.

- Okun's law relates cyclical unemployment and the output gap. According to this rule of thumb, each percentage point increase in cyclical unemployment is associated with about a 2 percent widening of a negative output gap, measured in relation to potential output.

WHY DO SHORT-TERM FLUCTUATIONS OCCUR? A PREVIEW AND A PARABLE

What causes periods of recession and expansion? In the preceding section, we discussed two possible reasons for slowdowns and speedups in real GDP growth. First, growth in potential output itself may slow down or speed up, reflecting changes in the growth rates of available capital and labor and in the pace of technological progress. Second, even if potential output is growing normally, actual output may be higher or lower than potential output—that is, expansionary or recessionary output gaps may develop.

In the chapter *Economic Growth*, we discussed some of the reasons that growth in potential output can vary, and the options that policymakers have for stimulating growth in potential output. But we have not yet addressed the question of how output gaps can arise or what policymakers should do in response. The causes and cures of output gaps will be a major topic of the chapters covering economic policy. Here is a brief preview of the main conclusions of those chapters:

1. In a world in which prices adjusted immediately to balance the quantities supplied and demanded for all goods and services, output gaps would not exist. However, for many goods and services, the assumption that prices will adjust immediately is not realistic. Instead, many firms adjust the prices of their output only periodically. In particular, rather than changing prices with every variation in demand, firms tend to adjust to changes in demand in the short run by varying the quantity of output they produce and sell. This type of behavior is known as "meeting the demand" at a preset price.

2. Because in the short run firms tend to meet the demand for their output at preset prices, changes in the amount that customers decide to spend will affect output. When total spending is low for some reason, output may fall below potential output; conversely, when spending is high, output may rise above potential output. In other words, *changes in economywide spending are the primary cause of output gaps*. Thus, government policies can help to eliminate output gaps by influencing total

spending. For example, the government can affect total spending directly simply by changing its own level of purchases.

3. Although firms tend to meet demand in the short run, they will not be willing to do so indefinitely. If customer demand continues to differ from potential output, firms will eventually adjust their prices to eliminate output gaps. If demand exceeds potential output (an expansionary gap), firms will raise their prices aggressively, spurring inflation. If demand falls below potential output (a recessionary gap), firms will raise their prices less aggressively or even cut prices, reducing inflation.

4. Over the longer run, price changes by firms eliminate any output gap and bring production back into line with the economy's potential output. Thus, the economy is "self-correcting" in the sense that it operates to eliminate output gaps over time. Because of this self-correcting tendency, in the long run actual output equals potential output, so that output is determined by the economy's productive capacity rather than by the rate of spending. In the long run, total spending influences only the rate of inflation.

These ideas will become clearer as we proceed through this text. Before plunging into the details of the analysis, though, let's consider an example that illustrates the links between spending and output in the short and long run.

AL'S ICE CREAM STORE: A TALE ABOUT SHORT-RUN FLUCTUATIONS

Al's ice cream store produces gourmet ice cream on the premises and sells it directly to the public. What determines the amount of ice cream that Al produces on a daily basis? The productive capacity, or potential output, of the shop is one important factor. Specifically, Al's potential output of ice cream depends on the amount of capital (number of ice cream makers) and labor (number of workers) that he employs, and on the productivity of that capital and labor. Although Al's potential output usually changes rather slowly, on occasion it can fluctuate significantly—for example, if an ice cream maker breaks down or Al contracts the flu.

The main source of day-to-day variations in Al's ice cream production, however, is not changes in potential output but fluctuations in the demand for ice cream by the public. Some of these fluctuations in spending occur predictably over the course of the day (more demand in the afternoon than in the morning, for example), the week (more demand on weekends), or the year (more demand in the summer). Other changes in demand are less regular—more demand on a hot day than a cool one, or when a parade is passing by the store. Some changes in demand are hard for Al to interpret: For example, a surge in demand for rocky road ice cream on one particular Tuesday could reflect a permanent change in consumer tastes, or it might just be a random, one-time event.

How should Al react to these ebbs and flows in the demand for ice cream? The basic supply and demand model that we introduced in the beginning of this book, if applied to the market for ice cream, would predict that the price of ice cream should change with every change in the demand for ice cream. For example, prices should rise just after the movie theater next door to Al's shop lets out on Friday night, and they should fall on unusually cold, blustery days, when most people would prefer a hot cider to an ice cream cone. Indeed, taken literally, the supply and demand model predicts that ice cream prices should change almost moment to moment. Imagine Al standing in front of his shop like an auctioneer, calling out prices in an effort to determine how many people are willing to buy at each price!

Of course, we do not expect to see this behavior by an ice cream store owner. Price setting by auction does in fact occur in some markets, such as the market for grain or the stock market, but it is not the normal procedure in most retail markets, such as the market for ice cream. Why this difference? The basic reason is that sometimes the economic benefits of hiring an auctioneer and setting up an auction exceed the costs of doing so, and sometimes they do not. In the market for grain, for example, many buyers and sellers gather together in the same place at the same time to trade large volumes of standardized goods (bushels of grain). In that kind of situation, an auction is an efficient way to determine prices and balance the quantities supplied and demanded. In an ice cream store, by contrast, customers come in by twos and threes at random times throughout the day. Some want shakes, some cones, and some sodas. With small numbers of customers and a low sales volume at any given time, the costs involved in selling ice cream by auction are much greater than the benefits of allowing prices to vary with demand.

Cost-Benefit

So how does Al, the ice cream store manager, deal with changes in the demand for ice cream? Observation suggests that he begins by setting prices based on the best information he has about the demand for his product and the costs of production. Perhaps he prints up a menu or makes a sign announcing the prices. Then, over a period of time, he will keep his prices fixed and serve as many customers as want to buy (up to the point where he runs out of ice cream or room in the store at these prices). This behavior is what we call "meeting the demand" at preset prices, and it implies that, *in the short run,* the amount of ice cream Al produces and sells is determined by the demand for his products.

However, *in the long run,* the situation is quite different. Suppose, for example, that Al's ice cream earns a citywide reputation for its freshness and flavor. Day after day Al observes long lines in his store. His ice cream maker is overtaxed, as are his employees and his table space. There can no longer be any doubt that at current prices, the quantity of ice cream the public wants to consume exceeds what Al is able and willing to supply on a normal basis (his potential output). Expanding the store is an attractive possibility, but not one (we assume) that is immediately feasible. What will Al do?

Certainly one thing Al can do is raise his prices. At higher prices, Al will earn higher profits. Moreover, raising ice cream prices will bring the quantity of ice cream demanded closer to Al's normal production capacity—his potential output. Indeed, when the price of Al's ice cream finally rises to its equilibrium level, the shop's actual output will equal its potential output. Thus, over the long run, ice cream prices adjust to their equilibrium level, and the amount that is sold is determined by potential output.

This example illustrates in a simple way the links between spending and output—except, of course, that we must think of this story as applying to the whole economy, not to a single business. The key point is that there is an important difference between the short run and the long run. In the short run, producers often choose not to change their prices, but rather to meet the demand at preset prices. Because output is determined by demand, in the short run total spending plays a central role in determining the level of economic activity. Thus, Al's ice cream store enjoys a boom on an unusually hot day, when the demand for ice cream is strong, while an unseasonably cold day brings an ice cream recession. But in the long run, prices adjust to their market-clearing levels, and output equals potential output. Thus, the quantities of inputs and the productivity with which they are used are the primary determinants of economic activity in the long run, as we saw in the chapter *Economic Growth.* Although total spending affects output in the short run, in the long run its main effects are on prices.

The Economic Naturalist 10.1

Why did Coca-Cola Co. test a vending machine that "knows" when the weather is hot?

According to *The New York Times* (October 28, 1999, p. C1), Coca-Cola Co. has quietly tested a soda vending machine that includes a temperature sensor. Why would Coca-Cola want a vending machine that "knows" when the weather is hot?

When the weather is hot, the demand for refreshing soft drinks rises, increasing their market-clearing price. To take advantage of this variation in consumer demand, the vending machines that Coca-Cola tested were equipped with a computer chip that gave them the capability to raise soda prices automatically when the temperature climbs. The company's chairman and chief executive, M. Douglas Ivester, described in an interview how the desire for a cold drink increases during a sports championship final held in the summer heat. "So it is fair that it should be more expensive," Ivester was quoted as saying. "The machine will simply make this process automatic." Company officials suggested numerous other ways in which vending machine prices could be made dependent on demand. For example, machines could be programmed to reduce prices during off-peak hours or at low-traffic machines.

In traditional vending machines, cold drinks are priced in a way analogous to the way Al prices his ice cream: A price is set, and demand is met at the preset price until the machine runs out of soda. The weather-sensitive vending machine illustrates how technology may change pricing practices in the future. Indeed, increased computing power and access to the Internet already have allowed some firms, such as airline companies, to change prices almost continuously in response to variations in demand. Conceivably, the practice of meeting demand at a preset price may someday be obsolete.

On the other hand, Coca-Cola's experiments with "smart" vending machines also illustrate the barriers to fully flexible pricing in practice. First, the new vending machines are more costly than the standard model. In deciding whether to use them, the company must decide whether the extra profits from variable pricing justify the extra cost of the machines. Second, in early tests, many consumers reacted negatively to the new machines, complaining that they take unfair advantage of thirsty customers. In practice, customer complaints and concerns about "fairness" make companies less willing to vary prices sensitively with changing demand.

◦ SUMMARY ◦

- Real GDP does not grow smoothly. Periods in which the economy is growing at a rate significantly below normal are called recessions; periods in which the economy is growing at a rate significantly above normal are called expansions. A severe or protracted recession, like the long decline that occurred between 1929 and 1933, is called a depression, while a particularly strong expansion is called a boom. *(LO1)*

- The beginning of a recession is called the peak because it represents the high point of economic activity prior to a downturn. The end of a recession, which marks the low point of economic activity prior to a recovery, is called the trough. Since World War II, U.S. recessions have been much shorter on average than booms, lasting between 6 and 16 months. The longest boom period in U.S. history began with the end of the 1990–1991 recession in March 1991, ending exactly 10 years later in March 2001 when a new recession began. *(LO1)*

- Short-term economic fluctuations are irregular in length and severity, and are thus hard to forecast. Expansions and recessions are typically felt throughout the economy and may even be global in scope. Unemployment rises sharply during recessions, while inflation tends to fall during or shortly after a recession. Durable goods industries tend to be particularly sensitive to recessions and booms, whereas services and nondurable goods industries are less sensitive. *(LO1)*

- Potential output, also called potential GDP or full-employment output, is the maximum sustainable amount of output (real GDP) that an economy can produce. The difference between the economy's actual output and its potential output, relative to potential output, at a point in time is called the output gap. When output is below potential, the gap is called a recessionary gap; when output is above potential, the difference is called an expansionary gap. Recessions can occur either because potential output is growing unusually slowly or because actual output is below potential. Because recessionary gaps represent wasted resources and expansionary gaps threaten to create inflation, policymakers have an incentive to try to eliminate both types of gap. *(LO2)*

- The natural rate of unemployment is the part of the total unemployment rate that is attributable to frictional and structural unemployment. Equivalently, the natural rate of unemployment is the rate of unemployment that exists when the output gap is zero. Cyclical unemployment, the part of unemployment that is associated with recessions and expansions, equals the total unemployment rate less the natural unemployment rate. *(LO3)*

- Cyclical unemployment is related to the output gap by Okun's law, which states that each extra percentage point of cyclical unemployment is associated with about a 2 percent widening of a negative output gap, measured in relation to potential output. *(LO4)*

- Our further study of recessions and expansions will focus on the role of economywide spending. If firms adjust prices only periodically, and in the meantime produce enough output to meet demand, then fluctuations in spending will lead to fluctuations in output over the short run. During that short-run period, government policies that influence aggregate spending may help to eliminate output gaps. In the long run, however, firms' price changes will eliminate output gaps—that is, the economy will "self-correct"—and total spending will influence only the rate of inflation. *(LO5)*

○ KEY TERMS ○

boom	Okun's law	recession (or contraction)
business cycles	output gap	recessionary gap
depression	peak	trough
expansion	potential output, Y^* (or potential	
expansionary gap	GDP or full-employment	
natural rate of unemployment, u^*	output)	

○ REVIEW QUESTIONS ○

1. Define *recession* and *expansion*. What are the beginning and ending points of a recession called? In the postwar United States, which have been longer on average: recessions or expansions? *(LO1)*

2. Which firm is likely to see its profits reduced the most in a recession: an automobile producer, a manufacturer of boots and shoes, or a janitorial service? Which is likely to see its profits reduced the least? Explain. *(LO1)*

3. Define *potential output*. Is it possible for an economy to produce an amount greater than potential output? Explain. *(LO2)*

4. How is each of the following likely to be affected by a recession: the natural unemployment rate, the cyclical unemployment rate, the inflation rate, the poll ratings of the president? *(LO1, LO3)*

5. True or false: When output equals potential output, the unemployment rate is zero. Explain. *(LO4)*

6. If the natural rate of unemployment is 5 percent, what is the total rate of unemployment if output is 2 percent below potential output? What if output is 2 percent above potential output? *(LO4)*

○ PROBLEMS ○

Visit your mobile app store and download the Frank: Study Econ app *today!*

1. Using Table 10.1, find the average duration, the minimum duration, and the maximum duration of expansions in the United States since 1929. Are expansions getting longer or shorter on average over time? Is there any tendency for long expansions to be followed by long recessions? *(LO1)*

2. From the homepage of the Bureau of Economic Analysis (www.bea.gov) obtain quarterly data for U.S. real GDP from three recessions: 1981–1982, 1990–1991, and 2001. *(LO1)*
   a. How many quarters of negative real GDP growth occurred in each recession?
   b. Which, if any, of the recessions satisfied the informal criterion that a recession must have two consecutive quarters of negative GDP growth?

3. Given below are data on real GDP and potential GDP for the United States for the years 2000–2013, in billions of 2009 dollars. For each year, calculate the output gap

as a percentage of potential GDP and state whether the gap is a recessionary gap or an expansionary gap. Also calculate the year-to-year growth rates of real GDP. Identify the recessions that occurred during this period? *(LO2)*

Year	Real GDP	Potential GDP
2003	13,271.1	13,520.3
2004	13,773.5	13,874.2
2005	14,234.2	14,203.6
2006	14,613.8	14,540.5
2007	14,873.7	14,890.2
2008	14,830.4	15,225.9
2009	14,418.7	15,495.4
2010	14,783.8	15,706.1
2011	15,020.6	15,922.3
2012	15,369.2	16,168.2
2013	15,710.3	16,431.4

SOURCE: Potential GDP, Federal Reserve Bank of St. Louis; real GDP, www.bea.gov.

4. From the homepage of the Bureau of Labor Statistics (www.bls.gov), obtain the most recent available data on the unemployment rate for workers aged 16–19 and workers aged 20 or over. How do they differ? What are some of the reasons for the difference? How does this difference relate to the decline in the overall natural rate of unemployment since 1980? *(LO3)*

5. Using Okun's law, fill in the four pieces of missing data in the table below. The data are hypothetical. *(LO4)*

Year	Real GDP ($ billions)	Potential GDP ($ billions)	Natural unemployment rate (%)	Actual unemployment rate (%)
2012	7,840	8,000	(a)	6
2013	8,100	(b)	5	5
2014	(c)	8,200	4.5	4
2015	8,415	8,250	5	(d)

6. Of the following, identify the incorrect statement. *(LO5)*
   a. Output gaps are caused by inflationary pressures generated by the unintended side effects of government policy.
   b. Low aggregate spending can make output fall below potential output.
   c. When spending is high, output may rise above potential output.
   d. Government policies can help to eliminate output gaps.

○ ANSWER TO CONCEPT CHECK ○

10.1 The actual unemployment rate in the first quarter of 2011 exceeded the natural rate by 4.6 percent. Applying Okun's law, actual output fell below potential output by 9.2 percent. *(LO4)*

CHAPTER 11

Spending, Output, and Fiscal Policy

Werner Dieterich/Getty Images

HOW ARE CONSUMER SPENDING AND GDP RELATED?

When one of the authors of this book was a small boy, he used to spend some time every summer with his grandparents, who lived a few hours from his home. A favorite activity of his during these visits was to spend a summer evening on the front porch with his grandmother, listening to her stories.

Grandma had spent the early years of her marriage in New England, during the worst part of the Great Depression. In one of her reminiscences, she remarked that, at that time, in the mid-1930s, it had been a satisfaction to her to be able to buy her children a new pair of shoes every year. In the small town where she and her family lived, many children had to wear their shoes until they fell apart, and a few unlucky boys and girls went to school barefoot. Her grandson thought this was scandalous: "Why didn't their parents just buy them new shoes?" he demanded.

"They couldn't," said Grandma. "They didn't have the money. Most of the fathers had lost their jobs because of the Depression."

"What kind of jobs did they have?"

"They worked in the shoe factories, which had to close down."

"Why did the factories close down?"

"Because," Grandma explained, "nobody had any money to buy shoes."

The grandson was only six or seven years old at the time, but even he could see that there was something badly wrong with Grandma's logic. On the one side were boarded-up shoe factories and shoe workers with no jobs; on the other, children without shoes.

LEARNING OBJECTIVES

After reading this chapter, you should be able to:

LO1 Identify the key assumption of the basic Keynesian model and explain how this affects the production decisions made by firms.

LO2 Discuss the determinants of planned investment and aggregate consumption spending and how these concepts are used to develop a model of planned aggregate expenditure.

LO3 Analyze, using graphs and numbers, how an economy reaches short-run equilibrium in the basic Keynesian model.

LO4 Show how a change in planned aggregate expenditure can cause a change in short-run equilibrium output and how this is related to the income-expenditure multiplier.

LO5 Explain why the basic Keynesian model suggests that fiscal policy is useful as a stabilization policy, and discuss the qualifications that arise in applying fiscal policy in real-world situations.

Efficiency

Why couldn't the shoe factories just open and produce the shoes the children so badly needed? He made his point quite firmly, but Grandma just shrugged and said it didn't work that way.

The story of the closed-down shoe factories illustrates in a microcosm the cost to society of a recessionary gap. In an economy with a recessionary gap, available resources, which in principle could be used to produce valuable goods and services, are instead allowed to lie fallow. This waste of resources lowers the economy's output and economic welfare, compared to its potential.

Grandma's account also suggests how such an unfortunate situation might come about. Suppose factory owners and other producers, being reluctant to accumulate unsold goods on their shelves, produce just enough output to satisfy the demand for their products. And suppose that, for some reason, the public's willingness or ability to spend declines. If spending declines, factories will respond by cutting their production (because they don't want to produce goods they can't sell) and by laying off workers who are no longer needed. And because the workers who are laid off will lose most of their income—a particularly serious loss in the 1930s, in the days before government-sponsored unemployment insurance was common—they must reduce their own spending. As their spending declines, factories will reduce their production again, laying off more workers, who in turn reduce their spending—and so on, in a vicious circle. In this scenario, the problem is not a lack of productive capacity—the factories have not lost their ability to produce—but rather *insufficient spending* to support the normal level of production.

The idea that a decline in aggregate spending may cause output to fall below potential output was one of the key insights of John Maynard Keynes (pronounced "canes"), a highly influential British economist of the first half of the twentieth century.[1] The goal of this chapter is to present a theory, or model, of how recessions and expansions may arise from fluctuations in aggregate spending, along the lines first suggested by Keynes. This model, which we call the *basic Keynesian model,* is also known as the *Keynesian cross,* after the diagram that is used to illustrate the theory.

We begin with a brief discussion of the key assumptions of the basic Keynesian model. We then turn to the important concept of total, or aggregate, *planned spending* in the economy. We show how, in the short run, the rate of aggregate spending helps to determine the level of output, which can be greater than or less than potential output. In other words, depending on the level of spending, the economy may develop an output gap. "Too little" spending leads to a recessionary output gap, while "too much" creates an expansionary output gap.

An implication of the basic Keynesian model is that government policies that affect the level of spending can be used to reduce or eliminate output gaps. Policies used in this way are called *stabilization policies.* Keynes himself argued for the active use of fiscal policy—policy relating to government spending and taxes—to eliminate output gaps and stabilize the economy. In the latter part of this chapter, we'll show why Keynes thought fiscal policy could help to stabilize the economy, and discuss the usefulness of fiscal policy as a stabilization tool.

The basic Keynesian model is not a complete or entirely realistic model of the economy, since it applies only to the relatively short period during which firms do not adjust their prices but instead meet the demand forthcoming at preset prices. Nevertheless, this model is an essential building block of leading current theories of short-run economic fluctuations and stabilization policies. We will later extend the basic Keynesian model to incorporate monetary policy, inflation, and other important features of the economy in other chapters.

THE KEYNESIAN MODEL'S CRUCIAL ASSUMPTION: FIRMS MEET DEMAND AT PRESET PRICES

The basic Keynesian model is built on a key assumption: In the short run, *firms meet the demand for their products at preset prices.* Firms do not respond to every change in the demand for their products by changing their prices. Instead, they typically set a price for

---

[1]A brief biography of Keynes is available at www.bbc.co.uk/history/historic_figures/keynes_john_maynard.shtml.

some period and then meet the demand at that price. By "meeting the demand," we mean that firms produce just enough to satisfy their customers at the prices that have been set.[2]

As we will see, the assumption that firms vary their production in order to meet demand at preset prices implies that fluctuations in spending will have powerful effects on the nation's real GDP.

The assumption that, over short periods of time, firms meet the demand for their products at preset prices is generally realistic. Think of the stores where you shop. The price of a pair of jeans does not fluctuate from moment to moment according to the number of customers who enter the store or the latest news about the price of denim. Instead, the store posts a price and sells jeans to any customer who wants to buy at that price, at least until the store runs out of stock. Similarly, the corner pizza restaurant may leave the price of its large pie unchanged for months or longer, allowing its pizza production to be determined by the number of customers who want to buy at the preset price.

Firms do not normally change their prices frequently because doing so would be costly. Economists refer to the costs of changing prices as **menu costs.** In the case of the pizza restaurant, the menu cost is literally just that—the cost of printing up a new menu when prices change. Similarly, the clothing store faces the cost of remarking all its merchandise if the manager changes prices. But menu costs also may include other kinds of costs—for example, the cost of doing a market survey to determine what price to charge and the cost of informing customers about price changes.

Menu costs will not prevent firms from changing their prices indefinitely. As we saw in the case of Al's ice cream store (in the chapter *Short-Term Economic Fluctuations*), too great an imbalance between demand and supply, as reflected by a difference between sales and potential output, will eventually lead firms to change their prices. If no one is buying jeans, for example, at some point the clothing store will mark down its jeans prices. Or if the pizza restaurant becomes the local hot spot, with a line of customers stretching out the door, eventually the manager will raise the price of a large pie.

Like many other economic decisions, the decision to change prices reflects a cost-benefit comparison: Prices should be changed if the benefit of doing so—the fact that sales will be brought more nearly in line with the firm's normal production capacity—outweighs the menu costs associated with making the change. As we have stressed, the basic Keynesian model developed in this chapter ignores the fact that prices will eventually adjust, and therefore should be interpreted as applying to the short run.

menu costs the costs of changing prices

Cost-Benefit

The Impact of New Technologies on Menu Costs   EXAMPLE 11.1

Will new technologies eliminate menu costs?

Keynesian theory is based on the assumption that menu costs are sufficiently large to prevent firms from adjusting prices immediately in response to changing market conditions. However, in many industries, new technologies have eliminated or greatly reduced the direct costs of changing prices. For example, the use of bar codes to identify individual products, together with scanner technologies, allows a grocery store manager to change prices with just a few keystrokes, without having to change the price label on each can of soup or loaf of bread. Airlines use sophisticated computer software to implement complex pricing strategies, under which two travelers on the same flight to Milwaukee may pay very different fares, depending on whether they are business or vacation travelers and on how far in advance their flights were booked. Online retailers such as booksellers have the ability to vary their prices by type of customer and even by individual customer, while other Internet-based companies such as eBay and Priceline allow for negotiation over the price of each individual purchase. As we discussed in

---

[2]Obviously, firms can meet the forthcoming demand only up to the point where they reach the limit of their capacity to produce. For that reason, the Keynesian analysis of this chapter is relevant only when producers have unused capacity.

"You thought we would offer lower fares? How insensitive."

Economic Naturalist 21.1, Coca-Cola experimented with a vending machine that automatically varied the price of a soft drink according to the outdoor temperature, charging more when the weather was hot.

Will these reductions in the direct costs of changing prices make the Keynesian theory, which assumes that firms meet demand at preset prices, less relevant to the real world? It's possible, but it is unlikely that new technologies will completely eliminate the costs of changing prices anytime soon. Gathering the information about market conditions needed to set the profit-maximizing price—including the prices charged by competitors, the costs of producing the good or service, and the likely demand for the product—will remain costly for firms. Another cost of changing prices is the use of valuable managerial time and attention needed to make informed pricing decisions. A more subtle cost of changing prices—particularly raising prices—is that doing so may lead regular customers to rethink their choice of suppliers and decide to search for a better deal elsewhere.

PLANNED AGGREGATE EXPENDITURE

In the simple Keynesian model, output at each point in time is determined by the amount that people throughout the economy want to spend—what we will refer to as *planned aggregate expenditure*. Specifically, **planned aggregate expenditure (*PAE*)** is total planned spending on final goods and services.

planned aggregate expenditure (*PAE*) total planned spending on final goods and services

The four components of spending on final goods and services were introduced in the chapter *Spending, Income, and GDP*:

1. *Consumption expenditure*, or simply *consumption* (*C*), is spending by households on final goods and services. Examples of consumption expenditure are spending on food, clothes, and entertainment and on consumer durable goods like automobiles and furniture.

2. *Investment* (*I*) is spending by domestic firms on new capital goods, such as office buildings, factories, and equipment. Spending on new houses and apartment buildings (residential investment) and increases in inventories (inventory investment) also are included in investment.[3]

3. *Government purchases* (*G*) are purchases by federal, state, and local governments of final goods and services. Examples of government purchases include new schools and hospitals, military hardware, equipment for the space program, and the services of government employees such as soldiers, police, and government office workers. Recall from the chapter *Spending, Income, and GDP* that *transfer payments* such as Social Security benefits and unemployment insurance and interest on the government debt are *not* included in government purchases.

4. *Net exports* (*NX*) equal exports minus imports. Exports are sales of domestically produced goods and services to foreigners. Imports are purchases by domestic residents of goods and services produced abroad that have been included in *C*, *I*, and *G* but must now be subtracted because they do not represent domestic production. Net exports therefore represent the net demand for domestic goods and services by foreigners.

Together, these four types of spending—by households, firms, the government, and the rest of the world—sum to total, or aggregate, spending.

PLANNED SPENDING VERSUS ACTUAL SPENDING

In the Keynesian model, output is determined by planned aggregate expenditure, or planned spending, for short. Could *planned* spending ever differ from *actual* spending?

---

[3]As we discussed earlier, we use "investment" here to mean spending on new capital goods such as factories, housing, and equipment, which is not the same as financial investment. This distinction is important to keep in mind.

The answer is yes. The most important case is that of a firm that sells either less or more of its product than expected. Note that additions to the stocks of goods sitting in a firm's warehouse are treated in official government statistics as inventory investment by the firm. In effect, government statisticians assume that the firm buys its unsold output from itself; they then count those purchases as part of the firm's investment spending.[4]

Suppose, then, that a firm's actual sales are less than expected, so that part of what it had planned to sell remains in the warehouse. In this case, the firm's actual investment, including the unexpected increases in its inventory, is greater than its planned investment, which did not include the added inventory. If this is true for the economy as a whole, we will find that $I > I^p$, where I^p equals the firm's planned investment, including planned inventory investment.

What if firms sell more output than expected? In that case, firms will add less to their inventories than they planned and actual investment will be less than planned investment, that is, $I < I^p$. The following example gives a numerical illustration.

Planned versus Actual Investment   EXAMPLE 11.2

What is the difference between planned investment and actual investment?

Fly-by-Night Kite Co. produces $5,000,000 worth of kites during the year. It expects sales of $4,800,000 for the year, leaving $200,000 worth of kites to be stored in the warehouse for future sale. During the year, Fly-by-Night adds $1,000,000 in new production equipment as part of an expansion plan. Fly-by-Night's planned investment, I^p, thus equals its purchases of new production equipment ($1,000,000) plus its planned additions to inventory ($200,000), for a total of $1,200,000 in planned investment. The company's planned investment does not depend on how much it actually sells.

If Fly-by-Night sells only $4,600,000 worth of kites, it will add $400,000 in kites to its inventory instead of the $200,000 worth originally planned. In this case, actual investment equals the $1,000,000 in new equipment plus the $400,000 in inventory investment, so $I = \$1,400,000$. We see that, when the firm sells less output than planned, actual investment exceeds planned investment ($I > I^p$).

If Fly-by-Night has $4,800,000 in sales, then it will add $200,000 in kites to inventory, just as planned. In this case, actual and planned investment are the same:

$$I = I^p = \$1,200,000.$$

Finally, if Fly-by-Night sells $5,000,000 worth of kites, it will have no output to add to inventory. Its inventory investment will be zero, and its total actual investment (including the new equipment) will equal $1,000,000, which is less than its planned investment of $1,200,000 ($I < I^p$).

With these assumptions, we can define planned aggregate expenditure by the following equation:

$$PAE = C + I^p + G + NX. \tag{11.1}$$

Equation 11.1 says that planned aggregate expenditure is the sum of planned spending by households, firms, governments, and foreigners.

To keep our analysis simple, we will assume that planned spending equals actual spending for households, the government, and foreigners. This is a reasonable assumption and does not affect the basic analysis. It also allows us to avoid using superscripts to distinguish between planned versus actual consumption, government purchases, or net exports.

[4]For the purposes of measuring GDP, treating unsold output as being purchased by its producer has the advantage of ensuring that actual production and actual expenditure are equal.

CONSUMER SPENDING AND THE ECONOMY

The largest component of planned aggregate expenditure is consumption spending. As already mentioned, consumer spending includes household purchases of goods such as groceries and clothing; services such as health care, concerts, and college tuition; and consumer durables such as cars, furniture, and home computers. Thus, consumers' willingness to spend affects sales and profitability in a wide range of industries. (Households' purchases of new homes are classified as investment, rather than consumption, but home purchases represent another channel through which household decisions affect total spending.)

What factors determine how much people plan to spend on consumer goods and services in a given period? While many factors are relevant, a particularly important determinant is their after-tax, or disposable, income. All else being equal, the higher the private sector's disposable income, the higher will be the level of consumption spending.

Figure 11.1 shows the relationship between real consumption expenditures and real disposable income in the United States for the period 1960–2012. Each point on the graph corresponds to a year between 1960 and 2012 (selected years are indicated in the figure). The position of each point is determined by the combination of relationship between aggregate consumption and disposable income.

FIGURE 11.1

The U.S. Consumption Function, 1960–2012.

Each point on this figure represents a combination of aggregate real consumption and aggregate real disposable income for a specific year between 1960 and 2012. Note the strong positive relationship between consumption and disposable income.

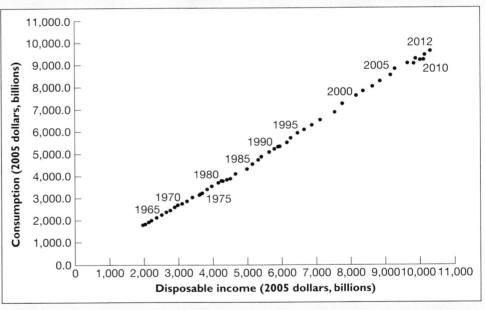

SOURCE: *Economic Report of the President,* March 2013, Table B-31, www.gpoaccess.gov/eop.

We can write this relationship between consumption and disposable income as a linear equation[5]

$$C = \overline{C} + (mpc)(Y - T). \tag{11.2}$$

consumption function

the relationship between consumption spending and its determinants, in particular, disposable income

This equation is known as the *consumption function.* The **consumption function** relates consumption spending (C) to disposable income ($Y - T$) and all other factors that might affect household spending.

Let's look at the consumption function more carefully. The right side of the equation contains two terms, $\overline{C}$ and $(mpc)(Y - T)$. The amount of consumption represented by $\overline{C}$

---

[5]You should review the material in the appendix to the chapter *Thinking Like an Economist* if you don't regularly work with linear equations.

is called **autonomous consumption** since it is consumption that is not related to (i.e., autonomous from) changes in disposable income. For example, suppose consumers became more optimistic about the future, so that they wanted to consume more and save less at any given level of their current disposable income. In this case, $\overline{C}$ will increase and consumption will increase even though disposable income has not changed.

We can imagine other factors that could affect autonomous consumption. Suppose, for example, that there is a boom in the stock market or a sharp increase in home prices, making consumers feel wealthier, and hence more inclined to spend, for a given level of current disposable income. This effect could be captured by assuming that $\overline{C}$ increases. Likewise, a fall in home prices or stock prices that made consumers feel poorer and less inclined to spend would be represented by a decrease in $\overline{C}$. Economists refer to the effects of changes in asset prices on consumption via changes in autonomous consumption as the **wealth effect.**

Finally, autonomous consumption also takes account of the effects that real interest rates have on consumption. In particular, higher real interest rates will make it more expensive to buy consumer durables on credit and so households may consume less and save more. $\overline{C}$ would thus decrease and consumption will fall even though disposable income has not changed. The opposite is also true: A decline in real interest rates will lower borrowing costs and the opportunity cost of saving, and so households may increase their autonomous consumption and therefore their total consumption spending.

autonomous consumption consumption spending that is not related to the level of disposable income

wealth effect the tendency of changes in asset prices to affect households' wealth and thus their consumption spending

Understanding Wealth Effects

EXAMPLE 11.3

How did the decline in U.S. stock market values from 2000–2002 affect consumption spending?

From March 2000 to October 2002, the U.S. stock market suffered a 49 percent drop in value as measured by the Standard and Poor's 500 stock index, a widely referenced benchmark of U.S. stock performance. According to MIT economist James Poterba, U.S. households owned roughly $13.3 trillion of corporate stock in 2000.[6] If households' stock market holdings reflect those of the Standard and Poor's stock index, the 49 percent drop in the value of the stock market wiped out approximately $6.5 trillion of household wealth in two years. According to economic models based on historical experience, a dollar's decrease in household wealth reduces consumer spending by 3 to 7 cents per year, so the reduction in stock market wealth had the potential to reduce overall consumer spending by $195 billion to $455 billion, a drop of approximately 3 to 7 percent. Yet, real consumption spending continued to rise from 2000 through 2002. Why did this happen?

Despite the start of a recession in March 2001, overall consumption spending remained strong during 2000–2002 for a variety of reasons. First, consumers' real after-tax income continued to grow into the fall of 2001, helping to maintain strong consumer spending despite the drop in the stock market. Furthermore, throughout 2001 and into early 2002, the Federal Reserve significantly reduced interest rates; we'll discuss how the Federal Reserve does this in another chapter. As we discussed, a reduction in interest rates helps to promote consumer spending, especially on durable goods such as automobiles, by reducing consumers' borrowing costs. Finally, housing prices rose significantly during this period, increasing consumers' housing wealth and partially offsetting their decline in stock-related wealth. Data on repeat house sales that measure the price of individual houses that are sold and resold over time indicate that housing prices rose by 20.1 percent between the first quarter of 2000 and the third quarter of 2002.[7]

[6]See Table 1 in James M. Poterba, "Stock Market Wealth and Consumption," *Journal of Economic Perspectives* 14 (Spring 2000), pp. 99–118.
[7]U.S. Office of Federal Housing Enterprise Oversight (OFHEO), www.ofheo.gov. House prices continued to rise from 2003 through mid-2006.

The total market value of household real estate was about $12 trillion in 2000, so house price appreciation added about $2.4 trillion to household wealth, offsetting about 37 percent of the decline in stock market wealth during this period.[8]

marginal propensity to consume (mpc) the amount by which consumption rises when disposable income rises by $1; we assume that $0 < mpc < 1$

The second term on the right side of Equation 11.2, $(mpc)(Y - T)$, measures the effect of disposable income, $Y - T$, on consumption. The **marginal propensity to consume (mpc),** a fixed number, is the amount by which consumption rises when current disposable income rises by one dollar. The intuition behind the marginal propensity to consume is straightforward: If people receive an extra dollar of income, they will consume part of the dollar and save the rest. That is, their consumption will increase, but by less than the full dollar of extra income. It is therefore realistic to assume that the marginal propensity to consume is greater than 0 (an increase in income leads to an increase in consumption) but less than 1 (the increase in consumption will be less than the full increase in income). Mathematically, we can summarize these assumptions as $0 < mpc < 1$.

Figure 11.2 shows a hypothetical consumption function, with consumption spending (C) on the vertical axis and disposable income on the horizontal axis.

FIGURE 11.2

A Consumption Function.

The consumption function relates consumption spending (C) to disposable income, (Y − T). The vertical intercept of the consumption function is autonomous consumption ($\overline{C}$), and the slope of the line equals the marginal propensity to consume (mpc).

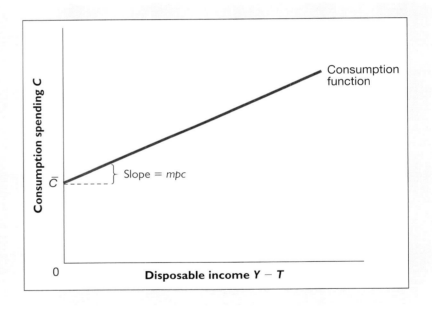

The intercept of the consumption function on the vertical axis equals autonomous consumption ($\overline{C}$), and the slope of the consumption function equals the marginal propensity to consume (mpc). To see how this consumption function fits reality, compare Figure 11.2 to Figure 11.1 (which shows the relationship between aggregate real consumption expenditures and real disposable income). Our theoretical relationship clearly fits with the actual relationship between disposable income and consumption.

PLANNED AGGREGATE EXPENDITURE AND OUTPUT

Thinking back to Grandma's reminiscences, recall that an important element of her story involved the links among production, income, and spending. As the shoe factories in Grandma's town reduced production, the incomes of both factory workers and factory

[8]Federal Reserve Board, Flow of Funds Accounts of the United States, www.federalreserve.gov.

owners fell. Workers' incomes fell as the number of hours of work per week were reduced (a common practice during the Depression), as workers were laid off, or as wages
were cut. Factory owners' income fell as profits declined. Reduced incomes, in turn,
forced both workers and factory owners to curtail their spending—which led to still lower
production and further reductions in income. This vicious circle led the economy further
and further into recession.

The logic of Grandma's story has two key elements: (1) declines in production
(which imply declines in the income received by producers) lead to reduced spending
and (2) reductions in spending lead to declines in production and income. In this
section, we look at the first part of the story, the effects of production and income on
spending. We return later in this chapter to the effects of spending on production and
income.

Why do changes in production and income affect planned aggregate spending? The
consumption function, which relates consumption to disposable income, is the basic
source of this relationship. Because consumption spending C is a large part of planned
aggregate spending, and because consumption depends on output Y, aggregate spending
as a whole depends on output.

Let's examine the link between planned aggregate expenditure and output in two ways.
We will begin by working with a specific numerical example so that you can see the relationship clearly. Next, we will plot the relationship on a graph so that you can see its general
shape and start working with these concepts using graphs.

Linking Planned Aggregate Expenditure to Output   EXAMPLE 11.4

What is the relationship between planned aggregate expenditure and output?

In a particular economy, the consumption function is

$$C = 620 + 0.8(Y - T),$$

so that the intercept term in the consumption function $\overline{C}$ equals 620 and the marginal
propensity to consume *mpc* equals 0.8. Also, suppose that we are given that planned investment spending $I^P = 220$, government purchases $G = 300$, net exports $NX = 20$, and
taxes $T = 250$.

Recall the definition of planned aggregate expenditure, Equation 11.1:

$$PAE = C + I^P + G + NX.$$

To find a numerical equation for planned aggregate expenditure, we need to find
numerical expressions for each of its four components. The first component of spending, consumption, is defined by the consumption function, $C = 620 + 0.8(Y - T)$.
Since $T = 250$, we can substitute for T to write the consumption function as
$C = 620 + 0.8(Y - 250)$. Now plug this expression for C into the definition of planned
aggregate expenditure above to get

$$PAE = [620 + 0.8(Y - 250)] + I^P + G + NX.$$

Similarly, we can substitute the given numerical values of planned investment I^P,
government purchases G, and net exports NX into the definition of planned aggregate
expenditure to get

$$PAE = [620 + 0.8(Y - 250)] + 220 + 300 + 20.$$

To simplify this equation, first note that $0.8(Y - 250) = 0.8Y - 200$, and then add together
all the terms that don't depend on output Y. The result is

$$PAE = (620 - 200 + 220 + 300 + 20) + 0.8Y$$
$$= 960 + 0.8Y.$$

The final expression shows the relationship between planned aggregate expenditure and output in this numerical example. Note that, according to this equation, a $1 increase in Y leads to an increase in PAE of $(0.8)(\$1)$, or 80 cents. The reason for this is that the marginal propensity to consume, mpc, in this example is 0.8. Hence, a $1 increase in income raises consumption spending by 80 cents. Since consumption is a component of total planned spending, total spending rises by 80 cents as well.

autonomous expenditure the portion of planned aggregate expenditure that is independent of output

induced expenditure the portion of planned aggregate expenditure that depends on output Y

expenditure line a line showing the relationship between planned aggregate expenditure and output

The specific equation we developed illustrates a general point: Planned aggregate expenditure can be divided into two parts, a part that depends on output (Y) and a part that is independent of output. The portion of planned aggregate expenditure that is independent of output is called **autonomous expenditure.** In the equation above, autonomous expenditure is the constant term and is equal to 960. This portion of planned spending, being a fixed number, does not vary when output varies. By contrast, the portion of planned aggregate expenditure that depends on output (Y) is called **induced expenditure.** In the equation above, induced expenditure equals $0.8Y$, the second term in the expression for planned aggregate expenditure. Note that the numerical value of induced expenditure depends, by definition, on the numerical value taken by output. Autonomous expenditure and induced expenditure together equal planned aggregate expenditure.

Figure 11.3 is a graph of the equation $PAE = 960 + 0.8Y$, which is a straight line with a vertical intercept of 960 and a slope of 0.8. This line, which shows the relationship between planned aggregate expenditure and output graphically, is called the **expenditure line**.

There are three properties of the expenditure line that are important to note. First, the slope of this line is equal to the marginal propensity to consume for our specific numerical example. This point holds in general: The slope of the expenditure line is equal to the marginal propensity to consume. Second, the vertical intercept is equal to autonomous expenditure for our example. This point also holds more generally: The vertical intercept of the expenditure line equals the level of autonomous expenditure. Third, changes in autonomous expenditure will shift the expenditure line: Increases in autonomous expenditure will shift the expenditure line up while decreases will shift the line down. We will apply all three of these properties in the rest of the chapter.

FIGURE 11.3

The Expenditure Line.

The line $PAE = 960 + 0.8Y$, referred to as the expenditure line, shows the relationship of planned aggregate expenditure to output.

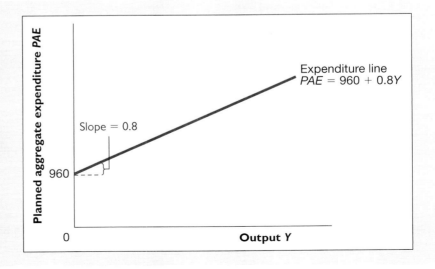

RECAP	PLANNED AGGREGATE EXPENDITURE

- Planned aggregate expenditure (*PAE*) is total planned spending on final goods and services. The four components of planned spending are consumer expenditure (*C*), planned investment (*I^p*), government purchases (*G*), and net exports (*NX*). Planned investment differs from actual investment when firms' sales are different from what they expected, so that additions to inventory (a component of investment) are different from what firms anticipated.

- The largest component of aggregate expenditure is consumer expenditure, or simply consumption. Consumption depends on disposable, or after-tax, income, according to a relationship known as the consumption function, stated algebraically as $C = \overline{C} + (mpc)(Y - T)$.

- The constant term in the consumption function, $\overline{C}$, captures factors other than disposable income that affect consumer spending. For example, an increase in housing or stock prices that makes households wealthier and thus more willing to spend—an effect called the wealth effect—could be captured by an increase in $\overline{C}$. The slope of the consumption function equals the marginal propensity to consume, *mpc*, where $0 < mpc < 1$. This is the amount by which consumption rises when disposable income rises by one dollar.

- Increases in output *Y*, which imply equal increases in income, cause consumption to rise. As consumption is part of planned aggregate expenditure, planned spending depends on output as well. The portion of planned aggregate expenditure that depends on output is called induced expenditure. The portion of planned aggregate expenditure that is independent of output is autonomous expenditure.

SHORT-RUN EQUILIBRIUM OUTPUT

Now that we have defined planned aggregate expenditure and seen how it is related to output, the next task is to see how output itself is determined. Recall the assumption of the basic Keynesian model: In the short run, producers leave prices at preset levels and simply meet the demand that is forthcoming at those prices. In other words, during the short-run period in which prices are preset, firms produce an amount that is equal to planned aggregate expenditure. Accordingly, we define **short-run equilibrium output** as the level of output at which output *Y* equals planned aggregate expenditure *PAE*:

$$Y = PAE. \tag{11.3}$$

Short-run equilibrium output is the level of output that prevails during the period in which prices are predetermined.

There are two approaches to finding the level of short-run equilibrium output in the simple Keynesian model. First, we can use a specific numerical example to show where equilibrium output equals planned spending. There are two ways to do this: We can use a table to find where $Y = PAE = 0$, or we can manipulate the equations directly. Each method illustrates an important point about the basic Keynesian model, so we apply both of them to the specific example we introduced in the previous section. Second, we can add a line to our graph of the expenditure line to find short-run equilibrium output. The resulting graph is called the Keynesian cross since it involves two lines intersecting. This technique is quite useful for generalizing the ideas we develop in the numerical example.

short-run equilibrium output the level of output at which output *Y* equals planned aggregate expenditure *PAE;* the level of output that prevails during the period in which prices are predetermined

FINDING SHORT-RUN EQUILIBRIUM OUTPUT: NUMERICAL APPROACH

Recall that in our previous example (Example 11.4), planned spending is determined by the equation

$$PAE = 960 + 0.8Y.$$

Thus, for instance, when $Y = 4,000$, $PAE = 960 + 0.8(4,000) = 4,160$. Table 11.1 shows the results of this calculation for different levels of output; column 1 shows various levels of output and column 2 lists the levels of planned aggregate expenditure (PAE) for the different levels of output given in column 1.

TABLE 11.1
Numerical Determination of Short-Run Equilibrium Output

(1) Output Y	(2) Planned aggregate expenditure $PAE = 960 + 0.8Y$	(3) $Y - PAE$	(4) $Y = PAE$?
4,000	4,160	−160	No
4,200	4,320	−120	No
4,400	4,480	−80	No
4,600	4,640	−40	No
4,800	4,800	0	**Yes**
5,000	4,960	40	No
5,200	5,120	80	No

In Table 11.1, notice that since consumption rises with output, total planned spending (which includes consumption) rises also. Specifically, compare columns 1 and 2, and see that every time output rises by 200, planned spending rises by only 160. That is because the marginal propensity to consume in this economy is 0.8, so that each dollar in added income raises consumption and planned spending by 80 cents.

Short-run equilibrium output is the level of output at which $Y = PAE$, or, equivalently, $Y - PAE = 0$. At this level of output, actual investment will equal planned investment and there will be no tendency for output to change. Looking at Table 11.1, we can see there is only one level of output that satisfies that condition, $Y = 4,800$. At that level, output and planned aggregate expenditure are precisely equal, so that producers are just meeting the demand for their goods and services.

In this economy, what would happen if output differed from its equilibrium value of 4,800? Suppose, for example, that output were 4,000. Looking at the second column of Table 11.1, you can see that, when output is 4,000, planned aggregate expenditure equals $960 + 0.8(4,000)$, or 4,160. Thus, if output is 4,000, firms are not producing enough to meet the demand. They will find that, as sales exceed the amounts they are producing, their inventories of finished goods are being depleted by 160 per year, and that actual investment (including inventory investment) is less than planned investment. Under the assumption that firms are committed to meeting their customers' demand, firms will respond by expanding their production.

Would expanding production to 4,160, the level of planned spending firms faced when output was 4,000, be enough? The answer is no because of induced expenditure. That is, as firms expand their output, aggregate income (wages and profits) rises with it, which in turn leads to higher levels of consumption. Indeed, if output expands to 4,160, planned spending will increase as well, to 960 + 0.8(4,160), or 4,288. So an output level of 4,160 will still be insufficient to meet demand. As Table 11.1 shows, output will not be sufficient to meet planned aggregate expenditure until it expands to its short-run equilibrium value of 4,800.

What if output were initially greater than its equilibrium value—say, 5,000? From Table 11.1, we can see that when output equals 5,000, planned spending equals only 4,960—less than what firms are producing. So at an output level of 5,000, firms will not sell all they produce, and they will find that their merchandise is piling up on store shelves and in warehouses (actual investment, including inventory investment, is greater than planned investment). In response, firms will cut their production runs. As Table 11.1 shows, they will have to reduce production to its equilibrium value of 4,800 before output just matches planned spending.

We can find short-run equilibrium output directly by using the equation for planned aggregate expenditure:

$$PAE = 960 + 0.8Y.$$

By definition, an economy is in short-run equilibrium when

$$Y = PAE.$$

So, using our equation for planned aggregate expenditure, we have

$$Y = 960 + 0.8Y.$$

Solving for Y, we have $Y = 4,800$, the same result we obtained using Table 11.1.

CONCEPT CHECK 11.1

Construct a table like Table 11.1 for an economy like the one we have been working with, assuming that the consumption function is $C = 820 + 0.7(Y - T)$ and that $I^P = 600$, $G = 600$, $NX = 200$, and $T = 600$.

What is short-run equilibrium output in this economy? (*Hint:* Try using values for output above 5,000.) Check your answer by finding short-run equilibrium output directly using the equation for planned aggregate expenditure.

FINDING SHORT-RUN EQUILIBRIUM OUTPUT: GRAPHICAL APPROACH

Figure 11.4 shows the graphical determination of short-run equilibrium output for the economy we analyzed numerically above. Output (Y) is plotted on the horizontal axis and planned aggregate expenditure (PAE) on the vertical axis.

The figure contains two lines. The blue line is the expenditure line, which we discussed earlier. This shows the amount of output people want to purchase at any given level of output. The red dashed line, extending from the origin, shows all of the points at which the variable on the horizontal axis (Y) equals the variable on the vertical axis (PAE). Since an economy is in short-run equilibrium where $Y = PAE$, the short-run equilibrium for our example must be somewhere along this line.

At which particular point on the $Y = PAE$ line will the economy be in short-run equilibrium? Only one point in the figure is on both the $Y = PAE$ line and the expenditure line: point E, where the two lines intersect. At point E, short-run equilibrium output equals 4,800, which is the same value that we obtained using Table 11.1.

What if the economy is above or below point E? At levels of output higher than 4,800, output exceeds planned aggregate expenditure. Hence, firms will be producing more than they can sell, which will lead them to reduce their rate of production. They will continue to reduce their production until output reaches 4,800, where output equals planned aggregate expenditure. By contrast, at levels of output below 4,800, planned aggregate expenditure exceeds output. In that region, firms will not be producing enough to meet demand, and

FIGURE 11.4

Determination of Short-Run Equilibrium Output (Keynesian Cross).

Short-run equilibrium output (4,800) is determined at point *E,* the intersection of the expenditure line and the equilibrium condition (*Y = PAE*). This type of diagram is known as a Keynesian cross.

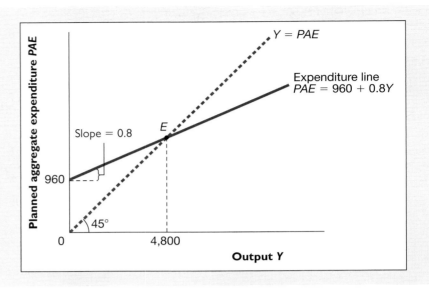

they will tend to increase their production. Only at point *E,* where output equals 4,800, will firms be producing enough to just satisfy planned spending on goods and services.

The diagram in Figure 11.4 is called the *Keynesian cross,* due to the fact that it is a crosslike, graphical model of Keynes's basic ideas. The Keynesian cross shows graphically how short-run equilibrium output is determined in a world in which producers meet demand at predetermined prices.

CONCEPT CHECK 11.2

Use a Keynesian-cross diagram to show graphically the determination of short-run equilibrium output for the economy described in Concept Check 11.1. What are the intercept and the slope of the expenditure line?

RECAP	**SHORT-RUN EQUILIBRIUM OUTPUT**

- Short-run equilibrium output is the level of output at which output equals planned aggregate expenditure, or, in symbols, *Y = PAE*. For a specific sample economy, short-run equilibrium output can be solved for numerically or graphically.

- The graphical solution is based on a diagram called the Keynesian cross. The Keynesian-cross diagram includes two lines: a 45° line that represents the condition *Y = PAE* and the expenditure line, which shows the relationship of planned aggregate expenditure to output. Short-run equilibrium output is determined at the intersection of the two lines. If short-run equilibrium output differs from potential output, an output gap exists.

PLANNED SPENDING AND THE OUTPUT GAP

We're now ready to use the basic Keynesian model to show how insufficient spending can lead to a recession. To illustrate the effects of spending changes on output, we will continue to work with the same example we've worked with throughout this chapter. We've shown that, in this economy, short-run equilibrium output equals 4,800. Let's now make the additional assumption that potential output in this economy also equals 4,800, or $Y^* = 4,800$, so that initially there is no output gap. Starting from this position of full employment, let's analyze how a fall in planned aggregate expenditure can lead to a recession.

A Fall in Planned Spending Leads to a Recession   EXAMPLE 11.5

Why does a fall in planned spending lead to a recession?

Suppose that consumers become pessimistic about the future, so that they begin to spend less at every level of current disposable income. We can capture this change by assuming that $\overline{C}$, the constant term in the consumption function, falls to a lower level. To be specific, suppose that $\overline{C}$ falls by 10 units, which in turn implies a decline in autonomous expenditure of 10 units.

We can see the effects of the decline in consumer spending on the economy using the Keynesian-cross diagram. Figure 11.5 shows the original short-run equilibrium point of the model (E), at the intersection of the 45° line, along which $Y = PAE$, and the original expenditure line, representing the equation $PAE = 960 + 0.8Y$. As before, the initial value of short-run equilibrium output is 4,800, which we have now assumed also corresponds to potential output Y^*.

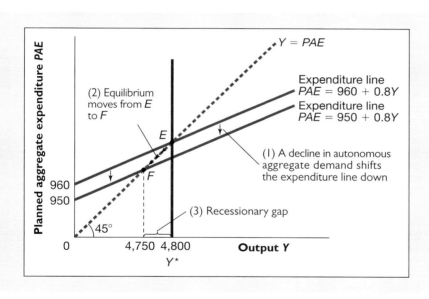

FIGURE 11.5

A Decline in Planned Spending Leads to a Recession.

(1) A decline in consumers' willingness to spend at any given level of output shifts the expenditure line down; (2) the short-run equilibrium point moves from *E* to *F*; (3) equilibrium output falls from 4,800 to 4,750; a recessionary gap of 50 is created.

Originally, autonomous expenditure in this economy was 960, so a decline of 10 units causes it to fall to 950. Instead of the economy's planned spending being described by the equation $PAE = 960 + 0.8Y$, as initially, it is now given by $PAE = 950 + 0.8Y$. What does this change imply for the graph in Figure 11.5? Since the intercept of the expenditure line (equal to autonomous expenditure) has decreased from 960 to 950, the effect of the decline in consumer spending will be to shift the expenditure line down in parallel fashion, by 10 units. Figure 11.5 indicates this downward shift in the expenditure line. The new short-run equilibrium point is at point *F*, where the new, lower expenditure line intersects the $Y = PAE$ line.

Point *F* is to the left of the original equilibrium point *E*, so we can see that output and spending have fallen from their initial levels. Since output at point *F* is lower than potential output, 4,800, we see that the fall in consumer spending has resulted in a recessionary gap in the economy. More generally, starting from a situation of full employment (where output equals potential output), any decline in autonomous expenditure leads to a recession.

Numerically, how large is the recessionary gap in Figure 11.5? To answer this question, we can use Table 11.2, which is in the same form as Table 11.1. The key difference is that in Table 11.2 planned aggregate expenditure is given by $PAE = 950 + 0.8Y$, rather than by $PAE = 960 + 0.8Y$, as in Table 11.1.

TABLE 11.2
Determination of Short-Run Equilibrium Output after a Fall in Spending

(1) Output Y	(2) Planned aggregate expenditure $PAE = 950 + 0.8Y$	(3) $Y - PAE$	(4) $Y = PAE$?
4,600	4,630	−30	No
4,650	4,670	−20	No
4,700	4,710	−10	No
4,750	4,750	0	**Yes**
4,800	4,790	10	No
4,850	4,830	20	No
4,900	4,870	30	No
4,950	4,910	40	No
5,000	4,950	50	No

As in Table 11.1, the first column of the table shows alternative possible values of output Y, and the second column shows the levels of planned aggregate expenditure PAE implied by each value of output in the first column. Notice that 4,800, the value of short-run equilibrium output found in Table 11.1, is no longer an equilibrium; when output is 4,800, planned spending is 4,790, so output and planned spending are not equal. As the table shows, following the decline in planned aggregate expenditure, short-run equilibrium output is 4,750, the only value of output for which $Y = PAE$. Thus, a drop of 10 units in autonomous expenditure has led to a 50-unit decline in short-run equilibrium output. If full-employment output is 4,800, then the recessionary gap shown in Figure 11.5 is $4,800 - 4,750 = 50$ units.

CONCEPT CHECK 11.3

In the economy described above, we found a recessionary gap of 50, relative to potential output of 4,800. Suppose that, in this economy, the natural rate of unemployment u^* is 5 percent. What will the actual unemployment rate be after the recessionary gap appears? (*Hint:* Recall Okun's law from the chapter *Short-Term Economic Fluctuations*.)

The example that we just worked through showed that a decline in autonomous expenditure, arising from a decreased willingness of consumers to spend, causes short-run equilibrium output to fall and opens up a recessionary gap. The same conclusion applies to declines in autonomous expenditure arising from other sources. Suppose, for instance, that firms become disillusioned with new technologies and cut back their planned investment in new equipment. In terms of the model, this reluctance of firms to invest can be interpreted as a decline in planned investment spending I^P. Under our assumption that planned investment spending is given and does not depend on output, planned investment is part of autonomous expenditure. So a decline in planned investment spending depresses autonomous expenditure and output, in precisely the same way that a decline in the autonomous part of consumption spending does. Similar conclusions apply to declines in other components of autonomous expenditure, such as government purchases and net exports, as we will see in later applications.

CONCEPT CHECK 11.4

Repeat the analysis of Example 11.5, except assume that consumers become *more* rather than less confident about the future. As a result, $\overline{C}$ rises by 10 units, which in turn raises autonomous expenditure by 10 units. Find the numerical value of the expansionary output gap.

The Japanese Recession of the 1990s	**EXAMPLE 11.6**

How did the deep Japanese recession of the 1990s affect the rest of East Asia?

During the 1990s, Japan suffered a prolonged economic slump. Japan's economic problems were a major concern not only of the Japanese but of policymakers in other East Asian countries, such as Thailand and Singapore. Why did East Asian policymakers worry about the effects of the Japanese slump on their own economies?

Although the economies of Japan and its East Asian neighbors are intertwined in many ways, one of the most important links is through trade. Much of the economic success of East Asia has been based on the development of export industries, and over the years Japan has been the most important customer for East Asian goods. When the economy slumped in the 1990s, Japanese households and firms reduced their purchases of imported goods sharply. This fall in demand dealt a major blow to the export industries of other East Asian countries.

Not just the owners and workers of export industries were affected, though; as wages and profits in export industries fell, so did domestic spending in the East Asian nations. The declines in domestic spending reduced sales at home as well as abroad, further weakening the East Asian economies. In terms of the model, the decline in exports to Japan reduced net exports *NX,* and thus autonomous expenditure, in East Asian countries. The fall in autonomous expenditure led to a recessionary gap, much like that shown in Figure 11.5.

Japan is not the only country whose economic ups and downs have had a major impact on its trading partners. Because the United States is the most important trading partner of both Canada and Mexico, the U.S. recession that began in 2001 led to declining exports and recessions in Canada and Mexico as well. East Asia, which exports high-tech goods to the United States, also was hurt by the U.S recession, with GDP in countries such as Singapore dropping sharply. Economic growth rebounded throughout most of East Asia after 2001, largely because of increased demand for exports to the United States and China.

The U.S. Recession of 2007–2009	**EXAMPLE 11.7**

What caused the 2007–2009 recession in the United States?

The house price bubble that burst in summer 2006 is a primary cause of the latest recession. The average price of American homes rose at a spectacular rate from the late 1990s until the summer of 2006; this phenomenon attracted both borrowers and lenders who wished to profit from the record real estate boom. This state of affairs was unprecedented in American history, as shown in Figure 11.6. The highest average annual rate of

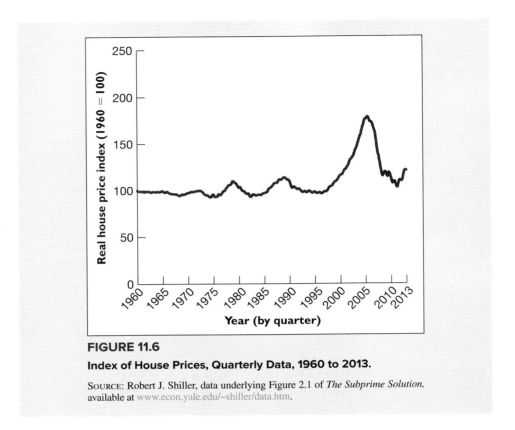

FIGURE 11.6

Index of House Prices, Quarterly Data, 1960 to 2013.

SOURCE: Robert J. Shiller, data underlying Figure 2.1 of *The Subprime Solution*, available at www.econ.yale.edu/~shiller/data.htm.

increase in house prices previously was the spike of 1976 to 1979, when house prices rose 4.7 percent per year. By contrast, from 2001 to 2006, average house prices rose by an average of 8.2 percent per year. This number masks the fact that over the period the rate of increase *itself* rose, starting at 4 percent in 2001 and peaking at an annual rate of 12 percent in 2004–2005.

We can use the rule of 72, discussed in the chapter covering economic growth, to put these numbers in context. At the growth rates experienced in the 1970s and 1980s, the average price of a house doubles in 15 to 19 years. By contrast, at the growth rates experienced in the recent house price boom, *the average price of a house doubles in about 10 years,* that is, between 50 percent and 100 percent faster than ever before.

The average home price peaked in July 2006. Prices at first fell gradually, declining by about 6 percent from July 2006 through May 2007. The decline accelerated, however, and between May 2007 and February 2009 the average home price dropped by over 20 percent.

The bursting of the housing bubble and the financial market crisis it induced caused both businesses and households to cut back on their spending in two ways. First, the financial market disruptions made it difficult for businesses to borrow funds for investment spending and for consumers to borrow funds for purchasing housing and automobiles. Second, the financial crisis increased the level of uncertainty about the future, which led to a reduction in autonomous spending, or spending independent of output.

Analytically, this situation can be represented as a downward shift in the planned aggregate expenditure (*PAE*) line as shown in Figure 11.7. At point *E*, planned spending and output are both equal to potential output Y^*. After the expenditure line shifts down, planned spending is less than actual output; the natural response of businesses is to reduce production until their output again meets demand (seen as the movement from point *E* to point *F* in Figure 11.7). At *F*, the economy is in a recession, with output below potential. Further, since output is below potential, Okun's law tells us that unemployment has now risen above the natural rate.

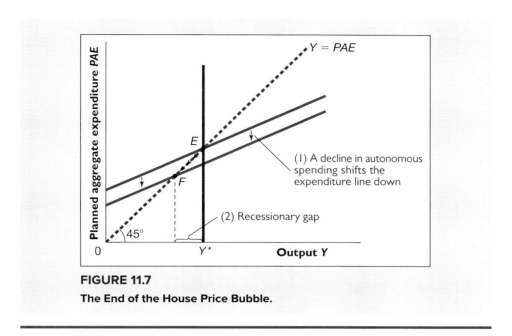

FIGURE 11.7
The End of the House Price Bubble.

THE MULTIPLIER

In Table 11.2 and Figure 11.5, we analyzed a case in which the initial decline in autonomous expenditure was only 10 units, and yet short-run equilibrium output fell by 50 units. Why did a relatively modest initial decline in consumer spending lead to a much larger fall in output?

The reason the impact on output was greater than the initial change in spending is the "vicious circle" effect suggested by Grandma's reminiscences about the Great Depression. Specifically, a fall in consumer spending not only reduces the sales of consumer goods directly; it also reduces the incomes of workers and owners in the industries that produce consumer goods. As their incomes fall, these workers and capital owners reduce their spending, which reduces the output and incomes of *other* producers in the economy. And these reductions in income lead to still further cuts in spending. Ultimately, these successive rounds of declines in spending and income may lead to a decrease in planned aggregate expenditure and output that is significantly greater than the change in spending that started the process.

The effect on short-run equilibrium output of a one-unit increase in autonomous expenditure is called the **income-expenditure multiplier,** or the *multiplier* for short. In our example economy, the multiplier is 5. That is, each 1-unit change in autonomous expenditure leads to a 5-unit change in short-run equilibrium output in the same direction. The idea that a change in spending may lead to a significantly larger change in short-run equilibrium output is a key feature of the basic Keynesian model.

What determines how large the multiplier will be? An important factor is the marginal propensity to consume (*mpc*). If the *mpc* is large, then falls in income will cause people to reduce their spending sharply, and the multiplier effect will then also be large. If the marginal propensity to consume is small, then people will not reduce spending so much when income falls, and the multiplier also will be small.

The appendix to this chapter provides more detail on the multiplier.

income-expenditure multiplier the effect of a one-unit increase in autonomous expenditure on short-run equilibrium output

RECAP	PLANNED SPENDING AND THE OUTPUT GAP

- Increases in autonomous expenditure shift the expenditure line upward, increasing short-run equilibrium output; decreases in autonomous expenditure shift the expenditure line downward, leading to declines in short-run equilibrium output. Decreases in autonomous expenditure that drive actual output below potential output are a source of recessions.

- Generally, a one-unit change in autonomous expenditure leads to a larger change in short-run equilibrium output, reflecting the working of the income-expenditure multiplier. The multiplier arises because a given initial increase in spending raises the incomes of producers, which leads them to spend more, raising the incomes and spending of other producers, and so on.

FISCAL POLICY AND RECESSIONS

According to the basic Keynesian model, inadequate spending is an important cause of recessions. To fight recessions, policymakers must find ways to stimulate planned spending. Policies that are used to affect planned aggregate expenditure, with the objective of eliminating output gaps, are called **stabilization policies.** Policy actions intended to increase planned spending and output are called **expansionary policies;** expansionary policy actions are normally taken when the economy is in recession. It is also possible, as we have seen, for the economy to be "overheated," with output greater than potential output (an expansionary gap). The risk of an expansionary gap, as we will see in more detail later, is that it may lead to an increase in inflation. To offset an expansionary gap, policymakers will try to reduce spending and output. **Contractionary policies** are policy actions intended to reduce planned spending and output.

The two major tools of stabilization policy are *monetary policy* and *fiscal policy.* We discussed long-run monetary policy in the chapter *Money, Prices, and Financial Intermediaries* and will analyze short-run monetary policy in the chapter *Monetary Policy and the Federal Reserve.* For the rest of this chapter, we will focus on how fiscal policy can be used to influence spending in the basic Keynesian model. **Fiscal policy** refers to decisions about how much the government spends and how much tax revenue it collects. We will start by looking at how changes in government spending affect short-run output, and then examine how variations in taxes can also affect spending and output. We will then focus in on the recession that began in 2007 and examine the fiscal policy actions taken by the Bush and Obama administrations.

GOVERNMENT PURCHASES AND PLANNED SPENDING

Decisions about government spending represent one of the two main components of fiscal policy, the other being decisions about taxes and transfer payments. Keynes himself felt that changes in government purchases were probably the most effective tool for reducing or eliminating output gaps. His basic argument was straightforward: Government purchases of goods and services, being a component of planned aggregate expenditure, directly affect total spending. If output gaps are caused by too much or too little total spending, then the government can help to guide the economy toward full employment by changing its own level of spending. Keynes's views seemed to be vindicated by the events of the 1930s, notably the fact that the Depression did not end until governments greatly increased their military spending in the latter part of the decade.

stabilization policies government policies that are used to affect planned aggregate expenditure, with the objective of eliminating output gaps

expansionary policies government policy actions intended to increase planned spending and output

contractionary policies government policy actions designed to reduce planned spending and output

fiscal policy decisions about how much the government spends and how much tax revenue it collects

Recessionary Gap

EXAMPLE 11.8

How can the government eliminate an output gap by changing its purchases of goods and services?

In our example economy, we found that a drop of 10 units in consumer spending creates a recessionary gap of 50 units. How can the government eliminate the output gap and restore full employment by changing its purchases of goods and services G?

Planned aggregate expenditure was given by the equation $PAE = 960 + 0.8Y$, so that autonomous expenditure equaled 960. The 10-unit drop in $\overline{C}$ implied a 10-unit drop in autonomous expenditure, to 950. Because the multiplier in that sample economy equaled 5, this 10-unit decline in autonomous expenditure resulted in turn in a 50-unit decline in short-run equilibrium output.

To offset the effects of the consumption decline, the government would have to restore autonomous expenditure to its original value, 960. Under our assumption that government purchases are simply given and do not depend on output, government purchases are part of autonomous expenditure, and changes in government purchases change autonomous expenditure one-for-one. Thus, to increase autonomous expenditure from 950 to 960, the government should simply increase its purchases by 10 units (for example, by increasing spending on military defense or road construction). According to the basic Keynesian model, this increase in government purchases should return autonomous expenditure and, hence, output to their original levels.

The effect of the increase in government purchases is shown graphically in Figure 11.8. After the 10-unit decline in the autonomous component of consumption spending, the economy is at point F, with a 50-unit recessionary gap. A 10-unit increase in government purchases raises autonomous expenditure by 10 units, raising the intercept of the expenditure line by 10 units and causing the expenditure line to shift upward in parallel fashion. The economy returns to point E, where short-run equilibrium output equals potential output ($Y = Y^* = 4{,}800$) and the output gap has been eliminated.

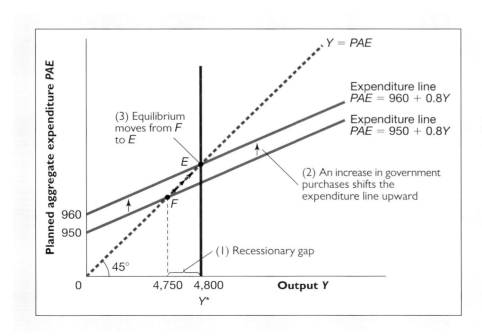

FIGURE 11.8

An Increase in Government Purchases Eliminates a Recessionary Gap.

(1) The economy is initially at point F, with a recessionary gap of 50; (2) a 10-unit increase in government purchases raises autonomous expenditure by 10 units, shifting the expenditure line up; (3) the new equilibrium is at point E, where output equals potential output. The output gap has been eliminated.

CONCEPT CHECK 11.5

In Concept Check 11.4, you considered the case in which consumers become more rather than less confident, leading to an expansionary output gap. Discuss how a change in government purchases could be used to eliminate an expansionary gap. Show your analysis graphically.

The Impact of Military Spending on the Economy **EXAMPLE 11.9**

Does military spending stimulate the economy?

An antiwar poster from the 1960s bore the message "War is good business. Invest your son." War itself poses too many economic and human costs to be good business, but military spending could be a different matter. According to the basic Keynesian model, increases in planned aggregate expenditure resulting from stepped-up government purchases may help bring an economy out of a recession or depression. Does military spending stimulate aggregate demand?

Figure 11.9 shows U.S. military spending as a share of GDP from 1940 to 2013. The shaded areas in the figure correspond to periods of recession as shown in Table 10.1. Note the spike that occurred during World War II (1941–1945), when military spending reached nearly 38 percent of U.S. GDP, as well as the surge during the Korean War (1950–1953). Smaller increases in military spending relative to GDP occurred at the peak of the Vietnam War in 1967–1969, during the Reagan military buildup of the 1980s, and during the wars in Afghanistan and Iraq.

Figure 11.9 provides some support for the idea that expanded military spending tends to promote growth in aggregate demand. The clearest case is the World War II era, during which massive military spending helped the U.S. economy to recover from the Great Depression. The U.S. unemployment rate fell from 17.2 percent of the workforce in 1939 (when defense spending was less than 2 percent of GDP) to 1.2 percent in 1944 (when defense spending was greater than 37 percent of GDP). Two brief recessions, in

---

FIGURE 11.9

U.S. Military Expenditures as a Share of GDP, 1940–2013.

Military expenditures as a share of GDP rose during World War II, the Korean War, the Vietnam War, the Reagan military buildup of the early 1980s, and during the wars in Afghanistan and Iraq. Increased military spending is often associated with an expanding economy and declining unemployment. The shaded areas indicate periods of recession.

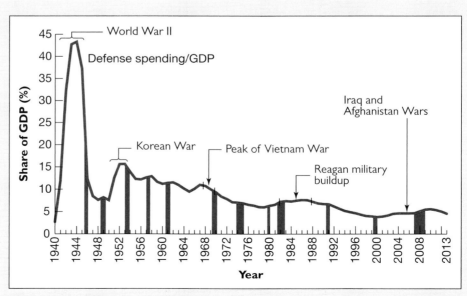

SOURCE: Bureau of Economic Analysis, www.bea.gov.

1945 and 1948–1949, followed the end of the war and the sharp decline in military spending. At the time, though, many people feared that the war's end would bring a resumption of the Great Depression, so the relative mildness of the two postwar recessions was something of a relief.

Increases in defense spending during the post–World War II period also were associated with economic expansions. The Korean War of 1950–1953 occurred simultaneously with a strong expansion, during which the unemployment rate dropped from 5.9 percent in 1949 to 2.9 percent in 1953. A recession began in 1954, the year after the armistice was signed, though military spending had not yet declined much. Economic expansions also occurred during the Vietnam-era military buildup in the 1960s and the Reagan buildup of the 1980s. Finally, on a smaller scale, increased government spending for homeland security and the wars in Afghanistan and Iraq probably contributed to the relative mildness of the U.S. recession in 2001 and the strength of the subsequent recovery. These episodes support the idea that increases in government purchases—in this case, of weapons, other military supplies, and the services of military personnel—can help to stimulate the economy.

TAXES, TRANSFERS, AND AGGREGATE SPENDING

Fiscal policy refers to the decisions governments make about how much to spend and tax. We have seen how changes in government spending affect short-run output. Now, we turn our attention to tax policy and its effects.

In the chapter *Saving, Capital Formation, and Financial Markets,* we defined net taxes (T) in the following way:

$$T = \text{Total taxes} - \text{Transfer payments} - \text{Government interest payments}.$$

Tax policy, as part of fiscal policy, involves the first two parts of net taxes: total taxes and transfer payments. Transfer payments, recall, are payments made by the government to the public, for which no current goods or services are received. Examples of transfer payments are unemployment insurance benefits, Social Security benefits, and income support payments to farmers.

The basic Keynesian model implies that, like changes in government purchases, changes in the level of taxes or transfers can be used to affect planned aggregate expenditure and thus eliminate output gaps. Unlike changes in government purchases, however, changes in taxes or transfers do not affect planned spending directly. Instead they work indirectly, by changing disposable income in the private sector. Recall that

"Your majesty, my voyage will not only forge a new route to the spices of the East but also create over three thousand new jobs."

disposable income is equal to $Y - T$. Net taxes will fall by one unit if *either* taxes are cut by one *or* transfers are increased by one. According to the consumption function, when disposable income rises, households should spend more. Thus, a tax cut or increase in transfers should increase planned aggregate expenditure. Likewise, an increase in taxes or a cut in transfers, by lowering households' disposable income, will tend to lower planned spending.

| **Using a Tax Cut to Close a Recessionary Gap** | **EXAMPLE 11.10** |

How can the government eliminate an output gap by cutting taxes?

In our hypothetical economy, an initial drop in consumer spending of 10 units creates a recessionary gap of 50 units. We showed that this recessionary gap could be eliminated by a 10-unit increase in government purchases. Suppose that, instead of increasing government purchases, fiscal policymakers decided to stimulate consumer spending by changing the level of tax collections. By how much should they change taxes to eliminate the output gap?

A common first guess is that policymakers should cut taxes by 10, but that guess is not correct. Let's see why.

The source of the recessionary gap is the reduction that households made in their consumption spending by 10 units at each level of output Y—that is, the constant term $\overline{C}$ in the consumption function is assumed to have fallen 10 units. To eliminate this recessionary gap, the change in taxes must induce households to increase their consumption spending by 10 units at each output level. However, if taxes T are cut by 10 units, raising disposable income $Y - T$ by 10 units, consumption at each level of output Y will increase by only 8 units.

Why? The reason is that the marginal propensity to consume in our example is 0.8, so that consumption spending increases by only 0.8 times the amount of the tax cut. (The rest of the tax cut is saved.) An increase in autonomous expenditure of eight units is not enough to return output to its full-employment level, in this example.

To raise consumption spending by 10 units at each level of output, fiscal policymakers must instead cut taxes by 12.5 units. This will raise the level of disposable income, $Y - T$, by 12.5 units at each level of output Y. Consequently, consumption will increase by the marginal propensity to consume times the increase in disposable income, or by $0.8(12.5) = 10$. Thus, a tax cut of 12.5 will spur households to increase their consumption by 10 units at each level of output.

These changes are illustrated in Table 11.3. Following the initial 10-unit drop in consumer spending, the equilibrium level of output fell to 4,750. When net taxes are equal to their initial level of 250, column 3 illustrates that disposable income equals $4,750 - 250 = 4,500$. After the drop in consumer spending, the consumption function becomes $C = 610 + 0.8(Y - T)$. Thus, when $Y = 4,750$ and $T = 250$, consumption will equal $610 + 0.8(4,750 - 250) = 610 + 0.8(4,500) = 4,210$, as shown in

TABLE 11.3
Initial Effect of a Reduction in Taxes of 12.5

(1) Output Y	(2) Net taxes T	(3) Disposable income $Y - T$	(4) Consumption $610 + 0.8(Y - T)$
4,750	250	4,500	4,210
4,750	237.5	4,512.5	4,220

column 4. If taxes are cut by 12.5 to 237.5, disposable income at that level of output will rise by 12.5 to $4,750 - 237.5 = 4,512.5$. Consumption at that level of output will rise by $0.8(12.5) = 10$ so that $C = 610 + 0.8(4,750 - 237.5) = 4,220$. This increase will just offset the initial 10-unit decrease in $\overline{C}$ and will bring the economy back to full employment.

Note that, since T refers to net taxes, the same result could be obtained by increasing transfer payments by 12.5 units. Because households spend 0.8 times any increase in transfer payments they receive, this policy also would raise consumption spending by 10 units at any level of output.

Graphically, the effect of the tax cut is identical to the effect of the increase in government purchases, shown in Figure 11.8. Because it leads to a 10-unit increase in consumption at any level of output, the tax cut shifts the expenditure line up by 10 units. Equilibrium is attained at point E in Figure 11.8, where output again equals potential output.

CONCEPT CHECK 11.6

In a particular economy, a 20-unit increase in planned investment moved the economy from an initial situation with no output gap to a situation with an expansionary gap. Describe two ways in which fiscal policy could be used to offset this expansionary gap. Assume the marginal propensity to consume equals 0.5.

The Economic Growth and Tax Relief Reconciliation Act of 2001	EXAMPLE 11.11

Why did the federal government send out millions of $300 and $600 checks to households in 2001?

On May 25, 2001, Congress passed the Economic Growth and Tax Relief Reconciliation Act (EGTRRA) of 2001, which President George W. Bush signed on June 7. The EGTRRA made significant cuts in income tax rates and also provided for one-time tax rebate checks of up to $300 for individual taxpayers and up to $600 for married taxpayers filing a joint return. Millions of families received these checks in August and September 2001, with payments totaling about $38 billion.

Although the 2001 recession was not officially "declared" until November 2001 (when the National Bureau of Economic Research announced that the recession had begun in March), there was clear evidence by spring 2001 that the economy was slowing. Congress and the president hoped that, by sending tax rebate checks to households, they could stimulate spending and perhaps avoid recession. In retrospect, the timing of the tax rebate was quite good, since the economy and consumer confidence were further buffeted by the terrorist attacks on New York City and Washington on September 11, 2001.

Did the tax rebates have their intended effect of stimulating consumer spending? In a study published in 2006, economists found that households spent about two-thirds of their rebates within six months of receiving them.[9] This suggests that the rebate had a substantial effect on consumer spending, which held up remarkably well during the last quarter of 2001 and into 2002.

---

[9]David S. Johnson, Jonathan A. Parker, and Nicholas S. Souleles, "Household Expenditure and the Income Tax Rebates of 2001," *American Economic Review,* December 2006, pp 1589–1610.

FISCAL POLICY AND THE RECESSION OF 2007–2009

Fiscal policy has been an important part of the U.S. government's response to the latest recession. Presidents Bush and Obama proposed and obtained congressional approval for packages of tax cuts, tax rebates, and spending increases designed to bolster private spending. The differences between the two policies illustrate how fiscal policy under two presidents can have a different emphasis yet the same ultimate goal.

The Economic Stimulus Act of 2008 was enacted during the last year of the Bush administration. The act called for roughly $100 billion in tax cuts and rebates and $60 billion in spending increases, spread over the course of 2008 and early 2009. By contrast, the American Recovery and Reinvestment Act of 2009, passed during the first month of the Obama administration, consisted of roughly $200 billion in tax cuts and $600 billion in additional government spending. Thus, the 2008 act was composed of roughly ⅔ tax cuts and ⅓ spending increases, while the 2009 act had ¼ tax cuts and ¾ spending increases.

The Congressional Budget Office (CBO) analyzed the effectiveness of both programs and found that they had the effects our basic Keynesian model predicts. Specifically, the CBO estimated that the 2008 legislation "raised the growth of consumption in the second and third quarters [of 2008] by 2.3 percent and 0.2 percent, respectively, but reduced it by 1.0 percent in the fourth quarter, when the distribution of the rebates ended." Similarly, the CBO found that real GDP was 1.2 to 3.2 percent higher in the third quarter of 2009 and 1.5 percent to 3.5 percent higher in the fourth quarter than it would have been without the 2009 act.[10]

Why did one president emphasize tax cuts while the other put more weight on spending increases? This is a deep question, to which we cannot do justice in this book. The disparity mostly boils down to differences in how each administration viewed the effects of tax cuts and spending increases on long-run growth rather than on short-run output. It also depends on problems that economists have identified with fiscal policy in general. We discuss these difficulties more generally in the next section.

FISCAL POLICY AS A STABILIZATION TOOL: THREE QUALIFICATIONS

The basic Keynesian model might lead you to think that precise use of fiscal policy can eliminate output gaps. But as is often the case, the real world is more complicated than economic models suggest. We close the chapter with three qualifications about the use of fiscal policy as a stabilization tool.

Fiscal Policy and the Supply Side

We have focused on the use of fiscal policy to affect planned aggregate expenditure. However, most economists would agree that *fiscal policy may affect potential output as well as planned aggregate expenditure.* On the spending side, for example, investments in public capital such as roads, airports, and schools can play a major role in the growth of potential output, as we discussed in the chapter *Economic Growth*. On the other side of the ledger, tax and transfer programs may well affect the incentives, and thus the economic behavior, of households and firms. Some critics of the Keynesian theory have gone so far as to argue that the *only* effects of fiscal policy that matter are effects on potential output. This was essentially the view of the so-called *supply-siders,* a group of economists and journalists whose influence reached a high point during the first Reagan term (1981–1985). Most economists now agree that fiscal policy affects *both* planned spending *and* potential output.

[10]The studies are "Did the 2008 Tax Rebates Stimulate Short-Term Growth?" "Estimated Impact of the American Recovery and Reinvestment Act on Employment and Economic Output as of September 2009," and "Estimated Impact of the American Recovery and Reinvestment Act on Employment and Economic Output from October 2009 through December 2009." All three studies are available at www.cbo.gov/publications/collections/collections.cfm?collect=12.

The Problem of Deficits

A second consideration for fiscal policymakers thinking about stabilization policies is *the need to avoid large and persistent budget deficits.* Recall from the chapter *Saving, Capital Formation, and Financial Markets* that the government's budget deficit is the excess of government spending over tax collections. Sustained government deficits can be harmful because they reduce national saving, which in turn reduces investment in new capital goods—an important source of long-run economic growth.

The need to keep deficits under control may make increasing spending or cutting taxes to fight a slowdown a less attractive option, both economically and politically. The policies of both the Bush and Obama administrations, for instance, contributed to large and rising budget deficits. It may be the case that the large budget deficits, and the increased debt resulting from these deficits, could make future administrations hesitant to apply fiscal policy during the next economic downturn.

The Relative Inflexibility of Fiscal Policy

The third qualification about the use of fiscal policy is that *fiscal policy is not always flexible enough to be useful for stabilization.* Our examples have implicitly assumed that the government can change spending or taxes relatively quickly in order to eliminate output gaps. In reality, changes in government spending or taxes must usually go through a lengthy legislative process, which reduces the ability of fiscal policy to respond in a timely way to economic conditions. For example, budget and tax changes proposed by the president must typically be submitted to Congress 18 months or more before they go into effect.

Another factor that limits the flexibility of fiscal policy is that fiscal policymakers have many other objectives besides stabilizing aggregate spending, from ensuring an adequate national defense to providing income support to the poor. What happens if, say, the need to strengthen the national defense requires an increase in government spending, but the need to contain planned aggregate expenditure requires a decrease in government spending? Such conflicts can be difficult to resolve through the political process.

This lack of flexibility means that fiscal policy is often less useful for stabilizing spending than the basic Keynesian model suggests. Nevertheless, most economists view fiscal policy as an important stabilizing force, for two reasons. The first is the presence of **automatic stabilizers,** provisions in the law that imply *automatic* increases in government spending or decreases in taxes when real output declines. For example, some government spending is earmarked as "recession aid"; it flows to communities automatically when the unemployment rate reaches a certain level. Taxes and transfer payments also respond automatically to output gaps: When GDP declines, income tax collections fall (because households' taxable incomes fall) while unemployment insurance payments and welfare benefits rise—all without any explicit action by Congress. These automatic changes in government spending and tax collections help to increase planned spending during recessions and reduce it during expansions, without the delays inherent in the legislative process.

The second reason that fiscal policy is an important stabilizing force is that, although fiscal policy may be difficult to change quickly, it may still be useful for dealing with prolonged episodes of recession. The Great Depression of the 1930s and the Japanese slump of the 1990s are two cases in point. The recession of 2007–2009 is another example; recall from the chapter *Short-Term Economic Fluctuations* that this is the longest recession since World War II. However, because of the relative lack of flexibility of fiscal policy in modern economies, governments first attempt to stabilize aggregate spending through monetary policy. Monetary policy can be enacted far more quickly than fiscal policy due to the fact that monetary policy changes can be made immediately by the Federal Reserve.

automatic stabilizers
provisions in the law that imply *automatic* increases in government spending or decreases in taxes when real output declines

RECAP	FISCAL POLICY AND PLANNED SPENDING

Fiscal policy consists of two tools for affecting total spending and eliminating output gaps: (1) changes in government purchases and (2) changes in taxes or transfer payments. An increase in government purchases increases autonomous expenditure by an equal amount. A reduction in taxes or an increase in transfer payments increases autonomous expenditure by an amount equal to the marginal propensity to consume times the reduction in taxes or increase in transfers. The ultimate effect of a fiscal policy change on short-run equilibrium output equals the change in autonomous expenditure times the multiplier. Accordingly, if the economy is in recession, an increase in government purchases, a cut in taxes, or an increase in transfers can be used to stimulate spending and eliminate the recessionary gap.

There are three important qualifications regarding fiscal policy.

- Changes in taxes and transfer programs may affect the incentives and economic behavior of households and firms;

- Governments must weigh the short-run effects of fiscal policy against the possibility of large and persistent budget deficits;

- Changes in spending and taxation take time and thus fiscal policy can be relatively slow and inflexible.

○ SUMMARY ○

- The basic Keynesian model shows how fluctuations in planned aggregate expenditure, or total planned spending, can cause actual output to differ from potential output. Too little spending leads to a recessionary output gap; too much spending creates an expansionary output gap. This model relies on the crucial assumption that firms do not respond to every change in demand by changing prices. Instead, they typically set a price for some period and then meet the demand forthcoming at that price. *(LO1)*

- Planned aggregate expenditure is total planned spending on final goods and services. The four components of total spending are consumption, investment, government purchases, and net exports. Actual investment may differ from planned investment because firms may sell a greater or lesser amount of their production than they expected. If firms sell less than they expected, for example, they are forced to add more goods to inventory than anticipated. And because additions to inventory are counted as part of investment, in this case actual investment (including inventory investment) is greater than planned investment. *(LO2)*

- The consumption function summarizes the relationship between disposable income and consumption spending. The amount by which consumption rises when disposable income rises by one dollar is called the marginal propensity to consume (mpc). The marginal propensity to consume is always greater than zero but less than one. *(LO2)*

- An increase in real output raises planned aggregate expenditure, since higher output (and, equivalently, higher income) encourages households to consume more. Planned aggregate expenditure can be broken down into two components: autonomous expenditure and induced expenditure. Autonomous expenditure is the portion of planned spending that is independent of output; induced expenditure is the portion of spending that depends on output. *(LO2)*

- In the period in which prices are fixed, short-run equilibrium output is the level of output that just equals planned aggregate expenditure. Short-run equilibrium can be determined numerically by a table that compares alternative values of output and the planned spending implied by each level of output and by using equations. Short-run equilibrium output also can be determined graphically in a Keynesian-cross diagram. *(LO3)*

- Changes in autonomous expenditure will lead to changes in short-run equilibrium output. In particular, if the economy is initially at full employment, a fall in autonomous expenditure will create a recessionary gap and a rise in autonomous expenditure will create an expansionary gap.

The amount by which a one-unit increase in autonomous expenditure raises short-run equilibrium output is called the multiplier. An increase in autonomous expenditure not only raises spending directly; it also raises the incomes of producers, who in turn increase their spending, and so on. Hence the multiplier is greater than one: A one-dollar increase in autonomous expenditure tends to raise short-run equilibrium output by more than one dollar. *(LO4)*

• To eliminate output gaps and restore full employment, the government employs stabilization policies. The two major types of stabilization policy are monetary policy and fiscal policy. Fiscal policy refers to the decisions governments make about how much to spend and tax. For example, an increase in government purchases raises autonomous expenditure directly, so it can be used to reduce or eliminate a recessionary gap. Similarly, a cut in taxes or an increase in transfer payments increases the public's disposable income, raising consumption spending at each level of output by an amount equal to the marginal propensity to consume times the cut in taxes or increase in transfers. Higher consumer spending, in turn, raises short-run equilibrium output. *(LO5)*

• Three qualifications must be made to the use of fiscal policy as a stabilization tool. First, fiscal policy may affect potential output as well as aggregate spending. Second, large and persistent government budget deficits reduce national saving and growth; the need to keep deficits under control may limit the use of expansionary fiscal policies. Finally, because changes in fiscal policy must go through a lengthy legislative process, fiscal policy is not always flexible enough to be useful for short-run stabilization. However, automatic stabilizers—provisions in the law that imply automatic increases in government spending or reductions in taxes when output declines—can overcome the problem of legislative delays to some extent and contribute to economic stability. *(LO5)*

○ KEY TERMS ○

automatic stabilizers
autonomous consumption
autonomous expenditure
consumption function
contractionary policies
expansionary policies

expenditure line
fiscal policy
income-expenditure multiplier
induced expenditure
marginal propensity to consume
 (*mpc*)

menu costs
planned aggregate expenditure
 (*PAE*)
short-run equilibrium output
stabilization policies
wealth effect

○ REVIEW QUESTIONS ○

1. What is the key assumption of the basic Keynesian model? Explain why this assumption is needed if one is to accept the view that aggregate spending is a driving force behind short-term economic fluctuations. *(LO1)*

2. Give an example of a good or service whose price changes very frequently and one whose price changes relatively infrequently. What accounts for the difference? *(LO1)*

3. Define *planned aggregate expenditure* and list its components. Why does planned spending change when output changes? *(LO2)*

4. Explain how planned spending and actual spending can differ. Illustrate with an example. *(LO2)*

5. Sketch a graph of the consumption function, labeling the axes of the graph. Discuss the economic meaning of (a) a movement from left to right along the graph of the consumption function and (b) a parallel upward shift of the consumption function. Give an example of a factor that could lead to a parallel upward shift of the consumption function. *(LO2)*

6. Sketch the Keynesian-cross diagram. Explain in words the economic significance of the two lines graphed in the diagram. Given only this diagram, how could you determine autonomous expenditure, induced expenditure, the marginal propensity to consume, and short-run equilibrium output? *(LO3)*

7. Using the Keynesian-cross diagram, illustrate the main cause of the 2007–2009 recession discussed throughout the chapter. *(LO3, LO4)*

8. Define the *multiplier.* In economic terms, why is the multiplier greater than one? *(LO4)*

9. The government is considering two alternative policies, one involving increased government purchases of 50 units, the other involving a tax cut of 50 units. Which policy will stimulate planned aggregate expenditure by more? Why? *(LO4)*

10. Discuss three reasons why the use of fiscal policy to stabilize the economy is more complicated than suggested by the basic Keynesian model. *(LO5)*

○ PROBLEMS ○

|ECONOMICS

Study Econ

McGraw-Hill

Visit your mobile app
store and download
the Frank: Study
Econ app *today!*

1. Acme Manufacturing is producing $4,000,000 worth of goods this year and expects to sell its entire production. It also is planning to purchase $1,500,000 in new equipment during the year. At the beginning of the year, the company has $500,000 in inventory in its warehouse. Find actual investment and planned investment if Acme actually sells
   a. $3,850,000 worth of goods.
   b. $4,000,000 worth of goods.
   c. $4,200,00 worth of goods.

   Assuming that Acme's situation is similar to that of other firms, in which of these three cases is output equal to short-run equilibrium output? *(LO1)*

2. Data on before-tax income, taxes paid, and consumption spending for the Simpson family in various years are given below. *(LO2)*

Before-tax income ($)	Taxes paid ($)	Consumption spending ($)
25,000	3,000	20,000
27,000	3,500	21,350
28,000	3,700	22,070
30,000	4,000	23,600

   a. Graph the Simpsons' consumption function and find their household's marginal propensity to consume.
   b. How much would you expect the Simpsons to consume if their income was $32,000 and they paid taxes of $5,000?
   c. Homer Simpson wins a lottery prize. As a result, the Simpson family increases its consumption by $1,000 at each level of after-tax income. ("Income" does not include the prize money.) How does this change affect the graph of their consumption function? How does it affect their marginal propensity to consume?

3. An economy is described by the following equations: *(LO2)*

$$C = 1,800 + 0.6(Y - T)$$
$$I^P = 900$$
$$G = 1,500$$
$$NX = 100$$
$$T = 1,500$$
$$Y^* = 9,000$$

   a. Find a numerical equation linking planned aggregate expenditure to output.
   b. Find autonomous expenditure and induced expenditure in this economy.

4. For the economy described in Problem 3: *(LO3)*
   a. Construct a table like Table 11.1 to find short-run equilibrium output. Consider possible values for short-run equilibrium output ranging from 8,200 to 9,000.
   b. Show the determination of short-run equilibrium output for this economy using the Keynesian-cross diagram.
   c. What is the output gap for this economy? If the natural rate of unemployment is 4 percent, what is the actual unemployment rate for this economy? (*Hint:* Use Okun's law.)

5. For the economy described in Problems 3 and 4, take as given that the multiplier for this economy is 2.5. Find the effect on short-run equilibrium output of *(LO4)*
   a. An increase in government purchases from 1,500 to 1,600.
   b. A decrease in tax collections from 1,500 to 1,400 (leaving government purchases at their original value).
   c. A decrease in planned investment spending from 900 to 800.

6. An economy is initially at full employment, but a decrease in planned investment spending (a component of autonomous expenditure) pushes the economy into recession. Assume that the *mpc* of this economy is 0.75 and that the multiplier is 4. *(LO4, LO5)*
   a. How large is the recessionary gap after the fall in planned investment?
   b. By how much would the government have to change its purchases to restore the economy to full employment?
   c. Alternatively, by how much would the government have to change taxes?
   d.* Suppose that the government's budget is initially in balance, with government spending equal to taxes collected. A balanced-budget law forbids the government from running a deficit. Is there anything that fiscal policymakers could do to restore full employment in this economy, assuming they do not want to violate the balanced-budget law?

7. An economy is described by the following equations:

$$C = 40 + 0.8(Y - T)$$
$$I^p = 70$$
$$G = 120$$
$$NX = 10$$
$$T = 150$$
$$Y^* = 580$$

   The multiplier in this economy is 5. *(LO4, LO5)*
   a. Find a numerical equation relating planned aggregate expenditure to output.
   b. Construct a table to find the value of short-run equilibrium output. (*Hint:* The economy is fairly close to full employment.)
   c. By how much would government purchases have to change in order to eliminate any output gap? By how much would taxes have to change? Show the effects of these fiscal policy changes in a Keynesian-cross diagram.
   d. Repeat part c assuming that $Y^* = 630$.
   e. Show your results for parts b through d on a Keynesian-cross diagram.

8.* An economy is described by the following equations: *(LO3, LO4, LO5)*

$$C = 3,000 + 0.5(Y - T)$$
$$I^p = 1,500$$
$$G = 2,500$$
$$NX = 200$$
$$T = 2,000$$
$$Y^* = 12,000$$

   a. For this economy, find the following: autonomous expenditure, the multiplier, short-run equilibrium output, and the output gap.
   b. Illustrate this economy's short-run equilibrium on a Keynesian-cross diagram.
   c. Calculate the amount by which autonomous expenditure would have to change to eliminate the output gap.
   d. Suppose that the government decided to close the output gap by reducing taxes. By how much must taxes be reduced in order to do this?

9.* An economy has zero net exports. Otherwise, it is identical to the economy described in Problem 7. *(LO3, LO4, LO5)*
   a. Find short-run equilibrium output.
   b. Economic recovery abroad increases the demand for the country's exports; as a result, *NX* rises to 100. What happens to short-run equilibrium output?
   c. Repeat part b, but this time assume that foreign economies are slowing, reducing the demand for the country's exports, so that $NX = -100$. (A negative value of net exports means that exports are less than imports.)
   d. How do your results help to explain the tendency of recessions and expansions to spread across countries?

*Denotes more difficult problem.

○ ANSWERS TO CONCEPT CHECKS ○

11.1 First we need to find an equation that relates planned aggregate expenditure *PAE* to output *Y*. We start with the definition of planned aggregate expenditure and then substitute the numerical values given in the problem:

$$PAE = C + I^P + G + NX$$
$$= [820 + 0.7(Y - 600)] + 600 + 600 + 200$$
$$= 1,800 + 0.7Y.$$

Using this relationship, we construct a table analogous to Table 11.1. Some trial and error is necessary to find an appropriate range of guesses for output (column 1).

Determination of Short-Run Equilibrium Output			
(1) **Output** *Y*	**(2)** **Planned aggregate expenditure** *PAE* **= 1,800 + 0.7Y**	**(3)** *Y = PAE*	**(4)** *Y = PAE?*
5,000	5,300	−300	No
5,200	5,440	−240	No
5,400	5,580	−180	No
5,600	5,720	−120	No
5,800	5,860	−60	No
6,000	6,000	0	**Yes**
6,200	6,140	60	No
6,400	6,280	120	No
6,600	6,420	180	No

Short-run equilibrium output equals 6,000, as that is the only level of output that satisfies the condition $Y = PAE$. Using the equation for planned aggregate

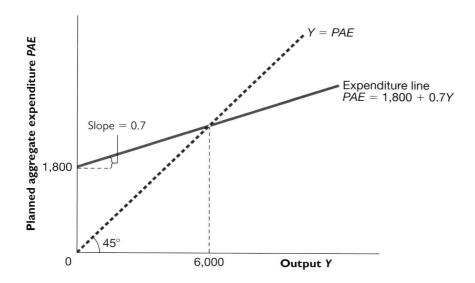

expenditure, in equilibrium we have $Y = 1,800 + 0.7Y$. Solving for Y, we find that $Y = 6,000$, just as we found using the table. *(LO2, LO3)*

11.2 The graph shows the determination of short-run equilibrium output, $Y = 6,000$. The intercept of the expenditure line is 1,800 and its slope is 0.7. Notice that the intercept equals autonomous expenditure and the slope equals the marginal propensity to consume. *(LO3)*

11.3 This problem is an application of Okun's law, introduced in the chapter *Short-Term Economic Fluctuations*. The recessionary gap in this example is $-50/4,800$, or about -1.04 percent, of potential output. By Okun's law, cyclical unemployment is one-half of the output gap (multiplied by -1), or 0.52 percent. As the natural rate of unemployment is 5 percent, the total unemployment rate after the recessionary gap appears will be approximately 5.52 percent. *(LO4)*

11.4 This exercise is just the reverse of the analysis in the text. An increase in $\overline{C}$ of 10 units raises autonomous expenditure and hence the intercept of the expenditure line by 10 units. The expenditure line shifts up, in parallel fashion, by 10 units, leading to an increase in output and an expansionary output gap. As output falls by 50 units in the text, it rises by 50 units, to 4,850, in the case analyzed here. To verify that short-run equilibrium output equals 4,850, note that an increase of 10 units in autonomous expenditure implies that PAE rises from $960 + 0.8Y$ to $970 + 0.8Y$. When $Y = 4,850$, then $PAE = 970 + 0.8(4,850) = 4,850$, so that we have $Y = PAE$. *(LO4)*

11.5 In Concept Check 11.4 we saw that a 10-unit increase in $\overline{C}$ increases autonomous expenditure and hence the intercept of the expenditure line by 10 units. The expenditure line shifts upward, in parallel fashion, by 10 units, leading to an expansionary output gap. To offset this gap, the government should reduce its purchases by 10 units, returning autonomous expenditure to its original level. The expenditure line shifts back down to its original position, restoring output to its initial full-employment level. The graph is just the reverse of Figure 11.8, with the expenditure line being shifted up by the increase in consumption and down (back to point E) by the offsetting reduction in government purchases. *(LO4, LO5)*

11.6 The 20-unit increase in planned investment is a 20-unit increase in autonomous expenditure, which will lead to an even greater increase in short-run equilibrium output. To offset the 20-unit increase in autonomous expenditure by means of fiscal policy, the government can reduce its purchases by 20 units. Alternatively, it could raise taxes (or cut transfers) to reduce consumption spending. Since the *mpc* = 0.5, to reduce consumption spending by 20 units at each level of output, the government will need to increase taxes (or reduce transfers) by 40 units. At each level of output, a 40-unit tax increase will reduce disposable income by 40 units and cause consumers to reduce their spending by 0.5 × 40 = 20 units, as needed to eliminate the expansionary output gap. *(LO4, LO5)*

The Multiplier in the Basic Keynesian Model

This appendix builds on the example economy used throughout the chapter to give a more complete explanation of the *income-expenditure multiplier* in the basic Keynesian model. In the chapter, we saw that a drop in autonomous expenditure of 10 units caused a decline in short-run equilibrium output of 50 units, five times as great as the initial change in spending. Hence, the multiplier in this example is 5.

To see why this multiplier effect occurs, note that the initial decrease of 10 in consumer spending (more precisely, in the constant term of the consumption function, $\bar{C}$) has two effects. First, the fall in consumer spending directly reduces planned aggregate expenditure by 10 units. Second, the fall in spending also reduces by 10 units the incomes of producers (workers and firm owners) of consumer goods. Since the marginal propensity to consume is 0.8, the producers of consumer goods will therefore reduce *their* consumption spending by 8, or 0.8 times their income loss of 10. This reduction in spending cuts the income of *other* producers by 8 units, leading them to reduce their spending by 6.4, or 0.8 times their income loss of 8. These income reductions of 6.4 lead still other producers to cut their spending by 5.12, or 0.8 times 6.4, and so on. In principle, this process continues indefinitely, although after many rounds of spending and income reductions, the effects become quite small.

When all these "rounds" of income and spending reductions are added, the *total* effect on planned spending of the initial reduction of 10 in consumer spending is

$$10 + 8 + 6.4 + 5.12 + \cdots.$$

The three dots indicate that the series of reductions continues indefinitely. The total effect of the initial decrease in consumption also can be written as

$$10[1 + 0.8 + (0.8)^2 + (0.8)^3 + \cdots].$$

This expression highlights the fact that the spending that takes place in each round is 0.8 times the spending in the previous round (0.8) because that is the marginal propensity to consume out of the income generated by the previous round of spending.

A useful algebraic relationship, which applies to any number x greater than 0 but less than 1, is

$$1 + x + x^2 + x^3 + \cdots = \frac{1}{1 - x}.$$

If we set $x = 0.8$, this formula implies that the total effect of the decline in consumption spending on aggregate demand and output is

$$10\left(\frac{1}{1 - 0.8}\right) = 10\left(\frac{1}{0.2}\right) = 10 \times 5 = 50.$$

This answer is consistent with our earlier calculation, which showed that short-run equilibrium output fell by 50 units, from 4,800 to 4,750.

By a similar analysis, we also can find a general algebraic expression for the multiplier in the basic Keynesian model. Recalling that *mpc* is the marginal propensity to consume out of disposable income, we know that a one-unit increase in autonomous expenditure raises spending and income by one unit in the first round; by $mpc \times 1 = mpc$ units in the second round; by $mpc \times mpc = mpc^2$ units in the third round; by $mpc \times mpc^2 = mpc^3$ units in the fourth round; and so on. Thus, the total effect on short-run equilibrium output of a one-unit increase in autonomous expenditure is given by

$$1 + mpc + mpc^2 + mpc^3 + \cdots.$$

Applying the algebraic formula given above, and recalling that $0 < mpc < 1$, we can rewrite this expression as $1/(1 - mpc)$. Thus, in a basic Keynesian model with a marginal propensity to consume of *mpc,* the multiplier equals $1/(1 - mpc)$. Note that if $mpc = 0.8$ then $1/(1 - mpc) = 1/(1 - 0.8) = 5$, which is the same value of the multiplier we found numerically above.

CHAPTER 12

Monetary Policy and the Federal Reserve

Jonathan Larsen/Getty Images

HOW DOES THE FEDERAL RESERVE AFFECT SPENDING AND OUTPUT IN THE SHORT RUN?

Financial market participants and commentators go to remarkable lengths to try to predict the actions of the Federal Reserve. For a while, the CNBC financial news program *Squawk Box* reported regularly on what the commentators called the Greenspan Briefcase Indicator. The idea was to spot the Fed chairman at that time, Alan Greenspan, on his way to meet with the Federal Open Market Committee, the group that determines U.S. monetary policy. If Greenspan's briefcase was packed full, presumably with macroeconomic data and analyses, the guess was that the Fed planned to change interest rates. A slim briefcase meant no change in rates was likely.

"It was right 17 out of the first 20 times," the program's anchor Mark Haines noted, "but it has a built-in self-destruct mechanism because Greenspan packs his [own] briefcase. He can make it wrong or right. He has never publicly acknowledged the indicator, but we have reason to believe that he knows about it. We have to consider the fact that he wants us to stop doing it because the last two times the briefcase has been wrong, and that's disturbing."[1]

The Briefcase Indicator is but one example of the close public scrutiny that the chairman of the Federal Reserve and other monetary policymakers face. Every speech, every congressional testimony, every interview from a member of the Board

[1]Robert H. Frank, "Safety in Numbers," *The New York Times Magazine,* November 28, 1999, p. 35.

LEARNING OBJECTIVES

After reading this chapter, you should be able to:

LO1 Describe the structure and responsibilities of the Federal Reserve System.

LO2 Analyze how changes in the federal funds rate and real interest rates affect planned aggregate expenditure and the short-run equilibrium level of output.

LO3 Show how the demand for money and the supply of money interact to determine the equilibrium nominal interest rate.

LO4 Discuss how the Fed uses its ability to control the money supply to influence nominal and real interest rates.

of Governors is closely analyzed for clues about the future course of monetary policy. The reason for the intense public interest in the Federal Reserve's decisions about monetary policy—and especially the level of interest rates—is that those decisions have important implications both for financial markets and for the economy in general.

In this chapter, we examine the workings of monetary policy, one of the two major types of *stabilization policy*. (The other type, fiscal policy, is discussed in another chapter.) Stabilizing policies are government policies that are meant to influence planned aggregate expenditure, with the goal of eliminating output gaps. Both types of stabilization policy, monetary and fiscal, are important and have been useful at various times. However, monetary policy, which can be changed quickly by a decision of the Federal Reserve's Federal Open Market Committee (FOMC), is more flexible and responsive than fiscal policy, which can be changed only by legislative action by Congress. Under normal circumstances, therefore, monetary policy is used more actively in the United States than fiscal policy to help stabilize the economy.

We begin this chapter by studying the Federal Reserve as an institution: how it came to be, how it responded to banking panics early in its history, and how it functions today. Next, we look at how monetary policy affects short-run output. Specifically, we first examine how changes in nominal interest rates, which the Fed can influence, affect real interest rates, which affect spending decisions. We then build on our analysis of the basic Keynesian model introduced in the chapter *Spending, Output, and Fiscal Policy* and show how, in the short run, changes in real interest rates change planned spending and thus short-run equilibrium output. We then look at some of the details of monetary policy by examining more closely the relationship between changes in the money supply and changes in nominal interest rates.

THE FEDERAL RESERVE

We first discussed the Federal Reserve in the chapter *Money, Prices, and Financial Intermediaries*. Recall that the Fed is the central bank of the United States, and that central banks in general have two main responsibilities. First, they are responsible for monetary policy, which means that a country's central bank determines how much money circulates in the economy. We'll see in this chapter that this responsibility implies that Federal Reserve actions affect the level of interest rates in the economy as well. Second, along with other government agencies, central banks in general, and the Fed in particular, have important responsibilities for the oversight and regulation of financial markets. In particular, central banks play important roles during periods of crisis in financial markets.

THE HISTORY AND STRUCTURE OF THE FEDERAL RESERVE SYSTEM

The Federal Reserve System was created by the Federal Reserve Act, passed by Congress in 1913, and began operations in 1914. Like all central banks, the Fed is a government agency. Unlike commercial banks, which are private businesses whose principal objective is making a profit, central banks like the Fed focus on promoting public goals such as economic growth, low inflation, and the smooth operation of financial markets.

The Federal Reserve Act established a system of 12 regional Federal Reserve banks, each associated with a geographical area called a Federal Reserve district. Congress hoped that the establishment of Federal Reserve banks around the country would ensure that different regions were represented in the national policymaking process. In fact, the regional Feds regularly assess economic conditions in their districts and report this information to policymakers in Washington. Regional Federal Reserve banks also provide various services, such as check-clearing services, to the commercial banks in their district.

*"I'm sorry, sir, but I don't believe you know us well enough
to call us the Fed."*

At the national level, the leadership of the Federal Reserve System is provided by its **Board of Governors.** The Board of Governors, together with a large professional staff, is located in Washington, D.C. The Board consists of seven governors, who are appointed by the president of the United States, subject to confirmation by the Senate, to 14-year terms. The terms are staggered so that one governor comes up for reappointment every other year. The president also appoints one of these Board members to serve as chairman of the Board of Governors for a term of four years. The Fed chairman, along with the secretary of the Treasury, is probably one of the two most powerful economic policymakers in the U.S. government, after the president. Recent chairmen, such as Paul Volcker and Alan Greenspan, have been highly regarded and influential.

Decisions about monetary policy are made by a 12-member committee called the **Federal Open Market Committee** (or **FOMC**). The FOMC consists of the seven Fed governors, the president of the Federal Reserve Bank of New York, and four of the presidents of the other regional Federal Reserve banks, who serve on a rotating basis. The FOMC meets approximately eight times a year to review the state of the economy and to determine monetary policy.

Board of Governors the leadership of the Fed, consisting of seven governors appointed by the president to staggered 14-year terms

Federal Open Market Committee (FOMC) the committee that makes decisions concerning monetary policy

THE FED'S ROLE IN STABILIZING FINANCIAL MARKETS: BANKING PANICS

The creation of the Fed in 1913 was promoted by a series of financial market crises that disrupted both the markets themselves and the U.S. economy as a whole. The hope of Congress was that the Fed would be able to eliminate or at least control such crises.

banking panic a situation in which news or rumors of the imminent bankruptcy of one or more banks leads bank depositors to rush to withdraw their funds

Banking panics were perhaps the most disruptive type of recurrent financial crisis in the United States during the nineteenth and early twentieth centuries. In a **banking panic,** news or rumors of the imminent bankruptcy of one or more banks leads bank depositors to rush to withdraw their funds.

Why do banking panics occur? An important factor that makes banking panics possible is the existence of fractional-reserve banking. As we discussed in the chapter *Money, Prices, and Financial Intermediaries,* in a fractional-reserve banking system, like that of the United States and all other industrialized countries, bank reserves are less than deposits, which means that banks do not keep enough cash on hand to pay off depositors if they were all to decide to withdraw their deposits at one time. Normally this is not a problem, as only a small percentage of depositors attempt to withdraw their funds on any given day. But if a rumor circulates that one or more banks are in financial trouble and may go bankrupt, depositors may panic, lining up to demand their money. Since bank reserves are less than deposits, a sufficiently severe panic could lead even financially healthy banks to run out of cash, forcing them into bankruptcy and closure. (Think of the scene in the movie *It's a Wonderful Life* when George Bailey tries to convince his depositors not to withdraw all of their deposits and close their accounts.)

The Federal Reserve was established in response to a particularly severe banking panic that occurred in 1907. The Fed was equipped with two principal tools to try to prevent or moderate banking panics. First, the Fed was given the power to supervise and regulate banks. It was hoped that the public would have greater confidence in banks, and thus be less prone to panic, if people knew that the Fed was keeping a close watch on bankers' activities. Second, the Fed was allowed to make loans to banks. The idea was that, during a panic, banks could borrow cash from the Fed with which to pay off depositors, avoiding the need to close.

No banking panics occurred between 1914, when the Fed was established, and 1930. However, between 1930 and 1933, the United States experienced the worst and most protracted series of banking panics in its history. Economic historians agree that much of the blame for this panic should be placed on the Fed, which neither appreciated the severity of the problem nor acted aggressively enough to contain it.

The Banking Panics of 1930–1933 and the Money Supply	EXAMPLE 12.1

How did the banking panics during the Great Depression affect the money supply?

The worst banking panics ever experienced in the United States occurred during the early stages of the Great Depression, between 1930 and 1933. During this period, approximately one-third of the banks in the United States were forced to close. This near-collapse of the banking system was probably an important reason that the Depression was so severe. With many fewer banks in operation, it was very difficult for small businesses and consumers during the early 1930s to obtain credit. Another important effect of the banking panics was to greatly reduce the nation's money supply.

During a banking panic, people are afraid to keep deposits in a bank because of the risk that the bank will go bankrupt and their money will be lost (this was prior to the introduction of federal deposit insurance, discussed below). During the 1930–1933 period, many bank depositors withdrew their money from banks, holding currency instead. These withdrawals reduced bank reserves. Recall from the chapter *Money, Prices, and Financial Intermediaries* that each extra dollar of currency held by the public adds $1 to the money supply; but each extra dollar of bank reserves translates into several dollars of money supply because in a fractional-reserve banking system each dollar of reserves can "support" several dollars in bank deposits. Thus, the public's withdrawals from banks, which increased currency holdings by the public but reduced bank reserves by an equal amount, led to a net decrease in the total money supply (currency plus deposits).

In addition, fearing banking panics and the associated withdrawals by depositors, banks increased their desired reserve-deposit ratios, which reduced the quantity of deposits that could be supported by any given level of bank reserves. This change in reserve-deposit ratios also tended to reduce the money supply.

Data on currency holdings by the public, the reserve-deposit ratio, bank reserves, and the money supply for selected dates are shown in Table 12.1. Notice the increase over the period in the amount of currency held by the public and in the reserve-deposit ratio, as well as the decline in bank reserves in 1931. The last column shows that the U.S. money supply dropped by about one-third between December 1929 and December 1933.

TABLE 12.1
Key U.S. Monetary Statistics, 1929–1933

	Currency held by public	Reserve-deposit ratio	Bank reserves	Money supply
December 1929	3.85	0.075	3.15	45.9
December 1930	3.79	0.082	3.31	44.1
December 1931	4.59	0.095	3.11	37.3
December 1932	4.82	0.109	3.18	34.0
December 1933	4.85	0.133	3.45	30.8

NOTE: Data on currency, the monetary base, and the money supply are in billions of dollars.

SOURCE: Milton Friedman and Anna J. Schwartz, *A Monetary History of the United States, 1863–1960* (Princeton, NJ: Princeton University Press, 1963), Table A-1.

Recall Equation 9.1:

Bank deposits = (Bank reserves)/(Desired reserve-deposit ratio).

Using this equation, we can see that increases in currency holdings by the public and increases in the reserve-deposit ratio both tend to reduce the money supply. These effects were so powerful in 1930–1933 that the nation's money supply, shown in the fourth column of Table 12.1, dropped precipitously, even though currency holdings and bank reserves, taken separately, actually rose during the period.

CONCEPT CHECK 12.1

Using the data from Table 12.1, confirm that the relationship between the money supply and its determinants is consistent with Equation 9.2 (Money supply = Currency held by public + Bank reserves/Desired reserve-deposit ratio). Would the money supply have fallen in 1931–1933 if the public had stopped withdrawing deposits after December 1930 so that currency held by the public had remained at its December 1930 level?

CONCEPT CHECK 12.2

According to Table 12.1, the U.S. money supply fell from $44.1 billion to $37.3 billion over the course of 1931. The Fed did use open-market purchases during 1931 to replenish bank reserves in the face of depositor withdrawals. Find (a) the quantity of reserves that the Fed injected into the economy in 1931 and (b) the quantity of reserves the Fed would have had to add to the economy to keep the money supply unchanged from 1930, assuming that public currency holdings and reserve-deposit ratios for each year remained as reported in the table. Why has the Fed been criticized for being too timid in 1931?

deposit insurance a system under which the government guarantees that depositors will not lose any money even if their bank goes bankrupt

When the Fed failed to stop the banking panics of the 1930s, policymakers decided to look at other strategies for controlling panics. In 1934 Congress instituted a system of deposit insurance. Under a system of **deposit insurance,** the government guarantees depositors—specifically, under current rules, those with deposits of less than $250,000—that they will get their money back even if the bank goes bankrupt. Deposit insurance eliminates the incentive for people to withdraw their deposits when rumors circulate that the bank is in financial trouble, which nips panics in the bud. Indeed, since deposit insurance was instituted, the United States has had no significant banking panics.

Unfortunately, deposit insurance is not a perfect solution to the problem of banking panics. An important drawback is that when deposit insurance is in force, depositors know they are protected no matter what happens to their bank, and they become completely unconcerned about whether their bank is making prudent loans. This situation can lead to reckless behavior by banks or other insured intermediaries. For example, during the 1980s, many savings and loan associations in the United States went bankrupt, in part because of reckless lending and financial investments. Like banks, savings and loans have deposit insurance, so the U.S. government had to pay savings and loan depositors the full value of their deposits. This action ultimately cost U.S. taxpayers hundreds of billions of dollars. To try to prevent such occurrences, the Federal Reserve and other government regulators examine banks to make sure they are lending prudently.

MONETARY POLICY AND ECONOMIC FLUCTUATIONS

We now examine how monetary policy can be used to eliminate output gaps and stabilize the economy. The basic idea is relatively straightforward. As we will see in this section, planned aggregate expenditure is affected by the level of the real interest rate prevailing in the economy. Specifically, a lower real interest rate encourages higher planned spending by households and firms, while a higher real interest rate reduces spending. By adjusting the real interest rate, the Fed can move planned spending in the desired direction. Under the assumption of the basic Keynesian model that firms produce just enough goods and services to meet the demand for their output, the Fed's stabilization of planned spending leads to stabilization of aggregate output and employment as well.

The Fed can control the economy's nominal interest rate through its control of the money supply. We will analyze how it does this later in the chapter; for now, we'll look at how control of the nominal interest rate leads to control of the real interest rate in the short run. We'll then look at how changes in the real interest rate affect planned spending and equilibrium output.

CAN THE FED CONTROL THE REAL INTEREST RATE?

Through its control of the money supply, the Fed can control the economy's *nominal* interest rate. But many important economic decisions, such as the decisions to save and invest, depend on the *real* interest rate. To affect those decisions, the Fed must exert some control over the real interest rate.

Most economists believe that the Fed can control the real interest rate, at least for some period. To see why, recall the definition of the real interest rate from the chapter *Inflation and the Price Level:*

$$r = i - \pi.$$

The real interest rate r equals the nominal interest rate i minus the rate of inflation π. The Fed can control the nominal interest rate quite precisely through its ability to determine the money supply. Furthermore, inflation appears to change relatively slowly in response to changes in policy or economic conditions, for reasons we discuss elsewhere in this text. Because inflation tends to adjust slowly, actions by the Fed to change the nominal interest rate generally lead the real interest rate to change by about the same amount.

The idea that the Fed can set the real interest rate appears to contradict our analysis in the chapter *Saving, Capital Formation, and Financial Markets.* There, we concluded that the real interest rate is determined by the condition that national saving must equal investment in new capital goods. *This apparent contradiction is rooted in a difference in the time frame being considered.* Because inflation does not adjust quickly, the Fed can control the real interest rate over the short run. In the long run, however—that is, over periods of several years or more—the inflation rate and other economic variables will adjust, and the balance of saving and investment will determine the real interest rate. Thus, the Fed's ability to influence consumption and investment spending through its control of the real interest rate is strongest in the short run.

THE ROLE OF THE FEDERAL FUNDS RATE IN MONETARY POLICY

Although thousands of interest rates and other financial data are easily available, the interest rate that is perhaps most closely watched by the public, politicians, the media, and the financial markets is the *federal funds rate*.

The **federal funds rate** is the interest rate commercial banks charge each other for very short-term (usually overnight) loans. For example, a bank that has insufficient reserves to meet its legal reserve requirements might borrow reserves for a few days from a bank that has extra reserves. Despite its name, the federal funds rate is not an official government interest rate and is not connected to the federal government.

Because the market for loans between commercial banks is tiny compared to some other financial markets, such as the market for government bonds, one might expect the federal funds rate to be of little interest to anyone other than the managers of commercial banks. But enormous attention is paid to this interest rate because, over most of the past 40 years, the *Fed has expressed its policies in terms of the federal funds rate.* Indeed, at the close of every meeting of the Federal Open Market Committee, the Fed announces whether the federal funds rate will be increased, decreased, or left unchanged. The Fed also may indicate the likely direction of future changes in the federal funds rate. Thus, more than any other financial variable, changes in the federal funds rate indicate the Fed's plans for monetary policy.[2]

Why does the Fed choose to focus on this particular nominal interest rate over all others? As we saw in the chapter *Money, Prices, and Financial Intermediaries,* in practice the Fed affects the money supply through its control of bank reserves. Because open-market operations directly affect the supply of bank reserves, the Fed's control over the federal funds rate is particularly tight. If, for example, the Fed wants the federal funds rate to fall, it conducts open-market purchases, which increase reserves, until the federal funds rate falls to the new desired level. However, if Fed officials chose to do so, they could probably signal their intended policies just as effectively in terms of another short-term nominal interest rate, such as the rate on short-term government debt.

Figure 12.1 shows the behavior of the federal funds rate from January 1970 through August 2014. As you can see, the Fed has allowed this interest rate to vary considerably in response to economic conditions. Note, however, how the federal funds rate has remained almost zero ever since the end of 2008, which is both considerably lower and more stable than the preceding 40-year period shown here.

In reality, not just one but many thousands of interest rates are seen in the economy. Because interest rates tend to move together (allowing us to speak of *the* interest rate), an action by the Fed to change the federal funds rate generally causes other interest rates to change in the same direction. However, the tendency of other interest rates (such as the long-term government bond rate or the rate on bonds issued by corporations) to

federal funds rate the interest rate that commercial banks charge each other for very short-term (usually overnight) loans; because the Fed frequently sets its policy in terms of the federal funds rate, this rate is closely watched in financial markets

---

[2] The Federal Open Market Committee's announcements are available on the Federal Reserve's website, www.federalreserve.gov.

FIGURE 12.1

The Federal Funds Rate, 1970–2014.

The federal funds rate is the interest rate commercial banks charge each other for short-term loans. It is closely watched because the Fed expresses its policies in terms of the federal funds rate. The Fed has allowed the federal funds rate to vary considerably in response to economic conditions.

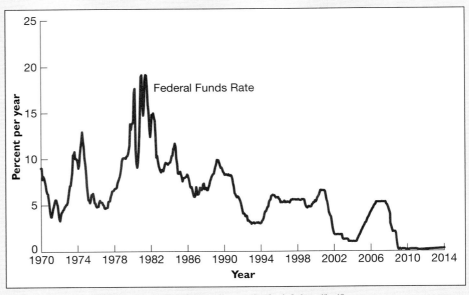

Source: Federal Reserve Bank of St. Louis, http://research.stlouisfed.org/fred2.

move in the same direction as the federal funds rate is only a tendency, not an exact relationship. In practice, then, the Fed's control of other interest rates may be somewhat less precise than its control of the federal funds rate—a fact that complicates the Fed's policymaking.

PLANNED AGGREGATE EXPENDITURE AND THE REAL INTEREST RATE

In the chapter *Spending, Output, and Fiscal Policy,* we saw how planned spending is affected by changes in real output Y. Changes in output affect the private sector's disposable income $(Y - T)$, which in turn influences consumption spending—a relationship captured by the consumption function. A second variable that has potentially important effects on aggregate expenditure is the real interest rate r.

In the chapter *Saving, Capital Formation, and Financial Markets,* we saw that the real interest rate influences both the saving decisions of households and the investment behavior of firms. For households, the effect of a higher real interest rate is to increase the reward for saving, which leads households to save more.[3] At a given level of income, households can save more only if they consume less. Thus, saying that a higher real interest rate *increases* saving is the same as saying that a higher real interest rate *reduces* consumption spending at each level of income.

The idea that higher real interest rates reduce household spending makes intuitive sense. Think, for example, about people's willingness to buy consumer durables such as automobiles or furniture. Purchases of consumer durables, which are part of consumption spending, are often financed by borrowing from a bank, credit union, or finance company. When the real interest rate rises, the monthly finance charges associated with the purchase of a car or a piano are higher, and people become less willing or able to make the purchase. Thus, a higher real interest rate reduces people's willingness to spend on consumer goods, holding constant disposable income and other factors that affect consumption.

When the real interest rate rises, financing a new car becomes more expensive and fewer cars are purchased.

[3]Because a higher real interest rate also reduces the amount households must put aside to reach a given savings target, a higher real interest rate could theoretically increase or decrease saving. However, empirical evidence suggests that higher real interest rates have a modest positive effect on saving.

Besides reducing consumption spending, a higher real interest rate also discourages firms from making capital investments. As in the case of a consumer thinking of buying a car or a piano, when a rise in the real interest rate increases financing costs, firms may reconsider their plans to invest. For example, upgrading a computer system may be profitable for a manufacturing firm when the cost of the system can be financed by borrowing at a real interest rate of 3 percent. However, if the real interest rate rises to 6 percent, doubling the cost of funds to the firm, the same upgrade may not be profitable and the firm may choose not to invest. We also should remember that residential investment—the building of houses and apartment buildings—is also part of investment spending. Higher interest rates, in the form of higher mortgage rates, certainly discourage this kind of investment spending as well.[4]

The conclusion is that, at any given level of output, *both consumption spending and planned investment spending decline when the real interest rate increases*. Conversely, a fall in the real interest rate tends to stimulate consumption and investment spending by reducing financing costs.

Planned Aggregate Expenditure and the Real Interest Rate

EXAMPLE 12.2

How does the interest rate affect planned aggregate expenditure?

In a certain economy, the components of planned spending are given by

$$C = 640 + 0.8(Y - T) - 400r,$$
$$I^P = 250 - 600r,$$
$$G = 300,$$
$$NX = 20,$$
$$T = 250.$$

This economy is similar to the one we worked with in previous chapters except that now the real interest rate r is allowed to affect both consumption and planned investment. For example, the final term in the equation describing consumption, $-400r$, implies that a 1 percentage point (0.01) increase in the real interest rate, from 4 percent to 5 percent—that is, from .04 to .05—reduces consumption spending by $400(0.01) = 4$ units. Similarly, the final term in the equation for planned investment tells us that in this example, a 1 percentage point increase in the real interest rate lowers planned investment by $600(0.01) = 6$ units. Thus, the overall effect of a 1 percentage point increase in the real interest rate is to lower planned aggregate expenditure by 10 units, the sum of the effects on consumption and investment. As in the earlier examples, disposable income $(Y - T)$ is assumed to affect consumption spending through a marginal propensity to consume of 0.8 (see the first equation), and government purchases G, net exports NX, and taxes T are assumed to be fixed numbers.

To find a numerical equation that describes the relationship of planned aggregate expenditure (PAE) to output, we can begin with the general definition of planned aggregate expenditure:

$$PAE = C + I^P + G + NX.$$

Substituting for the four components of expenditure, using the equations describing each type of spending, we get

$$PAE = [640 + 0.8(Y - 250) - 400r] + [250 - 600r] + 300 + 20.$$

[4]We discussed the relationship between the real interest rate and investment in the chapter *Saving, Capital Formation, and Financial Markets*. If you do not remember this material, you should review the section "Investment and Capital Formation."

The first term in brackets on the right side of this equation is the expression for consumption, using the fact that taxes $T = 250$; the second bracketed term is planned investment; and the last two terms correspond to the assumed numerical values of government purchases and net exports. If we simplify this equation and group together the terms that do not depend on output Y and the terms that do depend on output, we get

$$PAE = \left[(640 - 0.8 \times 250 - 400r) + (250 - 600r) + 300 + 20\right] + 0.8Y,$$

or, simplifying further,

$$PAE = \left[1{,}010 - 1{,}000r\right] + 0.8Y. \tag{12.1}$$

In Equation 12.1, the term in brackets is *autonomous expenditure,* the portion of planned aggregate expenditure that does not depend on output. *Notice that in this example autonomous expenditure depends on the real interest rate* r. Induced expenditure, the portion of planned aggregate expenditure that does depend on output, equals $0.8Y$ in this example.

The Real Interest Rate and Short-Run Equilibrium Output	EXAMPLE 12.3

How does the interest rate affect short-run equilibrium output?

Now, suppose that the Fed sets the real interest rate at 5 percent. Setting $r = 0.05$ in Equation 12.1 gives

$$PAE = \left[1{,}010 - 1{,}000(0.05)\right] + 0.8Y.$$

Simplifying, we get

$$PAE = 960 + 0.8Y.$$

So, when the real interest rate is 5 percent, autonomous expenditure is 960 and induced expenditure is $0.8Y$. Short-run equilibrium output is the level of output that equals planned aggregate spending. To find short-run equilibrium output, we could compare alternative values of output with the planned aggregate expenditure at that level of output. Short-run equilibrium output would be determined as the value of output such that output just equals spending, or

$$Y = PAE.$$

However, conveniently, when we compare this example with the example economy in the chapter *Spending, Output, and Fiscal Policy,* we see that the equation for planned aggregate expenditure, $PAE = 960 + 0.8Y$, is identical to what we found there. Thus, Table 11.1 applies to this example as well, and we get the same answer for short-run equilibrium output, which is $Y = 4{,}800$.

Short-run equilibrium output also can be found graphically, using the Keynesian-cross diagram. Again, since the equation for planned aggregate output is the same as in the chapter *Spending, Output, and Fiscal Policy,* Figure 11.4 applies equally well here.

CONCEPT CHECK 12.3

For the economy in Example 12.3, suppose the Fed sets the real interest rate at 3 percent rather than at 5 percent. Find short-run equilibrium output. (*Hint:* Consider values between 4,500 and 5,500.)

THE FED FIGHTS A RECESSION

We have now demonstrated that the following relationship holds between the real interest rate and equilibrium output:

$$\downarrow r \Rightarrow \uparrow \text{ planned } C \text{ and planned } I \Rightarrow \uparrow PAE \Rightarrow (\text{via the multiplier}) \uparrow Y.$$

A decrease in the real interest rate causes increases in both planned consumption and planned investment, which lead to an increase in planned spending. The increase in planned spending leads, through the multiplier, to an increase in short-run equilibrium output. Similarly,

$$\uparrow r \Rightarrow \downarrow \text{ planned } C \text{ and planned } I \Rightarrow \downarrow PAE \Rightarrow (\text{via the multiplier}) \downarrow Y.$$

That is, an increase in the real interest rate causes decreases in both planned consumption and planned investment, which lead to a decrease in planned spending. The decrease in planned spending leads, through the multiplier, to a decrease in short-run equilibrium output.

These two relationships are the key to understanding how monetary policy affects short-run economic activity. Let's first analyze how monetary policy can be used to fight a recession; then we will turn to how the Fed can fight inflation.

Suppose the economy faces a recessionary gap—a situation in which real output is below potential output, and planned spending is "too low." To fight a recessionary gap, the Fed should reduce the real interest rate, stimulating consumption and investment spending. According to the theory we have developed, this increase in planned spending will cause output to rise, restoring the economy to full employment.

Let's build on the example we worked through in the previous section. Suppose that potential output Y^* equals 5,000. As before, the Fed has set the real interest rate equal to 5 percent. The multiplier in this economy is 5.

We showed earlier that, with the real interest rate at 5 percent, short-run equilibrium output for this economy is 4,800. Potential output is 5,000, so the output gap ($Y - Y^*$) equals $5,000 - 4,800 = 200$. Because actual output is below potential, this economy faces a recessionary gap. To fight the recession, the Fed should lower the real interest rate, raising aggregate expenditure until output reaches 5,000, the full-employment level. That is, the Fed's objective is to increase output by 200. Because the multiplier equals 5, to increase output by 200, the Fed must increase autonomous expenditure by $200/5 = 40$ units.

By how much should the Fed reduce the real interest rate to increase autonomous expenditure by 40 units? Autonomous expenditure in this economy is $[1,010 - 1,000r]$, as you can see from Equation 12.1, so that each percentage point reduction in r increases autonomous expenditure by $1,000 \times (0.01) = 10$ units. To increase autonomous expenditure by 40, then, the Fed should lower the real interest rate by 4 percentage points, from 5 percent to 1 percent.

In summary, to eliminate the recessionary gap of 200, the Fed should lower the real interest rate from 5 percent to 1 percent. Notice that the Fed's decrease in the real interest rate increases short-run equilibrium output, as economic logic suggests.

The Fed's recession-fighting policy is shown graphically in Figure 12.2. The reduction in the real interest rate raises planned spending at each level of output, shifting the expenditure line upward. When the real interest rate equals 1 percent, the expenditure line intersects the $Y = PAE$ line at $Y = 5,000$, so that output and potential output are equal.

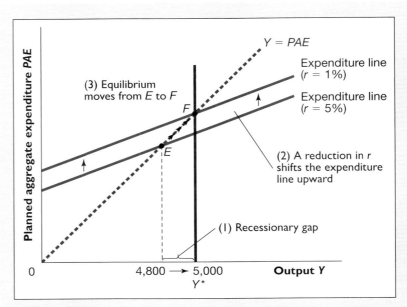

FIGURE 12.2

The Fed Fights a Recession.

(1) The economy is initially at point E, with a recessionary gap of 200;
(2) the Fed reduces the real interest rate from 5 percent to 1 percent,
shifting the expenditure line up; (3) the new equilibrium is at point F,
where output equals potential output. The output gap has been eliminated.

CONCEPT CHECK 12.4

Suppose that in Example 12.3 potential output is 4,850 rather than 5,000. By
how much should the Fed cut the real interest rate to restore full employment?
You may take as given that the multiplier is 5.

| The Fed and the Terrorist Attacks in 2001 | **EXAMPLE 12.4** |

How did the Fed respond to recession and the terrorist attacks in 2001?

The U.S. economy began slowing in the fall of 2000, with investment in high-tech equipment falling particularly sharply. According to the National Bureau of Economic Research, a
recession began in March 2001. To make matters worse, on September 11, 2001, terrorist attacks on New York City and Washington shocked the nation and led to serious problems in
the travel and financial industries, among others.

The Fed first began to respond to growing evidence of an economic slowdown at the
end of 2000. At the time, the federal funds rate stood at about 6.5 percent. (See Figure
12.1.) The Fed's most dramatic move was a surprise cut of 0.5 percentage point in the funds
rate in January 2001, between regularly scheduled meetings of the Federal Open Market
Committee. Further rate cuts followed, and by July the funds rate was below 4 percent.
By summer's end, however, there was still considerable uncertainty about the likely severity of the economic slowdown.

The picture changed suddenly on September 11, 2001, when the terrorist
attacks on the World Trade Center and the Pentagon killed almost 3,000 people.
The terrorist attacks imposed great economic as well as human costs. The physical
damage in lower Manhattan was in the billions of dollars, and many offices and

businesses in the area had to close. The Fed, in its role as supervisor of the financial system, worked hard to assist in the restoration of normal operations in the financial district of New York City. (The Federal Reserve Bank of New York, which actually conducts open-market operations, is only a block from the site of the World Trade Center.) The Fed also tried to ease financial conditions by temporarily lowering the federal funds rate to as low as 1.25 percent in the week following the attack.

In the weeks and months following September 11, the Fed turned its attention from the direct impact of the attack to the possible indirect effects on the U.S. economy. The Fed was worried that consumers, nervous about the future, would severely cut back their spending; together with the ongoing weakness in investment, a fall in consumption spending could sharply worsen the recession. To stimulate spending, the Fed continued to cut the federal funds rate.

By the time the recession officially ended in November 2001, the funds rate was at 2.0 percent, 4.5 percentage points lower than a year earlier. A number of factors made the 2001 recession relatively short and mild, including President Bush's tax cuts and increased government expenditures for homeland security and defense. Nevertheless, most economists agree that the Fed's quick actions helped to moderate the impact of the recession and the September 11 attacks.

THE FED FIGHTS INFLATION

To this point we have focused on the problem of stabilizing output, without considering inflation. In the chapter *Macroeconomic Policy*, we will see how inflation can be incorporated into our analysis. For now we will simply note that one important cause of inflation is an expansionary output gap—a situation in which planned spending, and hence actual output, exceeds potential output. When an expansionary gap exists, firms find that the demand for their output exceeds their normal rate of production. Although firms may be content to meet this excess demand at previously determined prices for some time, if the high demand persists, they ultimately will raise their prices, spurring inflation.

Because an expansionary gap tends to lead to inflation, the Fed moves to eliminate expansionary gaps as well as recessionary gaps. The procedure for getting rid of an expansionary gap—a situation in which output is "too high" relative to potential output—is the reverse of that for fighting a recessionary gap, a situation in which output is "too low." As we have seen, the cure for a recessionary gap is to reduce the real interest rate, an action that stimulates planned spending and increases output. The cure for an expansionary gap is to *raise* the real interest rate, which reduces consumption and planned investment by raising the cost of borrowing. The resulting fall in planned spending leads in turn to a decline in output and to a reduction in inflationary pressures.

Using the same example economy we've analyzed above, let's now assume that potential output is 4,600 rather than 5,000. At the initial real interest rate of 5 percent, short-run equilibrium output is 4,800, so this economy has an expansionary gap of 200.

As before, the multiplier in this economy is 5. Hence, to reduce total output by 200, the Fed needs to reduce autonomous expenditure by 200/5 = 40 units. From Equation 12.1, we know that autonomous expenditure in this economy is $[1,010 - 1,000r]$, so that each percentage point (0.01) increase in the real interest rate lowers autonomous expenditure by 10 units ($1,000 \times 0.01$). We conclude that to eliminate the inflationary gap, the Fed should raise the real interest rate by 4 percentage points (0.04), from 5 percent to 9 percent. The higher real interest rate will reduce planned aggregate expenditure and output to the level of potential output, 4,600, eliminating inflationary pressures.

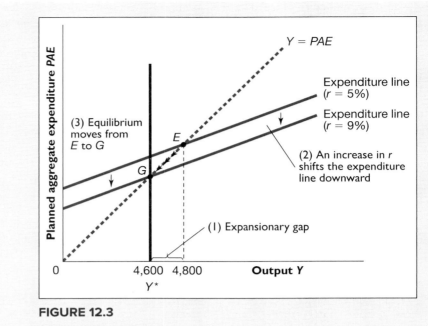

FIGURE 12.3

The Fed Fights Inflation.

(1) The economy is initially at point *E,* with an expansionary gap of 200;
(2) the Fed increases the real interest rate from 5 percent to 9 percent,
shifting the expenditure line down; (3) the new equilibrium is at point *G,*
where output equals potential output. The output gap has been eliminated.

The effects of the Fed's inflation-fighting policy are shown in Figure 12.3. With the
real interest rate at 5 percent, the expenditure line intersects the *Y* = *PAE* line at point *E* in
the figure, where output equals 4,800. To reduce planned spending and output, the Fed
raises the real interest rate to 9 percent. The higher real interest rate slows consumption and
investment spending, moving the expenditure line downward. At the new equilibrium
point *G,* actual output equals potential output at 4,600. The Fed's raising the real interest
rate—a contractionary policy action—has thus eliminated the expansionary output gap and,
with it, the threat of inflation.

"Personally, I liked this roller coaster a lot better before the Federal
Reserve Board got hold of it."

Raising Interest Rates

EXAMPLE 12.5

Why did the Fed raise interest rates in 2004 and 2005?

The Fed began tightening monetary policy in June 2004 when it increased the federal funds rate from 1.0 to 1.25 percent. (See Figure 12.1.) It continued to tighten by raising the federal funds rate by one-quarter percent at each successive meeting of the Federal Open Market Committee. By August 2006, after more than two years of tightening, the federal funds rate was 5.25 percent. Why did the Fed begin increasing the funds rate in 2004?

Because the recovery that began in November 2001 was slower than normal and marked by weak job growth, the Fed kept reducing the funds rate until it reached 1.0 percent in June 2003. Once the recovery took hold, however, this very low rate was no longer necessary. While employment had not risen as much during the recovery as it had in previous recoveries, real GDP grew at a rate of nearly 6 percent during the second half of 2003 and by 4.4 percent in 2004. Furthermore, by June 2004 the unemployment rate had fallen to 5.6 percent, not far above most estimates of the natural rate of unemployment. Although inflation began to rise in 2004, most of the increase was due to the sharp run-up in oil prices, and the rate of inflation excluding energy remained low. Nevertheless, the Fed began to raise the federal funds rate in order to prevent the emergence of an expansionary gap, which would result in higher inflation. Thus, the Fed's rate increases could be viewed as a preemptive strike against future inflation. Had the Fed waited until an expansionary gap appeared, a significant inflation problem could have emerged, and the Fed might have had to raise the federal funds rate by even more than it did.

The Fed's interest rate policies affect the economy as a whole, but they have a particularly important effect on financial markets. The introduction to this chapter noted the tremendous lengths financial market participants will go to in an attempt to anticipate Federal Reserve policy changes. The Economic Naturalist 12.1 illustrates the type of information financial investors look for, and why it is so important to them.

The Economic Naturalist 12.1

Why does news of inflation hurt the stock market?

Financial market participants watch data on inflation extremely closely. A report that inflation is increasing or is higher than expected often causes stock prices to fall sharply. Why does bad news about inflation hurt the stock market?

Investors in the financial markets worry about inflation because of its likely impact on Federal Reserve policy. Financial investors understand that the Fed, when faced with signs of an expansionary gap, is likely to raise interest rates in an attempt to reduce planned spending and "cool down" the economy. This type of contractionary policy action hurts stock prices in two ways. First, it slows down economic activity, reducing the expected sales and profits of companies whose shares are traded in the stock market. Lower profits, in turn, reduce the dividends those firms are likely to pay their shareholders.

Second, higher real interest rates reduce the value of stocks by increasing the required return for holding stocks. We saw in the chapter *Saving, Capital Formation, and Financial Markets* that an increase in the return financial investors require in order to hold stocks lowers current stock prices. Intuitively, if interest rates rise, interest-bearing alternatives to stocks such as newly issued government bonds will become more attractive to investors, reducing the demand for, and hence the price of, stocks.

SHOULD THE FEDERAL RESERVE RESPOND TO CHANGES IN ASSET PRICES?

The Federal Reserve's primary focus has been on reducing output gaps and keeping inflation low. In most instances, this has been a successful strategy. However, economists have recently started to question the Fed's focus on general economic conditions and have argued that it should pay attention to asset prices as well. The stock market boom and bust of the late 1990s and the housing bubble of the 2000s have prompted this discussion.

For example, many credit the Federal Reserve and its chairman at the time, Alan Greenspan, for effective monetary policymaking that set the stage for sustained economic growth and rising asset prices throughout the 1990s, especially during the second half of the decade. Between January 1995 and March 2000, the S&P 500 stock market index rose by a record-breaking 233 percent and the U.S. economy enjoyed a record-long business cycle expansion. Indeed, the stock market's strong, sustained rise helped to fuel additional consumer spending, which in turn promoted further economic expansion.

However, as stock prices fell sharply in the two years after their March 2000 peak, some people questioned whether the Federal Reserve should have preemptively raised interest rates to constrain investors' "irrational exuberance."[5] In this view, overly optimistic investor sentiment led to a speculative run-up in stock prices that eventually burst in 2000 as investors began to realize that firms' earnings could not support the stock prices that were being paid. Earlier intervention by the Federal Reserve, critics argued, would have slowed down the dramatic increase in stock prices and therefore could have prevented the resulting stock market "crash" and the resulting loss of consumer wealth.

At a symposium in August 2002, Alan Greenspan defended the Fed's monetary policymaking performance in the late 1990s, pointing out that it is very difficult to identify asset bubbles—surges in prices of assets to unsustainable levels—"until after the fact—that is, when its bursting confirm(s) its existence."[6] Even if such a speculative bubble could be identified, Greenspan noted, the Federal Reserve could have done little—short of "inducing a substantial contraction in economic activity"—to prevent investors' speculation from driving up stock prices. Indeed, Greenspan claimed, "the notion that a well-timed incremental tightening could have been calibrated to prevent the late 1990s bubble is almost surely an illusion." Rather, the Federal Reserve was focusing as early as 1999 on policies that would "mitigate the fallout when it occurs and, hopefully, ease the transition to the next expansion."[7]

Greenspan's remarks highlight two basic problems with using monetary policy to address "bubbles" in asset markets. First, doing so presupposes that the Federal Reserve is better than financial market professionals at identifying when asset prices are inappropriately high, relative to the asset's underlying value. In practice, however, the Fed does not have information about the stock market that is not also available to private-sector investors. Second, even if the Fed were sure that a "bubble" existed, monetary policy is not a very good tool for addressing the problem. The Fed could try to lower stock prices by raising the federal funds rate and slowing the economy. But if this policy led to a recession and rising unemployment, the outcome would be precisely the one that the Fed was trying to avoid in the first place. For these reasons, although the Fed monitors conditions in the stock market, when setting monetary policy it focuses on inflation, spending, and output, rather than stock prices themselves.

---

[5]Fed Chairman Alan Greenspan mentioned the possibility of "irrational exuberance" driving investor behavior in a December 5, 1996, speech, which is available online at www.federalreserve.gov/boarddocs/speeches/1996/19961205.htm.
[6]The text of Greenspan's speech is available online at www.federalreserve.gov/boarddocs/speeches/2002/20020830/default.htm.
[7]*The Federal Reserve's Semiannual Report on Monetary Policy,* testimony of Chairman Alan Greenspan before the Committee on Banking and Financial Services, U.S. House of Representatives, July 22, 1999. Available online at www.federalreserve.gov/boarddocs/hh/1999/July/Testimony.htm.

Economists have started to question whether these two problems are as serious as they seemed before the latest recession. Specifically, the rapid growth of house prices between 1999 and 2006 is now commonly referred to as "the housing bubble." Deep declines in output and steep increases in unemployment are clearly the result of this bubble popping, that is, the fact that the sharp rise in home prices was followed by swift declines in house prices during 2007 and 2008. As we discussed in the chapter *Spending, Output, and Fiscal Policy,* the decline in house prices led to decreases in planned aggregate expenditure both through the direct effects of less residential construction and through the indirect effects of reduced wealth on consumption spending. The view before 2008 was that it was difficult, if not impossible, to spot asset price bubbles, and that it was better to mitigate the effects of a collapsing bubble than to try to prevent the bubble in the first place. Now, after living through the consequences of a bubble, and seeing how difficult it is to clean up after a bubble pops, some economists are seriously reconsidering the role of monetary policy in preventing asset bubbles.

RECAP	MONETARY POLICY AND THE ECONOMY

- An increase in the real interest rate reduces both consumption spending and planned investment spending. Through its control of the real interest rate, the Fed is able to influence planned spending and short-run equilibrium output.

  To fight a recession (a recessionary output gap), the Fed lowers the real interest rate, stimulating planned spending and output. Conversely, to fight the threat of inflation (an expansionary output gap), the Fed raises the real interest rate, reducing planned spending and output.

- The Federal Reserve has not typically used monetary policy to affect asset prices. Rather, the Fed has focused on keeping prices stable and output near potential. The experience of the stock market bubble of the late 1990s tends to support this course of action, but the housing bubble of the 2000s provides evidence against it.

THE FEDERAL RESERVE AND INTEREST RATES

When we introduced the Federal Reserve System in the chapter *Money, Prices, and Financial Intermediaries,* we focused on the Fed's control of the *money supply,* that is, the quantity of currency and checking accounts held by the public. Determining the nation's money supply is the primary task of monetary policymakers. But if you follow the economic news regularly, you may find the idea that the Fed's job is to control the money supply a bit foreign because the news media nearly always focus on the Fed's decisions about *interest rates*. Indeed, the announcement the Fed makes after each meeting of the Federal Open Market Committee nearly always concerns its plan for a particular short-term interest rate, the *federal funds rate,* discussed earlier in this chapter.

Actually, there is no contradiction between the two ways of looking at monetary policy—as control of the money supply or as the setting of interest rates. As we will see in this section, the Fed changes the money supply to control the nominal interest rate. Thus, controlling the money supply and controlling the nominal interest rate are two sides of the same coin: Any value of the money supply chosen by the Fed implies a specific setting for the nominal interest rate, and vice versa. The reason for this close connection is that the nominal interest rate is effectively the "price" of holding money (or, more accurately, its opportunity cost). So, by controlling the quantity of money supplied to the economy, the Fed also controls the "price" of holding money (the nominal interest rate).

To better understand how the Fed determines interest rates, we will look first at the market for money, beginning with the demand side of that market. We will see that given the demand for money by the public, the Fed can control interest rates by changing the amount of money it supplies.

THE DEMAND FOR MONEY

Money refers to the set of assets, such as cash and checking accounts, that are usable in transactions. Money is also a store of value, like stocks, bonds, or real estate—in other words, a type of financial asset. As a financial asset, money is a way of holding wealth.

Anyone who has some wealth must determine the *form* in which he or she wishes to hold that wealth. For example, if Larry has wealth of $10,000, he could, if he wished, hold all $10,000 in cash. Or he could hold $5,000 of his wealth in the form of cash and $5,000 in government bonds. Or he could hold $1,000 in cash, $2,000 in a checking account, $2,000 in government bonds, and $5,000 in rare stamps. Indeed, there are thousands of different real and financial assets to choose from, all of which can be held in different amounts and combinations, so Larry's choices are virtually infinite. The decision about the forms in which to hold one's wealth is called the **portfolio allocation decision.**

What determines the particular mix of assets that Larry or another wealth holder will choose? All else being equal, people generally prefer to hold assets that they expect to pay a high *return* and do not carry too much *risk*. They also may try to reduce the overall risk they face through *diversification*—that is, by owning a variety of different assets.[8] Many people own some real assets, such as a car or a home, because they provide services (transportation or shelter) and often a financial return (an increase in value, as when the price of a home rises in a strong real estate market).

Here we do not need to analyze the entire portfolio allocation decision, but only one part of it—namely, the decision about how much of one's wealth to hold in the form of *money* (cash and checking accounts). The amount of wealth an individual chooses to hold in the form of money is that individual's **demand for money,** sometimes called an individual's *liquidity preference.* So if Larry decided to hold his entire $10,000 in the form of cash, his demand for money would be $10,000. But if he were to hold $1,000 in cash, $2,000 in a checking account, $2,000 in government bonds, and $5,000 in rare stamps, his demand for money would be only $3,000—that is, $1,000 in cash plus the $2,000 in his checking account.

How much money should an individual (or household) choose to hold? Applying the Cost-Benefit Principle, an individual should increase his or her money holdings only so long as the extra benefit of doing so exceeds the extra cost. The principal *benefit* of holding money is its usefulness in carrying out transactions. Larry's shares of stock, his car, and his furniture are all valuable assets, but he cannot use them to buy groceries or pay his rent. He can make routine payments using cash or his checking account, however. Because of its usefulness in daily transactions, Larry will almost certainly want to hold some of his wealth in the form of money. Furthermore, if Larry is a high-income individual, he will probably choose to hold more money than someone with a lower income would because he is likely to spend more and carry out more transactions than the low-income person.

Larry's benefit from holding money is also affected by the technological and financial sophistication of the society he lives in. For example, in the United States, developments such as credit cards, debit cards, and ATM machines have generally reduced the amount of money people need to carry out routine transactions, decreasing the public's demand for money at given levels of income. In the United States in 1960, for example, money holdings in the form of cash and checking account balances (the monetary aggregate M1) were about 28 percent of GDP. By 2013 that ratio had fallen to about 16 percent of GDP, with actual currency representing less than 7 percent of GDP.

portfolio allocation decision the decision about the forms in which to hold one's wealth

demand for money the amount of wealth an individual or firm chooses to hold in the form of money

Cost-Benefit

[8]We examined risk, return, and asset diversification in the chapter *Saving, Capital Formation, and Financial Markets.*

Although money is an extremely useful asset, there is also a cost to holding money—more precisely, an opportunity cost—that arises from the fact that most forms of money pay little or no interest. Cash pays zero interest, and most checking accounts pay either no interest or very low rates. For the sake of simplicity, we will assume that *the nominal interest rate on money is zero*. In contrast, most alternative assets, such as bonds or stocks, pay a positive nominal return. A bond, for example, pays a fixed amount of interest each period to the holder, while stocks pay dividends and also may increase in value (capital gains).

The cost of holding money arises because, in order to hold an extra dollar of wealth in the form of money, a person must reduce by one dollar the amount of wealth held in the form of higher-yielding assets, such as bonds or stocks. The opportunity cost of holding money is measured by the interest rate that could have been earned if the person had chosen to hold interest-bearing assets instead of money. All else being equal, the higher the nominal interest rate, the higher the opportunity cost of holding money, and hence the less money people will choose to hold.

Innovations such as ATM machines have reduced the amount of money that people need to hold for routine transactions.

We have been talking about the demand for money by individuals, but businesses also hold money to carry out transactions with customers and to pay workers and suppliers. The same general factors that determine individuals' money demand also affect the demand for money by businesses. That is, in choosing how much money to hold, a business, like an individual, will compare the benefits of holding money for use in transactions with the opportunity cost of holding a non-interest-bearing asset. Although we will not differentiate between the money held by individuals and the money held by businesses in discussing money demand, you should be aware that in the U.S. economy, businesses hold a significant portion—more than half—of the total money stock.

MACROECONOMIC FACTORS THAT AFFECT THE DEMAND FOR MONEY

In any household or business, the demand for money will depend on a variety of individual circumstances. For example, a high-volume retail business that serves thousands of customers each day will probably choose to have more money on hand than a legal firm that bills clients and pays employees monthly. But while individuals and businesses vary considerably in the amount of money they choose to hold, three macroeconomic factors affect the demand for money quite broadly: the nominal interest rate, real output, and the price level.

- *The nominal interest rate (i).* We have seen that the interest rate paid on alternatives to money, such as government bonds, determines the opportunity cost of holding money. The higher the prevailing nominal interest rate, the greater the opportunity cost of holding money, and hence the less money individuals and businesses will demand.

What do we mean by *the* nominal interest rate? As we have discussed, there are thousands of different assets, each with its own interest rate (rate of return). So can we really talk about *the* nominal interest rate? The answer is that, while there are many different assets, each with its own corresponding interest rate, the rates on those assets tend to rise and fall together. This is to be expected because if the interest rates on some assets were to rise sharply while the rates on other assets declined, financial investors would flock to the assets paying high rates and refuse to buy the assets paying low rates. So, although there are many different interest rates in practice, speaking of the general level of interest rates usually does make sense. In this book, when we talk about *the* nominal interest rate, what we have in mind is some average measure of interest rates.

The nominal interest rate is a macroeconomic factor that affects the cost of holding money. A macroeconomic factor that affects the *benefit* of holding money is:

- *Real income or output (Y).* An increase in aggregate real income or output—as measured, for example, by real GDP—raises the quantity of goods and services that people and businesses want to buy and sell. When the economy enters a boom, for example, people do more shopping and stores have more customers.

To accommodate the increase in transactions, both individuals and businesses need to hold more money. Thus higher real output raises the demand for money.

A second macroeconomic factor affecting the benefit of holding money is:

- *The price level (P).* The higher the prices of goods and services, the more dollars (or yen, or euros) are needed to make a given set of transactions. Thus, a higher price level is associated with a higher demand for money.

Today, when a couple of teenagers go out for a movie and snacks on Saturday night, they need probably five times as much cash as their parents did 25 years ago. Because the prices of movie tickets and popcorn have risen steeply over 25 years, more money (that is, more dollars) is needed to pay for a Saturday night date than in the past. By the way, the fact that prices are higher today does *not* imply that people are worse off today than in the past because nominal wages and salaries also have risen substantially. In general, however, higher prices do imply that people need to keep a greater number of dollars available, in cash or in a checking account.

THE MONEY DEMAND CURVE

money demand curve a curve that shows the relationship between the aggregate quantity of money demanded *M* and the nominal interest rate *i*; because an increase in the nominal interest rate increases the opportunity cost of holding money, which reduces the quantity of money demanded, the money demand curve slopes down

For the purposes of monetary policymaking, economists are most interested in the aggregate, or economywide, demand for money. The interaction of the aggregate demand for money, determined by the public, and the supply of money, which is set by the Fed, determines the nominal interest rate that prevails in the economy.

The economywide demand for money can be represented graphically by the *money demand curve* (see Figure 12.4). The **money demand curve** relates the aggregate quantity of money demanded *M* to the nominal interest rate *i*. The quantity of money demanded *M* is a nominal quantity, measured in dollars (or yen, or euros, depending on the country). Because an increase in the nominal interest rate increases the opportunity cost of holding money, which reduces the quantity of money demanded, the money demand curve slopes down.

If we think of the nominal interest rate as the "price" (more precisely, the opportunity cost) of money and the amount of money people want to hold as the "quantity," the money demand curve is analogous to the demand curve for a good or service. As with a standard demand curve, the fact that a higher price of money leads people to demand less of it is captured in the downward slope of the demand curve.

FIGURE 12.4

The Money Demand Curve.

The money demand curve relates the economywide demand for money to the nominal interest rate. Because an increase in the nominal interest rate raises the opportunity cost of holding money, the money demand curve slopes down.

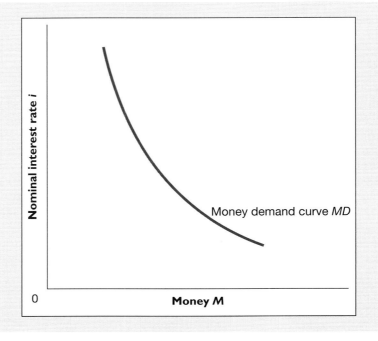

For a given nominal interest rate, any change that makes people want to hold more money will shift the money demand curve to the right, and any change that makes people want to hold less money will shift the money demand curve to the left. Thus, as in a standard demand curve, changes in factors other than the price of money (the nominal interest rate) cause the demand curve for money to shift. We have already identified two macroeconomic factors other than the nominal interest rate that affect the economywide demand for money: real output and the price level. Because an increase in either of these variables increases the demand for money, it shifts the money demand curve rightward, as shown in Figure 12.5. Similarly, a fall in real output or the general price level reduces money demand, shifting the money demand curve leftward.

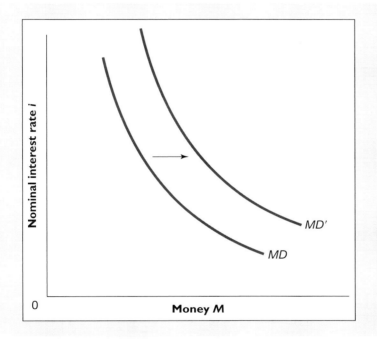

FIGURE 12.5

A Shift in the Money Demand Curve.

At a given nominal interest rate, any change that makes people want to hold more money—such as an increase in the general price level or in real GDP—will shift the money demand curve to the right.

The money demand curve also may shift in response to other changes that affect the cost or benefit of holding money, such as the technological and financial advances we mentioned earlier. For example, the introduction of ATM machines reduced the amount of money people choose to hold and thus shifted the economywide money demand curve to the left. The Economic Naturalist 12.2 describes another potential source of shifts in the demand for money, holdings of U.S. dollars by foreigners.

The Economic Naturalist 12.2

Why does the average Argentine hold more U.S. dollars than the average U.S. citizen?

Estimates are that the value of U.S. dollars circulating in Argentina exceeds $1,000 per person, which is higher than the per capita dollar holdings in the United States. A number of other countries, including those that once belonged to the former Soviet Union, also hold large quantities of dollars. In all, as much as $500 billion in U.S. currency—close to half the total amount counted as part of M1—may be circulating outside the borders of the United States. Why do Argentines and other non-U.S. residents hold so many dollars?

U.S. residents and businesses hold dollars primarily for transaction purposes, rather than as a store of value. As a store of value, interest-bearing bonds and dividend-paying stocks are a better choice for Americans than zero-interest money. But this is not necessarily the case for the citizens of other countries, particularly nations that are economically or politically unstable. Argentina, for example, endured many years of high and erratic inflation in the 1970s and 1980s, which sharply eroded the value of financial investments denominated in Argentine pesos. Lacking better alternatives, many Argentines began saving in the form of U.S. currency, which they correctly believed to be more stable in value than peso-denominated assets.

Argentina's use of dollars became officially recognized in 1990. In that year, the country instituted a new monetary system, called a currency board, under which U.S. dollars and Argentine pesos by law traded freely one for one. Under the currency board system, Argentines became accustomed to carrying U.S. dollars in their wallets for transaction purposes, along with pesos. However, in 2001 Argentina's monetary problems returned with a vengeance, as the currency board system broke down, the peso plummeted in value relative to the dollar, and inflation returned. Consequently, the Argentinian demand for dollars increased during the next few years.

After years of hyperinflation and price speculation in the African nation of Zimbabwe, the Zimbabwean dollar was effectively abandoned as an official currency on April 12, 2009. This followed a year when the growth in the money supply rose from 81,143 percent to 658 billion percent from January to December, and an egg was reportedly selling for Z$50 billion. On January 29, 2014, the Zimbabwe central bank announced that the U.S. dollar would be one of several foreign currencies that would be accepted as legal currency within that country.

Some countries, including a number formed as a result of the breakup of the Soviet Union, have endured not only high inflation but political instability and uncertainty as well. In a politically volatile environment, citizens face the risk that their savings, including their bank deposits, will be confiscated or heavily taxed by the government. Often they conclude that a hidden cache of U.S. dollars is the safest way to hold wealth. Indeed, an estimated $1 million in $100 bills can be stored in a suitcase. The ability to hold such wealth in a relatively small container is one reason why international criminals, most notably drug dealers, allegedly hold so many $100 bills. Now that the European currency, the euro, which is worth more than $1, can be held in the form of a 500-euro banknote, it has been suggested that drug dealers and other cash-hoarders may switch to holding 500-euro bills in even smaller suitcases. If they do, the demand for dollars would decline.

THE SUPPLY OF MONEY AND MONEY MARKET EQUILIBRIUM

Where there is demand, can supply be far behind? As we have seen, the *supply* of money is controlled by the central bank—in the United States, the Federal Reserve. As we discussed in the chapter *Money, Prices, and Financial Intermediaries*, the Fed's primary tool for controlling the money supply is *open-market operations*. For example, to increase the money supply, the Fed can use newly created money to buy government bonds from the public (an open-market purchase), which puts the new money into circulation.

Figure 12.6 shows the demand for and the supply of money in a single diagram. The nominal interest rate is on the vertical axis, and the nominal quantity of money (in dollars) is on the horizontal axis. As we have seen, because a higher nominal interest rate increases the opportunity cost of holding money, the money demand curve slopes downward. And because the Fed fixes the supply of money, we have drawn the *money supply curve* as a vertical line that intercepts the horizontal axis at the quantity of money chosen by the Fed, denoted M.

As in standard supply and demand analysis, equilibrium in the market for money occurs at the intersection of the supply and demand curves, shown as point E in Figure 12.6.

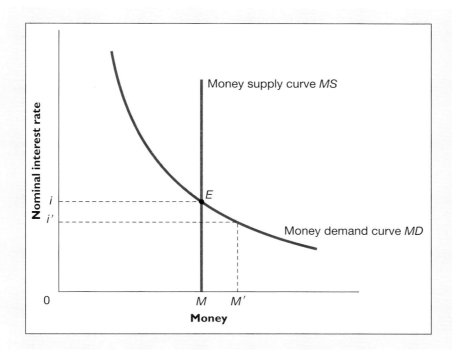

FIGURE 12.6

Equilibrium in the Market for Money.

Equilibrium in the market for money occurs at point *E*, where the quantity of money demanded equals the quantity of money supplied by the Federal Reserve. The equilibrium nominal interest rate, which equates the supply of and demand for money, is *i*.

The equilibrium amount of money in circulation, *M*, is simply the amount of money the Fed chooses to supply. The equilibrium nominal interest rate *i* is the interest rate at which the quantity of money demanded by the public, as determined by the money demand curve, equals the fixed supply of money made available by the Fed.

To understand how the market for money reaches equilibrium, it is helpful to recall the relationship between interest rates and the market price of bonds that was introduced in the chapter *Saving, Capital Formation, and Financial Markets*: The prices of existing bonds are *inversely related* to the current interest rate. Higher interest rates imply lower bond prices, and lower interest rates imply higher bond prices. With this relationship between interest rates and bond prices in mind, let's ask what happens if, say, the nominal interest rate is initially below the equilibrium level in the market for money—for example, at a value such as *i'* in Figure 12.6. At that interest rate, the public's quantity demanded of money is *M'*, which is greater than the actual amount of money in circulation, equal to *M*. How will the public—households and firms—react if the amount of money they hold is less than they would like? To increase their holdings of money, people will try to sell some of the interest-bearing assets they hold, such as bonds. But if everyone is trying to sell bonds and there are no willing buyers, then all the attempt to reduce bond holdings will achieve is to drive down the price of bonds, in the same way that a glut of apples will drive down the price of apples.

A fall in the price of bonds, however, is equivalent to an increase in interest rates. Thus, the public's collective attempt to increase its money holdings by selling bonds and other interest-bearing assets, which has the effect of lowering bond prices, also implies higher market interest rates. As interest rates rise, the quantity of money demanded by the public will decline (represented by a right-to-left movement along the money demand curve), as will the desire to sell bonds. Only when the interest rate reaches its equilibrium value, *i* in Figure 12.6, will people be content to hold the quantities of money and other assets that are actually available in the economy.

CONCEPT CHECK 12.5

Describe the adjustment process in the market for money if the nominal interest rate is initially above rather than below its equilibrium value. What happens to the price of bonds as the money market adjusts toward equilibrium?

RECAP	MONEY DEMAND AND SUPPLY

- For the economy as a whole, the demand for money is the amount of wealth that individuals, households, and businesses choose to hold in the form of money. The opportunity cost of holding money is measured by the nominal interest rate i, which is the return that could be earned on alternative assets such as bonds. The benefit of holding money is its usefulness in transactions.

- Increases in real GDP (Y) or the price level (P) raise the nominal volume of transactions and thus the economywide demand for money. The demand for money also is affected by technological and financial innovations, such as the introduction of ATM machines, that affect the costs or benefits of holding money.

- The money demand curve relates the economywide demand for money to the nominal interest rate. Because an increase in the nominal interest rate raises the opportunity cost of holding money, the money demand curve slopes downward.

- Changes in factors other than the nominal interest rate that affect the demand for money can shift the money demand curve. For example, increases in real GDP or the price level raise the demand for money, shifting the money demand curve to the right, whereas decreases shift the money demand curve to the left.

- In the market for money, the money demand curve slopes downward, reflecting the fact that a higher nominal interest rate increases the opportunity cost of holding money and thus reduces the amount of money people want to hold. The money supply curve is vertical at the quantity of money that the Fed chooses to supply. The equilibrium nominal interest rate i is the interest rate at which the quantity of money demanded by the public equals the fixed supply of money made available by the Fed.

HOW THE FED CONTROLS THE NOMINAL INTEREST RATE

We began this chapter by noting that the public and the press usually talk about Fed policy in terms of decisions about the nominal interest rate rather than the money supply. Indeed, Fed policymakers themselves usually describe their plans in terms of a specific value for the interest rate. We now have the necessary background to understand how the Fed translates the ability to determine the economy's money supply into control of the nominal interest rate. The Fed can control the money supply in three ways: through open-market operations, discount window lending, and directly affecting bank reserves.

OPEN-MARKET OPERATIONS

Figure 12.6 showed that the nominal interest rate is determined by equilibrium in the market for money. Let's suppose that for some reason the Fed decides to lower the interest rate. As we will see, to lower the interest rate, the Fed must increase the supply of money, which is usually accomplished by using newly created money to purchase government bonds from the public (an open-market purchase).

Figure 12.7 shows the effects of such an increase in the money supply by the Fed. If the initial money supply is M, then equilibrium in the money market occurs at point E in the figure, and the equilibrium nominal interest rate is i. Now suppose the Fed, by means

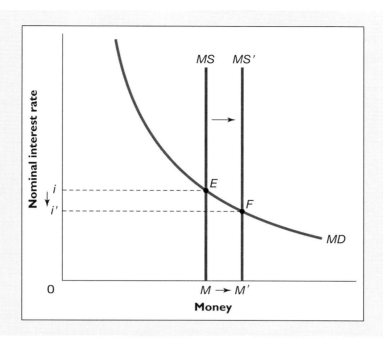

FIGURE 12.7

The Fed Lowers the Nominal Interest Rate.

The Fed can lower the equilibrium nominal interest rate by increasing the supply of money. For the given money demand curve, an increase in the money supply from M to M' shifts the equilibrium point in the money market from E to F, lowering the equilibrium nominal interest rate from i to i'.

of open-market purchases of bonds, increases the money supply to M'. This increase in the money supply shifts the vertical money supply curve to the right, which shifts the equilibrium in the money market from point E to point F. Note that at point F the equilibrium nominal interest rate has declined, from i to i'. The nominal interest rate must decline if the public is to be persuaded to hold the extra money that has been injected into the economy.

To understand what happens in financial markets when the Fed expands the money supply, recall once again the inverse relationship between interest rates and the price of bonds. To increase the money supply, the Fed typically buys government bonds from the public. However, if households and firms are initially satisfied with their asset holdings, they will be willing to sell bonds only at a price that is higher than the initial price. That is, the Fed's bond purchases will drive up the price of bonds in the open market. But we know that higher bond prices imply lower interest rates. Thus, the Fed's bond purchases lower the prevailing nominal interest rate.

A similar scenario unfolds if the Fed decides to raise interest rates. To raise interest rates, the Fed must *reduce* the money supply. Reduction of the money supply may be accomplished by an open-market sale—the sale of government bonds to the public in exchange for money.[9] (The Fed keeps a large inventory of government bonds, acquired through previous open-market purchases, for use in open-market operations.) But in the attempt to sell bonds on the open market, the Fed will drive down the price of bonds. Given the inverse relationship between the price of bonds and the interest rate, the fall in bond prices is equivalent to a rise in the interest rate. In terms of money demand and money supply, the higher interest rate is necessary to persuade the public to hold less money.

As Figures 12.6 and 12.7 illustrate, control of the interest rate is not separate from control of the money supply. If Fed officials choose to set the nominal interest rate at a

---

[9]The sale of existing government bonds by the Federal Reserve in an open-market sale should not be confused with the sale of newly issued government bonds by the Treasury when it finances government budget deficits. Whereas open-market sales reduce the money supply, Treasury sales of new bonds do not affect the money supply. The difference arises because the Federal Reserve does not put the money it receives in an open-market sale back into circulation, leaving less money for the public to hold. In contrast, the Treasury puts the money it receives from selling newly issued bonds back into circulation as it purchases goods and services.

particular level, they can do so only by setting the money supply at a level consistent with the target interest rate. The Fed *cannot* set the interest rate and the money supply independently, since for any given money demand curve, a particular interest rate implies a particular size of the money supply, and vice versa.

Since monetary policy actions can be expressed in terms of either the interest rate or the money supply, why does the Fed (and almost every other central bank) choose to communicate its policy decisions to the public by referring to the nominal interest rate rather than the money supply? One reason, which we analyzed earlier, is that the main effects of monetary policy on both the economy and financial markets are exerted through interest rates. Consequently, the interest rate is often the best summary of the overall impact of the Fed's actions. Another reason for focusing on interest rates is that they are more familiar to the public than the money supply. Finally, interest rates can be monitored continuously in the financial markets, which makes the effects of Fed policies on interest rates easy to observe. By contrast, measuring the amount of money in the economy requires collecting data on bank deposits, with the consequence that several weeks may pass before policymakers and the public know precisely how Fed actions have affected the money supply.

DISCOUNT WINDOW LENDING

The Fed controls the money supply, and hence the nominal interest rate, primarily by using open-market operations. However, the Fed can change the money supply with other tools that it uses much less frequently. One tool is called *discount window lending*. Recall from the chapter *Money, Prices, and Financial Intermediaries* that the cash or assets held by a commercial bank for the purpose of meeting depositor withdrawals are called its reserves. Its desired amount of reserves is equal to its deposits multiplied by the desired reserve-deposit ratio, as implied by Equation 9.1. When an individual commercial bank has insufficient reserves, it may choose to borrow reserves from the Fed. For historical reasons, lending of reserves by the Federal Reserve to commercial banks is called **discount window lending.** The interest rate that the Fed charges commercial banks that borrow reserves is called the **discount rate.** Loans of reserves by the Fed directly increase the quantity of reserves in the banking system, leading ultimately to increases in bank deposits and the money supply.

Be careful not to confuse the discount rate and the federal funds rate. The discount rate is the interest rate commercial banks pay to the Fed; the federal funds rate is the interest rate commercial banks charge each other for short-term loans.

RESERVE REQUIREMENTS

As we showed in the chapter *Money, Prices, and Financial Intermediaries* (in particular, Equation 9.2), the economy's money supply depends on three factors: the amount of currency the public chooses to hold, the supply of bank reserves, and the reserve-deposit ratio maintained by commercial banks. The reserve-deposit ratio is equal to total bank reserves divided by total deposits. If banks kept all of their deposits as reserves, the reserve-deposit ratio would be 100 percent, and banks would not make any loans. As banks lend out more of their deposits, the reserve-deposit ratio falls.

Within a certain range, commercial banks are free to set the reserve-deposit ratio they want to maintain. However, Congress granted the Fed the power to set minimum values of the reserve-deposit ratio for commercial banks. The legally required values of the reserve-deposit ratio set by the Fed are called **reserve requirements.**

Changes in reserve requirements can be used to affect the money supply, although the Fed does not usually use them in this way. For example, suppose that commercial banks are maintaining a legally mandated minimum 3 percent reserve-deposit ratio. If the Fed wants to expand the money supply, it could reduce required reserves to, say, 2 percent of deposits. This would allow banks to lend a greater portion of their deposits and keep a smaller percentage of deposits as required reserves. If banks wanted to make new loans, these new loans would generate additional deposits. A decline in the economywide reserve-deposit ratio would therefore cause the money supply to rise.

discount window lending the lending of reserves by the Federal Reserve to commercial banks

discount rate (or primary credit rate) the interest rate that the Fed charges commercial banks to borrow reserves

reserve requirements set by the Fed, the minimum values of the ratio of bank reserves to bank deposits that commercial banks are allowed to maintain

Suppose, on the other hand, the Fed wanted to contract the money supply. If the Fed raised required reserves to, say, 5 percent of deposits, commercial banks would need to raise their reserve-deposit ratio to at least 5 percent. This would lead to a contraction of loans and deposits, which would decrease the money supply.

INTEREST PAID ON RESERVES

In October 2008, the Federal Reserve added a new way of affecting bank reserves. Specifically, the Fed began paying interest on required reserve balances and on excess reserve balances (i.e., reserves over and above the required amount) held by commercial banks at the Federal Reserve. Before October 2008, these balances earned no interest, and thus banks had an incentive to keep these amounts to a minimum and loan out as much as they could above their legal reserves. Put another way, "The interest rate paid on required reserve balances is determined by the Board and is intended to eliminate effectively the implicit tax that reserve requirements used to impose on depository institutions."[10]

This gives the Fed another tool to control the money supply. Suppose, for example, that the Federal Reserve wants to decrease the money supply. It can increase the interest rate paid on reserves, thus increasing the reserve-deposit ratio since banks will want to hold more of these interest-bearing reserves relative to more risky loans that earn similar interest rates. This will cause the money supply to decrease and raise nominal interest rates in the economy more generally.

Many observers believe that this will be an important monetary policy tool as the economy recovers over the next few years. The Fed substantially increased the money supply during the latest recession, mostly by exchanging bonds and other financial assets held by banks for increased reserve balances held at the Fed. As the economy recovers, the banks will start to draw down their reserve balances and lend out these funds, causing the money supply to increase through the money-multiplier process. The Fed can slow down this process by increasing the interest rate it pays on reserves and thereby discouraging banks from turning their reserves into loans.

UNCONVENTIONAL MONETARY POLICY

Since the advent of the global financial crisis of 2007–2008, the U.S. Federal Reserve System has been undertaking a type of unconventional expansionary monetary policy known as quantitative easing. **Quantitative easing (QE)** refers to a central bank buying specified amounts of financial assets from commercial banks and other private financial institutions, thereby lowering the yield or return of those assets while increasing the money supply. Quantitative easing basically includes the same steps as regular open-market purchases, but is distinguished from these regular purchases in the type and term of the financial assets purchased as well as in the overall goal of the policy. While conventional expansionary policy usually involves the purchase of short-term government bonds in order to keep interest rates at a specified target value, quantitative easing is used by central banks to stimulate the economy by purchasing assets of longer maturity, thereby lowering longer-term interest rates. Since the peak of the financial crisis in 2008, the Federal Reserve has expanded its balance sheet dramatically, adding trillions of dollar's worth of longer-term treasury notes, commercial debt, and Mortgage Backed Securities (MBS) through several rounds of quantitative easing. By including commercial and private debt in these purchases, it has also been suggested that the Fed is providing *credit easing* by removing specific gridlocks that have been identified in certain credit markets. In 2014, the Federal Reserve started the process of slowing down or *tapering* its expansionary QE policies by gradually scaling back its monthly bond purchases from an existing level of $85 billion a month.

quantitative easing (QE)
An expansionary monetary policy in which a central bank buys financial assets from private financial institutions, thereby lowering the yield or return of those assets while increasing the money supply.

---

[10]See "Interest on Required Balances and Excess Balances" at www.federalreserve.gov/monetarypolicy/reqresbalances.htm.

RECAP	THE FEDERAL RESERVE AND INTEREST RATES

The Federal Reserve controls the nominal interest rate by changing the supply of money. An open-market purchase of government bonds increases the money supply and lowers the equilibrium nominal interest rate. An increase in discount window lending, a reduction in reserve requirements, a decrease in the interest rate paid on required reserves, or quantitative easing will all have the same effect. Conversely, an open-market sale of government bonds reduces the money supply and increases the nominal interest rate, as will a decrease in discount window lending, an increase in the interest rate paid on required reserves, or an increase in reserve requirements. The Fed can prevent changes in the demand for money from affecting the nominal interest rate by adjusting the quantity of money supplied appropriately.

○ SUMMARY ○

- The central bank of the United States is called the Federal Reserve System, or the Fed for short. The Fed's two main responsibilities are making monetary policy, which means determining how much money will circulate in the economy, and overseeing and regulating financial markets, especially banks. Created in 1914, one of the original purposes of the Federal Reserve was to help eliminate or control banking panics. A banking panic is an episode in which depositors, spurred by news or rumors of the imminent bankruptcy of one or more banks, rush to withdraw their deposits from the banking system. Because banks do not keep enough reserves on hand to pay off all depositors, even a financially healthy bank can run out of cash during a panic and be forced to close. *(LO1)*

- In the short run, the Fed can control the real interest rate as well as the nominal interest rate. Since the real interest rate equals the nominal interest rate minus the inflation rate, and because the inflation rate adjusts relatively slowly, the Fed can change the real interest rate by changing the nominal interest rate. In the long run, the real interest rate is determined by the balance of saving and investment (see the chapter *Saving, Capital Formation, and Financial Markets*). The nominal interest rate that the Fed targets most closely is the federal funds rate, which is the rate commercial banks charge each other for very short-term loans. *(LO2, LO4)*

- The Federal Reserve's actions affect the economy because changes in the real interest rate affect planned spending. For example, an increase in the real interest rate raises the cost of borrowing, reducing consumption and planned investment. Thus, by increasing the real interest rate, the Fed can reduce planned spending and short-run equilibrium output. Conversely, by reducing the real interest rate, the Fed can stimulate planned aggregate expenditure and thereby raise short-run equilibrium output. The Fed's ultimate objectives are to eliminate output gaps and maintain low inflation. To eliminate a recessionary output gap, the Fed will lower the real interest rate. To eliminate an expansionary output gap, the Fed will raise the real interest rate. *(LO2, LO4)*

- The nominal interest rate is determined in the market for money, which has both a demand side and a supply side. The money demand curve relates the aggregate quantity of money demanded to the nominal interest rate. Because an increase in the nominal interest rate increases the opportunity cost of holding money, which reduces the quantity of money demanded, the money demand curve slopes down. Factors other than the nominal interest rate that affect the demand for money (such as the price level of real GDP) will shift the demand curve to the right or left. The supply curve for money is vertical at the value of the money supply set by the Fed. Money market equilibrium occurs at the nominal interest rate at which money demand equals the money supply. *(LO3)*

- The Fed can reduce the nominal interest rate by increasing the money supply (shifting the money supply curve to the right) or increase the nominal interest rate by reducing the money supply (shifting the money supply curve to the left). *(LO4)*

- The Federal Reserve has several tools it can use to change the money supply. In open-market operations the Fed purchases or sells government bonds in order to increase (via purchases) or decrease (via sales) the money supply. Discount window lending allows commercial banks to borrow additional reserves directly from the Fed. The Fed can also affect bank reserves directly, either by changing reserve requirements or by adjusting the interest rate paid on reserve balances held at the Fed. *(LO4)*

○ KEY TERMS ○

banking panic
Board of Governors (of the Federal
  Reserve System)
demand for money
deposit insurance

discount rate
discount window lending
federal funds rate
Federal Open Market Committee
  (FOMC)

money demand curve
portfolio allocation decision
primary credit rate
quantitative easing (QE)
reserve requirements

○ REVIEW QUESTIONS ○

1. Why does the real interest rate affect planned aggregate expenditure? Give examples. *(LO2)*

2. The Fed faces a recessionary gap. How would you expect it to respond? Explain step by step how its policy change is likely to affect the economy. *(LO2)*

3. The Fed decides to take a contractionary policy action. Under what circumstances would this type of policy action be most appropriate? What would you expect to happen to the nominal interest rate, the real interest rate, and the money supply? *(LO2, LO3)*

4. Show graphically how the Fed controls the nominal interest rate. Can the Fed control the real interest rate? *(LO4)*

5. What effect does an open-market purchase of bonds by the Fed have on nominal interest rates? Discuss in terms of (a) the effect of the purchase on bond prices and (b) the effect of the purchase on the supply of money. *(LO4)*

○ PROBLEMS ○

1. The Federal Reserve System was created by the Federal Reserve Act, passed by Congress in 1913, and began operations in 1914. Like all central banks, the Fed is a government agency. Which of the following statements about the Fed is false? *(LO1)*
   a. The Fed has the power to supervise and regulate banks.
   b. The Fed's goals are to promote economic growth, maintain low inflation, and watch over a smooth operation of financial markets.
   c. The Fed is the "lender of last resort."
   d. The Fed is allowed to make a profit like commercial banks.

Visit your mobile app store and download the Frank: Study Econ app *today*!

2. An economy is described by the following equations:

$$C = 2,600 + 0.8(Y - T) - 10,000r$$
$$I^p = 2,000 - 10,000r$$
$$G = 1,800$$
$$NX = 0$$
$$T = 3,000$$

   The real interest rate, expressed as a decimal, is 0.10 (that is, 10 percent). *(LO2)*
   a. Find a numerical equation relating planned aggregate expenditure to output.
   b. Using a table (or algebra), solve for short-run equilibrium output.
   c. Show your result graphically using the Keynesian-cross diagram.

3. For the economy described in Problem 2 above, suppose that potential output Y^* equals 12,000. *(LO2)*
   a. What real interest rate should the Fed set to bring the economy to full employment? You may take as given that the multiplier for this economy is 5.
   b. Repeat part a for the case in which potential output Y^* equals 9,000.

c.* Show that the real interest rate you found in part a sets national saving equal to planned investment when the economy is at potential output. This result shows that the real interest rate must be consistent with equilibrium in the market for saving when the economy is at full employment. (*Hint:* Review the material on national saving in the chapter *Saving, Capital Formation, and Financial Markets*).

4.* Here is another set of equations describing an economy: *(LO2)*

$$C = 14,400 + 0.5(Y - T) - 40,000r$$
$$I^P = 8,000 - 20,000r$$
$$G = 7,800$$
$$NX = 1,800$$
$$T = 8,000$$
$$Y^* = 40,000$$

a. Find a numerical equation relating planned aggregate expenditure to output and to the real interest rate.
b. At what value should the Fed set the real interest rate to eliminate any output gap? (*Hint:* Set output Y equal to the value of potential output given above in the equation you found in part a. Then solve for the real interest rate that also sets planned aggregate expenditure equal to potential output.)

5. During the heavy Christmas shopping season, sales of retail stores, online sales firms, and other merchants rise significantly. *(LO3)*
a. What would you expect to happen to the money demand curve during the Christmas season? Show graphically.
b. If the Fed took no action, what would happen to nominal interest rates around Christmas?
c. In fact, nominal interest rates do not change significantly in the fourth quarter of the year, due to deliberate Fed policy. Explain and show graphically how the Fed can ensure that nominal interest rates remain stable around Christmas.

6. The following table shows Uma's estimated annual benefits of holding different amounts of money: *(LO3)*

Average money holdings ($)	Total benefit ($)
500	35
600	47
700	57
800	65
900	71
1,000	75
1,100	77
1,200	77

How much money will Uma hold on average if the nominal interest rate is 9 percent? 5 percent? 3 percent? Assume that she wants her money holding to be a multiple of $100. (*Hint:* Make a table comparing the extra benefit of each additional $100 in

*Denotes more difficult problem.

money holdings with the opportunity cost, in terms of forgone interest, of additional money holdings.)

7. How would you expect each of the following to affect the economywide demand for money? Explain. *(LO3)*
   a. Competition among brokers forces down the commission charge for selling holdings of bonds or stocks.
   b. Grocery stores begin to accept credit cards in payment.
   c. Financial investors become concerned about increasing riskiness of stocks.

8. For each of the scenarios described in Problem 7, what will happen to the nominal interest rate if the Fed does not change the money supply? Explain your reasoning using a supply and demand graph of the money market. *(LO3, LO4)*

○ ANSWERS TO CONCEPT CHECKS ○

12.1 Verify directly for each date in Table 12.1 that

$$\text{Money supply} = \frac{\text{Currency}}{\text{held by public}} + \frac{\text{Bank reserves}}{\text{Desired reserve-deposit ratio}}.$$

For example, for December 1929, we can check that $45.9 = 3.85 + 3.15/0.075$.

Suppose that the currency held by the public in December 1933 had been 3.79, as in December 1930, rather than 4.85, and that the difference $(4.85 - 3.79 = 1.06)$ had been left in the banks. Then bank reserves in December 1933 would have been $3.45 + 1.06 = 4.51$ and the money supply would have been $3.79 + (4.51/0.133) = 37.7$. The money supply would still have fallen between 1930 and 1933 if people had not increased their holdings of currency, but only by about half as much. *(LO1)*

12.2 Over the course of 1931, currency holdings by the public rose by $0.80 billion, but bank reserves fell overall by only $0.20 billion. Thus, the Fed must have replaced $0.60 billion of lost reserves during the year through open-market purchases. Currency holdings at the end of 1931 were $4.59 billion. To have kept the money supply at the December 1930 value of $44.1 billion, the Fed would have had to ensure that bank deposits equaled $44.1 billion − $4.59 billion, or $39.51 billion. As the reserve-deposit ratio in 1931 was 0.095, this would have required bank reserves of 0.095($39.51 billion), or $3.75 billion, compared to the actual value in December 1931 of $3.11 billion. Thus, to keep the money supply from falling, the Fed would have had to increase bank reserves by $0.64 billion more than it did. The Fed has been criticized for increasing bank reserves by only about half what was needed to keep the money supply from falling. *(LO1)*

12.3 If $r = 0.03$, then consumption is $C = 640 + 0.8(Y - 250) - 400(0.03) = 428 + 0.8Y$, and planned investment is $I^P = 250 - 600(0.03) = 232$. Planned aggregate expenditure is given by

$$PAE = C + I^P + G + NX$$
$$= (428 + 0.8Y) + 232 + 300 + 20$$
$$= 980 + 0.8Y.$$

To find short-run equilibrium output, we can construct a table analogous to Table 11.1. As usual, some trial and error is necessary to find an appropriate range of guesses for output (column 1).

Determination of Short-Run Equilibrium Output			
(1) Output Y	(2) Planned aggregate expenditure $PAE = 980 + 0.8Y$	(3) $Y - PAE$	(4) $Y = PAE$?
4,500	4,580	−80	No
4,600	4,660	−60	No
4,700	4,740	−40	No
4,800	4,820	−20	No
4,900	4,900	0	Yes
5,000	4,980	20	No
5,100	5,060	40	No
5,200	5,140	60	No
5,300	5,220	80	No
5,400	5,300	100	No
5,500	5,380	120	No

Short-run equilibrium output equals 4,900, as that is the only level of output that satisfies the condition $Y = PAE$.

The answer can be obtained more quickly by simply setting $Y = PAE$ and solving for short-run equilibrium output Y. Remembering that $PAE = 980 + 0.8Y$ and substituting for PAE, we get

$$Y = 980 + 0.8Y$$
$$Y(1 - 0.8) = 980$$
$$Y = 980/0.2 = 4,900.$$

So lowering the real interest rate from 5 percent to 3 percent increases short-run equilibrium output from 4,800 to 4,900. *(LO2)*

12.4 When the real interest rate is 5 percent, output is 4,800. Each percentage point reduction in the real interest rate increases autonomous expenditure by 10 units. Since the multiplier in this model is 5, to raise output by 50 units, the real interest rate should be cut by 1 percentage point, from 5 percent to 4 percent. Increasing output by 50 units, to 4,850, eliminates the output gap. *(LO2)*

12.5 If the nominal interest rate is above its equilibrium value, then people are holding more money than they would like. To bring their money holdings down, they will use some of their money to buy interest-bearing assets such as bonds. If everyone is trying to buy bonds, however, the price of bonds will be bid up. An increase in bond prices is equivalent to a fall in market interest rates. As interest rates fall, people will be willing to hold more money. Eventually interest rates will fall enough that people are content to hold the amount of money supplied by the Fed, and the money market will be in equilibrium. *(LO3)*

CHAPTER 13

Aggregate Demand, Aggregate Supply, and Business Cycles

Phillip Spears/Phillip Spears/Getty Images

HOW DO CHANGES IN HOUSE PRICES AFFECT CONSUMER SPENDING AND THE ECONOMY?

In December 2007, the U.S. economy entered its worst recession in 25 years. The depth of the recession, as measured by factors such as lost output and high unemployment, along with the financial panic that swept through the world in fall 2008, has led some to call it the Great Recession.

Three significant events are usually cited as causes of the Great Recession. First, the largest house price bubble in American history burst in July 2006 and average home prices fell 30 percent in the next 18 months. Higher home values had allowed households to increase their consumption, and when the housing bubble burst, consumer spending dropped as well. Second, a financial panic swept through the United States and Europe in fall 2008. The panic was in part a product of the collapsing house price bubble, but it had independent effects on the economy. Interest rates spiked during the crisis, making it difficult and even impossible for firms to borrow funds for investment spending. Third, an oil price shock sent the price of oil to its highest level in history. In summer 2008, for instance, gas prices reached historic highs, hitting $4 per gallon throughout the United States.

How did these factors trigger a deep recession? In this chapter, we develop the *aggregate demand–aggregate supply* (AD-AS) *model.* This model provides a framework for evaluating the possible causes of the Great Recession and helps us understand business cycles more generally. We build the model in three steps. First, we develop aggregate demand in a way that connects it to the analysis of the two chapters on planned aggregate expenditure, output, and the inflation rate, and their relationships with fiscal and monetary policy. Second, we develop aggregate supply by looking at how firms make price-setting decisions in reaction to changes in the demand for their products. Third, we put aggregate demand and aggregate supply together to see how output and the inflation rate are determined simultaneously.

Once we have a working understanding of the aggregate demand–aggregate supply model, we can put the model to work analyzing business cycles and examining how stabilization policy can be used to mitigate their effects. Along the way, we will pay close attention to the events of the past few years and how these events led to the Great Recession.

THE AGGREGATE DEMAND–AGGREGATE SUPPLY MODEL: A BRIEF OVERVIEW

The aggregate demand–aggregate supply (*AD-AS*) model is one of the most useful models in macroeconomics. It has two distinct advantages over the basic Keynesian model. First, we can use it to analyze fluctuations in both output *and* the inflation rate. In the basic Keynesian model we could not explain changes in inflation since our basic assumption was that the price level remained fixed. Second, the basic Keynesian model is a model of the short run, while the *AD-AS* model applies to both the short run and the long run.

Figure 13.1 shows the aggregate demand–aggregate supply (*AD-AS*) diagram. This is the tool we will use to apply the *AD-AS* model to real-world situations. The current inflation rate π is on the vertical axis and the current level of output Y is on the horizontal axis. The aggregate demand (*AD*) curve shows the relationship between planned

FIGURE 13.1

The Aggregate Demand–Aggregate Supply Diagram.

The aggregate demand (*AD*) curve slopes downward because a fall in the inflation rate causes an increase in planned spending and output. The aggregate supply (*AS*) curve is upward-sloping because an increase in the quantity of output supplied causes an increase in the inflation rate. The economy is in long-run equilibrium because the *AD* and *AS* curves intersect at the level of potential GDP Y^*.

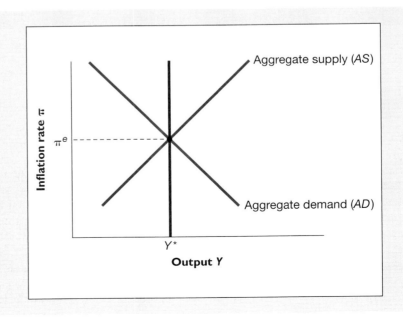

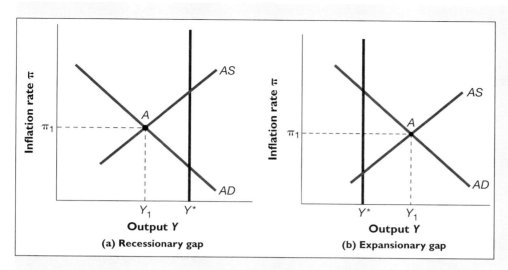

FIGURE 13.2
Short-Run Equilibrium.
The economy is in short-run equilibrium when the *AD* curve and the *AS* curve intersect at an output level that is below or above potential output. In panel (a), there is a recessionary gap because the current level of output Y_1 is below potential output Y^*. In panel (b), there is an expansionary gap because the current level of output Y_1 is above potential output Y^*.

spending and the inflation rate, holding all other factors constant. The aggregate supply (*AS*) curve shows the relationship between the amount of output firms want to produce and the inflation rate, holding all other factors constant. Potential output Y^* is shown in order to measure output gaps.

The economy shown in Figure 13.1 is in **long-run equilibrium.** An economy is in long-run equilibrium when the *AD* and *AS* curves intersect at potential output Y^*. The inflation rate in a long-run equilibrium is called the expected inflation rate π^e since this is the inflation rate that consumers, businesses, and government believe will prevail in the long run.

Figure 13.2 shows an economy in **short-run equilibrium.** A short-run equilibrium is a situation where the *AD* and *AS* curves intersect at a level of real GDP that is above or below potential. Shifts in either the *AD* curve or *AS* curve (or both) can push the economy out of long-run equilibrium. You can see this by comparing Figure 13.1 with Figure 13.2. Similarly, changes in aggregate demand and aggregate supply can move the economy from a short-run equilibrium toward a long-run equilibrium.

This is how we can use the *AD-AS* model to explain business cycles: shifts in the *AD* and *AS* curves push the economy out of long-run equilibrium, and shifts in the *AD* and *AS* curves bring the economy back as well. In the next two sections, we work through the reasoning behind the *AD* curve and the *AS* curve separately so that you understand why they are shaped the way that they are and why they shift. We can then apply the *AD-AS* model to real-world situations like the Great Recession.

long-run equilibrium a situation in which the *AD* and *AS* curves intersect at potential output Y^*

short-run equilibrium a situation where the *AD* and *AS* curves intersect at a level of real GDP that is above or below potential

THE AGGREGATE DEMAND CURVE

The **aggregate demand (*AD*)** curve shows the amount of output consumers, firms, government, and customers abroad want to purchase at each inflation rate, holding all other factors constant. In particular, the *AD* curve shows that, as the inflation rate rises, the quantity of planned spending and output demanded falls, holding other factors constant. Figure 13.3 shows a typical *AD* curve.

We need to answer two questions about the *AD* curve:

• Why does the *AD* curve slope downward?

• What factors shift the *AD* curve?

aggregate demand (*AD*) curve a curve that shows the amount of output consumers, firms, government, and customers abroad want to purchase at each inflation rate, holding all other factors constant

FIGURE 13.3

The Aggregate Demand (AD) Curve.

The *AD* curve slopes downward because a decrease in the inflation rate increases planned consumption, investment, and net exports, causing short-run output to rise.

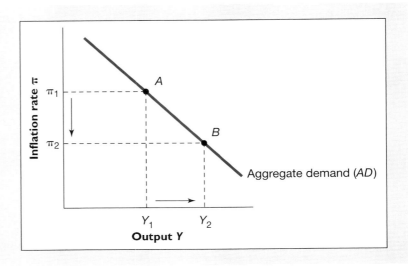

WHY DOES THE *AD* CURVE SLOPE DOWNWARD?

The *AD* curve slopes downward because, holding all else constant, an increase in the inflation rate π causes planned consumption C, investment I^P, and net exports NX to fall, resulting in decreased levels of planned spending *PAE* and short-run output Y. We can express this relationship as follows:

$$\uparrow \pi \Rightarrow \downarrow \text{planned } C, I^P, \text{ and } NX \Rightarrow \downarrow PAE \Rightarrow (\text{via the multiplier}) \downarrow Y.$$

We have already worked through the last three parts of this relationship. Specifically, we defined planned aggregate expenditure (*PAE*) as

$$PAE = C + I^P + G + NX.$$

Lower levels of planned consumption, investment, government spending, or net exports reduce planned spending. In the chapters on fiscal and monetary policy, we used the basic Keynesian model to show that a decrease in planned spending leads, through the multiplier, to a decrease in short-run equilibrium output. We can thus focus on the relationship between the inflation rate and the components of planned spending, knowing that a change in any of these components results in a change in short-run output. (For the moment, we ignore government spending as it is mostly determined by elected officials. We return to the effects of changes in government spending below.)

The inflation rate and planned spending are connected through the Federal Reserve's *monetary policy rule*. In particular, when inflation rises, the Federal Reserve increases the real interest rate, and a higher real interest rate causes consumption, investment, and net exports to fall. Similarly, when inflation falls, the Federal Reserve decreases the real interest rate, and a lower real interest rate causes consumption, investment, and net exports to rise.

The Fed's Monetary Policy Rule

monetary policy rule
a rule that describes how a central bank, like the Fed, takes action in response to changes in the state of the economy

A **monetary policy rule** describes how a central bank, like the Fed, takes action in response to changes in the state of the economy.

We will work with a particularly simple monetary policy rule: *When inflation rises, the Fed increases the real interest rate, and when inflation falls, the Fed decreases the real interest rate.* In symbols, we have

$$\uparrow \pi \Rightarrow \uparrow r \text{ and } \downarrow \pi \Rightarrow \downarrow r.$$

We actually developed this relationship in the previous chapter but did not call it a rule.[1] Let's review this analysis in order to understand why the Fed behaves this way. We will also see why the *AD* curve is sloped downward.

One of the primary responsibilities of the Fed is to maintain a low and stable rate of inflation. For example, in recent years, the Fed has tried to keep inflation in the United States in the range of 2 to 3 percent. How does the Fed carry out this responsibility? By using monetary policy to minimize output gaps. In particular, when the inflation rate π rises due to an expansionary gap, the Federal Reserve increases the real interest rate r in order to reduce consumption C and investment I. The decrease in consumption and investment reduces planned aggregate expenditure *PAE* and, through the multiplier process, this leads to a decrease in equilibrium output Y. The output gap starts to close as actual output Y falls relative to potential output Y^*. In symbols, we have

$$\uparrow \pi \Rightarrow \uparrow r \Rightarrow \downarrow \text{ planned } C \text{ and planned } I \Rightarrow \downarrow PAE \Rightarrow \text{(via the multiplier)} \downarrow Y.$$

Similarly, when a recessionary gap opens, inflation falls. The Federal Reserve reacts to the fall in inflation by decreasing the real interest rate, causing consumption, investment, and equilibrium output to rise. In symbols, we have

$$\downarrow \pi \Rightarrow \downarrow r \Rightarrow \uparrow \text{ planned } C \text{ and planned } I \Rightarrow \uparrow PAE \Rightarrow \text{(via the multiplier)} \uparrow Y.$$

We have now made the connection between change in inflation and the Fed's response in terms of changes in the real interest rate. Notice that we have also made a connection between inflation and output: using the endpoints of the two logic chains, we have

$$\uparrow \pi \Rightarrow \downarrow Y$$

and

$$\downarrow \pi \Rightarrow \uparrow Y.$$

We have thus shown that the *AD* curve must slope downward as shown in Figure 13.3.

WHAT FACTORS SHIFT THE *AD* CURVE?

The aggregate demand curve shows how the amount of planned spending and output varies with the inflation rate, holding all other factors constant. We need to examine these other factors to understand how and why they cause the *AD* curve to shift.

Before we dive into the details, we need some terminology. We did this in the chapter covering supply and demand, when we introduced the demand curve for a single market and distinguished between a change in the quantity demanded and a change in demand. Here, we need to focus on shifts in the *AD* curve. We define a **change in aggregate demand** as a shift of the *AD* curve.

Specifically, an increase in aggregate demand is a rightward shift in the *AD* curve, and a decrease in aggregate demand is a leftward shift of the *AD* curve. This is illustrated in Figure 13.4 for both an increase and a decrease in aggregate demand. We will use this language through the rest of the chapter, and we will refer to Figure 13.4 throughout this section.

change in aggregate demand a shift of the *AD* curve

Demand Shocks

Planned spending is affected by changes in output (e.g., consumption is a function of real GDP) and the inflation rate (e.g., consumption and investment rise or fall when the Fed reacts to a change in inflation by raising or lowering the real interest rate). However, many factors other than output or the inflation rate can have an effect on spending. For

[1]See the sections "The Fed Fights a Recession" and "The Fed Fights Inflation" in the chapter *Monetary Policy and the Federal Reserve*.

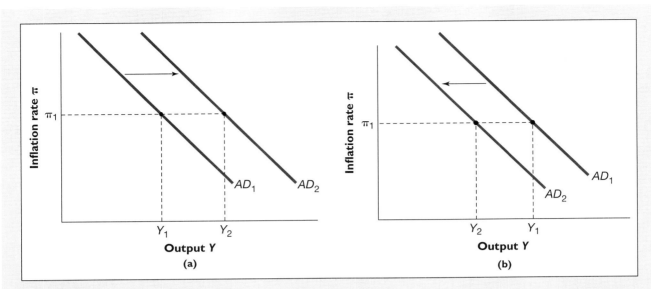

FIGURE 13.4

A Change in Aggregate Demand.

A change in aggregate demand is a shift of the *AD* curve. Panel (a) shows an increase in aggregate demand, and panel (b) shows a decrease in aggregate demand.

example, changes in consumer confidence and consumers' real wealth affect consumption spending even if there has been no change in output or the inflation rate. Decreased business confidence or new technological opportunities may lead firms to decrease or increase their planned investment.

demand shocks changes in planned spending that are not caused by changes in output or the inflation rate

Changes in planned spending that are not caused by changes in output or the inflation rate are called **demand shocks.** These events are termed shocks because they were not anticipated by households, businesses, government, or foreign buyers when those entities made their decisions about planned spending. Further, since demand shocks affect planned spending, they affect short-run output as well and therefore increase or decrease aggregate demand. Thus, demand shocks are one cause of shifts in the *AD* curve.

| **House Prices and Demand Shocks** | **EXAMPLE 13.1** |

Does an increase in house prices affect aggregate demand?

Suppose that the average price of homes begins to rise, as it did between 1999 and 2006 in the U.S. This will increase real household wealth and therefore cause consumption and planned aggregate expenditure to rise as well. How does this affect aggregate demand?

Go to Figure 13.4(a) and start with output Y_1 and inflation rate π_1. The increase in house prices causes planned expenditure to rise, which in turn raises output as well. Real GDP therefore moves from Y_1 to Y_2 while the inflation rate remains at π_1. Since we chose π_1 arbitrarily, output increases at every inflation rate and the *AD* curve shifts from AD_1 to AD_2. Hence, an increase in house prices increases aggregate demand.

The house price increase in Example 13.1(a) is called a *positive demand shock* because the *AD* curve shifts to the right as a result of the shock. A *negative demand shock* has the opposite effect and shifts the *AD* curve to the left. This is shown in Figure 13.4(b).

CONCEPT CHECK 13.1

Suppose that firms become extremely pessimistic about their business prospects over the next year or so. Is this a demand shock? If so, is it positive or negative? Explain your reasoning.

Stabilization Policy

Stabilization policies are government policies used to affect planned aggregate expenditure with the objective of eliminating output gaps. Recall that the two major tools of stabilization policy are fiscal policy and monetary policy. Fiscal policy refers to decisions about how much the government spends and how much tax revenue it collects. Monetary policy refers to decisions about the size of the money supply and hence the level of interest rates in the economy.

Stabilization policy in general, and changes in fiscal policy and monetary policy in particular, affects aggregate demand and shifts the *AD* curve. The Great Recession has seen active use of both fiscal and monetary policy, so it is worth taking a moment to understand how each affects aggregate demand.

Fiscal Policy: Changes in Government Spending and Taxes Fiscal policy affects the level of government purchases and taxes collected and thus influences total spending and output. For example, suppose that the government reduces its spending in order to decrease the budget deficit. This will cause spending to decrease at any given inflation rate and shift the *AD* curve to the left [as shown in Figure 13.4(b)]. Increases in government spending shift the *AD* curve to the right.

Changes in taxes also shift the *AD* curve. Suppose that the government cuts taxes; recall that this raises households' disposable income, leading them to increase their consumption spending. The higher level of consumption spending causes an increase in planned spending and real GDP. This process works at any given inflation rate, so a tax cut causes the *AD* curve to shift to the right as shown in Figure 13.4(a). Tax increases have the opposite effect: Disposable income falls, consumption and output fall, and the *AD* curve shifts to the left as in Figure 13.4(b).

Monetary Policy: Changes in the Real Interest Rate without Changes in Inflation We demonstrated earlier that the Fed's monetary policy rule is the reason why the *AD* curve slopes down. In this analysis, we implicitly assumed that the Fed had a target rate of inflation π^* and that the Fed increased the real interest rate when inflation rose above π^* and decreased the real interest rate when inflation fell below π^*. The Fed is, however, free to change the real interest rate even when inflation is stable. There are two possible reasons why the Feb might do this.

The first reason is that the Fed may decide to change its current target for the inflation rate. For instance, suppose the Fed considers its current target rate of inflation to be too high. To reduce inflation, the Fed needs to reduce planned spending and output by increasing the real interest rate. In terms of Figure 13.4(b), this means that, at an inflation rate such as π_1, output will fall from Y_1 to Y_2. We chose the inflation rate π_1 arbitrarily, so this means that a reduction in the Fed's inflation target will shift the *AD* curve to the left.

Now consider a situation in which the Fed realizes that its current target rate of inflation is too low. The Fed can now stimulate spending by decreasing the real interest rate. Using Figure 13.4(a), this means that, at inflation rate π_1, output will rise from Y_1 to Y_2. As in the previous case we chose the inflation rate π_1 arbitrarily, so we have demonstrated that an increase in the Fed's inflation target will shift the *AD* curve to the right.

The second reason the Fed may change interest rates is that it is concerned about the level of output itself relative to potential. For example, if the Fed believes that the current level of output is too low (e.g., the economy is in a deep recession), it can decrease the real interest rate and cause consumption, investment, and output to rise. This corresponds, once again, with the situation in Figure 13.4(a).

Stabilization Policy: Summarizing Its Effects on Aggregate Demand Let's summarize how the government can influence aggregate demand through stabilization policy. First, suppose that the government wants to increase aggregate demand. There are three tools it can employ (alone or in combination with one another):

- Increase government spending;
- Cut taxes;
- Decrease the real interest rate.

Second, if the government wants to decrease aggregate demand, it also has three options:

- Decrease government spending;
- Raise taxes;
- Increase the real interest rate.

RECAP	THE AGGREGATE DEMAND (*AD*) CURVE

- The aggregate demand (*AD*) curve shows the amount of output consumers, firms, government, and customers abroad want to purchase at each inflation rate, holding all other factors constant.

- The *AD* curve slopes downward because of the Fed's monetary policy rule: Higher inflation leads the Fed to raise the real interest rate, which reduces spending and thus short-run equilibrium output.

- Demand shocks (changes in planned spending that are not caused by changes in output or the inflation rate) shift the *AD* curve. Positive demand shocks shift the *AD* curve to the right, while negative demand shocks shift the *AD* curve to the left.

- Stabilization policy, that is, the use of fiscal and monetary policy to close output gaps, shifts the *AD* curve. Higher levels of government spending, lower taxes, and lower interest rates all increase aggregate demand, while decreased government spending, higher taxes, and higher interest rates all decrease aggregate demand.

THE AGGREGATE SUPPLY CURVE

So far, we have focused on the aggregate demand *(AD)* curve. The *AD* curve embodies the economic reasoning we developed in the two chapters on fiscal and monetary policy. Specifically, the basic Keynesian model tells us that, at a given price level, planned aggregate expenditure must equal short-run equilibrium output. The *AD* curve builds on this model and shows that when the inflation rate rises, the level of planned aggregate expenditure and short-run output falls, and when the inflation rate falls, planned spending and output rise.

This leaves us with an important, unanswered question: *What factors cause the inflation rate to rise or fall?* In this section, we develop the **aggregate supply (*AS*) curve** to help us answer this question. The *AS* curve shows the relationship between the level of output (real GDP) firms want to produce and the inflation rate, holding all other factors constant. Once we have worked through the details of the *AS* curve, we can use it along with the *AD* curve to analyze why the inflation rate rises and falls. A typical *AS* curve is shown in Figure 13.5.

aggregate supply (*AS*) curve a curve that shows the relationship between the amount of output firms want to produce and the inflation rate, holding all other factors constant

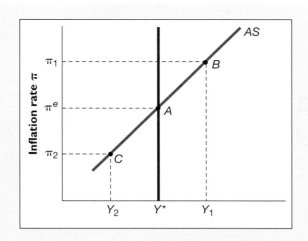

FIGURE 13.5

The Aggregate Supply (AS) Curve.

The *AS* curve slopes upward because, when firms increase their output, the inflation rate rises.

Just as we did with the aggregate demand (*AD*) curve, we must answer two questions about the *AS* curve:

- Why does the *AS* curve slope upward?

- What causes the *AS* curve to shift?

WHY DOES THE *AS* CURVE SLOPE UPWARD?

When we first developed the basic Keynesian model (in the chapter *Spending, Output, and Fiscal Policy*), we made a key assumption: In the short run, firms meet the demand for their products at preset prices. That is, firms do not always respond to changes in the demand for their products by changing their prices. Rather, many firms set their prices for some period and then meet the demand at those prices. We argued that this assumption is generally realistic over short periods of time due to a phenomenon known as menu costs. *Menu costs* refer to the fact that firms must incur costs in order to change their prices. Examples we gave in the chapter *Spending, Output, and Fiscal Policy* included the case of a restaurant, where the menu cost is literally the cost of printing up a new menu, and the cost a clothing store faces when it has to retag all its merchandise or reprogram its computer when the manager changes prices.

We can now relax the assumption that firms sell all of their output at preset prices and examine the relationship between output and the inflation rate. To do this, we must look at two important reasons why this relationship exists: inflation inertia and output gaps.

Inflation Inertia

Physicists have noted that a body will tend to keep moving at a constant speed and direction unless it is acted upon by some outside force—a tendency they refer to as inertia. Applying this concept to economics, many observers have noted that inflation seems to be inertial, in the sense that it tends to remain roughly constant as long as the economy is at potential output and there are no external shocks to the price level.

Economists refer to this phenomenon as *inflation inertia*. If the rate of inflation in one year is 2 percent, it may be 3 percent or even 4 percent in the next year. But unless the nation experiences very unusual economic conditions, inflation is unlikely to rise to 6 percent or 8 percent or fall to -2 percent in the following year. This relatively sluggish behavior contrasts sharply with the behavior of economic variables such as stock prices or commodity prices, which can change rapidly from day to day. For example, oil prices might well rise by 20 percent over the course of a year and then fall 20 percent over the next year. Yet since about 1992, the U.S. inflation rate has generally remained in the range of 2–4 percent per year.

Why does inflation tend to adjust relatively slowly in modern industrial economies? To answer this question, we must consider two closely related factors that play an important role in determining the inflation rate: the behavior of the public's *inflation expectations* and the existence of *long-term wage and price contracts.*

Inflation Expectations   Let's first consider the public's expectations about inflation. In negotiating future wages and prices, both buyers and sellers take into account the rate of inflation they expect to prevail in the next few years. As a result, today's *expectations* of future inflation may help to determine the future inflation rate. Suppose, for example, that office worker Fred and his boss Colleen agree that Fred's performance this past year justifies an increase of 2 percent in his real wage for next year. What *nominal,* or dollar, wage increase should they agree on? If Fred believes that inflation is likely to be 3 percent over the next year, he will ask for a 5 percent increase in his nominal wage to obtain a 2 percent increase in his real wage. If Colleen agrees that inflation is likely to be 3 percent, she should be willing to go along with a 5 percent nominal increase, knowing that it implies only a 2 percent increase in Fred's real wage. Thus, the rate at which Fred and Colleen *expect* prices to rise affects the rate at which at least one price—Fred's nominal wage—*actually* rises.

A similar dynamic affects the contracts for production inputs other than labor. For example, if Colleen is negotiating with her office supply company, the prices she will agree to pay for next year's deliveries of copy paper and staples will depend on what she expects the inflation rate to be. If Colleen anticipates that the price of office supplies will not change relative to the prices of other goods and services, and that the general inflation rate will be 3 percent, then she should be willing to agree to a 3 percent increase in the price of office supplies. On the other hand, if she expects the general inflation rate to be 6 percent, then she will agree to pay 6 percent more for copy paper and staples next year, knowing that a nominal increase of 6 percent implies no change in the price of office supplies relative to other goods and services.

Economywide, then, the higher the expected rate of inflation, the more nominal wages and the cost of other inputs will tend to rise. But if wages and other costs of production grow rapidly in response to expected inflation, firms will have to raise their prices rapidly as well in order to cover their costs. Thus, a high rate of expected inflation tends to lead to a high rate of *actual* inflation. Similarly, if expected inflation is low, leading wages and other costs to rise relatively slowly, actual inflation should be low as well.

CONCEPT CHECK 13.2

Assume that employers and workers agree that real wages should rise by 2 percent next year.

a.   If inflation is expected to be 2 percent next year, what will happen to nominal wages next year?

b.   If inflation is expected to be 4 percent next year, rather than 2 percent, what will happen to nominal wages next year?

c.   Use your answers from parts a and b to explain how an increase in expected inflation will affect the following year's actual rate of inflation.

The conclusion that actual inflation is partially determined by expected inflation raises the question of what determines inflation expectations. To a great extent, people's expectations are influenced by their recent experience. If inflation has been low and stable for some time, people are likely to expect it to continue to be low. But if inflation has recently been high, people will expect it to continue to be high. If inflation has been unpredictable, alternating between low and high levels, the public's expectations will likewise tend to be volatile, rising or falling with news or rumors about economic conditions or economic policy.

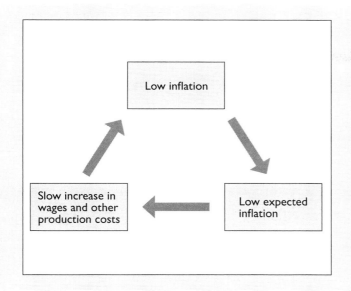

FIGURE 13.6

A Virtuous Circle of Low Inflation and Low Expected Inflation.

Low inflation leads people to expect low inflation in the future. As a result, they agree to accept small increases in wages and in the prices of the goods and services they supply, which keeps inflation—and expected inflation—low. In a similar way, high inflation leads people to expect high inflation, which in turn tends to produce high inflation.

Figure 13.6 illustrates schematically how low and stable inflation may tend to be self-perpetuating. As the figure shows, if inflation has been low for some time, people will continue to expect low inflation. Increases in nominal wages and other production costs thus will tend to be small. If firms raise prices only enough to cover costs, then actual inflation will be low, as expected. This low actual rate in turn will promote low expected inflation, perpetuating the "virtuous circle."

The same logic applies in reverse in an economy with high inflation: A persistently high inflation rate leads the public to expect high inflation, resulting in higher increases in nominal wages and other production costs. This in turn contributes to a high rate of actual inflation, and so on in a vicious circle. This role of inflation expectations in the determination of wage and price increases helps to explain why inflation often seems to adjust slowly.

Long-Term Wage and Price Contracts The role of inflation expectations in inflation inertia is strengthened by a second key element, the existence of long-term wage and price contracts. Union wage contracts, for example, often extend for three years into the future. Likewise, contracts that set the prices manufacturing firms pay for parts and raw materials often cover several years.

Long-term contracts serve to "build in" wage and price increases that depend on inflation expectations at the time the contracts were signed. For example, a union negotiating in a high-inflation environment is much more likely to demand a rapid increase in nominal wages over the life of the contract than would a union in an economy in which prices are stable.

To summarize, in the absence of external shocks, inflation tends to remain relatively stable over time—at least in low-inflation industrial economies like that of the United States. In other words, inflation is inertial (or, as some people put it, "sticky"). Inflation tends to be inertial for two main reasons. The first is the behavior of people's expectations of inflation. A low inflation rate leads people to expect low inflation in the future, which results in reduced pressure for wage and price increases. Secondly, a high inflation rate leads people to expect high inflation in the future, resulting in more rapid increases in wages and prices. The effects of expectations are reinforced by the existence of long-term wage and price contracts, which is the second reason inflation tends to be stable over time. Long-term contracts tend to build in the effects of people's inflation expectations.

CONCEPT CHECK 13.3

Using Figure 13.6, discuss why the Federal Reserve has a strong incentive to maintain a low inflation rate in the economy.

Output Gaps and Inflation

Just as a physical object will change speed if it is acted on by outside forces, so various economic forces can change the rate of inflation. An important factor influencing the rate of inflation is the output gap, which we defined in the chapter *Short-Term Economic Fluctuations* as the difference between the economy's actual output and its potential output, relative to potential output, at a point in time. At a particular time, the level of short-run equilibrium output may happen to equal the economy's long-run productive capacity, or potential output. But that is not necessarily the case. Output may exceed potential output, giving rise to an expansionary gap, or it may fall short of potential output, producing a recessionary gap. Let's consider what happens to inflation in each of these three possible cases: no output gap, an expansionary gap, and a recessionary gap.

No Output Gap: $Y = Y^*$ If actual output equals potential output, then by definition there is no output gap. When the output gap is zero, firms are satisfied in the sense that their sales equal their maximum sustainable production rates. As a result, firms have no incentive to either reduce or increase their prices relative to the prices of other goods and services. However, the fact that firms are satisfied with their sales does not imply that inflation—the rate of change in the overall price level—is zero.

To see why, let's go back to the idea of inflation inertia. Suppose that inflation has recently been steady at 3 percent per year, so that the public has come to expect an inflation rate of 3 percent per year. If the public's inflation expectations are reflected in the wage and price increases agreed to in long-term contracts, then firms will find their labor and materials costs are rising at 3 percent per year. To cover their costs, firms will need to raise their prices by 3 percent per year. Note that if all firms are increasing their prices by 3 percent per year, the relative prices of various goods and services in the economy—say, the price of ice cream relative to the price of a taxi ride—will not change. Nevertheless, the economywide rate of inflation equals 3 percent, the same as in previous years. We conclude that, if the output gap is zero, the rate of inflation will tend to remain the same.

Expansionary Gap: $Y > Y^*$ Suppose now that an expansionary gap exists, so that most firms' sales exceed their maximum sustainable production rates. As we might expect in situations in which the quantity demanded exceeds the quantity firms desire to supply, firms will ultimately respond by trying to increase their relative prices. To do so, they will increase their prices by more than the increase in their costs. If all firms behave this way, then the inflation rate will begin to rise more rapidly than before. Thus, when an expansionary gap exists, the rate of inflation will tend to increase.

Recessionary Gap: $Y < Y^*$ Finally, if a recessionary gap exists, firms will be selling an amount less than their capacity to produce, and they will have an incentive to cut their relative prices so they can sell more. In this case, firms will raise their prices less than needed to cover fully their increases in costs, as determined by the existing inflation rate. As a result, when a recessionary gap exists, the rate of inflation will tend to decrease.

DERIVING THE *AS* CURVE: GRAPHICAL ANALYSIS

We can now derive the *AS* curve by combining inflation inertia and the behavior of inflation when there are output gaps. In particular, we can summarize what we have learned in the following equation:

Current inflation (π) = Expected inflation (π^e)

$\qquad\qquad$ + Change in inflation caused by an output gap.

We label the first term on the right-hand side of the equation as expected inflation, rather than inflation inertia, because, as we discussed above, the primary cause of inflation inertia is agents' expectations of future inflation.

Let's begin with the situation where there is no output gap. Then,

$$\text{Current inflation } (\pi_1) = \text{Expected inflation } (\pi^e).$$

We show this situation as point *A* in Figure 13.7. Next, suppose that the economy has an expansionary gap. In this situation, the inflation rate will be equal to the amount of inertia in the economy plus some additional amount caused by the economy being above potential output level, that is,

$$\text{Current inflation } (\pi_2) > \text{Expected inflation } (\pi^e).$$

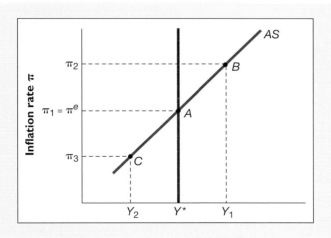

FIGURE 13.7

Deriving the *AS* Curve.

At point *A*, output is equal to potential output and so inflation is equal to expected inflation ($\pi_1 = \pi^e$). At point *B*, output is above potential, so inflation π_2 is above its expected level. At point *C*, output is below potential, so inflation π_3 is below its expected level.

This is shown as point *B* in Figure 13.7. Finally, suppose that there is a recessionary gap. In this case,

$$\text{Current inflation } (\pi_3) < \text{Expected inflation } (\pi^e).$$

Current inflation is lower than expected inflation because the recessionary gap encourages firms to reduce their prices and thus puts downward pressure on the inflation rate. Points *A, B,* and *C* in Figure 13.7 thus trace out the *AS* curve at the expected inflation level of π^e.

WHAT CAUSES THE *AS* CURVE TO SHIFT?

The aggregate supply (*AS*) curve shows the relationship between the amount of output firms want to produce and the inflation rate, holding all other factors constant. As we did with the *AD* curve, we next need to examine these other factors and understand how and why they cause the *AS* curve to shift.

Just as with aggregate demand, we need to cover some terms. A **change in aggregate supply** is a shift of the *AS* curve. An increase in aggregate supply is a rightward shift in the *AS* curve and a decrease in aggregate supply is shown by a leftward shift of the *AS* curve. Both cases are shown in Figure 13.8.

change in aggregate supply
a shift of the *AS* curve

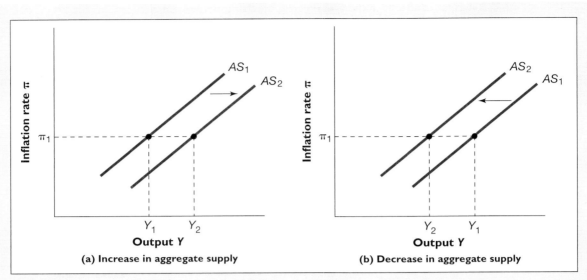

FIGURE 13.8

A Change in Aggregate Supply.

A change in aggregate supply is a shift of the *AS* curve. Panel (a) shows an increase in aggregate supply; panel (b) shows a decrease in aggregate supply.

Changes in Available Resources and Technology

If more resources become available in an economy, then firms can increase their capacity by hiring more labor, capital, natural resources, or some combination of all three at the given inflation rate. This is shown in Figure 13.8(a), where the economy begins at output Y_1 and inflation rate π_1, and output is increased to Y_2 while the inflation rate remains at π_1. Our choice of π_1 was entirely arbitrary, so the same reasoning applies to any inflation rate we choose, meaning that the entire *AS* curve shifts out when firms have more resources available to them.

Changes in technology have the same effect on aggregate supply as changes in resources. For example, suppose that, instead of hiring more workers or purchasing more machines, a manufacturer figures out a way to use its workers and machines more efficiently. This means that it can produce more using the same resources, and sell its production at the same prices as before. In general, technological improvements shift the *AS* curve outward.

Changes in Inflation Expectations

We discussed earlier how inflation expectations are formed and how either a virtuous or vicious cycle reinforces these expectations. (See Figure 13.6.) Why might inflation expectations change? What happens to the *AS* curve when inflation expectations change?

Suppose that wages and prices in certain industries begin to rise faster than workers and firms thought they would rise. This will cause the actual rate of inflation to be higher than what was expected and can lead people to revise upward their expected rate of inflation. Figure 13.9 shows what happens to the *AS* curve when expected inflation rises. Originally, AS_1 is the *AS* curve for the economy and expected inflation is at π^e_1. After inflation expectations rise, expected inflation is at π^e_2; the entire *AS* curve thus shifts left because output gaps still have the same effect on actual inflation.

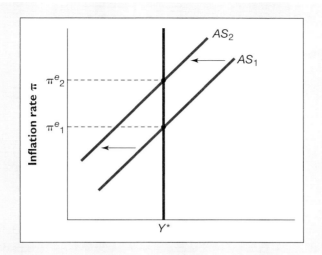

FIGURE 13.9

An Increase in Expected Inflation.

An increase in expected inflation from π^e_1 to π^e_2 shifts the *AS* curve left. Similarly, a decrease in expected inflation would shift the *AS* curve right.

CONCEPT CHECK 13.4

Draw an *AS* curve, being sure to label the current level of expected inflation. How will the *AS* curve be affected if inflation expectations fall?

Inflation Shocks

The second factor that can affect the inflation rate is a shock that directly affects prices, which we will refer to as an *inflation shock*. An inflation shock is a sudden change in the normal behavior of inflation, unrelated to the nation's output gap. A large increase in the price of imported oil, for example, raises the price of gasoline, heating oil, and other fuels, as well as of goods made with oil or services using oil.

A famous example of an inflation shock is the sudden increase in the price of oil that took place in the early 1970s. In late 1973, at the time of the Yom Kippur War between Israel and a coalition of Arab nations, the Organization of Petroleum Exporting Countries (OPEC) dramatically cut its supplies of crude oil to the industrialized nations, quadrupling world oil prices in a matter of months. The sharp increase in oil prices was quickly transferred to the price of gasoline, heating oil, and goods and services that were heavily dependent on oil, such as air travel. The effects of the oil price increase, together with agricultural shortages that increased the price of food, contributed to a significant rise in the overall U.S. inflation rate in 1974.

An inflation shock that causes an increase in inflation, like the large rise in oil prices in 1973, is called an *adverse* inflation shock and shifts the *AS* curve left. An inflation shock that reduces inflation, such as the sharp decline in oil prices that occurred in 1986, is called a *favorable* inflation shock and shifts the *AS* curve right.

inflation shock a sudden change in the normal behavior of inflation, unrelated to the nation's output gap

RECAP	THE AGGREGATE SUPPLY (AS) CURVE

- The aggregate supply (*AS*) curve shows the relationship between the amount of output firms want to produce and the inflation rate, holding all other factors constant.
- The *AS* curve slopes upward because actual inflation is related to expected inflation and also to the gap between actual output and potential output: When output is below potential, actual inflation is below expected inflation, and when output is above potential, actual inflation is above expected inflation.
- Changes in available resources and technology and changes in expected inflation shift the *AS* curve.
- Inflation shocks also shift the *AS* curve. Adverse inflation shocks shift the *AS* curve to the left and favorable inflation shocks shift the *AS* curve to the right.

UNDERSTANDING BUSINESS CYCLES

Now that you understand the basics of the *AD* curve and the *AS* curve we can put them together to analyze business cycles. Specifically, we will use the *AD-AS* model to answer two questions:

1. What are the fundamental causes of business cycles?

2. Is there a role for stabilization policy?

We address the first question in this section and then ask the second in the following section.

Let's return to Figures 13.1 and 13.2. Figure 13.1 shows the economy in long-run equilibrium: Output is at potential Y^* and the inflation rate is at its expected level π^e_1. Figure 13.2 shows the economy in short-run equilibrium, with panel (a) illustrating a recessionary gap and panel (b) displaying an expansionary gap. The question "What are the fundamental causes of business cycles?" can thus be rephrased as follows: What factors move the economy from the situation in Figure 13.1 to one of the scenarios in Figure 13.2? The short answer is that shifts in the *AD* curve and the *AS* curve push the economy out of long-run equilibrium and into either a recessionary gap or an expansionary gap. We examine each of these possibilities in turn.

DEMAND SHOCKS: SHIFTS IN THE *AD* CURVE

Figure 13.10 illustrates how shifts in the *AD* curve cause business cycles. Figure 13.10(a) shows the *AD* curve shifting to the left and opening a recessionary gap. By contrast, in Figure 13.10(b), the *AD* curve shifts to the right and opens an expansionary gap.

What would cause the *AD* curve to shift and push the economy out of long-run equilibrium? We identified three possibilities earlier in this chapter: demand shocks, changes in fiscal policy, and changes in monetary policy. Economists have found that demand shocks are the most common cause of business cycles that are induced by *AD* shifts. The following example illustrates this point.

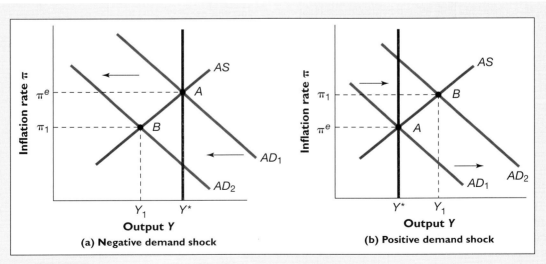

FIGURE 13.10

Demand Shocks and Business Cycles.
The economy begins in long-run equilibrium in each panel. Panel (a) shows a recessionary gap: A negative demand shock shifts the *AD* curve to the left, reducing both output (from Y^* to Y_1) and the inflation rate (from π^e to π_1). Panel (b) shows an expansionary gap: A positive demand shock shifts the *AD* curve to the right, increasing both output (from Y^* to Y_1) and the inflation rate (from π^e to π_1).

| The Impact of the Dot-Com Bubble on the U.S. Economy | EXAMPLE 13.2 |

How did the dot-com bubble affect the U.S. economy?

The dot-com bubble was a stock market boom that took place between 1995 and 2000. One of the driving forces of the boom was new stock issues by Internet companies such as Netscape.com, AOL.com, and Amazon.com. The Standard and Poor's (S&P) 500 stock index approximately doubled during this period, leading to a large increase in household wealth. This led to an increase in aggregate demand like that shown in Figure 13.10(b) and an expansionary gap.

The dot-com bubble burst in March 2000. By fall 2002, most of the gains reaped during the dot-com bubble had been wiped out and household wealth was greatly reduced. The result was a decrease in aggregate demand, like that shown in Figure 13.10(a), that caused the 2001 recession.

INFLATION SHOCKS: SHIFTS IN THE *AS* CURVE

Shifts in the *AS* curve can also cause business cycles, as shown in Figure 13.11. Figure 13.11(a) shows the *AS* curve shifting to the left and opening a recessionary gap, while Figure 13.11(b) shows the *AS* curve shifting to the right and opening an expansionary gap.

Changes in available resources and technology, changes in the expected inflation rate, and inflation shocks are reasons why the *AS* curve might shift. Economists have found that inflation shocks are the most frequent causes of shifts in the *AS* curve.

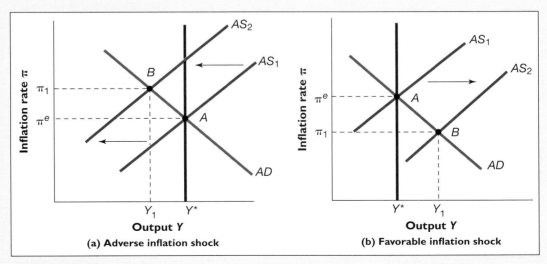

(a) Adverse inflation shock

(b) Favorable inflation shock

FIGURE 13.11

Inflation Shocks and Business Cycles.

The economy begins in long-run equilibrium in each panel. Panel (a) shows a recessionary gap: An adverse inflation shock shifts the *AS* curve to the left, reducing output (from Y^* to Y_1) and increasing the inflation rate (from π^e to π_1). Panel (b) shows an expansionary gap: A favorable inflation shock shifts the *AS* curve to the right, increasing output (from Y^* to Y_1) and reducing the inflation rate (from π^e to π_1).

The Impact of Oil Prices on the U.S. Economy	**EXAMPLE 13.3**

How did oil prices affect the U.S. economy in the 1970s and 1980s?

The U.S. experienced two "oil shocks," rapid increases in the price of oil, in 1973–74 and 1979. The price of oil tripled in the first case and then doubled in the second. Both of these acted as inflation shocks: aggregate supply decreased, as shown in Figure 13.11(a), pushing the economy into recessions in late 1973 and again in early 1980.

The price of crude oil reached a peak in early 1982. It then fell by 50 percent between 1982 and 1986, providing a favorable inflation shock to the U.S. economy. Aggregate supply rose during this period: first, reversing the adverse inflation shocks of the 1970s and then pushing the *AS* curve out further, causing an expansionary gap as seen in Figure 13.11(b).

USING THE *AD-AS* MODEL TO STUDY BUSINESS CYCLES

Examples 13.2 and 13.3 illustrate how the *AD-AS* model can be applied to real-world business cycles. Let's summarize the steps we followed in these examples and then apply them to the Great Recession.

Five Steps for Using the *AD-AS* Model to Study Business Cycles

In Examples 13.2 and 13.3, an event such as a stock market boom or an oil price shock occurred and we traced out the effect of that event on the economy's output and inflation rate. We can generalize our analysis in the following five steps:

Step 1: *Draw a diagram like Figure 13.1.* Be sure to mark the economy's long-run equilibrium, where output is at potential output Y^* and the inflation rate is at its expected rate π^e.

Step 2: *Ask whether the event affects the* AD *curve, the* AS *curve, or both.* This is where knowing the factors that shift the *AD* and *AS* curves pays off. You can write down the factors that shift the *AD* curve (demand shocks, fiscal policy, monetary policy) and the *AS* curve (changes in available resources and technology, changes in the expected inflation rate, inflation shocks), assign the event to one of the categories, and then ask what direction the event shifts the relevant curve.

Step 3: *Shift the curve(s) in the appropriate direction(s).*

Step 4: *Find the new short-run equilibrium.*

Step 5: *Compare the new short-run equilibrium to the original long-run equilibrium.* Be sure to compare the new level of output with potential output and the new inflation rate with the expected inflation rate.

Using *AD-AS* to Analyze the Great Recession

In 2009, U.S. real GDP was roughly 8 percent below potential output. Core inflation fell from 2.7 percent in 2007 to −0.7 percent in 2009.

We can now use the *AD-AS* model to understand the Great Recession. Three events are most often cited as causes: the decline in house prices that began in mid-2006, the sharp increase in the price of oil from early 2007 through mid-2008, and the worldwide financial panic in fall 2008. Here are the five steps:

Step 1: *Draw a diagram like Figure 13.1.* This is shown in panel (a) of Figure 13.12. The economy in 2007 is at point *A*.

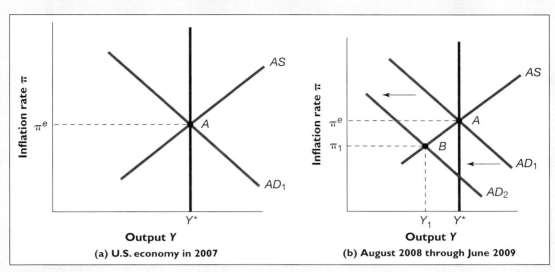

FIGURE 13.12

The Great Recession.

Panel (a) shows the U.S. economy in long-run equilibrium at point *A*. Panel (b) shows the economy moving into recession (from point *A* to point *B*). Declining house prices and a financial crisis caused consumption, investment, and net exports to fall, leading to a demand shock that shifted the *AD* curve to the left (AD_1 to AD_2). Output fell to Y_1 and the inflation rate π_1 was below its expected rate π^e. The *AS* curve does not shift in the picture because the sharp increase in oil prices from early 2007 to mid-2008 was offset by the rapid decline in oil prices from mid-2008 to early 2009.

Step 2: *Ask whether the event affects the* AD *curve, the* AS *curve, or both.* The decline in house prices and the worldwide financial panic were negative demand shocks. We have already referred to declines in house prices as causing a decline in household wealth, which leads to a fall in consumption spending and a decrease in aggregate demand. The worldwide financial panic was a negative demand shock because of its effects on investment spending. In particular, the financial crisis steeply increased the interest rates charged on corporate loans. This led directly to a fall in investment spending and a decrease in aggregate demand.

The price of oil approximately doubled between January 2007 and August 2008. From September 2008 to January 2009, however, oil prices approximately returned to their January 2007 levels. The U.S. economy, therefore, experienced an adverse inflation shock and a decrease in aggregate supply between early 2007 and mid-2008, and then a favorable inflation shock and an increase in aggregate supply from mid-2008 through early 2009.

Step 3: *Shift the curve(s) in the appropriate direction(s).* The negative demand shocks shifted the *AD* curve to the left; this is shown in Figure 13.12(b) by the movement from AD_1 to AD_2. The adverse inflation shock shifted the *AS* curve to the left but the favorable inflation shock shifted the *AS* curve to the right by an equal amount, so the *AS* curve remained roughly where it was in 2007.

Step 4: *Find the new short-run equilibrium.* The new short-run equilibrium is point *B* in Figure 13.12(b).

Step 5: *Compare the new short-run equilibrium to the original long-run equilibrium.* The economy moved from point *A* to point *B* in Figure 13.12(b). Actual output in 2009, Y_1, is below potential output Y^* and the actual inflation rate in 2009, π_1, is below the expected inflation rate π^e.

Thus, the story of the Great Recession is a story of negative demand shocks. The bursting of the housing bubble and the financial crisis of 2008 reduced aggregate demand and pushed the economy into a deep recession. The fluctuations in the price of oil may have been important at the microeconomic level, but at the macroeconomic level they did not have a lasting impact.

RECAP	UNDERSTANDING BUSINESS CYCLES

- Business cycles are caused by shifts in aggregate demand and aggregate supply.

- The primary causes of aggregate demand shifts are demand shocks, while the most frequent causes of aggregate supply shifts are inflation shocks.

- The *AD-AS* model can be used to study business cycles by applying a five-step process:

  - Show the economy in long-run equilibrium;

  - Identify how the *AD* and/or *AS* curves are affected;

  - Shift the *AD* and/or *AS* curves in the appropriate fashion;

  - Find the economy's new short-run equilibrium;

  - Compare the new short-run equilibrium with the initial long-run equilibrium to show how output and the inflation rate were affected.

- The Great Recession was the result of two negative demand shocks: declining house prices and the 2008 financial panic.

THE SELF-CORRECTING ECONOMY AND STABILIZATION POLICY

Governments apply fiscal and monetary policy to bring economies out of recessions or to slow down economies that are operating above potential output. We can study the effects of both types of policies using the *AD-AS* model. We will find that the nature of the shock that caused the recessions (i.e., a demand shock versus an inflation shock) matters greatly in how governments respond.

However, before we turn to stabilization policy, we first need to look at how the economy will behave if the government does *not* engage in stabilization policy. It turns out that this is a critical element in understanding how governments should use stabilization policy.

THE SELF-CORRECTING ECONOMY

In the basic Keynesian model, an output gap will not be eliminated unless one or more components of planned spending (consumption, investment, government spending, or net exports) change. The model implies that fiscal and monetary policies are crucial to closing output gaps. Without stabilization policy, the economy could sit below potential GDP indefinitely.

We built the basic Keynesian model on a crucial assumption: Firms meet the demand for their products at fixed prices. In the *AD-AS* model, we relaxed this assumption; now, the price level can vary and inflation can rise or fall due to shifts in aggregate demand and aggregate supply. This is a *very* important difference between the basic Keynesian model and the *AD-AS* model because, when the price level is no longer fixed, output gaps can be closed through rising or falling inflation. This is known as the economy's **self-correcting property.**

self-correcting property the fact that output gaps will not last indefinitely, but will be closed by rising or falling inflation

An Expansionary Gap

Figure 13.13 illustrates how an economy adjusts over time when it begins with an expansionary gap. The economy is initially in equilibrium with actual output Y_1 and actual inflation π_1. At this point, there is an expansionary gap since actual output Y_1 is greater than potential output Y^*. The AD curve will remain at AD_1 as long as there is no change in the Fed's monetary policy rule and there are no demand shocks.

Since the AD curve does not move, how will long-run equilibrium be restored? Graphically, the AS curve must shift to the left from AS_1 to AS_2 and inflation must rise from π_1 to π_2. But *why* does the AS curve shift to the left? What is the economics behind this shift?

As we discussed earlier in the chapter, changes in workers' and firms' expectations about inflation shift the AS curve, and this is the mechanism through which the economy adjusts from short-run equilibrium to long-run equilibrium. An expansionary gap causes both the actual and expected rates of inflation to rise as firms respond to high demand by raising their prices more rapidly than their costs are rising. Specifically, suppose that firms see that actual output is above potential output; this means that most firms will be experiencing excess demand for their products and they will respond by raising their prices. This will increase the inflation rate since not just one price relative to another is rising but the *general* level of prices is rising at a faster rate.

This is just the beginning of the story. Go to Figure 13.6 and look at the box marked "low inflation." If we change this box to "higher inflation" and follow the clockwise arrow to the next box, we will change "low expected inflation" to "higher expected inflation." Higher expected inflation shifts the AS curve to the left as wages and production costs begin to rise faster than before; that is, we change the box marked "slow increase in wages and other production costs" to "faster increases in wages and other production costs." The circle is now complete: Actual inflation continues to rise, causing expected inflation to rise, causing wages and production costs to increase at a faster rate.

This explains why inflation rises, but why does actual output fall to potential output? Remember the Fed's monetary policy rule: As inflation rises, the Fed increases the real interest rate. So, as inflation rises, the Fed will increase the real interest rate and spending will fall so that the economy moves along the AD curve and output falls while inflation is rising. We thus move from short-run equilibrium to long-run equilibrium, with actual output equal to potential output Y^* and actual inflation equal to expected inflation π_2.

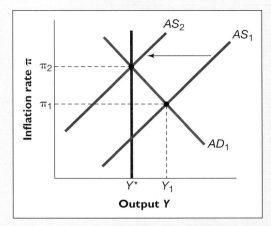

FIGURE 13.13

Adjustment to an Expansionary Gap.

The economy is initially in equilibrium with output Y_1 and inflation π_1. At this point, there is an expansionary gap. The AS curve shifts to the left from AS_1 to AS_2 as expected inflation rises and causes actual inflation to rise. The Fed follows its monetary policy rule and increases the real interest rate as inflation rises, so spending and output fall as inflation rises and the economy moves along the AD curve to long-run equilibrium at output Y^* and inflation π_2.

A Recessionary Gap

The economy's adjustment to a recessionary gap is similar to that for an expansionary gap. The adjustment of inflation in response to a recessionary gap is shown graphically in Figure 13.14. Again, the economy is initially in equilibrium with actual output Y_1 and actual inflation π_1. At this point, there is a recessionary gap since actual output Y_1 is less than potential output Y^*. The AD curve will remain at AD_1 as long as there is no change in the Fed's monetary policy rule and there are no demand shocks.

As was the case with an expansionary gap, the AS curve must shift, in this case to the right from AS_1 to AS_2, to close the gap as long as the AD curve is stable. Inflation will fall from π_1 to π_2 as workers' and firms' expectations about inflation fall due to the recessionary gap. (Again, as in the case of an expansionary gap, Figure 13.6 is helpful. In this case, lower inflation causes lower expected inflation and this in turn slows

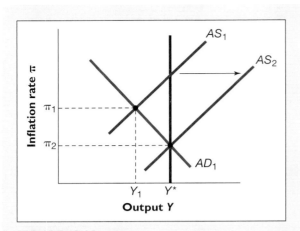

FIGURE 13.14

Adjustment to a Recessionary Gap.

The economy is initially in equilibrium with output Y_1 and inflation π_1. At this point, there is a recessionary gap. The AS curve shifts to the right from AS_1 to AS_2 as expected inflation falls and causes actual inflation to fall. The Fed follows its monetary policy rule and decreases the real interest rate as inflation falls, so spending and output rise as inflation falls and the economy moves along the AD curve to long-run equilibrium at output Y^* and inflation π_2.

the growth of wages and other production costs.) Actual output will rise from Y_1 to potential output Y^* because the Fed will follow its monetary policy rule and lower the real interest rate as inflation falls, stimulating increased levels of consumption and investment spending.

A ROLE FOR STABILIZATION POLICY?

Our analysis of Figures 13.13 and 13.14 makes an important general point: The economy tends to be *self-correcting* in the long run. In other words, given enough time, output gaps tend to disappear without changes in monetary or fiscal policy (other than the change in the real interest rate embodied in the Fed's policy rule). Expansionary output gaps are eliminated by rising inflation, while recessionary output gaps are eliminated by falling inflation. This result contrasts sharply with the basic Keynesian model, which does not include a self-correcting mechanism. The difference in results is explained by the fact that the basic Keynesian model concentrates on the short-run period, during which prices do not adjust, and does not take into account the changes in prices and inflation that occur over a longer period.

Does the economy's tendency to self-correct imply that aggressive monetary and fiscal policies are not needed to stabilize output? The answer to this question depends crucially on the *speed* with which the self-correction process takes place. If self-correction takes place very slowly, so that actual output differs from potential for protracted periods, then active use of monetary and fiscal policy can help to stabilize output. But if self-correction is rapid, then active stabilization policies are probably not justified in most cases, given the lags and uncertainties that are involved in policymaking in practice. Indeed, if the economy returns to full employment quickly, then attempts by policymakers to stabilize spending and output may end up doing more harm than good, for example, by causing actual output to "overshoot" potential output.

The speed with which a particular economy corrects itself depends on a variety of factors, including the prevalence of long-term contracts and the efficiency and flexibility of product and labor markets. However, a reasonable conclusion is that the greater the initial output gap, the longer the economy's process of self-correction will take. This observation suggests that stabilization policies should not be used actively to try to eliminate relatively small output gaps, but that they may be quite useful in remedying large gaps—for example, when the unemployment rate is exceptionally high. We will return to these issues in the chapter *Macroeconomic Policy*.

RECAP	*AD-AS* AND THE SELF-CORRECTING ECONOMY

- Inflation adjusts gradually to bring the economy into long-run equilibrium (a phenomenon called the economy's self-correcting tendency). Inflation rises to eliminate an expansionary gap and falls to eliminate a recessionary gap.

- The more rapid the self-correction process, the less need for active stabilization policies to eliminate output gaps. In practice, policymakers' attempts to eliminate output gaps are more likely to be helpful when the output gap is large than when it is small.

○ SUMMARY ○

- The aggregate demand (*AD*) curve shows the amount of output consumers, firms, government, and customers abroad want to purchase at each inflation rate, holding all the other factors constant. It slopes downward because of the Fed's monetary policy rule: Higher inflation leads the Fed to raise the real interest rate, which reduces spending and thus short-run equilibrium output. Demand shocks (changes in planned spending that are not caused by changes in output or the inflation rate) shift the *AD* curve: Positive demand shocks shift the *AD* curve to the right, while negative demand shocks shift the *AD* curve to the left. Stabilization policy also shifts the *AD* curve. *(LO1)*

- The aggregate supply (*AS*) curve shows the relationship between the amount of output firms want to produce and the inflation rate, holding all other factors constant. It slopes upward because actual inflation is related to expected inflation and also to the gap between actual output and potential output: When output is below potential, actual inflation is below expected inflation, and when output is above potential, actual inflation is above expected inflation. Changes in available resources and technology and changes in the expected inflation rate shift the *AS* curve. Inflation shocks also shift the *AS* curve: Adverse inflation shocks shift the *AS* curve to the left, and favorable inflation shocks shift the *AS* curve to the right. *(LO2)*

- Business cycles are caused by shifts in aggregate demand and aggregate supply. The primary causes of aggregate demand shifts are demand shocks, while the most frequent causes of aggregate supply shifts are inflation shocks. *(LO3)*

- The *AD-AS* model can be used to study business cycles by applying a five-step process: *(LO3)*
  1. Show the economy in long-run equilibrium;
  2. Identify how the *AD* and/or *AS* curves are affected;
  3. Shift the *AD* and/or *AS* curves in the appropriate fashion;
  4. Find the economy's new short-run equilibrium;
  5. Compare the new short-run equilibrium with the initial long-run equilibrium to show how output and the inflation rate were affected.

- In the absence of stabilization policy, output gaps will be closed through the economy's self-correcting property. The need to engage in active stabilization policy depends on the size of the output gap and the nature of the shock that created the output gap. *(LO4)*

○ KEY TERMS ○

aggregate demand (*AD*) curve
aggregate supply (*AS*) curve
change in aggregate demand

change in aggregate supply
demand shocks
inflation shock
long-run equilibrium

monetary policy rule
self-correcting property
short-run equilibrium

○ REVIEW QUESTIONS ○

1. What two variables are related by the aggregate demand (*AD*) curve? Explain why changes in the inflation rate affect the components of planned spending and cause the *AD* curve to slope downward. *(LO1)*

2. State how and why each of the following affects the *AD* curve: *(LO1)*
   a. An increase in government purchases.
   b. A tax increase.
   c. An increase in planned investment spending by firms caused by optimism about the future.
   d. A decrease in the Fed's inflation target.

3. Discuss the relationship between output gaps and inflation. How is this relationship captured in the *AS* curve? *(LO2)*

4. Sketch an *AD-AS* diagram depicting an economy in short-run equilibrium. Discuss how the economy reaches long-run equilibrium over a period of time without the use of stabilization policy, and show this on the diagram. *(LO3, LO4)*

○ PROBLEMS ○

1. Explain how and why each of the following events affects the AD curve. *(LO1)*
   a. An increase in consumer confidence leads to higher consumption spending.
   b. The government reduces income taxes.

2. Explain how and why each of the following events affects the AS curve. *(LO2)*
   a. The Fed raises its target rate of inflation.
   b. Oil prices drop sharply.

3. The Fed raises its target rate of inflation. Use an *AD-AS* diagram to show the short-run and long-run effects on output and the inflation rate. Assume the economy starts in the long-run equilibrium. *(LO1–LO4)*

4. Suppose that the government cuts taxes in response to a recessionary gap, but because of legislative delays the tax cut is not put in place for 18 months. Assuming that the government's objective is to return output and the inflation rate to their long-run levels, use an *AD-AS* diagram to illustrate how this policy action might actually prove to be counterproductive. *(LO1–LO4)*

5. Suppose that a permanent increase in oil prices both creates an inflation shock and, at the same time, reduces potential output. Use an *AD-AS* diagram to show the effects of the oil price increase on output and the inflation rate in the short run and the long run in the following two cases: *(LO2–LO4)*
   a. The government does not engage in stabilization policy.
   b. The government cuts taxes and increases government spending.

6. An economy is initially in recession. Using an *AD-AS* diagram, show how the economy returns to long-run equilibrium under each of the following policies. Discuss the costs and benefits of each approach in terms of output loss and inflation. *(LO1–LO4)*
   a. The Fed raises its target rate of inflation.
   b. The Fed does not change its target rate of inflation and follows its current monetary policy rule.

7. Suppose the economy is initially in long-run equilibrium. Now, due to a decline in house prices, consumers reduce their consumption spending. *(LO4)*
   a. Explain how the decline in consumer spending affects the *AD* curve.
   b. Explain how your answer to part a affects the economy's short-run equilibrium. Use an *AD-AS* diagram to illustrate your answer.
   c. Now, in addition to the decline in consumer spending, suppose that the economy experiences an adverse inflation shock.
      i. Explain how the adverse inflation shock affects the *AS* curve.
      ii. Discuss, using *AD-AS* diagrams, what choices the government now must make regarding stabilization policy.

8. True or false: The economy's self-correcting tendency makes active use of stabilization policy unnecessary. Explain in one to three paragraphs. *(LO4)*

○ ANSWERS TO CONCEPT CHECKS ○

13.1 Pessimism about the future will cause firms to decrease their investment spending. This will decrease aggregate demand because the decrease in investment spending is not associated with a change in the inflation rate. And, since aggregate demand decreases, businesses' pessimism is considered to be a negative demand shock. *(LO1)*

13.2 a. If inflation is expected to be 2 percent next year and workers are expecting a 2 percent increase in their real wages, then they will expect, and ask for, a 4 percent increase in their nominal wages.

b. If inflation is expected to be 4 percent next year, rather than 2 percent, workers will expect, and ask for, a 6 percent increase in their nominal wages.

c. If wage costs rise, firms will need to increase the prices of their goods and services to cover their increased costs, leading to an increase in inflation. In part b, when expected inflation was 4 percent, firms will be faced with larger increases in nominal wages than in part a, when expected inflation was only 2 percent. Thus, we can expect firms to raise prices by more when expected inflation is 4 percent than when expected inflation is 2 percent.

From this example, we can conclude that increased inflationary expectations lead to higher inflation. *(LO2)*

13.3 If the inflation rate is high, the economy will tend to stay in this high-inflation state due to expectations of high inflation and the existence of long-term wage and price contracts, while if the inflation rate is low, the economy will likewise tend to stay in this low-inflation state for similar reasons. However, since high inflation rates impose economic costs on society, as pointed out in the chapter *Inflation and the Price Level,* the Federal Reserve has an incentive to avoid the high-inflation state by keeping inflation low, which helps to maintain people's expectations of low inflation and leads to lower future inflation rates—perpetuating the "virtuous circle" illustrated in Figure 13.6. *(LO2)*

13.4 The graph should look the same as Figure 13.9 except that the *AS* curve shifts right. *(LO2)*

CHAPTER 14

Macroeconomic Policy

Ingram Publishing

IS MANAGING THE ECONOMY LIKE DRIVING A CAR?

LEARNING OBJECTIVES

After reading this chapter, you should be able to:

LO1 Discuss the policy options available to the Fed in response to demand shocks and inflation shocks.

LO2 Explain the roles played by the anchored inflationary expectations and central bank credibility in keeping inflation low.

LO3 Describe how fiscal policy can affect both aggregate demand and aggregate supply.

LO4 Address why macroeconomic policy is as much an art as a science.

In previous chapters, we have analyzed the basic economics underlying fiscal and monetary policy. We worked through examples showing how much policymakers would have to increase government spending, cut taxes, or engage in active monetary policy in order to eliminate a specific recessionary gap and restore output to its full employment level in the short run. While those examples are useful in understanding how fiscal and monetary policy works, they overstate the precision of policymaking.

In analyzing macroeconomic policy, one might be tempted to think of the economy as an automobile and the policymaker as its driver. By judiciously steering, braking, or accelerating at the appropriate times, the driver of a car can safely control it. She can steer it around obstacles. She can accelerate when the car is sluggish going up hills or if it needs an extra boost to pass another car. And she can step on the brake if the car is going too fast down a hill or if a hazard lies ahead.

Unfortunately, conducting macroeconomic policy is much more difficult than driving a car. The driver of a car typically knows exactly where she is at all times. She also knows her destination and can clearly see the road ahead. She has precise control over the accelerator, brake, and steering wheel. Finally, in most instances, she knows from experience how and when the car will respond to her actions. The real-world economy, on the other hand, is more complex because the economic policymaker has less information and control than the driver of a car. As one of us wrote, "If making monetary policy is like driving a car, then the car is one that has an unreliable speedometer, a foggy windshield, and a tendency to respond unpredictably and with a delay to the accelerator or the brake."[1]

In this chapter, we will examine both the art and science of macroeconomic policy. First, we use the *AD-AS* model to analyze stabilization policy in the face of shocks to aggregate demand and aggregate supply. Second, we focus on inflation and describe the ways in which monetary policy might be made more effective. Third, we examine the effects of fiscal policy on potential output and how policymakers must weigh the consequences of fiscal policy on both the short-run and the long-run performance of the economy. Finally, we return to the question: Is macroeconomic policy an art or a science?

WHAT IS THE ROLE OF STABILIZATION POLICY?

Previously, we discussed the economy's self-correcting property, which is the fact that output gaps will not last indefinitely but will be closed by rising or falling inflation rates. Does the economy's tendency to self-correct imply that aggressive monetary and fiscal policies are not needed to stabilize output? The answer to this question depends crucially on the speed with which the self-correction process takes place. If self-correction takes place very slowly, so that actual output differs from potential for protracted periods, then active use of monetary and fiscal policy can help to stabilize output.

On the other hand, if self-correction is rapid, active stabilization policies are probably not justified given the lags and uncertainties that are involved in policymaking. (For example, in the chapter *Spending, Output, and Fiscal Policy,* we identified these types of problems as they apply to fiscal policy.) Indeed, if the economy returns to full employment quickly, then attempts by policymakers to stabilize spending and output may end up doing more harm than good, for example, by causing actual output to go beyond potential output.

The speed with which a particular economy corrects itself depends on a variety of factors, including the prevalence of long-term contracts and the efficiency and flexibility of product and labor markets. Specifically, the self-correcting mechanism assumes that firms change their prices and/or alter their costs in response to output gaps. However, long-term contracts and market imperfections can slow this process and cause output gaps to persist for long periods of time.

In general, economists have found that the greater the initial output gap, the longer it will take the economy's self-correction process to return the economy to long-run equilibrium. This observation suggests that stabilization policies should not be used actively to try to eliminate relatively small output gaps, but that they may be quite useful in remedying large gaps such as the one created by the Great Recession.

[1] Ben S. Bernanke, "The Logic of Monetary Policy," December 2, 2004, www.federalreserve.gov/boarddocs/speeches/2004/20041202/default.htm.

The underlying causes of the output gap are also important in considering the role of stabilization policy. In particular, stabilization policy affects the economy in different ways depending on whether the economy was hit by a demand shock or an inflation shock.

STABILIZATION POLICY AND DEMAND SHOCKS

Suppose that a large negative demand shock knocks the economy out of its long-run equilibrium and into a deep recession; Figure 13.10(a) illustrates this situation. Notice that a negative demand shock pushes the inflation rate π_1 below its expected level π^e. In the absence of stabilization policy the economy's self-correcting mechanism will drive the AS curve downward and reestablish a long-run equilibrium at a lower expected inflation rate.

The self-correcting process could take many months or even years in the case of a large output gap. If the government recognizes this, it can employ fiscal or monetary policy to increase aggregate demand and bring the economy back to long-run equilibrium. This is shown in Figure 14.1.

As we discussed previously, the government can increase aggregate demand in two ways. First, Congress and the president can undertake expansionary fiscal policy through a combination of government spending increases and tax cuts. This will increase planned spending directly (through the increased government spending) and indirectly (through increased consumption induced by lower taxes and increased disposable income). Second, the Federal Reserve can apply expansionary monetary policy. This will lower interest rates, stimulate increased investment spending, and increase planned spending and output. Thus, in the case of a negative demand shock, active stabilization policy returns the economy to the output and inflation rate that prevailed before the recession.

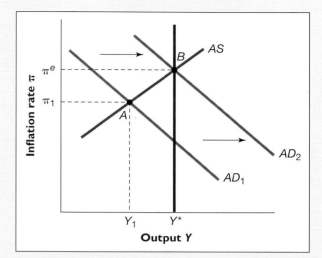

FIGURE 14.1

Stabilization Policy and Negative Demand Shocks.

The economy is in a recession at output Y_1 and inflation rate π_1. The current inflation rate is below its expected level π^e that prevailed before the recession. In this case, expansionary fiscal policy and/or expansionary monetary policy can be applied without causing inflation.

Federal Response to the 2001 Recession	EXAMPLE 14.1

How did the federal government respond to the 2001 recession?

We addressed this question in Examples 11.11 and 12.4 using the basic Keynesian model. Let's revisit it in the context of the AD-AS model. Recall that the bursting of the dot-com bubble was the primary cause of the 2001 recession. This was a negative demand shock that shifted the AD curve to the left, as in point B of Figure 13.10(a). The tax rebate checks sent out in 2001 increased households' disposable income and increased aggregate demand, as in point B of Figure 14.1.

The Federal Reserve began lowering interest rates even though there had been no change in inflation in late 2000. But, as we discussed in Example 12.4, the September 11, 2001, terrorist attacks prodded the Fed into a more active response. By November 2001, the federal funds rate was 4.5 percentage points lower than it had been one year earlier, stimulating an increase in both consumer and business spending. Expansionary monetary policy worked with fiscal policy to increase aggregate demand and push the economy back toward potential output.

STABILIZATION POLICY AND INFLATION SHOCKS

As we've seen, shocks in aggregate demand do not require the Fed to make a difficult choice between inflation and the stability of output. However, shocks to aggregate supply do create such a dilemma. If the Fed maintains the initial target inflation rate, the economy may experience a protracted recessionary or expansionary gap. If, on the other hand, it wants to hasten the return to potential GDP, it may have to change the inflation target.

We illustrate this dilemma in Figures 14.2 and 14.3. In both figures, the economy is initially in long-run equilibrium with output Y_1 equal to potential output and inflation π_1 equal to expected inflation and the Fed's long-run inflation target. An adverse inflation shock then shifts the AS curve from AS_1 to AS_2 in each figure. The Fed responds to the increase in inflation by following the monetary policy rule and increasing the real interest rate; the increase in the real interest rate causes planned spending to decline and output falls from Y_1 to Y_2.

Now, with the economy in a recession at output Y_2 and inflation rate π_2, the Fed faces a choice: engage in active monetary policy—that is, reduce the federal funds rate in order to increase aggregate demand—or follow its monetary policy rule and bring inflation back down to π_1. Figure 14.2 shows the consequences for output and inflation if the Fed loosens monetary policy. Specifically, the Fed raises the long-run inflation target to π_3, the level of inflation that workers and firms expect when the economy returns to potential output. The Fed thus lowers the real interest rate at each level of inflation and shifts the AD curve to the right, from AD_1 to AD_2. As the AD curve shifts to the right, the inflation rate rises toward the Fed's new long-run inflation target, π_3.

The rise in inflation validates the new level of expected inflation π_3: workers and firms expect inflation to continue rising, so they push for faster increases in wages and prices, which drives actual and expected inflation toward π_3. The AS curve thus remains

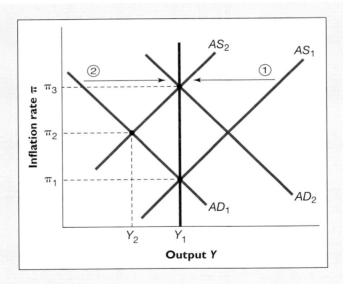

FIGURE 14.2

Accommodating an Inflation Shock.

The economy is initially in equilibrium with output Y_1 equal to potential output and inflation π_1 equal to expected inflation and the Fed's long-run inflation target. ① An adverse inflation shock shifts the AS curve from AS_1 to AS_2. The Fed responds to the increase in inflation by following the monetary policy rule and increasing the real interest rate; this causes output to fall from Y_1 to Y_2. ② The Fed accommodates the inflation shock by loosening monetary policy. Specifically, the Fed raises the long-run inflation target to π_3 since this is the inflation rate that workers and firms expect after the adverse inflation shock. The Fed thus lowers the real interest rate at every inflation rate and shifts the AD curve to the right from AD_1 to AD_2 and output returns to potential output Y_1. AS does not shift again since the Fed's action ratifies the increase in inflationary expectations.

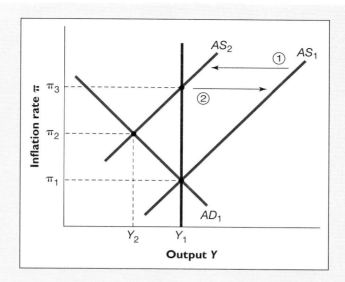

FIGURE 14.3

Maintaining Low Inflation after an Adverse Inflation Shock.

The economy is initially in equilibrium with output Y_1 equal to potential output and inflation π_1 equal to expected inflation and the Fed's long-run inflation target. ① An adverse inflation shock shifts the AS curve from AS_1 to AS_2. The Fed keeps the long-run inflation target at π_1 and raises interest rates in response to the adverse inflation shock. ② Inflation π_2 is lower than what people expect inflation to be after the inflation shock (π_3), so workers and firms reduce their inflationary expectations, shifting the AS curve to the right. This process continues until long-run equilibrium is restored at the Fed's long-run inflation target of π_1 and inflationary expectations are reduced to π_1 as well.

at AS_2 and the economy eventually returns to potential output with the new, higher long-run inflation rate π_3. Consequently, the higher inflation rate caused by the adverse inflation shock will be sustained and, in fact, increased by the Fed's monetary policy.

Economists use the term **accommodating policy** to describe a policy that allows the effects of a shock to occur. In this example, the Fed's accommodating policy is to allow the inflation shock to decrease output in the short run and inflation in the short run and the long run. There are two important implications of the Fed's accommodating policy. First, in the short run, the economy experiences a period of recession and higher inflation caused by the spending shock, followed by an increase in output with inflation rising even higher. Second, in the long run, the economy returns to potential output, where it began, but now has a higher inflation rate. A possibly shorter and shallower recession is paid for with a higher long-run inflation rate.

accommodating policy a policy that allows the effects of a shock to occur

The alternative to accommodating the adverse inflation shock is for the Fed to stick to the current long-run inflation target, π_1. To do this, the Fed must keep the real interest rate above the long-run target level and *not* lower it as when it accommodates the adverse inflation shock. Figure 14.3 illustrates this situation. The economy therefore remains at Y_2 for a longer time than when the Fed accommodates the shock—that is, the recession caused by the adverse inflation shock is longer than when the Fed lowers interest rates.

The Fed's willingness to keep interest rates high, and to not close the recessionary gap, will convince workers and firms that inflation will not rise to the level they expected, π_3. Expected inflation therefore starts to fall and the AS curve starts to shift back toward AS_1. Note how the Fed will react: As the AS curve shifts to the right, the actual inflation rate will fall and the Fed will follow the monetary policy rule and lower the real interest rate. The lower real interest rate will increase planned spending and output and reduce the recessionary gap and, eventually, the economy will return to potential output and the original level of inflation, π_1.

In deciding which of these two policy alternatives to follow, the Fed might like to know how long it would take for the economy to return to potential if it did not change monetary policy. The answer depends on the speed with which the aggregate supply curve shifts down when an adverse inflation shock creates a recessionary gap. If the AS curve shifts down quickly, the Fed is more likely to keep the target inflation rate unchanged at π_1 because any recession will probably be short. If, on the other hand, the AS curve shifts down very slowly, the Fed may be more inclined to increase the target inflation rate to avoid a lengthy recession.

Ironically, the speed with which the aggregate supply curve shifts back down following an adverse inflation shock depends partly on the public's expectation of how the Fed will act. If people are confident that the Fed will maintain the original target inflation rate, their expectations of future inflation will not change even if inflation rises temporarily. If this is the case, we describe people's expectations of inflation as being **anchored.** When an adverse inflation shock increases inflation, people with anchored expectations believe that the Fed will act to ensure that inflation quickly falls back to the initial level. Workers will then be less likely to ask for inflationary wage increases and firms will be less likely to raise prices. The second round of inflation will be eliminated, the aggregate supply line will shift back to AS_1 more rapidly, and output will return to potential more quickly. Because any recession will be shorter if inflationary expectations are anchored, the Fed also will be comfortable keeping the target inflation rate unchanged.

If, on the other hand, the Fed has frequently accommodated higher inflation rates in the past, expectations of inflation may not be anchored. If the public believes the Fed will raise the target inflation rate, expectations of future inflation will be higher. Workers will then demand larger wage increases and firms will raise prices more rapidly. In that event, the short-run aggregate supply line will shift down more slowly, and the return to full employment will be prolonged. Thus, the Fed has a stake in convincing the public that it will maintain its original target inflation rate.

> **anchored inflationary expectations** when people's expectations of future inflation do not change even if inflation rises temporarily

---

The Economic Naturalist 14.1

How was inflation conquered in the 1980s?

After reaching double-digit levels in the late 1970s and 13.5 percent in 1980, inflation in the United States fell all the way to 3.2 percent in 1983, and it remained in the 2–5 percent range for the rest of the decade. In the 1990s, inflation fell even lower, in the 2–3 percent range in most years. How was inflation conquered in the 1980s?

The person who was most directly responsible for the conquest of inflation in the 1980s was the Federal Reserve's chairman, Paul Volcker. Following an unusual and secret Saturday meeting he called on October 6, 1979, the Federal Open Market Committee agreed to adopt a strongly anti-inflationary monetary policy. The results of this policy change on the U.S. economy are shown in Table 14.1, which includes selected macroeconomic data for the period 1978–1985.

The data in Table 14.1 fit our analysis of anti-inflationary monetary policy quite well. First, as our model predicts, in the short run the Fed's maintenance of its low target rate of inflation and its unwillingness to accommodate inflation shocks led to a recession. In fact, two recessions followed the Fed's action in 1979, a short one in 1980 and a deeper one in 1981–1982. Note that growth in real GDP was negative in 1980 and 1982, and the unemployment rate rose significantly, peaking at 9.7 percent in 1982. Nominal and real interest rates also rose, a direct effect of the shift in monetary policy. Inflation, however, did not respond much during the period 1979–1981. All these results are consistent with the short-run analysis in Figure 14.3.

By 1983, however, the situation had changed markedly. The economy had recovered, with strong growth in real GDP in 1983–1985. In 1984 the unemployment rate, which tends to lag the recovery, began to decline. Interest rates remained relatively high, perhaps reflecting other factors besides monetary policy. Most significantly, inflation fell in 1982–1983 and stabilized at a much lower level. Inflation has remained low in the United States ever since.

TABLE 14.1
U.S. Macroeconomic Data, 1978–1985

Year	Growth in real GDP (%)	Unemployment rate (%)	Inflation rate (%)	Nominal interest rate (%)	Real interest rate (%)
1978	5.5	6.1	7.6	8.3	0.7
1979	3.2	5.8	11.4	9.7	−1.7
1980	−0.2	7.1	13.5	11.6	−1.9
1981	2.5	7.6	10.3	14.4	4.1
1982	−2.0	9.7	6.2	12.9	6.7
1983	4.3	9.6	3.2	10.5	7.3
1984	7.3	7.5	4.3	11.9	7.6
1985	3.8	7.2	3.6	9.6	6.0

SOURCE: *Economic Report of the President* (www.gpoaccess.gov/eop) and calculations by the authors.

The Economic Naturalist 14.2

What caused the Great Moderation?

From 1985 to 2007, both real GDP growth and inflation were much less volatile than they were prior to 1985. As shown in Figure 14.4, the variability in the growth rate of real GDP was about half of what it was prior to 1985. This trend has even continued

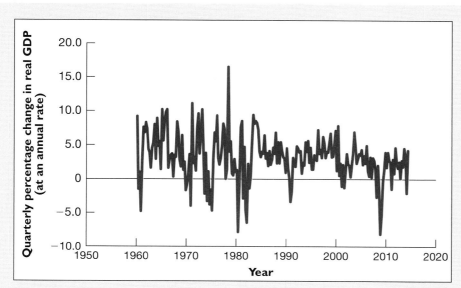

FIGURE 14.4

The Changing Volatility of Real GDP.

Between 1985 and 2014 there was a dramatic reduction in the volatility of real GDP.

SOURCE: Bureau of Economic Analysis (www.bea.gov).

after the significant volatility seen during the Great Recession between 2007 and 2009. In addition, the rate of inflation declined by two-thirds.[2] But why did macroeconomic volatility in the United States decline so markedly?

Reduced macroeconomic volatility has numerous benefits for the economy. It improves market functioning, makes economic and business planning easier, and reduces the resources devoted to managing inflation risks. More stable output and employment reduce the economic uncertainty confronting households and firms.

Many economists believe that better macroeconomic policy, especially monetary policy, was responsible for the reduced variability in both output and inflation. Prior to 1981, the Federal Reserve often allowed inflation to rise in response to shocks to aggregate demand and aggregate supply. This was followed by periodic attempts to rein in the inflation that followed. These swings in monetary policy from ease to tightness contributed to volatility in both output and inflation. Since the early 1980s, however, the Fed has been more consistent in its efforts to keep inflation from rising. These efforts have paid off by anchoring inflationary expectations, which, as we have just discussed, can stabilize not only inflation, but output, too.[3]

While most economists attribute the reduced variability in inflation to actions of the Fed, others believe that structural changes in the economy, and not the Fed, were largely responsible for the reduced variability in output. These structural changes included changes in technology, business practices, and other structural features that improved the ability of the economy to absorb shocks. Some examples of these changes include better management of inventories, deregulation, the shift away from manufacturing and toward services, and an increased openness to trade and international capital flows.

RECAP	THE ROLE OF STABILIZATION POLICY

In response to changes in spending that create shocks in aggregate demand, fiscal and monetary policy can be applied to return output to potential and inflation to its long-run expected rate. Shocks to aggregate supply (such as inflation shocks), however, force the Fed to choose between maintaining inflation and stabilizing output. If inflationary expectations are anchored, however, the return to potential output following an inflation shock will occur more rapidly. By monitoring the core rate of inflation, the Fed can determine whether an inflation shock has led to any second-round effects on inflation and can act accordingly.

INFLATIONARY EXPECTATIONS AND CREDIBILITY

As we saw in the last two Economic Naturalist examples, macroeconomic performance may be improved if inflationary expectations are anchored. But what determines whether expectations are anchored? Most economists believe that it depends on the **credibility of monetary policy,** which is the degree to which the public believes the central bank's promises to keep inflation low, even if doing so may impose short-run economic costs.

credibility of monetary policy the degree to which the public believes the central bank's promises to keep inflation low, even if doing so may impose short-run economic costs

[2]Olivier J. Blanchard and John A. Simon, "The Long and Large Decline in U.S. Output Volatility," *Brookings Papers on Economic Activity,* No. 1 (2001), pp. 135–64. Students who have taken statistics know that scientists generally use the variance of a variable (or its square root, called the standard deviation) to measure its variability.
[3]Ben Bernanke, "The Great Moderation," February 20, 2004, www.federalreserve.gov/boarddocs/speeches/2004/20040220/default.htm.

The importance of credibility was illustrated in our earlier analysis of an adverse inflation shock. In that case, the Fed's credibility as an inflation-fighter preempted the second-round effects of inflation and hastened the return to full employment at the original rate of inflation. Economists have identified several institutional characteristics that may affect the credibility of the central bank's pronouncements to keep inflation low and thus its ability to do so. These include the degree of central bank independence, the announcement of explicit inflation targets, and the establishment of a reputation for fighting inflation.

CENTRAL BANK INDEPENDENCE

The credibility of monetary policy may be enhanced if central bankers are insulated from short-term political considerations, a condition that is sometimes referred to as **central bank independence.** Independent central banks will be better able to take a long-term view of the economy. In particular, they can pursue anti-inflation policy when it is necessary, even if it leads to a temporary recession. Elected politicians, on the other hand, face frequent reelections, and they may be swayed by short-term political considerations to allow the economy to overexpand at the cost of higher inflation in the long run. Because of its enhanced credibility, an independent central bank may find it easier to anchor the public's expectations of inflation, reducing the duration of any inflationary or recessionary gap and promoting overall economic stability.

> **central bank independence** when central bankers are insulated from short-term political considerations and are allowed to take a long-term view of the economy

Various factors contribute to a central bank's independence. Among the many possible factors, we list four:

- The length of appointments to the central bank. Central banks are considered to be more independent if their central bankers are appointed for long terms, especially if the terms are staggered so that a single president or group of legislators cannot replace them all at once.

- Whether the central bank's actions are subject to frequent interference, review, or veto by the legislative branch. Central banks are considered to be more independent if their actions are not subject to frequent interference or review.

- Whether the central bank has the obligation, as it does in some countries, to finance the national deficit by buying newly issued government bonds. The obligation to do so reduces a central bank's independence.

- The degree to which the central bank's budget is controlled by the legislative or executive branch of government. Central banks are considered to be more independent if they are allowed to set and control their own budgets.

The U.S. Federal Reserve is generally considered to be a relatively independent central bank. The seven members of the Federal Reserve are appointed to staggered terms of 14 years, in contrast to the members of the U.S. House of Representatives, the president, and members of the Senate, who must face reelection every two, four, and six years, respectively. Although appointments to the Fed's Board of Governors must be approved by the Senate, and the Federal Reserve is subject to general oversight by the Congress, the daily policy actions of the Fed are not subject to review, approval, or veto by either the executive, legislative, or judicial branches of government. Finally, the Fed is under no obligation to finance the national deficit, and it controls its own budget. On the other hand, the law that created the Fed (the Federal Reserve Act) does not explicitly prohibit interference in monetary policy decisions by the legislative and executive branches of government. This prohibition is explicit in the central banking laws of many other countries.

Empirical evidence supports the proposition that countries should foster the independence of their central banks. Countries whose central banks are more independent have lower rates of inflation. More importantly, the lower inflation does not appear to come at the cost of lower output or higher unemployment, according to most studies. By enhancing a central bank's credibility, greater central bank independence leads to better overall economic outcomes.

ANNOUNCING A NUMERICAL INFLATION TARGET

Some economists believe that expectations are more firmly anchored and the central bank is perceived as more credible in those countries in which the central bank announces an explicit, numerical target for inflation. We have already introduced the idea of a target rate of inflation in our discussion of the monetary policy rule. Generally speaking, central banks must have an idea of the inflation rate they would like to achieve in order to make sensible policy. The more controversial question is whether central banks should announce their target inflation rate to the public. Proponents argue that announcing a numerical target for long-run inflation, and then sticking to it, will increase credibility and better anchor inflation expectations.

Many central banks publicly announce their inflation target. The Bank of Canada, for example, began announcing its inflation target in 1991. Since 1995, that target has been 2 percent. In March 2011, the Bank of England's inflation target was 2 percent, and the Central Bank of Brazil's target was 4.5 percent. Other central banks provide a range for their target rather than, or in addition to, a single number. The Bank of Israel and the Reserve Bank of New Zealand, for example, both had a 1–3 percent target range as of March 2011; in Chile the range was 2–4 percent.

Central banks that announce their targets typically provide additional information to the public. This information may include their forecasts of inflation, real GDP, and other variables, as well as some discussion of the specific policies that will be needed to meet their targets. Advocates believe that announcing inflation targets and accompanying them with supporting information enhances the credibility of the central bank and reduces uncertainty among households and firms. This helps to anchor inflationary expectations, keep inflation low, and maintain full employment.

Note that it makes sense for a central bank to announce a long-run inflation target, in that the central bank is able to control the rate of inflation in the long run. It would *not* make sense for a central bank to announce a long-run target for real GDP or employment because these variables are determined by a host of factors (such as productivity and the supply of labor) that are not under the control of the central bank.

Once an inflation target is announced, the central bank may choose to adhere to it strictly, or it may be more flexible. A central bank that sets a strict target tries to meet the target all the time without regard for the consequences for output. As we have seen, this policy keeps output at potential when the economy is beset by spending shocks, but it may result in a recession if the central bank acts to eliminate even the initial bulge in inflation following a shock to aggregate supply such as an inflation shock.

In practice, virtually all central banks that announce an inflation target are flexible inflation targeters—they try to hit their inflation target in the long run or on average over a long period while responding to short-term shocks to aggregate supply in a way that takes account of both output gaps and inflation. In these cases, the announced inflation targets correspond to the target inflation rate in the monetary policy rule.

Advocates of announcing explicit numerical targets believe that this practice reduces uncertainty in financial markets and among the public. Reduced uncertainty allows people to plan more effectively, save the resources used to protect themselves from unexpected inflation, and improve market functioning. By putting the prestige of the central bank behind its commitment to meet the target, the advocates also believe that explicit inflation targets enhance the central bank's credibility and anchor inflation expectations.

Supporters of inflation targets emphasize that the practice been successful in both developing and industrialized countries. They believe that explicit targets in Brazil, Chile, Mexico, and Peru are one important reason why the central banks in nine of the most populous Latin American countries were able to reduce their inflation rates from 160 percent per year in the 1980s and 235 percent during the first half of the 1990s to only 13 percent per year in 1995–1999 and less than 8 percent in the period 2000–2004.[4]

---

[4]Ben Bernanke, "Inflation in Latin America: A New Era?" February 11, 2005, www.federalreserve.gov/boarddocs/speeches/2005/20050211/default.htm.

Those central banks, such as the Federal Reserve, that do not announce an explicit target to the public still may have a target or range in mind when making policy. Instead of announcing a specific number to the public, however, these banks typically state that they are interested in keeping inflation low, without defining exactly what that means. Proponents of this approach believe that a system of publicly announced targets is too rigid and may reduce the flexibility of the central bank to deal with unexpected circumstances. They worry that having an explicit inflation target may lead the central bank to pay too much attention to inflation and not enough attention to stabilizing output and maintaining full employment. Finally, opponents of explicit inflation targeting for the United States emphasize that the Fed has achieved good results without having a publicly announced target. They suggest following the adage "If it ain't broke, don't fix it."

The Inflation Target   EXAMPLE 14.2

Why shouldn't the inflation target be zero?

Because central banks often state that they are in favor of stable prices, it would seem that the logical long-run target for inflation is 0 percent. However, most economists believe that an inflation target of zero is too low, and central banks that announce an explicit inflation target usually choose values that are low but above zero. Why shouldn't the inflation target be zero?

Several reasons have been offered. First, because hitting the target at all times is impossible in practice, an inflation target of 0 percent increases the risk that the economy will experience periods of deflation (negative inflation). The deflationary experiences of the United States in the 1930s and, more recently, in Japan in the 1990s illustrate that deflation can be difficult to stop once it starts, and it can lead to painful and persistent declines in real GDP, especially if people expect it to continue. Many policymakers prefer to reduce the risk of deflation by choosing an inflation target above 0 percent.

Second, there are times when the Fed may wish to counteract negative demand shocks to the economy with a negative real interest rate, but this requires that inflation be greater than zero. Recall that the real interest rate is equal to the nominal interest rate minus the rate of inflation. Thus, a negative real interest rate requires setting a nominal interest rate less than inflation. If inflation is zero (or less than zero), however, a negative real interest rate would require a negative nominal interest rate. But the federal funds rate cannot fall below zero because banks would rather keep their reserves than lend them out at a negative nominal interest rate. Consequently, a negative real interest rate must be accompanied by inflation greater than zero.

Third, as we saw in the chapter *Inflation and the Price Level,* some evidence suggests that the conventional measures of inflation tend to overstate the "true" rate of inflation by about one percentage point. Consequently, if the Fed wanted to maintain "true" price stability (that is, "true" inflation of 0 percent), this would require conventionally measured rates of inflation of at least 1 percent.

Finally, some economists believe that a small amount of inflation is necessary to "grease" our economic engine. The analysis in the chapter *Wages and Unemployment* indicated that technological change and shifts in product demand may require real wages in some industries or occupations to fall in an efficiently operating economy, even when real wages in other industries and occupations are rising. If inflation is positive, a worker's real wage will fall whenever her nominal wage rises by less than the rate of inflation. If, for example, her nominal wage rises by 4 percent but prices rise by 5 percent, her real wage (that is, the amount of goods and services she can buy with her earnings) will fall. If, however, inflation is 0 percent and prices are not changing, the only way in which a worker's real wage can fall is if her nominal wage itself falls. Some evidence suggests that workers will strenuously resist cuts in their nominal wages.[5] They seem

[5]This does not mean that nominal wages never fall. Many workers in the airline industry, for example, have had to accept lower nominal wages as their employers compete with newer low-cost airlines such as Southwest and Jet Blue.

to be less resistant to having their nominal wages rise by a smaller percent than inflation even though this, too, reduces their real wage. Consequently, inflation can provide the "grease" required to reduce real wages in some industries and achieve economic efficiency.[6] Critics of the "grease" theory, however, argue that workers will become less resistant to nominal wage cuts at very low or zero rates of inflation. In a low inflation environment, nominal wage cuts would, of necessity, be more common and workers would get used to the idea.

CENTRAL BANK REPUTATION

inflation hawk someone who is committed to achieving and maintaining low inflation, even at some short-run cost in reduced output and employment

inflation dove someone who is not strongly committed to achieving and maintaining low inflation

Ultimately, credibility can be won and maintained only by performance, and a central bank's performance will depend partly on its reputation as being an "inflation hawk" or an "inflation dove." An **inflation hawk** is someone who is committed to achieving and maintaining low inflation, even at some short-run cost in reduced output and employment. An **inflation dove** is someone who is not strongly committed to achieving and maintaining low inflation.

Inflation hawks believe that low and stable inflation allows the economy to grow more rapidly in the long run and therefore will be worth the possible short-run cost. Somewhat paradoxically, inflation hawks also may achieve more stable output and employment, even in the short run. Central banks that have acquired reputations as an inflation hawk will find it easier to anchor inflationary expectations. As we have learned, anchored expectations reduce the inflationary impact of an inflation shock by minimizing the second-round effects of that shock. Recall that anchored expectations also increase the speed with which short-run aggregate supply shifts down following an adverse inflation shock or demand shock. Consequently, by anchoring expectations, a central bank that is viewed as an inflation hawk may be better able to stabilize output at potential GDP, even in the short run.

But how does a central bank acquire a reputation as an inflation hawk? Some central bankers acquire this reputation only after conducting monetary policy like an inflation hawk. Sometimes, however, the president can select people to serve on the Fed who already have acquired reputations as inflation hawks, based on their professional or academic backgrounds. Jimmy Carter's appointment of Paul Volcker as chair of the Fed, which we discussed in Economic Naturalist 14.1, is a famous example of a chair coming to the Fed with a well-established reputation as an inflation hawk.

RECAP	INFLATIONARY EXPECTATIONS AND CREDIBILITY

Macroeconomic performance may be improved if expectations of inflation are anchored. Anchored expectations, in turn, depend on the extent to which a central bank's anti-inflation pronouncements are viewed as credible. Several institutional characteristics may help to enhance a central bank's credibility: the extent to which the central bank is independent from the executive and legislative branches of the government, the announcement of a numerical inflation target, and the reputation of the central bank as an "inflation hawk."

FISCAL POLICY AND THE SUPPLY SIDE

So far, we have focused on monetary policy and its effects. Now, we turn our attention to fiscal policy. Recall that in previous chapters we focused on the role of fiscal policy—government spending and taxes—in the determination of aggregate expenditure and aggregate demand. We saw, for example, that increased government spending or lower taxes

---

[6]George A. Akerlof, William T. Dickens, and George L. Perry, "The Macroeconomics of Low Inflation," *Brookings Papers on Economic Activity*, No. 1 (1996), pp. 1–76.

can expand the economy by increasing aggregate demand. However, most economists agree that fiscal policies affect the economy's productive capacity, or potential output, as well as aggregate demand. In general, a **supply-side policy** is a policy that affects potential output (the "supply side" of the economy). As we discuss here, fiscal policies are often supply-side policies in this sense.

supply-side policy a policy that affects potential output

For example, government expenditures on public capital increase aggregate spending, as we have already discussed. However, they also may increase the economy's potential output. The interstate highway system, begun under President Eisenhower, is a case in point: By lowering the costs of long-distance transportation, interstate highways made the U.S. economy more productive and increased potential output. Thus, spending on public capital may be a supply-side policy as well as an influence on aggregate demand.

Government tax and transfer programs affect the incentives, and thus the economic behavior, of households and firms. To the extent that changes in behavior in turn affect potential output, tax and transfer programs also have supply-side effects. A lower tax rate on interest income (as opposed to all income), for example, may increase people's willingness to save for the future. Although greater saving implies lower consumption expenditures and thus weaker aggregate demand in the short run, greater saving also leads to more investment in the long run and a faster rate of capital formation in the economy. As a result, potential output will grow more rapidly.

Tax and transfer policies also affect potential output by affecting the supply of labor. For example, lower tax rates on earnings may increase potential output by inducing people to work more hours. To illustrate, suppose that Tom earns $10 per hour before taxes and his tax rate is 40 percent. Thus, for each hour he works, Tom earns $10; pays 40 percent of $10, or $4, in taxes; and takes home $6 in after-tax earnings. Tom's situation is depicted in the first line of Table 14.2. Now suppose his tax rate is reduced to 30 percent. If Tom's before-tax wage rate remains equal to $10, his taxes on each hour of work fall to 30 percent of $10, or $3, and he takes home $7 in after-tax earnings, as illustrated in the second line of Table 14.2. Consequently, a *reduction* in Tom's tax rate from 40 percent to 30 percent *increases* his after-tax wage from $6 to $7 per hour.

TABLE 14.2
The Effects of a Reduction in Tax Rates on Tom's After-Tax Wage Rates

Pretax wage	Tax rate	Taxes paid	After-tax wage
$10	40% (= 0.40)	$4	$6
$10	30% (= 0.30)	$3	$7

Reductions in tax rates may increase the number of hours people want to work and reduce the amount of time they want to spend at home watching television and doing chores because the opportunity cost of staying home has risen. Tom's opportunity cost of watching an additional hour of television, for example, is equal to the amount of after-tax earnings he could have earned during that hour, which has risen from $6 to $7.

According to the Cost-Benefit Principle, individuals make decisions by comparing the extra benefits with the extra costs. In examining the effects of tax rates on economic incentives, therefore, economists focus on people's **marginal tax rate,** which is the tax rate on the *marginal* or extra dollar of income, or the amount by which taxes rise when before-tax income rises by one dollar. Someone's marginal tax rate can differ considerably from his **average tax rate,** which is calculated by dividing his total taxes by his total before-tax income to obtain the percentage of before-tax income he pays in taxes.

Although there was no difference between Tom's marginal and average tax rates in Table 14.2, this is not true for most people, as we show in Concept Check 14.1. In 2007 total taxes collected by federal, state, and local governments were about 30 percent of U.S. GDP,

Cost-Benefit

marginal tax rate the amount by which taxes rise when before-tax income rises by one dollar

average tax rate total taxes divided by total before-tax income

and many of these taxes, such as property taxes, do not depend on income. Most Americans, however, face marginal tax rates on their incomes that are greater than 30 percent.

CONCEPT CHECK 14.1

Suppose Tom pays no taxes on the first $10,000 of his income. Suppose, however, he has to pay taxes of 20 percent on any *additional* income. Thus, if he earns $11,000, he pays 0.20($11,000 − $10,000) = $200 in taxes. Similarly, if he earns $15,000, he pays 0.20($15,000 − $10,000) = $1,000 in taxes. Calculate Tom's average and marginal tax rates if he earns $5,000, $11,000, and $15,000.

Changes in marginal tax rates may affect other aspects of the labor supply decision besides the number of hours worked. For example, consider a student's decision about whether to invest the time and money necessary to become a doctor. From an economic perspective, the return to that investment in human capital is the extra income that the student will be able to earn as a doctor, relative to what he or she might earn without a medical degree. If the marginal tax rate on earnings is high, the economic incentive to become a doctor will be lower, and the student may decide not to make that investment. Likewise, a lower marginal tax rate increases the incentive for people to be entrepreneurial and to take risks—for example, by starting their own companies—since they know that they will be able to keep a larger portion of the returns to their efforts. As we discussed in the chapter *Economic Growth,* entrepreneurship is an important source of economic growth.

In Figure 14.5 we illustrate one scenario in which a cut in marginal tax rates increases both aggregate demand and aggregate supply. As before, the tax cut shifts the aggregate demand curve to the right, from AD_1 to AD_2. Now, however, the tax cut also increases potential output. As a result, real output will increase in both the short run and the long run. Whether the rate of inflation also will increase depends on the relative size of the two shifts. For simplicity, we have drawn them so that inflation remains constant, but this need not be the case.

Although economists agree that tax rates affect economic behavior, the magnitude and sometimes even the direction of the effects can be controversial. In our earlier example, we showed that a decline in Tom's tax rate implies an increase in his after-tax wage rate. As we

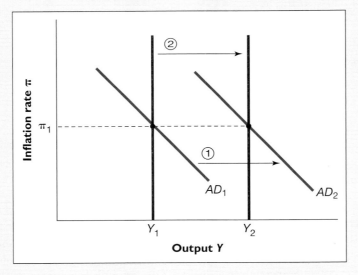

FIGURE 14.5

The Potential Effects of Tax-Rate Reductions on Aggregate Demand and Aggregate Supply.

The economy is initially in equilibrium with output Y_1 equal to potential output and inflation π_1 equal to expected inflation and the Fed's long-run inflation target. ① A reduction in tax rates shifts the *AD* curve from AD_1 to AD_2. ② If the supply-side effects of the tax-rate reduction are strong, inflation remains at π_1 and output rises from Y_1 to Y_2.

mentioned, the increase in Tom's after-tax wage gives him an incentive to work more hours and to watch less television because the opportunity cost of watching television instead of working has risen. On the other hand, the reduction in Tom's tax rate also might increase his after-tax wage to such an extent that he may feel that he can afford to work even fewer hours and still pay his bills.[7] Empirical studies of the labor market suggest that the responsiveness of an individual's labor supply to changes in taxes depends on many factors, including age, sex, marital status, and education. For example, married women have traditionally been more likely to move in and out of the labor force and appear to be more responsive to changes in after-tax wages than are their husbands, who have historically tended to remain in the labor market on a full-time basis even when tax rates change.

While many Americans may be dismayed by what they consider to be high taxes, Europeans generally have considerably higher marginal tax rates. In the following example, we examine the claim that the higher marginal tax rates in Europe are responsible for the fact that the typical European works many fewer hours each year than the typical American.

The Economic Naturalist 14.3

Why do Americans work more hours than Europeans?

The average American works many more hours than the average Western European. Not only is the average workweek longer in America, but Americans generally take fewer vacations, have fewer holidays, retire later, and experience less unemployment than Europeans. As indicated in Table 14.3, during the period 1993–1996, the average American worked 100/64 = 1.56 times as many hours as the average Italian, or 56 percent more hours. Similarly, the average American worked (100 − 75)/75 = 33 percent more hours than the average German. The average Japanese, on the other hand, worked (104 − 100)/100 = 4 percent more hours than the average American. Why?

TABLE 14.3
Hours Worked per Person and Marginal Tax Rates, 1993–1996

Country	Hours worked per person per year relative to the U.S. (U.S. = 100)	Marginal tax rate
Japan	104	37%
United States	100	40
United Kingdom	88	44
Canada	88	52
Germany	75	59
France	68	59
Italy	64	64

SOURCE: Edward C. Prescott, "Why Do Americans Work So Much More Than Europeans?" Federal Reserve Bank of Minneapolis *Quarterly Review,* July 2004, pp. 2–13.

Edward Prescott found that most of these differences can be explained by the variation in marginal tax rates on labor income among these countries.[8] The Japanese, for example, worked the most and had the lowest marginal tax rate of 37 percent, while the Italians worked the least and had the highest marginal tax rate of 64 percent.

---

[7]Students who have taken introductory microeconomics may recognize this as an example of substitution and income effects.
[8]Prescott's marginal tax rates include taxes on consumption as well as income.

Moreover, during the period 1970–1974, when the marginal tax rates in Europe were much closer to those in the United States, the average European worked as much as the average American. Prescott concludes that reductions in marginal tax rates in Europe would considerably increase both labor supply and potential output.

Most economists agree that higher tax rates help to explain why continental Europeans work fewer hours than Americans, but many note that there are other explanations as well. These explanations include Europe's higher unionization rates and government regulations that limit workweeks and the number of hours that stores may remain open. The differences in work-hours also may be related to more generous social security systems supporting the unemployed, the sick and disabled, and those who retire early in many European countries.[9]

Some observers also have suggested that Europeans simply have a greater taste for leisure and the "good life" than Americans do. However, as Prescott points out, people in most European countries worked much longer hours in the past (when, among other things, tax rates were lower) than they do today, which suggests that the underlying preferences of Europeans and Americans may not be all that different. Yet, the decrease in hours worked over time among a larger sample of European countries is only weakly related to the increase in tax rates.[10] Clearly, this remains a controversial issue.

If lower tax rates tend to increase potential output, why not reduce taxes to zero? The answer is that, ultimately, government expenditures can be paid for only through taxes. Of course, the government can run a deficit for a while, borrowing to cover the difference between what it spends and what it collects in taxes. But deficits can be harmful (they may reduce national saving, as we saw in the chapter *Saving, Capital Formation, and Financial Markets*), and in any case the government's borrowing eventually must be repaid with future taxes. Thus, in the long run, taxes should be set at a level commensurate with the government's rate of spending.

The important message is that fiscal policy can affect potential ouptut as well as aggregate demand. Thus, in making fiscal policy, government officials should take into account not only the need to stabilize aggregate demand but also the likely effects of government spending, taxes, and transfers on the economy's productive capacity.

RECAP	FISCAL POLICY AND THE SUPPLY SIDE

- A supply-side policy is a policy that affects potential output. Fiscal policies affect aggregate demand, but they also may be supply-side policies.

- Government expenditures on public capital—such as roads, airports, and schools—increase aggregate expenditure but also may increase potential output.

- Government tax and transfer programs affect the incentives, and thus the economic behavior, of households and firms.

- People may respond to reductions in their marginal tax rates by working more hours, investing more in education, and taking more entrepreneurial risks, all of which contribute to greater potential output. The size of the effect of tax changes on labor supply remains somewhat controversial.

- Fiscal policymakers should take into account the effects of spending and tax decisions on potential output as well as on aggregate demand.

[9]Stephen Nickell, "Employment and Taxes," London School of Economics Centre for Economic Performance Discussion Paper No. 634, May 2004, and Alberto Alesina, Edward Glaeser, and Bruce Sacerdote, "Work and Leisure in the U.S. and Europe: Why So Different?" National Bureau of Economic Research Working Paper No. 11278, April 2005.
[10]Olivier Blanchard, "The Economic Future of Europe," *Journal of Economic Perspectives* 18, No. 1 (2004), pp. 3–26.

POLICYMAKING: ART OR SCIENCE?

Perfect macroeconomic policy would require each of the following: (1) accurate knowledge of the current state of the economy, (2) knowledge of the future path of the economy if no policy changes are implemented, (3) the precise value of potential output to determine the existence and size of any output gap, (4) complete and immediate control over the tools of fiscal and monetary policy, and (5) knowledge of how and when the economy will respond to changes in policy.

Unfortunately, macroeconomic policy in reality is far from this ideal. The current levels of many macroeconomic indicators such as real GDP often are not known until several months later, and even after that they are subject to multiple revisions. Because policymakers do not have very precise knowledge of the current state of the economy, they may not be able to act decisively.

Further, policymakers are often unsure about the future path of the economy if no policy changes are implemented. If the economy will move to its potential level in the near future in the absence of any policy changes, it will be unnecessary and often unwise for policymakers to act now to eliminate an output gap. Instead of hastening the move back to full employment, policy changes may lead the economy to overshoot, necessitating a policy reversal in the future and potentially destabilizing the economy.

Economists are also unsure about the exact levels of potential output and the natural rate of unemployment. For example, most economists now believe that macroeconomic policy was often too expansionary (and, hence, too inflationary) during the 1970s because policymakers overestimated the potential level of output and hence underestimated the natural rate of unemployment.

Even when policy changes are needed, it can take a long time for policymakers to implement the appropriate policy changes. The **inside lag** of macroeconomic policy refers to the delay between the date a policy change is needed and the date that policy change is implemented. During this period, the policymakers' economic advisors must recognize that a persistent output gap exists and determine the correct policy change. The policymakers must then accept the desirability of that policy change and implement it.

inside lag (of macroeconomic policy) the delay between the date a policy change is needed and the date it is implemented

The inside lag for monetary policy is substantially shorter than the inside lag for fiscal policy. Once monetary policymakers accept the desirability of a change in the federal funds rate, they only have to wait until the next meeting of the Federal Open Market Committee. Since this committee meets eight times per year, the maximum delay is about seven weeks. In urgent situations, the committee has been known to act during conference calls in between meetings. And once the committee decides to change the federal funds rate, the Federal Reserve Bank of New York almost immediately conducts the open-market operations sufficient to move the rate to its desired level.

The inside lag for fiscal policy, on the other hand, is considerably longer. After the president proposes a change in tax rates or government spending, both houses of Congress must approve it. This process can take a long time, especially when one or both of the houses of Congress are controlled by the opposing political party. One of the reasons for these delays is that the exact form of a change in taxes or government spending can vary considerably. Should personal income taxes or business taxes be cut? Should defense spending or spending on education be increased? Even after Congress has approved the policy change and the president has signed the bill, it sometimes takes a long time to implement the tax changes or make the additional expenditures.

Finally, economists have only an approximate idea of the exact output effect of a change in policy. The marginal propensity to consume is not known with certainty and need not be the same for all changes in income. Similarly, Fed policymakers have only an approximate idea of the effect of a given change in the real interest rate on planned spending. Economists have constructed statistical models of the economy that track the historical performance of the economy reasonably well. Yet these same statistical models have often yielded disappointing and unreliable forecasts of the future path of the economy. Part of the problem is that it is difficult to predict the values of the exogenous variables in the economy, such as government spending or

outside lag (of macroeconomic policy) the delay between the date a policy change is implemented and the date by which most of its effects on the economy have occurred

tax rates. In addition, the economic structure of the economy itself occasionally changes over time. The extent to which investment responds to changing real interest rates, for example, has varied over time.

Furthermore, both fiscal and monetary policymakers are never sure about the length of time before the effects on planned spending will occur. The **outside lag** of macroeconomic policy refers to the delay between the date a policy change is implemented and the date by which most of its effects on the economy have occurred. Although fiscal policy has a longer inside lag than monetary policy, its outside lag may be shorter. Changes in government spending have an immediate effect on real GDP and the economy, although the multiplier effects continue into the future. Similarly, households often respond to tax cuts by increasing their consumption expenditures immediately. On the other hand, investment responds more slowly when the Fed changes the real interest rate since the interest rate is one among many factors that businesses look at before building a new factory or buying an expensive new machine.

Because our knowledge of the economy is imperfect, policymaking at its best also will be imperfect. In terms of our aggregate supply–aggregate demand model, policymakers don't know exactly how much or how fast the aggregate demand curve will shift in response to policy changes. They also don't know how fast the aggregate supply curve shifts up when output exceeds its potential level or how fast it shifts down if output is less than potential.

During the 1960s, economists were more confident about their ability to maintain output at its potential level using the appropriate monetary and fiscal policies. They believed they could compute the size of output gaps, and devise policies to eliminate these gaps. Many also believed they could easily predict the future path of the economy under alternate policy scenarios, and they were comfortable implementing frequent policy changes in order to "fine-tune" the economy. Finally, many economists mistakenly thought policymakers could deliver a permanently higher level of output with just a bit more inflation.

The experience of the past few decades has made economists more humble, even about identifying an output gap. Some economists believe that we are at potential output when the unemployment rate is 4.5 percent, while others believe the natural rate of unemployment is as high as 5.5 or even 6.0 percent. Consequently, whenever the actual unemployment rate lies between 4.5 and 6 percent, some economists think they see a recessionary gap while others see an expansionary gap.

Because of these uncertainties, macroeconomic policymakers tend to proceed cautiously. The Fed, for example, avoids large changes in interest rates and rarely raises or lowers the federal funds rate more than one-half of a percentage point (from 5 percent to 5.5 percent, for example) at any one time. Indeed, the typical change in the interest rate is one-quarter of a percentage point. Similarly, policymakers are now less likely to try to "fine-tune" the economy.

Is macroeconomic policymaking an art or a science, then? In practice it appears to be both. Scientific analyses, such as the development of detailed statistical models of the economy, have proved useful in making policy. But human judgment based on long experience—what has been called the "art" of macroeconomic policy—plays a crucial role in successful policymaking and is likely to continue to do so.

RECAP	POLICYMAKING: ART OR SCIENCE?

Macroeconomic policymaking is a difficult and inexact science. Policymakers do not know the precise state of the economy, the future path of the economy if no policy changes are implemented, or the precise level of potential output. They also have imperfect control over policy instruments and imprecise knowledge of the effects of any policy changes. The existence of inside and outside lags makes policymaking even more difficult. Consequently, macroeconomic policymaking is an art as well as a science.

○ SUMMARY ○

• Changes in exogenous spending shift the aggregate demand curve. In response, fiscal and monetary policy can be applied to return output to potential and inflation to its long-run expected rate. *(LO1)*

• Inflation shocks force the Fed to choose between maintaining inflation and stabilizing output. If inflationary expectations are anchored, the return to potential output following an inflation shock will occur more rapidly. *(LO1)*

• Anchored inflationary expectations will improve economic performance in the long run and also may reduce the volatility of output and inflation in the short run. Inflationary expectations are more likely to be anchored if the central bank's policies are viewed as credible and the public believes the central bank's promises to keep inflation low. *(LO2)*

• A central bank's credibility may be enhanced if it is insulated from short-term political considerations and is allowed to take a long-term view of the economy. Credibility also may be enhanced if the central bank publicly announces a numerical inflation target and if it has a reputation as an "inflation hawk." *(LO2)*

• A supply-side policy is a policy that affects potential output. Fiscal policies affect aggregate demand, but they also may be supply-side policies. Government expenditures on public capital increase aggregate expenditure but also may increase potential output. Government tax and transfer programs affect the incentives of households and firms. People may respond to reductions in their marginal tax rates by working more hours, investing more in education, and taking more entrepreneurial risks, all of which contribute to greater potential output. The size of the effect of tax changes on labor supply remains somewhat controversial. Fiscal policymakers should take into account the effects of spending and tax decisions on aggregate supply as well as on aggregate demand. *(LO3)*

• Economists now recognize that the analogy between driving a car and managing the economy is a poor one. Unlike driving a car, macroeconomic policymaking is an inexact science. Policymakers do not know the precise state of the economy, the future path of the economy if no policy changes are implemented, or the precise level of potential output. In addition, they have imperfect control over policy instruments and imprecise knowledge of the effects of any policy changes. During the past few decades, economic policymakers have become more humble about their ability to "fine-tune" the economy. *(LO4)*

○ KEY TERMS ○

accommodating policy
anchored inflationary expectations
average tax rate
central bank independence

credibility of monetary policy
inflation dove
inflation hawk
inside lag (of macroeconomic policy)

marginal tax rate
outside lag (of macroeconomic policy)
supply-side policy

○ REVIEW QUESTIONS ○

1. Suppose there is an increase in taxes. What is the short-run effect on output, inflation, and the real interest rate, assuming any supply-side effects are minimal? What will be the effect in the long run if the Fed chooses to adjust its target real interest rate to the new long-run real interest rate at which saving equals investment? *(LO1)*

2. How does the adoption of a tighter monetary policy, like that conducted by the Volcker Fed in the early 1980s, affect output, inflation, and the real interest rate in the short run? In the long run? *(LO1)*

3. Suppose there is a sudden increase in oil prices. What will be the effect on output and inflation in the short run? What is the "dilemma" faced by the Fed as a result of the adverse inflation shock? *(LO1)*

4. What are anchored inflationary expectations and how do they reduce the cost of an adverse inflation shock? *(LO2)*

5. What factors determine a central bank's independence? What are the benefits of having an independent central bank? *(LO2)*

6. How does a reduction in the marginal tax rate affect both aggregate demand and aggregate supply? *(LO3)*

○ PROBLEMS ○

|ECONOMICS

Visit your mobile app
store and download
the Frank: Study
Econ app *today!*

1. Suppose the economy is initially in long-run equilibrium and the Fed adopts a looser monetary policy and raises its long-run target for the inflation rate. *(LO1)*
   a. Explain how this change in monetary policy will affect the *AD* curve.
   b. Use your result for part a along with an *AD-AS* diagram to illustrate and explain what will happen to output and inflation in both the short run and the long run.

2. Suppose the economy is initially in long-run equilibrium and experiences a favorable inflation shock. *(LO1)*
   a. Explain how the *AS* curve is affected in the short run.
   b. Use your result for part a along with an *AD-AS* diagram to illustrate and explain what will happen to output and inflation in both the short run and the long run if the Fed accommodates the favorable inflation shock.
   c. Use your result for part a along with an *AD-AS* diagram to illustrate and explain what will happen to output and inflation in both the short run and the long run if the Fed does not accommodate the favorable inflation shock.

3. Suppose the economy is initially in long-run equilibrium. Due to a decline in house prices, suppose that consumers reduce their consumption spending. *(LO1)*
   a. Explain how the decline in consumer spending affects the *AD* curve.
   b. If the Fed does not change its monetary policy rule, how will the Fed react to the decline in consumer spending? Use an *AD-AS* diagram to illustrate and explain your answer.
   c. Now, in addition to the decline in consumer spending, suppose that the economy experiences an adverse inflation shock.
      i. Explain how the adverse inflation shock affects the *AS* curve.
      ii. Discuss, using *AD-AS* diagrams, what choices the Fed now must make regarding monetary policy. (*Hint:* Think about whether or not it should tighten monetary policy.)

4. Suppose there is a large increase in oil or food prices. *(LO2)*
   a. If the core rate of inflation remains unchanged, what might the Fed infer about inflationary expectations and the second-round effects of the inflation shock? How might it respond?
   b. If the core rate of inflation rises substantially, what might the Fed infer about inflationary expectations and the second-round effects of the inflation shock? How might it respond?

5. What are the advantages of having an independent central bank? Describe the institutional features that make a central bank independent. *(LO2)*

6. Suppose the economy is initially in long-run equilibrium and the government reduces the marginal tax rate. *(LO3)*
   a. Use a graph like Figure 14.5 to illustrate and explain what will happen to output and inflation in both the short run and the long run if the effects of the tax cuts are stronger on aggregate demand than on aggregate supply.
   b. How would your conclusions in part a be affected if the effects of the tax cuts are stronger on aggregate supply than on aggregate demand? Explain using a graph like Figure 14.5.

7. Using the theory presented in this chapter, explain why the adoption of a tighter, more anti-inflationary monetary policy might be politically unpopular. *(LO4)*

8. Explain how the recognition that macroeconomic policymaking is an inexact science affects your recommended policy response to the following situations: *(LO4)*
   a. Your estimate of the natural rate of unemployment is 5 percent, and the actual unemployment rate is 5.5 percent.
   b. Your estimate of the natural rate of unemployment is 5 percent, and the actual unemployment rate is 8 percent.

○ ANSWER TO CONCEPT CHECK ○

14.1 If Tom earned $5,000, he would pay no taxes, so his average tax rate would be 0 percent. If he earned $5,001, he would still pay no taxes, so his marginal tax rate also would be 0 percent.

If Tom earned $11,000, he would pay 0.20($11,000 − $10,000) = $200 in taxes, so his average tax rate would be $200/$11,000 = 0.018, or 1.8 percent. If his income rose by $1 so that he earned $11,001, his taxes would be 0.20($11,001 − $10,000) = $200.20. Thus, he would pay an additional $0.20 in taxes and his marginal tax rate would be 20 percent.

If Tom earned $15,000, he would pay 0.20($15,000 − $10,000) = $1,000 in taxes, and his average tax rate would be $1,000/$15,000 = 0.067, or 6.7 percent. If his income rose by $1 to $15,001, he would pay an additional $0.20 in taxes, so his marginal tax rate would still be 20 percent. *(LO3)*

CHAPTER 15

Exchange Rates, International Trade, and Capital Flows

Maria Toutoudaki/Getty Image

WHAT DETERMINES EXCHANGE RATES IN THE SHORT RUN AND LONG RUN?

LEARNING OBJECTIVES

After reading this chapter, you should be able to:

LO1 Define the nominal exchange rate and discuss the advantages and disadvantages of flexible versus fixed exchange rates.

LO2 Use supply and demand to analyze how the nominal exchange rate is determined in the short run.

LO3 Define the real exchange rate, summarize the law of one price, and understand how purchasing power parity determines the long-run real exchange rate.

LO4 Analyze the factors that determine international capital flows to understand how domestic saving, the trade balance, and net capital inflows are related.

Two Americans visiting London were commiserating over their problems understanding English currency. "Pounds, shillings, tuppence, thruppence, bob, and quid, it's driving me crazy," said the first American. "This morning it took me 20 minutes to figure out how much to pay the taxi driver."

The second American was more upbeat. "Actually," he said, "since I adopted my new system, I haven't had any problems at all."

The first American looked interested. "What's your new system?"

"Well," replied the second, "now, whenever I take a taxi, I just give the driver all the English money I have. And would you believe it, I have got the fare exactly right every time!"

Dealing with unfamiliar currencies—and translating the value of foreign money into dollars—is a problem every international traveler faces.[1] The traveler's problem is

---

[1]However, British money today is less complicated to understand than suggested by the introductory story. In 1971 the British switched to a decimal monetary system, under which each pound is worth 100 pence. At that time, the traditional British system, under which a pound equaled 20 shillings and each shilling equaled 12 pence, was abandoned.

complicated by the fact that *exchange rates*—the rates at which one country's money trades for another—may change unpredictably. Thus, the number of British pounds, Russian rubles, Japanese yen, or Australian dollars that a U.S. dollar can buy may vary over time, sometimes quite a lot.

The economic consequences of variable exchange rates are much broader than their impact on travel and tourism, however. For example, the competitiveness of U.S. exports depends in part on the prices of U.S. goods in terms of foreign currencies, which in turn depend on the exchange rate between the U.S. dollar and those currencies. Likewise, the prices Americans pay for imported goods depend in part on the value of the dollar relative to the currencies of the countries that produce those goods. Exchange rates also affect the value of financial investments made across national borders. For countries that are heavily dependent on trade and international capital flows—the majority of the world's nations—fluctuations in the exchange rate may have a significant economic impact.

This chapter discusses exchange rates, international trade, and international capital flows, and their effects on the broader economy. We will start by introducing the nominal exchange rate—the rate at which one national currency trades for another. Next we will turn to the question of how exchange rates are determined in the short run. Exchange rates may be divided into two broad categories: flexible and fixed. The value of a flexible exchange rate is determined freely in the market for national currencies, known as the foreign exchange market. In contrast, the value of a fixed exchange rate is set by the government at a constant level. We show that a country's monetary policy plays a particularly important role in determining the exchange rate. Furthermore, in an open economy with a flexible exchange rate, the exchange rate becomes a tool of monetary policy, in much the same way as the real interest rate.

We focus on flexible exchange rates because most countries allow market forces to determine their nominal exchange rate. However, many small and developing economies fix their exchange rates, so we will also consider the relative merits of fixed and flexible exchange rates. We close our discussion of exchange rates by introducing the real exchange rate—the rate at which one country's goods trade for another's—and discussing how exchange rates are determined in the long run.

Finally, we examine data on U.S. international trade in goods and services, and analyze how trade in goods and services is directly connected with international capital flows. Specifically, we analyze how for many countries, including the United States, foreign saving provides an important supplement to domestic saving as a means of financing capital formation.

EXCHANGE RATES

The economic benefits of trade between nations in goods, services, and assets are similar to the benefits of trade within a nation. In both cases, trade in goods and services permits greater specialization and efficiency, whereas trade in assets allows financial investors to earn higher returns while providing funds for worthwhile capital projects. However, there is a difference between the two cases. Trade in goods, services, and assets *within* a nation normally involves a single currency—dollars, yen, pesos, or whatever the country's official form of money happens to be—whereas trade *between* nations usually involves dealing in different currencies. So, for example, if an American resident wants to purchase an automobile manufactured in South Korea, she (or more likely, the automobile dealer) must first trade dollars for the Korean currency, called the won. The Korean car manufacturer is then paid in won. Similarly, an Argentine who wants to purchase shares in a U.S. company (a U.S. financial asset) must first trade his Argentine pesos for dollars and then use the dollars to purchase the shares.

TABLE 15.1
Nominal Exchange Rates for the U.S. Dollar

Country	Foreign currency/U.S. dollar	U.S. dollar/foreign currency
United Kingdom (pound)	1.631	0.613
Canada (Canadian dollar)	1.089	0.918
Mexico (peso)	13.068	0.077
Japan (yen)	104.940	0.010
China (yuan)	6.140	0.163
European Monetary Union (euro)	1.296	0.772

SOURCE: Federal Reserve Statistical Release H.10 for September 5, 2014.

NOMINAL EXCHANGE RATES

The rate at which two currencies can be traded for each other is called the **nominal exchange rate,** or more simply the *exchange rate,* between the two currencies. For example, if one U.S. dollar can be exchanged for 90 Japanese yen, the nominal exchange rate between the U.S. and Japanese currencies is 90 yen per dollar. Each country has many nominal exchange rates, one corresponding to each currency against which its own currency is traded. Thus, the dollar's value can be quoted in terms of English pounds, Swedish kronor, Israeli shekels, Russian rubles, or dozens of other currencies.

nominal exchange rate the rate at which two currencies can be traded for each other

Table 15.1 gives exchange rates between the dollar and six other important currencies as of the close of business in New York City on September 5, 2014. As Table 15.1 illustrates, an important point to keep in mind about exchange rates: They can be expressed either as the amount of foreign currency needed to purchase one U.S. dollar (left column) or as the number of U.S. dollars needed to purchase one unit of the foreign currency (right column). These two ways of expressing the exchange rate are equivalent: Each is the reciprocal of the other.

Exchange Rates   **EXAMPLE 15.1**

What is the exchange rate between the Canadian dollar and the British pound?

We can also use the data in Table 15.1 to find the exchange rate between any pair of countries in the table. For example, suppose that you need to find the exchange rate between the British pound and the Canadian dollar. The table tells us that we can purchase one U.S. dollar for 1.089 Canadian dollars; it also tells us that we can buy one U.S. dollar for 1.631 British pounds. This implies that

$$1.089 \text{ Canadian dollars} = 1.631 \text{ British pounds.}$$

Thus, we can find the exchange rate between British pounds and Canadian dollars in two ways. First, we can find out how much one Canadian dollar is worth in terms of British pounds by dividing both sides of the above equation by 1.089:

$$1 \text{ Canadian dollar} = \frac{1.631}{1.089} \text{ British pounds} = 1.498 \text{ British pounds.}$$

Alternatively, we can divide both sides of the first equation by 1.631:

$$1 \text{ British pound} = \frac{1.089}{1.631} \text{ Canadian dollar} = 0.668 \text{ Canadian dollar.}$$

CONCEPT CHECK 15.1

From the business section of a newspaper or an online source (try the Federal Reserve Bank of St. Louis FRED database, http://research.stlouisfed.org/fred2), find recent quotations of the value of the U.S. dollar against the British pound, the Canadian dollar, and the Japanese yen. Based on these data, find the exchange rate (a) between the pound and the Canadian dollar and (b) between the Canadian dollar and the yen. Express the exchange rates you derive in two ways (e.g., both as pounds per Canadian dollar and as Canadian dollars per pound).

Figure 15.1 shows the nominal exchange rate for the U.S. dollar from 1973 to 2013. Rather than showing the value of the dollar relative to that of an individual foreign currency, such as the Japanese yen or the British pound, the figure expresses the value of the dollar as an average of its values against other major currencies. This average value of the dollar is measured relative to a base value of 100 in 1973. So, for example, a value of 120 for the dollar in a particular year implies that the dollar was 20 percent more valuable in that year, relative to other major currencies, than it was in 1973.

You can see from Figure 15.1 that the dollar's value has fluctuated over time, sometimes increasing (as in the period 1980–1985) and sometimes decreasing (as in 1985–1987 and 2002–2011). An increase in the value of a currency relative to other currencies is known as an **appreciation**; a decline in the value of a currency relative to other currencies is called a **depreciation**. So we can say that the dollar appreciated in 1980–1985 and depreciated in 1985–1987 and 2002–2011.

We will use the symbol e to stand for a country's nominal exchange rate. Table 15.1 shows that we can express the exchange rate as either foreign currency units per unit of domestic currency or vice versa. The choice is arbitrary, but it is important because you need to be consistent whenever you are analyzing exchange rates. Thus, we define e as the number of units of foreign currency that each unit of domestic currency will buy. For example, if we treat the United States as the "home" or "domestic" country and Japan as the "foreign" country, e is the number of Japanese yen that one

appreciation an increase in the value of a currency relative to other currencies

depreciation a decrease in the value of a currency relative to other currencies

FIGURE 15.1

The U.S. Nominal Exchange Rate, 1973–2013.

This figure shows the value of the dollar as an average of its values against other major currencies, relative to a base value of 100 in 1973.

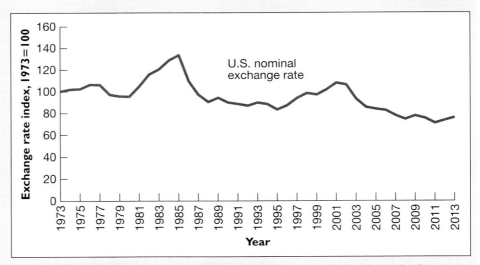

SOURCE: Federal Reserve Bank of St. Louis, FRED database, http://research.stlouisfed.org/fred2.

U.S. dollar will buy. The advantage of defining the nominal exchange rate this way implies that an *increase* in *e* corresponds to an *appreciation,* or a strengthening, of the home currency since each unit of domestic currency will then buy more units of foreign currency. Similarly, a *decrease* in *e* implies *depreciation,* or weakening, of the home currency since each unit of domestic currency will buy fewer units of foreign currency.

FLEXIBLE VERSUS FIXED EXCHANGE RATES

Figure 15.1 shows that the exchange rate between the U.S. dollar and other currencies isn't constant but varies continually. Indeed, changes in the value of the dollar occur daily, hourly, even minute by minute. Such fluctuations in the value of a currency are normal for countries like the United States, which have a *flexible* or *floating exchange rate.* The value of a **flexible exchange rate** is not officially fixed but varies according to the supply and demand for the currency in the **foreign exchange market**—the market on which currencies of various nations are traded for one another. We will discuss the factors that determine the supply and demand for currencies shortly.

    Some countries do not allow their currency values to vary with market conditions but instead maintain a *fixed exchange rate.* The value of a **fixed exchange rate** is set by official government policy. (A government that establishes a fixed exchange rate typically determines the exchange rate's value independently, but sometimes exchange rates are set according to an agreement among a number of governments.) Some countries fix their exchange rates in terms of the U.S. dollar (Hong Kong, for example), but there are other possibilities. Many African countries fix the value of their currencies in terms of the euro, the currency of the European Union. Under the gold standard, which many countries used until its collapse during the Great Depression, currency values were fixed in terms of ounces of gold.

flexible exchange rate an exchange rate whose value is not officially fixed but varies according to the supply and demand for the currency in the foreign exchange market

foreign exchange market the market on which currencies of various nations are traded for one another

fixed exchange rate an exchange rate whose value is set by official government policy

SHOULD EXCHANGE RATES BE FIXED OR FLEXIBLE?

We will focus on the case of flexible exchange rates since it is the relevant case for most countries. However, an alternative approach is to fix an exchange rate. Fixed exchange rates have been quite important historically and are still used in many countries, especially small or developing nations.

    Should countries adopt fixed or flexible exchange rates? In briefly comparing the two systems, we will focus on two major issues: (1) the effects of the exchange rate system on monetary policy and (2) the effects of the exchange rate system on trade and economic integration.

    The type of exchange rate a country has strongly affects the central bank's ability to use monetary policy to stabilize the economy. A flexible exchange rate actually strengthens the impact of monetary policy on aggregate demand. However, a fixed exchange rate prevents policymakers from using monetary policy to stabilize the economy because they must instead use it to keep the exchange rate's market equilibrium value at its official value.

    In large economies like that of the United States, giving up the power to stabilize the domestic economy via monetary policy makes little sense. Thus, large economies should nearly always employ a flexible exchange rate. However, in small economies, giving up this power may have some benefits. An interesting case is that of Argentina, which for the period 1991–2001 maintained a one-to-one exchange rate between its peso and the U.S. dollar. Although prior to 1991 Argentina had suffered periods of hyperinflation, while the peso was pegged to the dollar, Argentina's inflation rate essentially equaled that of the United States. By tying its currency to the dollar and giving up the freedom to set its monetary policy, Argentina attempted to commit itself to avoiding the inflationary policies of the past, and instead placed itself under the "umbrella" of the Federal Reserve.

Unfortunately, early in 2002, investors' fears that Argentina would not be able to repay its international debts forced Argentina to abandon its fixed exchange rate and let the peso float. The peso depreciated, and Argentina experienced an economic crisis from which it has not yet fully recovered. The lesson is that a fixed exchange rate alone cannot stop inflation in a small economy if other policies are not sound as well. Large fiscal deficits financed by foreign borrowing ultimately pushed Argentina into crisis.

The second important issue is the effect of the exchange rate on trade and economic integration. Proponents of fixed exchange rates argue that fixed rates promote international trade and cross-border economic cooperation by reducing uncertainty about future exchange rates. For example, a firm that is considering building up its export business knows that its potential profits will depend on the future value of its own country's currency relative to the currencies of the countries to which it exports. Under a flexible-exchange-rate regime, the value of the home currency fluctuates with changes in supply and demand and is therefore difficult to predict far in advance. Such uncertainty may make the firm reluctant to expand its export business. Supporters of fixed exchange rates argue that if the exchange rate is officially fixed, uncertainty about the future exchange rate is reduced or eliminated.

One problem with this argument, which has been underscored by episodes like the East Asian crisis of the late 1990s and the Argentine crisis, is that fixed exchange rates are not guaranteed to remain fixed forever. Although they do not fluctuate from day to day as flexible rates do, a fixed exchange rate that is set above the market's equilibrium exchange rate may lead suddenly and unpredictably to a large and sudden fall in the value of the country's currency. For instance, in 1997, the Thai currency (the baht) depreciated by over 67 percent in just two weeks. Thus, a firm that is trying to forecast the exchange rate 10 years into the future may face as much uncertainty if the exchange rate is fixed as if it is flexible.

The potential instability of fixed exchange rates has led some countries to try a more radical solution to the problem of uncertainty about exchange rates: the adoption of a common currency.

The Euro: A Common Currency for Europe

Since World War II, the nations of western Europe have worked to increase economic cooperation and trade among themselves. European leaders recognized that a unified and integrated European economy would be more productive and perhaps more competitive with the U.S. economy than a fragmented one. As part of this effort, these countries established fixed exchange rates in the 1970s under the auspices of a system called the European Monetary System (EMS). Unfortunately, the EMS did not prove stable. Numerous devaluations of the various currencies occurred, and in 1992 severe problems maintaining their exchange rates forced several nations, including Great Britain, to abandon the fixed-exchange-rate system.

In December 1991, in Maastricht in the Netherlands, the member countries of the European Community (EC) agreed to a pact known as the Maastricht Treaty. One of the major provisions of the treaty, which took effect in November 1993, was the member countries would strive to adopt a common currency. Effective January 1, 1999, 11 western European nations, including France, Germany, and Italy, adopted a common currency, called the euro. In several stages, the euro replaced the French franc, the German mark, the Italian lira, and other national currencies. The process was completed in early 2002, when the old currencies were completely eliminated and replaced by euros.

The advent of the euro means that Europeans no longer have to change currencies when trading with other European countries, much as Americans from different states can trade with each other without worrying that a "New York dollar" will change in value relative to a "California dollar." The euro has helped to promote European trade and cooperation while eliminating the necessity of individual countries maintaining fixed exchange rates.

Since so many European countries now have a common currency, they also need to have a common monetary policy. The EC members agreed that European monetary policy would be put under the control of a new European Central Bank (ECB), a multinational institution located in Frankfurt, Germany. The ECB, in effect, has become "Europe's Fed."

One potential problem with having a single monetary policy for many different countries is that different countries may face different economic conditions, so a single monetary policy cannot respond to all of them. For example, in recent years, some countries in Europe (such as Greece, Ireland, Portugal, and Spain) have faced financial crises due to large government budget deficits, while other countries (such as Germany) have been concerned about increases in inflation. The former set of countries would prefer an easier monetary policy, while the latter countries would argue in favor of tighter monetary policy. Because the ECB can choose only a single monetary policy for all the countries using the euro, conflicts of interest may arise among the member nations of the European Union, and the International Monetary Fund has had to aid countries such as Greece, Ireland, and Portugal directly.

RECAP	NOMINAL EXCHANGE RATES

- The nominal exchange rate between two currencies is the rate at which the currencies can be traded for each other. More precisely, the nominal exchange rate e for any given country is the number of units of foreign currency that can be bought for one unit of the domestic currency.

- An appreciation is an increase in the value of a currency relative to other currencies (a rise in e); a depreciation is a decline in a currency's value (a fall in e).

- An exchange rate can be either flexible—meaning that it varies freely according to supply and demand for the currency in the foreign exchange market—or fixed, meaning that its value is established by official government policy.

EXCHANGE RATE DETERMINATION IN THE SHORT RUN

Countries that have flexible exchange rates, such as the United States, see the international values of their currencies change continually. What determines the value of the nominal exchange rate at any point in time? In this section, we use supply and demand analysis to answer this question for the short run. Later in the chapter we discuss the determination of exchange rates in the long run.

A SUPPLY AND DEMAND ANALYSIS

In this section, we analyze the foreign exchange market and discuss the factors that affect the supply of and demand for dollars, and thus the U.S. exchange rate. As we will see, dollars are demanded in the foreign exchange market by foreigners who seek to purchase U.S. goods, services, and assets. Similarly, dollars are supplied by U.S. residents who need foreign currencies to buy foreign goods, services, and assets. The market equilibrium exchange rate is the value of the dollar that equates the number of dollars supplied and demanded in the foreign exchange market.

Before proceeding, we need to be careful about our terminology. In the chapter *Monetary Policy and the Federal Reserve*, we analyzed how the supply of money (controlled by the Fed) and the demand for money by the public determine the nominal interest rate. However, the supply of and demand for money in the domestic economy, as presented in that chapter, are *not* equivalent to the supply and demand for dollars in the foreign exchange market. The foreign exchange market is the market in which the currencies of various nations are traded for one another. The supply of dollars to the foreign exchange market is *not* the same as the money supply set by the Fed; rather, it is the number of dollars U.S. households and firms offer to trade for other currencies. Likewise, the demand for dollars in the foreign exchange market is *not* the same as the domestic demand for money, but is the number of dollars holders of foreign currencies seek to buy.

To understand the distinction, keep in mind that, while the Fed determines the total supply of dollars available in the U.S. economy, a dollar is not supplied to the foreign exchange market until a holder of dollars, such as an American household or firm, offers to trade it for foreign currency.

The Supply of Dollars

Anyone who holds dollars, from an international bank to a Russian citizen whose dollars are buried in the backyard, is a potential supplier of dollars to the foreign exchange market. In practice, however, the principal suppliers of dollars to the foreign exchange market are U.S. households and firms.

Why would a U.S. household or firm want to supply dollars in exchange for foreign currency? There are two major reasons. First, a U.S. household or firm may need foreign currency to *purchase foreign goods or services*. For example, a U.S. automobile importer may need yen to purchase Japanese cars, or an American tourist may need yen to make purchases in Tokyo. Second, a U.S. household or firm may need foreign currency *to purchase foreign assets*. For example, an American mutual fund may wish to acquire stocks issued by Japanese companies, or an individual U.S. saver may want to purchase Japanese government bonds. Because Japanese assets are priced in yen, the U.S. household or firm will need to trade dollars for yen to acquire these assets.

The supply of dollars to the foreign exchange market is illustrated by the upward-sloping curve in Figure 15.2. We will focus on the market in which dollars are traded for Japanese yen, but bear in mind that similar markets exist for every other pair of traded currencies. The vertical axis of the figure shows the U.S.–Japanese exchange rate as measured by the number of yen that can be purchased with each dollar. The horizontal axis shows the number of dollars being traded in the yen–dollar market.

The supply curve for dollars is upward-sloping, indicating that the more yen each dollar can buy, the more dollars people are willing to supply to the foreign exchange market. Why? At given prices for Japanese goods, services, and assets, the more yen a dollar can buy, the cheaper those goods, services, and assets will be in dollar terms.

FIGURE 15.2

The Supply and Demand for Dollars in the Yen–Dollar Market.

The supply of dollars to the foreign exchange market is upward-sloping because an increase in the number of yen offered for each dollar makes Japanese goods, services, and assets more attractive to U.S. buyers. Similarly, the demand for dollars is downward-sloping because holders of yen will be less willing to buy dollars the more expensive they are in terms of yen. The *market equilibrium exchange rate e** equates the quantities of dollars supplied and demanded.

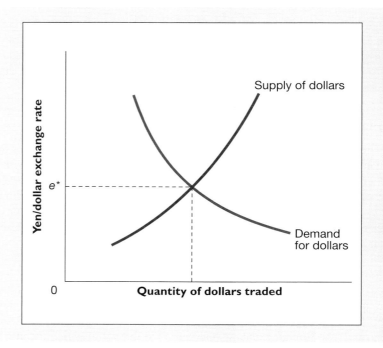

The Impact of the Exchange Rate on the Price of Imported Goods

EXAMPLE 15.2

How does the exchange rate affect the price of imported goods?

Suppose a video game costs 5,000 yen in Japan and a dollar can buy 100 yen; the dollar price of the video game will be

$$5,000 \text{ yen} \times \$1/100 \text{ yen} = \$50.^2$$

If, however, the yen price of a dollar rises to 200 yen, the dollar price of the same video game that costs 5,000 yen in Japan will then be

$$5,000 \text{ yen} \times \$1/200 \text{ yen} = \$25.$$

If lower dollar prices will induce Americans to increase their total dollar expenditures on Japanese goods, services, and assets, a higher yen–dollar exchange rate will increase the supply of dollars to the foreign exchange market. Thus, the supply curve for dollars is upward-sloping.

The Demand for Dollars

In the yen–dollar foreign exchange market, demanders of dollars are those who wish to acquire dollars in exchange for yen. Most demanders of dollars in the yen–dollar market are Japanese households and firms, although anyone who happens to hold yen is free to trade them for dollars. Why demand dollars? The reasons for acquiring dollars are analogous to those for acquiring yen. First, households and firms that hold yen will demand dollars *so that they can purchase U.S. goods and services.* For example, a Japanese firm that wants to license U.S.-produced software needs dollars to pay the required fees, and a Japanese student studying in an American university must pay tuition in dollars. The firm or the student can acquire the necessary dollars only by offering yen in exchange. Second, households and firms demand dollars *in order to purchase U.S. assets.* The purchase of Hawaiian real estate by a Japanese company or the acquisition of Microsoft stock by a Japanese pension fund are two examples.

The demand curve for dollars will be downward-sloping, as illustrated in Figure 15.2. The quantity of dollars demanded will be low when dollars are expensive in terms of yen and high when dollars are cheap in terms of yen.

The Impact of the Exchange Rate on the Price of Exported Goods

EXAMPLE 15.3

How does the exchange rate affect the price of exported goods?

Suppose the licensing fee for a piece of U.S.-produced software is $30. If it costs a Japanese business 200 yen to buy $1, the software will cost the Japanese

$$\$30 \times 200 \text{ yen}/\$1 = 6,000 \text{ yen}.^3$$

If, however, the price of a dollar falls to 100 yen, the yen price of the same software that costs $30 in the United States will then be

$$\$30 \times 100 \text{ yen}/\$1 = 3,000 \text{ yen}.$$

[2]Recall that an exchange rate of one dollar per 100 yen is the same as 100 yen per dollar. We are writing it the first way in this example so that the yen will cancel when we perform the multiplication and we are left with the dollar price.
[3]In this calculation, we use the yen-per-dollar exchange rate so that the dollars cancel when we perform the multiplication and we are left with the price in yen.

As the yen price per dollar falls, U.S. goods, services, and assets become cheaper and more attractive to the Japanese. They respond by buying more U.S. goods, services, and assets and thereby demanding more dollars.

The Market Equilibrium Value of the Dollar

As mentioned earlier, the United States maintains a flexible, or floating, exchange rate, which means that the value of the dollar is determined by the forces of supply and demand in the foreign exchange market. In Figure 15.2, the equilibrium value of the dollar is e^*, the yen–dollar exchange rate at which the quantity of dollars supplied equals the quantity of dollars demanded. In general, the **market equilibrium value of the exchange rate** is not constant but changes with shifts in the supply of and demand for dollars in the foreign exchange market.

market equilibrium value of the exchange rate the exchange rate that equates the quantities of the currency supplied and demanded in the foreign exchange market

CHANGES IN THE SUPPLY OF DOLLARS

Recall that people supply dollars to the yen–dollar foreign exchange market in order to purchase Japanese goods, services, and assets. Factors that affect the desire of U.S. households and firms to acquire Japanese goods, services, and assets therefore will affect the supply of dollars to the foreign exchange market. Some factors that will *increase* the supply of dollars, shifting the supply curve for dollars to the right, include:

Supplying dollars, demanding yen.

Gallo Images - Richard Keppel-Smith/ Getty Images

- An increased preference for Japanese goods. For example, suppose that Japanese firms produce some popular new consumer electronics. To acquire the yen needed to buy these goods, American importers will increase their supply of dollars to the foreign exchange market.

- An increase in U.S. real GDP. An increase in U.S. real GDP will raise the incomes of Americans, allowing them to consume more goods and services (recall the relationship between consumption and income we discussed in the chapter *Spending, Output, and Fiscal Policy*). Some part of this increase in consumption will take the form of goods imported from Japan. To buy more Japanese goods, Americans will supply more dollars to acquire the necessary yen.

- An increase in the real interest rate on Japanese assets or a decrease in the real interest rate on U.S. assets. Recall that U.S. households and firms acquire yen in order to purchase Japanese assets as well as goods and services. With other factors, such as risk, held constant, the higher the real interest rate paid on Japanese assets (or the lower the real interest rate paid on U.S. assets), the more Japanese assets Americans will choose to hold. To purchase additional Japanese assets, U.S. households and firms will supply more dollars to the foreign exchange market.

Conversely, reduced demand for Japanese goods, a lower U.S. GDP, a lower real interest rate on Japanese assets, or a higher real interest rate on U.S. assets will *reduce* the number of yen Americans need, in turn reducing their supply of dollars to the foreign exchange market and shifting the supply curve for dollars to the left.

Suppose, for example, that Japanese firms come to dominate the video game market, with games that are more exciting and realistic than those produced in the United States. All else being equal, how will this change affect the relative value of the yen and the dollar?

The increased quality of Japanese video games will increase the demand for the games in the United States. To acquire the yen necessary to buy more Japanese video games, U.S. importers will supply more dollars to the foreign exchange market. As Figure 15.3 shows, the increased supply of dollars will reduce the value of the dollar. In other words, a dollar will buy fewer yen than it did before. At the same time, the yen will increase in value: A given number of yen will buy more dollars than it did before.

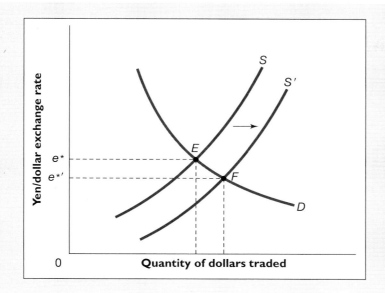

FIGURE 15.3

An Increase in the Supply of Dollars Lowers the Value of the Dollar.

Increased U.S. demand for Japanese video games forces Americans to supply more dollars to the foreign exchange market to acquire the yen they need to buy the games. The supply curve for dollars shifts from S to S', lowering the value of the dollar in terms of yen. The market equilibrium value of the exchange rate falls from e^* to $e^{*'}$.

CONCEPT CHECK 15.2

The United States goes into a recession, and real GDP falls. All else equal, how is this economic weakness likely to affect the value of the dollar?

CHANGES IN THE DEMAND FOR DOLLARS

The factors that change the demand for dollars in the foreign exchange market, and thus shift the dollar demand curve, are analogous to the factors that affect the supply of dollars. Factors that will *increase* the demand for dollars include:

- An increased preference for U.S. goods by foreign customers. For example, Japanese airlines might find that U.S.-built aircraft are superior to others, and decide to expand the number of American-made planes in their fleets. To buy the American planes, Japanese airlines would demand more dollars on the foreign exchange market.

- An increase in real GDP abroad, which implies higher incomes abroad, and thus more demand for imports from the United States.

- An increase in the real interest rate on U.S. assets or a reduction in the real interest rate on Japanese assets, which would make U.S. assets more attractive to foreign savers. To acquire U.S. assets, Japanese savers would demand more dollars.

DOES A STRONG CURRENCY IMPLY A STRONG ECONOMY?

Politicians and the public sometimes take pride in the fact that their national currency is "strong," meaning that its value in terms of other currencies is high or rising. Likewise, policymakers sometimes view a depreciating ("weak") currency as a sign of economic failure.

Contrary to popular impression, there is no simple connection between the strength of a country's currency and the strength of its economy. For example, Figure 15.1 shows that the value of the U.S. dollar relative to other major currencies was greater in 1973 than in the year 2007, though U.S. economic performance was considerably better in 2007 than in 1973, a period of deep recession and rising inflation. Indeed, the one period shown in Figure 15.1 during which the dollar rose markedly in value, 1980–1985, was a time of recession and high unemployment in the United States.

One reason a strong currency does not necessarily imply a strong economy is that an appreciating currency (an increase in e) tends to hurt a country's net exports. For example, if the dollar strengthens against the yen (that is, if a dollar buys more yen than before), Japanese goods will become cheaper in terms of dollars. The result may be that Americans prefer to buy Japanese goods rather than goods produced at home. Likewise, a stronger dollar implies that each yen buys fewer dollars, so exported U.S. goods become more expensive to Japanese consumers. As U.S. goods become more expensive in terms of yen, the willingness of Japanese consumers to buy U.S. exports declines. A strong dollar therefore may imply lower sales and profits for U.S. industries that export, as well as for U.S. industries (like automobile manufacturers) that compete with foreign firms for the domestic U.S. market.

MONETARY POLICY AND THE EXCHANGE RATE

Of the many factors that could influence a country's exchange rate, among the most important is the monetary policy of the country's central bank. Monetary policy affects the exchange rate primarily through its effect on the real interest rate.

Suppose the Fed is concerned about inflation and tightens U.S. monetary policy in response. The effects of this policy change on the value of the dollar are shown in Figure 15.4. Before the policy change, the equilibrium value of the exchange rate is e^*, at the intersection of supply curve S and the demand curve D (point E in the figure). The tightening of monetary policy raises the domestic U.S. real interest rate r, making U.S. assets, such as bonds, more attractive to both foreign and American financial investors. The increased willingness of foreign investors to buy U.S. assets increases the demand for dollars, shifting the demand curve rightward from D to D'. The willingness of American investors to buy more U.S. assets (and presumably fewer foreign assets) decreases the supply of dollars and shifts the supply curve leftward from S to S'. The equilibrium moves from point E to point F, and the market equilibrium value of the dollar rises from e^* to $e^{*'}$.

In short, a tightening of monetary policy by the Fed raises the demand for dollars and reduces the supply of dollars, causing the dollar to appreciate. By similar logic, an easing of monetary policy, which reduces the real interest rate, would make U.S. assets, such as bonds, less attractive to both Americans and foreigners. This would weaken the demand for dollars but increase the supply of dollars (as Americans buy more foreign assets), causing the dollar to depreciate.

FIGURE 15.4

A Tightening of Monetary Policy Strengthens the Dollar.

Tighter monetary policy in the United States raises the domestic real interest rate, increasing the demand for U.S. assets by foreign and American savers. An increased demand for U.S. assets by foreigners increases the demand for dollars, shifting the demand curve rightward from D to D'. An increased demand for U.S. assets by American savers decreases the supply of dollars, shifting the supply curve to the left. The exchange rate appreciates from e^* to $e^{*'}$.

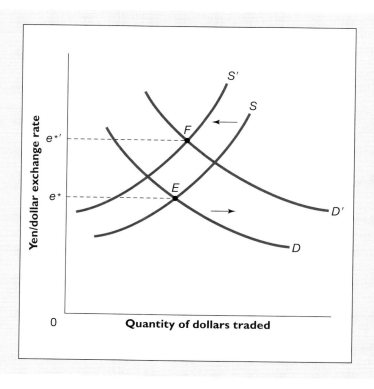

The appreciation of the dollar in the first half of the 1980s and the depreciation of the dollar between 2002 and 2011 were primarily the result of U.S. monetary policy. In particular, the Fed responded to the surge in inflation in the late 1970s by raising the real interest rate sharply in hopes of reducing aggregate demand and inflationary pressures. As a result, the real interest rate in the United States rose from negative values in 1979 and 1980 to more than 5 percent in 1983 and 1984 (see Figure 5.3). Attracted by these high real returns, U.S. and foreign savers rushed to buy U.S. assets, driving the value of the dollar up significantly. The Fed's attempt to bring down inflation was successful. By the middle of the 1980s, the Fed was able to ease U.S. monetary policy. The resulting decline in the real interest rate reduced the demand for U.S. assets, and thus for dollars, at which point the dollar fell back almost to its 1980 level.

Similarly, Figure 15.1 shows that the dollar depreciated substantially starting in early 2002. There are several reasons for this depreciation, but we will focus on two. First, the U.S. economy grew faster during this period than that of most of the countries to which it exports (Canada, Mexico, and Japan). Consequently, the supply of dollars (to pay for imports) increased. Second, as we discussed in the chapter *Monetary Policy and the Federal Reserve,* the Fed reduced the federal funds rate from 6 percent in early 2001 to 1 percent in June 2003 and then down to almost zero percent in 2009 after a short increase between 2004 and 2008. All else equal, the decline in U.S. real interest rates reduced the attractiveness of U.S. bonds to both Americans and foreigners. Consequently, the supply of dollars rose and the demand for dollars fell, contributing to the depreciation of the dollar.

The Exchange Rate as a Tool of Monetary Policy

In a closed economy, monetary policy affects aggregate demand solely through the real interest rate. For example, by raising the real interest rate, a tight monetary policy reduces consumption and investment spending. In an open economy with a flexible exchange rate, the exchange rate serves as another channel for monetary policy, one that reinforces the effects of the real interest rate.

To illustrate, suppose that policymakers are concerned about inflation and decide to restrain aggregate demand. To do so, they increase the real interest rate, reducing consumption and investment spending. But, as Figure 15.4 shows, the higher real interest rate also increases the demand for dollars and reduces the supply of dollars, causing the dollar to appreciate. The stronger dollar, in turn, further reduces aggregate demand. Why? As we saw in discussing the exchange rate, a stronger dollar reduces the cost of imported goods, thereby increasing imports. It also makes U.S. exports more costly to foreign buyers, which tends to reduce exports. Recall that net exports—or exports minus imports—is one of the four components of aggregate demand. Thus, by reducing exports and increasing imports, a stronger dollar (more precisely, a higher exchange rate) reduces aggregate demand.[4]

In sum, when the exchange rate is flexible, a tighter monetary policy reduces net exports (through a stronger dollar) as well as consumption and investment spending (through a higher real interest rate). Conversely, an easier monetary policy weakens the dollar and stimulates net exports, reinforcing the effect of the lower real interest rate on consumption and investment spending. Thus, relative to the case of a closed economy we studied earlier, *monetary policy is more effective in an open economy with a flexible exchange rate.*

The tightening of monetary policy under Fed Chairman Volcker in the early 1980s illustrates the effect of monetary policy on net exports. As we discussed above, Volcker's tight-money policies were a major reason for the 50 percent appreciation of the dollar during 1980–1985. In 1980 and 1981, the United States enjoyed a trade surplus, with exports that modestly exceeded imports. Largely in response to a stronger dollar, the U.S. trade balance fell into deficit after 1981. By the end of 1985, the U.S. trade deficit was about 3 percent of GDP, a substantial shift in less than half a decade.

---

[4]We are temporarily assuming that the prices of U.S. goods in dollars and the prices of foreign goods in foreign currencies are not changing.

RECAP	EXCHANGE RATE DETERMINATION IN THE SHORT RUN

- Supply and demand analysis is a useful tool for studying the short-run determination of the exchange rate. U.S. households and firms supply dollars to the foreign exchange market to acquire foreign currencies, which they need to purchase foreign goods, services, and assets. Foreigners demand dollars in the foreign exchange market to purchase U.S. goods, services, and assets. The market equilibrium exchange rate equates the quantities of dollars supplied and demanded in the foreign exchange market.

- An increased preference for foreign goods, an increase in U.S. real GDP, an increase in the real interest rate on foreign assets, or a decrease in the real interest rate on U.S. assets will increase the supply of dollars on the foreign exchange market, lowering the value of the dollar. An increased preference for U.S. goods by foreigners, an increase in real GDP abroad, an increase in the real interest rate on U.S. assets, or a decrease in the real interest rate on foreign assets will increase the demand for dollars, raising the value of the dollar.

- A tight monetary policy raises the real interest rate, increasing the demand for dollars, reducing the supply of dollars, and strengthening the dollar. A stronger dollar reinforces the effects of tight monetary policy on aggregate spending by reducing net exports, a component of aggregate demand. Conversely, an easy monetary policy lowers the real interest rate, weakening the dollar.

EXCHANGE RATE DETERMINATION IN THE LONG RUN

In this section, we discuss how exchange rates are determined in the long run. In our short-run analysis, we assumed that both the dollar price of U.S. goods and the foreign currency price of foreign goods (for example, the price of Sony PlayStations in yen) did not change. In discussing the long run, we relax this assumption. The theory we use to discuss the long-run determination of the exchange rate is called the theory of *purchasing power parity*. In order to explain this theory, we must first introduce the real exchange rate.

THE REAL EXCHANGE RATE

The nominal exchange rate tells us the price of the domestic currency in terms of a foreign currency. As we will see in this section, the *real exchange rate* is the price of the average domestic *good or service* in terms of the average foreign *good or service*.

Purchasing a Domestic versus Imported Good	EXAMPLE 15.4

Should you purchase a domestic good or an imported good?

Suppose that you are in charge of purchasing for a U.S. corporation that is planning to acquire a large number of new computers. The company's computer specialist has identified two models, one Japanese-made and one U.S.-made, that meet the necessary specifications. Since the two models are essentially equivalent, the company will buy the one with the lower price. However, since the computers are priced in the currencies of the countries of manufacture, the price comparison is not straightforward. Your mission—should you decide to accept it—is to determine which of the two models is cheaper.

To complete your assignment, you will need two pieces of information: the nominal exchange rate between the dollar and the yen and the prices of the two models in terms of the currencies of their countries of manufacture.

Suppose that a U.S.-made computer costs $2,400, and a similar Japanese-made computer costs 242,000 yen. If the nominal exchange rate is 110 yen per dollar, which computer is the better buy? To make this price comparison, we must measure the prices of both computers in terms of the same currency. To make the comparison in dollars, we first convert the Japanese computer's price into dollars. The price in terms of Japanese yen is ¥242,000 (the symbol ¥ means "yen"), and we are told that ¥110 = $1. As we did earlier, we find the dollar price of the Japanese computer by observing that, for any good or service,

Price in yen = Price in dollars × Value of dollar in terms of yen.

Note that the value of a dollar in terms of yen is just the yen–dollar exchange rate. Making this substitution and solving, we get

$$\text{Price in dollars} = \frac{\text{Price in yen}}{\text{Yen–dollar exchange rate}}$$

$$= \frac{¥242,000}{¥110/\$1} = \$2,200.$$

Notice that the yen symbol appears in both the numerator and the denominator of the ratio, so it cancels out. Our conclusion is that the Japanese computer is cheaper than the U.S. computer at $2,200, or $200 less than the price of the U.S. computer, $2,400. The Japanese computer is the better deal.

CONCEPT CHECK 15.3

Using the same information presented in Example 15.4, compare the prices of the Japanese and American computers by expressing both prices in terms of yen.

The fact that the Japanese computer was cheaper implied that your firm would choose it over the U.S.-made computer. In general, a country's ability to compete in international markets depends in part on the prices of its goods and services *relative* to the prices of foreign goods and services, when the prices are measured in a common currency. In the hypothetical example of the Japanese and U.S. computers, the price of the domestic (U.S.) good relative to the price of the foreign (Japanese) good is $2,400/$2,200, or 1.09. So the U.S. computer is 9 percent more expensive than the Japanese computer, putting the U.S. product at a competitive disadvantage.

More generally, economists ask whether *on average* the goods and services produced by a particular country are expensive relative to the goods and services produced by other countries. This question can be answered by the country's *real exchange rate*. Specifically, a country's **real exchange rate** is the price of the average domestic good or service *relative* to the price of the average foreign good or service, when prices are expressed in terms of a common currency.

> **real exchange rate** the price of the average domestic good or service *relative* to the price of the average foreign good or service, when prices are expressed in terms of a common currency

To obtain a formula for the real exchange rate, recall that e equals the nominal exchange rate (the number of units of foreign currency per dollar) and that P equals the domestic price level, as measured, for example, by the consumer price index. We will use P as a measure of the price of the "average" domestic good or service. Similarly, let P^f equal the foreign price level. We will use P^f as the measure of the price of the "average" foreign good or service.

The real exchange rate equals the price of the average domestic good or service relative to the price of the average foreign good or service. It would not be correct, however, to define the real exchange rate as the ratio P/P^f because the two price levels are expressed in different currencies. As we saw in our example of U.S. versus Japanese computers, to convert foreign prices into dollars, we must divide the foreign price by the exchange rate. By this rule, the price in dollars of the average foreign good or service equals P^f/e. Now we can write the real exchange rate as

$$\text{Real exchange rate} = \frac{\text{Price of domestic good}}{\text{Price of foreign good, in dollars}}$$

$$= \frac{P}{P^f/e}.$$

To simplify this expression, multiply the numerator and denominator by e to get

$$\text{Real exchange rate} = \frac{eP}{P^f}, \tag{15.1}$$

which is the formula for the real exchange rate.

To check this formula, let's apply it to the situation we analyzed in Example 15.4. For the sake of argument, imagine that computers are the only good produced by the United States and Japan, so the real exchange rate becomes just the price of U.S. computers relative to Japanese computers. In that example, the nominal exchange rate e was ¥110/$1, the domestic price P (of a computer) was $2,400, and the foreign price P^f was ¥242,000. Applying Equation 15.1, we get

$$\text{Real exchange rate (for computers)} = \frac{(\yen110/\$1) \times \$2,400}{\yen242,000}$$

$$= \frac{\yen264,000}{\yen242,000}$$

$$= 1.09,$$

which is the same answer we got earlier.

The real exchange rate is an important economic variable. It incorporates both the nominal exchange rate and the relative prices of goods and services across countries: When the real exchange rate is high, domestic goods are on average more expensive than foreign goods (when priced in the same currency). A high real exchange rate implies that domestic producers will have difficulty exporting to other countries (domestic goods will be "overpriced"), while foreign goods will sell well in the home country (because imported goods are cheap relative to goods produced at home).

Since a high real exchange rate tends to reduce exports and increase imports, we conclude that *net exports will tend to be low when the real exchange rate is high.* Conversely, if the real exchange rate is low, then the home country will find it easier to export (because its goods are priced below those of foreign competitors), while domestic residents will buy fewer imports (because imports are expensive relative to domestic goods). *Thus, net exports will tend to be high when the real exchange rate is low.*

In our earlier analysis, we showed how an increase in the nominal exchange rate e will reduce net exports by making exports more expensive to foreigners and by making imports cheaper for Americans. Equation 15.1 shows that an increase in e also will increase the real exchange rate, all other things equal, most notably, the ratio P/P^f. And an increase in the real exchange rate will again reduce net exports.

A SIMPLE THEORY OF EXCHANGE RATES: PURCHASING POWER PARITY (PPP)

law of one price if transportation costs are relatively small, the price of an internationally traded commodity must be the same in all locations

The most basic theory of how nominal exchange rates are determined in the long run is called *purchasing power parity*, or PPP. To understand this theory, we must first discuss a market equilibrium economic concept, called *the law of one price*.

The **law of one price** states that if transportation costs are relatively small, the price of an internationally traded commodity must be the same in all locations. For example, if transportation costs are not too large, the price of a bushel of wheat ought to be the same in Bombay, India, and Sydney, Australia. Note that this condition implies that the real exchange rate must equal one in the long run.

Suppose that were not the case. For instance, imagine that the price of wheat in Sydney were only half the price in Bombay. In that case, grain merchants would have a strong incentive to buy wheat in Sydney and ship it to Bombay, where it could be sold at double the price of purchase. As wheat left Sydney, reducing the local supply, the price of wheat in Sydney would rise, while the inflow of wheat into Bombay would reduce the price in Bombay.

According to the Equilibrium Principle, the international market for wheat would return to equilibrium only when unexploited opportunities to profit had been eliminated—specifically, only when the prices of wheat in Sydney and in Bombay became equal or nearly equal (with the difference being less than the cost of transporting wheat from Australia to India). Let's look at a specific example.

| Equilibrium |

The Relationship between Goods Prices and the Real Exchange Rate

EXAMPLE 15.5

How is the price of wheat related to the real exchange rate?

Suppose that a bushel of wheat costs 5 Australian dollars in Sydney and 150 rupees in Bombay. If the law of one price holds for wheat, what is the nominal exchange rate between Australia and India? Because the market value of a bushel of wheat must be the same in both locations, we know that the Australian price of wheat must equal the Indian price of wheat, so that

$$5 \text{ Australian dollars} = 150 \text{ rupees}.$$

Dividing by 5, we get

$$1 \text{ Australian dollar} = 30 \text{ Indian rupees}.$$

Thus, the nominal exchange rate between Australia and India should be 30 rupees per Australian dollar.

Alternatively, if we use Equation 15.1 and the PPP assumption that the real exchange rate will equal one,

$$1 = \frac{eP}{P^f}$$

and

$$e = P^f/P = 150 \text{ Indian rupees}/5 \text{ Australian dollars}$$
$$= 30 \text{ Indian rupees per 1 Australian dollar}.$$

CONCEPT CHECK 15.4

The price of gold is $300 per ounce in New York and 2,500 kronor per ounce in Stockholm, Sweden. If the law of one price holds for gold, what is the nominal exchange rate between the U.S. dollar and the Swedish krona?

These examples illustrate the concept of purchasing power parity. According to the **purchasing power parity (PPP)** theory, nominal exchange rates are determined as necessary for the law of one price to hold.

A particularly useful prediction of the PPP theory is that, in the long run, the *currencies of countries that experience significant inflation will tend to depreciate*. To see why, let's extend our analysis of the price of wheat in India and Australia.

purchasing power parity (PPP) the theory that nominal exchange rates are determined as necessary for the law of one price to hold

Purchasing Power Parity   **EXAMPLE 15.6**

How does inflation affect the real exchange rate?

Suppose India experiences significant inflation so that the price of a bushel of wheat in Bombay rises from 150 to 300 rupees. Australia has no inflation, so the price of wheat in Sydney remains unchanged at 5 Australian dollars. If the law of one price holds for wheat, what will happen to the nominal exchange rate between Australia and India?

We know that the market value of a bushel of wheat must be the same in both locations. Therefore,

$$5 \text{ Australian dollars} = 300 \text{ rupees.}$$

Equivalently,

$$1 \text{ Australian dollar} = 60 \text{ rupees.}$$

The nominal exchange rate is now 60 rupees per Australian dollar. Before India's inflation, the nominal exchange rate was 30 rupees per Australian dollar. So, in this example, inflation has caused the rupee to depreciate against the Australian dollar. Conversely, Australia, with no inflation, has seen its currency appreciate against the rupee.

This link between inflation and depreciation makes economic sense. Inflation implies that a nation's currency is losing purchasing power in the domestic market. Analogously, exchange rate depreciation implies that the nation's currency is losing purchasing power in international markets.

Figure 15.5 shows annual rates of inflation and nominal exchange rate depreciation for the 10 largest South American countries from 1995 to 2004.[5] Inflation is measured as

FIGURE 15.5

Inflation and Currency Depreciation in South America, 1995–2004.

The annual rates of inflation and nominal exchange rate depreciation (relative to the U.S. dollar) in the 10 largest South American countries varied considerably during 1995–2004. High inflation was associated with rapid depreciation of the nominal exchange rate. (Data for Ecuador refer to the period 1995–2000.)

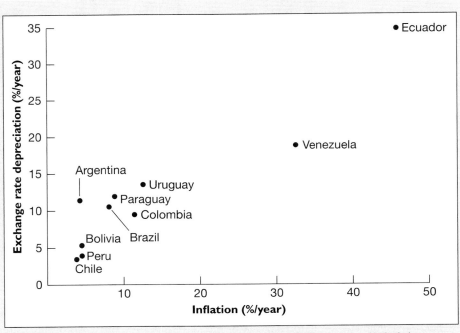

SOURCE: International Monetary Fund, *International Financial Statistics,* and authors' calculations.

[5]Since Ecuador, the tenth country, adopted the U.S. dollar as its currency in 2000, the data for Ecuador refer to the period 1995–2000.

the annual rate of change in the country's consumer price index; depreciation is measured relative to the U.S. dollar. As you can see, inflation varied greatly among South American countries during the period. For example, Chile's inflation rate was within two percentage points of the inflation rate of the United States, while Venezuela's inflation was 33 percent per year.

Figure 15.5 shows that, as the PPP theory implies, countries with higher inflation during the 1995–2004 period tended to experience the most rapid depreciation of their currencies.

SHORTCOMINGS OF THE PPP THEORY

Empirical studies have found that the PPP theory is useful for predicting changes in nominal exchange rates over the relatively long run. In particular, this theory helps to explain the tendency of countries with high inflation to experience depreciation of their exchange rates, as shown in Figure 15.5. However, the theory is less successful in predicting short-run movements in exchange rates.

A particularly dramatic failure of the PPP theory occurred in the United States in the early 1980s. Figure 15.1 shows that, between 1980 and 1985, the value of the U.S. dollar rose nearly 50 percent relative to the currencies of U.S. trading partners. This strong appreciation was followed by an even more rapid depreciation during 1986 and 1987. PPP theory could explain this roller-coaster behavior only if inflation were far lower in the United States than in U.S. trading partners from 1980 to 1985, and far higher from 1986 to 1987. In fact, inflation was similar in the United States and its trading partners throughout both periods.

Why does the PPP theory work less well in the short run than the long run? Recall that this theory relies on the law of one price, which says that the price of an internationally traded commodity must be the same in all locations. The law of one price works well for goods such as grain or gold, which are standardized commodities that are traded widely. However, *not all goods and services are traded internationally*, and *not all goods are standardized commodities*.

Many goods and services are not traded internationally because the assumption underlying the law of one price—that transportation costs are relatively small—does not hold. For example, for Indians to export haircuts to Australia, they would need to transport an Indian barber to Australia every time a Sydney resident desired a trim. Because transportation costs prevent haircuts from being traded internationally, the law of one price does not apply to them. Thus, even if the price of haircuts in Australia were double the price of haircuts in India, market forces would not necessarily force prices toward equality in the short run. (Over the long run, some Indian barbers might emigrate to Australia.) Other examples of nontraded goods and services are agricultural land, buildings, heavy construction materials (whose value is low relative to their transportation costs), and highly perishable foods.

In addition, some products use nontraded goods and services as inputs: A McDonald's hamburger served in Moscow has both a tradable component (frozen hamburger patties) and a nontradable component (the labor of counter workers). In general, the greater the share of nontraded goods and services in a nation's output, the less precisely the PPP theory will apply to the country's exchange rate.[6]

The second reason the law of one price and the PPP theory sometimes fail to apply is that not all internationally traded goods and services are perfectly standardized commodities, like grain or gold. For example, U.S.-made automobiles and Japanese-made automobiles are not identical; they differ in styling, horsepower, reliability, and

[6]Trade barriers, such as tariffs and quotas, also increase the costs associated with shipping goods from one country to another. Thus, trade barriers reduce the applicability of the law of one price in much the same way that physical transportation costs do.

other features. As a result, some people strongly prefer one nation's cars to the other's. Thus, if Japanese cars cost 10 percent more than American cars, U.S. automobile exports will not necessarily flood the Japanese market since many Japanese will still prefer Japanese-made cars even at a 10 percent premium. Of course, there are limits to how far prices can diverge before people will switch to the cheaper product. But the law of one price, and hence the PPP theory, will not apply exactly to nonstandardized goods.

RECAP	EXCHANGE RATE DETERMINATION IN THE LONG RUN

- The real exchange rate is the price of the average domestic good or service relative to the price of the average foreign good or service, when prices are expressed in terms of a common currency. A useful formula for the real exchange rate is eP/P^f, where e is the nominal exchange rate, P is the domestic price level, and P^f is the foreign price level.

- An increase in the real exchange rate implies that domestic goods are becoming more expensive relative to foreign goods, which tends to reduce exports and stimulate imports. Conversely, a decline in the real exchange rate tends to increase net exports.

- The most basic theory of nominal exchange rate determination in the long run, purchasing power parity (PPP), is based on the law of one price. The law of one price states that if transportation costs are relatively small, the price of an internationally traded commodity must be the same in all locations. According to the PPP theory, the nominal exchange rate between two currencies can be found by setting the price of a traded commodity in one currency equal to the price of the same commodity expressed in the second currency.

- A useful prediction of the PPP theory is that the currencies of countries that experience significant inflation will tend to depreciate over the long run. However, the PPP theory does not work well in the short run. The fact that many goods and services are nontraded, and that not all traded goods are standardized, reduces the applicability of the law of one price, and hence of the PPP theory.

INTERNATIONAL CAPITAL FLOWS AND THE BALANCE OF TRADE

trade balance (or net exports) the value of a country's exports less the value of its imports in a particular period (quarter or year)

trade surplus when exports exceed imports, the difference between the value of a country's exports and the value of its imports in a given period

trade deficit when imports exceed exports, the difference between the value of a country's imports and the value of its exports in a given period

In the chapter *Spending, Income, and GDP,* we introduced the term *net exports (NX),* the value of a country's exports less the value of its imports. An equivalent term for the value of a country's exports less the value of its imports is the **trade balance.** Because exports need not equal imports in each quarter or year, the trade balance (or net exports) need not always equal zero. If the trade balance is positive in a particular period so that the value of exports exceeds the value of imports, a country is said to have a **trade surplus** for that period equal to the value of its exports minus the value of its imports. If the trade balance is negative, with imports greater than exports, the country is said to have a **trade deficit** equal to the value of its imports minus the value of its exports.

Figure 15.6 shows the components of the U.S. trade balance since 1960. The blue line represents U.S. exports as a percentage of GDP; the red line, U.S. imports as a percentage of GDP. When exports exceed imports, the vertical distance between the two lines gives the U.S. trade surplus as a percentage of GDP. When imports exceed exports, the vertical distance between the two lines represents the U.S. trade deficit.

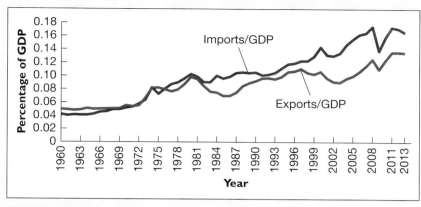

FIGURE 15.6

The U.S. Trade Balance, 1960–2013.

This figure shows U.S. exports and imports as a percentage of GDP. Since the late 1970s, the United States has run a trade deficit, with imports exceeding exports.

SOURCE: Bureau of Economic Analysis, www.bea.gov.

Figure 15.6 shows first that international trade has become an increasingly important part of the U.S. economy in the past several decades. In 1960, only 5 percent of U.S. GDP was exported, and the value of imports equaled 4.2 percent of U.S. GDP. By 2008, almost 13 percent of U.S. production was sold abroad and imports were over 17 percent of U.S. GDP. The steep decline in imports and exports in 2009 was the result of the worldwide recession that began in late 2007 and spread from the U.S. to the rest of the world in late 2008 and early 2009. As the recession ended, both U.S. exports and imports have once again increased, but the trade deficit has diminished somewhat compared to the levels seen during the mid 2000s.

INTERNATIONAL CAPITAL FLOWS

Like the production of goods and services, saving and investment opportunities are not necessarily restricted by national boundaries. The most productive use of a U.S. citizen's savings might be located far from U.S. soil, in helping to build a factory in Thailand or starting a small business in Poland. Likewise, the best way for a Brazilian saver to diversify her assets and reduce her risks could be to hold bonds and stocks from a number of different countries. Over time, extensive financial markets have developed to permit cross-border borrowing and lending. Financial markets in which borrowers and lenders are residents of different countries are called *international financial markets*.

International financial markets differ from domestic financial markets in at least one important respect: Unlike a domestic financial transaction, an international financial transaction is subject to the laws and regulations of at least two countries, the country that is home to the lender and the country that is home to the borrower. Thus, the size and vitality of international financial markets depend on the degree of political and economic cooperation among countries. For example, during the relatively peaceful decades of the late nineteenth and early twentieth centuries, international financial markets were remarkably highly developed. Great Britain, at the time the world's dominant economic power, was a major international lender, dispatching its savings for use around the globe. However, during the turbulent years 1914–1945, two world wars and the Great Depression substantially reduced both international finance and international trade in goods and services. The extent of international finance and trade returned to the levels achieved in the late nineteenth century only in the 1980s.

international capital flows purchases or sales of real and financial assets across international borders

capital inflows purchases of domestic assets by foreign households and firms

capital outflows purchases of foreign assets by domestic households and firms

net capital inflows capital inflows minus capital outflows

In thinking about international financial markets, it is useful to understand that lending is economically equivalent to acquiring a real or financial asset, and borrowing is economically equivalent to selling a real or financial asset. For example, savers lend to companies by purchasing stocks or bonds, which are financial assets for the lender and financial liabilities for the borrowing firms. Similarly, lending to a government is accomplished in practice by acquiring a government bond—a financial asset for the lender and a financial liability for the borrower, in this case the government. Savers also can provide funds by acquiring real assets such as land; if I purchase a parcel of land from you, though I am not making a loan in the usual sense, I am providing you with funds that you can use for consuming or investing. In lieu of interest or dividends from a bond or a stock, I receive the rental value of the land that I purchased.

Purchases or sales of real and financial assets across international borders are known as **international capital flows.** From the perspective of a particular country, say the United States, purchases of domestic (U.S.) assets by foreigners are called **capital inflows;** purchases of foreign assets by domestic (U.S.) households and firms are called **capital outflows.** To remember these terms, it may help to keep in mind that capital inflows represent funds "flowing in" to the country (foreign savers buying domestic assets), while capital outflows are funds "flowing out" of the country (domestic savers buying foreign assets). The difference between the two flows is expressed as **net capital inflows**—capital inflows minus capital outflows.

From a macroeconomic perspective, international capital flows play two important roles. First we will discuss how they allow countries whose productive investment opportunities are greater than domestic savings to fill in the gap by borrowing from abroad. Later, we will see how capital flows allow countries to run trade imbalances; a trade deficit is matched by net capital inflows and a trade surplus is matched by net capital outflows.

THE DETERMINANTS OF INTERNATIONAL CAPITAL FLOWS

The existence of international capital flows begs the question: Why would foreigners want to acquire U.S. assets, and, conversely, why would Americans want to acquire assets abroad?

The basic factors that determine the attractiveness of any asset, either domestic or foreign, are *return* and *risk.* Financial investors seek high real returns; thus, with other factors (such as the degree of risk and the returns available abroad) held constant, a higher real interest rate in the home country promotes capital inflows by making domestic assets more attractive to foreigners. By the same token, a higher real interest rate in the home country reduces capital outflows by inducing domestic residents to invest their savings at home. Thus, all else being equal, a higher real interest rate at home increases net capital inflows. Conversely, a low real interest rate at home tends to reduce net capital inflows (by increasing net capital outflows), as financial investors look abroad for better opportunities.

Figure 15.7 shows the relationship between a country's net capital inflows and the real rate of interest prevailing in that country. When the domestic real interest rate is high, net capital inflows are positive (foreign purchases of domestic assets exceed domestic purchases of foreign assets). But when the real interest rate is low, net capital inflows are negative (that is, the country experiences net capital outflows).

The effect of risk on capital flows is the opposite of the effect of the real interest rate. For a given real interest rate, an increase in the riskiness of domestic assets reduces net capital inflows, as foreigners become less willing to buy the home country's assets, and domestic savers become more inclined to buy foreign assets. For example, political instability, which increases the risk of investing in a country, tends to reduce net capital inflows. Figure 15.8 shows the effect of an increase in risk on capital flows: At each value of the domestic real interest rate, an increase in risk reduces net capital inflows, shifting the capital inflows curve to the left.

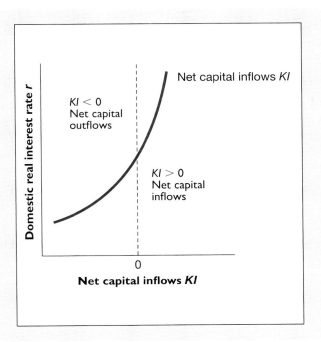

Net capital inflows KI

FIGURE 15.7

Net Capital Inflows and the Real Interest Rate.

Holding constant the degree of risk and the real returns available abroad, a high real interest rate in the home country will induce foreigners to buy domestic assets, increasing capital inflows. A high real rate in the home country also reduces the incentive for domestic savers to buy foreign assets, reducing capital outflows. Thus, all else being equal, the higher the domestic real interest rate r, the higher will be net capital inflows KI.

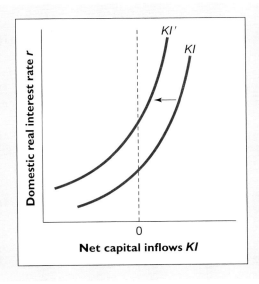

FIGURE 15.8

An Increase in Risk Reduces Net Capital Inflows.

An increase in the riskiness of domestic assets, arising, for example, from an increase in political instability, reduces the willingness of foreign and domestic savers to hold domestic assets. The supply of capital inflows declines at each value of the domestic real interest rate, shifting the KI curve to the left.

CONCEPT CHECK 15.5

For given real interest rate and riskiness in the home country, how would you expect net capital inflows to be affected by an increase in real interest rates abroad? Show your answer graphically.

SAVING, INVESTMENT, AND CAPITAL INFLOWS

As mentioned earlier in this section, the trade balance represents the difference between the value of goods and services exported by a country and the value of goods and services imported by the country. Net capital inflows represent the difference between purchases of domestic assets by foreigners and purchases of foreign assets by domestic residents.

There is a precise and very important link between these two imbalances: In any given period, the trade balance and net capital inflows sum to zero. It's convenient to write this relationship as an equation:

$$NX + KI = 0, \tag{15.2}$$

where NX is the trade balance (i.e., net exports) and KI stands for net capital inflows. The relationship given by Equation 15.2 is an identity, meaning that it is true by definition.[7]

This relationship between the trade balance and net capital inflows makes an important point that policymakers ignore at their peril: A country with a trade deficit also must be receiving capital inflows. That is, Equation 15.2 tells us that if a trade deficit exists (that is, $NX < 0$), then it must be true that net capital inflows are positive (i.e., $KI > 0$). Thus, policies that aim to restrict trade in goods and services, and thus reduce the trade deficit, have a clear cost since they will reduce the flow of international capital.

Trade Balance and Net Capital Inflows	**EXAMPLE 15.7**

What can a Japanese company do with U.S. dollars?

Suppose that a U.S. resident purchases an imported good, say, a Japanese automobile priced at $20,000. The U.S. buyer pays by check so that the Japanese car manufacturer now holds $20,000 in an account in a U.S. bank.

What will the Japanese manufacturer do with this $20,000? Basically, there are two possibilities. First, the Japanese company may use the $20,000 to buy U.S.-produced goods and services, such as U.S.-manufactured car parts or Hawaiian vacations for its executives. In this case, the United States has $20,000 in exports to balance the $20,000 automobile import. Because exports equal imports, the U.S. trade balance is unaffected by these transactions (for these transactions, $NX = 0$). Because no assets are bought or sold, there are no capital inflows or outflows (that is, $KI = 0$). So under this scenario, the condition that the trade balance plus net capital inflows equals zero, as stated in Equation 15.2, is satisfied.

Alternatively, the Japanese car producer might use the $20,000 to acquire U.S. assets such as a U.S. Treasury bond or some land adjacent to a manufacturing plant it owns in the United States. In this case, the United States compiles a trade deficit of $20,000 because the $20,000 car import is not offset by an export (that is, $NX = -\$20,000$). And there is a corresponding capital inflow of $20,000, reflecting the purchase of a U.S. asset by the Japanese company (that is, $KI = \$20,000$). Once again, the trade balance and net capital inflows sum to zero and Equation 15.2 is satisfied.

In fact, there is a third possibility, which is that the Japanese car company might swap its dollars to some other party outside the United States. For example, the company might trade its dollars to another Japanese firm or individual in exchange for Japanese yen. However, the acquirer of the dollars would then have the same two options as the car company—to buy U.S. goods and services or acquire U.S. assets—so that the equality of net capital inflows and the trade deficit would continue to hold.

International capital flows have a close relationship to domestic saving and investment. As we will see next, capital inflows augment the domestic saving pool, increasing the funds available for investment in physical capital, while capital outflows reduce the

---

[7]Technically, Equation 15.2 is not quite correct. The current account (CA) consists of net exports plus net factor income (that is, the net flow of income on investments abroad) plus international transfers (that is, nonmarket transfers from citizens of one country to citizens of another). Thus, the precise relationship is $CA + KI = 0$. However, net factor income plus international transfers is less than 10 percent of the current account. Since it will make the discussion easier, it is better to use net exports in Equation 15.2 rather than the current account.

amount of saving available for investment. Thus capital inflows can help to promote economic growth within a country, and capital outflows, to restrain it.

To derive the relationship among capital inflows, saving, and investment, recall from the chapter *Spending, Income, and GDP* that total output or income Y must always equal the sum of the four components of expenditure: consumption (C), investment (I), government purchases (G), and net exports (NX). Writing out this identity, we have

$$Y = C + I + G + NX.$$

Next, we subtract $C + G + NX$ from both sides of the identity to obtain

$$Y - C - G - NX = I.$$

In the chapter *Saving, Capital Formation, and Financial Markets* we saw that national saving S is equal to $Y - C - G$. If we make this substitution in the preceding equation, we obtain

$$S - NX = I. \tag{15.3}$$

Now recall that Equation 15.2 describes the relationship between the trade balance NX and net capital inflows KI. In particular, the trade balance plus capital inflows equals zero, or $NX + KI = 0$. This also can be written as $KI = -NX$. If we make this substitution in the above equation, we find that

$$S + KI = I. \tag{15.4}$$

Equation 15.4, a key result, says that the sum of national saving S and net capital inflows from abroad KI must equal domestic investment in new capital goods, I. In other words, in an open economy, the pool of saving available for domestic investment includes not only national saving (the saving of the domestic private and public sectors) but funds from savers abroad as well.

In the chapter *Saving, Capital Formation, and Financial Markets* we introduced the saving-investment diagram, which shows that, in a closed economy, the supply of saving must equal the demand for saving. A similar diagram applies to an open economy, except that the supply of saving in an open economy includes net capital inflows as well as domestic saving.

Figure 15.9 shows the open-economy version of the saving-investment diagram. The domestic real interest rate is shown on the vertical axis and saving and investment flows on the horizontal axis. As in a closed economy, the downward-sloping curve I shows the demand for funds by firms that want to make capital investments. The curve marked $S + KI$ shows the total supply of saving, including *both* domestic saving S and net capital inflows from abroad KI. Since a higher domestic real interest rate increases both domestic saving and net capital inflows, the $S + KI$ curve is upward-sloping. As Figure 15.9 shows, the equilibrium real interest rate in an open economy, r^*, is the level that sets the total amount of saving supplied (including net capital inflows from abroad) equal to the amount of saving demanded for purposes of domestic capital investment.

Figure 15.9 also indicates how net capital inflows can benefit an economy. A country that attracts significant amounts of foreign capital flows will have a larger pool of total saving and, hence, both a lower real interest rate and a higher rate of investment in new capital than it otherwise would. The United States and Canada both benefited from large inflows of capital in the early stages of their economic development, as do many developing countries today. Because capital inflows tend to react very sensitively to risk, an implication is that countries that are politically stable and safeguard the rights of foreign investors will attract more foreign capital and thus grow more quickly than countries without those characteristics.

FIGURE 15.9

The Saving-Investment Diagram for an Open Economy.

The total supply of saving in an open economy is the sum of national saving S and net capital inflows KI. An increase in the domestic real interest rate will increase both S and KI. The domestic demand for saving for purposes of capital investment is shown by the curve labeled I. The equilibrium real interest rate r^* sets the total supply of saving, including capital inflows, equal to the domestic demand for saving.

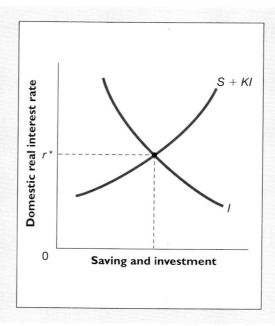

THE SAVING RATE AND THE TRADE DEFICIT

What causes trade deficits? Stories in the media sometimes claim that trade deficits occur because a country produces inferior goods that no one wants to buy or because other countries impose unfair trade restrictions on imports. Despite the popularity of these explanations, however, there is little support for them in either economic theory or evidence. For example, the United States has a large trade deficit with China, but no one would claim U.S. goods are generally inferior to Chinese goods. And many developing countries have significant trade deficits even though they, rather than their trading partners, tend to impose the more stringent restrictions on trade.

Economists argue that, rather than the quality of a country's exports or the existence of unfair trade restrictions, *a low rate of national saving is the primary cause of trade deficits.*

We have already seen the relationship between national saving and the trade balance in Equation 15.3, $S - NX = I$, which we rewrite as

$$S - I = NX. \tag{15.5}$$

According to Equation 15.5, if we hold domestic investment (I) constant, a high rate of national saving S implies a high level of net exports NX, while a low level of national saving implies a low level of net exports. Furthermore, if a country's national saving is less than its investment, or $S < I$, then Equation 15.5 implies that net exports NX will be negative. That is, the country will have a trade deficit. The conclusion from Equation 15.5 is that, holding domestic investment constant, low national saving tends to be associated with a trade deficit ($NX < 0$), and high national saving is associated with a trade surplus ($NX > 0$).

Why does a low rate of national saving tend to be associated with a trade deficit? A country with a low national saving rate is one in which households and the government have high spending rates, relative to domestic income and production. Since part of the spending of households and the government is devoted to imported goods, we would expect a low-saving, high-spending economy to have a high volume of imports. Furthermore, a low-saving economy consumes a large proportion of its domestic production, reducing the quantity of goods and services available for export. With high imports and low exports, a low-saving economy will experience a trade deficit.

A country with a trade deficit also must be receiving capital inflows. (Recall that Equation 15.2 tells us that if a trade deficit exists, $NX < 0$, then it must be true that net capital inflows are positive, $KI > 0$.) Is a low national saving rate also consistent with the existence of net capital inflows? The answer is yes. A country with a low national saving rate will not have sufficient saving of its own to finance domestic investment. Thus, there likely will be many good investment opportunities in the country available to foreign savers, leading to capital inflows. Equivalently, a shortage of domestic saving will tend to drive up the domestic real interest rate, which attracts capital flows from abroad.

U.S. Trade Deficit   EXAMPLE 15.8

Why is the U.S. trade deficit so large?

As shown by Figure 15.6, U.S. trade was more or less in balance until the mid-1970s. Since the late 1970s, however, the United States has run large trade deficits, particularly in the mid-1980s and since the latter part of the 1990s. Indeed, in 2006 and 2007 the trade deficit equaled 5.7 percent of U.S. GDP. Why is the U.S. trade deficit so large?

Figure 15.10 shows national saving, investment, and the trade balance for the United States from 1960 to 2013 (all measured relative to GDP). Note that the trade balance has been negative since the late 1970s, indicating a trade deficit. Note also that trade deficits correspond to periods in which investment exceeds national saving, as required by Equation 15.5.

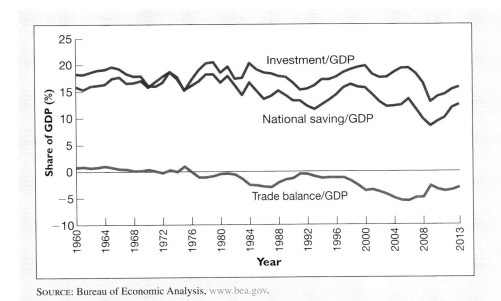

FIGURE 15.10

National Saving, Investment, and the Trade Balance in the United States, 1960–2013.

Since the 1970s, U.S. national saving has fallen below domestic investment, implying a significant trade deficit.

SOURCE: Bureau of Economic Analysis, www.bea.gov.

U.S. national saving and investment were roughly in balance in the 1960s and early 1970s, and, hence, the U.S. trade balance was close to zero during that period. However, U.S. national saving fell sharply during the late 1970s and 1980s. One factor that contributed to the decline in national saving was the large government deficits of the era. Because investment did not decline as much as saving, the U.S. trade deficit ballooned in the 1980s, coming under control only when investment fell during the recession of 1990–1991. Saving and investment both recovered during the 1990s, but in the latter part of the 1990s, national saving dropped again. This time the federal government was not at fault since its budget showed a healthy surplus. Rather, the fall in national saving reflected a decline in private saving, the result of a powerful upsurge in consumption spending. Much of the increase in consumption spending was for imported goods and services, which increased the trade deficit. In 2002, however, the federal government again began to have large budget deficits. This reduced national saving even more and led to a record trade deficit in 2006 (as a percentage of GDP).

Is the U.S. trade deficit a problem? The trade deficit implies that the United States is relying heavily on foreign saving and net capital inflows to finance its domestic capital formation. These foreign loans must ultimately be repaid with interest. If the foreign savings are well invested and the U.S. economy grows, repayment will not pose a problem. However, if economic growth in the United States slackens, repaying the foreign lenders will impose an economic burden in the future.

"But we're not just talking about buying a car—we're talking about confronting this country's trade deficit with Japan."

RECAP	INTERNATIONAL CAPITAL FLOWS AND THE BALANCE OF TRADE

- Purchases or sales of assets across borders are called *international capital flows*. If a person, firm, or government in (say) the United States borrows from abroad, we say that there is a capital inflow into the United States. In this case, foreign savers are acquiring U.S. assets. If a person, firm, or government in the United States lends to someone abroad, thereby acquiring a foreign asset, we say that there has been a capital outflow from the United States to the foreign country. Net capital inflows to a given country equal capital inflows minus outflows.

- If a country imports more goods and services than it exports, it must borrow abroad to cover the difference. Likewise, a country that exports more than it imports will lend the difference to foreigners. Thus, as a matter of accounting, the trade balance *NX* and net capital inflows *KI* must sum to zero in every period.

- The funds available for domestic investment in new capital goods equal the sum of domestic saving and net capital inflows from abroad. The higher the return and the lower the risk of investing in the domestic country, the greater will be the capital inflows from abroad. Capital inflows benefit an economy by providing more funds for capital investment, but they can become a burden if the returns from investing in new capital goods are insufficient to pay back the foreign lenders.

- An important cause of a trade deficit is a low national saving rate. A country that saves little and spends a lot will tend to import a greater quantity of goods and services than it is able to export. At the same time, the country's low saving rate implies a need for more foreign borrowing to finance domestic investment spending.

○ SUMMARY ○

- When the exchange rate is flexible, a tight monetary policy increases the demand for the currency, reduces the supply of currency, and causes it to appreciate. The stronger currency reinforces the effects of the tight monetary policy on aggregate demand by reducing net exports. Conversely, easy monetary policy lowers the real interest rate and weakens the currency, which in turn stimulates net exports. *(LO1)*

- The nominal exchange rate between two currencies is the rate at which the currencies can be traded for each other. A rise in the value of a currency relative to other currencies is called an appreciation; a decline in the value of a currency is called a depreciation. *(LO2)*

- Supply and demand analysis is a useful tool for studying the determination of exchange rates in the short run. The equilibrium exchange rate, also called the market equilibrium value of the exchange rate, equates the quantities of the currency supplied and demanded in the foreign exchange market. *(LO2)*

- A currency is supplied by domestic residents who wish to acquire foreign currencies to purchase foreign goods, services, and assets. An increased preference for foreign goods, an increase in the domestic GDP, an increase in the real interest rate on foreign assets, or a decrease in the real interest rate on domestic assets all will increase the supply of a currency on the foreign exchange market and thus lower its value. A currency is demanded by foreigners who wish to purchase domestic goods, services, and assets. An increased preference for domestic goods by foreigners, an increase in real GDP abroad, an increase in the domestic real interest rate, or a decrease in the foreign real interest rate all will increase the demand for the currency on the foreign exchange market and thus increase its value. *(LO2)*

- The real exchange rate is the price of the average domestic good or service *relative* to the price of the average foreign good or service, when prices are expressed in terms of a common currency. The real exchange rate incorporates both the nominal exchange rate and the relative levels of prices among countries. An increase in the real exchange rate implies that domestic goods and services are becoming more expensive relative to foreign goods and services, which tends to reduce exports and increase imports. Conversely, a decline in the real exchange rate tends to increase net exports. *(LO3)*

- A basic theory of nominal exchange rate determination in the long run, the purchasing power parity (PPP) theory, is based on the law of one price. The law of one price states that if transportation costs are relatively small, the price of an internationally traded commodity must be the same in all locations. According to the PPP theory, we can find the nominal exchange rate between two currencies by setting the price of a commodity in one of the currencies equal to the price of the commodity in the second currency. The PPP theory correctly predicts that the currencies of countries that experience significant inflation will tend to depreciate in the long run. However, the fact that many goods and services are not traded internationally, and that not all traded goods are standardized, makes the PPP theory less useful for explaining short-run changes in exchange rates. *(LO3)*

- The trade balance, or net exports, is the value of a country's exports less the value of its imports in a particular period. Exports need not equal imports in each period. If exports exceed imports, the difference is called a trade surplus, and if imports exceed exports, the difference is called a trade deficit. *(LO4)*

- A low rate of national saving is the primary cause of trade deficits. A low-saving, high-spending country is likely to import more than a high-saving country. It also consumes more of its domestic production, leaving less for export. Finally, a low-saving country is likely to have a high real interest rate, which attracts net capital inflows. Because the sum of the trade balance and net capital inflows is zero, a high level of net capital inflows always accompanies a large trade deficit. *(LO4)*

• The higher the real interest rate in a country, and the lower the risk of investing there, the higher its net capital inflows. The availability of capital inflows expands a country's pool of saving, allowing for more domestic investment and increased growth. A drawback to using capital inflows to finance domestic capital formation is that the returns to capital (interest and dividends) accrue to foreign financial investors rather than domestic residents. *(LO4)*

○ KEY TERMS ○

appreciation
capital inflows
capital outflows
depreciation
fixed exchange rate
flexible exchange rate

foreign exchange market
internationl capital flows
law of one price
market equilibrium value of
 the exchange rate
net capital inflows

nominal exchange rate
purchasing power parity (PPP)
real exchange rate
trade balance (net exports)
trade deficit
trade surplus

○ REVIEW QUESTIONS ○

1. Under a flexible exchange rate, how does an easing of monetary policy (a lower real interest rate) affect the value of the exchange rate? Does this change in the exchange rate tend to weaken or strengthen the effect of the monetary ease on output and employment? Explain. *(LO1)*

2. Why do U.S. households and firms supply dollars to the foreign exchange market? Why do foreigners demand dollars in the foreign exchange market? *(LO2)*

3. Japanese yen trade at 110 yen per dollar and Mexican pesos trade at 10 pesos per dollar. What is the nominal exchange rate between the yen and the peso? Express in two ways. *(LO2)*

4. Define *nominal exchange rate* and *real exchange rate.* How are the two concepts related? *(LO2, LO3)*

5. Explain with examples why, in any period, a country's net capital inflows equal its trade deficit. *(LO4)*

6. How are capital inflows or outflows related to domestic investment in new capital goods? *(LO4)*

○ PROBLEMS ○

|ECONOMICS

Visit your mobile app store and download the Frank: Study Econ app *today!*

1. If the government follows an easy monetary policy and the exchange rate is flexible, which of the following will likely be the result? *(LO1)*
   a. A falling real interest rate but higher net exports.
   b. A higher real interest rate but lower net exports.
   c. A strong currency that helps stimulate exports.
   d. Increases in the demand for the currency and decreases in the supply of the currency.

2. Using the data in Table 15.1, find the nominal exchange rate between the Mexican peso and the Japanese yen. Express in two ways. How do your answers change if the peso appreciates by 10 percent against the dollar while the value of the yen against the dollar remains unchanged? *(LO2)*

3. Suppose a French bottle of champagne costs 20 euros. *(LO2)*
    a. If the euro–dollar exchange rate is 0.8 euro per dollar, so that a dollar can buy 0.8 euro, how much will the champagne cost in the United States?
    b. If the euro–dollar exchange rate rises to 1 euro per dollar, how much will the champagne cost in the United States?
    c. If an increase in the euro–dollar exchange rate leads to an increase in Americans' dollar expenditures on French champagne, what will happen to the amount of dollars supplied to the foreign exchange market as the euro–dollar exchange rate rises?

4. Consider an Apple iPod that costs $240. *(LO2)*
    a. If the euro–dollar exchange rate is 1 euro per dollar, so that it costs a European 1 euro to buy a dollar, how much will the iPod cost in France?
    b. If the euro–dollar exchange rate falls to 0.8 euro per dollar, how much will the iPod cost in France?
    c. Consequently, what will happen to French purchases of iPods and the amount of dollars demanded in the foreign exchange market as the euro–dollar exchange rate falls?

5. How would each of the following be likely to affect the value of the dollar, all else being equal? Explain. *(LO2)*
    a. U.S. stocks are perceived as having become much riskier financial investments.
    b. European computer firms switch from U.S.-produced software to software produced in India, Israel, and other nations.
    c. As East Asian economies grow, international financial investors become aware of many new high-return investment opportunities in the region.

6. Between last year and this year, the CPI in Blueland rose from 100 to 110 and the CPI in Redland rose from 100 to 105. Blueland's currency unit, the blue, was worth $1 (U.S.) last year and is worth 90 cents (U.S.) this year. Redland's currency unit, the red, was worth 50 cents (U.S.) last year and is worth 45 cents (U.S.) this year.

    Find the percentage change from last year to this year in Blueland's *nominal* exchange rate with Redland and in Blueland's *real* exchange rate with Redland. (Treat Blueland as the home country.) Relative to Redland, do you expect Blueland's exports to be helped or hurt by these changes in exchange rates? *(LO2, LO3)*

7. A British-made automobile is priced at £20,000 (20,000 British pounds). A comparable U.S.-made car costs $26,000. One pound trades for $1.50 in the foreign exchange market. Find the real exchange rate from the perspective of the United States and from the perspective of Great Britain. Which country's cars are more competitively priced? *(LO3)*

8. How do each of the following transactions affect (1) the trade surplus or deficit and (2) capital inflows or outflows for the United States? Show that in each case the identity that the trade balance plus net capital inflows equals zero applies. *(LO4)*
    a. A U.S. exporter sells software to Israel. She uses the Israeli shekels received to buy stock in an Israeli company.
    b. A Mexican firm uses proceeds from its sale of oil to the United States to buy U.S. government debt.
    c. A Mexican firm uses proceeds from its sale of oil to the United States to buy oil drilling equipment from a U.S. firm.

9. Use a diagram like Figure 15.9 to show the effects of each of the following on the real interest rate and capital investment of a country that is a net borrower from abroad. *(LO4)*
    a. Investment opportunities in the country improve owing to new technologies.
    b. The government budget deficit rises.
    c. Domestic citizens decide to save more.
    d. Foreign investors believe that the riskiness of lending to the country has increased.

○ ANSWERS TO CONCEPT CHECKS ○

15.1 Answers will vary, depending on when the data are obtained. *(LO1)*

15.2 A decline in U.S. GDP reduces consumer incomes and hence imports. As Americans are purchasing fewer imports, they supply fewer dollars to the foreign exchange market, so the supply curve for dollars shifts to the left. Reduced supply raises the market equilibrium value of the dollar. *(LO2)*

15.3 The dollar price of the U.S. computer is $2,400, and each dollar is equal to 110 yen. Therefore, the yen price of the U.S. computer is (110 yen/dollar) × ($2,400), or 264,000 yen. The price of the Japanese computer is 242,000 yen. Thus, the conclusion that the Japanese model is cheaper does not depend on the currency in which the comparison is made. *(LO3)*

15.4 Since the law of one price holds for gold, its price per ounce must be the same in New York and Stockholm:

$$\$300 = 2{,}500 \text{ kronor.}$$

Dividing both sides by 300, we get

$$\$1 = 8.33 \text{ kronor.}$$

So the exchange rate is 8.33 kronor per dollar. *(LO3)*

15.5 An increase in the real interest rate abroad increases the relative attractiveness of foreign financial investments to both foreign and domestic savers. Net capital inflows to the home country will fall at each level of the domestic real interest rate. The supply curve of net capital inflows shifts left, as in Figure 15.8. *(LO4)*

A

Absolute advantage. One person has an absolute advantage over another if he or she takes fewer hours to perform a task than the other person.

Accommodating policy. A policy that allows the effects of a shock to occur.

Aggregate demand (*AD*) curve. A curve that shows the amount of output consumers, firms, government, and customers abroad want to purchase at each inflation rate, holding all other factors constant.

Aggregate supply (*AS*) curve. A curve that shows the relationship between the amount of output firms want to produce and the inflation rate, holding all other factors constant.

Anchored inflationary expectations. When people's expectations of future inflation do not change even if inflation rises temporarily.

Appreciation. An increase in the value of a currency relative to other currencies.

Assets. Anything of value that one *owns*.

Attainable point. Any combination of goods that can be produced using currently available resources.

Automatic stabilizers. Provisions in the law that imply *automatic* increases in government spending or decreases in taxes when real output declines.

Autonomous consumption. Consumption spending that is not related to the level of disposable income.

Autonomous expenditure. The portion of planned aggregate expenditure that is independent of output.

Average benefit. The total benefit of undertaking *n* units of an activity divided by *n*.

Average cost. The total cost of undertaking *n* units of an activity divided by *n*.

Average labor productivity. Output per employed worker.

Average tax rate. Total taxes divided by total before-tax income.

B

Balance sheet. A list of an economic unit's assets and liabilities on a specific date.

Bank reserves. Cash or similar assets held by commercial banks for the purpose of meeting depositor withdrawals and payments.

Banking panic. A situation in which news or rumors of the imminent bankruptcy of one or more banks leads bank depositors to rush to withdraw their funds.

Barter. The direct trade of goods or services for other goods or services.

Bequest saving. Saving done for the purpose of leaving an inheritance.

Board of Governors. The leadership of the Fed, consisting of seven governors appointed by the president to staggered 14-year terms.

Bond. A legal promise to repay a debt, usually including both the principal amount and regular interest, or coupon, payments.

Boom. A particularly strong and protracted expansion.

Business cycles. Short-term fluctuations in GDP and other variables.

Buyer's reservation price. The largest dollar amount the buyer would be willing to pay for a good.

Buyer's surplus. The difference between the buyer's reservation price and the price he or she actually pays.

C

Capital gains. Increases in the value of existing assets.

Capital good. A long-lived good that is used in the production of other goods and services.

Capital inflows. Purchases of domestic assets by foreign households and firms.

Capital losses. Decreases in the value of existing assets.

Capital outflows. Purchases of foreign assets by domestic households and firms.

Cash on the table. An economic metaphor for unexploited gains from exchange.

Central bank independence. When central bankers are insulated from short-term political considerations and are allowed to take a long-term view of the economy.

Change in aggregate demand. A shift of the *AD* curve.

Change in aggregate supply. A shift of the *AS* curve.

Change in demand. A shift of the entire demand curve.

Change in the quantity demanded. A movement along the demand curve that occurs in response to a change in price.

Change in the quantity supplied. A movement along the supply curve that occurs in response to a change in price.

Change in supply. A shift of the entire supply curve.

Comparative advantage. One person has a comparative advantage over another if his or her opportunity cost of performing a task is lower than the other person's opportunity cost.

Complements. Two goods are complements in consumption if an increase in the price of one causes a leftward shift in the demand curve for the other (or if a decrease causes a rightward shift).

Compound interest. The payment of interest not only on the original deposit but on all previously accumulated interest.

Constant (or parameter). A quantity that is fixed in value.

Consumer price index (CPI). For any period, a measure of the cost in that period of a standard basket of goods and services relative to the cost of the same basket of goods and services in a fixed year, called the *base year*.

Consumption expenditure (or consumption). Spending by households on goods and services such as food, clothing, and entertainment.

Consumption function. The relationship between consumption spending and its determinants, in particular, disposable income.

Contraction. *See* **Recession.**

Contractionary policies. Government policy actions designed to reduce planned spending and output.

Core rate of inflation. The rate of increase of all prices except energy and food.

Coupon payments. Regular interest payments made to the bondholder.

Coupon rate. The interest rate promised when a bond is issued; the annual coupon payments are equal to the coupon rate times the principal amount of the bond.

Credibility of monetary policy. The degree to which the public believes the central bank's promises to keep inflation low, even if doing so may impose short-run economic costs.

Cyclical unemployment. The extra unemployment that occurs during periods of recession.

D

Deadweight loss. The reduction in economic surplus that results from adoption of a policy.

Deflating (a nominal quantity). The process of dividing a nominal quantity by a price index (such as the CPI) to express the quantity in real terms.

Deflation. A situation in which the prices of most goods and services are falling over time so that inflation is negative.

Demand curve. A schedule or graph showing the quantity of a good that buyers wish to buy at each price.

Demand for money. The amount of wealth an individual or firm chooses to hold in the form of money.

Demand shocks. Changes in planned spending that are not caused by changes in output or the inflation rate.

Dependent variable. A variable in an equation whose value is determined by the value taken by another variable in the equation.

Deposit insurance. A system under which the government guarantees that depositors will not lose any money even if their bank goes bankrupt.

Depreciation. A decrease in the value of a currency relative to other currencies.

Depression. A particularly severe or protracted recession.

Diminishing returns to capital. If the amount of labor and other inputs employed is held constant, then the greater the amount of capital already in use, the less an additional unit of capital adds to production.

Diminishing returns to labor. If the amount of capital and other inputs in use is held constant, then the greater the quantity of labor already employed, the less each additional worker adds to production.

Discount rate (or **primary credit rate**). The interest rate that the Fed charges commercial banks to borrow reserves.

Discount window lending. The lending of reserves by the Federal Reserve to commercial banks.

Discouraged workers. People who say they would like to have a job but have not made an effort to find one in the past four weeks.

Diversification. The practice of spreading one's wealth over a variety of different financial investments to reduce overall risk.

Dividend. A regular payment received by stockholders for each share that they own.

Duration. The length of an unemployment spell.

E

Economic efficiency. *See* **Efficiency.**

Economic surplus. The benefit of taking an action minus its cost.

Economics. The study of how people make choices under conditions of scarcity and of the results of those choices for society.

Efficiency (or **economic efficiency**). A condition that occurs when all goods and services are produced and consumed at their respective socially optimal levels.

Efficient point. Any combination of goods for which currently available resources do not allow an increase in the production of one good without a reduction in the production of the other.

Entrepreneurs. People who create new economic enterprises.

Equation. A mathematical expression that describes the relationship between two or more variables.

Equilibrium. A balanced or unchanging situation in which all forces at work within a system are canceled by others.

Equilibrium price and **equilibrium quantity.** The price and quantity at the intersection of the supply and demand curves for the good.

Equity. *See* **Stock.**

Excess demand (or **shortage**). The amount by which quantity demanded exceeds quantity supplied when the price of a good lies below the equilibrium price.

Excess supply (or **surplus**). The amount by which quantity supplied exceeds quantity demanded when the price of the good exceeds the equilibrium price.

Expansion. A period in which the economy is growing at a rate significantly above normal.

Expansionary gap. A positive output gap, which occurs when actual output is higher than potential output ($Y > Y*$).

Expansionary policies. Government policy actions intended to increase planned spending and output.

Expenditure line. A line showing the relationship between planned aggregate expenditure and output.

F

Federal funds rate. The interest rate that commercial banks charge each other for very short-term (usually overnight) loans; because the Fed frequently sets its policy in terms of the federal funds rate, this rate is closely watched in financial markets.

Federal Open Market Committee (FOMC). The committee that makes decisions concerning monetary policy.

Federal Reserve System (or **the Fed**). The central bank of the United States.

Final goods or services. Goods or services consumed by the ultimate user; because they are the end products of the production process, they are counted as part of GDP.

Financial intermediaries. Firms that extend credit to borrowers using funds raised from savers.

Fiscal policy. Decisions about how much the government spends and how much tax revenue it collects.

Fisher effect. The tendency for nominal interest rates to be high when inflation is high and low when inflation is low.

Fixed exchange rate. An exchange rate whose value is set by official government policy.

Flexible exchange rate. An exchange rate whose value is not officially fixed but varies according to the supply and demand for the currency in the foreign exchange market.

Flow. A measure that is defined *per unit of time.*

Foreign exchange market. The market on which currencies of various nations are traded for one another.

Fractional-reserve banking system. A banking system in which bank reserves are less than deposits so that the reserve-deposit ratio is less than 100 percent.

Frictional unemployment. The short-term unemployment associated with the process of matching workers with jobs.

Full-employment output. *See* **Potential output, $Y*$.**

G

Government budget deficit. The excess of government spending over tax collections $(G - T)$.

Government budget surplus. The excess of government tax collections over government spending $(T - G)$; the government budget surplus equals public saving.

Government purchases. Purchases by federal, state, and local governments of final goods and services; government purchases do *not* include *transfer payments,* which are payments made by the government in return for which no current goods or services are received, nor do they include interest paid on the government debt.

Gross domestic product (GDP). The market value of the final goods and services produced in a country during a given period.

H

Hyperinflation. A situation in which the inflation rate is extremely high.

I

Income-expenditure multiplier (or **multiplier**). The effect of a one-unit increase in autonomous expenditure on short-run equilibrium output.

Independent variable. A variable in an equation whose value determines the value taken by another variable in the equation.

Indexing. The practice of increasing a nominal quantity each period by an amount equal to the percentage increase in a specified price index. Indexing prevents the purchasing power of the nominal quantity from being eroded by inflation.

Induced expenditure. The portion of planned aggregate expenditure that depends on output Y.

Inefficient point. Any combination of goods for which currently available resources enable an increase in the production of one good without a reduction in the production of the other.

Inferior good. A good whose demand curve shifts leftward when the incomes of buyers increase and rightward when the incomes of buyers decrease.

Inflation dove. Someone who is not strongly committed to achieving and maintaining low inflation.

Inflation hawk. Someone who is committed to achieving and maintaining low inflation, even at some short-run cost in reduced output and employment.

Inflation-protected bonds. Bonds that pay a nominal interest rate each year equal to a fixed real rate plus the actual rate of inflation during that year.

Inflation shock. A sudden change in the normal behavior of inflation, unrelated to the nation's output gap.

Inside lag (of macroeconomic policy). The delay between the date a policy change is needed and the date it is implemented.

Intermediate goods or services. Goods or services used up in the production of final goods and services and therefore not counted as part of GDP.

International capital flows. Purchases or sales of real and financial assets across international borders.

Investment. Spending by firms on final goods and services, primarily capital goods.

L

Labor force. The total number of employed and unemployed people in the economy.

Law of one price. If transportation costs are relatively small, the price of an internationally traded commodity must be the same in all locations.

Liabilities. The debts one *owes.*

Life-cycle saving. Saving to meet long-term objectives such as retirement, college attendance, or the purchase of a home.

Long-run equilibrium. A situation in which the AD and AS curves intersect at potential output Y^*.

M

M1. The sum of currency outstanding and balances held in checking accounts.

M2. All the assets in M1 plus some additional assets that are usable in making payments but at greater cost or inconvenience than currency or checks.

Macroeconomics. The study of the performance of national economies and the policies that governments use to try to improve that performance.

Marginal benefit. The increase in total benefit that results from carrying out one additional unit of an activity.

Marginal propensity to consume (*mpc*). The amount by which consumption rises when disposable income rises by \$1; we assume that $0 < mpc < 1$.

Marginal tax rate. The amount by which taxes rise when before-tax income rises by one dollar.

Market. The market for any good consists of all buyers or sellers of that good.

Market equilibrium. Occurs in a market when all buyers and sellers are satisfied with their respective quantities at the market price.

Market equilibrium value of the exchange rate. The exchange rate that equates the quantities of the currency supplied and demanded in the foreign exchange market.

Market interest rate. *See* **Nominal interest rate.**

Maturation date. The date at which the principal of a bond will be repaid.

Medium of exchange. An asset used in purchasing goods and services.

Menu costs. The costs of changing prices.

Microeconomics. The study of individual choice under scarcity and its implications for the behavior of prices and quantities in individual markets.

Monetary policy. Determination of the nation's money supply.

Monetary policy rule. A rule that describes how a central bank, like the Fed, takes action in response to changes in the state of the economy.

Money. Any asset that can be used in making purchases.

Money demand curve. A curve that shows the relationship between the aggregate quantity of money demanded M and the nominal interest rate i; because an increase in the nominal interest rate increases the opportunity cost of holding money, which reduces the quantity of money demanded, the money demand curve slopes down.

Multiplier. *See* **Income-expenditure multiplier.**

Mutual fund. A financial intermediary that sells shares in itself to the public and then uses the funds raised to buy a wide variety of financial assets.

N

National saving. The saving of the entire economy, equal to GDP less consumption expenditures and government purchases of goods and services, or $Y - C - G$.

Natural rate of unemployment, u^*. The part of the total unemployment rate that is attributable to frictional and structural unemployment; equivalently, the unemployment rate that prevails when cyclical unemployment is zero, so the economy has neither a recessionary nor an expansionary output gap.

Net capital inflows. Capital inflows minus capital outflows.

Net exports. Exports minus imports. (*See also* **Trade balance.**)

Nominal exchange rate. The rate at which two currencies can be traded for each other.

Nominal GDP. A measure of GDP in which the quantities produced are valued at current-year prices; nominal GDP measures the *current dollar value* of production.

Nominal interest rate (or **market interest rate**). The annual percentage increase in the nominal value of a financial asset.

Nominal quantity. A quantity that is measured in terms of its current dollar value.

Normal good. A good whose demand curve shifts rightward when the incomes of buyers increase and leftward when the incomes of buyers decrease.

Normative economic principle. One that says how people should behave.

O

Okun's law. Each extra percentage point of cyclical unemployment is associated with about a 2 percentage point increase in the output gap, measured in relation to potential output.

100 percent reserve banking. A situation in which banks' reserves equal 100 percent of their deposits.

Open-market operations. Open-market purchases and open-market sales.

Open-market purchase. The purchase of government bonds from the public by the Fed for the purpose of increasing the supply of bank reserves and the money supply.

Open-market sale. The sale by the Fed of government bonds to the public for the purpose of reducing bank reserves and the money supply.

Opportunity cost. The value of what must be forgone to undertake an activity.

Output gap. The difference between the economy's actual output and its potential output at a point in time, $(Y - Y^*)/Y^*$.

Outside lag (of macroeconomic policy). The delay between the date a policy change is implemented and the date by which most of its effects on the economy have occurred.

Outsourcing. A term increasingly used to connote having services performed by low-wage workers overseas.

P

Parameter. *See* **Constant.**

Participation rate. The percentage of the working-age population in the labor force (that is, the percentage that is either employed or looking for work).

Peak. The beginning of a recession; the high point of economic activity prior to a downturn.

Planned aggregate expenditure (*PAE*). Total planned spending on final goods and services.

Portfolio allocation decision. The decision about the forms in which to hold one's wealth.

Positive economic principle. One that predicts how people will behave.

Potential output, Y^* (or potential GDP or full-employment output). The maximum sustainable amount of output (real GDP) that an economy can produce.

Precautionary saving. Saving for protection against unexpected setbacks such as the loss of a job or a medical emergency.

Price ceiling. A maximum allowable price, specified by law.

Price index. A measure of the average price of a given class of goods or services relative to the price of the same goods or services in a base year.

Price level. A measure of the overall level of prices at a particular point in time as measured by a price index such as the CPI.

Primary credit rate. *See* **Discount rate.**

Principal amount. The amount originally lent.

Private saving. The saving of the private sector of the economy is equal to the after-tax income of the private sector minus consumption expenditures $(Y - T - C)$; private saving can be further broken down into household saving and business saving.

Production possibilities curve. A graph that describes the maximum amount of one good that can be produced for every possible level of production of the other good.

Public saving. The saving of the government sector is equal to net tax payments minus government purchases $(T - G)$.

Purchasing power parity (PPP). The theory that nominal exchange rates are determined as necessary for the law of one price to hold.

Q

Quantity equation. Money times velocity equals nominal GDP: $M \times V = P \times Y$.

R

Rate of inflation. The annual percentage rate of change in the price level, as measured, for example, by the CPI.

Rational person. Someone with well-defined goals who tries to fulfill those goals as best he or she can.

Real exchange rate. The price of the average domestic good or service *relative* to the price of the average foreign good or service, when prices are expressed in terms of a common currency.

Real GDP. A measure of GDP in which the quantities produced are valued at the prices in a base year rather than at current prices; real GDP measures the actual *physical volume* of production.

Real interest rate. The annual percentage increase in the purchasing power of a financial asset; the real interest rate on any asset equals the nominal interest rate on that asset minus the inflation rate.

Real quantity. A quantity that is measured in physical terms—for example, in terms of quantities of goods and services.

Real wage. The wage paid to workers measured in terms of purchasing power; the real wage for any given period is calculated by dividing the nominal (dollar) wage by the CPI for that period.

Recession (or **contraction**). A period in which the economy is growing at a rate significantly below normal.

Recessionary gap. A negative output gap, which occurs when potential output exceeds actual output ($Y < Y^*$).

Relative price. The price of a specific good or service *in comparison to* the prices of other goods and services.

Reserve-deposit ratio. Bank reserves divided by deposits.

Reserve requirements. Set by the Fed, the minimum values of the ratio of bank reserves to bank deposits that commercial banks are allowed to maintain.

Rise. *See* **Slope.**

Risk premium. The rate of return that financial investors require to hold risky assets minus the rate of return on safe assets.

Run. *See* **Slope.**

S

Saving. Current income minus spending on current needs.

Saving rate. Saving divided by income.

Self-correcting property. The fact that output gaps will not last indefinitely, but will be closed by rising or falling inflation.

Seller's reservation price. The smallest dollar amount for which a seller would be willing to sell an additional unit, generally equal to marginal cost.

Seller's surplus. The difference between the price received by the seller and his or her reservation price.

Short-run equilibrium. A situation where the *AD* and *AS* curves intersect at a level of real GDP that is above or below potential.

Short-run equilibrium output. The level of output at which output *Y* equals planned aggregate expenditure *PAE*; the level of output that prevails during the period in which prices are predetermined.

Shortage. *See* **Excess demand.**

Skill-biased technological change. Technological change that affects the marginal products of higher-skilled workers differently from those of lower-skilled workers.

Slope. In a straight line, the ratio of the vertical distance the straight line travels between any two points *(rise)* to the corresponding horizontal distance *(run)*.

Socially optimal quantity. The quantity of a good that results in the maximum possible economic surplus from producing and consuming the good.

Stabilization policies. Government policies that are used to affect planned aggregate expenditure, with the objective of eliminating output gaps.

Stock. A measure that is defined *at a point in time.*

Stock (or equity). A claim to partial ownership of a firm.

Store of value. An asset that serves as a means of holding wealth.

Structural unemployment. The long-term and chronic unemployment that exists even when the economy is producing at a normal rate.

Substitutes. Two goods are substitutes in consumption if an increase in the price of one causes a rightward shift in the demand curve for the other (or if a decrease causes a leftward shift).

Substitution effect. The change in the quantity demanded of a good that results because buyers switch to or from substitutes when the price of the good changes.

Sunk cost. A cost that is beyond recovery at the moment a decision must be made.

Supply curve. A graph or schedule showing the quantity of a good that sellers wish to sell at each price.

Supply-side policy. A policy that affects potential output.

Surplus. *See* **Excess supply.**

T

Total surplus. The difference between the buyer's reservation price and the seller's reservation price.

Trade balance (or **net exports**). The value of a country's exports less the value of its imports in a particular period (quarter or year).

Trade deficit. When imports exceed exports, the difference between the value of a country's imports and the value of its exports in a given period.

Trade surplus. When exports exceed imports, the difference between the value of a country's exports and the value of its imports in a given period.

Transfer payments. Payments the government makes to the public for which it receives no current goods or services in return.

Trough. The end of a recession; the low point of economic activity prior to a recovery.

U

Unattainable point. Any combination of goods that cannot be produced using currently available resources.

Unemployment rate. The number of unemployed people divided by the labor force.

Unemployment spell. A period during which an individual is continuously unemployed.

Unit of account. A basic measure of economic value.

V

Value added. For any firm, the market value of its product or service minus the cost of inputs purchased from other firms.

Variable. A quantity that is free to take a range of different values.

Velocity. A measure of the speed at which money changes hands in transactions involving final goods and services, or, equivalently, nominal GDP divided by the stock of money. Numerically, $V = (P \times Y) / M$, where V is velocity, $P \times Y$ is nominal GDP, and M is the money supply whose velocity is being measured.

Vertical intercept. In a straight line, the value taken by the dependent variable when the independent variable equals zero.

W

Wealth. The value of assets minus liabilities.

Wealth effect. The tendency of changes in asset prices to affect households' wealth and thus their consumption spending.

Worker mobility. The movement of workers between jobs, firms, and industries.

Page numbers followed by n refer to notes.